PUBLICATIONS OF THE INSTITUTE OF BUSINESS AND ECONOMIC RESEARCH

Recent publications in this series:

ANTITRUST IN THE MOTION PICTURE INDUSTRY
By Michael Conant (1960)

ECONOMIC DOCTRINES OF KNUT WICKSELL
By Carl G. Uhr (1960)

A THEORY OF ACCOUNTING TO INVESTORS
By George J. Staubus (1961)

ORGANIZATION, AUTOMATION, AND SOCIETY
By Robert A. Brady (1961)

HOUSING POLICY—THE SEARCH FOR SOLUTIONS
By Paul F. Wendt (1962)

COMPETITION, REGULATION, AND THE PUBLIC INTEREST
IN NONLIFE INSURANCE
By Roy J. Hensley (1962)

THE SIX-LEGGED DOG: MATTEI AND ENI—A STUDY IN POWER
By Dow Votaw (1964)

A HISTORY OF RUSSIAN ECONOMIC THOUGHT: NINTH THROUGH EIGHTEENTH CENTURIES

PUBLICATIONS OF THE INSTITUTE OF BUSINESS AND ECONOMIC RESEARCH
UNIVERSITY OF CALIFORNIA

A History of Russian Economic Thought: Ninth through Eighteenth Centuries

EDITED AND WITH A FOREWORD BY

John M. Letiche

Translated with the collaboration of Basil Dmytryshyn and Richard A. Pierce

Original Russian Edition edited by Corresponding Member of the Academy of Sciences of the USSR, A. I. Pashkov

UNIVERSITY OF CALIFORNIA PRESS / BERKELEY AND LOS ANGELES / 1964

UNIVERSITY OF CALIFORNIA PRESS
BERKELEY AND LOS ANGELES, CALIFORNIA

CAMBRIDGE UNIVERSITY PRESS,
LONDON, ENGLAND

LIBRARY OF CONGRESS CATALOG CARD NUMBER: 64-18641

FOREWORD

This volume is intended to serve Western scholars as a basic reference on the ideological and historical sources of Soviet thought.

In our time the United States and the Soviet Union both look at important problems from the standpoint of the totality of national and worldwide interest. This implies that in an era of fundamental political instability every act of defense—intellectual as well as military—on the part of one nation is interpreted as a potential act of aggression by the other. To reduce misunderstanding, error and miscalculation, a knowledge of the history of ideas of both countries is clearly indispensable.

Since the Second World War, American scholars and statesmen have made increasing efforts to formulate and communicate the concepts underlying the relationships of American democracy to its world environment. This research has been enriched by the continued appearance of private memoirs, freer access to archives, and the excellent work of American scholarship in the study and analysis of these materials. Soviet scholars and statesmen have also made a concentrated effort to analyze and to present the fundamental relationships of Marxist-Leninist thought to its world environment. The present volume contains important contributions to this endeavor.

The essays were written by distinguished Soviet economists. Their exhaustive research has been based on voluminous primary and secondary sources. The history of Russian economic thought from the ninth to the eighteenth century has been thoroughly reappraised. Within the context and limitations of soviet ideology, the quality of the work is of high order. The reader will discover much new information and interpretation, especially pertaining to the interdependence of early Russian history and economic thought.

The marshaling and treatment of the material indicate that this book was primarily intended for the use of Russian scholars. It reflects the conclusion reached by Soviet economists that previous interpretations of the history of Russian economic thought have seriously underrated the role of Russian conditions and ideas, and have grossly exaggerated the impact of Western ideas on Russian thought. I shall have occasion to appraise these and related issues elsewhere. It should be noted here, however, that one of the major contributions of this volume to Western readers lies in the insights which it provides into Soviet beliefs regarding past and future world developments. Although a study of these views will not necessarily lead to a more sympathetic understanding of them, it reveals the wide gulf between Soviet and Western social thought. Scholarship can contribute to the bridging of this gulf if, as we assume, it is the responsibility of social scientists to provide the theoretical foundations for social action, rather than the other way round. Assessment of the mutual influence of theory and action is complicated by the awareness of scholars the world over that vested interests and established institutions have ways of generating ideas congenial to themselves. Nevertheless, in a period of serious mixed conflict and cooperation between two civilizations, a knowledge of which issues are at the time fundamentally in conflict and which lend themselves to further cooperation is a primary requisite for the endless process of resolution.

Modern pluralistic societies such as the United States and, to a developing extent, the Soviet Union allow the individual to have allegiances to a variety of interests, groups, and institutions. In this respect they contrast with traditional feudal social structures. With more and freer intellectual interchange and with greater access to the ideas and ideals of other nations, individuals in otherwise conflicting societies can share a growing proportion of these interests and pursuits. Wherever a genuine mutuality of interests exists, the further extension of such interests across national boundaries should promote the achievement of their goals. In this way, preservation of the accomplishments of the human race may be enhanced. It is hoped that the present volume can contribute in a small way to the realization of this objective and that it can serve as a basis for genuine problem-solving rather than mere debate.

In preparing this translation, my collaborators and I often had to choose between a concise style and an accurate rendering of the authors' nuances. We have endeavored to maintain the spirit of the original. Refinement of exposition would at times have called for greater conciseness, but fair representation of the authors' intended emphasis precluded severe economy of words.

As regards transliteration from Cyrillic to Roman characters, we have adhered, with minor exceptions, to the Library of Congress system. Russian terms not readily translatable have been defined in order of appearance and a glossary of unfamiliar expressions has been provided on pp. 637-640. An index (not present in the Russian original) has also been supplied.

Although subsequent Russian volumes have appeared, it is not presently our intention to translate them. Our main objective has been to provide English-speaking readers with the flavor of Soviet economic thought and it is hoped that this aim has been achieved by the publication of this volume.

Thanks are due to the Institute of Business and Economic Research, and to the Center for Slavic Studies, both of the University of California, Berkeley, which provided the funds for research assistants and furnished the typing facilities.

JOHN M. LETICHE

University of California, Berkeley
July 20, 1964

LIST OF AUTHORS

The authors of the first part of Volume I of *A History of Russian Economic Thought* are: A. I. Pashkov, Corresponding Member of the Academy of Sciences of the USSR, I. S. Bak, Doctor of Economic Science, and E. V. Prikazchikova and E. S. Iarantseva, Candidates of Economic Science.

The chapters of the book were written as follows:

Introduction	A. I. Pashkov, editor
Chapters 1-7	A. I. Pashkov
Chapters 8-9	E. S. Iarantseva
Chapters 10-12	A. I. Pashkov
Chapter 13	
Sections on Saltykov and Volynskii	A. I. Pashkov
Section on Tatishchev	I. S. Bak
Chapters 14-15	I. S. Bak
Chapter 16	
Sections on the "Nakaz" of Catherine II and on Sumarokov	I. S. Bak
Section on Shcherbatov	E. V. Prikazchikova
Chapter 17	I. S. Bak
Chapter 18	E. V. Prikazchikova
Chapters 19-20	I. S. Bak
Chapter 21	E. V. Prikazchikova

E. V. Prikazchikova participated in editing the volume. V. S. Vilenskaia, S. M. Kots, and E. F. Kosheleva took part in the technical preparation of the book for the press. N. A. Tsagolov, Doctor of Economic Science, is editor of the publishing house.

CONTENTS

THE ACADEMY OF SCIENCES OF THE USSR.

INSTITUTE OF ECONOMICS

A HISTORY OF RUSSIAN ECONOMIC THOUGHT

Vol. I

The Epoch of Feudalism

Part I

IX to XVIII Centuries

Edited by Corresponding Member of
the Academy of Sciences of the USSR
A. I. PASHKOV

THE STATE PUBLISHING HOUSE OF POLITICAL LITERATURE
MOSCOW, 1955

INTRODUCTION

The Great October Socialist Revolution inaugurated a new era in the history of human society. The elimination of man's exploitation of man, the victory of socialism in our country, the decisive role of the Soviet people in the destruction of German fascism and Japanese militarism, and the great successes of the USSR in all walks of life after the Second World War have clearly shown the world the mighty strength of the Soviet system which was created by the October Revolution and the greatness of the Soviet people.

During the Socialist Revolution, and as a result of the victory of socialism, a Soviet culture was created in our country, socialist in content and national in form, a culture which represents basically a new, higher level in the development of world civilization.

Among all the peoples of the Soviet State, the great Russian people are the leading ones. They are justifiably proud of their enormous contribution to the struggle for freedom and the happiness of the toiling masses and of their invaluable contribution to world culture. During the course of their centuries-old history the Russian people have produced numerous brilliant and famed representatives of advanced thought, creators of advanced science in the most diverse fields of knowledge. The contribution of the Russian people to the science of economics has been equally great.

Even during the early history of the Russian people advanced Russian economic thought played an enormous and positive role in the development of our country. During the fifteenth and sixteenth centuries such important statesmen of Russia as Ivan III and Ivan the Terrible were advocates of economic progress. The activities of Afanasii Nikitin, Ivan Peresvetov, and Ermolai-Erazm also influenced the development of Russian economic thought during this period.

Later, still under conditions of the feudal-serf system, the Russian people produced a number of important and original thinkers and statesmen distinguished by their profound understanding of economic life and considered among the foremost representatives of contemporary world economic thought. Such were Ordyn-Nashchokin in the seventeenth century; Peter I and Pososhkov; the first Russian revolutionary, Radishchev, in the eighteenth century; the Decembrists Turgenev and Pestel'; and the revolutionary democrats Herzen and Chernyshevskii in the nineteenth century. Radishchev, the ardent fighter against serfdom and autocracy, was at the same time an important economist, while Pestel', the distinguished revolutionary, worked out an original plan for a solution of the agrarian problem in Russia.

The economic writings of the great Russian revolutionary democrats were important in the development of advanced economic thought, not only for Russia but for the entire world. The works of Chernyshevskii —unstinting defender of the interests of the oppressed peasantry, brilliant critic of serfdom, capitalism, and bourgeois political economy— occupied a high position in the Russian economic thought of the pre-Marxian political economy. The economic teachings of the revolutionary democrats paved the way for the adoption and assimilation of Marxism by advanced representatives of Russian social thought. And Plekhanov laid the foundations for the Marxist stage in the development of Russian economic thought.

The Russian people gave mankind *Leninism*—the highest achievement of contemporary thought. The Soviet people rightfully take pride in the fact that our motherland nurtured Leninism—a new and higher stage of *Marxism,* and the acme of Russian culture.

V. I. Lenin, the founder of the Communist party and of the Soviet state and the brilliant successor to the work of Marx and Engels, defended revolutionary science from the attack of bourgeois ideologies and all kinds of revisionists and opportunists. He fully developed Marxism to conform to the new conditions of the class struggle—to the conditions of the epoch of imperialism and of proletarian revolutions. He added a new chapter to Marxist political economy—the study of modern capitalist-imperialism. Lenin developed the bases of the theory of the general crisis of capitalism, created a new theory of socialist revolution, and laid the foundations of the political economy of socialism. In his studies he worked out scientifically the basic problems of building socialism and communism. Marxist-Leninist economic teaching was further developed and enriched in the works of Lenin's great companion-in-arms and pupil, I. V. Stalin. This body of thought is creatively developed in the decisions of the Communist party of the Soviet Union and in the writings of its leaders as well as in the works of the leaders of the communist and workers' parties of other countries.

Soviet economists and Marxist economists of the people's democracies and capitalist countries have taken an active part in the scientific solution of the problems of political economy. The Marxist-Leninist economic theory serves as the guiding star, as a banner of the toilers in their struggle for liberation, as a mighty weapon of the revolutionary struggle of the working class for the overthrow of the capitalist system, and for the victory of the new system—Communism.

The theory of historical materialism, especially the Marxist-Leninist teaching about the base and the superstructure, is the key to a correct understanding of the history of social thought, including economic thought, and to an explanation of its origins and significance. The origin of the spiritual life of society, of social ideas, theories, and views must be sought not in ideas, theories, and views, but in the conditions of the material life of society and the social existence which they reflect. The basis of society—that is, the economic system of society at a given stage of development—determines its superstructure, its political, legal, religious, artistic, and philosophical views, and its corresponding political, legal, and other institutions. Hence the base of any society has a necessarily corresponding superstructure. When the base is altered, immediately the superstructure changes and liquidates itself; and, with the emergence of a new base, a corresponding superstructure is born. V. I. Lenin wrote, "Exactly as man's perception reflects independently from his existing nature, that is, from his organic, developing material, so man's *social perception* (that is, the various views and philosophical, religious, political, and other teachings) reflects the *economic order* of society." [1]

The diversity of economic ideas and theories in various epochs in the history of society is stipulated by, and can hence be explained by, the diverse conditions of the material life of society in these epochs. In the study of the history of economic thought, a correct understanding of the base is therefore of prime significance. One must seek the roots of the economic viewpoints, ideas, and theories, by examining the nature of the economic order prevailing in a given country at a given time.

It should also be noted that all the various fields of social ideology, economic views, ideas, and theories are determined most directly by the base. This does not mean, of course, that the economic viewpoint of one or another people always reflects only the basis of society and nothing else. Marx warned against such an erroneous understanding of the question. "One and the same economic base—one and the same from the standpoint of the main conditions—thanks to the endless variety of empirical conditions, natural conditions, and racial relations acting outside of historical influences, can be manifested in end-

[1] V. I. Lenin, *Sochineniia* [Works] (Moscow: Gospolitizdat, 1941–9), XIX, 5.

less variations and gradations which can be understood only through analysis of these empirical, given conditions." [2]

The historian of economic thought is obliged, consequently, to show concretely the effect of these various empirical circumstances, of various conditions, influences, and so forth, in order to define explicitly their nature and degree of influence on the economic scene under study.

In the study of the history of economic thought still another aspect of historical materialism has fundamental significance: the superstructure, being born of and determined by the base of society, in turn acts upon it and exerts a definite influence on the base. Economic and all other ideas, theories, and views do not merely reflect passively the base of society, but in one way or another act upon it. The character and extent of this influence depend on many factors, but first of all on how these ideas, theories, and views are related to the prevailing system of production and to the base of society, and again on their relationship to the demands of the economic law of compulsory conformity of productive relations to the nature of the productive forces of society.

The classics of Marxism-Leninism emphasize the need to distinguish between the old theories which have outlived their time and have served the interests of outmoded forces of society and new, advanced ideas and theories which serve the interests of the advanced forces of society and its development and progress, furthering the solution of pressing problems of the development of the material life of society. New ideas, theories, and views arising out of new tasks imposed by the development of the material life of society have important organizing, mobilizing, and transforming significance. The superstructure rises out of the base, but "once emerged, it becomes a great active force, definitely helping its base to form and strengthen itself, and it takes all measures to help the new order finish off and liquidate the old base and the old classes." [3]

To understand correctly the *origin* of economic ideas, theories, and views and their social *significance,* it is important to study the concrete conditions of the effect of the economic law of compulsory conformity of productive relations on the nature of the productive forces of society at that stage of historical development to which are related the ideas, theories, and views which we study. Their social significance, their nature and degree of effect on the base of society, will vary depending on whether these ideas receive scope or, on the other hand, aid the preservation of conditions hindering the operation of this law.

---

[2] K. Marx, *Kapital* [Capital] (Moscow: Gospolitizdat, 1953), III, 804.

[3] I. V. Stalin, *Marksizm i voprosy iazikoznaniia* [Marxism and Problems of Linguistics] (Moscow: Gospolitizdat, 1952), p. 7.

In a class society economic ideas are inevitably of a class nature. They reflect immediately the most pressing interests of people and their material concerns. Therefore, the class nature of social ideas and theories is most clearly visible in economic theories and views. As in other countries, so in Russia, economic thought has developed along with the real development of social contradictions and class struggle. Lenin wrote that "the history of ideas is the history of the replacement and *consequently the struggle* of ideas." [4]

Russian economic thought of the past is the complex result of the development of contradictions and the struggle of various classes of society at different stages in the development of this society. One must not look upon it, therefore, as something homogeneous. Lenin taught that in a class society there are two nations in each nation, two national cultures in each national culture, that in Russia there was a Great Russian culture of exploiters and a Great Russian culture of the oppressed and exploited class.[5] The spokesmen of the Russian ruling classes—the feudalists (*boyars* and *pomeshchiks*) and the bourgeoisie—used their ideas and theories to strengthen both the position of the economic order of society and the exploiting classes which they represented. The spokesmen of the oppressed and exploited classes of Russia on the other hand—the peasants and the working class (the proletariat)—expressed with their economic ideas and theories the protest of the exploited against the oppressors and their state and summoned the oppressed to struggle against the exploiters.

In its historical development, Russian economic thought has reflected not only the contradictions and the class struggle between the exploited and the exploiters, but also, in one form or another, the contradictions and struggle between the various classes and groups amongs the exploiters themselves—between the pomeshchiks and the bourgeoisie, between the manufacturing and the trading bourgeoisie, and so on.

Economic thought has not been a simple reflection of the views of the spokesmen of various social classes and groups, but a mighty weapon of class struggle. Therefore, one of the basic conditions of a scientific study of the history of Russian economic thought is the analysis of the class structure of society, of the various contradictions peculiar to it, the condition of the class struggle, the form of political institutions, and the power of the state.

The victory of socialism in the USSR brought about for the first time in history a moral-political unity of society. In the USSR, Marxist-

[4] Lenin, *op. cit.*, XX, 237.
[5] *Ibid.*, XX, 16.

Leninist economic science, which expresses the interests of the toilers and is led by the Communist party, rules indivisibly and is constantly developing.

The study of the history of Russian economic science poses the task of disclosing the outstanding significance of *advanced* economic ideas; the interests of advanced forces of society in its historical development are served by showing the role of economic ideas in the struggle of *progressive* forces of social development against conservative, reactionary forces. It is particularly important to show the great role of *revolutionary* economic ideas in the various stages of the movement to liberate the toilers of Russia: to bring out the inner historical connection and succession, the progressive movement of Russian *revolutionary* economic thought from Radishchev to the Decembrists and from them to the revolutionary democrats headed by the great Russian economist of the pre-Marxian period, Chernyshevskii; and, to go further, to the Russian Marxists—the social-democrats—whose forerunners, as Lenin indicated, were the revolutionary democrats, Belinskii, Herzen, Chernyshevskii, and Dobroliubov. These most important stages in the development of Russian revolutionary economic science have been marked by the *qualitative* changes of Russian economic thought in conformity with the changes in the conditions of material life of society and the class struggle.

The appearance and development in Russia of Marxist economic science has had worldwide historical significance of extensive importance. This is indicated by the formation of a *fundamentally new* stage in the development of Russian economic science as the product of a new stage of revolutionary struggle—the struggle between hired labor and capital. This new stage is connected indissolubly with the unfolding in Russia of the revolutionary workers' movement and with the preparation and direction of the revolution in our country. The Communist party, leading the struggle of the working class and the peasantry of Russia for liberation from oppression and exploitation, was armed by advanced revolutionary science—by Marxism-Leninism.

V. I. Lenin's economic teaching, which was continued by I. V. Stalin and creatively developed in the resolutions of the Communist party of the Soviet Union and its leaders, is the further development of the economic science of Marx-Engels, and, at the same time, the continuation and development of the outstanding achievements of Russian revolutionary economic science.

A very significant task of scientific study of the history of Russian economic thought consists in revealing the conditions of its conception and in showing the process of its development in our country and the great worldwide historical significance of this new, higher stage of Marxist political economy.

Economic thought serves as one of the important weapons, not only in the class struggle within a country, but also in the struggle for a state's independence. The history of Russian social thought shows that the national tasks of Russia—the development of productive forces and the guarantee of the country's independence and might—were posed long ago in one form or another by the foremost representatives of the Russian people. One must not forget, however, that the understanding by the earlier spokesmen and public figures of Russia of the problems of the country's economic development and the guaranteeing of her independence always came through the prism of their *class* consciousness. In speaking of the comprehension by one economist or another of the national tasks of Russia, in speaking of the patriotism of the advanced Russian economists, one must always have in mind *which* Russia these economists cared for and *which* class they represented in the vanguard of Russia's movement along the path of progress.

Russia's technical-economic backwardness in the past was early recognized as an evil. Many Russian economists and progressive public figures proposed various measures directed toward the struggle with the country's backwardness. But the view of this problem by the spokesmen of the nobility and the bourgeoisie inevitably had limited scope. Not one of the old classes could solve the problem of Russia's backwardness; with the passing of centuries it was eliminated only on the basis of socialist construction, as a result of the liquidation of the exploiting classes and the victory of socialism in our country.

Although progressive for their time, the programs for the economic development of Russia put forth by such enlightened persons as Ordyn-Nashchokin, Peter I, and Pososhkov show that their understanding of the way to correct the economic backwardness of feudal Russia was historically limited. These statesmen carried on the struggle against Russia's backwardness and for its independence from other countries which had already developed on a higher basis—the basis of capitalist productive relations—within the framework of the feudal-serfdom system then prevailing in our country, the existence of which they did not criticize.

An entirely different formulation of the question is to be seen in Radishchev and the Decembrists, who considered that the liquidation of Russia's backwardness and the guarantee of her might and glory were possible only by eliminating the basic cause for this backwardness—the existence of the serf system.

The revolutionary democrats—Belinskii, Herzen, Chernyshevskii, and Dobroliubov—believed it necessary to liberate the Russian people not only from feudal-serfdom but also from capitalist exploitation, seeing in this liberation the basic condition of the development of the economic power of their country. But their proposals regarding the ways to liberate Russia from capitalist exploitation were still utopian.

Lenin, the leader of the proletarian revolution, revealing the causes of our country's centuries-old backwardness, showed that only a socialist revolution could guarantee the removal of this backwardness and create the right conditions for independence and growth and a strong country. To overtake and surpass economically the advanced capitalist countries, to perish or to forge ahead at full steam: thus history poses the problem, said V. I. Lenin about Russia on the eve of the October Revolution.[6] In order to go forward Russia could only look to socialism.

Under the leadership of the Communist party the toilers of our country overthrew the centuries-old yoke of the pomeshchiks and bourgeoisie, created the Soviet state, and, effecting socialist industrialization of the country and collectivization of agriculture, transformed the formerly backward Russia into a mighty, independent, socialist state.

An important condition for scientific study of the development of economic thought is a strictly historical approach toward the analysis of ideas and theories and the explanation of concrete historical conditions under which these ideas and theories were formulated. Such an approach to the understanding of economic and political roots, as well as class structure, is basic to the understanding of society. It is clear, for example, that the equally positive attitudes of various spokesmen and statesmen toward serfdom in Russia have entirely different social significances and must receive different evaluations by the historian, depending upon the degree of development of the feudal-serf order to which their activity is related—whether to a time when feudal productive relationships still corresponded to the productive forces of society, or to a period when such correspondence had already disappeared.

The failure to recognize this elementary requirement of historical study can result in the practice of mechanically asserting that views progressive for their time may be equally advanced for later epochs with entirely different social conditions and tasks. Likewise, economic

---

[6] *Ibid.*, XXV, 338.

theories appearing advanced and progressive under certain conditions at one stage of social development can appear backward and reactionary in other social situations. On the other hand, it would be entirely incorrect and anti-historical if we should approach the thinkers and statesmen of the past by appraising their significance in terms of more modern standards. As Lenin wrote: "Historical merits must be judged not by what the historical figures *did not contribute* compared with modern demands, but by what they *contributed* that was new in comparison with their predecessors." [7]

In the study of the history of Russian economic thought it is very important to establish a correct perspective. In bourgeois literature the periodization of Russian economic thought has customarily been designated as arising from certain *sources of influence:* periods of "English influence," "French influence," "German influence," or such "epochs" as "mercantilism in Russia," "physiocracy in Russia," "Smithianism in Russia," and so on. Such "periodization" is utterly worthless. (See, for example, the works of Sviatlovskii.) It represents an inseparable part of the lying and harmful assertions of the alleged dependent nature of the development of Russian economic science. It ignores economic facts and the conditions of class struggle which determine the appearance and development of one or another ideology. This arbitrary approach to the development of economic thought results in idealistically altering the sources of "adaptation." In foreign bourgeois literature this perverse "periodization" of the history of Russian economic thought persists to this day.

Inasmuch as the roots of all kinds of economic ideologies lie in real economic relations and in the class contradictions which develop from them, the scientific Marxist periodization of the history of Russian economic thought must begin with the periodization of the history of our country's economic development. The development of economic thought must be studied first of all in separate, historically interchangeable socio-economic formations. In conformity with the history of Russian economic thought one can speak of the necessity of strict demarcation of the development of this thought: first, in the epoch of feudalism; second, in the epoch of capitalism; and, third, in the epoch of socialism.

Whatever the nature of the class struggle, the historical role of separate classes and of their ideologies in various stages of development of one and the same socio-economic formations have fundamentally changed. Therefore the periodization of the history of economic

[7] *Ibid.*, II, 166.

thought cannot be limited to major epochs defined by socio-economic formations. It is necessary to consider also the most essential periods and stages in the development of each formation. The differences between these various periods and the phases within each socio-economic formation are in their turn stipulated by varying degrees of maturity of social productiveness, that is, of economic relationships determining a given formation, of diverse stages of development of class contradictions and of class struggle in society, changes in the political order, the nature of the state and of the ruling power (feudal disunity, the centralized state, absolutism), and by other conditions determining development of economic thought.

The periodization of the history of our country's economic development gives, of course, only the basis of the periodization of the history of Russian economic thought. It is necessary to consider the conformity of the development of economic thought itself to laws of economic development as a definite form of social consciousness. Its roots must be sought in economic conditions and in the class struggle, and its ideal material must to one degree or another be connected also with the preceding development of social consciousness. The periodization must reflect the continuity of Russian economic thought, the main landmarks of its progressive movement, and must simultaneously reveal those features which characterize it in each stage of development in order to show the deep, qualitative changes that it has undergone. The periodization of the history of this thought must help disclose the succession of various stages and trends in the economic thought of each of the contending classes of Russian society.

The object of our study is this historical development of thought. Economic thought reflects human consciousness of the socio-productive —that is, the economic—relations of people; in other words, of those relationships which accumulate among people in the course of the production of material goods. But the economic thought of a people over a prolonged period is extremely varied, and the historian of economic thought must naturally make a definite choice of material for his study. As a criterion for such a selection one must take, obviously, the most typical aspect of economic thought, that which was most characteristic of given classes over a given period of the history of society. Out of all the abundance of the monuments of economic thought of pre-October Russia which have come down to us one must pick those which in the greatest measure characterize the economic points of view and trends of thought of the spokesmen of the various classes of feudal and bourgeois Russia.

With the development of economic points of view, not only the content, but also the form of expression has changed and developed. During the first centuries of its history, economic thought in Russia is difficult to separate from other forms of ideology with which it was then intrinsically connected. As in other countries, economic ideas remained for a long time fragmentary, broken, closely linked with legal monuments, church literature, and so on. One of the earliest manifestations of economic thought lies in measures of state economic policy. Thus, for example, the economic policy of the Kievan princes, determining in its content the economic order and class structure of Kievan Rus, presupposed the princes' definite attention to questions of the country's economy, to the economic side of the relations of the princes with the population, and, above all, to means of obtaining income for the treasury.

As the economy of the Russian state developed, attempts were made to formulate the principles of economic policy and to devise methods and forms for their implementation.

In connection with the establishment of measures of economic policy, the necessity arises to analyze economic relationships and formulate laws for their development. In this process *economic science* is born and develops. The beginning of economic science, the first attempts to disclose the existence of economic phenomena and their conformity to law, took place in Russia as early as the eighteenth century. For example, in the first quarter of the eighteenth century we have I. T. Pososhkov's *Book on Poverty and Wealth,* and Radishchev's writings in the last third of the same century were outstanding.

In the study of the history of Russian economic thought it is particularly important to show the process of the rise and development of *economic science* in our country, to reveal the legitimate development of *scientific* economic thought, the moving forces of its development, and to show the practical (broadly speaking) significance of economic science in the various stages of its development in Russia.

Russian thinkers gradually became more and more interested in the economics and economic policy not only of Russia but also of other countries. The economic-geographic study of Russia developed, and the application of the statistical method of study of economic life grew.

At the end of the eighteenth century and particularly during the nineteenth, Russian economic science not only became broader and deeper, but also noticeably differentiated; it branched out into a number of more or less independent, isolated scientific disciplines. Along with political-economic works, there now appeared more often special works on the history of national economy or on economic statistics. Financial science and agricultural economics became special branches. Works on the economics of transport, on trade, and of other activities began to emerge.

The study of the history of Russian economic thought demands that the researcher should not limit himself to the framework of economic works (in the narrow sense of the word) of thinkers, but that he review a whole series of documents and various publications which characterize the economic views of their respective authors. On the other hand, even strictly economic works have various natures: the description and analysis of the country's economics, its past, present, and prospective future development, the basis of concrete measures of state economic policies, the manifestation of conformity to law, and the jurisprudential facets of the economic development of society indicate some of the ramifications. Study and analysis of all these sources are needed in the characterization of economic thought.

The history of economic thought is broader in its content than the history of political economy. Political economy is an exalted stage of the theoretical understanding of economic life. But however high this stage of perception, political economy is inseparably connected with the course of class struggle; it utilizes for its enrichment the material of works which determine the tasks, methods, and principles of economic policy; it analyzes the economies of various countries, describes the history of economic development, and reveals its perspectives.

The study of the real process of development of Russian economic thought, like that of any other country, cannot therefore be limited to the study of the history of political economy alone—an error into which economic historians often fall. The ignoring, for example, of specific Russian problems, studied by Russian economists of former times, has led to the minimization of the significance of Russian economic thought in the development of world economic science. The enrichment of political economy by Russian economists was inseparably connected with the analysis of the economic condition of Russia and with their desire to determine paths of development for their motherland. Often in conjunction with this there have arisen, and have been scientifically proven by leading Russian economists, a number of new theoretical positions and laws. These had not only prime significance for the fate of our country's development, but were also valuable contributions to political economy, endowing it with new and important chapters.

Scientific study of the history of economic thought thus inescapably presupposes the study of the whole sum of basic ideas, arising and developing with the founding of the principles of economic policies, in connection with the analysis of the past, present, and future development of the country's economics. Therefore before and after the rise of political economy in the proper sense, the study of economic thought can be fruitful only if all of its above stated forms are covered.

A simultaneous study of Russian economic thought of the past with the internal and inextricable connections between all its fundamental forms—that is, political economy, concrete analysis of the country's economic situations and the perspectives of its development, and the theoretical foundations of the principles of the state's economic policy—reveals not only the true significance of economic ideas and teachings in the social life of our motherland, the concrete understanding of their economic class roots, and the determining role of economics in relation to economic ideas, but also the active role of ideas and their reverse action upon the economic system.

Russian economic thought did not develop in isolation but in close association with the economic thought of other countries with whom Russia had economic, political, and cultural relations. It would be incorrect to look upon the history of Russian economic thought in fragments, in isolation from the history of the development of economic science in the rest of the world. It is necessary to show the influence of Russian economic thought on that of other countries; and it is extremely important to disclose and evaluate the contribution of advanced Russian economists to world economic science, assertions made by bourgeois cosmopolitans to the contrary notwithstanding.

One of the most important tasks of the scientific study of the history of Russian economic thought is to unmask and totally destroy the slanderous fabrications about the alleged nonindependent nature of Russian economic thought in general and about the "imported" nature of Russian economic science. The roots of these slanderous fabrications must be sought, on the one hand, in the mercenary interests of the reactionary nationalists of other countries and, on the other hand, in the grovelling servility before western bourgeois culture of the reactionary spokesmen of the ruling classes of Tsarist Russia—the landowners and capitalists.

In Tsarist Russia the reactionary falsehoods about the "dependence" of Russian culture and of Russian science upon the culture and science of other lands were heartily propagated by the conservative spokesmen of the nobility and bourgeoisie. This was one of the forms of expression of these proponents' grovelling servility to the nobility and to the bourgeois culture of the West, and it served at the same time as a means of ideological struggle against the progressive, advanced social forces of the country, the struggle for the preservation of the ruling classes.

In the realm of economic science in the nineteenth century we see in the works of two ardent defenders of autocracy and class privilege, V. P. Bezobrazov [8] and N. Kh. Bunge,[9] the debasement of Russian economic thought before the bourgeois West. Later V. V. Sviatlovskii, the author of a number of special works published in the twentieth century before and after the October Revolution, reflected the history of Russian economic thought in the curved mirror of bourgeois cosmopolitanism. This bourgeois historian, appearing under a Marxist mask, during the first years of Soviet power minimized earlier Russian economic thought and regarded it as a simple imitation of Western European economic views.[10]

Failure to understand the enormous significance of Russian economic thought and its resultant minimization were peculiar to the Mensheviks. G. V. Plekhanov gave an incorrect evaluation of Russian economic science in works written during the period of Menshevism, particularly in research on the history of Russian social thought. Plekhanov erroneously characterized the economic structure of Russia as another type of "oriental slavery." Therefore, in the Plekhanov interpretations of the economics and class structure of feudal Russia, the relations of the basic classes—the pomeshchiks and peasants—did not receive the primary place and *importance* which they actually merited. Plekhanov proceeded from the incorrect assumption that in a country with a backward economy, backward economic thought was unavoidable.

Plekhanov's analysis of Russian social thought was carried on primarily from the viewpoint of relations between "East" and "West," between Russia and Europe. He saw the source of the intellectual movements in Russia in the ideologies of the West, an influence which he believed determined the entire development of Russian social thought. In Plekhanov's treatment leading Russian spokesmen are not presented as original thinkers, but only as popularizers and propagandists of the best ideas of the West.

---

[8] See V. P. Bezobrazov, "O vliianii ekonomicheskoi nauki na gosudarstvennuiu zhizn v sovremennoi Evrope" [On the Influence of Economic Science on State Life in Contemporary Europe], *Russkii Vestnik* [Russian Herald], January, 1867, p. 139.

[9] See N. Kh. Bunge, *Ocherki politiko-ekonomicheskoi literatury* [Outlines of Political-Economic Literature] (St. Petersburg: 1895), pp. 199–200.

[10] See V. V. Sviatlovskii, *Istoriia ekonomicheskikh idei v Rossii* [History of Economic Ideas in Russia] (Petrograd: 1923), vol. I, and others of his works.

Although Plekhanov took upon himself the task of revealing the class nature of Russian social, as well as economic, thought, his work actually consists mainly of a purely formal analysis of economic teachings and a logical comparison of one teaching with another. As a result, Plekhanov gave an untrue evaluation of the content of economic teachings in Russia and their social significance. He did not understand, for example, the nature and importance of the views of Chernyshevskii and other Russian revolutionary democrats and their role in the development of Russian social and economic thought. Plekhanov identified the views of Chernyshevskii and other Russian revolutionary democrats with the ideas of Western European utopian socialism and did not see in the ideas of the Russian revolutionary democrats the primary consideration—their revolutionary democratism, born of specifically Russian conditions of the class struggle of the peasantry, a factor which placed these advanced Russian thinkers on a much higher plane than that of the socialist-utopians of Western Europe.

Writing a brilliant criticism of populism, the *narodnik* movement, Plekhanov, like all the Mensheviks, did not show, however, the ambiguity and contradiction of the narodnik program and the ties between this ambiguity and contradiction and the socio-economic nature of the peasantry; he did not show the peasantry's position in a country where capitalism was developing in the presence of great remnants of serfdom. Correctly revealing the reactionary side of the narodnik program, Plekhanov saw the other side of it, in which he found reflected the revolutionary-democratic aspirations of the peasantry.

After the Great October Socialist Revolution, the bourgeois scholars, the Mensheviks, the Trotskyites, the Menshevist idealists, the historians of the "Pokrovskii school," and so forth, tried to introduce cosmopolitan distortions of the history of Russian science and culture. In his work on the history of Russian economic thought, reissued in 1923, V. V. Sviatlovskii repeated in full all of his bourgeois-cosmopolitan conceptions of the history of Russian economic thought.

Incorrect and distorted interpretations also appeared in the works of several Soviet economists. Thus, for instance, I. G. Bliumin, in his book *Outlines of Economic Thought in Russia in the First Half of the Nineteenth Century*, appearing in 1940, failed to refute the falsehoods about the alleged lack of independence of Russian economic science. Contrary to reality, he maintained that economic thought in Russia in the first half of the nineteenth century was nothing but simple borrowing and "importation" of ready-made economic ideas from the West. Having assumed such an incorrect position, this author failed to reveal the outstanding scientific import of the works of Mordvinov, the Decembrists Pestel and Turgenev, and other original Russian economic thinkers of the first half of the nineteenth century. Further, any indication of the outstanding significance of Russian economic thought of the past is lacking in the works of D. I. Rozenberg on the history of political economy.

In the modern stage of the historical development of mankind—during the gradual transition of the USSR to communism and of the successful building of socialism in the countries of the peoples' democracies, on the one hand, and the deep *social crisis* of the entire capitalist system on the other—bourgeois political economy ardently serves the futile aspirations of the bourgeoisie to preserve the capitalist order. It is an ideological weapon in the struggle of the imperialists against the USSR and the countries of the peoples' democracies and against the toiling masses and the progressive forces in the capitalist countries themselves.

The reactionary bourgeois economists of the USA are now the ardent troubadours of the aggressive, usurping policies of the American imperialists who head the antidemocratic, imperialist camp and prepare to drag humanity into a new world war.

In the aggressive struggle of the reactionary imperialist forces of the USA for world dominance, the preaching of the ideas of bourgeois cosmopolitanism is an ideological weapon. One of the tools of the reactionary bourgeois economists of the USA and of their apprentices in Western Europe is the minimization of the cultural achievements of the Soviet people. The hired defenders of the corrupt "culture" of the imperialist obscurants do not even hesitate to direct ideological falsification in the field of the history of the culture of the Russian people.

Thus, in 1945 in New York a work was published entitled *The Spirit of Russian Economics.*[11] J. Normano, the author of this booklet, slanderously maintains that Russian economic thought of the past was not the product of the independent creativeness of the Russian people, but was only the adaptation and elaboration of the economic thought of the "advanced" peoples of the West. Minimizing Russian economic thought of the past, this spokesman of bourgeois cosmopolitanism, in another of his books, *The Spirit of American Economics,* exalts American economic "science" and strenuously attempts to show its great significance, although it is well known that in the development of economic science the bourgeois economists of the USA have contributed nothing of significance; they have only caught up "the last word" of

[11] J. Normano, *The Spirit of Russian Economics* (New York: 1945).

the vulgar economy of Western Europe and adapted it to the taste and demands of the American bourgeois.[12]

In their services to the American aggressors, who are aspiring to deprive other peoples of sovereignty and to subjugate the whole world, several economists have not even stopped at attempts to show the dependence of Russian economic thought of the past on America. Thus, for example, David Hecht, author of the book, appearing in the USA in 1947, *Russian Radicals Look to America,*[13] crudely distorting the facts, tries to show that the revolutionary democrats of Russia—Belinskii, Herzen, Dobroliubov, and Chernyshevskii—considered America to have the ideal social order and highly esteemed the social thought of the USA.

Yet it is well known that representatives of Russian revolutionary democracy were very critical of American bourgeois democracy and unmasked the vulgar American economy. They hit not only at Russian serfdom, but also at the then widespread slavery in America. Unmasking the myth of bourgeois democracy, they showed that the capitalist system is one of exploitation of hired labor, a system in which the elements of crying poverty of the majority of the population and the luxury of the minority are inescapable.

The task of the present work is to unmask the slanderous fabrications of the bourgeois cosmopolitans regarding the history of Russian economic thought and to show the great contribution of the latter.

The foremost spokesmen of our country have shown the greatness of the Russian people and their mighty creative powers; they have foreseen the great future of the Russian people and have struggled for the attainment of this future. Advanced Russian economists have approached the attempts and the ideas of other peoples, not as students but as thinkers and statesmen, independently and creatively developing the science to conform to the daily problems of their country.

The Great October Socialist Revolution eliminated all forms of de-

---

[12] Marx acknowledged the contribution of B. Franklin, famous American scientist and political statesman (XVIII century) in formulating the labor theory of value at the beginning stage of its development. At the same time Marx wrote that the analysis of exchange value offered by Franklin did not influence directly the general trend of economic science. Franklin examined only individual problems of political economy in connection with fixed practical motives. (See K. Marx, *K kritike politicheskoi ekonomii* [On the Criticism of Political Economy] (Moscow: Gospolitizdat, 1953), p. 46). A destructive criticism of the representatives of vulgar political economy of the XIX century, including a trivial apologist of capitalism, an American, Carey, is given in the works of Marx and of the great Russian economist Chernyshevskii.

[13] D. Hecht, *Russian Radicals Look to America* (Cambridge: Harvard University Press, 1947).

pendence of our land on the bourgeois states. The Communist party smashed the bourgeois and petty-bourgeois theories harmful to the affairs of the toilers and with them the antipopular "theory" of the dependence of Russian culture and of Russian social thought.

Interest in the history of political economy in general and in the history of national economic science in particular begins to be noticeable in Russia only in the nineteenth century. It is displayed first of all in the published works of the Russian thinkers and statesmen of the past who were occupied with economic problems. Thus in 1842 Pososhkov's *Book on Poverty and Wealth* appeared for the first time; in 1854 A. Volynskii's "Instructions" was printed in *Moskovitianin* [Moscovite]. At the same time a special literature developed in Russia, and attempts were made to show the significance of these works and the place of their authors in the development of Russian economic science, and also to compare them with the economists of other countries.

Of the Russian economists of past centuries Pososhkov has aroused great interest. Even in the nineteenth century a comparatively large Russian literature existed about him. The name of Pososhkov as an original Russian economist of the eighteenth century appears also in a number of works by foreign authors on the history of political economy (Roscher, John Ingram, L. Cosse, and others). But they remained stubbornly silent regarding Russian economists of a revolutionary tendency, especially of Radishchev.

The well-known interest in economic thought in Russia was manifested also in the fact that in the courses in political economy and the general history of political economy offered by Russian economists of the nineteenth century and in the Russian translations of foreign books on the history of political economy lists of well-known names of Western European economists and their works usually were supplemented by names and works of the most outstanding Russian economists.[14]

One of the earliest endeavors to attract atention to Russian economic thought of the past was an article in *Sovremennik* [Contemporary] for 1851 devoted to the contents of the first Russian journal, *Ezhemesiachnye sochineniia* [Monthly Works], published from 1755 to

[14] See T. Stepanov, *Zapiski o politicheskoi ekonomii* [Notes on Political Economy] (St. Petersburg: 1844), Pt. I and (Kharkov: 1848), Pt. II; I. Vernadskii, *Ocherk istorii politicheskoi ekonomii* [An Outline of the History of Political Economy] (St. Petersburg: 1858); Ad. Blanqui, *Istoriia politicheskoi ekonomii v Evrope s drevneishego do nastoiashchego vremeni* [History of Political Economy in Europe from Ancient to Present Times]. Translated from the French. (St. Petersburg: 1869), Vol. II.

1764. Here are given short notes on the articles in *Ezhemesiachnye sochineniia* concerning political economy.[15] Among those deserving "particular attention" is the short work of Rychkov, "A Correspondence Between Two Friends About Commerce."

At the same time, the first attempts at a general analysis of the history of Russian economic thought also appeared. The article by Professor V. Leshkov of Moscow University, "Ancient Russian Science Regarding National Wealth and Welfare," was published in 1855 in the jubilee collection of the university.[16] It presents a comparative analysis of three works of Russian thought of past centuries, the *Domostroi,* Poshkov's *Book on Poverty and Wealth,* and A. Volynskii's *Instructions.* This article considers the indigenous character of Russian economic thought and shows the points of similarity and difference of the three above-mentioned works and the characteristic traits of each. The article, however, has no scientific significance. Leshkov belonged to the circle of clearly expressed conservatives. His views of economic thought are full of worship of the old times, the Tsar, and the Orthodox Church. He characterizes the contents of the above-mentioned works as "true Christian philosophy."

The noble and bourgeois historiography of Russia could not create a scientific history of Russian economic thought during all of its long period of development; it was unable to conduct any sort of valuable research in the various stages of development of Russian economic thought and the individual economists. Undoubtedly this fact is connected with the servility of the ruling circles of Tsarist Russia toward the bourgeois culture of the West and their minimization of the significance of the country's science.

During the entire second half of the nineteenth century one can find in Russian literature only a few articles which mention the historical process of the development of Russian economic thought and which attempt to analyze the various stages of its development. V. A. Goltsev's article, "The Development of Russian Economic Science," printed in the third volume of the journal, *Russkaia mysl* [Russian Thought] for 1855, belongs to this type of work. The author, who later became

---

[15] See "Ocherki russkoi zhurnalistiki, preimushchestvenno staroi" [Outlines of Russian Journalism, Primarily the Ancient], *Sovremennik* [Contemporary], No. 3, Section II (1851), pp. 15–20.

[16] See *V vospominanie 12 ianvaria 1855 g. Ucheno-literaturnye stati professorov i prepodavatelei imperatorskogo Moskovskogo universiteta, izdannye po sluchaiu ego stoletnego iubileia* [In Memory of January 12, 1855. Scientific-Literary Articles of Professors and Lecturers of the Imperial Moscow University Published in Commemoration of Its One Hundredth Anniversary] (Moscow: 1855).

a well-known bourgeois figure and publicist of a liberal viewpoint, gives a running account of the condition of Russian economic science for the previous twenty years and shows the rapid growth in Russia of independent economic research. The epoch of liberation of the peasants, he notes, brought increased attention to economic problems and gave rise to writers such as Chernyshevskii, Ziber, Kovalevskii, and Chuprov, who might have occupied an honorable place even among the political economists of the West.

A work of similar nature was a series of articles under the general heading of "Contemporary Russian Economists," [17] published in *Nauchnoe obozrenie* [Scientific Review] for 1899 and 1900, written by M. Filippov, the editor of the same journal. The author examines the economic works of Ziber, the criticism by Zhukovskii of Marx, the economic views of Nikolai-on (N. Danielson), Mikhailovskii, V. V. (Vorontsov), and other narodniks, and the works of Chuprov. Filippov discloses the presence in Russian economic literature of a definite scientific tradition and a succession of original ideas. He considers one of the characteristic traits of the development of Russian economic science during the last third of the nineteenth century to be that "any outstanding writer on economic questions appearing among us from the beginning of the 1870's in one way or another had to concern himself with the teachings of Marx . . ." [18] He notes the "parallels between the development of political economy among us and in the West—parallels not excluding, of course, the individual traits of Russian science found in connection with the particular conditions of the development of social thought among us." [19]

Examining the correlation between the theories of the Russian economists of that day and the teachings of the economists of classical bourgeois political economy, the author writes: "True, even in Russian economic literature we find abundant examples of the vulgarization of political economy; but through its best representatives Russian science has always adhered to the traditions of Adam Smith and Ricardo and at the same time was already prepared to receive the teachings of Marx—at the very least in the fundamental positions." [20]

Filippov noted and examined a number of real, characteristic traits of Russian economic thought of the period and was critical of narodnik viewpoints; but his whole analysis reflected the bourgeois-objective

---

[17] See *Nauchnoe obozrenie* [Scientific Review], Nos. 7–12 (1899) and No. 3 (1900).

[18] *Ibid.*, No. 7 (1899), p. 1346.

[19] *Ibid.*, pp. 1346-7.

[20] *Ibid.*, p. 1348.

positions of "legal Marxism," of which he was a representative. Like Struve, Tugan-Baranovskii, and other "critics" of Marx, Filippov openly came out against "the dogmatism of orthodox Marxists." Truly scientific analysis of the development of Russian economic thought cannot be found in Filippov's articles.

Tugan-Baranovskii also sets forth the history of Russian economic thought in the spirit of bourgeois objectivism in a brief article in the Brockhaus and Efron *Encyclopedic Dictionary* (1899) ("Rossiia," Vol. 55). His account of the history of economic science in Russia begins with a reference to the translation of Adam Smith's *The Wealth of Nations* into Russian at the beginning of the nineteenth century. The long history of the development of Russian economic thought before the nineteenth century remains entirely out of this author's range of vision; it is, in effect, ignored. He lauds the works of lesser authorities on economic thought—Storch, Haxthausen, and others—but fails to recognize the characteristics of the representatives of Russian science. The statements of Tugan-Baranovskii on the problems of the history of Russian economic thought in the book, *The Russian Factory in Past and Present* (1898), also indicate the author's bourgeois-apologetic position.

In the twentieth century publication of, and commentary on, various works of early Russian economic thought continued. A general analysis of the development of Russian economic thought from ancient times was given in the articles of V. Sviatlovskii, then published as a collection under the title *On the History of Political Economy and Statistics in Russia* (1906).

Sviatlovskii's work is the first attempt at a systematic survey of the entire history of Russian economic science. The reader can learn from Sviatlovskii's work the names of many of the old Russian economists and the titles of their works. But his analysis of the history of Russian economic thought, torn from the real conditions of economics and of the class struggle in Russia, is entirely incorrect. Sviatlovskii examines Russian economic science primarily in the light of the "influence" on it of Western European science and tries to fit Russian economic science artificially into the scheme of development of Western European science. The class and national character of Russian economic science, its deep roots in Russian reality, its diverse importance in the historical development of Russia, and the world significance of Russian economic science are not shown by this bourgeois historian.

Some, although quite inadequate, attention to the history of our science found expression in university courses in political economy and in histories of political economy which occasionally contained chapters published in Russia on the history of Russian economic thought.[21]

During the first World War an attempt of a group of bourgeois economists (Zheleznov, Manuilov, Bulgakov, among others), uniting in the "Moscow Scientific Institute in Memory of the Nineteenth of February, 1861," to prepare for publication a separate volume on the history of Russian economic thought,[22] failed.

As a rule Western European and American bourgeois historians of political economy ignore Russian economic science. Thus in James Ingram's *History of Political Economy* Russian political economy is represented only by Pososhkov, and in Ch. Gide and Ch. Rist's *History of Economic Science* by three authors, Bakunin, Kropotkin, and Nechaev. In L. Cosse's work on the history of economic teachings of the world, Russian thought is but a meager adjunct to the economic thought of the Scandinavian and Hungarian peoples, and the very reference has the character of a bibliographical note.[23]

The history of Russian economic thought of the nineteenth and twentieth centuries is presented in a false light in the work, *Contemporary Economic Theory,* published in Vienna under the direction of Hans Meier. Two articles from this collective multi-volume work by bourgeois economists are devoted to Russian economic thought: one of them (by Professor Zheleznov) gives a quite cursory and superficial survey of Russian economic thought from the beginning of the nineteenth century; [24] another (by Professor Ivantsov) is devoted to the state of economic theories in the USSR after the October Revolution.[25] The sparse modern foreign literature on the history of Russian economic thought usually presents a greatly distorted picture.

During the first years after the Great October Socialist Revolution we gave little attention to the study of the history of Russian economic thought. In 1923 the revised book of V. Sviatlovskii, *The History of Economic Ideas in Russia,* was published, and it reproduced all of the basic errors of the author's previous works.

---

[21] See I. Ivaniukov, *Politicheskaia ekonomiia kak uchenie o protsesse razvitiia ekonomicheskikh iavlenni* [Political Economy as a Study of the Process of Development of Economic Phenomena] (Moscow: 1891); A. A. Manuilov, *Politicheskaia ekonomiia* [Political Economy] (1st edition, Moscow: 1914).

[22] V. Ia. Zheleznov and A. A. Manuilov, ed. *Istoriia ekonomicheskoi mysli* [History of Economic Thought] (1st edition, Moscow: 1916), Foreword to Vol. I.

[23] See L. Cosse, *Istoriia ekonomicheskikh uchenii* [History of Economic Teachings] (1900), pp. 385-6, 392-7.

[24] See *Die Wirtschaftstheorie der Gegenwart* [Contemporary Economic Theories] (Vienna: 1927), Part I.

[25] See *ibid.,* (Vienna, 1928), Part IV.

In the 1930's, the works of Pososhkov, N. I. Turgenev, Flerovskii, Ziber, Chernyshevskii, and other Russian economists of the past were republished in the USSR. Studies of these and of other Russian economists appeared. Attempts were made toward Marxist illumination of the development of Russian economic thought for the various periods of Russian history and the inclusion of Russian economic thought in a general course on the history of political economy. But, as mentioned above, in the understanding of the nature and significance of Russian economic science of the past those Soviet economists who especially occupied themselves with the study for a long time retained harmful, anti-national positions of servility and grovelling before the bourgeois economic science of the West, and they lowered and underestimated the significance of Russian economic science.

The unmasking and crushing by the Communist party of the harmful ideology of bourgeois cosmopolitanism and the false theories of the "importation" into Russia of Western European teachings put the study of the history of Russian economic thought on the right track at last—theoretically and politically.

During recent years Soviet economists have published a number of works on various outstanding Russian economists of the past. These works, based on concrete materials, indicate the great significance of Russian economic thought and its role in the life of the Russian people and in world economic science.

There is an urgent need for writings which will give a Marxist-Leninist analysis of the development of the entirety of Russian economic thought during its long history.

The present work is devoted to the study of the history of the economic thought of the Russian people. Russian economic science has developed in close connection with the economic thought of other peoples of the USSR, and it is necessary to study the history of economic thought of the Ukrainian, White Russian, Georgian, Armenian, and other peoples to show the mutual ties and the influence which advanced Russian revolutionary thought has had on the development of economic thought among the other peoples of the Soviet Union, thus allowing the creation of a scientific history of the economic thought of the entire great Soviet people.

PART I
THE PERIOD OF EARLY FEUDALISM

CHAPTER 1. *Economic Thought in Kievan Rus and Its Class Differentiation.*

The Economy of Kievan Rus. The Class Structure of Society.

The formation of the Kievan state was preceded by a long history of the Slavic peoples in the eastern expanses of Europe. The eastern Slavs lived in a primitive-communal order which gradually declined. The process of decomposition of this order began long before the ninth century. Even before the formation of the Kievan state there were state combinations of various eastern Slavic tribes, which were formed as a result of the decomposition of the primitive-communal order and the division of the population into classes. In the ninth century, feudal means of production were already in existence. During this same century the feudal Kievan state was formed.

The basic occupation of the population of Kievan Rus was agriculture. Soil cultivation played the leading role, particularly in the southern and central regions of the country, where wheat, rye, millet, barley, oats, hemp, and flax were grown. The population also engaged in cattle herding, apiculture, hunting, and fishing. Hunting was most widespread in the forested regions of the north.[1]

[1] See *Ocherki istorii SSSR. Period feodalizma. IX-XV vv.* [Outlines of the History of the USSR. Period of Feudalism, IX-XV centuries] (Moscow: Academy of Sciences USSR, 1953), Pt. I; *Istoriia kultury drevnei Rusi* [History of the Culture of Ancient Rus] (Moscow-Leningrad: Academy of Sciences USSR, 1948); B. D. Grekov, *Kievskaia Rus* [Kievan Rus] (Moscow: Uchpedgiz, 1949); P. I. Liashchenko, *Istoriia narodnogo khoziaistva SSSR* [History of the National Economy of the USSR] (Moscow: Gospolitizdat, 1952), Vol. I; N. Aristov, *Promyshlennost drevnei Rusi* [Industry of Ancient Rus] (St. Petersburg: 1866). Hereafter publications of the Academy of Sciences will be documented: AS USSR.

The small-scale production of industrial goods [2] was relatively widely developed for that time. Ore was extracted from bogs, iron was smelted by craftsmen in special furnaces—with the draft supplied by hand bellows (finery iron)—and there was domestic production of iron in ordinary cooking stoves. Blacksmiths produced agricultural tools, instruments for craftsmen, household utensils, and arms. High craftsmanship was achieved in Kievan Rus in jewelry making, and pottery making was widely developed. Eastern Slavs were familiar with the making of glass and glass wares; tanning, weaving, and wood and stone working also were developed.

The transition of the eastern Slavs from the primitive-communal to the feudal system occurred through the development of more productive methods. The old hand-tilling type of agriculture was replaced by the plow. From the seventh and eighth centuries they began to use horses as draft animals. As a result of this new productivity, a process of disintegration of the clan order began; private ownership arose and developed, and society divided into classes. During this period the level of development of productive forces was higher among the Eastern European Slavs than in the slave-owning societies. The eastern Slavs passed from the primitive-communal state to the feudal, bypassing the slave-owning stage of development. They took an active part in the struggle with the slave-owning world. Slave labor was widespread in Kievan Rus, but slave-owning relationships were not dominant.

The productive relationships in Kievan Rus were more progressive not only in comparison with the primitive-communal, but also with the slave-owning order. They corresponded to the nature and level of development of means of production, aided their further development, and gave ample scope to their growth.

The bulk of the rural population of Kievan Rus was made up of the *smerdy,* or small husbandmen. These were divided into two groups: one was independent, had its own tools, possessed parcels of land, and had its own households; the other group had lost its independence and had fallen under the domination of the big landowners.

Originally all smerdy were free farmers and were organized in communes. In time the communal lands which they used were declared the property of the Grand Prince and were considered *"okniazhennoi,"* and the smerdy began to fulfill various obligations of the feudal state. Gradually they lost their economic independence and became dependent on the big landowners, who enslaved them. By the eleventh

[2] See B. A. Rybakov, *Remeslo drevnei Rusi* [Crafts of Ancient Rus] (Moscow: AS USSR, 1948).

century a considerable number of the smerdy had already lost their independence.[3]

There were various forms and degrees of feudal enslavement in Kievan Rus. The feudally dependent people included, for example, the so-called *"riadovichi," "zakupy," "izgoi,"* and *"kholopy"* (not *"obel'nye,"* or complete kholopy, who were personal slaves). The riadovichi were bondsmen working for a master in accordance with a legally formulated agreement, *"riad."* A variety of riadovichi were the so-called "zakupy." These were the recent smerdy, deprived of the means of production and forced to seek earnings from big landowners. The *"kupa"* was a sum of money which the zakup received from the master upon concluding an agreement with him. The zakup performed various kinds of work for the master. If he wanted to leave, his pay was to be returned.[4] The zakup who tried to flee from his master became a kholop. Izgoiy were former kholopy—personal slaves, who, after voluntary release or redemption, became feudal-dependent people. They were bound to an owner and to the soil.[5]

The Kievan state was a feudal state corresponding to the early stages of development of a fedual society. Being a superstructure, it aided the strengthening of its base of feudal productive relations. The foundation of feudal productive relations is the feudalists' possession of land, which under feudalism is the most important means of production. In developed feudalism there is also partial ownership by the feudalist of the worker—the bound serf, whom the feudalist can buy and sell.

Alongside feudal ownership are the individual peasants and craftsmen owning their own tools of production and their own private homesteads, based on individual labor.

In the feudal system of economy the immediate producer—the peasant—is allotted the means of production, including land, and he is bound to the soil. The peasant who was allotted land had to be personally dependent on the landowner. Thus the system of feudal economy gives rise to "extra-economic compulsion," serfdom, legal dependence, inequality, and so forth.[6]

As in all other countries where the feudal order prevailed, particularly in the early stages of development, the economy in Kievan Rus

---

[3] See B. D. Grekov, *Krestiane na Rusi s drevneishikh vremen do XVII veka* [Peasants in Rus from Ancient Times to the XVII Century]. 2nd ed. (Moscow: AS USSR, 1952), Bk. I: *Ocherki istorii SSSR,* Pt. I.

[4] See Grekov, *Krestiane na Rusi,* p. 179.

[5] *Ibid.,* pp. 220–1.

[6] Lenin, *Sochineniia,* XV, 66.

was basically natural, and the products produced by agriculture were directly consumed by the peasants and the feudalists who exploited them.

The feudal exploitation of the peasantry was based mainly on the primitive "working out of rents." As Marx wrote, worked-out rent occurred "when the direct producer works on the land actually belonging to him one part of the week, with the aid of instruments of production (plow, livestock, and so on) belonging to him actually or legally, and the remaining days of the week works for nothing on the estate of the landowner, for the landowner . . ."[7] The product of the dependent peasant's surplus labor went in its natural form to the land's proprietor—the feudal lord—and satisfied the needs of the lordly manor.

Although both agriculture and farm products had basically a natural character, Kievan Rus had also a considerably developed trade, both domestic and foreign, and there was trade and money lending. Russian merchants exported honey, wax, and furs to Byzantium and other countries and purchased there gold, expensive carpets, wine, spices, and arms. Russian merchants also purchased goods in the West for resale in the eastern lands. The rivers crossing the East European plain formed important highways for the international trade of the time, first with Arabia and then with Byzantium.

In the period from the eighth to the tenth century the eastern Slavs carried on extensive trade with the Arabs, mainly along the Volga and its tributaries. Beginning with the ninth century, the new trade route "from the Varangians to the Greeks," that is, from the Baltic to the Black Sea, acquired great importance. Internal trade existed mainly in the form of small and scattered local markets.

Towns began to rise among the eastern Slavs even before the formation of the Kievan state, mainly along the water routes from the Baltic to the Black Sea. Among them were Novgorod, Beloozero, Smolensk, Kiev, Liubech, Pereiaslavl', Chernigov, and others. Kievan princes built many new fortified towns: Ladoga, Iziaslavl', Belgorod, Suzdal', Murom, Iaroslavl', and Vladimir-on-Kliazma, among others. The towns were settled by military people, artisans, and tradesmen. Kiev, the capital of the government and the trading center of the country, and Novgorod, a rich trading city with well developed crafts, became particularly important.

After the adoption of Christianity, large church and monastery land acquisitions began in Kievan Rus, the result of princely gifts to the churches and monasteries and other means. Along with the exploita-

[7] Marx, *Kapital,* III, 802.

tion of the people by feudalists, there existed also that by the merchants and money lenders, particularly of the town population.

The growth of feudal exploitation inevitably produced class struggle, which often took the form of violence such as the well known uprising of the Drevliani in 945, the popular uprisings of 996, the uprising in the Suzdal' land in 1024, in Kiev in 1068, in the Rostov land in 1071, in Kiev and its vicinity in 1113. The struggle of the popular masses against feudal exploitation was interwoven with the struggle against money lenders, merchants, and princely rule.

The Kievan state in its most flourishing period (tenth to eleventh centuries) was one of the two mightiest states of the early Middle Ages (the second was the empire of Charlemagne) and in extent was the largest state in Europe. It had enormous historical significance. "Just as the empire of Charlemagne preceded the formation of France, Germany, and Italy, so the empire of the Ruriks preceded the formation of Poland, Lithuania, the Baltic colonies, Turkey, and the state of Moscow itself," wrote Marx.[8]

The epoch of Kievan Rus witnessed a great rise of Russian culture. United in the Kievan state, the Russians emerged as a great people, an equal participant in the economic and political life of all Europe, an active participant in the creation of a world culture.

Economic Concepts of the Eastern Slavs

In Russia, as in all other countries, economic thought developed along with the development of productive relations, social contradictions, and class struggle. For a long time it existed not as a particular, clearly limited field of ideology, but in inseparable connection with the religious views of the people, their legal concepts, and so forth. Therefore the economic thought of ancient Russia has to be studied in general historical writings—chronicles, treaties, princely edicts, *Russkaia Pravda,* church literature, and in the various forms of oral and written works of the people.

From the dawn of human society the knowledge of people has been determined by their social surroundings, in which the deciding role is played by the conditions of material life, primarily by the means of production of material goods. Thought and language themselves arose in connection with the collective labor of people, on the basis of labor. Therefore the economic ideas of people and their perception in one way or another of the conditions of their economic activity are al-

[8] Karl Marx, *Secret Diplomatic History of the Eighteenth Century* (London: 1899), p. 75.

ready related to the very earliest stages of the development of society.

As with other forms of ideology, economic concepts, ideas, and theories are not connected directly with production and the productive activity of man, but through means of the base, that is, of the economic system and of the joint productive relations of the given society. Economic concepts, ideas, and theories are formed under the direct influence of productive relations, class struggle, and the actions of state authority.

In the undeveloped condition of material production and economic relationships of people in primitive society, the ideas of people concerning their mutual relations in the process of the production of material goods, just as with all their other notions and ideas, are determined by conditions of material life, by means of production of material goods, more directly than in the later, higher levels of social development. Marx and Engels stated that "the creation of ideas, concepts and knowledge at first are directly interrelated with the material activity and communality of the people; it is therefore the language of real life. At this stage of development, ideas and spiritual ties flow directly from the material relationships of the people." [9]

The economic concepts of people were bound up inseparably with the general awareness of people of their immediate environment, with their realization of their limiting ties with other peoples and things, and with their view of nature as a strange, all-powerful and unconquerable force.

The first form of the ideas of people about the external world, and in significant degree about their society, was animism. Man, powerless before the forces of nature, did not distinguish himself from them. He spiritualized them, identified himself with them, and believed that the world around him was peopled by supernatural forces. Later, with the emergence of clan organization, primitive religion unfolded in the form of totemism, magic, the cult of nature, the cult of ancestors, and in other forms.

"Every type of religion," wrote Engels, "appears as nothing other than a fantastic reflection in the minds of people of those external forces which rule over them in their daily life—a reflection in which terrestrial forces assume the form of the celestial. In the beginning of history the objects of this reflection are first of all the forces of nature . . . But soon, along with the forces of nature, appear also social forces . . ." [10]

---

[9] K. Marx and F. Engels, *Nemetskaia ideologiia* [German Ideology] (Moscow: Partizdat, 1934), p. 16.

[10] F. Engels, *Anti-Düring* (Moscow: Gospolitizdat, 1953), p. 299.

Primitive religion was also a reflection of the form of the economic ideas of people, ideas which typified the extreme weakness of mankind before the forces of nature. As a consequence, the original form of the collective production of material goods came into being.

Kievan Rus was a feudal society which arose as a result of the decline of the primitive-communal order. Therefore, not only for centuries immediately preceding the formation of the Kievan state, but in the period of the Kievan state itself, the economic notions of the eastern Slavs were still strongly influenced by the religion of primitive society.

The close connection of the ideas of the people with their productive activity appears graphically in the pagan outlook of the eastern Slavs and also in the monuments of Russian folklore of the period of Kievan Rus. The pagan religion of the eastern Slavs, like religions of other peoples in early stages of development, was characterized by worship of the forces of nature. The weak development of productive forces, the low level of the productivity of labor, and the enormous dependence on the blind forces of nature all led to the deification of nature and homage to it.

The pre-Christian religion of the Slavs was based on the cult of agriculture. The main gods were the sun and the earth. After the adoption of Christianity the cult of agriculture was preserved, but appeared in another form: for example, spring was portrayed as the Mother of God, arriving on a wooden plow at the Feast of the Annunciation (March 25); "Saints" Elijah, George, and Michael replaced the former heathen gods, the protectors of agricultural labor, the patrons of the farmer.[11] Further, the ceremonies, songs, and holidays of the ancient heathen Slavs were to a significant degree connected with agriculture.

The dependence of people on the blind forces of nature caused them to aspire to assist their labor by influencing nature through various types of ceremonies, incantations, and songs. Of such a character, for example, were the ceremonies of singing magic wishes during the winter caroling and the songs of spring, summer, and fall. Many Russian games received names connected with various labor processes—"to sow millet," "to spool yarn," "to weave," and so forth.[12]

The religious beliefs of the Slavs were connected also with industry

---

[11] See N. M. Nikolskii, *Istoriia russkoi tserkvi* [History of the Russian Church], 2nd ed. (Moscow-Leningrad: 1931), pp. 50–1 ff.; E. V. Anichkov, *Iazychestvo i drevniaia Rus* [Paganism and Ancient Rus] (St. Petersburg: 1914), Chapt. XII; *Istoriia kultury drevnei Rusi,* Chapt. III.

[12] See *Istoriia russkoi literatury* [History of Russian Literature] (Moscow-Leningrad: AS USSR, 1941), I, 224–5; *Istoriia kultury drevnei Rusi,* II, Chapter V.

and crafts. Some researchers maintain that the goddess Mokosh', established in Kiev by Vladimir, was considered the protectress of spinning and weaving.[13] Many beliefs and ceremonies were connected with blacksmithing. Blacksmiths were considered unusual people, sorcerers, and their protector was the heathen god Svarog; (later Svarog was transformed into the Christian "saints," Kuz'ma and Dem'ian).[14] The heathen god Volos (Veles) was the "cattle god," the protector of cattle. With the spread of Christianity in Rus, Volos became Vlasiia. On the basis of the fact that where Volos is mentioned in the early chronicles the word *"skot"* is still used in the designation of money, Kliuchevskii puts forth the theory that Volos might also have been the god of wealth.[15] This proposal seems plausible. Because Volos was the god of wealth and trade, his image stood in Kiev in the market, the Podole. It is possible that the Slavic merchants—the "guests," described by the Arabic writers Ibn-Rusta (Ibn-Dasta) and Ibn-Fadlan, among others—prayed to this god.[16]

Fairy tales were also developed in antiquity. Their ideas according to M. Gorkii, "resulted from the aspiration of the ancient working people to lighten their labors, to increase their productivity, to arm themselves against four-legged and two-legged enemies and, by the power of words, by means of 'charms' and 'incantations,' to influence the elemental, hostile phenomena of nature." [17] In the tales and songs which have come down to us "we hear the echoes of works on the domestication of animals, the discovery of medicinal herbs, and the invention of the tools of labor." [18] The dreams of people to lighten their toil produced the "flying carpet" and the "quick shoemaker." The tale about Vasilisa the Wise, of the possibility of sewing in one

---

[13] See A. Afanasev, *Poeticheskie vozzreniia slavian na prirodu* [Poetic Views of the Slavs on Nature] (Moscow: 1868), II, 266–7; *Pamiatniki tserkovno-uchitelnoi literatury* [Monuments of Religious-Educational Literature] (St. Petersburg: 1897), Issue III, pp. 195–9, 316–20; Anichkov, *op. cit.*, pp. 313–5, 327; *Istoriia kultury drevnei Rusi*, II, 69.

[14] *Ibid.*, II, 70–99; Anichkov, *op. cit.*, pp. 291–2.

[15] See V. Kliuchevskii, *Kurs russkoi istorii* [The Course of Russian History] (Moscow: Sotsekgiz, 1937), Pt. I, p. 114.

[16] See D. A. Khvolson, *Izvestiia o khozarakh, burtasakh, bolgarakh, madiarakh, slavianakh i rusakh Ibn-Dasta* [Reports About the Khazars, Burtasy, Bulgars, Magyars, Slavs and Russians by Ibn-Dast] (St. Petersburg: 1869), p. 31; *Puteshestvie Ibn-Fadlana na Volgu* [Ibn-Fadlan's Travels Along the Volga] (Moscow-Leningrad: AS USSR, 1939), pp. 79–80. See also *Ocherki istorii SSSR*, I, 104.

[17] M. Gorkii, "O literature. Literaturno-kriticheskie stati" [On Literature. Literary-critical Articles], *Sovetskii pisatel* [Soviet Writer] (Moscow: 1953), pp. 693–4.

[18] *Ibid.*, p. 693.

night an enormous amount of cloth, is connected with the invention of spinning wheels and primitive hand looms.[19]

The worship of the elemental forces of nature and the cults of agriculture and handicrafts were inseparably connected with the work and economic activity of the people and were the earliest forms of economic ideas of the eastern Slavs. These ideas were still primitive. They reflected the low level of development of the productive forces of society and the undeveloped nature of social relations.

The Principles of Economic Policy of the Kievan Princes

In the study of the social thought of ancient Rus the chronicles have great significance. They are a very rich source of information, not only of living conditions in ancient Rus, but of political ideas and concepts and the ideology of the Russian people. The viewpoints of the compilers of chronicles serve as one of the most important sources for the study of the history of the development of the ideology of Russian society. The chronicles are permeated with the spirit of ardent patriotism; they glorify the Russian people and constantly put forth the idea of the necessity of their solidarity for a common struggle against external foes.

The chronicles are also significant for the study of Russian economic thought. True, the events of economic life occupy a modest place in the chronicles; they are lost in the abundant material about the political life of the country, military events, the genealogy of the Russian princes, the history of the Russian Church, and other subjects. In the chronicles we are informed of the concluding of treaties by the princes and the exacting of tribute from the population. There are descriptions of the country's economic condition, for example, of famine and other misfortunes suffered by the people. In the Novgorod chronicle there are numerous mentions of crop failures, severe shortages of bread, and, in connection with this, sharp rises in the price of bread.[20] Descriptions in the chronicles of the economic measures of the Russian princes give some material for judging the economic ideas of those times.

The division of society into classes and the rise and development of the state were also responsible for class differences in the economic

---

[19] *Ibid.*

[20] See *Novgorodskaia pervaia letopis starshego i mladshego izvodov* [Early and Late Editions of the First Novgorod Chronicle] (Moscow-Leningrad: AS USSR, 1950).

views of the Russian people. With the rise and development of the Kievan state, there appears and develops the field of economic thought, directly connected with the economic policy of the state.

One of the earlier tasks of the economic policy of the princes was the problem of finding means to support the court and military retinue and to carry on warfare. These means were collected from the population in the form of tribute and *obrok.* The chronicles are full of references to the exaction of tribute by the Kievan princes from the various conquered Slavic tribes. Quite early, however, the Kievan princes learned that abuse of the collection of tribute was at their own peril, that it was necessary to set up definite organized forms of taxation. [Prince Igor, attempting to collect tribute twice in succession, was killed by the angry Drevliani]. Princess Olga was subsequently forced to reorganize and regularize the taking of tribute. As the chronicler puts it, after pacifying the Drevliani, Olga went about their land and set up "laws, quit-rents, and tributes," [21] that is, she determined the amount of the tributes and the terms and place of their payment by the people. According to the chronicle, tribute was paid on plows and on households.

To fill their treasury, the Kievan princes employed the right of vengeance inherited from the primitive system, at first on a limited, but after a time on a full, scale; the prince received the *vira,* i.e., fine for killing a man, and the so-called *prodazha,* a fine for other crimes.

In the eleventh century, the princes also took customs duties. They levied various obligations in kind on the people, and they forced them to work on the construction of fortifications and other projects. In the ninth and tenth centuries the Kievan princes sometimes transferred their right to collect tributes from the population of certain lands to vassal princes and the military retinue. Marx characterized this system of relationships in Kievan Russia as vassal dependence without fiefs (fees), consisting of only the payment of tributes.[22]

Questions of tax policy occupied an important place in the economic activity of the Kievan princes. The organization of the monetary system and the circulation of money also entered into their economic policy. In Kievan Rus money was coined from silver and gold. The beginning of coinage of gold money in Russia is connected with the name of the Kievan prince Vladimir (the First). Silver money of large denomination was coined in Kievan Rus hundreds of years earlier than in Western Europe, and the coining of gold began much earlier than

---

[21] See *Povest vremennykh let* [The Tale of Bygone Years] (Moscow-Leningrad: AS USSR, 1950), Pt. I, p. 43.

[22] Marx, *Secret Diplomatic History,* p. 76.

in England and Germany.[23] The attempt of the Kievan princes to coin their own money and to introduce a uniform monetary system was directed, along with their other measures, toward the strengthening of the Kievan state and its unity.[24] The active policy of the Kievan princes in the field of money economy is also shown in the prohibition by Vladimir Monomakh's son, Prince Mstislav the Great, of the export of gold and silver from the country.[25]

The economic policy of Kievan princes also encompassed the field of trade. Questions of foreign trade interested the Kievan princes above all from the point of view of safeguarding their own interests and those of their military retinue. Part of the products received by the princes from levies on the people were exchanged and sold in other countries. In the treaties concluded by the Kievan princes with the Greeks (the treaties of Oleg in 907 and 911, Igor in 944, and Sviatoslav in 971) questions of trade occupied first place. These treaties testify to the fact that the Kievan princes wanted to set up permanent and regularized relations on a basis of complete equality with the most influential state of that time, Byzantium. The military expeditions to Constantinople were motivated in large degree by the wish to obtain the best conditions for Rus in trade with Byzantium and other countries. Prince Sviatoslav wanted to establish himself on the Danube in the city of Pereiaslavets, a very convenient trade center, "Where all riches are concentrated: gold, silks, wine, and various fruits from Greece, silver and horses from Hungary and Bohemia, and from Rus furs, wax, honey, and slaves." [26]

The treaties of the Kievan princes with Byzantium strictly defined the nature of trade relations. They strengthened the privileges of the Russian princes in this commerce, clearly foresaw the economic interests of the trading participants, and set down provisions which were designed to prevent clashes between the Russian and Greek peoples in the discharge of their trade operations. The treaties established a procedure for safeguarding goods salvaged from shipwrecks, the compulsory return of fugitives and kidnapped serfs to their masters, the administration of the estates of those who died abroad, and other ques-

---

[23] See F. I. Mikhalevskii, *Ocherki istorii deneg i denezhnogo obrashcheniia* [Outlines of the History of Money and Money Circulation] (Moscow: Gosfinizdat, 1948), pp. 239–40; A. V. Oreshnikov, *Denezhnye znaki domongolskoi Rusi* [Money Symbols of the Pre-Mongol Rus] *Trudy Gosudarstvennogo istoricheskogo muzeia* [Works of the State Historical Museum] (Moscow: 1936).

[24] See *Istoriia kultury drevnei Rusi,* I, 387.

[25] See *Istoricheskii arkhiv* [Historical Archives] (Moscow: AS USSR, 1951), VII, 412.

[26] *Povest vremennykh let,* I, 48.

tions connected with foreign trade relations. The treaty of 907 proclaimed the right of Russians to trade freely with the Greeks with no payment of duties or taxes on anything.[27]

The interests of the treasury forced the Kievan princes to encourage and to regulate the trade of the Rus with other peoples. Thus in 1006 the Kievan prince Vladimir concluded a trade treaty with the Volga Bulgars. In this treaty the Bulgar merchants were permitted by a special "seal" from the prince to trade in all the towns on the Oka and Volga, and Russian merchants with seals from the "viceroys" could go freely to the Bulgars to buy and sell goods. The Bulgar merchants were allowed to trade with the Russian merchants only in the towns; they were forbidden to go to the villages and trade with *tiunami, virnikami, ognishchanami,* and smerdy.[28] Prince Mstislav the Great not only forbade the export of gold and silver from the state, but placed a duty on the import of arms and also issued a mercantile code for the Novgorodians.[29]

As the literary monuments of the epoch testify, several Kievan princes interfered very actively in trading affairs to advance their own personal interests. Outstanding in this regard was Sviatopolk (1093-1113). For example, by not admitting merchants with salt from Galich and Peremyshl he caused a shortage of salt in the country and a sharp rise in its price. Sviatopolk then appropriated for himself the salt monopoly.[30] He also traded in grain.

The agricultural policy of the Kievan princes and the relations between the ruling and the exploited classes of society had particular significance. The process of the development of feudal relations in Kievan Rus was completed, of course, through the workings of economic laws in the development of society. But in this process the economic policy of the Kievan princes also played an important role by hastening it and giving it legal sanction and form. The princes appropriated territory for themselves. Land with smerdy living on it was organized and distributed to their *druzhennik-boyars.* [In time, druzhenniki were settled on the land to become landed aristocrats (boyars).] The prince and the boyars carried on the economy with the work of *"cheliad,"* kholopy (slaves), dependent smerdy, izgoiy, and

---

[27] *Ibid.,* I, 25.

[28] See V. N. Tatishchev, *Istoriia Rossiiskaia* [Russian History] (Moscow: 1773), Bk. II, pp. 88–9.

[29] *Istoricheskii arkhiv,* VII, 412.

[30] See "Paterik Kievskogo Pecherskogo monastyria" [Paterikon of the Kiev-Crypt Monastery], *Pamiatniki Slaviansko-russkoi pismennosti* [Monuments of Slavic-Russian Literature] (St. Petersburg: 1911), pp. 108, 207–8.

other dependent people. More and more the possession of land was concentrated in the hands of the monasteries and churches.

The dependence of the exploited upon the feudalists, based on feudal ownership of the land, was strengthened by the ruling power representing the interests of the big landowners, the princes and boyars. The extra-economic compulsion to work—the use of the forced labor of kholopy, dependent smerdy, and others—demanded state interference in the relations between the feudalist and the exploited worker. The state put down attempts at resistance by the exploited and issued laws guaranteeing the daily exploitation of their labor by the feudalists. This assistance to large feudal landowners, both secular and church, played an important part in the economic policy of the Kievan princes.

The scarcity of historical documents makes it impossible to paint a complete picture of the viewpoints and principles of the economic policy of the various Kievan princes; the chronicles give only a fragmentary account. Of the Kievan Prince Vladimir (the First) the chronicler states that he loved his *druzhina* and consulted it on "matters of administration, wars, and government." [31] Under Yaroslav, (Vladimir's son) appears the first written Russian civil code—*Russkaia Pravda* (short edition). With the name of Vladimir Monomakh are associated a number of new and important articles of *Russkaia Pravda* having to do with purchases and interest. The most significant of the literary works left by him, the *"Pouchenie"* ("Testament") contains several interesting economic ideas.

The "Pouchenie" of Vladimir Monomakh portrays a form of ideal ruler and gives instruction on how to rule. The author exhorts his children to love work, to look after everything, not counting on others, and to learn what one does not know. The druzhina of the prince must be considerate toward the people of its country and not ruin them. "When journeying anywhere by road through your domain, do not permit your followers to harm your own or the people of others be they in villages or fields so that they will not curse you." [32] Particular attention should be given to "guests." "Wherever you go, as often as you halt, give the beggar something to eat and to drink. Furthermore, honor the stranger, if not with a gift, at least with food and drink, whensoever he comes to you, be he simple or noble or an emissary. For travellers give a man a universal reputation as generous or nig-

---

[31] *Povest vremennykh let,* I, 86.

[32] "Pouchenie" [Instruction]—See A. S. Orlov, *Vladimir Monomakh* (Moscow-Leningrad: AS USSR, 1946), p. 139.

gardly."[33] In the "Pouchenie" there is counsel of broad social significance, not to forget the poor, the orphan and the widow: "Permit the mighty to destroy no man."[34] This same motif is repeated in a more definite form in which the author uses himself as an example: "I did not allow the mighty to distress the smerd or the poverty-stricken widow; I interested myself in church administration and service."[35] Taking upon himself the role of a protector of the smerdy, Vladimir Monomakh had in view, evidently, his legislative activity, expressed in the supplement to the *Russkaia Pravda* containing new articles on loans and interest. The true meaning of this "care" of the Kievan prince for the smerdy will be described below.

The Economic Ideas in Russkaia Pravda

Russkaia Pravda is an outstanding monument of Russian social thought of the Kievan Rus period. It also has great significance for the study of economic thought. The numerous copies of the text which have come down to us are divided into two groups different in form and content. Among scholars, one of these collections has received the title of the "Short Pravda," and the other, the "Extensive Pravda."[36]

Russkaia Pravda was not compiled all at once but was developed over several centuries. In part it reflects the customary law of the eastern Slavs, and in part it is the fruit of the legislation of the princes. The latter is noted directly in the chronicles, where the text of this code of ancient laws was written.[37] One of the parts of *Russkaia Pravda,* the so-called Yaroslav's Pravda, appeared in the 1030's; another part, the Pravda of Yaroslav's Descendants, in the 1070's. The articles of the "Code of Vladimir Vsevolodich" belong around 1113.

Marx stressed that "both political and civil laws have always only reflected and borne out the demands of economic relations."[38] Such an example was *Russkaia Pravda,* which was the codified civil law of the Kievan state. This most valuable historical document not only ac-

---

[33] *Ibid.*

[34] *Ibid.,* p. 137.

[35] *Ibid.,* p. 149.

[36] The third edition of the text known as the *Abbreviated Pravda* has been preserved. Most scholars consider it to be an excerpt from the *Extensive Pravda* while some view it as an independent edition of *Pravda Russkaia* along with the *Short Pravda* and *Extensive Pravda.* (See M. N. Tikhomirov, *Issledovanie o Russkoi Pravde* [*Studies About Russian Pravda*] (Moscow-Leningrad: AS USSR, 1941), pp. 183–7.

[37] B. D. Grekov, *ed. Pravda Russkaia. Teksty* [Russian Pravda. Texts] (Moscow-Leningrad: 1940), I, 402, 403, 424 ff.

[38] K. Marx and F. Engels, *Sochineniia* [Works] (Moscow: 1953), V, 342.

quaints us with the legal ideas, norms, and organization of the court in Kievan Rus, but it also gives the modern scholar a wealth of material on the economic and political structure of society, ideas, and concepts of that time. *Russkaia Pravda* reflects most completely the economic ideas of the ruling social class in Kievan Rus, which expressed in legislation its understanding of economic and social questions and defended its class interests with all its might.

The central place in *Russkaia Pravda* is occupied by the questions of economic and property relationships: the determination of responsibility for crimes in this field—theft, breaking of field boundaries, and others—and also the establishment of norms for types of property relations—for loans, inheritance of property, and others.

If separate articles of *Russkaia Pravda* are grouped by their content, almost half of the articles of the Short Pravda—twenty out of forty-two—refer to the responsibility for violation of the right of property and other questions of an economic character. Of the 121 articles of the Extensive Pravda, eighty-seven articles are devoted to economic problems. This testifies to the increased attention in the legislation of Kievan Rus to problems of an economic nature. The articles of *Russkaia Pravda* speak of the preservation and guarantee of the right of property ownership, of slaves and persons of a semi-slave status, and first and foremost of the protection of the property of the princes and the feudal hierarchy and the guarantee of their right to exploit the labor of others.

The explicit fiscal role of the princely court in Kievan Rus is striking. The "vira" and "prodazha"—monetary fines for crimes against individuals and property—were established after the prohibition of blood vengeance and stipulated that the guilty had to pay fines to the prince. On rare occasions the guilty had to pay the injured party for the "insult." [39]

The state authority in the person of the Kievan princes guarded vigilantly the private property of the ruling classes. *Russkaia Pravda* served as a weapon for the defense of the interests of the exploiters. A "servant [cheliadin] was looked upon in *Russkaia Pravda* as the prop-

[39] "Concern about the prince and his revenues runs through the entire text of the 'Extensive Pravda' . . . A memorial like 'Extensive Pravda' was designated not only to regulate the legal practice of ancient Rus, but primarily to protect the interests of the prince. The interests of ancient society, which was familiar with the payments for 'insult' reflected in 'Ancient Pravda,' were relegated to secondary place in the 'Extensive Pravda' behind the interests of the prince and the princely administration. Intensified attention to high vira and prodazha are main characteristics of the 'Extensive Pravda,' " justly writes Tikhomirov, *op. cit.*, p. 219.

erty of the lord on a level with livestock and inanimate objects, and a definite fine was set for the theft of a servant or for the concealment of a fugitive servant.[40] A number of articles of the "Extensive Pravda" are dedicated to the protection of land ownership and land holding; these articles define the responsibility for the violation of field boundaries and markers. The "Extensive Pravda" also devotes great attention to the order of inheritance.

In eight articles of *Russkaia Pravda* mention is made of loans and interest, the preservation and order of guaranteeing the property interests of the creditor, the conditions under which the demand of the return of the loan has legal force, the order for exacting payment of debts, and similar subjects. Money lending, as is evident, was quite widespread in Kievan Rus. Credit relations here are called *"dolog"* and interest *"rez."* The establishing of a money loan is designated as the giving of *"kun v rez"* (Article 50). Money given in loan for interest, in *Russkaia Pravda,* bears the term *"isto"* (in the text of the other edition, *"istoe"*) (Article 53). Besides money loans, *Russkaia Pravda* discusses debt obligations in natural produce: *"nastav v med," "zhito v prisop"* (in another edition, *"vo prosop"*), the payment in products with the condition that they be returned with interest (Article 50).[41]

It is interesting to note that *Russkaia Pravda* also defines the amount of the "rez," that is, the percent of interest on a money loan (Articles 51 and 53). Article 53, called the "Code of Vladimir Vsevolodich," mentions that Prince Vladimir (Vladimir Monamakh) gathered his druzhina in Berestov, and at this meeting it was declared that the money lender, lending his money for interest, *"v tret' kuny,"* had the right to collect this interest only twice, after which he could receive only his capital, the money loaned. If the lender received such interest three times he lost the right to receive his capital from the debtor. To take interest in the sum of ten kun out of a *grivna* per year was not forbidden.[42]

Consequently, the maximum amount of interest was defined by law. The exact size of this maximum remains unclear,[43] but it is entirely clear that loan interest in Kievan Rus was very high, and the princely

---

[40] See *Pravda Russkaia,* I, 125–6.

[41] The term *"vo prosop,"* from the verb *"prisypat,"* means the lending of grain with the stipulation that it be returned with interest.

[42] See *ibid.,* I, 424.

[43] See *Pravda Russkaia. Kommentarii* [Russian Pravda. Commentaries] (Moscow-Leningrad: AS USSR, 1947), pp. 426–8; S. G. Strumilin, *Dogovor zaima v drevnerusskom prave* [A Credit Agreement in Ancient Russian Law] (Moscow: 1929), p. 3.

power was forced to regulate it by means of legislation in order to lower it somewhat.

Historians consider, on good grounds, that only the struggle of the toiling masses against money lenders forced Vladimir Monomakh to take an important step in the field of economic policy not directly connected with his fiscal interests: namely, the legislative regulation of the maximum interest on loans. Vladimir Monomakh's legislation concerning loans, zakupy and kholopy "must be labelled an act of self-defence of the upper social classes in the face of the pressure of the common people's irritation." [44]

The social policy of the Kievan princes may be judged by their legislation concerning zakupy and kholopy. As was stated above, the zakup was one of the various types of dependent people in ancient Rus; the zakup was a smerd forced to resort to a loan (in money or in agricultural inventory) which he had to work out in the household of the lender, who thus became the master of the zakup. As a result of the ruin of the smerdy, the zakup system became ever more widespread. Another type of zakup was the *roleinyi* zakup, that is, the zakup who worked in the master's fields, in contrast to the ordinary zakup, who worked in the master's house.

The articles of the "Extensive Pravda" on zakupy can be looked upon as a type of "Zakupy Code." Not only did they protect the interests of the lord, but they also strictly defined the extent of his power over the zakup, set the degree of his rights over the zakup, and defined the zakup's status.

In the "Extensive Pravda" the conditions under which the zakup is transformed into a complete slave (obelnyi kholop) are exactly defined, for example, in case the zakup escapes from his master or in case the zakup steals something from another and the master pays for what is stolen. The zakup had the right to leave his master in order to earn money and the right to petition the prince or judges regarding a complaint against his master. Herein lies the real difference between the positions of the zakup and the kholop.

The "Extensive Pravda" strictly defines the responsibility of the roleinyi zakup for the property of his master: the zakup is obliged to compensate his master only for those losses which are the result of his own carelessness and negligence. The "Extensive Pravda" concretely establishes the master's responsibility in case he exceeds his power over the zakup: for confiscating money or personal property belonging to

---

[44] A. Presniakov, *Kniazhoe pravo v drevnei Rusi* [Princely Law in Ancient Rus] (St. Petersburg: 1909), p. 248.

the zakup, for selling the zakup as his slave, or for beating him without cause.

Historians directly connect the Kiev uprising of 1113 with the articles in *Russkaia Pravda* concerning the arbitrariness of the master's relationship to the zakup, just as the articles concerning the rez established the level of interest on loans. Academician B. D. Grekov writes: "Traces of the revolutionary origin of legislation about the zakupy are very noticeable. The zakup was guaranteed the right to go to court with his master and the right to leave the master to earn money. Instances of the zakup's responsibility for the master's property are well defined, and the property and personal rights of the zakup are significantly protected. Outstanding, in a political sense, is the explicitness of some articles concerning the zakup: unless he wishes to incur punishment, the master cannot beat the zakup without cause, senselessly, or while drunk. In all these guarantees one feels clearly the hopeless position of the zakup before the uprising of 1113 and the desire of the legislator to set limits, although sometimes merely verbal, on the arbitrariness of the master." [45]

A large part of the "Extensive Pravda" (16 articles) is devoted to the question of kholopy—the most unjustly treated group of the population of Kievan Rus. Scholars call this part of the "Extensive Pravda" the "Kholopy Code." In the "Extensive Pravda" are defined the conditions under which the free person becomes a slave. According to Article 110, complete bondage is based on three conditions: 1) the purchase of a man in the presence of witnesses, even if for only a half grivna, with the giving of the money in the presence of the kholop himself; 2) marriage to a slave without any sort of stipulation; if someone marries conditionally that person retains any rights agreed upon; 3) becoming a *tiun* or *kliuchnik* without stipulation; if conditions are concluded, rights agreed upon are retained. The next (111th) article establishes that the contract worker is not a kholop. It is forbidden to make a man a kholop either in return for sustenance or for furnishing household objects. If the worker serving for a stated period wants to leave before the expired term, he is not to be prevented if he returns to the master the money received.

Articles 112-115 of the "Extensive Pravda" define the criminal responsibility for giving aid to a fugitive kholop and the reward for the apprehension of a fugitive. Article 118 defends the interests of the master whose kholop has sold himself to another master, concealing his previous bondage. Articles 116, 117, and 119 define the master's

[45] Grekov, *Kievskaia Rus*, p. 197.

responsibility for the money taken from anyone by deception as a loan by his kholop, pretending to be a free man; the master's responsibility for credit received by the kholop when he has permitted him to trade; and the right of the master to goods obtained by his fugitive kholop. In other articles are established the master's responsibility for thefts perpetrated by his kholop, the kholop's responsibility for striking a free man, and the master's responsibility for not surrendering a kholop who has struck a free man.

Such is the content of *Russkaia Pravda* in that part which is of interest for the study of the history of Russian economic thought. We see that *Russkaia Pravda,* particularly the "Extensive Pravda," reflected the interests of the exploiting classes, supported private property in general, the property of merchants and money lenders, and particularly feudal property. It defended the interests of the wealthy ruling classes, that is, the interests of the exploiters and was directed against the lower social classes, the poor and the needy, the kholopy, zakupy, and smerdy.

Russkaia Pravda devoted particular attention to the defense of the property of the masters, first of all of the princes and the boyars. For a transgression against the property of the prince, for example, the theft of the prince's horse, *Russkaia Pravda* set up a fine one-and-a-half times greater than for stealing the horse of a common man—a smerd (Art. 45). For the slaying of a princely tiun an extremely high fine of eighty grivny was set up (Art. 12). For killing an official of the prince in a fight, if the murderer was not found, the commune was obliged to pay a fine of eighty grivny, while for the killing of a *liudina,* or a simple free man, forty grivny was exacted (Art. 3). For the murder of a smerd or kholop the fine was fixed at five grivny (Art. 16). This sum was also set for the killing of a simple servant, a contract servant (Art. 14), but for the killing of a prince's servant, groom, or cook, the penalty was forty grivny (Art. 11). The class nature of the legislation of early Rus is entirely evident.

V. O. Kliuchevskii considered *Russkaia Pravda* to be primarily a "code of capital." "Capital," he wrote, "is the object of particularly intensive attention for the legislator; labor itself, that is, man, is looked upon as a tool of capital; one can say that 'capital' is the most privileged character in *Russkaia Pravda.*" Kliuchevskii's opinion of *Russkaia Pravda* as a "code of capital" is shared by many other historians. V. V. Sviatlovskii, for example, wrote that in general *Russkaia Pravda* is a "code for the protection of early Russian capitalism." "The basic socio-economic task, so to speak, and the essence of these documents [46] [the

[46] Kliuchevskii, *op. cit.,* I, 253.

trade treaties of Kiev with Byzantium and *Russkaia Pravda*—A.P.], is the defense of the emerging trade-capital interests, its middle men, and goods." [47]

Such an interpretation of the class nature of *Russkaia Pravda* is incorrect. It is based, first of all, on a faulty understanding of the character of the economics of Kievan Rus—on an exaggeration of the degree of development of trade and trade capital in early Rus; and, secondly, on a lack of understanding of the nature of "capital" itself. Kliuchevskii's conception of capital simply identifies it with private property and, in general terms, with all sorts of private property.

The defense of the property and political interests of the ruling classes, the restraint of the exploited masses, and the suppression of their resistance are the main functions of any state in a society where antagonistic classes exist and where one class oppresses and exploits others. The principle of the defense of private property, first of all of feudal property, appears again and again through all the legislation of princely and tsarist Russia, from Kievan Rus down to the revolutionary overthrow of the landowners and bourgeoisie in 1917.

Russkaia Pravda was the first code of laws of the Russian state. Its content not only reflected the feudal productive relationships existing in Kievan Rus, but also served as a tool for their formation, a tool for strengthening the ruling positions and privileges of the feudal aristocracy. The legal norms set in *Russkaia Pravda* mirrored the *economic policy* of the Kievan state—the policy of exalting the feudal aristocracy, of defending and strengthening *feudal ownership*. The fixing in *Russkaia Pravda* of feudal right was one of the most important elements in the superstructure of feudal society; it helped to form its base and aided the strengthening and development of this base.

Russkaia Pravda is a clear monument of the economic concepts, notions, and ideas existing in Kievan Rus. Here we meet the concepts of usurious capital ("istoe"), of interest ("rez"), *"tovara,"* [48] of the rural commune (*"verv"*), the concept of the "riadovich," the "zakup," the "kholop," and others. The economic lexicon of *Russkaia Pravda* is very rich (for that period, of course), which testifies to the complexity and multiformed economic relationships existing in Kievan Rus.

Economic terms in *Russkaia Pravda* express a number of economic relationships which later, thanks to the country's further development, altogether disappeared ("riadovich," "zakup," "roleinyi zakup," "che-

---

[47] V. V. Sviatlovskii, *Istoriia ekonomicheskikh idei v Rossii* [History of Economic Ideas in Russia] (Petrograd: 1923), I, 9, 11.

[48] The word *tovar* [goods] in ancient Rus was used variedly: 1) size, baggage, 2) property, 3) product sold on the market.

liad'," "obelnyi kholop," among others). Many economic relationships which were preserved in altered form during the next stages of our country's development subsequently received other names: "istoe" and "rez," for example, began to be called "capital" and "interest."

"Istoe, "rez," "tovar," "riadovich," *"naimit"* (servant), "obel'nyi kholop", and other economic terms found in *Russkaia Pravda* still cannot be looked upon as *economic categories,* that is, as *theoretical* expressions of productive relationships. Only after several centuries did Russian economic thought begin to establish the existing productive relations of society and to analyze and formulate these relationships theoretically. In their time other Slavic countries also had "codes of law" like *Russkaia Pravda,* for example, the *"Zakon Sudnyi liudem"* (Legal Code of the People), the *"Polskaia Pravda"* (Polish Law), and the ancient Czech codes. Many other peoples of Western Europe had them as well, for example, the "Westgoth Pravda" [Law], the "Burgundian Pravda," and the "Salic Law" of the Germanic tribes. A comparative analysis of the economic ideas contained in these legal monuments of various countries is of interest in the study of the general history of economic thought. Such an analysis would reveal the similarity of some and the differences between other economic ideas in the codes of various countries. A comparison of codes of law would disclose real similarities and differences in the living conditions of feudal countries.

Russkaia Pravda was the sum of the internal socio-economic development of the eastern Slavs and the early Russian people. The views of some noble-bourgeois cosmopolitans that the contents of *Russkaia Pravda* were "borrowed" from other peoples is a fiction and a slander.[49]

The Church in the Service of the Feudal Order

With the Slavic acceptance of Christianity the church acquired great significance in the social life of Rus. It emerged as a great ideological force, utilized by the princes for the consolidation of their power, for the strengthening of feudal relationships. The new religion called upon the people to obey the princely authority and sanctified this power with the authority of God. It preached: "There is no power save that given by God."

In comparison with heathendom, Christianity represented progress.

---

[49] On this see B. D. Grekov, "Russkaia Pravda i ee slavianskoe okruzhenie" [Russian Pravda and Its Slavic Environment], *Izvestiia Akademii Nauk SSSR. Seriia istorii i filosofii* [News of the Academy of Sciences of the USSR. Historical and Philosophical Series], IX, No. 2 (1952), pp. 105–14.

Along with Christianity the Slavs received some elements of the higher Byzantine culture, and the church and the monasteries played a significant role in the development of literacy and education in Kievan Rus.

Having made Christianity the ruling religion, the Kievan princes gave a decisive rebuff to the insistent attempts of Byzantium to use this religion for the political and ideological subjugation of the Kievan state. In this struggle of the young Russian state for independence the Russian church also played a positive role. In an outstanding literary monument of that epoch, "Essay on Law and Prosperity" written by Ilarion, the presbyter of the Yaroslav rural court church (who later became the first Russian metropolitan), the idea of the equality of peoples is established. Contrary to Byzantine theories, which maintained that only the Greek people were chosen of God, Ilarion glorified the Russian people and declared that the exclusive right of the New Rome to universal rule was unfounded. Ilarion looked upon world history as a gradual adoption of Christian culture by all peoples, and he declared the equality of Kiev and Constantinople.[50]

The Christian religion was an ideology corresponding to the growing complexity in Kievan Rus of the economic and political order of feudalism. Engels characterized the Christian church as the most general synthesis and the most general sanction of the existing feudal order.[51] Marx argued that the social principles of Christianity justified ancient slavery, exalted medieval serfdom, and defended the oppression of the proletariat. These principles preach the necessity of the existing classes of rulers and enslaved and the transfer to Heaven as the promised reward for all abominations borne on earth. At the same time, they justify the continuation of these abominations on earth, accompanied by all the enormities of the oppressors against the oppressed, whether by just punishment for offenses or by ordeals which the master wantonly inflicts upon the people. The social principles of Christianity exalt cowardice, self-contempt, self-abnegation, subjugation, and meekness.[52]

This subordinate role of Christianity as an ideological weapon in the hands of the exploiting classes also appears graphically in the history of Kievan Rus. From the church literature of this period which has been preserved, it is evident that the church by its authority sanc-

---

50 See D. S. Likhachev, *Natsionalnoe samosoznanie drevnei Rusi* [National Consciousness of Ancient Rus] (Moscow-Leningrad: AS USSR, 1945), p. 30.

51 See F. Engels, *Krestianskaia voina v Germanii* [Peasant War in Germany] (Moscow: Gospolitizdat, 1953), p. 34.

52 Marx and Engels, *Sochineniia,* V, 173.

tioned and justified the complexity of the division of society into rich and poor, of exploiters and exploited.

The church not only aided by its ideology the strengthening of feudal productive relationships, but was itself an immediate exploiter of the toiling mass. Receiving from the princes land with smerdy living on it, the church became a large landowner.

The churchmen called upon the faithful to obey God and the princes, urged them to submit resignedly to their masters, and taught that submission to their landlord was one of the virtues of a true Christian. Amid conditions of growing contradictions and class struggle the churchmen persistently preached the idea, advantageous for the ruling class, of social peace between the rich and poor, between the exploiters and the exploited. They called upon the poor and the exploited to be resigned to their lot; and the rich and the exploiters were urged not to abuse their power over the poor people and to give them crumbs from their wealth. This idea of class peace is clearly expressed, for example, in the outstanding monument of church literature of the period of Kievan Rus—Sviatoslav's "Collection" of 1076.[53] "Hold your prince in great awe with all your might." "Bow your head before every rich man; humble yourself," it is ordered in the introduction of the "Collection." [54]

Poor people were urged to practice submission, patience, humility, and industry, for which they were promised the heavenly kingdom. Beggars should not envy the rich. The admonition to labor was insistently repeated, and laziness was adjudged a sin, unworthy of the Christian. "Work always, for God sees thy labor and sends thee his aid; if you do this you will dwell in the kingdom of God," [55] we read in the "Instructions of Saint Feodora to Her Children."

Under the conditions of a society divided into classes with feudal and slave-owning forms of exploitation existing, the church's insistent urgings to labor, not to be lazy, had a definite class sense: they meant the religious sanction of the appropriation by the ruling classes of the labor and products of the labor of the poor, the call to toil for the exploiters.

---

[53] See V. Shimanovskii, *Sbornik Sviatoslava 1076 g.* [Sviatoslav's Collection of 1076] (Warsaw: 1894). An interesting analysis of the social nature of this memorial is offered by I. U. Budovnits, "Izbornik Sviatoslava 1076 g. i Pouchenie Vladimira Monomakha i ikh mesto v istorii russkoi obshchestvennoi mysli" [Sviatoslav's Collection of 1076 and Vladimir Monomakh's Instructions and their Place in the History of Russian Social Thought] *Trudy otdela drevnerusskoi literatury* (Moscow-Leningrad: AS USSR, 1954), X, 44–75.

[54] See *Pamiatniki drevnerusskoi tserkovno-uchitelnoi literatury,* p. 7.

[55] *Ibid.,* p. 38.

On the other hand, churchmen counselled the rich not to abuse the dependent and the poor, not to bring them to "wrath." Slaves had to be fed and clothed. The church recommended that the disobedient slave be punished, but in the process the master was not to forget that the slave was also a man, given by God to serve his master. Churchmen condemned the slaying of a slave by his master, because for the killing of a slave the master bore responsibility before God. The rich were obligated to give alms to the poor. For all of this they were promised heavenly bliss.

In the article "Socialism and Religion," V. I. Lenin wrote: "Religion is one of the forms of spiritual oppression everywhere lying on the popular masses, forced to eternal labor for others, to need and solitude. The powerlessness of the exploited classes in the struggle with the exploiters also inescapably gives rise to faith in a better life beyond the grave, just as the powerlessness of the savage in the struggle with nature gives rise to faith in gods, devils, miracles, and so on. To those who work all their life and are in need, religion preaches docility and patience during the earthly life, with the hope for a heavenly reward. And to those who live by the labor of others, religion teaches charity during the earthly life, offering them a very cheap justification for all of their exploiting existence and selling at a low price their tickets to heavenly bliss." [56]

Urging the well-to-do and rich not to resort to the extremity of oppressing the toilers, churchmen sometimes give a clear picture of just how greatly labor was exploited. For example the Abbot Feodosii tells the Kievan prince Iziaslav: "Your slaves . . . work quarreling, fighting, and cursing each other and often are beaten by stewards, and thus all of their service is being performed in sin." [57] The Testament of the Bishop of Turov, Cyril, states that the masters by their cruelty in relations with their slaves often drive them to suicide: "They do not give them sufficient food and clothing and force upon them work and other miseries and beat them uselessly and throw them into water, and because of this oppression they commit suicide." [58]

Christianity was implanted forcibly by the princes. The opposition of the toiling masses to the growing feudal exploitation and the struggle against money lenders were bound up with the struggle against the new religion. Almost simultaneously with the adoption of Christianity

[56] Lenin, *op. cit.*, X, 65–6.

[57] *Paterik Kievskogo Pecherskogo monastyria*, p. 40.

[58] See M. N. Tikhomirov, *Istochnikovedenie istorii SSSR s drevneishikh vremen do kontsa XVIII v.* [Source Material for the History of the USSR from Ancient Times to the End of the XVIII Century] (Moscow: Sotsekgiz, 1940), p. 91.

in Rus "heresies" appeared. At the head of the revolting people often stood the sorcerers—the ardent champions of the ousted heathendom. The popular uprisings forced the Kievan princes to set certain limits to the exploitation of the toilers, which, as we have seen, were reflected in various sections of the princely legislation *Russkaia Pravda.*

One can also judge the economic views of the churchmen of the period of Kievan Rus by their attitude toward money lending and interest. In the Western European countries, the Catholic church, as is known, regarded the taking of interest negatively; it forbade the taking of interest not only by church officials, but by all believers. In the church literature of Kievan Rus interest is condemned in general, and the church officials are forbidden to act as money lenders. Church officials who lent money at high interest were defrocked. High interest rates were proclaimed a sin, on the same level as robbery; moderate interest rates were recommended.[59]

Some historians have exaggerated the role of the church in questions of the interrelations between exploiters and the exploited. The church in Russia during the period of the early development of slavery was characterized by A. Shchapov, for example, as if it were the sole carrier which "mightily held back the aspiration of material force against enslavement and abetted a desire to improve the lot of the enslaved." [60]

In reality, one cannot speak of any serious "restraint" by the early Russian church with regard to the exploitation of one person by others. The development of feudal forms of exploitation in Kievan Rus, as in later periods of the history of Russia, was bound up with objective laws of social development. The history of Kievan Rus indicates that the only real force actually upholding "the aspiration of material power against enslavement" was that of the popular masses themselves, their uprisings, and their stubborn resistance to their exploiters. The church, already a mighty ideological force, truly served the class of exploiters and in fact existed at the expense of the people's labor.

By adopting Christianity and making it the state religion, Vladimir levied upon the people the costs of supporting the church officials. For the church constructed in Kiev he set aside "a tithe of all the lands of Rus and from the principality . . . from all princely courts every tenth [squirrel] fur, and from trade every tenth week, and from households

[59] See *Pamiatniki drevnerusskogo kanonicheskogo prava* [Memorials of Ancient Russian Canon Law], Pt. I; *Russkaia istoricheskaia biblioteka* [Russian Historical Library], 2nd ed. (St. Petersburg: 1908), VI, 24–5; *Pamiatniki drevnerusskoi tserkovno-uchitelnoi literatury,* I, 91–2.

[60] A. Shchapov, *Golos drevnei Russkoi tserkvi ob uluchshenii byta nesvobodnykh liudei* [A View of the Ancient Russian Church on the Improvement of Conditions of Non-Free People] (Kazan: 1859), p. 12.

every year a tenth of all the herds, and from all grain . . ." [61] He also set up a special church court, the income from which went for the support of the church.

It is interesting to note that Vladimir (the First) imposed on the churches the obligation to observe the exactitude of trading measures and weights. "Town and trade and all kinds of measures, *merila, spudy, izvesy, stavila,* set justly by God should be upheld by churchmen and be neither increased nor decreased." Samples of weights and measures were kept in the church.[62]

Economic Ideas in the Folklore of the People

The views of the people themselves regarding the most important phenomena of social life were reflected in their folk tales. Scholars assign the rise of the Russian folk tale to the ninth and tenth centuries. The folk tales display the socio-political mood of the Russian people, the attitude of the broad masses of the toilers toward events and various aspects of existence. They give clear expression to the patriotic ideas of struggle for state unity and for independence of the Russian people. At the same time their content also permits one to judge the attitudes of the popular masses toward the representatives of the ruling class. They show a high evaluation by the people of their role in their country's fate.

The conflict of legendary heroes with Prince Vladimir and his boyars portrayed in the folk tales is an artistic depiction of the antagonistic contradictions between the exploiting classes and the people.[63] The folk tales often stress the superiority of popular heroes over princes and "fat-bellied boyars." The chief hero of the Russian epic, the "son of a peasant" Il'ia Muromets, is glorified not only as the defender of his country and the preserver of the unity and might of the Russian land, but as the defender of "widows and orphans" and of the toilers.

The folk tales epitomize not only military prowess, but also the peaceful labor of the Russian people. In this regard the well known story of Mikula Selianinovich is particularly interesting. The events described in it, judging by the text, relate to the time of the reign in Kiev of Vladimir (the First or Monomakh; it cannot be definitely determined). The folk tale depicts the meeting of the worker on the field

[61] *Novgorodskaia pervaia letopis starshego i mladshego izvodov,* p. 480.

[62] *Ibid.,* p. 479. *Merila* means the measure of length (*arshini, sazheni*); *spudy* means the measure of volume (*chetveriki*); *izvesy* means scale; *stavila* means weights.

[63] See *Istoriia russkoi kultury* [History of Russian Culture] (Moscow-Leningrad: AS USSR, 1941), I, 247.

of the *ratai* (husbandman), Mikula Selianinovich, with the representatives of the other social classes of Kievan Rus—with the prince's son Volga and his wife—and Mikula Selianinovich's clash with the town "highwaymen."

Mikula Selianinovich is a legendary hero, a husbandman. In clear poetic forms the folk tale tells of the great significance for all society of the husbandman's labor. The difficulty of agricultural labor is depicted here in very vivid colors. The tale describes the unusual strength and heroism of the agriculturalist Mikula Selianinovich and his superiority over the princely druzhenniki and the city "highwaymen." Mikula speaks to the prince with ease and boldly calls the druzhenniki *Khleboiastsy,* that is, parasites. The tale of Mikula Selianinovich also indicates the existence of antagonisms between town and country even in that early period of our country's history. Going to town for salt, Mikula Selianinovich is forced into a cruel fight with the town "highwaymen," who demand from him, one may suppose, various types of trade duties and customs.

Giving attention to the "most profound, clear, and artistically ideal types of heroes created by folk lore, by word-of-mouth of the toiling people," M. Gorkii stresses the "perfection of such forms as Hercules, Prometheus, Mikula Selianinovich, Sviatogor . . . and Vasilisa the Wise. . . ."[64] These forms, says Gorkii, harmoniously blend thought and feeling.

Other folk tales reflect the toilers' views on prevailing social relations. In the well-known story of Sadko, created in Novgorod and probably relating to a later time, the twelfth century, is shown the conflict of a common man, a bold and talented representative of the freedom-loving Novgorodian people, with the rich merchants. The popular hero here resists "Great Novgorod" with all its wealth. He summons all the merchants of Novgorod to competition and vanquishes them.[65]

Among the literary monuments of Kievan Rus, coming from the pen of churchmen, the "Life and Journey of Daniel" to Palestine is of particular interest.[66] The author of this work was an abbot of a monastery. Together with a group of other Russians, he lived in Jerusalem from 1106 to 1108. Such journeys of believers to the "Holy Land" were widespread. The possibility cannot be excluded, however, that the

---

[64] Gorkii, *op. cit.*, p. 698.

[65] See *Russkoe narodnoe poeticheskoe tvorchestvo* [Russian National Poetic Creativeness] (Moscow-Leningrad: AS USSR, 1953), I, 230–4.

[66] See *Zhitie i khozhene Danila Russkyia zemli igumena 1106–1108 g.* [Life and Journey of Daniel, An Abbot of Russian Lands, 1106–1108] (St. Petersburg: 1896).

great prince Sviatopolk Iziaslavich used Daniel's pilgrimage for diplomatic purposes.[67]

Daniel visited Jerusalem soon after the end of the first crusade, during the reign of Baldwin I, when the Crusaders still occupied a considerable part of Palestine. The "Life and Journey of Daniel" describes in detail what Daniel saw in Palestine. The gracious reception by the king, as well as an acquaintance with the venerable Sratsinskii, made it possible for Daniel to visit spots inaccessible to other travellers.

Along with the basic content of "Life and Journey of Daniel," which contains detailed descriptions of the Christian temples seen by him, a rich characterization of the nature and economy of Palestine is included. Daniel describes its agriculture (the cultivation of various grains and fruit and horticulture) and other branches of the economy. He speaks of the fertility of the land around Jerusalem, tells of the artificial irrigation near Jericho, and discusses the economic condition and the wealth of various towns of Palestine. The abundance of economic-geographic information favorably sets apart the "Life and Journey of Daniel" from contemporary and even later descriptions of Palestine by other travelers. It should be considered the first literary work reflecting the Russian people's knowledge of the economic geography of other countries.

Thanks to the precise description of Palestine, the "Life and Journey of Daniel" enjoyed great popularity in Russia for several centuries and served as a type of guidebook; this work was also known in a number of other European countries.

We have briefly characterized here the basic traits of Russian economic thought during the earliest period of the historical life of the great Russian people—the period of Kievan Rus. As with all other peoples at the dawn of their historical development, in the process of their economic activity the eastern Slavs inescapably created definite ideas involving their productive relations and social forms of economy.

The helplessness of people before the forces of nature compelled them to deify these forces, to worship them. The heathen faith of the eastern Slavs reflected their ideas of the economic side of their life. The beginnings of definite economic thought are to be seen also in popular tales and ceremonies. The close and immediate connection of the religious viewpoints of the eastern Slavs with the nature of their agricul-

---

[67] See V. B. Danilov, "K kharakteristike 'Khozhdeniia igumena Daniila' " [Comments on the Travels of Abbot Daniel], *Trudy otdela drevnerusskoi literatury,* X, 92–105.

tural and industrial activity is preserved later in somewhat complex forms in the Christian religion of the Russian people.

Along with their economic, political, and cultural growth, the eastern Slavs developed a wealth of economic thought. The growth of production and trade, the division of society into antagonistic classes, the formation of the Kievan state, and the adoption of Christianity by the eastern Slavs aided in that state the spread of literacy and education and also produced considerable economic thought.

The economic ideas of the ruling classes of ancient Rus were expressed in the economic policy of the Kievan princes, in the code of laws of the Kievan princes—*Russkaia Pravda*—and in the insistent preachings of the church officials directed at the toilers, to submit without reservation to their masters.

At the same time the rich and clear oral poetic creation of the Russian people in the popular epic expressed the opinion of the toiling masses of the importance of agricultural labor, the toil of the peasantry, for the entire life of society. Numerous uprisings of the popular masses clearly show their attitude toward the exploiting class and toward exploitation.

Thus, even in this period of the historical life of the Russian people, appears the class differentiation of economic thought, expressing and defending economic interests of various classes of society. Russian economic thought during the period of Kievan Rus was an important element in the entire social ideology.

Reflecting the economic and political processes achieved in the life of the Russian people, the economic viewpoints of the representatives of the ruling class, being one of the elements of the superstructure of society, played a great role in the formation and strengthening of the feudal order: By its social content Russian economic thought of this epoch reflected the division of society into classes, the conflict of class interests and the struggle of the classes in Kievan Rus.

The population of Kievan Rus was an ancient Russian population, formed from separate Slavic tribes. From it emerged the great Russian, the Ukrainian, and the White Russian nationalities. Thus the economic thought in Kievan Rus established the general basis and the point of departure of economic thought in Russia, in the Ukraine, and in White Russia.

PART II
THE PERIOD OF THE COUNTRY'S FEUDAL DISUNITY

CHAPTER 2. *Economic Thought in the Period of Feudal Disunity.*

The Character of the Economy. Classes and the Class Struggle.

The flowering of the Kievan state occurred in the tenth and eleventh centuries. In the second half of the eleventh century the political decline of Kiev began, and in the second half of the twelfth century it had already ceased to be a capital city and had lost its former significance as the political, economic, and cultural center of Rus.

The Kievan state did not represent a stable whole. The predominance of a natural economy meant that the political unity of the various parts of the great state still had no permanent economic basis insofar as a broad development of a social division of labor and exchange were concerned.

In place of the single former Kievan Rus, feudal independent semi-states now appeared: the Rostov-Suzdal, Murom-Riazan, Smolensk, Kiev, Chernigov, Seversk, Pereiaslav, Volyn, Galich, Polotsk, and Turov-Pinsk principalities. They in turn consisted of a number of smaller appanage principalities. Novgorod became an autonomous feudal republic in which the power belonged to the boyars. A new period began in the life of the Russian people—the period of feudal disunity.

During this period an incessant struggle for power and territory took place between the Russian princes, while the Russian people had to contend with numerous enemies—the Polovtsy, Mongols, Germans, and Swedes—who tried to profit from the political disunity of Rus.

The political disunity of the land was the result of further development of the feudal means of production, an inexorable stage in historical development. It arose on the basis of the completed processes in the economic order of society, viz., on the basis of the productive relationships of feudalism. The country's political disunity was the result of its economic disunity, caused by economic rivalry among neighboring principalities, and the development of class struggle. A rapid growth occurred in large princely, boyar, and monastic feudal landownership; the bondage of the smerdy was also strengthened. The increase of feudal landholding served as the main form of seizure by princes, boyars, and monasteries of communal lands formerly belonging to the free small producers.

The economic interests of the feudalists demanded an increase of their immediate and direct power over the dependent population, complete correspondence of the state apparatus with the feudal economy, a transformation in force which exerted universal and daily pressure on the enslaved peasantry.

Among the factors leading to the country's feudal disunity, the growth of the economic and political strength of the towns also played a great role. Great Novgorod, whose vast territories extended from the Baltic coast to the Urals, stood out in particular.

The feudal-dependent small husbandmen of this period were the "orphans," "field hands," and, in general, "Christians." From the beginning of the fifteenth century there appeared new groups of peasants, the so-called "old timers" and "new comers" with various degrees of dependence on the landowner. Obligations incurred by the peasants in the form of loans to be repaid by the performance of various works on the feudal estate rather than by payment of interest were widespread. The peasant's dependence upon the landowner was also established by "usurious" silver, that is, loans of money to the peasant with interest.

During this period feudal rents were paid predominantly in products —natural obrok—(payment in kind of a serf's dues). The tillage of the princes, boyars, and monasteries themselves was insignificant; it was carried on mainly by the labor of kholopy and other enslaved persons. In part the labor of the dependent peasantry was utilized. At the end of this period the use of money rent increased. The peasant's obligations in kind to the state and to the landowner began to be replaced by cash payments. The exploitation of the peasant grew. Extra-economic compulsion began to take the form of direct limitations by the state authority on the transfer of dependent peasants from one feudalist to another.

Feudal landowning existed in two basic forms: that of the *"votchina,"*—characterized by boyar or monastic ownership of the land—and that of *"zhalovanie"* (grant)—conditional landowning, connected with the rendering of specific services by one feudalist to a higher feudalist. The "zhalovanie" could not be sold, given away, or bequeathed by the owner.

In the "votchinas" the feudalists themselves governed the population and collected revenues for the prince's treasury and for themselves. In the towns and in the *"chernye volosti"* (black lands) local and district administrators ruled; they received payment from the population in kind, hence they were called *"kormlenshchiki."*

Feudal disunity weakened the country and lessened resistance to the attacks of external foes. From the twelfth century on ruinous assaults by the Polovtsy on Russian soil became frequent. In the thirteenth century the Russian people were subjected to their severest trial—enslavement by the Tartar-Mongol conquerors.

For almost two and a half centuries, the Tartar-Mongol yoke inflicted extreme misery. The conquerors murdered, plundered and ruined towns and villages and levied heavy tribute in the form of head taxes and various duties. Already suffering from feudal exploitation, the peasantry now had to endure the still more difficult burden of the Tartar-Mongol yoke, which, "not only suppressed but also outraged and consumed the very spirit of the people who were its victim." [1]

The weight of Tartar-Mongol oppression fell largely on the toiling masses who, because of this, often revolted. Thus in 1259 "The Great Rebellion" occurred in Novgorod and in the volosti; in 1262 there were uprisings in Rostov, Suzdal, and Yaroslav; in 1327, in Tver and other areas.

As a result of the Tartar-Mongol yoke the productive forces of the country suffered a great loss. Agriculture, industry, and trade were dealt a heavy blow. Town craftsmanship suffered particularly. The development of Russian industry, which had been at a high level, was halted by the Tartar-Mongol invasion. The Russian people bore the brunt of the Tartar-Mongol blow and thereby saved Western Europe from ruin and suppression.

Her western neighbors—the German knights of the Livonian and Teutonic orders and the Swedes—also carried on an aggressive policy with regard to Russia, but the freedom-loving Russian people decisively repelled these aggressors. In 1240 Russian warriors led by Alexander Nevskii completely crushed the Swedes on the Neva, and in 1242 the German knights on the ice of Lake Chud "so that the scoundrels were finally pushed over the Russian border." [2]

The increase of feudal oppression, the feudal wars of the Russian

---

[1] Marx, *Secret Diplomatic History*, p. 78.

[2] K. Marx, "Khronologicheskie vypiski" [Chronological Excerpts] *Arkhiv Marksa i Engelsa* [An Archive of Marx and Engels], V (1938), p. 344.

princes, and the attacks of the Polovtsy and Mongols led to the economic desolation of the lower Dnepr region. The peasants left for more northerly, forested areas.

The changing of trade routes which took place after the conquest of Constantinople by the Crusaders in 1204 also had a negative effect on the economic position of the southern Russian towns. The main highway of European trade with the countries of the east now shifted to the Mediterranean Sea, and the former route "from the Varangians to the Greeks" lost its significance. But trade, internal and external, continued to develop. The merchants of Novgorod, Pskov, and Moscow carried on extensive commerce with the countries of Western Europe and Asia.

Novgorod became the center of the external trade of the Russian princes. The big merchants were organized into *"sotni"* (groups of 100) having a certain similarity to the merchant guilds of Western Europe.

The growth and deepening of feudal exploitation and the increase of trade capital and moneylending led to the sharpening of class contradictions and often to popular rebellions. Particularly sharp class antagonisms appeared in Novgorod, where popular movements often occurred against the boyar magnates and the big merchants. Thus, according to the chronicles, in 1209, "the Novgorodians called a *veche* (assembly) to deal with Mayor Dmitrii"; he was accused of allowing "the confiscation of silver from the Novgorodians and of doing all kind of ill in the volost', such as the requisition of chickens and of wagons." The household and villages of the mayor were divided and long inventories comprising "limitless wealth" were given to the Prince for his examination.[3]

Along with the growth of towns, industry, and trade within the bosom of feudal society, economic ties among the various parts of the Russian land were also strengthened. The need to unite forces in the struggle with the external foe and the increasing resistance of the toiling masses against the feudal exploiters forced the princes still farther along the path of political centralization. The growth of economic ties among the various principalities served as a material basis for the unfolding struggle to centralize state power. The necessity of defense against the enslaving Tartars and other foes hastened this process.

In the fourteenth and fifteenth centuries the grand princes strengthened their power at the expense of the appanaged princes; that is, they

[3] See "Troitskaia letopis" [Chronicle of Troitsk], *Polnoe sobranie russkikh letopisei* [Complete Collection of Russian Chronicles] (St. Petersburg: 1846), I, 210.

centralized political power within the bounds of the various grand principalities. At the same time a cruel struggle took place when the grand princes attempted to unite under their rule the greatest possible part of the Russian territories and population. However, during the fourteenth and fifteenth centuries the country began to emerge from its economic and political disunity.

In the struggle for the country's political centralization the Moscow principality had a leading role. It was under Ivan Kalita that "the foundation of the *might of Moscow* was laid." [4] As I. V. Stalin stated, "the service of Moscow consists first of all in that it became the basis of the unity of disunited Rus into one state with one government, and with one leadership." [5]

The growth of political centralization strengthened the Russian people in its struggle against the aggressors. In 1380, under the leadership of Dmitrii Donskoi, the Tartar-Mongol enslavers were dealt a crushing blow on the field of Kulikovo. But not for another century did the Russian people throw off the Tartar-Mongol yoke completely.

The Principles of the Economic Policy of the Princes

The development of feudal productive relationships in this period, along with the sharpening of class contradictions and class struggle, determined the further development of Russian economic thought and the increase of its class differentiation.

During this period the content and forms of Russian economic thought indicate the great influence exerted by the political disunity of the country and the cruel feudal struggle among the princes. The liberating struggle of the Russian people against the Tartar-Mongol enslavers and other aggressors was also manifest. Russian economic thought appears in this period as one of the most important ideological weapons of struggle for the liquidation of the feudal disunity of the country and for the liberation of the people from foreign aggressors.

Advanced Russian social thought of the whole period of feudal disunity is characterized by progressive ideas concerning the necessity of the unity of the Russian people and by patriotic ideas for the liberation of the Russian people from foreign domination.

Sources which aid the study of Russian economic thought of this period are various literary and other monuments. The characterization of this thought must begin with the basic traits of the economic policy of the Russian princes. Besides the chronicles, the *economic policy* of

[4] *Arkhiv Marksa i Engelsa,* VIII (1946), 149.

[5] *Pravda,* September 7, 1947.

the Russian princes of this period was expressed in various legal documents, such as the grant charter, the testaments and agreements of the grand and appanage princes, legal charters, codes, and treaties between Great Novgorod and Pskov.

The policy of the princes on the question of the relations between the chief classes of feudal society—the feudalists and the exploited toiling masses—is of greatest import. The princes' socio-economic policy is reflected in the resulting process of the enslavement of the toiling masses by the great feudalists, a policy which at the same time aided this process. Thus the significance of the policies of the princes is particularly clear in the grant charters of the princes and the agreements between these princes.

The grant charters of the princes endowed the secular feudalists, monasteries, and churches with various types of immunities and privileges, limiting the right of the local princely power to the land given the feudalists, and according them the right to rule and judge the population and to collect various taxes and duties from them. The majority of the grant charters which have come down to us are of the fourteenth and fifteenth centuries.[6]

The grant charters of the Russian princes of the thirteenth to sixteenth centuries, which guaranteed the holders of votchiny extensive judicial and tax privileges, expressed and formulated the institution of immunities then in existence in Western Europe.[7] The grant charters defined the relationship of the feudalist to the prince and that of the population on the territory of the given secular or clerical feudalist to the princely power and to the feudalist. Enjoying certain immunities, the feudalist found himself immediately dependent on the supreme power of the prince. The feudalist bypassed the local power stemming from the prince so that, in effect, the whole population was subject only to the feudalist, its master. Fully applicable to the Russia of this era

---

[6] On grant-charters see A. N. Gorbunov, "Lgotnye gramoty, zhalovannye monastyriam i tserkvam v XIII, XIV i KV vv." [Exemption Charters Granted to Monasteries and Churches in the XIII, XIV, and XV Centuries], *Arkhiv istoricheskikh i prakticheskikh svedenii, otnosiashchikhsia do Rossii* [An Archive of Historical and Practical Information Related to Russia] edited by N. Kalachov. (St. Petersburg: 1860, Bk. I, 1863, Bk. V, 1869, Bk. VI); D. M. Meichik, *Gramoty XIV i XV vv. Moskovskogo arkhiva Ministerstva iustitsii* [Charters of the XIV and XV Centuries of the Moscow Archive of the Ministry of Justice] (Moscow: 1883); N. P. Pavlov-Silvanskii, *Immunitet v udelnoi Rusi* [*Immunity in Appanaged Rus*] (St. Petersburg: 1900).

For a list of works which contain publications of various grant-charters, see, S. V. Bakhrushin, ed., *Dukhovnye i dogovornye gramotoy kniazei velikikh i udelnykh* [Testaments and Agreement Charters of the Grand and Appanaged Princes] (Moscow: 1909), p. vii–viii.

[7] Pavlov-Silvanskii, *Immunitet v udelnoi Rusi,* p. 3 ff.

are the words of Marx: "in the feudal epoch the higher power in military and legal affairs was the attribute of land ownership." [8]

Judicial and tax immunity was inseparably connected with the large feudal landholdings. The historians, K. A. Nevolin,[9] N. P. Pavlov-Silvanskii,[10] and A. E. Presniakov,[11] stated that immunity was the primordial customary right of big landowners, existing independently from princely grants. These feudalists had long since enjoyed court and administrative rights over the populations of their domains. But the strengthening of the princely power was incompatible with the immunities of the big feudalists. Therefore the princes aspired to place the privileges of the feudalists under their control. They proclaimed the effectiveness only of those privileges which were supported by their grant charters: "that which formerly belonged to the votchinnik by votchina right was now guaranteed to the biggest votchiniki by the grant charter as a particular priority." [12]

A different and incorrect point of view on the question of the origin of immunity was developed by S. B. Veselovskii, who tried to show that the judicial and tax privileges of the landowners were based only on the grant charters of the princes and were not connected with the landownership by private persons according to customary law.[13]

In reality, in the majority of cases the grant charters of the princes only sanctioned the privileges of the feudalists, who had long since possessed them as feudal landowners. In other cases, by means of the grant charters the princes gave privileges to landowners not enjoyed by them earlier.[14] In all cases the grant charters played a great role in strengthening the feudal order and in increasing the exploitation of the peasantry.

The grant charters issued by the princes to the feudalists recognized the latter's right of judgment in all the territory of the given landholding and the right to collect taxes and duties, and the representatives of local authorities were forbidden in the feudal domain. "And my peasants shall not enter on the territory of a monastery . . . neither shall

---

[8] Marx, *Kapital,* I, 339.

[9] See K. A. Nevolin, *Istoriia rossiiskikh grazhdanskikh zakonov* [History of Russian Civil Laws] (St. Petersburg: 1857), IV, 150–1.

[10] See N. P. Pavlov-Silvanskii, *Feodalizm v udelnoi Rusi* [Feudalism in Appanaged Rus] (St. Petersburg: 1910), p. 293 ff.

[11] See A. E. Presniakov, *Moskovskoe tsarstvo* [Moscovite Tsardom] (Petrograd: 1918), p. 39 ff.

[12] Nevolin, *op. cit.,* IV, 151.

[13] See S. B. Veselovskii, *K voprosu o proiskhozhdenii votchinnogo rezhima* [On Origins of the Votchina Regime] (Moscow: 1926), p. 27.

[14] See I. I. Smirnov, "Sudebnik 1550 goda" [The Code of 1550] *Istoricheskie zapiski* [Historical Notes], No. 24 (1947), pp. 296–312.

our volost' administrators, tribute and tax collectors enter . . . No one shall be sent to monasteries for anything."[15] These or similar stipulations appeared in all the grant charters.

The scope of the judicial rights of the landholder, foreseen in the grant charters, varied in the principalities, and also changed with time. The Tver princes, for example, gave the monasteries the right of judgment on all matters, both civil and criminal, without exception. Pavlov-Silvanskii observed that such an order was in effect from earliest times in both Moscow and other principalities of the Rostov-Suzdal lands.[16]

The same diversity existed in the extent of the tax privileges given by the princely grant charters. In comparatively rare cases the population of domains having grant charters were freed completely from payment of all taxes. Usually tax immunities referred only to several separate forms of imposts and had a provisional character for a term of two to ten years, and in a few instances of fifteen to twenty years.[17]

One of the aims of the temporary liberation of the votchina populations from imposts was the stimulation of peasant movement to deserted lands. In such cases new settlers were extended immunities for a specified period only; old settlers were not granted such privileges. Occasionally princes abolished general taxes on monasteries and substituted a definite obrok.

The freeing of the population of the votchina from the prince's taxes did not mean liberation from taxes and collections in general. In many cases, for example the judicial dues, payment went to the landholder. But in cases where the taxes continued to go to the prince, the grant charters indicated an extremely essential fact: these taxes were collected from the population by representatives, not of the princely power, but of the feudalists, who then deposited them in the prince's treasury.

Possession of judicial and tax immunities guaranteed the feudalist enormous power over the population. The feudalist's economic power as a landholder was supplemented by this public power, which served in his hands as an important lever for extra-economic compulsion. The big feudalist was not only a landholder, but, also, like a prince, a sov-

---

[15] See Pavlov-Silvanskii, *Immunitet v udelnoi Rusi,* p. 5; V. Miliutin, *O nedvizhimikh imushchestvakh dukhovenstva v Rossii* [On the Immovable Properties of the Clergy in Russia] (Moscow: 1862), Chapt. V; Gorbunov, *op. cit.,* Bk. I and V; M. Gorchakov, *O zemelnikh vladeniiakh vserossiiskikh mitropolitov, patriarkhov i sv. Sinoda 988–1738* [On Land Holdings of Russian Metropolitans, Patriarchs, and the Holy Synod (988–1738)] (St. Petersburg: 1871).

[16] See Pavlov-Silvanskii, *Immunitet v udelnoi Rusi,* p. 13.

[17] Gorbunov, *op. cit.,* Bk. V, pp. 38–9.

ereign in his votchina, a holder of political power. By giving grant charters the prince at the same time increased the extra-economic dependence of the peasant on the feudalist.

While acknowledging the determining significance of feudal landownership as the basis for feudal exploitation, it would be incorrect to underestimate the great importance of the socio-economic policies of the princes heading the feudal semi-state—policies directed at the further elevation of the feudalist class and the still greater subordination of the toilers and the exploited mass to the feudalists. These policies in particular appear clearly in the grant charters of the grand and appanage princes.

Where the grant charter set up immunity for the first time, that is, transferred into the hands of the feudalist judicial power and the right to collect taxes, the enormous effect of princely policy upon the growth of the peasant's dependence on the feudalist is evident. But where the grant charter only fixed the condition existing earlier, the princely power by this means gave the *de facto* relationship legal force, formulated it into law, and further strengthened the peasants' dependence upon the monasteries, churches, and secular feudalists.

The agreements of the great and the appanage princes, concluded by them with the aim of setting up general foreign policies and regulating mutual relations, are an important source for the study of the economic policies of the princes.[18] Many of the interprincely agreements have been preserved, the very earliest of which is the agreement between the Grand Prince Semen Ivanovich of Moscow and his brothers, the Princes Ivan and Andrei, written about 1350–1351.[19]

The interprincely agreements show clearly the country's political disunity, which, in turn, was the result and consequence of its economic disunity. The agreements were concluded between princes as equal parties and stressed the independence of the agreeing sides, the sovereign rights of the princes entering into the agreements, and the principle of noninterference of one prince in the affairs of another. "You are master on your votchina, and I am master on my votchina," is usually stated in the agreements.

---

[18] See *Dukhovnye i dogovornye gramoty velikikh i udelnykh kniazei XIV-XVI vv* [Testament and Agreement Charters of the Grand and Appanaged Princes of the XIV-XV Centuries] (Moscow-Leningrad: AS USSR, 1950); L. V. Cherepnin, *Russkie feodalnye arkhivy XIV-KV vv.* [Russian Feudal Archives of the XIV-XV Centuries] (Moscow-Leningrad: AS USSR, 1948), Pt. I, and (Moscow: 1951), Pt. II.

[19] See *Dukhovnye i dogovornye gramoty velikikh i udelnykh kniazei XIV-XVI vv.*, pp. 11–3

Entering into treaty relations between themselves which stressed their independence with regard to each other, the princes at the same time provided in the agreements for economic measures which could also preserve and guarantee their future mutual independence.

The treaty texts show that the princes understood well the direct and close connection between the political and economic independence of their principalities, and they attempted by all means to preserve and strengthen this economic independence. The insistent mutual demands of the princes and their mutual obligations included in the treaties did not permit *economic intrusions* in the feudal domains of their principalities by the other agreeing principalities. The princes mutually promised that neither they nor their boyars would buy villages, nor hold mortgagees or tax-obligated people in the other contracting principality. "And you, my younger brother, shall not purchase villages in my appanage, nor your boyars, nor shall you have mortgagees nor tax-obligated people. On my part I shall not buy villages in your appanage, nor shall my boyars, and I shall not have mortgagees nor tax-obligated people," [20] states an agreement of the grand Prince Dmitrii Ivanovich (Donskoi) with the Prince of Serpukhov and Borov, Vladimir Andreevich, concluded about 1367.

The rationale of this agreement regarding the nonpurchase of villages in another principality is clear: the princes wanted to have strong economic support in their own principalities and anticipated the possibility of this support being weakened by such peaceful economic means as the buying up by other princes or their boyars of villages and votchiny in their principalities.

The references to mortgages in the agreement are equally significant. The economic existence of the mortgage and its original importance in ancient Rus are not clear to this day. Only one thing is certain: the mortgagee was a person in a dependent position with relation to another.[21] By including in the treaty a mutual obligation not to receive mortgages from the people of other treaty principalities, the princes forestalled the possibility of the population of their principalities becoming dependent on the princes and boyars of other principalities.

Where possible, the princes not only tried in advance to prevent the sale of villages to the princes and boyars of other principalities, but also to liquidate all similiar transactions accomplished earlier. This is found, for example, in another agreement of Grand Prince Dmitrii Ivanovich (Donskoi) and the Prince of Serpukhov and Borov,

---

[20] *Ibid.*, p. 20.

[21] See Grekov, *Krestiane na Rusi*, pp. 404–12.

Vladimir Andreevich, concluded in 1389. The Grand Prince proposed that former holders of votchiny in his principality, sold earlier to Prince Vladimir Andreevich and his boyars, buy them back. If the former holders could not do this, the new owners were to assume responsibility to serve the Moscow principality; otherwise, the agreement stated, the land should be taken from the new owners and given to the peasants without payment.[22]

Concern over the preservation of economic independence appears clearly in the treaties between Novgorod and the princes. As a boyar republic Novgorod at the same time had princes who were obliged to perform judicial and administrative functions and to defend the possessions of Novgorod from the enemy. The Grand Prince Vladimir usually served as the prince of Novgorod. Relations with the prince were defined by an agreement.

The Novgorodians jealously guarded the unity and independence of their territories. "And in Bezhitse, neither you, prince, nor your princess, nor your boyars, nor your nobles are allowed to hold or purchase villages, nor to accept them as a gift, throughout the entire volost of Novgorod," [23] states the treaty of Novgorod with the Grand Prince Yaroslav Yaroslavich of Tver (1266). The treaty also forbade the prince to take into his land people from Novgorod: "And from Bezhitse, prince, you shall not take people into your land, nor from any other volost of Novgorod, nor shall you give them charters, nor shall you, or your princess, or your boyars, or your nobles acquire mortgagees: neither smerd nor *kuptsiny*." [24]

These points are repeated in later agreements of Novgorod with the princes.[25] Novgorod demanded the return of its mortgagees from Novgorodian land taken by princes, by princesses, or by their retainers. The treaty with the Grand Prince Mikhail Aleksandrovich of Tver in 1371 not only stipulated that the prince, his boyars and retainers would thereafter not acquire villages in the Novgorodian land, but that lands acquired by them earlier were to be returned to Novgorod.[26]

The agreements between princes show their aspiration to strengthen and to make permanent the country's political disunity by the preservation of the economic independence of their principalities. Political disunity, however, weakened the Russian people in the face of external

---

22 See *Dukhovnye i dogovornye gramoty velikikh i udelnykh kniazei XIV-XVI vv.*, p. 32.

23 *Gramoty Velikogo Novgoroda i Pskova* [Charters of Great Novgorod and Pskov] (Moscow-Leningrad: AS USSR, 1949), p. 11.

24 *Ibid.*

25 *Ibid.*, pp. 12, 15, 21–2, 27–8, 29, and 35.

26 *Ibid.*, p. 29.

danger. By entering into political agreements among themselves and by concluding treaties, the princes tried to reduce the unfavorable side of this disunity, to unite their strength in the struggle with the Tartars and other external foes. "And we both shall be united. And whoever is your friend, Grand Prince, is my friend. And whoever is your enemy is my enemy. And I shall not side with anyone without you . . . And you too will not side with anyone without my knowledge." [27] This formula of general policy appears typical. In addition, many charters speak directly of the general policy of the agreeing princes with relation to the Tartar khans.

Two basic functions characterize the activity of the state in the exploiting social structure, said I. V. Stalin: "the internal (the main one) is to hold the exploited majority in check and the external one (not the main one) is to expand the territory of the ruling class at the expense of the territories of other states or to defend the territories of their state from the attacks of other states." [28]

The political agreements were necessary to the princes in order to set up a general policy and to unite against the external foe; they were also dictated by the need of the feudalists to join forces against the resistance of the exploited mass. By means of these agreements the princes desired to establish unity not only in questions of foreign policy, relations with the Tartar conquerors and other foreign aggressors, but also in important problems of the domestic and social policies of the principalities.

An important point, therefore, repeated in all the interprincely agreements, anticipated the mutual safeguarding of the class rights and privileges of the feudalists. The political disunity of the country and the mutual struggle of the princes for land and power did not hinder them from setting up a general line in the question of the peasantry providing for joint forces to cut off attempts by the toiling masses to emerge from feudal bonds.

The feudalists' service to the prince was voluntary. The boyars, "boyar sons," and free retainers could at any time leave their prince and transfer their allegiance to the service of another. In their agreements [among themselves] the princes strictly preserve this right of the boyars and of free retainers. In the inter-princely agreements the usual statement was: "And the boyars and free retainers shall have freedom:

---

[27] *Dukhovnye i dogovornye gramoty velikikh i udelnykh kniazei XIV–XVI vv.*, pp. 75–6, 81.

[28] I. V. Stalin, *Voprosy leninizma* [Problems of Leninism] (Moscow: 1952), p. 644.

whoever shall depart from us to you, grand prince, or from you to us, shall not be restrained."[29]

In later agreements the mutual obligations of the princes not to hinder the transfer of the boyars from the service of one prince to another were supplemented by the obligation to completely preserve the interests of the boyars transferring from the service of one principality to another. "And your boyars and retainers who live in my votchina I shall treat as my own. And my boyars and retainers who live in your votchina and in the Grand Principality you shall treat as your own,"[30] is stated in the agreement of Prince Iurii Dmitrievich of Halich with the Grand Prince Vasilii Vasil'evich (1433).

The votchiny of the boyars transferring to another principality remained theirs, but the taxes and collections from such votchiny continued to go to the prince on whose territories these votchiny were located. The latter was specified by a point of the treaties: "And court [fees] shall be collected from land and water."

The agreements included important points touching on the peasants: the princes mutually obligated themselves not to receive *"pismennykh,"* that is, persons registered on lists of taxpayers, and *"tiaglykh"* people, that is, persons who had been assessed definite obligations in kind and in money. This agreement of the princes substantially injured the interests of the peasants. The latter were deprived of the possibility of improving their position by transfer from one principality to another. The agreement of the princes not to accept each others' "registered" and "assessed" people was actually the first legal limitation on the right of the peasants to leave the land, binding them to the principality within whose boundaries they found themselves. These measures were dictated by the care of the princes for the interests both of their feudalist–landholders, and the princely treasury: the departure of the "registered" and "assessed" people from the bounds of the principality meant the departure of taxpayers.

The treaties also reflected policy concerning kholopy. The Novgorodians jealously guarded their right to possess slaves. Their agreements with the princes systematically stated that: "And if a kholop or slave makes a complaint against the master, do not believe it."[31]

The inter-princely agreements also disclosed the *trade* policy of the princes. Trade provisions appear constantly in these agreements.

[29] *Dukhovnye i dogovornye gramoty velikikh i udelnykh kniazei XIV–XVI vv.*, pp. 13, 20, and 27.
[30] *Ibid.*, p. 77.
[31] *Gramoty Velikogo Novgoroda i Pskova,* pp. 13, 16, and 36.

Measures were provided for aiding development of trade between the populations of the agreeing principalities: provisions were made for freedom of transit of merchants from one principality to the territories of another, and uniform levies on the merchants of both agreeing principalities were set up with the prohibition of supplemental levies upon them.

A standard formula of the treaties is the point: "And between us our people and merchants shall have a clear way without boundary," that is, the freedom of movement of the trading people in the territories of the agreeing principalities was provided for. "And you shall collect customs and duties from our guests and merchants on the basis of the old tax. And you shall not obstruct their travel, as it was not obstructed under the Grand Prince Ivan, our grandfather, under the Grand Prince Semeon, our uncle, and under our father, the Grand Prince Ivan. And you shall not levy new taxes and duties," [32] states the treaty of the Grand Prince Dmitrii Ivanovich with the Grand Prince of Tver, Mikhail Aleksandrovich (1375).

Many agreements stipulate precisely the manner and rates of collecting duties and taxes levied on trade, with concrete provisos as to the degree of *myto* (transit and marketing tax), *tamga* (levying of a tax on a commodity as a percentage of its value [*ad valorem*]), and *kostka* (a 'head tax' on persons accompanying the goods).[33]

As the richest trading town of Rus, Novgorod was particularly interested in having for its merchants *"a clear way without bounds"* in other principalities. This point appears therefore in all of Novgorod's agreements with princes. With the aid of these agreements Novgorod guaranteed for its merchants not only the right of free trade in the Russian principalities, but other interests as well.

Novgorod diligently guarded its position as a trade intermediary between the Russian principalities and western countries. In all the agreements the statement occurs that the prince must not trade directly with the Germans, but only through Novgorodian merchants. "And in the German settlement, you, prince, trade through our brethren; you shall not close down the settlement, and you shall not appoint any inspectors." [34] It was specially stated that the prince could not impose his myto on the Novgorodian land. The prince could sell tribute collected on the Novgorodian land only to Novgorodians and did not

---

[32] *Dukhovnye i dogovornye gramoty velikikh i udelnykh kniazei XIV–XVI vv.*, p. 28.

[33] *Ibid.*, p. 188.

[34] *Gramoty Velikogo Novgoroda i Pskova*, pp. 13, 16, 22 and 28.

have the right to send it beyond Volok. The prince's nobles were forbidden to take merchants' carts except for military needs.[35]

The policy of protection of trade, as it was expressed in the agreements, was dictated first of all, of course, by the fiscal interests of the princes. The growth of trade meant the growth of princely incomes. This policy reflected at the same time the process of growth of economic and trade ties between the various Russian principalities, notwithstanding the country's political disunity. The economic interests of the princes forced them to set up measures which minimized the hindrances to trade between various principalities, unavoidable under the political disunity of the land. The formula "a clear way without bounds" reflected the progressive tendency of the growth of the country's economic unity, serving in its further development as the foundation for overcoming political disunity and the creation of a centralized Russian state. This formula showed the contradiction between the growing market and the country's political disunity and simultaneously served to resolve the contradictions pointed out above at the particular stage of its development.

The Moscow princes began early to appreciate the significance of the growth of trade as a factor contributing to the country's political unity. They tried to guarantee a normal trade with other principalities, not only with the measures stated above, but also, where necessary, they did not stop short of such measures as complete liberation of some merchants from all forms of levies on trade. In the statutory charter of the Dvina land, given by the Grand Prince of Moscow Vasilii Dmitrievich in 1397, it is stipulated "And wherever the Dvina merchants go, they shall not have to pay throughout my votchina or in the Grand Principality, neither tamga, myto, kostka, *gostinoe, iavka,* nor any other taxes." [36]

From the agreement between the Grand Prince Dmitrii Ivanovich of Moscow with Prince Vladimir Andreevich of Serpukhov and Borov (1389) it is evident that the Moscow princes considered it necessary to protect guests (merchants), and textile traders and therefore did not subject them to princely service.[37]

As has been said, Novgorod occupied the most important place in the trade of Rus with the Western European countries. Novgorod's foreign trade policy is evident from its agreements with the West.[38]

---

[35] *Ibid.*, pp. 16, 22, and 28.

[36] *Ibid.*, pp. 145–6.

[37] *Dukhovnye i dogovornye gramoty velikikh i udelnykh kniazei XIV–XVI vv.*, p. 32.

[38] See *Gramoty Velikogo Novgoroda i Pskova,* pp. 55–136.

These agreements state the mutual right of the parties to visit their territories freely and carry on trade without hindrance; measures are provided to guarantee the personal rights and preserve the property of merchants, the order and degree of taxation of trade, and so on. "Novgorodian ambassadors and all Novgorodians have the right to go in peace into the German land and to the Gotland shore; so too, the Germans and the Goths may go to Novgorod without danger or harm from anyone," [39] stipulates the treaty of Novgorod with the Gotland shore and the German towns (1189–1199).

Novgorod's agreements with the German towns included a clause forbidding the arrest of German merchants in Novgorod and of Novgorodians in German lands; they provided for holding merchants' property as security for the payment of their debts; they recognized the individual responsibility of the merchant for debt or for crimes and the inadmissibility of the seizure of the property of persons not participating in the affair; they stressed the prime importance of the right of the foreign merchant to collect money from the Novgorodian buying goods from the foreigner who proves to be insolvent; they defined responsibility for crimes against the persons of Novgorodians in German lands and of German merchants in Novgorod, and they provided for the composition of a special mixed court in Novgorod for foreign merchants. There are also other items touching on trade relations of Novgorod with foreigners.[40]

Although foreign merchants could freely enter Novgorod, and could travel beyond the limits of the town, Novgorod nevertheless set its trade within narrow limits. As in all other countries at that time, the trade activity of foreigners in Novgorod and in its territory was strictly regulated. Foreign merchants could live only in the special Gothic and German settlements; and the places and times of trade were strictly defined.

As may be judged from the materials, Novgorod firmly held to the principle of forbidding trade between foreign merchants on her territory; the role of intermediary in this trade was retained firmly for Novgorodian merchants, in distinction to other countries, where the Hanseatic League members succeeded in securing the right of direct trade with foreigners without intermediaries.[41] Evidently Novgorod did not accord the members of the Hanseatic League the right of retail

[39] *Ibid.*, p. 55.
[40] *Ibid.*, pp. 60–1.
[41] See I. M. Kulisher, *Istoriia russkogo narodnogo khoziaistva* [History of Russian National Economy] (Moscow: 1925), I, 169.

trade, in contrast to a number of other countries where they possessed this right.

An important field of economic policy of the princes was their *financial policy*—taxes, monetary system, and so on. The Grand Princes established their financial policy independently within each principality. In the fourteenth century the coining of small silver money was resumed in Rus. In Moscow the initiative for this was taken by the Grand Prince Dmitrii Ivanovich (Donskoi), who began to remint the Tartar silver coin, the *denga.* During the second half of the fourteenth century the Moscow, Suzdal'-Nizhegorod, and Riazan principalities coined their own money; in the beginning of the fifteenth century, Tver; and at the end of the fourteenth or the beginning of the fifteenth century, the Rostov principality. The growth of trade dictated the need for their own coinage.

Later (in the fifteenth century) silver money was coined in Novgorod, where previously foreign money was widely used. The adulterated coinage of counterfeiters, the reduction in value of silver money caused by clipping, the recoining of old clipped money into new—all these practices severely affected the interests of the populace and caused uprisings. In the Novgorodian chronicle of 1446 it was written that: "In that year the people began to abuse silver money. All the Novgorodians looked suspiciously at each other, since poverty, hatred, and upheaval prevailed among them. The mayor and the *tisiatsky* (military official) and all the five appointed Novgorod minters began to recoin old money, and new money was to be coined on the following terms: four old coins to one new coin and one grivna made one *poludengi.* The peasants suffered greatly; much loss was brought on the city and on the volost', so that this shall not be forgotten by succeeding generations." [42]

The main form of exploitation of the Russian people by the Tartar-Mongol conquerors was the exacting of heavy tribute and permanent and extraordinary taxes and collections. The order and amount of the levies of these taxes on the population and their collection and transfer to the Golden Horde were the most burning and acute socio-economic questions in Rus during the period of the Tartar-Mongol yoke.

At first the tribute was collected by tax farmers, mainly Moslem merchants, who mercilessly plundered the population and lorded it over them. People who were unable to pay the tribute were put in bondage by the tax farmers and subsequently sold into slavery. Popular

[42] *Novgorodskaia pervaia letopis starshego i mladshego izvodov,* pp. 426–7.

uprisings in Rostov, Vladimir, Suzdal, Yaroslav, and other cities in 1262 forced the Horde to abolish this system of tribute collection, to change first to collection by means of tribute collectors sent for this purpose, and then to transfer the collection of the Horde's tribute to the Russian princes. From this time the collection of the Tartar tribute became one of the most important levers of policy of the princes both in their relations with the Golden Horde and in their relations among themselves.

The tie with the Golden Horde and the responsibility to it for the payment of "Tartar vykhod" (tribute) strengthened the position of the Grand Prince in respect to the appanage princes, who were barred from immediate relations with the Horde. The collection of the Tartar tribute was one of the most important sources of the Grand Princes for filling their own treasuries, as they collected much more than they paid the Horde.

This collection of Tartar tribute by the Russian princes freed the population from the plunder and arbitrariness of the tax farmers, but at the same time it served to increase the feudal oppression of the toiling masses in Rus.

The elevation of the Moscow princes took place because important economic powers were concentrated in their hands. The Moscow Prince Ivan Danilovich, who laid the foundations for the might of Moscow, distinguished himself by displaying great economic ability. "By industriousness and purchases" he zealously acquired lands which yielded much revenue, and hence he was nicknamed "Kalita," or "money bags."

Some materials on the characteristics of the economic policies of the Russian princes and the city-republics, and, at the same time, of Russian economic thought in this period are given us by the Dvina statutory charter and the Pskov court charter.

The Dvina statutory charter was granted by Grand Prince Vasilii Dmitrievich of Moscow to the inhabitants of the Dvina lands in 1397 after the conquest of these lands from Novgorod. The charter was given in connection with the appointment of the Grand Prince's viceroy and was intended to lay the basis of the new administration. It was in effect only for a few months, as the Dvina lands were soon reconquered by the Novgorod army.[43]

---

[43] A text of the Dvina patent charter can be found in *Gramoty Velikogo Novgoroda i Pskova,* pp. 144–6. On princely patent charters whose major portion refers to the subsequent period of Russian history, the period of the creation of a centralized state, see N. Zagoskin, *Ustavnye gramoty XIV–XVI*

We have already noted above one of the points of the Dvina statutory charter, shedding light on the trade policy of the Moscow princes. The provision of this charter concerning the kholopy is significant. "And if the master becomes angry, strikes his kholop or slave, and death should result, the viceroy will not judge or place him in blame," [44] that is, for the unintentional killing of his kholop the master bears no sort of responsibility. This shows the complete lack of rights of the kholopy in the Dvina land in the fourteenth century, as a master could proclaim any sort of killing of kholop unintentional.

There were court charters then in each principality. They defined the right of the court in criminal and civil affairs, and the organization of the judicial process. The significant content of the Pskov court charter, differing from other documents of this type by its abundance of articles, detail, and care in elaborating the legal norms, is of particular interest. It is a collection of legal norms and rules, employed in the court of the Pskov land and is closely related in its purpose to the early all-Russian document, *Russkaia Pravda.*[45]

The time of compilation of the Pskov court charter has not been definitely established. It is supposed that it covers the long period of 1397–1467 in the course of which were compiled various parts of the charter.[46] Similar to *Russkaia Pravda,* the Pskov court charter included articles regulating economic relations.

The Pskov court charter expresses in legal norms economic relations on another level of development than those of *Russkaia Pravda.* It shows the characteristics of the Pskov principality, one of the most advanced Russian regions of that time. As a result of Pskov's border position, the Pskov court charter does not mention the kholopy, differing in this respect not only from *Russkaia Pravda,* but also from the contemporary court charters of other principalities. The Pskov land served as a refuge for kholopy fleeing from other areas.[47]

In contrast to *Russkaia Pravda,* the Pskov court charter contains

---

vv., opredeliaiushchie poriadok mestnogo pravitelstvennogo upravleniia [Patent Charters of the XIV–XVI Centuries Determining the Order of Local Administration] (Kazan: 1875–6), Pt. I and II.

[44] *Gramoty Velikogo Novgoroda i Pskova,* p. 145.

[45] The Lenin Moscow State Pedagogical Institute has published the text of the charter in *Uchenye zapiski* [Scientific Notes] (Moscow: Uchpedgiz, 1952), LXV. It can also be found in I. D. Martysevich, *Pskovskaia sudnaia gramota* [Pskov Court Charter] (Moscow: University, 1951). Translation of the text into modern Russian and commentaries to it by L. V. Cherepnin and A. I. Iakovlev have been published in *Istoricheskie zapiski* [Historical Notes], No. 6 (1940).

[46] See *ibid.,* p. 255 ff.

[47] *Ibid.,* p. 259.

points regulating the purchase, sale, and taxation of land and the transfer of land by bequest. It includes the first article establishing the element of time as the basis for the acquisition of the right of ownership of immovable property (Art. 9).

The Pskov court charter shows the difference between possession and ownership of land. The person using another's land loses this right if he tries to use it as his own—to sell or mortgage it. The right of ownership of the land is described as "land or pure water"; ownership received by inheritance as "pure fold."

The Pskov court charter regulates the mutual relations of the feudalists and persons dependent on them, utilizing the lands or reservoirs—field hands, gardeners, fishermen. Here, for the first time, the right of small landholders to leave the feudalist on whom they are dependent is legally limited. According to Article 42 of the charter, the field hand, gardener, and fisherman can leave his master only at one strictly defined time of the year—the *"Filippovo zagoven'e"* (14 November). This limitation was two-sided: the feudalist could refuse the field hand, gardener, and fisherman work on land or on water only at this same time. The violation of this rule brought retribution on the guilty party: the master refusing work except at the set time lost the right to receive the part of the product destined for him.

Unlike the *Russkaia Pravda,* the Pskov court charter devoted considerable attention to the personal hiring agreement, which figures here in connection with domestic workers, carpenters, and masters for teaching crafts to apprentices. The charter establishes responsibility of the participants of the agreement for the observance of the set period of employment.

A large part of the Pskov court charter is devoted to the question of credit relations. In part, unlike *Russkaia Pravda,* in which for the making of loans exceeding a set minimum it was necessary to have twelve witnesses present, the Pskov court charter demands only a formal document. A number of articles guaranteed the interest of the creditor. Interest in the Pskov court charter is called *"gostinets"* (Art. 73). The amount of interest is not regulated.

As in the Kievan state, the economic thought of Rus during the period of feudal disunity was determined immediately by the economic, political, and cultural conditions of the life of the Russian people. Russian economic thought in these periods does not show in content or in form any signs of foreign influence. An exception must be made, however, with respect to the economic views of Russian churchmen. In their sermons and teachings a direct and strong influence of the Greek church is noticeable, but even here, as we have seen, concrete expression of the general dogmas of the Christian religion was to a significant degree determined by the economic and political conditions of the life of early Rus.

The lack of influence of other countries on the economic policy of the Russian princes is by no means explained by the isolation of Rus from other countries. Many Kievan princes were educated people, and several of them were distinguished by unusual breadth of knowledge, as, for example, the Princes Yaroslav the Wise and Vladimir Monomakh. The Kievan princes carried only lively relations with a number of more influential courts of Europe, and several had family ties with them. Also a number of foreign manuscripts dealing with various fields of knowledge were translated into Russian.

Translations of works of an economic or primarily economic content relating to the period of Kievan Rus are unknown, and there were almost none during the period of feudal disunity, for there was nothing to translate. In the countries of Western Europe economic thought then stood on a level no higher than in Rus. Special economic works were extremely rare and were devoted first of all to the acute problem of money. The widespread practice among the kings of issuing money which was not of full value and the defacing of money were subject to criticism, and to these ends special treatises on money were written. In his works, one written in 1300 and a second in 1306, the Frenchman Philip Dubois rebuked King Philip the Fair for defacing money and warned him of the danger connected with this. Also in the fourteenth century (supposedly in 1373) the French bishop Nicholas Orezmius, the teacher of Charles V, wrote a work, outstanding for that time, in which he examined the questions of money circulation. The author stated that the king did not have the right to obtain income from the coining of money. Orezmius' treatise was originally distributed in manuscript copies. It was first printed in Paris at the beginning of the sixteenth century.

Studying the history of Russian economic thought during the epoch of feudal disunity, one must not overlook one translated literary monument whose content has, to a significant degree, an economic character. This is the "Laws Agricultural" or, as they are otherwise called, "Agricultural Code and Peasant Law." [48]

The "Agricultural Code" is a translation from the Greek. A student

[48] See A. Pavlov, ed., *"Knigi zakonnye," soderzhashchie v sebe, v drevnerusskom perevode, vizantiiskie zakony, zemledelcheskie, ugolovnye, brachnye i sudebnye* [Law Books Containing in Old Russian Translation Byzantine Land, Penal, Marriage, and Judicial Codes] (St. Petersburg: 1885).

of this monument, V. Vasilevskii, believed that the Russian translation of the "Agricultural Code" could be ascribed to the eleventh or the twelfth centuries,[49] but A. Pavlov's supposition that the translation belongs to the end of the twelfth or the beginning of the thirteenth century appears more likely.[50]

The "Law Books," which include the "Agricultural Code," have several parts: 1. The foreword to the law books, "which should serve as a guide to all orthodox princes in their administration"; 2. "Laws of agriculture from Justinian's Books on landowners"; 3. "Law of the Exchecquer"; 4. "Law of Divorce"; 5. "Chapters on *poslusekh*" (that is, concerning witnesses).

The "Laws of Agriculture" consists of detailed regulations concerning economic relationships between agriculturalists, anticipating the various types of disputes between them. In it are defined the conditions and nature of the responsibility of the person guilty of transgressing the economic interests of another: for example, in the case of a neighbor's violation of the bounds of a plowed area or arbitrary sowing on another's land or a dispute of two villages over boundaries. It defines also the conditions of transfer of plowed areas either temporarily or permanently; the conditions of use of another's plot of plowed land—a payment of every tenth and a half sheaf. It sets forth the responsibility of the guilty party for the theft of a plow or plowshare, or of grain and other products, for the injury or killing of another's livestock, for intentional and accidental firing of another's grainfield, garden, and so forth.

The document deals exclusively with husbandmen and their mutual relations. Nothing is said of the relations characteristic of colonist's or of serf's law. The central figures dealt with herein are the husbandman-landowner and the husbandman leasing land from other husbandmen. A number of articles discuss the master's responsibility for an action of the kholop causing loss to a third party. In several articles the code mentions the relations of the husbandman and the commune.

Scholars suppose that the "Agricultural Code" was created in

---

49 See V. G. Vasilevskii, "Zakonodatelstvo ikonobortsev" [The Legislation of the Iconoclasts], *Zhurnal Ministerstva narodnogo prosveshcheniia* [Journal of the Ministry of National Education], October, 1878, pp. 258–309, and November, 1878, pp. 95–129; see also his article on A. Pavlov, *Knigi zakonnye* in *ibid.*, February, 1886, pp. 317–51.

50 See *Knigi zakonnye;* A. Pavlov, "Po voprosu o vremeni, meste i kharaktere pervonachalnogo perevoda vizantiiskogo zemledelcheskogo ustava na slavianskii iazyk" [On the Question of the Time, Place, and Nature of the First Translation of the Byzantine Agricultural Code Into the Slavic Language], *Zhurnal Ministerstva narodnogo prosveshcheniia,* September, 1886, pp. 98–125.

Byzantium in connection with Slavic colonization of the Balkan peninsula during the spread of Slavic settlement into the territories of the Empire in the sixth and seventh centuries.

The majority of early scholars (among them the Russian authors V. Vasilevskii, A. Pavlov, and others) considered the "Agricultural Code" an act of state legislation of eighth century Byzantium, attributing it to the time of the Byzantine emperor-iconoclasts—Leo and Constantine. Another view of the origin and practical significance of the Greek original of the "Agricultural Code" was set forth by B. A. Panchenko.[51] The latter regarded the "Agricultural Code" as a *supplement* to the general civil legislation of Justinian or the iconoclasts, as a supplementary record of customary law from peasant practice dedicated to the needs of the peasant, which had not previously found expression in law. The "Peasant Law" was a record of customary practices and an official record of popular peasant customs.[52]

The content of the Code clearly shows that agrarian relations and the economic structure it reflects did not coincide with those in Rus in the twelfth and thirteenth centuries: for by this time feudal relations already reigned in Rus, big landowners had arisen, and peasants were dependent upon them; whereas the "Agricultural Code" in no way depicts such relations.

This provides an answer to the question of the role of the "Agricultural Code" in ancient Rus. The assertion of some scholars of the possible practical application of the "Agricultural Code" in Rus appears complete conjecture without any factual basis. To such forms of conjecture belongs the theory of A. Pavlov that the Moscow Grand Prince Ivan Kalita might formally have recognized the Byzantine "Agricultural Code" and actively put it into practice in the Moscow principality.[53]

The lack of direct or serious indirect testimony, the comparatively insignificant number of preserved fragments of this code and the fact that in the *Ulozhenie* of 1649 [Code of 1649], where there are refer-

[51] See B. A. Panchenko, "Krestianskaia sobstvennost v Vyzantii. Zemledelcheskii zakon i monastyrskie dokumenty" [Peasant Ownership in Byzantium. Agricultural Law and Monastic Documents], *Izvestiia Russkogo arkheologicheskogo instituta v Konstantinopole* [Bulletin of the Russian Archeological Institute in Constantinople] (Sofia: 1904), IX, 1–234.

[52] See *ibid.*, pp. 4, 27, and 86. According to the opinion of a contemporary scholar, the Agricultural Law represented an original codification of Slavic customary law merged with the Byzantine. (See E. E. Lipshitz, "Vizantiiskoe krestianstvo i slavianskaia kolonizatsiia" [Byzantine Peasantry and Slavic Colonization], *Vizantiiskii sbornik* [Byzantine Collection] (Moscow-Leningrad: AS USSR, 1945), pp. 141–3).

[53] See *Knigi zakonnye*, pp. 35–9.

ences to former laws, nothing whatever is said of the "Agricultural Code" convincingly shows that this monument had, in general, little practical importance in Rus, although the translator of the "Law Books" defines and recommends them as volumes which "should serve as a guide to all orthodox princes in their administration" (from the heading of the foreword to the "Law Books" in the old Russian translation).

Of real significance and definite interest is A. Pavlov's suggestion that the translator of the "Agricultural Code" possibly tried to russify the Byzantine laws, adapting them to the Russian way of life and concepts. "The translator," writes A. Pavlov, "not only transposes to Russian terms or 'meanings' various Byzantine terms of technical significance, but also makes various changes, abbreviations, and additions in the text of the foreign laws." Thus the word "tsar" is always accompanied by the addition, "or prince"; the Greek word signifying treasury is translated "public treasury," "lord's treasury," or "lord's public treasury," with an explanation in one case of the phrase, "to the public treasury," with the words, "that is, to the prince"; the Greek word signifying "state pay to officials" is translated by paraphrase "honor and power and food coming from the prince," which evidently refers to the Russian system of "kormlenie." [54]

Economic Problems in the Literature of the Churchmen. The Heresy of the "Shearers' sect"

In the preceding chapter the social role of the church in Kievan Rus was shown and the class content of the utterances of the churchmen on socio-economic problems explained. The Christian religion is one of the forms of the ideological superstructure strengthening the base of the feudal society. Completely supporting the feudal form of exploitation of labor and slaveowning, sanctifying with the dogmas of the Christian religion the division of society into exploiters and exploited, the churchmen at the same time came out against the extremes of this exploitation and recognized in this a means of strengthening the feudal structure and, along with it, the authority of the church. They wanted to present the church to the toiling masses as if it were the defender of the interests of the exploited.

The same must be said also of the literature of the churchmen during the period of feudal disunity. As earlier, the church not only sancti-

[54] *Ibid.*, p. 20.

fied with its authority the feudal exploitation of the toiling masses, but also itself took an active part in this exploitation as a large feudal landowner. As before, the church officials called on the poor people to abase themselves unconditionally before their masters, and the masters were exhorted not to display extreme cruelty to their slaves. There is no particular need to set forth here the statements of the churchmen on these questions related to this given period, inasmuch as the sense and real significance of them was the same as in the period of Kievan Rus examined by us above. It is important, however, to note that the statements of the churchmen on socio-economic problems sometimes prominently reflect the further sharp aggravation of the class contradictions in Rus.

As earlier, in the period of Kievan Rus, the churchmen condemned any gain by means of moneylending and cheating in trade. Sharp condemnation of *"rezoimstvo"* (moneylending) is seen, for example, in the statements of the Bishop Serapion of Vladimir, an outstanding preacher of the thirteenth century.[55] "The money lenders eat their brothers' blood," said the metropolitan Nikifor in his teachings. However he demanded, not the abolition of interest, but only its lowering to 20 per cent—*"na piat shestoia."*

From the fourteenth century the colection of translated and Russian teachings under the title of *"Izmaragd"* increased. Among many other admonitions and injunctions there are those which relate directly to the economic aspects of life.

Thus, for example, the author of "Words on the Wealthy and Merciless" condemns wealth which is earned by way of plunder or which finds its way into the hands of the speculator, contrasting it to wealth earned honestly and found in the hands of a good man. In "A Word on the Rebellion of the Human Life," Gold—allegorized and depicted as being concealed by the wealthy—complains of its fate and persistently asks to be allowed to go to the poor people: "O wealthy gold lovers, why do you make me a nuisance? Why don't you accept me as a true friend, and stop treating me as a thief, tying me up firmly or burying me in the ground, and shifting me from the darkness of one fist to another? If you want me to see the light again, let me go into the hands of lower people, I beg you." [56]

The negative attitude of the church to moneylending was also ex-

---

[55] See E. Petukhov, *Serapion Vladimirskii, russkii propovednik XIII veka* [Serapion of Vladimir, Russian Preacher of the XIII Century] (St. Petersburg: 1888), Appendix, pp. 2, 4.

[56] See *Istoriia russkoi literatury,* II, 160.

pressed in the tale of the Novgorod mayor Shchilo, who lent money for interest and was punished for this practice by God.[57]

As earlier, the church personnel and monasteries occupied in trade and moneylending were subjected to particularly sharp censure. "And those abbots or priests or monks who trade or lend silver for interest," wrote the Metropolitan Fotius to the Novgorodians (1410), "no matter from what sources, should stop it: Because the holy apostles were not addicted to it, nor is it blessed by the Holy Fathers, and it is dangerous." [58]

The churches received definite advantage from the development of trade in the country. As stated in the preceding chapter, a tenth share of the trading collections was set aside for the support of the church. In Kiev, Novgorod, and in other towns, the church was entrusted with the important function of supervising trading weights and measures and the obligation of watching over their accuracy.[59] The monasteries themselves carried on trade, several of them to a great extent. The persistent exhortations of the churchmen, directed at the abbots, priests, and monks, not to engage in trade and moneylending indicate that the latter were widely engaged in this their own personal interests.

In the fourteenth century new traits are noted in the relations of the propertied classes toward the slaves and slave labor. In the testament [will] of Ivan Kalita (about 1339), the slaves and all of the prince's property are transferred to his heirs. In the will of the Grand Prince Semen Ivanovich (1353) slaves are to be freed upon the death of the prince. "As regards my working people, or those who were purchased or obtained because of debt, also my servants, peasants, housekeepers, and elders, and whoever shall be married to these people, I give all these people freedom to go wherever they wish. These people are unnecessary to either my brothers or my princess." [60] A similar provision regarding the liberation of the slaves after the death of the prince is repeated in the wills of later princes.[61]

In spite of the assertions of the church apologists the ideological

---

[57] See N. Gudzii, *Khrestomatiia po drevnei russkoi literature XI–XVII vv.* [Anthology of Early Russian Literature XI–XVII Centuries] (Moscow: Uchpedgiz, 1947), pp. 195–6.

[58] *Pamiatniki drevnerusskogo kanonicheskogo prava,* Pt. I; *Russkaia istoricheskaia biblioteka* [Russian Historical Library] (2nd edition, St. Petersburg: 1908), VI, 275.

[59] See M. F. Vladimirskii-Budanov, ed., *Khrestomatiia po istorii russkogo prava* [Anthology of the History of Russian Law]. (4th edition, 1889), pp. 226–37.

[60] *Dukhovnye i dogovornye gramoty velikikh i udelnykh kniazei XIV–XVI vv.,* p. 14.

[61] *Ibid.,* pp. 17, 25, 57, and 198.

influence of the church may be seen least of all in these actions. As stated, the church adopted the slaveowning form of exploitation and condemned only the cruelty of a lord in relation to slaves and the extreme exploitation of them.

Beginning in the fourteenth century the liberation of slaves by the princes had its economic basis, for it had been increasingly discovered that the productivity of the kholopy was low and that it had disadvantages in comparison with the other basic forms of compulsory labor —the labor of the feudally dependent peasants.

In this difficult period of the history of the Russian people the church not only sanctified with its authority the feudal and slave-owning exploitation of the toiling masses, but also offered prayers for the Khan's family and called the people to humility and submission before the Tartar-Mongol enslavers. In return, the church received from the Golden Horde full freedom from tribute and from all other collections and obligations. The *yarlyks* [letters] of the Khans protected the churchmen not only from the Tartars, but from the Russian princes as well, who could not enter church lands. The church thus became independent of princely authority.

It is not within the scope of this work to make any sort of detailed and systematic comparison of the historical process of the development of Russian economic thought and of the economic thought of the peoples of other countries. The unfolding of a comparative analysis of the history of the development of economic thought in Russia and in other lands of Western Europe and the Orient demands an enormous preliminary work. In the *Theories of Surplus Value,* Marx's *Capital,* and other works of the founders of scientific socialism the history of the development of *bourgeois* political economy is brilliantly shown. Marx critically analyzes the most important stages of the development of bourgeois political economy in the principal capitalist countries, beginning with its appearance. There are no analogous works regarding the economic thought of feudal society. Moreover, a comparative analysis of the historical process of the development of economic thought in various countries in the period of feudalism requires a differentiated study of this process in various stages of the development of feudalism and of the presentation of the economic thought of the spokesmen of various classes and social groups of feudal society. That which is now in existence in this field comes mainly from the pens of bourgeois economists and touches only on certain periods and various parts of economic thought. Thus, for example, even the work of the famous French historian of the nineteenth century, Ad.

Blanqui, *History of Political Economy in Europe From the Earliest to the Present Time,* attempts to illuminate such questions as the "political economy of Charlemagne" and the economic side of his Capitularies. Reference is made to the "upheaval produced in the development of political economy during the reign of Charles V," [62] But the works of the bourgeois economists merely skim the actual history of economic thought and give nothing for comparative analysis. The comparison of the development of Russian economic thought with the economic thought of other countries, therefore, inescapably bears a fragmentary character in our book.

Returning to the question of the economic viewpoints of the Russian churchmen, one can, it seems to us, note still another important trait. Although the ideological role of the economic thought of the Russian churchmen was influential in strengthening the base of society—the feudal-serf productive relations—in feudal Russia, it nevertheless did not have such direct influence on the social life of the country as it had in the countries of Western Europe in the medieval period. First of all we have here the influence of the economic views of the churchmen on civil legislation with respect to such important questions of economic life as price, trade profit, and interest on capital. It is known that these questions also occupy an important place in the works of the medieval writers—the theologians and canonists—of western Europe.

Economic problems, like philosophic, legal and, other problems of social life were examined in the Middle Ages by scholastics from the point of view of their relationship to the dogmas of the "Holy Scripture." Economic problems were treated as religious-ethical norms of economic activity, determined by church authorities.

Canonists created the theory of the so-called "just price." This theory did not reveal the objective law lying at the base of commodity prices, but set up norms for the conduct of people in the market: goods *must* be sold only at a "just price." As "just price" the medieval scholastics understood a price which would reflect the amount of labor expended in the production of the goods and the social position of the producer of the goods, which would give the seller the ability to live in accordance with his position in the class feudal society. The theory of the "just price" had a broad practical significance in Western Europe. Corresponding organs set up firm, fixed prices on various goods, and these fixed prices had to be strictly observed by sellers and buyers.

The views of the writers—the theologians and canonists—on money

---

[62] See Blanqui, *Istoriia politicheskoi ekonomii v Evrope,* I, pp. 130–41, 245–55; and II.

lending also had practical application. At first the church forbade only the clergy to engage in moneylending. Beginning in the ninth century this prohibition began to extend also to laymen. At the end of the twelfth century Pope Alexander III threatened money lenders with excommunication and deprivation of Christian burial. Gregory X ordered moneylenders to be expelled from communes, corporations, and towns and took from them the right to make wills. The Synod of 1311 applied the prohibition of moneylending to secular legislation. The secular laws which contradicted the church decrees on interest were proclaimed inoperative. Secular legislation also began to prohibit usury. The prohibition of interest was a church dogma, doubt of which was proclaimed a "heresy" and persecuted as a heresy. The Catholic church considered the lending of money for interest to be as serious and punishable a crime as theft, robbery, and murder; it sternly controlled the civilian trade turnover and credit transactions, hindering their development.

The contradictions between the dogmatists of the Catholic church and objective conformity to the principles of the economic development of society, expressed in the growth of commodity production and the market as well as in the expansion of commodity and financial loans, led to evasion of the laws forbidding usury and trade profits in many ways, including the use of these practices by churchmen themselves. On the other hand, the theologians and canonists increasingly tried to justify theoretically these manifestations of economic life, making corrections in their categorical demands and permitting digressions from them.

In this regard Thomas Aquinas (thirteenth century), who tried in some measure to adapt the teachings of the canonists to the demands of life, is particularly characteristic. He condemned only speculative trade and rejected high profit, but permitted moderate profit. Trying to justify moderate usury, he compared interest with land rent, which had always been permitted. Taking interest was proclaimed a reward for loss or for nonreceived profit. However it may have been, the prohibition on interest continued in the civil legislation of the countries of Western Europe until the sixteenth century, when it was removed by the Reformation. In the sixteenth century works appeared justifying the taking of interest (Calvin, Diumulen).[63]

---

[63] See W. J. Ashley, *Ekonomicheskaia istoriia Anglii v sviazi s ekonomicheskoi teoriei* [Economic History of England in Connection with Economic Theory] (Moscow: 1897), Pt. I and II; A. I. Chuprov, *Istoriia politicheskoi ekonomii* [History of Political Economy] (Moscow: 1918); V. V. Sviatlovskii, *Ocherki po istorii ekonomicheskikh vozzrenii na Zapade i v Rossii* [Outlines

In Russia the theories of "just price" did not exist at all, and no prohibtion of interest was reflected in civil legislation. The prohibition of interest by the church extended only to the clergy; acceptance of usury by laymen was condemned only morally.

The roots of this important economic outlook of Russian churchmen toward usury evidently lie in the difference in relations between the church and the state authority in Russia and in the countries of Western Europe: the Catholic church preached and tried to embody the theoretical idea of church supremacy, the spiritual authority over secular authority; whereas the Greek orthodox church—the dogmas of which were adopted by the Russian clergy—insisted on the subordination of the church to the state authority. In addition, the negative attitude of Orthodox church officials toward usury did not have the extremely sharp character which it had among Catholic officials.

To the fourteenth century belongs the appearance of the sectarian movement of "the shearers' sect" (*strigolniki*) which became widespread in Novgorod and Pskov in the last quarter of the fourteenth and the first quarter of the fifteenth century. Information concerning this movement has come down to us mainly from the charters of the church authorities issued in Novgorod and Pskov and from entries in the chronicles. The strigolniki repudiated the established church rituals and came out resolutely against all church exactions and against ordainment. They repudiated ordainment because they believed that simple laymen could perform the church service.

The strigolnik Karp, states Bishop Stefan of Perm in an accusing epistle against the strigolniki, "began to tell the people: it is neither dignified to sing over the dead, nor to mention them; nor to bring offerings for the dead to the church; nor to have feasts; nor to give alms for the soul of the departed." [64] The nature of the strigolnik movement is seen from the following words of the same Bishop Stefan's teachings: "Of the strigolniki illiterate people say: those neither steal nor collect wealth." [65]

Attacking the ruling church and its rituals, the strigolniki also criticized the feudal order. If one takes the immediate economic aspect of views of the strigolniki, they mainly protested against the supplementary exploitation of the toiling masses by the church in the form of

---

of the History of Economic Views in the West and in Russia] (St. Petersburg: 1913), Pt. I.

[64] *Pamiatniki drevnerusskogo kanonicheskogo prava*, Pt. I; *Russkaia istoricheskaia biblioteka*, VI, 224.

[65] *Ibid.*, VI, 226.

various collections gathered from the believers. To this movement apply the words of Engels regarding the "burgher heresies" of the Middle Ages in the West: "burgher opposition struggled very seriously against the priests' idle, luxurious life and their debauched ways, which called forth the greatest discontent." [66] "The heresy of the cities—and it is particularly the official heresy of the Middle Ages—was directed mainly against the priests and their wealth and political position, which it attacked . . . the medieval burghers demanded first of all a cheap church . . . reactionary in form, as every heresy, which in further development of the church and dogmas was able to see only distortion; the burgher heresy demanded restoration of the simple order of the early Christian church and the abolition of the special class of ecclesiasts." [67]

Against the strigolniki who encroached on the propertied well-being of the church, the latter directed all its ideological and administrative force. In numerous epistles to the clergy and inhabitants of Novgorod and Pskov the church leadership tried to discredit the movement of the strigolniki idealistically, with reference to the Scriptures, proving the correctness of the church in receiving its income.[68]

But the matter was not limited to ideological struggle. The strigolniki were excommunicated, persecuted, driven from the towns, or simply killed. The chronicles state that in Novgorod, "the heretic strigolniki were beaten; deacon Nikita and Parishioner Karp and a third man with them were thrown from the bridge."

Marx wrote in the preface to the first volume of *Capital:* "The English Established Church will more readily pardon an attack on thirty-eight of its Thirty-nine Articles than on a thirty-ninth of its income." By the fourteenth and fifteenth centuries the Russian church had in effect to endure the first attacks on its income. For the time being this took place in only one part of Russia—the rich and developed feudal town-republics.

In addition to the epistles aimed directly at the heresy of the strigolniki, the appeals of leaders of the Russian church to the Novgorodians and Pskovians have been preserved from the end of the fourteenth and beginning of the fifteenth century. They consist of insistent admonitions and demands to leave the church and monastery property inviolate, that is, in the full ownership of the churches and monasteries. This testifies to the fact that even at so early a date members of

---

[66] Engels, *Krestianskaia voina v Germanii,* p. 28.

[67] *Ibid.,* p. 35.

[68] See *Pamiatniki drevnerusskogo kanonicheskogo prava,* Pt. I, pp. 191–8, 211–28.

the "flock" in Novgorod and Pskov made persistent assaults not only on the current income of the church, but also on church domains in general. In the struggle against these attacks on its wealth, the Russian church ardently defended the theory of the inviolability and inalienability of church property.

The doctrine of the inviolability of church property is shown in the charter of the Metropolitan Cyprian to the Novgorodian Archbishop Ioann (1392), specifically devoted to just this question: "No peasant should interfere with church yards, villages, lands, waters, and taxes obtained by the Holy Church, or purchased or bequeathed in return for prayer of the soul; and God's rules will not bless whomever should interfere." [69] "And no one shall interfere with either church taxes, or lands, or waters, and still observe the holy rules; whoever does so shall cease instantly." [70]

In 1395 similar admonitions are repeated in the epistle of the Metropolitan Cyprian to Pskov.[71] The inviolability of church properties is mentioned in the teachings of the Metropolitan Fotius to the Grand Prince Vasilii Dmitrievich (about 1410).[72] The Novgorodian archbishop Simeon instructs the Pskovians in 1419: "do not injure the Church of God . . . in lands, in waters, in courts, in press and in all duties of the Church do not interfere." [73] The same is repeated in the epistles of the Metropolitan Feodosii to Novgorod in 1463 [74] and in his epistles to the Pskovians in 1463–1465.

Later, in the sixteenth century, church landholdings became one of the most acute problems, inaugurating a long and stubborn struggle.

Economic Questions in Secular Literature. Afanasii Nikitin and His "Journey Beyond Three Seas"

The monuments of secular literature of this period reflected the most important events in the life of the Russian people.

A great work of old Russian literature, the "Tale of the Host of Igor," belonging to the end of the twelfth century, tells of the unsuccessful Russian expedition against the Polovtsy in 1185. "The sense of the poem," wrote Marx of the "Tale," "is the call of the Russian princes to unite on the eve of the Mongol invasion." [75] The "Tale" supports the defense of the entire Russian land.

[69] *Ibid.*, Pt. I, pp. 229–30.
[70] *Ibid.*, Pt. I, pp. 230–1.
[71] *Ibid.*, Pt. I, pp. 231–2.
[72] *Ibid.*, Pt. I, pp. 289–304.
[73] *Ibid.*, Pt. I, p. 402.
[74] *Ibid.*, Pt. I, pp. 695–8.
[75] Marx and Engels, *Sochineniia*, XXII, 122.

The "Tale of the Host of Igor" has some significance also for the study of the history of Russian economic thought. Various poetic descriptions are dedicated to agricultural work, evidently well known to the author. "On the Nemige sheaves are stacked as heads, and they flail with tempered chains; the body is placed on the threshing floor, and the soul is winnowed from the body." [76]

Remembering the times of Oleg Sviatoslavich, the grandfather of Prince Igor, the author reproaches Oleg for promoting discord, which led to the destruction of people and wealth: "In those days the ploughmen rarely shouted at the horses, but ravens croaked often when they divided the dead bodies among themselves . . ." [77]

In the "Tale" the author's attitude toward slave labor is also revealed. Appealing to the Grand Prince Vsevolod and inviting him to struggle with the Polovtsy, the author says: "For you could dry up the Volga with your oars, and empty the Don with your helmets. If you were here, a [Polovtsy] slave girl would be worth a dime, and a man slave, half a ruble." [78] The existence of slaves appears to be a fully normal phenomenon to the author. His imagination is captivated by the prospect of an abundance of slaves from the prisoners and of their cheapness. This attitude toward slaves corresponds fully to the viewpoints of the representatives of the ruling class of Kievan Rus and the beginning of the period of feudal disunity. Later, as we have already said, this attitude began to change.

A number of outstanding literary works of the time throw light upon the Tartar-Mongol bondage and the heroic struggle of the Russian people for liberation: "The Tale of the Ruin of the Land of Rus," "Trans-Don," and others. In "The Song of Shchelkan Diudent'evich" the cruelty of the enslavers is clearly depicted, as is the suffering of the Russian people under the Tartar-Mongol yoke.[79]

Among the monuments of secular literature in which the socioeconomic ideas of the epoch were reflected, "The Prayer of Daniel Zatochnik" is of some significance in the study of the history of Russian economic thought. This work is preserved in two editions, one of which the literary historians attribute to the twelfth century and the other to the 13th. Who the author of the work was and for what reason it was written is unknown. Some believe that "The Prayer" was written by a scribe formerly in the service of the prince and then exiled

---

[76] *Slovo o polku Igoreve* [Tale of Igor's Host], Biblioteka poeta, Malaia seriia. [Poet's Library, Small Series] (2nd edition, Leningrad: 1949), p. 105.

[77] *Ibid.*, p. 97.

[78] *Ibid.*, p. 102.

[79] See *Istoricheskie pesni* [Historical Songs], Biblioteka poeta, Malaia seriia [Poet's Library, Small Series] (2nd edition, Leningrad: 1951), pp. 66–70.

or imprisoned; others assume that the author of "The Prayer" was a courtier, a princely retainer.[80] A third sees in the author a kholop of a boyar, a view which in general has little likelihood if we take into consideration the author's great erudition and literary experience. Finally, the academician M. N. Tikhomirov, who not long ago discovered a new copy of a work by Daniel Zatochnik called in the manuscript "Notes," suggests that the author was an artisan-silversmith who had fallen into poverty and had been punished for theft.[81] The one thing certain is that the "Prayer" was written by a dependent person who was discontented with his position and requested aid of the prince.

In "The Prayer," the antagonism between the poor and the rich and the author's opposition to boyardom and monastacism clearly appear. This antagonism is expressed, for example, in the words: "They do not have their households close to the Tsar's, and they do not have villages close to the princely ones: his servants are like a fire loaded with explosives, and his common people are like sparks. You may save yourself from fire, but from sparks you cannot." "When the rich man speaks everyone is silent, and then his words are elevated to the clouds; but when the poor man speaks, everyone calls out to him. For the discourses of those are honored whose garments are clean." [82]

Daniel Zatochnik compares his poor life to that of the rich prince: "While you consume various foods, remember me [who am] eating dry bread; while you enjoy sweet drinks, dressed in your beautiful garments, remember me [he who] lies in dirty rags; while you sleep on a soft bed remember me [who am] lying under one cover, whose body the raindrops penetrate like arrows, and who is dying in winter." [83]

"The Prayer" is characterized by the author's sharply negative attitude toward monks and the monastic life. Daniel rejects the thought of shedding his poverty-stricken position by becoming a monk. He would rather end his life in poverty than to lie to God by accepting monasticism. Many monks, he writes, return again to their worldly life, go around the village and the houses of the worldly well-to-do "as

---

[80] See V. M. Gussov, "Istoricheskaia osnova 'Moleniia Danila Zatochnika' " [Historical Foundation of 'the Supplication of Daniel the Exile], *Trudy otdela drevnerusskoi literatury* [Works of the Department of Ancient Russian Literature], VII (1949), 410–18.

[81] See M. N. Tikhomirov, " 'Napisanie' Danila Zatochnika" [The Writing of Daniel the Exile], *ibid.*, X (1954), 278.

[82] "Slovo Danila Zatochnika po redaktsiiam XII i XIII vv. i ikh peredelkam" [Discourses of Daniel the Exile from Twelfth and Thirteenth Century Redactions and Their Recastings], *Pamiatniki drevnerusskoi literatury* [Monuments of Ancient Russian Literature] (3rd issue, Leningrad: AN USSR, 1932), pp. 11, 21.

[83] *Ibid.*, p. 66.

flattering dogs." Wherever there are marriages and feasts, there are monks and nuns in transgression; they have an angelic appearance and a sinful way, "they possess holy orders, but indecent customs." The author of the "Prayer" insistently asks the prince to take him into service as a counsellor.

The view to the effect that Daniel Zatochnik was a spokesman for the kholop position, expressed in literature for the first time and very clearly reflected in "The Prayer," has been justly refuted as unfounded.[84] The text of the memorial shows that its author regards the kholop with extreme contempt.

Finally we will examine the remarkable literary monument created by one of the Russian merchants, Afanasii Nikitin, "A Journey Beyond Three Seas."[85] The merchant Afanasii Nikitin, together with other Russian merchants from Tver and Moscow and Bukhara merchants returning from Rus, set out with goods in 1466 down the Volga to the sea and, as far as can be judged, to the Shirvan independent khanate found in the ciscaspian Transcaucasus in northeast Azerbaidzhan. Russian merchants then engaged in a lively trade with the eastern countries, including Shirvan. A particularly large trade was carried on by the Tver merchants, who were favored by their advantageous geographical position on the Volga trade route.

Below Astrakhan the small caravan of boats with which Afanasii Nikitin sailed was plundered by Tartars. Nikitin and the other merchants reached Derbent, one of the towns of the Shirvan khanate, but their attempts to obtain material aid from the Shah of Shirvan in order to return to Rus, were unsuccessful. "And we, weeping, dispersed wherever we could: those who had something in Rus went to Rus, and those who were indebted there went wherever their eyes could lead them; others remained in Shemakh [a town in Shirvan, one of the residences of the shahs of Shirvan—A. P.], and others went to work in Baku."[86]

Among the latter was Nikitin. In the winter of 1467 he set out from Baku across the Caspian Sea to Persia. Russian merchants had carried on trade with Persia for a long time. There they obtained mainly silk, in exchange for furs and other goods. Nikitin stayed there for about

---

[84] See Tikhomirov, *Istochnikovedenie istorii SSSR,* I, 86–7.

[85] The text *Khozhenie za tri moria* [A Journey Across Three Seas] is in two copies: the Troitsk copy and the Undolskii copy of the XVII century. For a translation of *Journey* into modern Russian, scholarly analysis and commentaries see B. D. Grekov and V. P. Adrianova-Perets, eds., *Khozhenie za tri moria Afanasiia Nikitina (1466–1472)* [A Journey Across Three Seas of Afanasii Nikitin (1466–1472)] (Moscow-Leningrad: AS USSR, 1948).

[86] *Ibid.,* p. 55. Hereinafter the contemporary translation is cited.

a year and a half and visited many parts of the country, evidently in connection with his business transactions.

In April, 1469, he set out from Ormuz, the last Persian port on the road to India beyond the "Indian Sea," as the Indian Ocean was then called. Nikitin remained in India almost three years. He was homesick throughout his long trip. In the beginning of 1472 Nikitin left India and set out for the motherland. By way of the "Indian Sea" he went to Persia, crossed the Black Sea, arrived in Balaklava, and proceeded to Kafa (now Feodosiia), then a Crimean colony of the Genoese republic. In Kafa at that time there were also Russian merchants and a Russian monastery-inn.

"The Three Seas," the journey across which Nikitin describes, were thus the Caspian, Indian, and Black Seas. From Kafa, Nikitin set out for Tver through the Lithuanian principality, the route then usually used by Russian merchants trading with Crimea, but before reaching Smolensk he died. In 1475 Russian merchants arriving in Moscow from Lithuania brought back the notebook containing Afanasii Nikitin's account. They gave it to the clerk of the Grand Prince, who turned it over to the chronicler to enter in the chronicle for that year.

Nikitin describes the route of his journey in detail, carefully enters in the notebook his impressions of the places he visited, and recounts events which he witnessed personally, or of which he had heard from others. He describes the nature and population of India, its economic activity, customs, religion, and military affairs.

Nikitin was the first Russian to describe India, which until then was known to Russians only by tales, mainly of a fantastic character. At the same time his description of India was generally one of the first eyewitness accounts of this land by a European. Nikitin departed from India twenty-five years before the Portuguese traveller Vasco de Gama arrived there by sea, (1497–1499). The latter described the sea route to India, but not India itself. In its wealth of material and the accuracy of its description of the various aspects of the life of the country Nikitin's record takes first place among the few descriptions of India of that time. It is thus of worldwide significance.

In the account of his journey, Afanasii Nikitin appears as a man of broad outlook and exact observation, extremely curious to see essential facts and events. His narrative is permeated by a feeling of patriotism, and fervent love for the Russian land. The Tver principality was at that time still an independent grand principality, but Nikitin felt himself in India as a representative of all Rus.

At the same time, it is evident from his accounts that he was dissatisfied with the situation in Russia and with the injustice of the boyars. "And the Russian land God protects," he writes, "in this world there is no land like it, although the wealthy ones (boyars) of the Russian land are unjust (not good). But the Russian land builds itself, and there will be justice in it." [87]

In the study of Russian economic thought of this period it is particularly significant that problems of the economy of India, primarily of its trade, occupy a large place in Nikitin's description of his "Journey Beyond Three Seas." Nikitin was struck by the abundance of towns in India. He indicates the distance between various places, and the nature of the communications between them, "on land" or "by sea." He describes the towns he visited, the ports in various parts of India, and he carefully notes such details as the kind of goods, their prices, where and how trade is carried on, the rate of duties, and so on.

All of this Nikitin examines in the light of the possibility of trade between Rus and India. He feels himself there as a trade representative of Rus and explains the economic potentialities and the conditions of Russian-Indian trade. "The *psy busurmane* (Moslem dogs) deceived me," writes Nikitin of his first impressions on arrival in India. "They spoke of the abundance of goods, but it turned out that there was nothing here for our land. All pure commodities are only for Moslem lands. Pepper and indigo are cheap. Some carry goods by sea; others do not pay duty for it. But they will not give it to us without duties. And the duty is large, and there are many pirates on the sea." [88]

Visiting the great Indian city of Bidar, Nikitin writes: "In Bidar there is trade in horses and in goods; damask, silk, and all other such commodities; one can also buy black people here [Negro slaves]. There is nothing else to buy. Their commodities are all Indian. As for food, everything is fruit: No commodities here for Russia." [89]

Nikitin describes, further, a place 120 versts from Bidar "where once a year there is a bazaar whither all the Indian land comes to trade, and they trade there ten days." "In India this is a good trading place." [90]

Nikitin was greatly impressed by Ormuz, where a great trade was carried on with the participation of merchants of many different countries. "Ormuz is a great port. The people of all the world visit it, and various commodities are found here. Whatever grows in the world is found at Ormuz. The duty is high; on everything they take a tithe." [91]

Nikitin describes the port of Calcutta—"a port for the entire Indian Sea." He writes of the products that are found there—pepper, ginger,

[87] *Ibid.*, p. 68.
[88] *Ibid.*, p. 58.
[89] *Ibid.*
[90] *Ibid.*, p. 59.
[91] *Ibid.*, pp. 63–4.

nutmeg, cinnamon, cloves, spices, and others. "And all of it is cheap." [92] He indicates that Ceylon "is a large port on the Indian Sea," and enumerates in detail the products that are manufactured there. For several of the wares Nikitin indicates also the means of measuring them: "an arm's length," and a "weight." He also describes the port of Shabat, Peg, and others.[93]

Problems relating to India's agriculture did not attract much of Nikitin's attention; he speaks very little about them in his notes. "For four months," he writes, "everywhere there was water and mud, both day and night." "Then they plow and sow wheat, tuturgan, peas, and everything edible." [94]

The material condition of the inhabitants of India did not escape Nikitin's observing eye. He notes the great difference in the condition of various groups, of classes of society. "The land is densely populated; the peasants are very poor, and the boyars rich and luxurious." [95]

The "Journey Beyond Three Seas," entered, as has been said, in the chronicle, enriched the knowledge of the Russian people concerning a great land almost entirely unknown to them until that time.

The economic thought of this period reflects the process of development in feudal productive relationships, the increase of feudal exploitation, and the accentuation of class contradictions. At the same time it shows the economic and political disunty of the country and the struggle that was occurring to overcome the feudal disunity of the land and to create a unified Russian state.

Economic thought of the period of feudal disunty revealed the struggle of the Russian people against the Tartar-Mongol enslavers and other usurpers. The church literature, continuing to play the same social role as it had in the preceding period, the ideal of sanction and sanctification of feudal exploitation, objectively reflected in its various works the further, and then sharp accentuation of, class contradictions and class struggle.

In this period the first clearly expressed opposition to the exploitation of the popular masses by the church appeared. Demands arose to deprive the churchmen of their unearned income and to take from the church its immovable property.

At the end of this period the representatives of a new, growing class appear on the scene in literature—the merchants.

---

92 *Ibid.*, p. 64.
93 *Ibid.*, pp. 64–5.
94 *Ibid.*, pp. 56–7.
95 *Ibid.*, pp. 59–60.

PART III
THE PERIOD OF LIQUIDATION OF THE COUNTRY'S DISUNITY

CHAPTER 3. *The Economic Policy of Ivan III.*

Changes in the Economy and Formation of the Russian Centralized State.

The last decades of the fifteenth and the [entire] sixteenth century represent a very important transition period in the history of Rus. This period witnessed the conclusion of the long and complicated process, begun under Ivan Kalita, of the consolidation of the lands around Moscow, the liquidation of the country's feudal disunity, and the formation of the centralized Russian state. This era represents one of the most important stages in Russian social history.

The creation of the centralized state meant a change in the relative power of the various groups within the ruling feudal class: the weakening of the role of the boyars and the hereditary feudal nobles on the one hand, and the elevation of the *dvorianstvo* [nobility] on the other. The formation of the centralized state was accomplished by strengthening the autocratic power of the sovereign, with the support of the nobility.

The unification of the Russian lands around Moscow and the strengthening of the power of the Moscow princes led to the weakening of the dependence of the Russian people on the Tartar-Mongol enslavers. In Russia, wrote Engels, "the conquest of the appanage princes went hand in hand with liberation from the Tartar yoke and finally was rendered permanent by Ivan III." [1] In 1480 Russia completely liberated herself from the Tartar-Mongol domination, which had been smothering the Russian people for almost two and a half centuries.

[1] Marx and Engels, *Sochineniia,* XVI, Pt. I, 450.

Beginning approximately in the middle of the fifteenth century, a new rise of productive forces became noticeable in the northeastern regions of the country. The rise of agriculture was accomplished on the basis of a broad application of the three-field system, which already dominated a large part of the country in this period. The establishment of the three-field system and increase in the use of fertilizers significantly raised the productivity of agricultural labor.

Important changes took place in the forms of feudal exploitation. Until the sixteenth century the feudal landowners had comparatively little plowland, and their land was worked mainly by kholopy. In the sixteenth century seigniorial plowland greatly increased, and the working of seigniorial land was accomplished by the labor of feudally dependent peasants. Bread was produced on the feudal estate not only for immediate consumption, but also for sale. The exploitation of the peasants increased.

From the end of the fifteenth century cases of the replacement of natural obrok by money became more frequent on the estates employing the obrok system; that is, money rent appeared, which again was connected with the growth of markets and of money-commodity relationships. For the payment of obrok the peasants sold part of their produce on the market. Taxes to the state were also paid in money. The labor of kholopy was constantly being replaced by the labor of the dependent peasant. At the end of the fifteenth century a new form of dependent labor appeared—*sluzhilaia kabala* (serving obligation).

With the formation of the centralized state a particular group of subservient landowners, the dvoriane (nobles), formed within the class of feudalists. *Pomestie* landowning, connected with the bearing of military service to the Moscow prince and the tsar, became widespread.

During the fifteenth and sixteenth centuries monastery landowning grew very rapidly. Great masses of land, about a third of all the appropriated territories according to contemporaries, belonged to the clergy, mainly to the monasteries, which also exploited the peasantry.

Industry, as in the preceding period, continued to bear a primarily domestic character, remaining inseparably connected with agriculture and consisting mainly of domestic processing of agricultural products. The role of the handicraftsmen, working on order and for the local market, gradually expanded. Handicrafts, which suffered extraordinarily from the Tartar-Mongol invasion, now revived, and developed to a more important status. Old towns were revitalized and new settlements arose. More than two hundred different handicraft specialties appeared in the Russian towns of the sixteenth century. The growth in productivity of agricultural labor in connection with the spread of the three-field system, reinforced the separation of industry from agriculture. Small handicraft production was concentrated not only in *posada* (towns), but in rural areas as well. The products of these handicraft centers were sold locally and in more distant markets.

In fifteenth and sixteenth century Russia heavy industrial production for the market, such as salt-boiling, ironsmelting, and potash-making, was already under way. It was accomplished in the votchiny and the large monasteries. Cannons and other types of arms were produced in state factories.

The number of towns in which trade-industrial activity was concentrated increased; and local markets—various *torzhki* (trade fairs) of the monasteries and villages—multiplied. Internal trade not only grew quantitatively, but important qualitative changes also became noticeable. From the beginning of the sixteenth century trade connections between various towns and *oblasti* were established on a wide scale. The way was prepared for the formation of the all-Russian market.[2] Salt, extracted mainly in the north, was distributed throughout Russia. Grain and other goods were transported for long distances. In the sixteenth century direct trade relations were inaugurated between Russia and the Western European market by way of the White Sea. Trade with eastern lands also increased.

In Western Europe the formation of centralized states coincided with, on the one hand, disintegration of the feudal means of production and with the capitalistic development of those countries, on the other hand. In Russia political union of the country under the rule of the Moscow princes was accomplished on an economic basis as a result of the growth of the social division of labor, of money-commodity relationships, and of the growth of towns and strengthening of the ties between various oblasti and principalities. But the Russian centralized state, in contrast to the Western European countries, was formed before the dissolution of the feudal means of production and before the beginning of capitalistic development. In Russia, as in other countries of Eastern Europe, the process of the formation of a centralized state was hastened by the struggle against external dangers and by the necessity of defense against the incursions of the Turks, Mongols, and other peoples of the East.

---

[2] See S. V. Bakhrushin, "Predposylki 'vserossiiskogo rynka' v XVI v." [Prerequisites for "an all-Russian market" in the XVI Century] *Uchenye zapiski Moskovskogo gosudarstvennogo universiteta* [Scientific Notes of Moscow State University] (87th Issue, Moscow: 1946), pp. 38–65.

The Russian centralized state acted as a political superstructure over the feudal productive relationships then becoming consolidated in the country, which constituted the base of society. It was from the very beginning a multi-national state, a mixed state uniting diverse peoples not yet formed into nations.[3] This multi-national state was a *Russian* state, because "in Russia the role of welder-of-nationalities was assumed by the Great Russians headed by the aristocratic military bureaucracy, which had been historically formed and was powerful and well organized." [4]

During this period the class struggle continued to be aggravated by the growth of feudal exploitation of the peasantry and the increase of trade and moneylending.

At the end of the fifteenth century and at the beginning of the sixteenth the movement of the "heretics" unfolded anew in Rus. Uprisings occurred among the town poor in Novgorod and Pskov during the struggle of the Moscow grand prince to unite Novgorod with Moscow, and in 1483–1485 unrest was evident among the peasant-smerdy of Pskov. The class struggle was sharply aggravated in the middle of the sixteenth century, when uprisings in Moscow, Pskov, and other places occurred.

Growing opposition of the toilers to feudal exploitation was one of the important factors forcing the ruling class to form a centralized state. Centralization of political power in the hands of the autocratic monarch strengthened the feudal class in its struggle against the exploited mass and guaranteed suppression by the feudalists of the ever-increasing peasant opposition. Creation of a centralized state was accomplished in the very struggle a new class of feudalists—the dvorianstvo (nobility)—made against the boyars and their reactionary separatist tendencies. Ivan IV, completing the formation of the Russian centralized state, leaned on the then progressive dvorianstvo and also on the towns. The elevation of the dvorianstvo was a consequence of its violent struggle for land and for labor—that is, for the peasantry.

In the 1570's and 1580's, as a result of the hard and prolonged war with Livonia and the mass ruin of peasant holdings during the *oprichnina,* the national economy of Russia experienced a deep decline: sowings were sharply curtailed, the old oblasti of the country became

[3] See I. V. Stalin, *Sochineniia* [Works] (Moscow: Gospolitizdat, 1953), V, 34; see V. Pashuto and L. Cherepnin, "O periodizatsii istorii Rossii epokhy feodalizma [On the Periodization of Russian History of the Period of Feudalism], *Voprosy Istorii* [Problems of History], No. 2 (1951), pp. 66–7; "Ob itogakh diskusii o periodizatsii istorii SSSR" [On the Results of the Discussion about Periodization of the History of the USSR], *ibid.*, No. 3 (1951), p. 57.

[4] Stalin, *Sochineniia,* II, 304.

desolate, and the population, burdened by taxes and obligations for the pomeshchiki and the military needs of the state, moved to new locations, into the southeast of the country.

In the interests of the nobility, which supported the autocratic power in the sixteenth century under Ivan IV and his successors, the binding of the peasant to the land was legally formalized. This represented a very important stage in the development of feudal exploitation.

In answer to this was the growth of the class struggle of the peasantry. In the last decade of the sixteenth century a rebellion flared up in Uglich in which the peasantry of the surrounding countryside took part; a number of other peasant and town uprisings took place; and anti-feudal movements of peasants of non-Russian peoples occurred in the Volga and the Kama regions. The groundwork was laid for the widespread peasant war which took place at the beginning of the seventeenth century under the leadership of Bolotnikov.

The formation of a centralized state had great progressive significance for the future of Russia. It strengthened the Russian people in their struggle for the independence of the country and for a guarantee of its national interests; it opened the way for further growth of the productive forces of the country and for the development of the culture of the Russian people. As I. V. Stalin wrote, "Only a country united in one centralized state can count on the possibility of serious cultural-economic growth, on the possibility of maintaining its independence." [5]

With the liquidation of feudal disunity the Russian state entered the international arena as a major power. "A dumbfounded Europe, which in the beginning of the reign of Ivan III hardly suspected the existence of Moscovy, squeezed between the Lithuanians and the Tartars as it was, was stupefied by the sudden appearance of the colossal empire on its eastern borders." [6]

The formation of a centralized state indicated at the same time a new and therefore extremely important strengthening of the rule of the feudalists over the toiling masses of the country. The enserfment of the peasantry in the last decade of the sixteenth century was accomplished by a centralized feudal state.

The period of the formation of a centralized Russian state was accompanied by a great surge in Russian social thought, including economic thought. The circle of people actively responding in one form or another to the burning questions of social life was broadened; the number of documents or social thought which have come down to

[5] *Pravda,* September 7, 1947.
[6] Marx, *Secret Diplomatic History,* p. 81.

us increased; and the composition of the documents of this period is significantly richer and more varied than in the preceding periods.

Social issues attracted the attention of progressive people more and more. Publicists at the end of the fifteenth century and during the sixteenth examined fundamental questions of the social-political life of Russia: the political union of the feudal principalities into one centralized state; the stabilization of the power of the tsar; the right and obligation of the sovereign to all of Russia; the right and obligation of the Russian princes and the boyars; the place of the Russian state among other states; the interrelations of the various classes (*soslovii*) of Russia and the relationship of the state to each of them; the relations of the state and the church; monastery landownership; and other questions of prime importance.

In the process of the struggle with feudal disunity and the creation of a centralized state the idea of the unity of the Russian land receives clear expression. National self-consciousness grows with the aspiration to comprehend theoretically, to base answers on fundamental, moving questions of the political, economic, and spiritual life of a country. In this rise of Russian social thought a great and important place was occupied by economic thought.

The struggle for the liquidation of feudal disunity and the creation of a centralized state explained the transfer of Russian economic thought to a new level of development significantly higher than that of preceding periods. Economic thought appears now as a serious ideological weapon in deciding the fundamental political tasks of the Russian people. The qualitative change of economic thought in this period and the raising of its practical significance is evident first of all in the economic policy of the Moscow princes. Together with the formation of a centralized state there emerges a definite economic policy of the state, distinguished not only by high activity, but great complexity, multi-sided in its content.

Ivan III, the energetic unifier of the Russian lands, actively carried on an economic policy directed at the liquidation of the remnants of feudal disunity. Ivan IV, under whom the formation of the Russian centralized state was completed, insistently put into practice in the field of agrarian relations, finances, and trade a consistent system of measures directed at the solution of the fundamental political problems of the period.

In the various classes of society appear a number of active figures and original thinkers, who pose great and complex questions of economic life and who consider these questions broadly, in the light of the interests of the various classes of society and the tasks of the entire state.

Such individuals as, for example, Ivan Peresvetov and Ermolai-Erazm, attempted to found a harmonious system of proposals in the field of politics and economics.

In the struggle of the "non-covetous" and the "Josephites," one of the most pressing questions of that time—the question of monastery landholding—was subjected to broad examination; the acquisition of slave labor received sharp condemnation from representatives of various social groups, and for the first time a demand was raised for the abolition of this form of labor. From among the churchmen (Ermolai-Erazm) came an original project for deciding a number of different questions of state economic policy. In the person of Peresvetov appeared a spokesman of the new group of the feudalist class—the serving nobility—with its definite political and economic pretensions. In Ivan IV's correspondence with Prince Kurbskii the struggle of the new, progressive and the old, reactionary directions of social development and of social thought was clearly expressed. In the publicist writings of the sixteenth century was first posed the question of the peasantry, its economic position, and the role of peasant labor for society (Ermolai-Erazm) and the "non-covetous." The "heresies" of the sixteenth century expressed the enmity of the oppressed, exploited mass toward the feudal order (Feodosii Kosoi).

In that part of the *Domostroi* (which was compiled in this period) dealing with questions of economic life, the ideas of several circles of Russian society are expressed regarding problems and rules of household management.

The Economic Policy and Principles of Ivan III

Russian economic thought of this period is expressed primarily in the specific principles of *economic policy* promulgated by the grand princes of Moscow, Ivan III (reigned 1462–1505) and Vasilii III (reigned 1505–1533).

Under Ivan III, the "sovereign of all Rus," the lands around Moscow were united and the foundations of a centralized state in the form of a feudal monarchy were begun. He inaugurated a centralized state apparatus in the form of *prikazy* (departments); a military force was organized immediately subordinate to the Moscow prince, and the foundations of a uniform state legislation (The *Sudebnik* [Code] of 1497) were laid. During his reign Russia's dependence on the Tartar khans ended. Ivan III also conducted an independent, active, and skillful foreign policy.

The struggle with Lithuania and Poland for the uniting of ancient

Russian, Belorussian, and Ukrainian lands was dictated by the urgent demands of the economic and cultural development of the state and by the interests of its defense. The Livonian Order, Lithuania, and Sweden, in an effort to halt the might of the young Russian state, wanted to deny Moscow access to the Baltic Sea and to close the direct route between Moscow and the Western European countries. Ivan III struggled for the liberation of the Russian lands from Lithuanian-Polish rule. He carried on a war with the Livonian Order and with the Baltic countries for free access to the Baltic Sea. In the south and southeast the struggle was carried on for liberation from the Tartar-Mongol yoke, for the expansion of the boundaries of the state, and for the development of trade connections.

Ivan III also inaugurated an economic policy for the Russian centralized state wide in content and strong in purpose. It aided the liquidation of the remnants of feudal disunity, the creation and consolidation of the centralized state, and the solution of foreign and domestic political problems. To this basic problem was subordinated Ivan III's policy regarding landholding, finances, trade, and relations between feudalists and peasantry.

As was shown in the preceding chapter, the economic foundations of the country's feudal disunity was the rule of the big feudal owner, the concentration of great masses of land and peasantry in the hands of the feudal aristocracy, secular and ecclesiastical, the princes, boyars, and the churches and monasteries. The liquidation of the country's feudal disunity, the suppression of the separatist aspirations of the princes and boyars, and the creation of a united centralized state headed by an autocratic monarch were accomplished by undermining the economic might of the princes and boyars, by changing the form of landownership, and by creating the corresponding social and class bases of the autocracy, the serving nobility.

Ivan III set up a domestic system of land ownership which in subsequent centuries played an enormous role in the development of feudal exploitation, the consolidation of the autocracy, and the growth of the social life of the country. The creation of the pomestie system of landownership was inextricably linked with the formation of the Russian centralized state. As compared with the votchiny, representing full feudal ownership of the land, the pomestie constituted conditional ownership, connected with the feudalist's military or state service to the Grand Prince and later to the tsar of the Moscovite state. The pomestie was given only for service and at the time of service. It passed on to the son only on condition of his entering the service of the prince.

The feudal state in the person of the Grand Prince—the Tsar—was considered the supreme owner of the land.

In the period of feudal disunity conditional landownership was already in existence. The feudalist negotiated with a more powerful counterpart to exchange service to the latter on the basis of vassalage in exchange for land and peasants. But under Ivan III the pomestie acquired another meaning. It now became a means of material security for persons in military or other service to the Moscow prince, depending upon and serving only him. These people were, in effect, the nobles: they provided military force and social support to the Moscow prince in his struggle against other princes, boyars, and external foes; they also supplied the force to suppress the opposition of the exploited masses.

Ivan III almost ceased granting lands as votchiny and lavishly gave out pomestia to serving people from among the small landholders, free persons, and former kholopy of the boyars—on court lands of the Moscow prince, on confiscated lands of the boyars in the annexed regions, and in the "black volosti," that is, the lands of hitherto free peasants.

With the aim of liquidating the separatist tendencies of the boyars in the lands annexed to the Moscow principality, Ivan III adopted the "transplanting" of local, and particularly big, landowners and some of the merchants, confiscating their land. After the Novgorod republic was annexed to the Moscow state the "transplanting" from the Novgorodian lands was especially widespread. Here confiscation was imposed on more than half of the feudal holdings, including a large portion of church and monastery lands. The large and medium-sized Novgorodian landholdings were destroyed, and the feudalists were resettled on territory of the Moscow principality. On the confiscated Novgorodian lands Ivan III settled about two thousand pomeshchiki sent from the Moscow principality. Thus the large and medium-sized feudal landholders of the Novgorodian republic were replaced by subservient people who would provide permanent support to the Moscow princes.

A similar operation of "transplanting" boyars and ceding their lands to faithful people serving the Moscow prince was carried out in the Viatka land after its annexation by the Moscow state. Ivan III's successor, Grand Prince Vasilii III, employed the same practices in Pskov. In the second half of the sixteenth century the Moscow Tsar Ivan IV performed a similar operation on a large scale with regard to the entire boyar class (the oprichnina). The pomestie system of landowning became the economic basis of the Russian feudal state and its military organization.

Striking a blow at the economic might of the boyars on the lands annexed to the Moscow state, Ivan III at the same time reduced the economic position and political influence of the big feudalists in the entire Moscow Grand Principality. This weakening was accomplished by limiting the rights of immunity of the big feudalists; by shifting further judicial power, financial functions, and so forth, from the big feudalists to the centralized feudal state; and by restricting the power of viceroys and district officials.

While he reduced the rights of the feudalists as fixed in the petition charters, Ivan III gave the immunities to the newly created class of feudalists, that is, to the serving nobility, the pomeshchiki, and thus increased the number of persons enjoying this privilege. He demanded military service from landowners, large and small. They were no longer vassals as in the epoch of feudal disunity, but subjects of the Great Moscow Prince, obligated to serve him.

Ivan III's *financial policy* also served the purpose of creating a centralized state. With the unification of Russian lands, finances were also consolidated. The collection of taxes for the princely treasury was accomplished earlier by the viceroys, who in effect independently administered the towns. In the beginning of the sixteenth century these functions were transferred to the "town bailiffs." This reform marked the centralization of financial affairs and the beginning of a national financial system. In his testament to his eldest son Vasilii, who had been proclaimed heir to the Grand Prince, Ivan III left not only the greater part of the towns, among them some of the largest, but also the major portion (72 per cent) of the income of the treasury (the residue having been distributed among the other four sons).

In the fifteenth century an important change occurred in the field of direct taxation—the transition from head and household taxation to that of the plowland, in which the tax unit was the *sokha*. Mention of the sokha as a tax unit appears as early as the thirteenth century. Tatishchev wrote that in 1275 the Grand Prince Vasilii Yaroslavich paid the Horde a tribute of half a grivna per sokha, and a sokha "represented a holding worked by two men." From this record some historians believe that the sokha, a unit of account representing the output of two workers, was the basis of taxation in the first Tartar census.[7] The majority of scholars believe, however, that the tribute established by the Tartar-Mongols was calculated in terms of numbers, that is, a "head tax." In the fifteenth century the sokha as a tax base

---

[7] See P. Miliukov, *Spornye voprosy finansovoi istorii Moskovskogo gosudarstva* [Disputed Problems of Financial History of the Muscovite State] (St. Petersburg: 1892), p. 18.

evidently represented a definite amount of work: that of two or three peasants.[8]

The transfer to *plowland taxation,* as far as may be judged, was accomplished in the Grand Principality of Moscow earlier than elsewhere and from there spread to lands annexed by the principality. The chronicler notes for 1492 that Grand Prince Ivan III sent officials into various lands—Tver, Novgorod, and others—"to take Moscow's census on the basis of the sokha." [9] This measure was an integral part of his policy designed to centralize the financial system.

During the period of feudal disunity money was coined in many grand principalities, and this activity was one of the characteristics of the sovereignty of these semi-states. In his will Ivan III left the sole right to coin money to his eldest son, the heir to the throne.

Ivan III also furthered the development of internal *trade* in the country. The liquidation of feudal disunity, which by removing the political boundaries between the various principalities lifted the former trade barriers between the various Russian towns and oblasti, was of prime importance in this regard.

In the field of foreign trade Ivan III aimed at establishing direct trade relations with the West; he put through measures directed at the defense of the southeastern part of the Gulf of Finland and adjoining territories belonging to Russia which served as an outlet to the Baltic Sea. The Hanseatic League wanted to preserve control of all of Russia's foreign trade with the West, however the Livonian knights and merchants tried to block the attempts of Russian merchants to set up direct trade connections with the West. In retaliation for the killing of Novgorodian merchants in Reval organized by the Hansa, Ivan III closed the German trade center in Novgorod. Through his ambassador Ivan III obtained from the Turkish Sultan priority for Russian traders in Constantinople. He maintained trade relations with Azov and Kafa.

In the last half of the fifteenth century and during the sixteenth, handicrafts developed noticeably. The Russian masters of this period left many excellent examples of fine art in various branches—architecture, painting, and so on. Ivan III hired mining experts from other countries, as well as gold and silver craftsmen, cannon founders, architects, artillery experts, and other specialists. During his reign the manufacture of cannon was established in Moscow. In the 1490's Ivan III sent people to Pechora to search for silver ore.[10]

---

[8] *Ibid.*

[9] *Polnoe sobranie russkikh letopisei* [Complete Collection of Russian Chronicles] (St. Petersburg: 1911), XXII, 507–8.

[10] *Ibid.,* XXII, 508.

Ivan III's struggle for the creation of a centralized state was also clearly expressed in the issuing of the Sudebnik (Code) of 1497. This Code for the entire Russian state replaced the former legal charters of the various principalities. The Code of 1497 set up an order of court procedures and legal norms, binding uniformly on all parts of the united Moscow state; it clearly helped to strengthen the central authority.

The sources for the compilation of the Sudebnik of 1497 were *Russkaia Pravda,* the Pskov legal charter, the princely charters which determined the order of local administration and courts, and also customary law. A significant part of the Code of 1497 was devoted to judicial procedure. A number of articles defined the property rights and economic relations of the people—loans, the departure of peasants, the conditions of bondage, hirelings, among other subjects.[11]

The article of the Code on kholopy reflected the tendency of the Moscow princes to limit the conditions of complete bondage. In the "Extensive Pravda" one of the sources of full kholopstvo (slavery) was recognized as the entering into service as a tiun or steward. According to the Sudebnik of Ivan III the service as a tiun steward led to kholopstvo only in the village (Art. 66). The inclusion of sections on "hirelings" in the Sudebnik of 1497 showed the growth of the adoption of hired labor by both secular landowners and the monasteries. Hired labor took on various forms: the labor of the so-called harvest hirelings, hirelings for plowland, labor hirelings, hired fishermen, and others. The Sudebnik of 1497 guarded the interests of the hirer by decreeing that the *naimit* (hired laborer) who left the hirer sooner than the agreed term was to lose his pay (Art. 54).

As was said above (see the preceding chapter), during the period of feudal disunity the princes in their agreements assumed the obligation not to admit into their realms peasants from other principalities, actually binding the peasant to the feudalist within the confines of the principality. With the liquidation of feudal disunity these restrictions on the peasant transfer from one principality to another lost their *raison d'être;* and yet the process of serfdom continued to develop.

Ivan III's Sudebnik set a limit on the peasant's departure; that is, the right of the peasant to transfer from one owner to another. He was only permitted to do so one day in the year, St. George's Day. This limitation had been put into effect in various regions of Northeastern Rus even before the Sudebnik of 1497. In the 1450's and 1460's the

---

[11] See "Sudebnik 1497 g." [The Code of 1497] in *Sudebniki XV-XVI vekov* [Codes of the XV–XVI Centuries] (Moscow-Leningrad: AS USSR, 1952), pp. 19–29.

Moscow prince granted charters to various monasteries (Troitse-Sergievskii and Kirillo-Belozerskii) and secular feudalists limiting the peasant's right to departure to St. George's Day (November 26th).

By the Sudebnik of 1497 this restraint on peasant mobility became a national norm, transformed into law. Article 57 of the Sudebnik "On Peasant Departure" states: "And the peasant may leave the volost and may go from one village to another once a year, a week before [St.] George's Day in the fall, and a week after [St.] George's Day in the fall."

Moreover, the Sudebnik of 1497 established the obligation of the departing peasant to pay the feudalist *pozhiloe* (rent) for the use of his house—one ruble per house in localities without forests and a *poltina* in forested localities; it was indicated that the peasant living under a feudalist for one year paid on departure a fourth part of the rent, for two years he paid a half, three years, three-fourths, and for four years he paid the rent in full.[12]

The legislative limitation in the Sudebnik of 1497 on the time of departure of the peasant for the whole country and the setting up of the payment of rent on departure meant a further and, at the same time, extremely fundamental expansion of the rights of the feudalist and a limitation on the rights of the peasant. It was an important step in the legal formulation of serf relations in Russia. This measure strengthened the interests of the pomeshchiki. The forces of the newly created centralized state were directed toward defending the interests of the feudalists and suppressing the opposition of the exploited peasantry.

These regulations were utilized by the pomeshchiki to increase the exploitation of the peasants. The Sudebnik of 1497, being the first code of feudal laws of the Russian centralized state, served as a mighty weapon for the defense and strengthening of feudal landownership and for the appropriation of the surplus labor of the peasants by the feudalists. The political superstructure—the centralized state—became a great force; it actively served and strengthened its economic base, feudal productive relationships, and aided their formation.

Such were the basic highlights of the economic policies of Ivan III. His successor, Grand Prince Vasilii III, characterized by a chronicler as "the last gatherer" of the Russian lands, continued to carry on his father's economic policy. This policy, however, attained clearest expression and completion in the intense state activity of Ivan the Terrible.

---

[12] *Ibid.*, p. 27. On the significance of Article 57 of the Code of 1497, see *ibid.*, pp. 91–7.

CHAPTER 4. *The Ideological Struggle over Monastery Landownership. The Economic Content of the "Heresies" of the Sixteenth Century.*

The Struggle over Monastery Landholding

During this period, as in the preceding eras of Russian history, economic thought was also expressed in the literature of the churchmen, and lively controversies were carried on in this literature. Disputes over monastery landholdings were the most acrimonious.

In the 1470's a new "heresy" arose in Novgorod known as the "heresy of the Judaizers." Later it became widespread not only in Novgorod, but in Moscow as well. Leading the struggle against the "heretics," Joseph Volotskii wrote, "Many have learned from them to chastise the Holy Scriptures, and in the markets and in the homes they carry on a lively criticism of the faith and entertain doubts." [1]

The "heretics" repudiated church ceremonies, refused to acknowledge the icons and saints, and were critical of church writings. They denounced the parasitism of the monks and monastery landholding. The class basis of the movement was not homogeneous; its strength was derived from two sources. One was the mass of the town population, including the merchant class of Novgorod and the peasantry of the Novgorod villages. Leaders were representatives of the "white clergy"—Novgorodian priests, deacons, and laymen. Since this source signified the struggle of the lower classes against feudal exploitation—expressed in the form of a religious struggle—it represented a progressive tendency in Russian social thought. The second source obtained expression through various court representatives of the higher clergy. It was reactionary in character. Criticism of church dogmas and monastery landownership was utilized by representatives of the boyar

[1] *Prosvetitel, ili oblichenie eresi zhidovstvuiushchikh. Tvorenie prepodobnogo ottsa nashego Iosifa, igumena Volotskogo* [Educator, or a Disclosure of the Judaizers' Heresy. The Work of Our Father, the Reverend Joseph, Abbot of Volotsk] (Kazan: 1855), pp. 59–60.

reaction in this struggle against the centralization of state power and to preserve feudal disunity.[2]

In the church councils of 1490 and 1504 the "heresy of the Judaizers" was condemned. The "heretics" were burned at the stake or confined to monasteries.

By their repudiation of monastery landowning the "heretics" adhered to the movement of the so-called "non-covetous," which included some Russian churchmen.

We can see an extremely active manifestation of economic thought in the then unfolding political and idealistic struggle concerning the question of monastery landowning. In the preceding chapter it was pointed out that in Novgorod and Pskov the problem of church properties had previously become acute. Frequently the leaders of the church had to warn the Novgorodians and Pskovians that property and income of churches and monasteries must be inviolable; that intrusion on them by a layman was a terrible sin, for which there would be severe punishment.

At the end of the fifteenth century and in the sixteenth, the struggle over monastery landholdings acquired enormous scope. This question became one of the most pressing issues of state policy. Kliuchevskii has written that in this period the problem of monastery landowning was discussed with the same intensity as the question of freeing serfs in the nineteenth century, viz., on the eve of the reforms of 1861.

The issue was whether the monasteries had the right to own villages and hamlets, to utilize compulsory labor of the peasants, or whether these should constitute the privilege of secular feudalists. Should the monasteries be allowed to retain their villages and hamlets, or should they be confiscated? On this question the economic and political interests of various classes and groups of the ruling class—churchmen, boyars, nobles, and the grand princely power dependent upon them—clashed sharply.

The larger monasteries owned tens and even hundreds of thousands of *desiatiny* of land and villages, often scattered in various places.

Monastery landowning was established and grew as a result of princely grants, the donations of feudalists and of other rich people "for prayers for the soul," and donations from princes, boyars, nobles and merchants becoming monks. It grew partly through purchase of monastery lands in the north and in several other places, through the

[2] See A. A. Zimin, "O politicheskoi doktrine Iosifa Volotskogo" [The Political Doctrine of Joseph of Volotsk], *Trudy otdela drevnerusskoi literatury,* IX (1953), pp. 164–5.

acquisition of new lands, and often through crude seizure by monasteries of lands already owned by peripheral peasants.[3]

The economy of the monasteries depended upon the forced labor of the peasants. The monasteries displayed great greed, lent money to the peasants at exorbitant interest rates, and ruined the peasants in case of nonpayment of loans. Constant land disputes and lawsuits took place between the monasteries and the "black" peasants and peasant communes, particularly over parcels owned jointly by the monasteries and the peasant communes.

In the very monasteries themselves the positions of various groups of monks were different: on the one hand, there was a privileged upper class, the abbots, monastery elders, and monks who had taken their vows from among the boyars and other upper layers of society; on the other, there was the main mass of the ordinary monks, sharply differing in their position from the privileged leadership.

In this period the question of monastery landowning became extremely acute in connection with the formation of the centralized state. It was closely interwoven with the political problem of the relationship between the Russian church and the Moscow princes, with the question of the relationship between various classes within the class of feudalists —the feudal magnates and boyars on the one side, and the serving nobility on the other—and with the question of the power of the Grand Prince of Moscow and the emerging centralized state in general.

With the growth of the serving nobility and the necessity to guarantee its lands, the question as to the source from which to take lands for the endowment of the retainers of the Moscow princes acquired great significance.

For this purpose Ivan III confiscated the lands not only of the secular feudalists of Novgorod, but of the ecclesiastics as well. In 1478 he confiscated from the Novgorod archbishop ten *volosti,* all of his Novyi Torzhok lands, and also half of the votchiny of the Novgorod monasteries. In 1500, as retribution for the treason of the Novgorodian archbishop against the Moscow prince, Ivan III again confiscated lands of the Novgorod clergy. In other newly annexed lands he instituted certain limitations on the growth of monastery landholding; for example, he forbade the serving people of the former appanage princes of Suzdal, Yaroslav, and Starodub to cede their lands to the monasteries.

In preceding chapters we have spoken of the important functions of the Christian religion in feudal society as an ideological sanction

---

[3] See Kliuchevskii, *Kurs russkoi istorii, II, Chapts. XXXIV-XXXVI;* I. U. Bubovnits, *Russkaia publitsistika XVI veka* [Russian Publicity of the XVI Century] (Moscow-Leningrad: AS USSR, 1947), pp. 9–14.

and ideal defense of feudal exploitation of the masses. The church faithfully served the exploiters—the feudalists and feudal state in the period of Kievan Rus and in the period of feudal disunity. The support by the leadership of the Russian church of the policy of the Moscow princes, aimed at consolidating the Russian lands around Moscow and liquidating feudal disunity, played a decisive role in the successes of the Moscow princes. And now, when the gathering of the Russian lands around Moscow was for the most part finished, there arose in its turn the task of elevating and strengthening the power of the Moscow princes in the entire state at the expense of the power of the big feudalists, the boyars. The question of what position the Russian church would occupy, of whether it would support the Moscow prince in his aspiration to set up an autocratic rule, had great significance.

The feudal upper class, the boyars, struggled against the autocracy of the Moscow prince in order to preserve political power in their own hands. They naturally wanted full preservation of their lands, and they considered it expedient to satisfy the need of the prince for land reserves for grants to retainers at the expense of the "black" peasantry and the monasteries. Therefore the idea of "non-covetousness" emanating from monastery circles was seized upon by the reactionary boyars and utilized by them as a weapon of struggle for their economic and political interests.

Besides being opponents of monastery landholding, the "non-covetous" defended the idea of the independence of the church from princely rule and were opponents of the strengthening of autocratic power. In their relation to the Grand Prince's authority the "covetous" were dependent on the position which the Grand Prince of Moscow took on the question of the landholding of monasteries and in the struggle with the "heretics."

The attitude of the Grand Prince toward the question of monastery landholding was contradictory: the church and monastery lands were extremely necessary to him for grants to retainers, but to confiscate these lands from the churches and monasteries would mean depriving himself of a strong ally and would swell the ranks of his opponents. The Grand Prince of Moscow needed the support of the church, and the churches needed defense from the claims on their wealth. These mutual interests became the foundation for a union between the Prince and the church at this time. Leaders of the "covetous," convinced that the Prince would leave monastery properties inviolate, actively took his side and began to argue the necessity of the autocracy and the subordination of the church to princely power. From the name of the most active defender of monastery landholding, Joseph Volotskii, the abbot of the Volokolamsk monastery, the group of the "covetous" became known as Josephites.

Criticizing monastery landholding, the "non-covetous" painted a vivid picture of the exploitation of the peasants by the monasteries. But their criticism was limited; they did not touch upon the entire feudal system of economy prevailing in the country. At the same time, on the basic political question of this period of the creation of a centralized state and the strengthening of autocratic power—the monarchy—the "non-covetous" took reactionary positions expressing the interests of the boyars. The "covetous," defending monastery landholding, protected their own mercenary class interests, but, at the same time, on the question of strengthening the centralized state they took a progressive position corresponding to the national interests of the development of the Russian people. This also determined the outcome of the struggle between the "non-covetous" and the "Josephites"; the "Josephites" won.

But the progressiveness of the political positions of the "covetous" was relative and limited: the preservation of church and monastery landowning which they defended hindered the process of strengthening the centralized state inasmuch as a vast expanse of land, concentrated in the economies of the monasteries and churches, remained outside the disposition of Moscow's Grand Prince, who headed the struggle for the formation and strengthening of the centralized state.[4] The ferocious struggle of the "covetous" with the "heretics" was also conservative. Under a religious cloak the toilers protested against feudal exploitation, and the ruling feudal church defended it. The question of their relation to the "heretics" occupied a significant place in the struggle between the "covetous" and the "non-covetous." The "Josephites" jealously guarded the dominant position of the Orthodox church from all attacks made on it by the "heretics." They demanded and obtained severe retribution against the "Judaizers" and other representatives of the church opposition.

The outstanding spokesmen of the "non-covetous" were Nil Sorskii and Vassian Kosoi. Nil Sorskii (1433–1508) was the ideological leader of the "non-covetous." It is believed that he came from a boyar family. Nil took the monastic vows in the Cirillo-Belozerskii monastery and later visited Constantinople and Mount Athos. Returning to the monastery he retired to the river Sor, where he founded a hermitage. Here he wrote a number of works for his students. Nil Sorskii stressed the necessity of spiritual perfection, retirement from the world, and non-

---

[4] Zimin, *op. cit.*

interference in worldly affairs. He condemned human sins, particularly avarice. The main sin, according to Nil Sorskii, was the appropriation of the fruits of labor of another, that is, robbery. He argued that monks should live by their labor and follow the words of the apostle Paul: "if any would not work, neither should he eat."

This principle Nil strictly established in his hermitage, obliging all the monks to occupy themselves with physical labor. He preached the necessity of an ascetic life for a monk and condemned the giving of alms: A poor man cannot give alms, and alms given by a covetous one are inefficacious. Warning the monks of the sinfulness of greed, Nil Sorskii argued the inadmissibility of monasteries owning land and appropriating peasant labor. "Covetousness . . . which is satisfied from the work of others will not bring us any benefit." [5]

At the Church Council of 1503 in Moscow, when the work of the Council was already finished and part of the participants had left, Nil Sorskii made a fiery speech against monastery landowning.[6] "And elder Nil began to say that the monasteries should have no villages, and that monks should live in hermitages, and should support themselves by handicrafts: the Belozerskii hermits sided with him." [7]

By order of Ivan III the Council continued its work, but, notwithstanding the sympathy of the Grand Prince toward the proposition of Nil Sorskii and the insistent desire to guarantee him victory, the Council condemned the "non-covetous" and confirmed the right of the monasteries to own land.

Like other of the "non-covetous," Nil Sorskii was by no means a reformer, let alone an opponent of the feudal order. As a result he made no attempt to change contemporary society, to pose the question of the abolition of feudal landowning in general, or to criticize feudal exploitation of labor. Guided by aspirations for the spiritual perfection of mankind and painting an ideal of monastic life, he saw only the narrow question of monastery landowning and of the labor of peasants in monastery votchiny.

After the death of Nil Sorskii the struggle of the "non-covetous" was led by his student Vassian Patrikeev (nicknamed Kosoi). The latter was the son of an influential boyar and a close relative of the Grand

---

[5] "Nila Sorskogo predanie i ustav" [The Arraignment and Church-Punishment of Nil Sorskii], *Pamiatniki drevnei pismennosti i iskusstva* [Monuments of Ancient Literature and Art] (Issue 179, St. Petersburg: 1912), p. 6.

[6] Vipper writes that this appearance of Nil Sorskii took place on orders of Ivan III (P. Iu. Vipper, *Ivan Groznyi* [Ivan the Terrible] (Moscow-Leningrad: AS USSR, 1944), p. 28.

[7] *Pribavleniia k izdaniiu tvorenii sv. ottsov* [Appendixes to the Works of the Holy Fathers] (Moscow: 1851), Pt. 10, p. 505.

Prince, and he fulfilled important tasks for the Grand Prince in the diplomatic and military fields. In 1499, in connection with the court struggle over the succession to the throne, the Patrikeev princes fell into disfavor, and Prince Vasilii was forced to take vows as a monk, under the name of Vassian.

Prince-monk Vassian found himself in Nil Sorskii's hermitage accepting the teaching of "non-covetousness," which he transformed into a weapon of the political struggle of the boyars for their class interests.

In his polemical writings, directed against the "Josephites," Vassian persistently attacked the "covetous" and rejected the attempts of the latter to refer to the Scriptures for support of their positions. "Where in the Bible or the apostolic or the [holy] father's sermons are monks allowed to have an abundance of wealth, namely through the acquisition of populated villages and the enslavement of peasants and their brothers, unjustly collecting from them silver and gold, and still go about the *mir*?" [8]

Vassian accused the monks of avarice and love of glory. Poverty, charity, brotherhood, and suffering should be inherent in the monastic life, he wrote. God prohibited selling estates, and we, even after entering monasteries, acquire villages and estates, begging them from magnates or buying them. Instead of living by labor we "travel constantly from one city to another, look into the hands of the rich and employ various flattering devices to receive from them a village, or a hamlet, or money, or livestock." [9] By moneylending the monasteries appropriated the property of the poor; they argued in court with the poor about overdue payments on loans and disputed with neighbors over the borders of their adjoining villages.[10] The princes gave the monasteries their estates for saving their souls; the monks on the other hand increased their surpluses or concealed them in order to sell them in lean years at a high price.[11]

In antiquity, he writes, monks lived in the monasteries by their labor and did not look to strange hands, did not fatten on Christian blood, and did not engage in moneylending.[12]

---

[8] "Slovo otvetno protivu kleveshchushchikh istinu evangelskuiu i o inochskom zhitii i ustroenii tserkovnem" [A Discourse Against Slanders Directed at the Gospel's Truth, Monastic Life, and Church Organization] *Pravoslavnyi sobesednik* [Orthodox Conversationalist], Pt. III (1863), p. 105.

[9] *Ibid.*, Pt. III (1863), p. 109.

[10] *Ibid.*, Pt. III (1863), p. 110.

[11] See "Sobranie Vasiana, uchenika Nila Sorskogo, na Iosifa Volotskogo ot pravil sviatykh Nikanskikh ot mnogikh glav" [Collection of Vasian, Nil Sorskii's Pupil, Against Joseph of Volokolam About His Departure From Many Sacred Rules], *ibid.*, Pt. III (1863), p. 187.

[12] *Ibid.*, Pt. III (1863), p. 190.

With severe words Vassian flayed the cruel treatment of the peasants by the monasteries and the heartless plundering of the latter. The Lord ordered distribution of estates to the poor; "We, however, are money lovers and are overcome by greed, while our living brothers are poor in our own villages and are being variously abused; we impose on them cajolery and usurious interest, and we never show any mercy towards them should they be unable to pay usurious interest; we tax their property mercilessly, requisition their cow or horse and take them far away from their lands with their wife and children." "We," Vassian writes further, "do wrong and steal, sell peasants, our brothers, and we punish them with sticks mercilessly, attacking their bodies like wild beasts." [13]

Although Vassian denounced monastery ownership of land and peasants and moneylending by the monasteries, he did not oppose in general the existence of monasteries. In his verbose and biting discourses on the position of the peasant masses in the monastery holdings and their oppression and ruin by the monasteries Vassian was least of all concerned about the oppressed peasantry.

This defender of the boyars understood well the role of the clergy and the church as weapons for the ideological enslavement of the toiling masses. Fighting for the confiscation of the lands and peasants from the monasteries, Vassian wanted, on the one hand, to protect the boyar holdings from the encroachments of the Grand Prince and, on the other, to avoid the danger of the church losing its prestige in the eyes of the toiling masses. As may be supposed, depriving the monasteries of the right to utilize the labor of others and to engage in moneylending operations would put an end, in Vassian's view, to the religious wavering beginning among the people, would strengthen the trust of the people toward the church, and would at the same time increase the then dominant feudal means of production.

It should be admitted, however, that Vassian, like other of the "non-covetous," coming out as an opponent of monastery landowning, considered at the same time that council and secular churches should own land as formerly, but that all church wealth should be handled not by the bishops and priests but by special *"ikonomy"* (that is, "economists") and that the revenues of the churches from their holdings should be spent not only on the salaries of the churchmen, but also on the aid of the poor and the ransom of prisoners.[14]

Vassian revised the *"Kormchaia,"* corrected it and, in the interests of the struggle with the "Josephites," furnished commentaries in the spirit of the "non-covetous." The Metropolitan Daniel obtained a council

---

[13] *Ibid.*, Pt. III (1863), pp. 109–110.
[14] *Ibid.*, Pt. III (1863), p. 207.

judgment against Vassian (in 1531), whom he had first accused of correcting the *"Kormchaia."* Vassian was then imprisoned in the Volokolamsk monastery, where he soon died.

A critical depiction of monastery landholding and of the cruel exploitation of the peasants in the monastery votchiny, showing their ruin by the usurious operations of the monks, is also contained in the works of Maxim the Greek. He had arrived in Moscow from Mount Athos in 1518 in response to a request by the Grand Prince Vasilii Ivanovich for a learned translator of books.[15]

The criticism of the greediness of the monasteries in the works of Maxim the Greek is in the same vein as that of his partisan and coworker in the struggle with the "Josephites," Vassian Patrikeev, who exerted important influence upon him in this regard.[16]

During this period not only churchmen and monks criticized monastery landowning; a sharp condemnation of this practice and an extended discourse on the necessity of its liquidation are contained in a sixteenth century work specially dedicated to this theme entitled *Conversation of Saints Sergei and Herman, the Miracle-Workers.*[17] Neither the author of this book nor the date of its writing is known. Only one thing is sure—the work belongs to the sixteenth century, when the question of monastery landowning became particularly acute. The social group to which the author belongs remains unclear.

The author's views are in opposition to the interests of the monasteries and "communes," which he considers volosti "with peasants."

---

[15] See *Sochineniia Maksima Greka v russkom perevode* [Works of Maxim the Greek in Russian Translation] (Troitsk-Sergeev Monastery: 1910), Parts I and II; V. S. Ikonnikov, *Maksim Grek i ego vremia* [Maxim the Greek and His Time] 2nd edition, Kiev: 1915); V. F. Rzhiga, "Opyty po istorii russkoi publitsistiki XVI veka. Maksim Grek kak publitsist" [Essays On the History of Russian Publicity of the XVI Century. Maxim the Greek as Publicist], *Trudy otdela drevnerusskoi literatury,* I (1934), pp. 5–110.

[16] The role of Maxim the Greek's works in the development of social thought in Russia in the XVI century is exaggerated by many historians. Thus, for instance, V. S. Ikonnikov, in his monumental study *Maksim Grek i ego vremia,* even considers that "The literary movement of the XVI century on the important church-social problems is directly associated with the works of Maxim the Greek and stems from them." (p. 559). In reality, however, the utterances of Maxim the Greek on the question of monastic landownership as well as on other problems of social life were met by the Russians with considerable interest because their author touched problems which were then acute and which concerned the Russians long before the arrival of Maxim the Greek in Russia.

[17] "Beseda prepodobnykh Sergeia i Germana, Valaamskikh chudotvortsev" [A Conversation of Fathers Sergei and Herman, Valaam Thaumaturgists] *Letopis zaniatii Arkheograficheskoi komissii* [A Chronicle of Works of the Archeographic Commission] (St. Petersburg: 1895), Issue X, Pt. II, pp. 1–32.

Monasteries are looked upon as a force alien and hostile to the peasants.

The idea of the inviolability of monastery landowning is argued against very insistently in the *Conversation.* Unlike Nil Sorskii and Vassian Patrikeev, who appeal to the monks and exhort them to renounce the use of the fruits of labor of dependent peasants in order to save their souls, the author of the *Conversation* challenges the Tsar and warns him not to give land to the monasteries. "It is undignified for the Tsar to grant villages and volosti with peasants to monasteries, nor can such actions of the Tsar be approved." [18] He sharply condemns the tsars for distributing volosti with peasants to the monasteries. The denial of monastery landowning is closely connected with the thought that clerics, priests, and monks in general must not take part in lay affairs, especially the administration of state matters.[19] The Tsar must rule together with the princes, boyars, and other laymen, and not with "unburied corpses," which are what monks are in the view of this author.

The monks must feed themselves "from their own labor and sweat by direct exertion and not from the Tsar's bounty nor by Christian tears." Those monks who do not do so are "not Pilgrims of God, but iconoclasts," and they should be sent into the Tsar's service.[20] The author considers monks parasites living at the expense of toilers; he is troubled that in monasteries monks build themselves palaces "and gold-plated designs with multicolored flowers"; cells are painted like the Tsar's apartments, and monks have the best food and drink, taking them from those who actually labor to create these blessings and who should utilize them: "and by [the right] of inheritance food and drink and everything good belong to laymen and toilers, but not to us monks, and I repeat, but not to us." [21]

It is difficult to believe that the author of this sharp criticism of monasticism belonged to a religious order. More likely he was a layman, hiding his original name under the pseudonym of "Saints Sergius and Herman."

It is necessary to note that he does not limit himself to questions of monastery landowning. He also poses the question of the relationship of the Tsar (state) to the toiling masses. Condemning the receipt of unearned income by the monks, the author of the *Conversation* reminds the Tsar twice of the need to take measures for the aid of his subjects:

---

[18] *Ibid.,* p. 4.
[19] *Ibid.,* p. 12.
[20] *Ibid.,* p. 12.
[21] *Ibid.,* pp. 15–6.

"The Tsar should collect all taxes from the mir with reason and administer with mercy, and not in anger or with extensive torture." [22]

Historians studying the *Conversation* usually consider that its author belonged to the circle of "non-covetous" boyars. They are supported by such statements as: the Tsar must rule, counselling with his princes and boyars, and with other laymen, but not with monks.

Another conception of the problem has been expressed by the historian I. I. Smirnov. Analyzing the content of the *Conversation,* he arrived at the conclusion that this manuscript is a propaganda piece, coming from the midst of the black volost population of North Russia.[23] In the sixteenth century the main social force in the North was the black volost peasantry, and the main form of big feudal holdings was that of monastery landownership. Deep contradictions and a sharp ideological struggle prevailed between the monasteries and the "black peasantry." "One of the ideological expressions of this struggle was the *Conversation*—the first early Russian propaganda piece expressing the interests of the northern black peasantry." [24] Such a view of the problem is debatable, however.[25]

It has been noted above that the most zealous defender of monastery landowning was Joseph Volotskii, born Sanin, the abbot of a monastery not far from Volokolamsk. Under his leadership the monastery quickly grew, with villages and hamlets received from the prince of Volotsk, from the Novgorod archbishop, and from rich landowners of the neighborhood. Eminent neophytes brought money, livestock, and other valuables to the monastery. Joseph Volotskii was thus an outstanding coveter in practice. It is not surprising that he headed the camp of the "covetous," ardently defending the economic privileges of the monasteries. He carried on a fierce struggle against the "heretics," assuming an extremely intransigent position. He sought to adopt the very severest measures against them, down to their physical annihilation. He wrote works directed at refuting the statements of the Novgorodian "heretics" and in defense of the dogma of the Orthodox church.

As has already been observed the Church Council of 1503 rejected

---

[22] *Ibid.,* pp. 21 and 23.

[23] See I. I. Smirnov, "Beseda Valaamskikh chudotvortsev" i ee mesto v russkoi publitsistike XVI veka" ["Conversation of the Valaam Thaumaturgists" and Its Place in the History of Russian Publicistics of the XVI Century], *Istoricheskie Zapiski* [Historical Notes], No. 15 (1945), pp. 247–61.

[24] *Ibid.,* No. 15 (1945), p. 258.

[25] See *Izvestiia Akademii nauk USSR. Seriia istorii i filosofii* [Bulletin of the Academy of Sciences of the USSR. Series of History and Philosophy], III, No. 4 (1946), pp. 387–8.

and condemned the projosal of Nil Sorskii; in its report to the Grand Prince the Council proclaimed the principle of the inviolability and inalienability of monastery holdings: "church acquisitions are God's acquisitions, imposed, designated, and given to God and can never be sold, given away, or appropriated by anyone for eternity; and, untouched, they should be preserved as holy for God, and it should be pleasant and praiseworthy. And we, humble, praise, glorify, and protect it." [26]

Facing the danger of a break with the church, Ivan III had to retreat and leave the state of affairs unchanged. However, the struggle of the "non-covetous" and the "Josephites," continued.

About 1507 Joseph Volotskii wrote a special tract in defense of monastery landholdings.[27] Referring to texts of the Holy Scripture, he insistently warns the reader that monastery holdings must remain inviolate. He does not spare words to increase church wealth, and he ascribes to it a great social role. Church wealth, asserts Joseph Volotskii, is the wealth of the lower classes, the orphans, and the aged.[28] The Holy Scriptures do not permit injuring even the poor people, still less the church. Joseph Volotskii wanted to persuade his readers that no sort of attack on the rule of the church and monasteries would remain unpunished. Anyone who assails this property is subject to damnation. He inescapably awaits the severest punishment from God, not only in the world beyond the grave, but, without fail, here on earth. From the church books Joseph Volotskii takes terrible "examples" of such punishments. As far as possible the chief design of his work is to instill mortal fear in people, to convince them of the inevitable responsibility for encroachment on the property of the churches and monasteries.

The very selection of "cases" taken from church literature of crimes against monastery property and the punishment that follows is curious. All of these "cases" grouped together constitute a definite and, at the same time, sufficiently full system of various types of encroachment on the economic interests of the churches and monasteries, evidently well known to the abbot-coveter. Here figure the most diverse categories of wrongdoers against the monasteries, beginning with the prince and ending with ordinary bandits.

---

[26] See A. Pavlov, *Istoricheskii ocherk sekuliarizatsii tserkovnykh zemel v Rossii* [Historical Outline of the Secularization of Church Lands in Russia] (Odessa: 1871), Pt. I, p. 47.

[27] It is published in Appendixes in V. Malinin, *Starets Eleazarova monastyria Filofei i ego poslaniia* [Elder Philopheus of the Eleazarov Monastery and His Teachings] (Kiev: 1901), pp. 128–44.

[28] *Ibid.*, p. 144.

Various types of violation against the interests of the churches and monasteries are foreseen. In describing all possible "cases" of crimes against the property interests of the church and their punishment, it is not by chance that Joseph Volotskii begins with the prince. He is eager to prove that all suffer cruel punishment for crimes against church property, among them and above all the prince. Joseph begins his examples with a description of how the Prince of Antioch, named Marapa, a prince over all princes, an orthodox and virtuous man, "once upon a time began, at Satanic instigation, to acquire property from monasteries under his rule, being ignorant of the Holy Scriptures." Saint Nikon, learning of this, wrote the Prince an accusatory epistle in which he stated that the Prince should not encroach on the church and monastery property or God would judge him sacrilegious, and he and all of his family would incur cruel punishment from Him. Prince Marapa repented of his sin, and, as it "was small and he was ignorant of holy writings," he was forgiven by God. Other princes, perpetrating similar sins, received great punishment; they were doomed to writhe in eternal fire.

The tract of Joseph Volotskii on monastery landownership was a direct product of the encroachments of the Volotsk appanage prince on the wealth of the monasteries. But this tract had wider significance. Joseph Volotskii gave his mercenary defense of the property interests of his monastery as the basis in principle for the inviolability of the right of the monasteries to the ownership of land and the free labor of the peasants working it. The "example" of the prince's injuring the monasteries and then repenting could be applied not only to the appanage prince under whose rule the Volokolamsk monastery found itself at that time, but to the Grand Princes of Moscow, who also had "sinned" no little in this matter.

Considering that the acquisition of monastery lands or property by the princes could also take place by the external voluntary action of the abbot, Joseph insistently stressed the idea that the abbot did not have the right to dispose of the monastery property to its detriment. The abbot who squandered church property, he wrote, was a sacrilegious person and subject to expulsion from the monastery. The bishop could sell a village not giving income or sell something else for payment of a church debt only with the permission of the metropolitan.

Thus the spokesman of Orthodoxy defended the church and declared monastery land ownership holy and inviolate. In Novgorod the "Sinodik," which annually proclaimed the first week of Lent, included the following words: "anyone doing injury to holy God's churches and monasteries, taking from them villages and vineyards, if he does not cease such injury, will be damned." The example of Novgorod was followed by other archdioceses.[29]

Volotskii's works also posed other sharp contemporary questions: of the rule of the Moscow princes and of the interrelation of the church and secular authority.

Joseph Volotskii was the spokesman of a powerful militant church. For a long time when his monastery was under the rule of the appanage princes of Volotsk, he defended and developed the reactionary theory of the supremacy of the ecclesiastical power over the secular. After the Volokolamsk monastery was transferred (in 1507) to the patronage of Moscow's Grand Prince, Joseph Volotskii began to praise the princely power and to develop the thought of the theocratic character of the rule of the Grand Prince. He wrote that the Tsar was like God in his power, and therefore the power of the prince was higher than that of the church. Consequently it was necessary to submit to the prince as the higher representative of God on earth. In turn the Moscow prince should actively struggle with the enemies of the church, strictly observe Orthodoxy, root out "heresies," and preserve the wealth of the churches and monasteries.[30] Thus the strong power of the Moscow Tsar was necessary to the churchmen for the preservation of their own interests and for the defense of the Russian Church against the inroads of the "heretics."

After Joseph Volotskii's death (1515) the party of the "covetous" was headed by Daniel, who replaced Joseph in the role of abbot of the Volokolamsk monastery and who was from 1522 to 1539 metropolitan of all Rus.

The defense of monastery landownership, the basis of the inviolability of church and monastery property, and the obligation of the abbots and bishops strictly to safeguard church property also appeared in a number of other works of this period, for example such works of unknown authorship as: "A Brief Treatise Against Those Who Interfere with Sacred Property Acquired by the Church," [31] (end of the fifteenth or beginning of the sixteenth century) and "About God's Holy

---

[29] In Novgorod at a sermon annually preached on the first Sunday of Lent the following words were spoken: "All those who command and insult the Holy Churches and monasteries and who requisition villages and vineyards granted to them be cursed if they do not discontinue it." Novgorod's example was followed by other dioceses. See Pavlov, *op. cit.*, pp. 50–1.

[30] See Zimin, *op. cit.*, pp. 159–77.

[31] *Chteniia v Obshchestve istorii i drevnostei rossiiskikh* [Readings in the Society of History and Russian Antiquities] (Moscow: 1902), Bk. 2, Pt. 2, pp. 1–60.

Churches and the Imposed Acquisitions of the Holy Church and their Protection from Violators." [32]

The "non-covetous"—including Nil Sorskii, Vassian, and Maxim the Greek—criticized only monastery landholding, leaving aside the large secular feudal landownership. To criticize large secular landowning would have meant rejecting the entire socio-economic structure of society existing at that time, which churchmen, serving the ruling feudal structure ideologically, were incapable of doing.

The restriction of criticism by the "non-covetous" to large landownership and exploitation of the peasantry within the bounds of the monastery votchiny was noticed by several of their opponents from the camp of the "covetous" and utilized by them as one of the essential arguments against the "non-covetous." Zinovei Otensky, in a work written in the 1560's criticizing the "non-covetous," wrote that God's commandments to which they referred were obligatory for all Christians and concerned not only monasteries, but also villages and towns, that is, secular landholders. "Why did Vassian and Maxim [the Greek] criticize monasteries as being violators of biblical commandments and differentiate them from cities and villages? There is no evidence [in the Bible] to support such action." [33]

The struggle concerning monastery landholding which was released with such force in sixteenth century Russia was not peculiar to the social life of our land. In the Middle Ages the churches and monasteries in the Western European countries owned tremendous expanses of land (a third of the national territories, and sometimes even more) and received enormous incomes.[34] Monasticism was a parasitic form of life. From numerous circles of society arose protests and demands to deprive the churches and monasteries of their privileges. At various times both individuals and entire social groups in the Western European countries denounced church property. In England in the fourteenth century John Wycliffe called for confiscation of the rich holdings of the monasteries. In Italy at the end of the fifteenth century Savonarola made passionate accusations against church-monastery property owning.

---

[32] V. Druzhin, "Neskolko neizvestnykh literaturnykh pamiatnikov iz sbornika XVI v." [A Few Unknown Literary Monuments From a XVI Century Collection], *Letopis zaniatii Arkheograficheskoi komissii za 1908 g.* (St. Petersburg: 1909), Issue 21, pp. 36–8.

[33] *Istiny pokazanye k voprosivshim o novom uchenii. Sochinenie inoka Zinoviia* [Truths Shown to Those Who Inquired About the New Teaching, the Work of the Monk Zinovei] (Kazan: 1863), p. 890.

[34] See Ikonnikov, *op. cit.*, p. 372.

Economic Content of the "Heresies" of Matvei Bashkin and Feodosii Kosoi

In the 1560's "heresies" flared up in Russia with new vigor. The church and state authorities carried on a bitter struggle against them, and a number of church councils were convened to consider charges against "heretics," many of whom were banished to imprisonment in monasteries. Again and again the "heretics" raised burning contemporary socio-economic questions such as the encroachments of the monasteries and kholopy.

In their socio-economic content the Russian "heresies" of the feudal period paralleled the "heretical" movements in Western Europe in the Middle Ages, which were disguised as religious struggles, but were actually protests against feudal oppression and the sanctified feudal exploitation of the ruling church.

In *The Peasant War in Germany* F. Engels treats comprehensively the social significance of the religious "heresies" and shows them as the inescapable form of struggle against feudalism and the church's defense of it during the Middle Ages. The priests had a monopoly on intellectual education, and education itself bore a primarily theological character. Theology reigned in all fields of intellectual activity; the dogmas of the church were at the same time political axioms. This was "a consequence of the position which the church occupied as the most general force for coordinating and sanctioning existing feudal domination."

It is obvious that under such conditions all general and overt attacks on feudalism, expressed primarily as attacks on the church, as well as all social and political revolutionary doctrines, necessarily became religious heresies. To attack the existing social conditions it was necessary to tear from them the aura of sanctity.

Revolutionary opposition to feudalism endured throughout the Middle Ages. It appeared, according to the conditions of the times, in the form of mysticism, as open heresy, or as armed insurrection." [35]

Engels states further that the content and social significance of the "heresies" varied. Thus, for example, the "heresy" of the Waldenses was expressed in the reaction of the patriarchal Alpine herdsmen against the encroachments of feudalism, which became a reactionary attempt to fence themselves off from historical development. The "heresy" of the Albigense was an opposition to feudalism by towns growing up within its framework, while the opposition of John Ball

[35] Engels, *Krestianskaia voina v Germanii,* p. 34.

was an open insurrection. Furthermore, in the "heresies" expressing the opposition of the towns to feudalism there were contradictions between the opposition of burgher and that of peasant. The "heresy" of the towns was directed mainly against the priests, whose wealth and political position they attacked: the medieval burghers demanded first of all an inexpensive church. Their opposition to the feudal structure appears only in the form of opposition to church feudalism, for the town could struggle against secular feudalism with the aid of its privileges, weapons, or class-oriented meetings. On the other hand, the "heresy" taking the form of open uprisings by the peasants bore an altogether different character. It went immeasurably beyond the demands of the burgher "heresy" in relation to the priests, the Papacy, and the restoration of the early Christian church structure. It demanded the restoration of early Christian equality and acknowledgement of this equality as a norm for the secular world as well. In the "equality of the children of God" it saw an implication as to civil equality and partly also as to equality of property. To make the nobility equal to the peasants, the patricians and the privileged middle-class equal to the plebians; to abolish serfdom, ground rents, taxes, privileges, and at least the most flagrant abuses of property—these were the demands put forth with more or less definiteness, and they were regarded as emanating naturally from the teaching of early Christian doctrine.[36]

Engels' views make it possible to understand the social content of the "heresies" in Russia. First one must note that, in consequence of the specific historical development of feudal Russia, "heresies" did not play as important a role in the class struggle against feudalism here as in Western European countries.

In feudal Russia the class struggle of the enserfed peasantry and the town poor usually took place under slogans expressing entirely secular, material demands; and religious motives were either completely lacking or were of no significance. However, where "heresies" took place, they undoubtedly served as a form of protest against the feudal order (for example, the "heresy" of the strigolniki, the "Judaizers," "schismatics" in the seventeenth century).

The social content and significance of various "heresies" in Russia, as we have already said, were not identical. For one and the same or similar demands with relation to the church dogmas, ceremonies, and so forth, among the various "heretics" not infrequently concealed far from uniform demands in questions concerning the social organization of life.

[36] *Ibid.*, p. 36.

Among the "heretics" in Russia in the middle of the sixteenth century were people who went no farther than to protest against church feudalism. But there were also "heretics" for whom criticism of the dogmas of the ruling church was only an approach to criticism, concealing censure, of various other aspects of the feudal order or even of the feudal system as a whole. For the characteristics of this latter trend of the "heretical" movements, the greatest interest is represented by Matvei Bashkin and Feodosii Kosoi.

Matvei Bashkin was, as may be deduced from the extremely scanty information about him, a man of substance. Bashkin read a great deal. Among other questions he was much concerned with the problem of "how we ourselves should live and maintain people without complaint." He was distressed by the lack of conformity between what the commandments and sacred books taught and what was practiced in life.

After much thought Bashkin arrived at a complete rejection of the use of the labor of kholopy (slaves). He believed in the necessity of replacing the labor of kholopy with freely hired labor. The Blagoveshchensk priest Semeon, to whom Matvei Bashkin turned with his doubts, stated that Bashkin told him that God's commandment taught one "to love your neighbor as yourself." "But we hold peasants as slaves," he said. "Christ called every man a brother, but we call some slaves, others fugitives, and still others trim, and some fat. I tore up everything, and I remain as master by the peasants' free choice; if one has virtue, he stays; if not, he goes wherever he wants; none of you, fathers, need trouble to visit us from time to time and tell us how we should live and hold people." [37] The Council of 1553 condemned Bashkin and he was confined to the Volokolamsk monastery.

We have seen that the churchmen, accepting slavery as a form of labor, sometimes protested against the extremes of exploitation of the kholopy and appealed to the feudalists to treat their slaves charitably. This attitude toward slave labor also remained characteristic of the churchmen in the sixteenth century. Joseph Volotskii, the leader of the camp of the "covetous," in an epistle to a magnate rebuked him for uncharitable treatment of his "slaves and house orphans," who suffered very much from the extreme lack of food and clothing, from nakedness and hunger. Joseph Volotskii stated that such treatment of slaves by a master was contrary to the Scriptures.[38]

---

[37] "Moskovskie Sobory na eretikov XVI veka. Zhalobnitsa blagoveshchenskogo popa Simeona" [Moscow's Church Councils Against Heretics of the XVI Century. A Complaint of Simeon, a Priest of the Annunciation], *Chteniia v Obshchestve istorii i drevnostei rossiiskikh* (Moscow: 1847), Bk. 3, Pt. 2, p. 22.

[38] See *Dopolneniia k aktam istoricheskim* [Addenda to Historical Acts] (St. Petersburg: 1846), I, 360–1; Grekov, *Krestiane na Rusi,* p. 223.

Matvei Bashkin did not belong to the church circle. In him we see in principle another formulation of the question. Bashkin demands not mollification of the exploitation of slave labor, but complete abolition of this form of forced labor, even though he feels it necessary to supplement his arguments with theses from the Holy Scripture. Bashkin's testimony that he released his own kholopy and used only hired labor suggests that his view of the question of slave labor was practical and efficient, his appeals to the Holy Scripture notwithstanding.

His complete rejection of slavery and preference for hired labor is a remarkable fact in the history of the development of Russian economic thought, and it is directly connected with the sharp decline of the economic importance of slave labor which significantly appeared in the sixteenth century.

Bashkin was not an exception on this question: the need to liquidate slavery was developed a little earlier by Ivan Peresvetov, who proceeded from entirely different considerations. The priest Silvester also released all of his slaves and replaced them with hired laborers, setting this as an example for others to follow.

Of course, Bashkin was not condemned for releasing his slaves. Instead, in a number of allegations he was accused of heresy. But as slavery was still in wide use, the spread of the idea that the institution of slavery (kholopstvo) was contradictory to the Scriptures was appraised by the church and by the Tsar, who took part in the trial of the "heretics," as one of the elements of "heresy."

As far as can be judged from the scanty surviving evidence stemming from the camp of the ruling church, various "heretics" went far in their negative attitude toward the socio-economic and political structure which then prevailed in the country.

Feodosii Kosoi was a slave who fled from his master and took the vows in a trans-Volga hermitage. Along with other "trans-Volga elders," Feodosii was transferred to Moscow in connection with the trial of Matvei Bashkin, but he soon fled to Lithuania.

Not one of Feodosii Kosoi's works has come down to us. Information about him, his life and his teachings is preserved mainly in the works of the monk Zinovei Otensky, which are devoted to the criticism of Feodosii Kosoi. Zinovei is sharply hostile to Kosoi's views, and his discussion is, of course, biased. As is evident from the account of Feodosii Kosoi's teachings in Zinovei Otensky's book, Feodosii rejected all the external attributes of the Orthodox church—churches, icons, prayers, and basic dogmas and ceremonies.

Kosoi's attitude toward religion bore a rationalist character. He considered the Christian faith an "unjust faith." Icons are useless, as no sort of miracle comes from them; worshipping icons, people bow to wood instead of God; prayers, confession, fasts, the Communion—none of these are ordered by God, and so they are unnecessary. The saints are ordinary mortals; they must not be substituted for the real God. Christ was only an ordinary human being.

Feodosii Kosoi rejected monasticism, monasteries, and churches. Referring to the Scriptures, he opposed church and monastery landowning. "It is not written in the Bible or in the Apostles' Creed that monasteries or churches should take over villages; all this is human tradition." [39] He also referred to the Prince-monk Vassian and to Maxim the Greek, who condemned the monastery ownership of villages. However, he went much farther than these preachers of "non-covetousness." Unlike them, Feodosii Kosoi rejected not only monastery, but also church landowning and, more than that, the very existence of churches and monasteries. He sharply attacked church officials and maintained that priests and bishops are deceivers and hypocrites. They use idol worship instead of the true faith; in their mercenary interests they purposely hide the true God. Feodosii called upon people to disobey the churchmen, not to read their books, and not to listen to their sermons.

By thus attacking the Orthodox church, Feodosii Kosoi boldly snatched away the pall of sanctity from all of its dogmas, ceremonies, and external attributes, and exposed the mendacity, hypocrisy, and greed of the church officials. He dealt the feudal church an idealistic blow of great force by dethroning it in the eyes of the believers. The attack upon the feudal church, an institution which occupied a dominant position in the country, was in effect an attack upon the social order of which the church was the defender.

But Feodosii did not limit himself to criticism of the church. He attacked the entire social structure of Russia. As seen from the writings of Zinovei, Feodosii's criticism of the ruling church was inseparable from, and closely interwoven with, a criticism of the economic and political system, as well as every other facet of contemporary social life. His call for disobedience of the church authorities developed into propaganda urging the people to refuse to obey all authorities; it unmasked the parasitism of the monks and of church-monastery landownership; in short, it was a criticism of the entire economic order of Russia. He taught that not only should one not bow to icons, saints, and priests, but to rulers in general: "Why should the Orthodox bow to the might of the righteous and their icons? Kosoi said that it is

[39] *Istiny pokazanie k voprosivshim o novom uchenii,* p. 923.

undignified to bow, not only to the dead, but also to the living." [40] "One should obey neither a civil official nor a priest." [41] "In the churches priests teach from books and rules that are man-made; they order us to listen to them and to fear civil authorities and to pay them tribute. Christianity recognizes neither civil authority nor war." [42]

In criticizing the social order of contemporary Russia Feodosii looked at the entire system. He rejected not only slavery, as had his contemporary Bashkin, but all domination and oppression in general of one group of persons by another, that is, all of the then existing feudal economic and political order.

Thus Feodosii is in his time the first embodiment known to us of that decisive and ideal representative of the oppressed and exploited masses, struggling against the entire feudal structure while still clothed in the dress of theological heresy.

As far as can be judged from the writings of Zinovei Otenskii, Feodosii Kosoi's positive program remained unclear. One can only make conjectures about it. Kosoi evidently sought the ideal of social life in the books of early Christianity. In his view the sole authority for humanity is God; hence there is no need of human authority. Society must not tolerate the existence of rich and poor. The wealthy should relinquish their wealth and give it to the "apostles," that is, one may suppose, to the adherents of the new teaching. "And anyone who understands us will bring us property, for as it is written in the Acts: 'For as many as were possessors of lands or houses sold them, and brought the prices of the things that were sold, and laid them down at the apostles' feet.' " [43]

From this one may deduce that Feodosii aspired toward absolute equality with regard to property. According to him, all people are equal because they are equal before God. For that reason there must be equality not only between Christians, but between peoples of various languages and faiths: "All people are equal before God, the Tartars, the Germans, and persons of other languages, for, as the Apostle Peter said, "God is no respecter of persons: but in every nation he that feareth him, and worketh righteousness, is accepted with him." [44]

Analyzing the medieval "heresies" in Western Europe, Engels stated that the dream of a future communist society began with the expres-

---

[40] *Ibid.*, p. 501.

[41] "Poslanie mnogoslovnoe. Sochinenie inoka Zinoviia" [A Prolix Message. The Work of the Monk Zinovei], *Chteniia v Obshchestve istorii i drevnostei rossiiskikh* (Moscow: 1880), Bk. 2, p. xvii.

[42] *Ibid.*, p. xvi.

[43] *Ibid.*, p. xvii.

[44] *Ibid.*, p. xv.

sion of the demands of the real social groups by Thomas Muenzer and his party in Germany in the sixteenth century, thanks to the participation of the plebeians in this movement. The plebeians were a class apart from official society. They were outside the feudal, as well as the middle-class, organization. "They had neither privileges nor property; they were deprived even of the possessions owned by peasant or petty bourgeois, and burdened with crushing duties as heavy as they could bear; they were deprived of property and rights in every respect; they lived in such a manner that they did not even come into direct contact with the existing institutions, which ignored them completely. They were a living symptom of the dissolution of the feudal and guild middle-class societies, and were at the same time the first precursors of modern bourgeois society." [45]

Even though the socio-economic conditions of sixteenth century Russia differed from those of Germany, nevertheless Engels' characterization of the struggle of Thomas Muenzer and his party, which reveals the real content of the plebs' demands, explains the significance of Kosoi's views as well.

Although Feodosii Kosoi's view of the future was very obscure and leaned heavily on an interpretation of the New Testament and the rest of the Bible, it did reflect the demands of real social groups within Russia. It incorporated the kholop's dream of a society where none would be without rights and property and where all would be equal. His vision also expressed the protest of the oppressed peasantry against the crying inequality of feudal society, the division into oppressors and oppressed, rich and poor. Thus in criticizing the feudal order, Kosoi voiced the interests of the contemporary oppressed masses of Russia: the kholopy and the peasantry.[46]

It is evident from Zinovei's book that the "heretical" teaching of Feodosii Kosoi found wide response and sympathy in certain circles. Zinovei quotes the Monk Feodor, who said that the instruction of Kosoi "is being praised, accepted and loved by many and recognized as a truly new teaching . . ." [47]

Feodosii's doctrines concerned the very foundations of the dominant social order of Russia and presented a great danger for the feudalists. Consequently, criticism was launched against his teachings in the special works of Zinovei Otenskii.

---

[45] Engels, *Krestianskaia voina v Germanii,* pp. 37–8.

[46] See R. G. Lapshina, "Feodosii Kosoi–ideolog krestianstva XVI veka" [Feodosii Dosoi–A Spokesman of the Peasantry of the XVI Century], *Trudy otdela drevnerusskoi literatury,* IX (1953), pp. 235–50.

[47] *Istiny pokazanie k voprosivshim o novom uchenii,* p. 15.

Zinovei was a fervent apologist for the Orthodox religion. He had been a student of Maxim the Greek, and after Maxim's confinement to the monastery, Zinovei was banished to the Novgorod Otenskii monastery, where he remained until his death (1568). Zinovei's basic works are dedicated to "unmasking" and "overthrowing" Kosoi's teachings.[48] He also criticizes the "non-covetous" teaching of Maxim the Greek and Vassian Patrikeev. In this criticism, and in his defense of monastery landownership Zinovei evinces little originality; he repeats the conclusions of the "covetous" noted above.

It is interesting to note, however, that he detects an inconsistency in the works of Vassian and Maxim the Greek: The Holy Scripture, Zinovei writes, does not distinquish between landownership by secular and clerical persons, whereas Maxim the Greek and Vassian depict only monastery greed, being silent with respect to secular people. Zinovei portrays colorfully the hard labor and scant diet of ordinary monks in the monasteries and contrasts this regimen with the luxurious life of the "non-covetous" Vassian, who made abundant use of munificent benefits from the Tsar's court.

Zinovei presents Feodosii Kosoi and his work in the most derogatory manner. Kosoi's teaching, he states, cannot be correct, because Feodosii himself is a slave, and slaves by law cannot bear witness. (The fact that Feodosii Kosoi, who was formerly a slave, fled from his master to a trans-Volga hermitage with his own belongings Zinovei utilizes to discredit Feodosii in the eyes of his co-believers.) In this connection Zinovei depicts the basic difference between the slave and the hired worker: "The work of a free man and a slave is not the same. The slave's work is different from that of a hired man. The hired person is free. He wants to work by hiring himself out, and whoever wishes may hire him; a slave cannot work for whomever he desires nor for whomever might like to hire him, because a slave has his master and a slave belongs to his master and to no one else; and though he works for his master he gets no remuneration nor does he pay a tax. Should he not wish to work for his master, a slave is wounded and beaten. And therefore a slave has nothing of his own, and whatever he has belongs to his master; . . . and should a slave appropriate something, that, too, belongs to his master and not to him." [49] Zinovei thus characterizes the difference between a slave and a hired laborer in order to condemn Feodosii's flight from his master as a crime and the seizure of his property as theft.

Zinovei Otenskii emerges as a fierce apologist for the exploitation of

[48] *Ibid.*

[49] *Ibid.*, p. 30.

slave labor. Unlike Bashkin, Zinovei looks upon slavery as an entirely normal phenomenon.[50] At the same time, this defender of the exploiters displays great fear of the slaves, maintaining that: "History shows the great magnitude of the evil perpetrated by slaves; if ever the slave should rule, the country would experience a great upheaval." [51]

---

[50] See F. Kalugin, *Zinovii, inok Otenskii i ego bogoslovsko-polemicheskie i tserkovno-uchitelnye proizvedeniia* [Zinovei, An Otensk Monk, and His Religious-Polemic and Church-Informative Works] (St. Petersburg: 1894), p. 126.

[51] *Istiny pokazanie k voprosivshim o novom uchenii,* p. 25.

CHAPTER 5. *The Spokesmen of the Landed Nobility.*

I. S. Peresvetov

Ivan Semenovich Peresvetov was a prominent representative of Russian social thought in the sixteenth century. In his works he described an idealistic basis for performing the main political tasks of the Russian state and set before Ivan IV reform programs in various fields of Russian social life, including economics.

But scanty information on the personality of Peresvetov can be drawn from his works. He traced his family to the monk, Peresvet, who fell in the battle of Kulikovo Plain. Being the subject of the King of Poland, I. Peresvetov, with the King's permission, and together with other Polish nobles, entered the "noble service" of the Hungarian king for three years, and then served with the King of Bohemia for an equal length of time. Between these periods Ivan served under the Wallachian *voevoda* (Moldavian lord) Peter for five months.

At the end of the 1530's "Ivashko Semenov, son of Peresvetov," as he then called himself in a petition written to the Tsar, arrived in Moscow from Lithuania to offer his services to the sovereign of Moscow. He was accepted and received an estate from the Tsar. But this estate was "barren," and Peresvetov's means were soon spent: "As a result of insults and delays" by influential persons, he fell into great misery and was "naked, barefoot, and pedestrian." More than once he tried to appeal to the Tsar with a request for aid and defense "from the abuse of strong persons." [1] His further fate is unknown.

I. Peresvetov wrote a number of short works intended for Ivan IV: "The Tale of Tsar Constantine," "The Tale of the Books," "The Tale of Sultan Mohammed," "The Prophesies of Philosophers and Doctors," "First Petition," "Second Petition," and others.[2] It is not known precisely when these works were written, but judging from several events mentioned in them, V. F. Rzhiga has determined that they could have been written between 1546 and 1549.[3]

[1] V. F. Rzhiga, *I. S. Peresvetov, publitsist XVI veka* [I. S. Peresvetov, A Publicist of the XVI Century] (Moscow: 1908), pp. 79–81.

[2] Rzhiga's two-volume work contains Peresvetov's writings in its addenda.

[3] *Ibid.,* Chapter II.

In his works Peresvetov strongly criticizes various facets of social and particularly political life in contemporary Russia, and recommends to Tsar Ivan IV a definite program of action.

Peresvetov's works have an unusual form: the criticism of existing orders in Russia and the proposal of indispensable reforms are made not in the name of the author, but allegorically, in the form of "speeches" and "writings" of sage rulers and learned persons—the Turkish Sultan Mohammed, the Wallachian voevoda Peter, and "wise philosophers and doctors" in the service of Peter. For precedent to his ideas, I. Peresvetov sets forth many examples from the history of Byzantium and Turkey. He usually criticizes indirectly the state of affairs in Russia or the policy of Ivan IV by referring to the unsatisfactory conditions of Byzantium or the policy of the Byzantine Emperor Constantine, under whom Constantinople was conquered by the Turks. He recommends wise measures through positive evaluations of the policy of the Turkish Sultan Mohammed II, conqueror of Constantinople, by citing "wise speeches" of this Sultan or those of the voevod Peter and other "philosophers and doctors."

Peresvetov clearly expresses in his works the ideology and interests of the nobility, as well as its political and economic demands, during the period of the formation of the centralized state. Peresvetov points out to the Tsar that in governing the country he must lean not on the big feudalists—the well-to-do magnates—but on the small and medium retainers—the nobles, the "warriors." This idea is central to Peresvetov in all his works.

He challenges the "magnates," that is, the boyars and the big feudalists, maintaining that their rule cannot guarantee the unity of the country and its political, military, and economic might, but will inescapably bring the country to ruin. The root of the country's shortcomings and misfortunes, he continues, stems from the ruling position of the magnates. These "lazy rich" [4] do not truly serve their sovereign, but betray him, "impoverish" the state, and attempt to limit or to tame their sovereign. "The magnates of the Russian Tsar enrich themselves, are indolent, and weaken his Tsardom; they join his [military] service with ostentatious equestrian display, servants in tow; they neither stand firmly for Christian faith nor bravely fight against enemies, thus lying to God and sovereign." [5]

Peresvetov considers the rule of the magnates, their arbitrariness and enrichment, and their undermining of the autocracy and military

[4] *Ibid.*, p. 71.
[5] *Ibid.*, p. 62.

might of the Tsar to have been the main reasons for the downfall of Byzantium. He warns the Tsar of the need for a large and strong army and urges close ties with the "warriors," that is, the serving nobility: "The warriors make the Tsar strong and glorious," [6] he writes, stressing the particular importance of the warriors to the state and the obligation to care for them in every way. It is necessary, he counsels, "to keep a military man and pet him like a falcon, always make his heart joyful, and under no conditions allow him to be sorrowful." [7] He advises the Tsar to surround himself with devoted, brave, and wise "warriors," to elevate them, to increase their salaries, and to love and trust them in all generosity. The Tsar should, writes Peresvetov, gather around him and elevate men for their personal worth, for their services, even if they are of undistinguished origin.

Peresvetov considered the ideal political order for contemporary Russia to be the unlimited autocracy of the Tsar. The Tsar, he believed, should not give in to the will of the magnates; he should be stern, for without sternness it would be impossible to hold the kingdom. This severity must be directed first of all against the big feudalists. The magnates, intimate with the Tsar for reasons neither of military service nor of wisdom, but who exert influence on him by sorcery and distract him from military affairs," should be burned [at the stake] and subjected to other horrible deaths to prevent the multiplication of evil." [8]

Peresvetov's understanding of the role of the boyars and nobles in the state, his appeal to the Tsar to depend on the nobles in a merciless struggle against the big feudalists, and the idea of unlimited and stern rule by the Tsar coincide completely with Ivan IV's views on these same questions as formulated by Ivan the Terrible after the time to which I. Peresvetov's works relate.

Peresvetov's political ideal was opposed to the reactionary views of the boyars concerning the organization of the country. The boyars opposed the strengthening of the sovereign's authority, as they aspired to retain political and economic power in their own hands.

Peresvetov gave much thought to the Tsar's obligation to guarantee justice in the country; he stressed that justice was higher than faith: "God loves not faith, but justice." Justice (the absence of force and arbitrariness in the magnates' decisions, an honest court, and others), writes Peresvetov, gives the Tsar great strength and wisdom. He proposes replacing the unjust, venal court of the viceroys with honest

6 *Ibid.*, p. 65.
7 *Ibid.*, p. 62.
8 *Ibid.*, p. 65.

judges who should be guaranteed salaries from the treasury, and if they judge unjustly they should receive the heaviest penalty—death.

Insistently urging upon the Tsar the necessity of eliminating the ruling position in the country of the big feudalists—the magnates—and the general elevation of the "warriors" of the nonmagnate families—the nobility—I. Peresvetov passes by in complete silence the question of the toiling masses, the basic class of the feudal society—the peasantry. The feudal exploitation of the peasantry evidently appeared to him a fully normal and natural phenomenon.[9] Speaking decisively against the single, ruling part of the class of feudalist-exploiters—against the boyars and the big feudalists—I. Peresvetov urged the elevation of another portion of the same class of feudalist-exploiters, the loyal nobility. This spokesman for the nobility wanted to crowd the big feudalists out of the ruling economic and political positions, to clear these positions for another sector of the same class.

Though evading the question of the mutual relations of the feudalists and peasants, I. Peresvetov at the same time took an extremely radical position in relation to the labor of the kholop-slaves. He came forth with strong demands for complete elimination of slavery (kholopstvo) in Russia.

The conclusions on which Peresvetov based his demands for the elimination of slavery are curious. We have seen above that the "heretic" Bashkin, arguing the inadmissibility of slavery, tried to appeal to the "Holy Scriptures": the possession of kholopy, Bashkin held, was completely contrary to the teaching of the Gospel regarding the equality of men. Peresvetov also referred to the "Holy Scriptures": "God created man self-ruling and ordered him to be a ruler and not a slave," he wrote.[10] "One God over the entire universe, and that means that those who enslave others for eternity sin and please the devil." [11]

But, as in other questions, the argument based on the "Holy Scriptures" played no substantial role with Peresvetov. He argued the necessity of complete abolition of slavery in Russia because of his own fundamental political idea—the destruction of the power and arbitrariness of the big feudalists in the country, the elevation of the nobles and "warriors," and the establishment of an unlimited and stern rule of the Tsar supported by the serving nobility. Peresvetov connected the very existence of slavery directly with the presence of the "magnates" in the

[9] To understand Peresvetov's views on the peasantry one must remember that he wrote his works during the period when there already existed a limitation on a peasant's transfer from the *pomeshchik* to one period a year (St. George's Day), but as yet there did not exist complete enserfment.

[10] *Ibid.*, p. 34.

[11] *Ibid.*

country. The magnates enslaved the entire country. In the Byzantine Empire, he wrote, the magnates "enslaved the Christians." Under the Byzantine Tsar Constantine "all the empire depended on his magnates . . . When the land was enslaved, in that land all evils were perpetrated: theft, robbery, and outrage, and the entire empire was greatly impoverished . . ." [12] Greece [Byzantium], writes Peresvetov, perished from the pride of the magnates and their enslavement of the people.[13] In Peresvetov's view, the elimination of slavery was necessary so that the Tsar could have a strong and brave army at his disposal. The kholopy served the magnates. The Tsar must have an army directly subordinate only to him. The kholop could not be a brave soldier. "In a kingdom in which people are enslaved, in that kingdom the people are not brave and not bold in battle against an enemy: the enslaved person does not fear disgrace and does not strive for honor, whether strong or not, as he believes that: No matter what happens I shall remain a slave." [14] Peresvetov advised burning the *kabalnye* books [slave registers].

Peresvetov's strongly negative attitude toward the existence of kholopstvo in Russia is understandable if one takes into consideration that in the middle of the sixteenth century the transition of small landholders into kholopy of the big feudalists was widespread. The economic significance of the work of the kholopy during this period declined sharply. Peresvetov evidently believed that the economic interests of the noble landowners could be fully satisfied by the exploitation of the peasantry and that the elimination of the kholopstvo would both undermine the power of the big feudalists and aid the strengthening of the nobility and the autocratic power of the Tsar. In this way Peresvetov attempted to solve the question of the kholopy in the light of his understanding of the basic political problems of the time. Although as a whole kholopstvo continued to exist in Russia long after Peresvetov sent Ivan IV his advice, it is important to note that the Tsar's Code of 1550 forbade the conversion of [petty] nobles into kholopy.

An important link in I. S. Peresvetov's program was the demand for the abolition of administration through viceroys and for reforms in the financial system of the Moscow state. The administration of the country by viceroys and the existence of the system of kormlenie Peresvetov considers harmful to both the Tsar's power and to the whole country. The system of the viceroys and kormlenie was utilized by the magnates

---

[12] *Ibid.*, p. 67.
[13] *Ibid.*
[14] *Ibid.*, p. 75.

for the consolidation of their power and the weakening of the authority of the sovereign, for their enrichment at the price of the "impoverishment" of the country. It concealed within its framework the threat of feudal wars. Peresvetov condemns the system by which the Tsar "gives towns and volosti to the rule of magnates, and the magnates enrich themselves from the tears and blood of Christians by iniquitous collection, and they sustain themselves from kormlenie, from towns, and from volosti, and unjustly appropriate lands, and in so doing on both sides many sins are committed." [15]

Peresvetov advises the abolition of the viceroy system and kormlenie; the income from the whole country should go to the treasury, and all the officials, judges and warriors should receive salaries from the treasury in accordance with their service. This eliminates the possibility of wrongdoing by the magnates and judges and will aid the establishment of justice in the land. The magnates cannot then enrich themselves and "impoverish" the Tsar's treasury. The greater part of the state income should go to the support of the army.

Peresvetov cites the example of Sultan Mohammed, who, in Peresvetov's words, "ordered that the revenue from the entire empire go to his treasury and allowed none of his magnates to acquire a post of viceroy, in order to prevent them from making prejudiced judgments. He paid his magnates salaries from his treasury on the basis of dignity, introduced courts throughout the empire, and established fees in order to prevent judges from attempting to give out unjust sentences." [16]

Peresvetov's proposal to liquidate the system of *namestnichestvo* and kormlenie reflected the growing demands of the centralized Russian feudal state. Only a few years after Peresvetov wrote to the Tsar about this, the kormlenie system was abolished, and Ivan IV subsequently realized the centralization of the state's financial systems.

I. Peresvetov also raises the question of the merchants and trade, although his formulation has a narrowly noble viewpoint. He wants to protect the interests of the warriors, that is, the nobles, from the greed of the merchants and to set up state regulation of prices on goods sold by the merchants to the warriors. This is reflected in his reasoning that in Constantinople" the warriors are impoverished and ruined, while the moneylenders are enriched." [17] "The Byzantine court was unjust, and their trade was unfair; the merchants could not set prices on their goods, and they were taxed in an unfair fashion." [18] This

[15] *Ibid.*, p. 61.
[16] *Ibid.*, p. 72.
[17] *Ibid.*, p. 65.
[18] *Ibid.*, pp. 65–6.

negative picture Peresvetov contrasts with a positive one: Sultan Mohammed, he writes, "introduced great justice in his empire, and the merchants were allowed to trade; they bought and sold without difficulty even up to one thousand rubles." [19]

The substance of these reflections by Peresvetov on merchants and trade is not clear. It is only certain that he wanted state regulation of trade in the interests of warriors. He also advised the Tsar to regulate the merchants' sale of goods to warriors during campaigns. Here he definitely recommends that the sale of goods be established "so that all prices be set . . . by order of the Tsar." [20] For selling goods to the warrior at a price "greater than that ordered by the Tsar" and for cheating in weighing the merchant should get the death penalty, just as the warrior does who takes goods and does not pay the price set for them.[21]

Thus in Peresvetov's works are expressed the contradictions not only between the nobility and the powerful feudalists, but also between the nobility and commercial capital, although less clearly. Peresvetov defends the interests of the nobility from both the boyars and the merchants.

He considered it necessary to carry on an active foreign policy, and he advised the Tsar to conquer the kingdom of Kazan [Kazan Tartars]. As a representative of the nobility he is interested first of all in the "very fertile land," similar to "the promised land." [22] This part of Peresvetov's program soon was realized: after the conquest of Kazan its lands were distributed among the Russian pomeshchiki (nobles). With regard to Crimea, Peresvetov advised a defensive policy. Peresvetov also believed that the Russian Tsar should aid the peoples of the Balkan peninsula, the Greeks and Serbs, to free themselves from the Turkish yoke.[23]

Such were the political and economic views of I. Peresvetov, clearly expressing the ideology and interests of the Russian nobility of the period concerning the formation of the centralized state. Peresvetov's program was particularly significant because it was formulated not long before Ivan IV began to institute reforms in various fields, and before he introduced the special royal domain. The works of Peresvetov were, as may be judged from his petition, known to the Tsar and, one may think, exerted influence on Ivan IV's policy. One must not, of course,

[19] *Ibid.*, p. 66.
[20] *Ibid.*, p. 75.
[21] *Ibid.*, pp. 75–6.
[22] *Ibid.*, p. 68.
[23] *Ibid.*, p. 63.

exaggerate their possible role in this respect, but they raised such real questions and illuminated them in such a way that they could not but attract his attention. In his works Ivan Peresvetov gave a broad theoretical basis to the policy which was later introduced by Ivan the Terrible—the policy towards the boyars and nobility, in the field of finances, among others.

Ermolai-Erazm

Among the Russian churchmen of the sixteenth century who diligently considered the essential problems of Russian socio-economic life and attempted solutions to them a special and outstanding place is occupied by Ermolai-Erazm.

Biographical information on Ermolai-Erazm is scanty. It is known only that he was a priest of the Moscow court church, Savior of the Hill, and that he later became a monk under the name of Erazm. Ermolai-Erazm ardently defended the dogmas of orthodoxy and struggled against heresies. As a priest he evidently was subjected to insults and persecution by influential persons. He writes Tsar Ivan IV a letter in which he asks the Tsar to defend him against the machinations of enemies and from slander which has been raised against him. Offering his literary services to the Tsar and writing to him in the form of a religious-moral work, Ermolai proclaims his readiness to write a composition for the Tsar in which would be set forth and illuminated questions of social life and state administration: "Should Your Majesty allow me to write on worldly matters, on the well-being of the land and decrease of arbitrariness, I possess a written chapter which I would be glad to reveal to your Tsarist Majesty." [24] Evidently the Tsar agreed, for there appeared a political and economic work by Ermolai-Erazm significant for those times, entitled "Regulation and Land Surveying [Decree] by the Benevolent Tsar."

Ermolai was an educated person with broad interests. He belonged to a circle of learned churchmen gathered around the Metropolitan Makarii who engaged themselves in writing original theological compositions and translating literature from the Greek. He wrote a number of theological and moral compositions: "A Word on the Consideration of Love and Truth and of the Victory over Enmity and Lies," a "Book about the Holy Trinity," a religious-historical "Novel about Peter and Febronius of Murom," "Illuminating Easter," and others. The greater

---

[24] V. F. Rzhiga, "Literaturnaia deiatelnost Ermolaia-Erazma" [Literary Activity of Ermolai-Erazm] *Letopis zaniatii Arkheograficheskoi komissii za 1923–1925 gg.* Issue 33 (1926), pp. 157–8.

part of Ermolai-Erazm's works was dedicated to theological and moral themes; but in them he raised and elucidated questions of a pressing social character.

In his political views Ermolai was an opponent of boyar arbitrariness. His works clearly show his antiboyar feelings. At the same time, on another political question of enormous significance at the time—the strengthening of the centralized state as an autocratic monarchy which would affect the relations of the secular and spiritual authority—Ermolai stood for independence of the church from the Tsar's authority. In effect, he espoused the supremacy of spiritual rule over that of the Tsar. While the Tsar's authority over man was temporal, Ermolai wrote, and was exerted only on the body, spiritual power over man's soul endured through life and after death.

This theory did not aid the consolidation of autocracy as the sole possible form of centralized state under the existing historical conditions. However this part of Ermolai's views was not as clearly expressed as were his other tenets, *viz.*, his antiboyar tendency.

In his works Ermolai raised the question of wealth, which he considered, however, not from the economic but from the religious-ethical point of view. In his study, "A Word on the Judgment of Love and Justice . . . ," Ermolai spoke against the pride of eminent persons and magnates as well as their wealth. He considered the highest virtue of man to be love of God and neighbors; but this virtue was incompatible with the accumulation of wealth. Poverty was superior to wealth, since wealth was achieved not by one's own labor, but by craft and force. It is difficult, he states, quoting the Scriptures, for the rich to enter into the kingdom of God: "Because we collect all our wealth forcibly by the prevailing trickery or cunning; for from one's own labor one cannot acquire much wealth." [25] The magnates had nothing by virtue of their own labor, but fed and clothed themselves by the labor of others: "for magnates have produced nothing by their own labor, but they eat and clothe themselves from the labor of others." [26]

He accuses wealth of being always connected with injury to others. Sincere love, writes Ermolai, is incompatible with the appropriation of profit from others: "He who believes in love cannot desire a gain of any sort from others; he does not defeat, steal, beat, commit violence, or appropriate the property of others." [27]

He condemns the enrichment of the merchant through extraordinary profits and also through moneylending. This argument against money-

---

[25] *Ibid.*, p. 181.
[26] *Ibid.*
[27] *Ibid.*, p. 161.

lending is curious: only animal and plant life can grow, he writes, and not silver. "And if you are a merchant and you purchased only a little you cannot expect to gain much from it in a short time, for this would destroy love . . . similarly when you give your silver for interest that, too, will destroy love, this because every living thing grows by God's will; garden products grow because of God's will from the sun's warmth; your silver God meant not to grow. You are trying to oppose God by allowing a non-growing thing to grow." [28]

Ermolai's work, "Regulation and Land Surveying [Decree] by the Benevolent Tsar," was the first definite economic and political treatise in Russia.[29] The word "regulation" is used here in the sense of "guide." The work is thus a guide for the Tsar in ruling the kingdom and in land surveying. The comparison of the proposals contained in Ermolai's "Regulation" with the events taking place in the sixteenth century suggests that this work was written in the 1540's or early 1550's.

In his works Ermolai counsels the Tsar to establish a system of important measures directed at the solution of actual problems of the time. This system includes the following measures: 1) reduction by legislative enactment of the peasants' obligations to the landowners; 2) reform with respect to the monetary needs of the Tsar; 3) change in the field of postal obligations; 4) reform in land surveying; 5) abolition of the kormlenie system; 6) regulation of military obligations.

The question of the position of the peasant masses occupies a central place in the work. Ermolai writes that the Russian Tsar is obligated to care not only for the magnates, but for all of his subjects, even to the very least. The magnates, he writes, of course are needed, but they do not support themselves with their own labor. The peasants are the most indispensable subjects, for by their labor they supply bread, the product most urgently needed by all persons: "Magnates are needed, but they do not support themselves with their own labor. Peasants are needed above all, as from their labor there is bread—the most precious item: during a Mass bread is offered to God, which is transformed into Christ's body, and finally the entire country from the Tsar to the commoner seeks their [the peasants'] work." [30]

Proclaiming the primary significance of the peasantry for the life of society, Ermolai points out their difficult, poverty-stricken position, burdened with more than one yoke: "They always remain in sad agitation inasmuch as they carry the burden of more than one yoke." [31]

---

[28] *Ibid.*, p. 162.
[29] *Ibid.*, pp. 193–9.
[30] *Ibid.*, p. 193.
[31] *Ibid.*

It would be enough for them to have to bear only one yoke a year, for even the birds and beasts molt only once a year, in the summer, but the peasant must always bear various obligations, money taxes, postal obligations, and others.

Those sent to the peasants to collect the Tsar's taxes, writes Ermolai, drink at the cost of the peasant and collect much extra for themselves; large sums are taken from the peasant for postal expenditures. Many offenses are inflicted on them by the Tsar's surveyors, working slowly and eating much of their grain. Ermolai considers such behavior toward the peasantry entirely abnormal: "I have read much about various kingdoms, but I have not encountered such a custom," [32] he remarks.

In his deliberations concerning the mutual relations of the peasantry and the landowners, Ermolai begins with the feudal relationships then existing in the land, that is, the division of people into landowners having the right to appropriate the product of the labor of other people and peasants obliged to fulfill specific obligations for the benefit of the landowners. But he proposes an important reform in this field: the setting up of a specific degree of obligation of the peasant to the landowner. The peasant must give the landowner only a fifth of the product he obtains, for example, grain, hay, firewood, and nothing more.

Why a fifth? Ermolai refers to a biblical example: Joseph proposed in Egypt to take a fifth part of the harvest for the use of the Pharaoh; Ermolai calls on Ivan IV to follow this example.

Ermolai considers it necessary to free the peasant from all types of money payments to the landowner. The peasant must fulfill his obligation to the landowner only in the form of a "natural tax" of a stated amount. Russia, writes Ermolai, is an agricultural country; the peasants here produce grain and with grain must fulfill their obligations. The need of obtaining money puts the peasant in an extremely difficult position. "In all lands everyone pays his emperor or master a tax from the fruits of his land: where gold or silver is found, there they give gold or silver; where livestock is found, there they give livestock; and where wild beasts, they give beasts. Here in Russia, neither gold and silver, nor livestock is found; but by God's grace we have grain for man's livelihood. A tribute in grain from the peasants to the Tsar and magnates is sufficient, and these tributes should be set at a fifth, as was Joseph's in Egypt." [33]

One must not, he writes, demand silver of the peasants and at the

[32] *Ibid.*, p. 194.
[33] *Ibid.*

same time weary them with torment: "They do not eat silver, but bread. Therefore they should be allowed to pay in bread, on the basis of Joseph's fair code. A fifth part, also, of hay and firewood is sufficient." [34]

Ermolai knew, of course, that besides products the feudalists needed money—gold and silver. This money, he believed, the landowner could receive by duty-free sales of part of his products on the market to town inhabitants, who also needed bread.

One must remember that Ermolai's proposals concerning the amount of the peasants' obligation—a fifth part of the product produced by them—was much less than the share the peasant had to give the landowner in the mid-sixteenth century in the form of taxes.

Ermolai writes only about the obrok and omits entirely the question of the *barshchina.* Academician B. D. Grekov explains this omission by the fact that the barshchina was not yet a widespread phenomenon.[35]

Ermolai also proposed that the Tsar fundamentally change the system of collecting revenue to cover general state expenditures. Here too he proposed, in effect, the very principles which he placed at the foundation of the interrelation between the feudalist and the peasant. He urged the abolition of all sorts of money taxes and collections for the Tsar's treasury from the peasantry, as demands of money from the peasants were a burden on them. For the creation of revenue necessary to the sovereign, a definite amount of land should be set aside in various parts of the country; the peasants working this land should pay the Tsar a fifth of the harvest of grain. From forested lands they should tender animals and money, and from rivers, fish and beaver.

Thus the Tsar would receive products in kind; part of the collected grain could be sold, and the Tsar would have the money he needed, "and not one peasant would be tearful and troubled by insufficiencies . . ." [36]

In trying to lighten their position, Ermolai also proposed liberating the peasantry from postal obligations. A postal service, he writes, should connect towns. Expenditures for this service should be imposed on the city merchants, inasmuch as they become rich from the buying and selling of goods. In return city merchants should be freed from duties and other payments.[37]

---

[34] *Ibid.,* p. 197.

[35] Grekov, *Krestiane na Rusi,* pp. 217–8.

[36] *Letopis zaniatii Arkheograficheskoi komissii za 1923–1925 gg.* Issue 33 (1926), p. 126.

[37] *Ibid.,* p. 194.

With the aim of lightening the peasants' burden and setting in order the allotment of lands to the serving people, Ermolai suggested a reform of the units of land measurement. He considered that the existing unit of land measurement—the *"chetvert"* (a half desiatina)—was burdensome to the peasant; this small unit necessitated prolonged labor by the Tsar's land surveyors and scribes who in this work "consumed much of the peasants' food," and "peasants sustained considerable loss from this consumption."

Ermolai proposed adopting a much larger unit, the "square field," an area equal to one thousand *sazhens* (one sazhen being equal to seven square feet). The square field would be equal to 833 chetverts, with 250 chetverts in each of three smaller fields and 83 chetverts in hayfields and woods. Reform into this large unit of measurement, thought Ermolai, would hasten the work of land surveyors tenfold and lessen the causes of litigation.[38]

In Ermolai's view, the square field should become a normal noble assessment, and this area should consist of twenty complete peasant portions.[39] He also recommended the square field as a land measurement for the Tsar in state expenditures and for the retainers—the boyars, voevodas, and the military.

If, considered Ermolai, someone was of greater worth than others, he should be given more land and peasants—to one twice as much, to another three times, and to others seven to eight times as much. This would make it possible for worthy people to be voevodas and boyars. But they would not behave like masters in relation to other warriors. "Since they collect enough from their peasants, it is superfluous to collect silver from other strangers for reasons of wealth and pride." [40] Whoever needs money can obtain it by selling surpluses of his grain. In these reflections of Ermolai the scholar sees the proposal to abolish the system of kormlenie then existing in the country.[41]

To Ermolai the "boyar," "voevoda," and "warrior" were retainers, and they could and should receive land and peasants from the Tsar only as a material guarantee of their service to the state. "Should the magnates need anything, they have their own peasants and should be satisfied; they receive from every peasant a fifth part of the produce and in return they perform service for the Tsar." [42] The amount of security of various persons would differ with regard to the official worth of

---

[38] *Ibid.*, pp. 195–6.
[39] *Ibid.*, p. 197.
[40] *Ibid.*
[41] *Ibid.*, pp. 153–4.
[42] *Ibid.*, p. 194.

each. However, Ermolai limited the amounts of the grant. In his view the greatest grant should consist of four fields, the least, a half field. In this way the greatest guarantee would not exceed the least by more than eight times. The amount of this grant should be sufficient to guarantee conscientious service, but by no means enough to permit surplus wealth. Ermolai rejected the unearned wealth of magnates as unjust.

Further, he proposed to establish a direct connection between the military service of the feudalist and his material guarantee. Whoever received from the Tsar land in the amount of one square field should have one servant in armor in service. If anyone were given more land, he should supply one soldier from every ten complete peasant allotments.[43] In order for the Tsar to be able to collect an army quickly, Ermolai suggested that the warriors be forbidden to live in villages and hamlets, but that they settle in towns, where the peasants would bring them grain, hay, and firewood.[44]

To raise the morale of the country Ermolai advised the Tsar to institute measures against drunkenness and robbery. He recommended closing inns everywhere, as they were the centers of drunkenness and other sins, banning the distribution of hops, and also forbidding blacksmiths to make knives with sharp points.[45]

Such was the content of the economic and political treatise of Ermolai-Erazm. The treatise is an interesting monument in the history of Russian economic thought.

Ermolai tries here to solve the problem of the formation of the economic base of the centralized Russian state. This base he sees in the pomestie system of land tenure. The boyars, "voevodas" and warriors were to serve the Russian state and for this duty were to receive from the Tsar land with peasants to work it. In his conception of the basic social relations of this period—the relation of the feudalists and peasants—Ermolai stands firmly on the position of acceptance of the then existing feudal social order. In all of his reflections he never goes beyond the framework of this system, based on the exploitation by the landowners of the labor of the peasants dependent on them.

It is characteristic of Ermolai's conception of the rights of the landowners to the labor of the peasants and the obligation of the peasants with regard to the landowners that he connects the right of one and the obligation of others directly to the bearing of military and state service by the landowner. In his conception of the feudal rights of the follower

---

[43] *Ibid.*, p. 197.
[44] *Ibid.*
[45] *Ibid.*, p. 198–9.

of the Tsar and of the feudal obligations of the peasants, Ermolai assumes a position characteristic of Ivan III, who established the pomestie system of landowning, and Ivan IV, who completely adhered to the same system.

Ermolai looks upon the right of the feudalists to landownership and to peasant labor as only the reverse side of their obligation to serve the Tsar. Thus the implications of his views are evident both as to the basis of mutual relations of the class of feudalists and peasants in the economic position of Russia during the sixteenth century and as to the political process of the formation and consolidation of a centralized state.

With regard to the "magnates," Ermolai was critical. Although his position on this question was far from being as clear and consistent as Peresvetov's, nevertheless in his project of reform with respect to large feudal landownership he reflected primarily the interests of the new progressive part of the class of feudalists—the subservient nobility. The reforms he proposed to the Tsar in the field of landownership—the distribution of lands and peasants to the nobility, dictated by problems of forming and strengthening the centralized state—directly answered the interests of the nobility and went contrary to those of the hereditary boyars.

One must note that in his detailed presentation of the bases for his proposed reforms, Ermolai said not a word about monastery landownership as one of the possible sources of the land fund for the nobility. In his project he deals simply with the "military," without indicating on whose lands the loyal followers of the Tsar would be settled. Ermolai's silence on this question can best be interpreted as agreement with the contemporary state of affairs, that is, with the inviolability of monastery landownership.

Ermolai's proposal of material guarantees for the nobility by way of allocating land to them was directed toward the strengthening of the feudal centralized state and in this sense had a progressive significance. Ivan IV established exactly such a policy on a wide scale. Ermolai emerges as the spokesman and reflector of the immediate interests of the serving nobility.

But this characterization of Ermolai-Erazm's class position is not complete. He differs from Ivan IV and from other spokesmen of the nobility, such as Peresvetov, by reason of his great attention to the needs of the oppressed peasantry. Their interests and the wish to ease their lot runs through all of Ermolai's treatises.

He stresses the great significance of peasant labor for the country, depicts the difficult position of the peasantry, and proposes a system of measures directed at improving the lot of the peasant mass. But in all of his aspirations to improve their position Ermolai-Erazm remains unalterably the spokesman of the serving nobility and not the advocate and representative of the interests of the peasants, as several scholars have maintained.[46] It is incorrect to label the views of Ermolai as democratic and populist. "Democracy" and "populism" are conceptions which are in no way applicable to the thinkers and statesmen of Russia of the sixteenth century, promoting as they did the consolidation of unlimited monarchy and its economic base, feudal pomestie landownership. Likewise, one cannot, as does R. Iu. Vipper, regard Ermolai's aspiration to aid the peasant masses simply as the result of his acquaintance with the legislation of the Byzantine emperors.[47]

Ermolai tried to reconcile the interests of the various classes of feudal society—clearly an unrealizable task. He wanted to guarantee the material demands of the centralized state so that the real interests of all classes of society would be protected—the serving nobility, the peasantry, and the merchants—to the detriment only of the interests of the eminent boyars. He hoped to harmonize the interests of the nobility and the peasants. Such an ambition indicates the utopian nature of his project in this central point of his proposals.

While Ermolai's proposal to guarantee free goods to the serving nobility was realized wisely in the policy of Ivan IV—free goods obtained from the feudally dependent peasants—his desire to improve the peasants' lot remained an idle wish. Reality worked toward ever greater oppression of the peasant masses by the feudalists and the feudal state, not toward their betterment. As regards guaranteeing the interests of the serving nobility, Ermolai showed himself a true politician, but as to the interests of the peasantry he was no more than a utopian. He wanted to reconcile the irreconcilable—the interests of the exploited peasantry, on the one hand, with the interests of the exploiter-nobles and the feudal state, on the other.

Ermolai desired to curtail significantly the share of the peasants' labor-product going to the feudalist. With the development of commodity production, however, the feudalists increased their pretensions to gratuitous peasant labor. The growth of the barshchina meant greater exploitation of the peasants. Similarly, Ermolai's demands to abolish all money payments by the peasantry to the feudalists and the state were unrealistic. With the growth of the market Ermolai's demand to return entirely to natural levies on the peasantry was not

---

[46] *Ibid.*, p. 188; see also Vipper, *Ivan Groznyi*, p. 38; Budovnits, *Russkaia publitsistika XVI veka*, p. 221.

[47] Vipper, *op. cit.*, p. 39.

only utopian, but in essence reactionary: it was contrary to the progressive economic forces of expansion of money-commodity relationships in the country. His proposals to free the peasants from postal obligations also remained unrealized.

Ermolai's proposals for enlarging the units of land measurement and abolishing the system of kormlenie had a different significance. Historians have noted the connection between these proposals and the reforms of Ivan IV in the 1550's. Ermolai's project to replace the small unit of land measurement, the "fourth," with the larger unit, the "square field," possibly exerted some influence on Ivan IV. It was during the land census taken in the middle of the sixteenth century that a new larger unit of tax levy was introduced, the so-called *"bolshaia sokha"* (large land). This measure approximates the one which Ermolai proposed.[48] One thing is certain: Ermolai's proposal for reform of the units of land measurement dealt with the practical side of the question, and he realistically pointed the way toward its solution.

The proposal for the abolition of the system of kormlenie was also realistically conceived; this was accomplished by Ivan IV in 1555.

Such were the economic views of Ermolai-Erazm. As we have shown, in his original treatise he developed interesting, comprehensive views on the critical issues of his time. His project of material guarantees for the serving nobility was dictated by a progressive desire to create and strengthen the centralized Russian state. Also progressive were his proposals to abolish the system of kormlenie and to increase the unit of land measurement.

The measures proposed by Ermolai-Erazm for the improvement of the position of the peasantry, however, also bore a utopian character, for he considered it possible to improve the position of the peasantry while preserving the bases of feudal exploitation.

---

[48] See Miliukov, *Spornye voprosy finansovoi istorii Moskovskogo gosudarstva,* p. 76.

CHAPTER 6. *Ivan the Terrible's Principles of Economic Policy.*

The Policy of Landownership. The Strengthening of Serf Law.

Ivan the Terrible occupies an outstanding place in the history of the development of the Russian state. He struggled persistently against the remnants of feudal disunity and fought for the consolidation and might of Russia. The reforms he introduced in the 1550's were of great significance in effecting the formation of a centralized state.

In order to strengthen the state apparatus, he created new prikazy; he initiated local administrative reform with the aim of increasing the role of central organs; he discontinued local administration by viceroys and district officials; he inaugurated judicial reform. With the creation of a new Sudebnik (1550), a uniform procedure was inaugurated for the entire country. Reforms in the field of finance were introduced, and the system of kormlenie was abolished. With the conquest of the Kazan and Astrakhan khanates the threat of Tartar forays was reduced, and the security of the eastern and southeastern borders of Russia was guaranteed.

In establishing the oprichnina [Ivan's personal and select military force] (1565–1572), Ivan the Terrible dealt a crushing blow to the reactionary feudal aristocracy—those princely and boyar notables with their separatist aspirations. At the same time, a new group of the feudalist class—the serving nobility—was elevated. The oprichnina army played an historically progressive role.

Ivan IV carried out an active and bold foreign policy. He struggled resolutely for the liquidation of the western barrier formed by Poland, Livonia, and Sweden, and for the establishment of a direct route from Russia to Western Europe. Marx wrote of Ivan the Terrible: "He was insistent in his pressures against Livonia: *the conscious goal was to give Russia an outlet to the Baltic Sea and to open communications with Europe.* That is why Peter I admired him so!" [1]

[1] Marx, *Arkhiv Marksa i Engelsa,* VIII (1946), p. 165.

Ivan IV was a well-informed person, one of the best educated Russians of that time. His remarkable letters to the traitor, Prince A. Kurbskii, revealed the basic cause of his struggle against the reactionary boyars for establishment of unlimited autocratic rule. The interests of the Russian state, he declared, motivated his actions.

The many-sided economic policy of Ivan the Terrible was subordinated to two basic aims: consolidation of the Russian state and strengthening of the autocratic power of the Tsar. The political views and economic policy of Ivan IV were expressed in the Tsar's Sudebnik of 1550,[2] in the "Tsarist inquiries" of the *Stoglav* Council (1551),[3] in various decrees which determined the reforms of the 1550's and thereafter; [4] in his codes and customs charters; and in the institutions of the oprichnina.[5]

Among Ivan the Terrible's literary works, his first letter to Prince Kurbskii (1565), his letter to the English queen, Elizabeth (1570), and his letter to the Kirillo-Belozerskii monastery (1573) are of the greatest significance in the history of Russian economic thought.[6]

In the system of various closely related economic measures put into effect by Ivan IV, the most important are those in the field of large feudal landownership. Ivan IV's land policy was directed toward strengthening the serving nobility which contributed to the social support of the feudalists. He thus continued the economic policy inaugurated by Ivan III. The essence of Ivan IV's land policy was the forcible establishment of pomestie landownership. One of the first major undertakings in this direction was the *ispomeshchenie* [grants of pomestia] made in 1550 to 1,070 of the "best servants" around Moscow. This so-called "selected thousand" was comprised mainly of the town serving people, and provincial "petty boyars."

Okol'nichi [petty courtiers] were also in their rank. From the fund of the Tsar's court they were presented with pomestia. The size of the pomestia varied: the boyars and okol'nichi who did not have their own votchiny near Moscow were granted pomestia to the amount of

---

2 See *Sudebniki XV–XVI vekov,* pp. 135–77.

3 See *Stoglav* (Kazan: 1862) and other editions; I. N. Zhdanov, "Materialy dlia istorii Stoglavogo sobora" [Materials for the History of the Stoglav Council], *Sochineniia* [Works] (St. Petersburg: 1904), I, 171–272.

4 See Vladimirskii-Budanov, ed., *Khrestomatiia po istorii russkogo prava,* pp. 1–42; M. Diakonov, *Ocherki obshchestvennogo i gosudarstvennogo stroia drevnei Rusi* [Outlines of the Social and State System of Ancient Rus] (Iuriev: 1907), I, 222–4.

5 Zagoskin, *Ustavnye gramoty XIV–XVI vekov,* Issue I and II.

6 See *Poslaniia Ivan Groznogo* [Letters Of Ivan the Terrible] (Moscow-Leningrad: AS USSR, 1951).

200 chetverts of plowland in a field, that is, 300 desiatiny in three fields; the nobles and the petty boyars were given 200, 150 and 100 chetverts in each field, according to their rank. The "selected thousand" were made part of the sovereign's court; they occupied command posts in the army and had important duties in the state apparatus.[7] The allotment of lands around Moscow to the serving people was one of the reforms put into effect in the 1550's. The essence of that reform centered in the legal establishment of a direct tie between large landholding and military service to the state, and the amount of this service depended upon the land owned.

The working of the land by peasant labor, in accordance with the land fund for the material guarantee of the serving people under the system of natural economy, had great significance and explains the attention Ivan IV gave to the question of landownership. In fact he completed the formation of the pomestie landownership system.

The success of putting through the reforms of feudal landownership was naturally contingent upon the amount of the land which the Tsar could command and, hence, grant as pomestia to the serving people. At the Stoglav Council of 1551 Ivan IV spoke of the necessity of surveying all the lands in the state, regardless of who might own them. He wished to know exactly who owned what, and how much, land, from which land service was fulfilled, and from which it was not:

"I have decided to send out scribes into all of my possessions to take inventory and to survey [estates] belonging to me, the Tsar and grand prince, and to metropolitans, bishops, monasteries, churches, princes, boyars, votchiny, pomestia; blackland, obrok, cleared fields, wastelands, villages, and all other lands regardless of who owns them. They will survey and record plowed and nonplowed land, meadows and forests and all kinds of property—rivers, lakes, ponds, obrok hunting areas; also pales, hives, weights, tolls, bridges, carriages, shops, and markets; merchant lands, churches, mansions, and gardens. And should I grant something to someone, then the grant charters should record such deeds, word for word, to prevent future court litigations over land or water. Whatever one gets, of this he should be master. And should anyone be burdened somewhat he must refer this matter to me, the Tsar and Grand Prince. And should anyone petition me, I will know what to grant to whom, who needs it, who performs a service for what;

---

[7] See *Tysiachnaia kniga 1550 goda i Dvorovaia tetrad 50-kh godov XVI veka* [Book One Thousand of the Year 1550 and a Court Copy-Book of the '50s of the XVI Century] (Moscow-Leningrad: AS USSR, 1950). For a decree on the removal, see L. Maksimovich, ed., *Ukazatel Rossiiskikh zakonov* [A Guide to Russian Laws] (Moscow: 1803), Pt. I, p. 106.

and I shall know about both productive and unproductive pursuits." [8] Ivan IV's proposal was the first of its kind to result in a detailed description of the land resources of the entire country. For the accounting of the votchiny, the Tsar proposed the establishment of special votchina records to register accurately the buying and selling of land, exchanges, and transfers to monasteries.[9] Pomestia were also to be registered.

Thus a broad surveying and accounting program for all lands in the country was planned with the aim of setting land tenure in order, carrying it out in accordance with the goals of the centralized feudal state. The redistribution of lands among the feudal rulers and the transfer of surplus lands to other serving people were also foreseen.

This program was put into effect in the 1550's. In 1551 surveying and description of the lands were undertaken. The rules of measurement were defined in a special decree which served as a guide for the scribes.[10] The surveying of the land was dictated also by the financial needs of the state. A uniform and larger unit of taxation was introduced, the so-called "large Moscow sokha."

In 1555 (or 1556) the Code concerning service from votchiny and pomestia was published. The votchinniki were obligated to bear military or other state service in the same manner as the pomeshchiki. The size of the land grant was determined in various ways, according to the genealogy of the serving person and his rank in service. For the nobles of the lower ranks the grant was set at an amount of 300 chetverts (150 desiatiny) in three fields; the maximum grant was 6000 chetverts (for some boyars). In addition to land grants, a money allowance was fixed. The size of the land grant determined the amount of military obligation. From each one hundred chetverts of land in one field one person had to appear on horseback and in armor and was obligated to provide two horses for any distant expedition.

A redistribution of lands was introduced among the pomeshchiki. The L'vov chronicles report: "Regarding this, the sovereign decreed the following: for those magnates and all military men and others who hold many lands but who have become impoverished because of service, not having been paid by the sovereign, though performing service from their votchiny, the sovereign adjusted their pomestia on the basis of their service in such a fashion that surpluses were given to those who had little, and service from pomestia and votchiny was henceforth to be as follows: from a hundred chetverts of good land, the service of one

[8] See Zhdanov, *op. cit.*, I, 186.
[9] *Ibid.*, I, 182–3.
[10] *Ibid.*, I, 186–7.

man with a horse and full equipment, and for long expeditions one man and two horses." [11]

After the death of a person serving the Tsar, the pomestie was transferred to his son together with the obligation of service. Thus by granting such persons pomestia and by drawing the votchinniki into service Ivan IV strove to insure that the lands "did not leave service" or fall into hands incapable of performing either military or other state service.

An important feature of Ivan IV's land program was his policy towards votchina landownership. He instituted measures limiting the ownership rights of the votchinniki. This restriction was effected by narrowing, on the one hand, the circle of persons having the right to acquire votchiny, and, on the other, the right of the votchinnik to dispose of his votchina. Some limitations on the right of disposal of the family votchiny had been established by Ivan III and Vasilii III. Ivan IV went much farther, however, and historians disagree as to the social aim of that part of Ivan IV's Sudebnik which deals with the votchina.

In the Sudebnik of 1550 a special article on the votchiny defined the conditions of sale and purchase, exchange, mortgaging and redemption of family votchiny. (Art. 85). The old Sudebnik (1497) had no similar article. But Ivan III and Vasilii III had issued decrees on votchina redemption. These decrees, and the appearance in the Sudebnik of 1550 of articles normalizing the sale and purchase, exchange, mortgaging, and redemption of family votchiny show that these economic operations were already quite widespread. It also testifies to the aspirations of the Moscow sovereigns and particularly to Ivan IV's ambition to influence the direction these operations would take.

The lengthy Sudebnik article on the votchiny deals in the main with the guarantee of the interests of various participants in economic transactions with the votchiny. To give a more concrete definition of its sense, or an indication of its political direction in the light of the opposing interests of the various parts of the feudal class—the princes and boyars, the nobles and higher clergy—is extremely difficult to view of the excessively general character of the positions formulated in this article.

An attempt to define more exactly the political significance of Article 85 of the Sudebnik of Ivan IV was made by I. I. Smirnov.[12] The

---

[11] *Polnoe sobranie russkikh letopisei,* XX, 571.

[12] See I. I. Smirnov, "Sudebnik 1550 goda" [The Code of 1550], *Istoricheskie zapiski* [Historical Notes], No. 24 (1947), pp. 318–22.

right of family redemption, writes I. I. Smirnov, was one of the most important privileges of the landowning votchinniki and was one of the foundations of their power, as it gave them the ability to resist the threat of transfer of the votchina estates through purchase-sale into other hands. According to I. I. Smirnov, Article 85 of the Sudebnik substantially limited the right of family redemption. Striking at the interests of the votchinniki, weakening the hereditary ties of the boyar and princely families, it facilitated the mobilization of votchina lands and stimulated their transfer into new hands. I. I. Smirnov defined the article of the Sudebnik of 1550 on votchiny as a measure directed against the princes and boyars, the expression of the anti-boyar land policy of Ivan IV.[13]

Such an interpretation of the political meaning of this article of the Sudebnik on the votchiny was criticized by B. A. Romanov.[14] In the view of the latter the section in the Sudebnik on votchiny cannot be looked upon as a weapon for the defense of the interests of the pomeshchiki against the princes and boyars. By including Article 85 in the Sudebnik Tsar Ivan protected the interests of the secular votchinniki in general, and not the interests of the pomeshchiki against the boyars and princes, as I. I. Smirnov, somewhat anticipating the course of events, maintains.[15]

The position of B. A. Romanov appears convincing. At the same time, viewing the right of family redemption historically, it would be incorrect, it seems to us, to ignore the gradual change in the significance of this right. In the sixteenth century, with the developing market and money economy, the right of family redemption was an inconvenience in disposing of the votchina and not a privilege of the owner, inasmuch as this right actually required personal agreement of the kinsmen to the sale of the votchina. Its holder could sell the votchina only when the buyer was convinced that the family of the seller would not buy it back and that it would remain permanently in his hands.

Article 85 of the Sudebnik not only established the right of family redemption, that is, in effect restricted the right of the votchinnik to dispose of his votchina, but also strictly defined who could utilize the right of family redemption; in other words, this limitation on the right of the votchinnik to dispose of his votchina was specifically defined: the long-existing law of family redemption was recognized now

[13] *Ibid.*, p. 322.

[14] See B. A. Romanov, "K voprosu o zemelnoi politike Izbrannoi rady" [On the Question of Land Policy of the Chosen Council], *ibid.*, No. 38 (1951). See also commentaries to Article 85 of the Code of 1550 in *Sudebniki XV–XVI vekov, pp.* 297–319.

[15] See Romanov, *op. cit.*, p. 269.

only for a definite narrow circle of relatives and, of these, only ones who had not been witnesses in the sale of the votchina.

Article 85 says nothing of the social position of the buyer of the votchina, that is, of his position in the feudal centralized state. Moreover, the basic direction of the land policy of the Moscow sovereigns did not move toward general limitation or increase of the right of family redemption of the votchiny, but toward ever-increasing *outright prohibition of the sale of votchiny* and approximating them to conditional land owning—the pomestia. It is in this field of Ivan IV's legislation that the antinoble and antiboyar character of his policy concerning votchina landownership is displayed.

As was pointed out above, the treaties of Russian princes of the period of feudal disunity prohibited purchase of votchiny in other contracting principalities. This meant that the big feudalist could not sell his land to a person living in another principality. Such restrictive ownership rights of the feudalist were dictated, as has been said, by the aspiration of the princes to protect their sovereignty and independence from other princes.

The limitation on the right of the votchinnik took on another character and significance during the formation and strengthening of the Russian centralized state under Ivan III, Vasilii III, and Ivan the Terrible. Now all forms of limitations on ownership rights of the votchinnik were aimed at the strengthening and consolidation of the power of the head of the centralized state and the reduction of the power of the feudalist votchinnik. Not the preservation of the existing positions, not the mutual guarantees of rights of the various agreeing parties, as during the period of feudal disunity, but the increase of the political might of the Moscow Prince-Tsar by weakening the power and importance of the large feudalist-votchinnik—such was the essence of the policy of the Moscow sovereigns. Their basic idea in relation to the votchina was that the votchina land should serve the Moscow sovereign, and not be a basis of separatist aspirations of the large feudalists—the princes and boyars.

The limitations of the votchina right by the Moscow sovereigns affected in the first place those big feudalists from whom this separatism might most be expected: the descendants of the former appanage princes, now serving the Moscow sovereign, and the serving people in areas newly annexed to Moscow. Under Ivan III both had already been forbidden to transfer their votchiny into non-serving hands.[16] This prohibition was repeated by Vasilii III. The latter forbade all the

[16] See Pavlov, *Istoricheskii ocherk sekuliarizatsii tserkovnykh zemel v Rossii*, p. 122.

owners of votchiny in several districts—Tver, Mikulin, Torzhok, Obolensk, Beloozero, and Riazan—to sell votchiny to people of other districts or to give their votchiny *"na pomin dushi"* [for having a prayer said for the souls of the dead] to monasteries without reporting it to the Grand Prince. Suzdal, Yaroslav, and Starodub princes in particular were forbidden to sell their votchiny to anyone whomsoever, except their relatives, or to give them to monasteries without permission of the Grand Prince.

By the Sobor decree of May 11, 1551, the votchinniki of the districts listed above were again denied the privilege to sell their votchiny to persons of other districts, and the princes of Suzdal, Yaroslav, and Starodub were also forbidden any sort of sales of their votchiny without the Tsar's knowledge. It was decreed that the votchiny sold in violation of this decree would be taken from the votchinnik and the money of the purchaser forfeited. All of the votchinniki in general (and not only in the stated districts) were forbidden to grant their votchiny to monasteries *"na pomin dushi"* without the Tsar's permission under the threat of confiscation of the transferred votchiny.[17]

The Tsar's decree of January 15, 1562, prohibited the sale, exchange, or the granting as dowry of the family votchiny of the princes. Princes could sell a votchina only to close relatives—brothers or nephews. The votchina of a dead prince, as of a boyar or boyar's son, who died without children or near relatives was to revert to the Tsar. A prince without a son could leave his votchina to his brother, a nephew, or any of his other near relatives, but only in that circle of the family within which intermarriage was forbidden. This disposition, however, could be executed only by decree of the sovereign. The votchinnik had the right to bequeath the votchina, or part of it, to his wife, but only for lifetime ownership.[18]

The decree of 1562 which significantly limited the right of the princes to dispose of their votchiny, is particularly noteworthy in that it was issued in a year close to the time of the formation of the oprichnina by Ivan IV.

The limitations of the right of disposal of votchiny were confirmed and strenghtened by the law of October 9, 1572. Its provisions concerned not only the votchiny of the princes, but also those of the boyars. It differentiated between the old family votchiny, and the votchiny granted by the sovereign, while the conditions established by the law of 1562 referred only to family votchiny. The law of 1572 stated that a votchina received by the Tsar's charter went, on the death of its

[17] See *Stoglav*, pp. 430–4.

[18] See Vladimirskii-Budanov, *op. cit.*, pp. 28–32.

owner, to his wife, children, and family only if this was provided for in the granting charter; otherwise it reverted to the sovereign, even though the owner of the votchina left children. The law of 1572 also restricted the right of inheritance of the family votchina to those relatives no farther removed than the third generation ("and do not give votchiny to those farther removed than grandchildren"). It was forbidden to give the votchiny *"na pomin dushi"* to great monasteries which possessed many votchiny.[19] All these limitations on the rights of the owner regarding the disposal of his votchina meant at the same time the strengthening of the Tsar's right with regard to the votchiny and led to the ever closer tie between votchina and pomestie as the two forms of feudal landownership.

The aim of Ivan IV's legislation was to force the votchinniki to perform service for the state. It implanted the pomestie system of landownership and limited the expansion of votchina. The establishment of the pomestie system of landownership and the effacement of the distinctions between the votchina and the pomestie were dictated by the tasks of consolidating the unity of the state and the autocratic power of the Tsar. Votchina landowning, which served during the period of feudal disunity as the economic basis of the political strength of the appanage princes and boyars, was now extremely circumscribed, not only in quantitative ratio to the pomestie, but also in the scope of the rights of the votchinnik.

Votchina landowning became increasingly conditional, and was connected with the service of the votchinnik. This dependence was expressed also in the evolution of the petitioning charters. The granting of petitioning charters by the Moscow princes was in itself linked, as noted above, with the limitation not only of the circle of feudalists enjoying the right of immunity, but also with the extent of privileges allowed the feudalists receiving these charters. The immunity of the votchinniki to regulation by the prince-sovereign was incompatible with the full political unity of the feudal state and with the autocracy of the sovereign. The consolidation of the political unity of the country and the centralization of the political power in the form of an autocratic monarchy demanded the elimination of the immunities of the feudalist votchinnik. Struggling to eliminate the remnants of feudal disunity and to consolidate his autocratic power, Ivan IV followed a policy of liquidation of those immunities. His purpose was clearly expressed in the Sudebnik of 1550. Article 43 stated: "Privileges henceforth will be given to no one; and the old privilege charters will

---

[19] *Ibid.*, pp. 32–4.

be taken from everyone." [20] In accordance with this article, "exemption," "regulation," and future "yearly" charters would henceforth be given only by order of the Tsar.

P. P. Smirnov held that the aim of the privilege charters was the exemption from payment of the transit and trade duties and taxes and services; whereas the holders of exemption, regulation, and yearly charters received only immunity and paid a determined amount in installments.[21]

Even under Tsar Fedor Ivanovich, the Sobor of 1584 abolished the privileges for the church institutions.

Liquidation of the privileges dealt a strong blow to large feudal, privileged, landowning.[22]

The culmination of domestic (including land) policies of Ivan IV was the formation of the oprichnina (1565–1572). The oprichnina marked a special new stage in Ivan IV's votchiny policy. The political and economic significance of the institution of the oprichnina is revealed in Soviet historical literature.[23] The historically progressive importance of the oprichnina centered in the crushing of the princely-boyar aristocracy, the destruction of the boyars' power, the liquidation of the remnants of feudal disunity, and the consolidation of a centralized Russian state. Ivan IV's suppression of the princely-boyar magnates was accompanied by the growth and strengthening of the nobility. The oprichnina is, therefore, of great interest in the study of the history of Russian economic thought, inasmuch as the oprichnina was an integral part of the economic policy of Ivan IV.

The hereditary votchina formed the economic basis of the political power of the princes and boyars and of their aspirations to remain independent of the tsarist power and to participate in the administration of the country. In attempting to destroy the political power of the feudal aristocracy and to consolidate his autocracy, Ivan IV used the oprichnina to deal an economic blow to the princes and boyars—a blow to their great hereditary votchina. During the period of the oprichnina mass confiscation of the princely-boyar votchiny took place.

---

[20] *Sudebniki XV–XVI vekov,* p. 153.

[21] See P. P. Smirnov, *Posadskie liudi i ikh klassovaia borba do serediny XVII veka* [Settlers and Their Class Struggle Before the Middle of the XVII Century] (Moscow-Leningrad: AS USSR, 1947), p. 113.

[22] On immunity see also I. I. Smirnov, *op. cit.;* and B. A. Romanov, "Sudebnik Ivana Groznogo" [The Code of Ivan the Terrible] *Istoricheskie zapiski* [Historical Notes], No. 29 (1949).

[23] See Vipper, *Ivan Groznyi;* S. F. Platonov, *Ivan Groznyi* (Petrograd: 1923); S. Bakhrushin, "Ivan Groznyi," *Bolshevik,* No. 13 (1943); P. A. Sadikov, *Ocherki po istorii oprichniny* [Outlines of the History of the Oprichnina] (Moscow-Leningrad: AS USSR, 1950).

Enormous territories, about half of the entire state, including the central and important districts embracing many of the old princely and boyar votchiny, was taken over by the oprichnina.[24]

The princes and boyars, jealously defending their power from the pretensions of the Tsar's authority, were ousted from their family homes, the votchiny. Some were physically annihilated, others transferred to new areas of the country where they could not present a real threat to the state. The princely-boyar lands were confiscated and distributed as pomestia to petty service officials devoted to the Tsar. As a result of the oprichnina a great shift in feudal landholding ensued. The oprichnina destroyed the economic base of the power of the princes and boyars.

The change in the superstructure—the formation of a centralized Russian state in place of the many disunited "half-states" which existed earlier—was determined by the transformations which were achieved in the base of the society—the feudal productive relationships. In its turn the superstructure, the centralized feudal state, was utilized for the further strengthening of the base of society, the feudal economic system, imposition of pomestie landownership, and expansion of the serf exploitation of the peasantry.

By undermining decisively the very basis of the political power of the princes and boyars, Ivan IV emerged as a major political figure who saw clearly the problems of his times and unswervingly struggled for their solution. However the extinction of the big feudal princely-boyar votchina did not lead to the annihilation of feudal landownership in general, but to the growth of another form of it, viz., the landownership of the serving nobility and further enslavement of the peasantry.

Ivan IV's policy concerning landownership by the clerical feudalists —the metropolitans, bishops and monasteries—was much less decisive and significant. With respect to this aspect of feudal landownership, his policy, like that of his grandfather and father, was ambiguous. The church was an important ally of autocratic power in the struggle to achieve a centralized state. Ivan IV, therefore, did not wish to confiscate the great land reserves of the church and monasteries for state purposes. Nevertheless, he increased state control over the monastery economy and endeavored to put an end to the further growth of monastery landholding.

The Grand Prince Vasilii III had already actively interfered in the

---

[24] *Ibid.*, pp. 21 ff.

internal affairs of the monasteries. In effect he had transformed the administration of monastery economy. He appointed abbots to the monasteries, gave them orders on "how to protect the treasury and satisfy the brotherhood," demanded from them stern accountability in the expenditure of money, and to that end introduced a system of inventory of monastery property compiled by the scribes of the Grand Prince. "Under Vasilii Ivanovich the monasteries for the first time were subjected to a *correct* state control, which, in the final analysis, led to their complete economic dependence on the government."[25] This control by the state, however, almost ceased in the years before Ivan IV became of age.

In the Stoglav Sobor in 1551 Ivan IV made a clearly accusatory speech, in the form of "questions" addressed to the monastery superiors, indicting them in the spirit of the "non-covetous" of illegal expenditure of monastery funds, of crude violation of the monastic code of living, and of aspirations to exist at the expense of the state.

In the monasteries, said Ivan IV, some monks and priests take their vows in order to enjoy physical comforts and carousals, and wander about the monastery villages for their pleasure. Some archimandrites and abbots "purchase" their positions, are ignorant of the church rituals, of the brotherhood, of the general altar [ceremony], and take their ease in their cells with guests. They establish their relatives in the monasteries and villages at the monastery's expense, and drive out old servants and donors, thus desolating the monasteries. The monasteries receive votchiny *"na pomin dushi"* [in return for prayers for the souls of the dead]. They themselves buy votchiny and villages, seek lands from the Tsar, and have privileged exemption and immunity charters. Meanwhile, he accused, the food and drink of the monks become inferior, no new buildings are erected, and the old ones are deserted. "Where are the profits and who pocketed them?"[26]

The Sobor adopted a decree for the monasteries in which control over their treasuries and the audit of their expenditures were entrusted to the Tsar's officials, stewards, and clerks.

Ivan IV spoke before the Sobor against moneylending by the church and monasteries. The church and monastery treasuries, he said, are augmented by interest payments, although the Lord's writing forbade moneylending even to laymen, and more particularly to churches.[27] In response to this speech the Sobor suggested that the bishops and monasteries lend their peasants bread and money without interest "so

---

[25] Pavlov, *op. cit.*, pp. 100–1.
[26] See *Stoglav*, pp. 54–6, 60.
[27] *Ibid.*, p. 61.

that peasants can live there and their villages will not be deserted"[28]—in other words, so that the peasants need not flee from the monastery lands.

The basic problem before the Sobor, however, was the question of monastery landownership. Heeding the urgent need of the state for a free land reserve from which to grant pomestia to the serving people, Ivan IV endeavored to curtail the growth of monastery landownership in the country. At the same time he did not infringe seriously upon the existing church and monastery land holdings nor make serious onslaughts on the wealth of the church and monasteries. By the Sobor agreement of May, 1551 the archbishops and monasteries were forbidden either to buy votchiny, or to accept them as bequests without permission of the Tsar. The votchiny which in the future were bought or received through wills by bishops and monasteries in violation of this order would go to the sovereign without compensation, that is, they would be confiscated.

Votchiny bequeathed to monasteries prior to the Sobor agreement of 1551, in violation of the previous decree of Ivan III, were subject to confiscation by the sovereign, but with payment to the monasteries equal to their value; while votchiny bequeathed to the monasteries before 1551, but not referred to in the decree of Vasilii III, were retained by the monasteries.

The Sobor decreed the return to their former owners by inquiry of those pomestia and "black lands" which had been confiscated by the archbishops and monasteries from petty boyars and peasants who had fallen into debt, or those which had been acquired by monasteries through improper registration by the scribes. It was also decreed that the villages, volosti, fishing and obrok villages given to the archbishops and monasteries by boyars during the minority of Ivan IV should be confiscated and returned to whomever they had belonged under Vasilii III.[29]

The fact that more than one tsarist decree concerning monastery landownership was later required shows that the Sobor decision of 1551 forbidding the increase of monastery lands by purchase and bequest was not being carried out. This restriction was repeated in 1562 and 1572 and was finally made effective in 1580.

On October 9, 1572, a Sobor of the clergy and boyars decreed: "And big monasteries, which have many votchiny, shall henceforth acquire no votchiny; and should some votchiny be available, they will not be registered in the pomestie office, but will be given to a family of serving

28 *Ibid.*, p. 345.

29 *Ibid.*, pp. 430–4.

people, so *that there will be no loss in service, and the land will not be outside the service.*" [30]

The prohibition on giving votchiny to monasteries involved only the great monasteries. The smaller ones, which had little land, were allowed to receive votchiny even later, but only upon report to the sovereign and by boyar consent.

But even this law was badly administered. The monasteries continued to acquire lands by purchase, by bequest, and by mortgage. Disgraced boyars who became monks by custom had to bring with them part of their votchiny. Votchinniki, fearing disgrace and the possibility of being forever deprived of their holdings, entered into secret arrangements with the monasteries in order to preserve something for themselves and their families. Under the disguise of prayer for souls, votchiny were acquired in payment for debts; they were also obtained as a prerequisite deposit in becoming a monk—in reality this constituted purchase of land.[31] Even the Tsar himself often gave the monasteries votchina lands.

Even after becoming monks the boyars tried to occupy a special, privileged position. In 1572 Ivan IV wrote one of his most outstanding literary contributions—"Letter to the Kirillo-Belozerskii monastery." [32] Angrily he attacked the flagrant violations of the code of monastic life and accused primarily the eminent boyar-monks. Monasteries should practice equality and brotherhood; there was no place here for differentiation between freeman and slave, boyar and kholop. In reality, even in the monasteries the boyars enjoyed all sorts of favors. "And here is yet another example: he who is famous is high and mighty—there is no brotherhood here. When people are equal, then there is brotherhood, but when they are not, what kind of brotherhood can there be? Surely this is not the life for a monk! The boyars with their vices have disrupted order in all the monasteries." [33] He condemned the monasteries for wooing boyars and justifying this "by the shameful words" that if the monasteries did not admit boyars, they (the monasteries) would receive no gifts and grow poor. The boyar-monks, wrote Ivan IV, should observe the code of monastic life like others and not represent themselves as influential protectors of the monasteries.

Ivan IV's letter to the Kirillo-Belozerskii monastery "to a significant degree was directed against the transformation of the monasteries into

[30] Vladimirskii-Budanov, *op. cit.*, p. 34. (Italics mine—A.P.)
[31] Pavlov, *op. cit.*, pp. 149–50.
[32] See *Poslaniia Ivana Groznogo*, pp. 351–69.
[33] *Ibid.*, p. 365.

boyar vassals or into disguised boyar votchiny," justly writes Ia. S. Lur'e in commentaries on the "Letters."[34]

At the Sobor of 1580 Ivan IV again demanded cessation of the increase of monastery lands and justified this action by pointing to the poor condition of the country, which was exhausted by wars. At a time, said the Tsar, when all social layers except the clergy bore sacrifices, the clergy used their influence and wealth to increase their holdings. A Sobor decree of January 15, 1580, proclaimed the inviolability of the churches' and monasteries' properties received by bequests which had already been made; but at the same time it categorically forbade the archbishops and monasteries to augment their land holdings by any means—by purchase, mortgage, or bequest. All such acquisitions by the churches and monasteries henceforth were to be confiscated by the sovereign without payment. But poor monasteries, even in the future, retained the right to petition the Tsar to grant them land. The votchinniki were given the right to bequeath money to the monasteries in amounts corresponding to the value of their votchiny, to be paid by the heirs of the donor. All votchiny purchased or taken in mortgage by the archbishops and monasteries from serving people prior to January 15, 1580, were subject to confiscation by the sovereign.[35]

Summing up this problem, one may say that the policy of Ivan IV on the question of monastery landownership had little real effect. Even in the past century A. Pavlov, who studied the relationships between social thought and the policies of the state in the sixteenth century concerning landownership by the Russian church, stressed the necessity "in general not to exaggerate the *actual* significance of the legislative measures of Ivan IV on the question of monastery and church votchiny. Not only did he not save Russia from the trend toward the acquisition of monastery property, as some have maintained, but he assisted the extraordinary enrichment of the monasteries with lands almost as much as all of his predecessors combined."[36]

The formation and consolidation of the centralized state were of great significance for the destiny of the Russian people: such a unification guaranteed the preservation of the country's independence, the growth of its productive forces, and the flowering of Russian culture.

---

[34] *Ibid.*, p. 480.

[35] See *Sobranie gosudarstvennykh gramot i dogovorov* [Collection of State Charters and Agreements] (Moscow: 1813), Pt. I, No. 200, pp. 583–5; Pavlov, *op. cit.*, pp. 144–5.

[36] *Ibid.*, p. 151. One has in mind forceful transfer by the votchinniki of their lands to monasteries as well as Ivan IV's distribution of votchini to monasteries.

Simultaneously, it was connected with the political and economic elevation of a new layer of the feudalist class, the nobility, and with the enserfment of the broad mass of the toilers, the peasantry. The strengthening of the serving nobility's position and the crushing of the princely-boyar aristocracy were accompanied by a sharp deterioration in the economic and political status of the peasantry. The centralized state greatly exalted the feudalist class in relation to the peasantry and served as a means of holding in check the actual producers. More than ever the peasantry had to bear the burden for the benefit of the feudalists and of the feudal state. Writing of the most important events of 1547, of the great fire in Moscow and the subsequent antiboyar uprising, the chronicler informs us that "in the same winter the Tsar and Grand Prince ordered tribute to be taken at twelve rubles per sokha, *which caused great hardship for the peasants.*" [37]

Appearing before boyars, courtiers, court nobility, and exchequers in 1549 at the so-called "Sobor of settlement," Ivan IV rebuked them for the fact that "prior to his coming of Tsarist age they and their people greatly maltreated the petty boyars and the peasants, sold their lands, abused kholopy, and so on." [38] The Tsar warned the boyars not to commit offenses against the petty boyars and the peasants and threatened the offenders with disgrace and imprisonment. In other words, he pledged his protection against the force and arbitrariness of these groups, not only toward the "petty boyars," that is, the lower layer of the feudalists, but also toward the "peasants." This part of the declaration, however, remained mere verbiage, since in actuality only the petty boyars and the nobility became the objects of Ivan IV's attention and care.

Ivan IV's policy on the peasant question followed the line of increasing subordination of the peasant to the pomeshchiki, and was determined and directed mainly by the interests of the nobility. The most important measures of his policy relating to the peasantry were: 1) the Sudebnik of 1550; 2) the distribution of the "black" lands to the pomeshchiki; 3) the oprichnina, and 4) the abolition of St. George's Day.

The Sudebnik of 1550 (Art. 88) reiterated in its entirety the stand of the Sudebnik of 1497 concerning peasants' departure. At the same time it introduced some corrections and supplements in the corresponding article of the former Sudebnik: it increased the amount and defined more accurately the manner of taking "household rent"; it added regu-

---

[37] *Polnoe sobranie russkikh letopisei,* XXII, Pt. I, p. 527 (Italics mine—A. P.)

[38] *Ibid.,* XXII, Pt. I, pp. 528–9 (Italics mine—A. P.)

lations concerning "land grain," that is, the winter field sowed by a departing peasant. The peasant retained the right to harvest from the field which he had sowed, but with the obligation to pay rent on this land. In addition he was obligated to pay the landowner for "transport," that is, to compensate the latter for transport charges incurred by the peasant during the winter.[39] Thus the Sudebnik of 1550 not only confirmed the existing limitations regarding the peasant's right to leave during one period of the year, but increase the economic difficulties of his doing so, inasmuch as he had to pay more than formerly.

Ivan IV established noble pomestia in Russia, not only at the expense of the crown lands and boyar votchiny, but also at the expense of the black peasantry. He also gave pomestia to the serving people from the lands of the free peasant communes. The black peasant volosti were preserved only in the northern districts. In 1582 it was required in other districts that the black lands be added to those of the crown, handed out as pomestia, or distributed to the riflemen, cannoneers, and other serving people of the lower ranks.[40]

The introduction of the oprichnina had a strong impact on the position of the peasantry. The oprichniki ruined not only the votchiny of the princes and boyars, but also the households of their peasants. With the breakdown of the large votchiny into small pomestia, the peasant "communes" working on these lands were also broken up and parcelled out. In the search for workers the oprichniki-landowners often forcibly carried off their neighbors and peasants. By seizing peasant lands and expanding the pomestie plowland at the expense of the peasant lands within the pomestia and by increasing the pomestie collections the pomeshchniki-oprichniki sharply multiplied the pressures on the peasantry. Not infrequently the peasant was simply robbed without any concern for his future.[41] According to the testimony of contemporaries, he had to pay the oprichnik-pomeshchik as much in one year as he was supposed to pay in the course of ten. The oprichnina thus further increased the feudal exploitation of the peasantry and constituted a new stage in the development of serfdom.[42] Within a short period the development of feudal landownership broke up the princely-boyar, as well as the mass-propagated pomestie estates and brought about a deterioration in the position of the peasantry.

---

[39] See *Sudebniki XV–XVI vekov,* pp. 172–3; I. I. Smirnov, *op. cit.,* pp. 330–3.

[40] See D. Samokvasov, *Istoriia russkogo prava* [History of Russian Law] (Moscow: 1906), pp. 517–8.

[41] See Sadikov, *op. cit.,* pp. 44 ff.

[42] See I. I. Smirnov, *Vosstanie Bolotnikova, 1606–7* [Bolotnikov's Uprising, 1606–7] (Moscow: Gospolitizdat, 1951), pp. 44 ff.

It was also on the shoulders of the peasantry that all the weight of the long Livonian war fell.

In the 1570's and 1580's a deep economic crisis engulfed the entire country. It manifested itself in an enormous decline in the economy of the central, northwestern and western districts of the Russian state. The peasant economy was ruined by pomeshchiki and by Tsarist taxes. The peasants departed for the eastern and southern regions of the country, the plowland was sharply curtailed, and the villages and hamlets were deserted. Trade declined and the condition of the treasury deteriorated. Under these circumstances the sharpest struggle unfolded among the feudalists for workers and for free peasant labor. The economic advantage was on the side of the rich, strong, and eminent feudalists and the secular and monastery estates, against which the small pomestie could not successfully compete. The peasants preferred to live under the affluent landowners and under the monasteries, thus enjoying the various privileges such tenure involved. The eminent feudalists often forcibly carried off peasants from the pomeshchiki.

A number of additional measures were intended to strengthen the economic position of the nobility. An important one was the abolishment of St. George's Day. In 1580 a law of "forbidden years," that is, years during which peasant departures were banned, was promulgated. The first "forbidden year" was 1581. The abolition of the right of peasant departure was proclaimed a temporary measure. It is possible that this was done, as some historians maintain, as a tactical measure to prevent a peasant explosion against the law.

The law of 1580 was an act of great historic significance: it meant the official confirmation of serfdom in Russia. Serfdom, which actually had existed for a long time and which was prepared for by the entire process of the economic and political development of the country, now received full legal sanction. With regard to the peasants, the feudal state introduced the strongest form of extra-economic compulsion. The superstructure—the state power—was utilized by the ruling class, the nobility, to strengthen the base of society—the feudal-productive relationships. In the law of 1580, the class-oriented nature of the policy of Ivan IV—a policy of elevation of the nobility—found its clearest expression. It bound the peasants closer to the land and thus opened the way to the increased exploitation of peasant labor.

Also beginning in 1581, and continuing until 1592, a new general census of the country's lands was undertaken. In the census records the peasants were registered on those lands on which they happened to be during the "forbidden years." Registration in these records served as testimony of the right of the landowner over the peasants living on his land. And in 1597 a law dealing with the search for fugitive peasants was issued. Under this law peasants fleeing from landowners in the period after 1592 were returned to their former owners. Thus serfdom was finally formalized in Russia. The enserfment of the peasantry and the growth of its exploitation at the end of the sixteenth century paved the way for the great antifeudal war which erupted at the beginning of the seventeenth century under the leadership of Ivan Bolotnikov.[43]

One of the questions which greatly attracted the attention of social thought in this period was that of the kholopy. Increasingly voices were raised concerning the need for complete abolition of this form of forced labor. The economic basis of this trend of social thought is stated above. What, then, was the attitude of the state towards this question? Ivan IV pursued a policy of gradual limitation of the sources of slavery. Even small landowners often became kholopy of the big feudalists. The Sudebnik of 1550 (Art. 81) forbade taking petty boyars and their children into service as kholopy.[44] This measure prevented the nobility from evading service by becoming kholopy. At the same time it protected small serving persons from loss of personal freedom and thus directly countered the class interests of the nobility.

As was stated above, the Sudebnik of 1497 had effectively narrowed the sources of complete slavery. Service as a tiun or steward no longer led to slavery except in the villages. By virtue of the Sudebnik of 1550 service by tiun and steward even in the village thwarted another source of kholopstvo—with the exception of slavery by agreement. Moreover, it was established that the kholop could not sell sons born before he became a slave; nor could parents who entered monasteries or convents sell their children. (Art. 76.)[45]

A number of articles of the Sudebnik of 1550 reflected the growth of the use of hired labor in the national economy of Russia. In these articles the tendency of the state to fix legally the difference between hired labor (free persons) and all forms of dependent labor and to prevent the transformation of free persons working for personal hire into kholopy, is evident. In this regard, Article 78 of the Tsar's Sudebnik, devoted to the question of enslaved persons (serving kabala), is of great interest.

Unlike full kholopy, who were slaves, the kabala persons were formally free men accepting the obligation to work for (serve) the master for a definite and agreed upon period of time in place of a payment

---

[43] See Grekov, *Krestiane na Rusi,* pp. 231–3; Smirnov, *Vostanie Bolotnikova,* Chapter I.

[44] See *Sudebniki XV–XVI vekov,* p. 170.

[45] *Ibid.,* p. 168.

of interest on a loan.[46] With the growth of a commodity production, markets, and the increased role of money, the serving kabala became widespread in the sixteenth century and increasingly crowded out the older forms of slavery.

In the Sudebnik of 1497 nothing is said of kabala persons, evidently because of the insignificant proportion at that time of this form of dependent labor. The Sudebnik of 1550, on the other hand, did contain definite state regulation of kabala dependence: the conclusion of kabala agreements was controlled by the state. First, a maximum sum of fifteen rubles was set on which kabala could be taken; second, it was made obligatory that a boyar or a clerk officially record the serving kabala; third, only free persons could accept kabala–fugitive kholopy and former kholopy could not do so. (Art. 78.) [47]

The Sudebnik of 1550 did not call kabala persons kholopy. Actually a kabala person worked for shares for a master and lived with him. The former usually received food and clothing, and with no possibility of liquidating his debt he continued to work for the master all of his life. Although his dependence was in form temporary and conditional, in practice the position of the kabala persons approached that of the kholop. The fixing of a maximum sum of money as the indebtedness in a kabala agreement was evidently intended to preserve kabala service as a special form of labor and to prevent the merging of this form of forced labor, made necessary by the country's economic development, with kholopstvo.[48]

The tendency of the legislation of Ivan IV legally to sanction the existence of voluntarily hired labor in various branches of the economy and to prevent the transformation of this labor into the forced labor of the kholop is also evident in other official documents. The Ukaz of 1555 forbade the transformation of hired servants into kholopy. The voluntary servant could leave his master when he wished. In practice there were evidently many cases in which the master, not wanting to release a servant working for him voluntarily, would try to accuse the departing servant of theft. Taking this practice into consideration, the Ukaz of 1555 ordered the courts thenceforth not to accept any attempts to introduce such cases "because the servants served the master voluntarily." [49]

Other measures were also adopted against the compulsory transfor-

---

[46] Grekov, *op. cit.*, pp. 114 ff.

[47] *Sudebniki XV–XVI vekov,* p. 169.

[48] Grekov, *op. cit.*, pp. 113–32 and 310–4; I. I. Smirnov, "Sudebnik 1550 goda," *Istoricheskie zapiski,* No. 24 (1947), pp. 333–6.

[49] See Vladimirskii-Budanov, *op. cit.*, pp. 4–5.

mation of the free person into a kholop. In 1558 the death penalty was set for a master or official who attempted to ensnare a free person into serfdom.[50] In 1560 slavery for debts was abolished: it was decreed that insolvent debtors could not enter into full kholopstvo to their creditors, even with agreement of the debtors themselves.[51] But kholopstvo as a special form of forced labor continued to exist for a long time in Russia.

At the end of the sixteenth century the legal position of the kabala person grew worse. By the Ukaz of 1597 he lost the right to leave his master even after payment of his debt. Kabala kholopy were obliged to live with their master until the latter's death, after which they and their wives and children became free without payment. This process was closely connected with the general approach of the feudal state to the enserfment of the peasantry.

Increase in the use of hired labor in the sixteenth century necessitated definite state regulation of this form of economic relationship. The Sudebnik of 1497 (Art. 54) established that the naimit (hired laborer) leaving his "master" before the agreed upon period lost his right to receive the naim, or payment. Preserving this norm, the Sudebnik of 1550 (Art. 83) at the same time augmented the responsibility of the hirer: if the latter were convicted of refusing to give the worker naim, then as a consequence a double naim was exacted from him.[52]

Trade Principles and Financial Policies

The *trade policy* of Ivan IV encompassed broad economic and political aims.

Russia carried on the long and burdensome Livonian war in order to establish direct ties with the countries of Western Europe by the easiest and most convenient route—across the Baltic Sea. The dire need for this route was dictated first of all by the economic development of the country. Russia required free import from the West of industrial goods, including arms, and free export of agricultural products to the West.

In the sixteenth century Russia already possessed the embryo of big industry. Besides the activities of private persons, like the salt manufactures of the Stroganovs and those of various monasteries participating in the commercial extraction of salt, potash, and other products, industrial enterprises were also created by state initiative. The treasury supported the production of arms, including cannon, and of other war

[50] *Ibid.*, pp. 24–5.
[51] *Ibid.*, pp. 26–7.
[52] See *Sudebniki XV–XVI vekov*, p. 170.

materiel such as, for example, saltpeter. Measures were adpoted for the organization of the extraction of ores and the smelting of iron. To further these ends, Ivan IV considered the admission of foreign capital desirable. English merchants were permitted to search for ore, to construct mills on the Vychegda, and to export iron to England after the payment of duties. In return, English masters were obligated to teach Russians the metallurgical arts, and English merchants to sell iron to the treasury at a fixed price.

As long as Russia's import and export of goods, as well as her solicitation of specialists, had been under the control of Livonia, Sweden, and Poland, she had been economically dependent on her western neighbors. Consequently she fought stubbornly to break the barrier for an exit to the Baltic Sea. This problem, however, was not solved under Ivan IV.

In 1558 at the very beginning of the Livonian wars, the Russians seized Narva, which remained in Russia's hands until 1581. Ivan IV tried to utilize Narva as a base from which to trade with the western countries and to transform it into the main Russian port on the Baltic so as to counterbalance Reval, whose merchants, members of the German Hanseatic League, were trying to monopolize the trade of the West with Russia. Narva merchants were given the right of duty-free trade in the entire Russian state and of unhindered trade relations with Germany. As a result of this policy, Narva began to grow rich, while the commerce of Reval ceased almost entirely. In the interests of the broad development of Russian foreign trade on the basis of equality of parties and the denial of monopoly positions to merchants of any other country, Ivan IV admitted merchants of various countries to Narva and thus assured competition.

He tried to promote the sea route through the White Sea for trade relations with the West and accorded English merchants great advantages. In 1555 they were given the right of free passage into and out of the Russian state and the right of duty-free trade in border towns. Although England formally granted Russian merchants similar rights, the latter were unable to make use of these, since Russia did not have a merchant fleet. In 1567 a company of English merchants was given a monopoly on trade at the mouth of the Northern Dvina and duty-free trade in Kazan, Astrakhan, Narva and Dorpat and was also permitted free transit of goods to Bukhara and China. Later the English company was allowed duty-free trade in all Russian territories, the right of transit of goods to Persia, and other privileges.

In granting extensive privileges to English merchants, Ivan IV had political aims in mind. He hoped to secure from the English government a military-political alliance against the coalitions of Baltic states hostile to Russia. His trade policy in relation to England was thus subordinated to the general foreign policy objectives of Russia. When he realized that the English government did not favor such an alliance and that it supported only the mercenary commercial interests of its merchants, these privileges were discontinued.

In a letter to Queen Elizabeth (1570) Ivan IV pointed out that he had given England extensive concessions in the hope of friendly and helpful relations between England and Russia, but that Elizabeth thought only of the interests of her merchants. The sovereign, wrote Ivan IV, should be concerned with the needs and welfare of the entire state, and not only with the privileges of a particular group. "We thought that in your state you governed alone and cared for your state's honor and advantages. That is why we inaugurated these talks. But it seems apparent that in your country, besides you, other persons have a voice in government—and not only people, but merchants who do not worry about their sovereign's honor and their country's advantages but seek their own commercial profits. You are just like any other woman." [53]

The letter, written in a difficult period in the life of the country, was pervaded with a consciousness of Russia's greatness. "Let those individuals who have scorned the honor and officials of our state and the advantages of our country worry about trade matters and see how they will trade! The Moscow state is not poor, even without English goods." [54] The Tsar declared null and void all of his commercial charters granted to Englishmen.

Later, trade privileges were restored to the English, but in curtailed form (for real aid, that is, the furnishing of arms, they now had to pay half-rates of duty). England's plans to make Russia a colony were divined by Ivan IV. After Narva was lost to Russia he no longer permitted English merchants to enjoy a monopoly on the White Sea, where merchants of other countries, including the Dutch, now travelled.

Ivan IV's ambition to enter into active trade relations with western countries on a parity basis is shown by his agreements with Sweden and Denmark. After peace with Sweden was concluded, Swedish merchants were granted the right to go to Moscow, to Kazan, to Astrakhan, and also across Russia to India and China. In turn, Russian merchants could go from Sweden to Lubeck, Antwerp, and Spain. By agreement with the King of Denmark, Russians were permitted to trade freely in

---

[53] *Poslaniia Ivana Groznogo,* pp. 332–3.
[54] *Ibid.,* p. 333.

all Danish towns. They were to travel unhindered with their commodities from Copenhagen to the maritime states, and foreign merchants were to be freely permitted to pass through the Danish kingdom via the Sound.

In the development of Russian trade with the Caucasus and Central Asia the conquest of the Kazan and Astrakhan khanates, guaranteeing free travel on the Volga, was of great significance.

An important aspect of Ivan IV's commercial policy was the establishment of a state trade monopoly in grain, hemp, rhubarb, potash, resin, caviar, and other products. Only the Tsar and the treasury could deal in these "protected" commodities. In 1555 the export of beeswax and salt to Livonia was prohibited. Export of wax, tallow, flax, and hemp to Sweden was forbidden. Some goods—furs, beeswax, honey, tallow, and the like—were often purchased for the Tsar's trade at rates set by the treasury and then resold at a higher price abroad or within the country. Sometimes the population was forbidden to dispose of its commodities until such goods in the Tsar's warehouses had been sold.

The monoply character of trade was reflected also in the Tsar's right to purchase any goods imported into Russia by foreigners before they were placed on the open market. Merchants bringing goods into the country were not allowed to sell them to anyone until they had been examined by the Tsar's officials and the latter had selected goods for the Crown. Evidently, this did not apply to all goods in general, but mainly to luxury items. This practice was given legal sanction: the Customs Charter of 1571 provided: "And the Tsar, lord [and] Grand Prince ordered that [customs officials] see to it that visitors, all foreign merchants, and everyone else who brings velvets, damasks, and other ornaments, and horses, first supply the sovereign with whatever he needs. And when a visitor brings some commodity into the country, customs officials shall report it to [the Tsar's] clerk. And until a report and inspection are made and it is determined what the sovereign needs, that commodity shall not be released by customs officials nor be sold." [55] Goods were purchased not only for the Tsar's personal use, but for resale as well.[56]

Among the measures introduced by Ivan in the field of foreign trade one must also note his prohibition of the export of money, as well as of gold and silver objects. In the same Customs charter it is stated: "And customs officials shall vigilantly prevent Moscow's visitors and merchants of all cities of the Moscovite State, Moscow, Novgorod, and

---

[55] *Sobranie gosudarstvennykh gramot i dogovorov,* Pt. II, pp. 57–8.

[56] See Fletcher, *O gosudarstve russkom* [On the Russian State] (St. Petersburg: 1905), p. 51.

the Moscovite lands, from taking money, silver, and gold, or silver and gold dishes in trunks, boxes, or chests, from Novgorod, into Lithuania or Germany, or other cities." [57] This measure was dictated by the growing demand of the national economy for money. It coincided in its aims with the policies of western European states of the Middle Ages and was the first stage in the development of mercantilism. Concern for the increase in the amount of money in the country was shown by an administrative prohibition of the export of money and of precious metals in general. Ivan IV was the first (if one does not count the analogous measures of the Kievan prince Mstislav the Great in the twelfth century) to put into effect in this field a measure which was systematically repeated by Russia in the seventeenth, eighteenth, and even nineteenth centuries and which, rather than being an isolated measure, contributed along with others to the increase in the amount of money and precious metals in the country.

State policy in relation to the towns was of great importance for the development of trade and urban handicrafts. The struggle of the Moscow princes for the liquidation of feudal disunity and for the formation of a centralized state led to the transfer of cities belonging to individual feudalists to the Moscow prince. Ivan III and Vasilii III persistently carried out a policy of collecting towns under their rule—to "deboyar" them. The towns were taken from the feudal landowners and placed directly under the rule of the Grand Prince of Moscow. Towns annexed by the Moscow state were not distributed to, and thus became independent of, the various local feudalists.

This had not only great political significance, as it increased the dependence of the population on the Moscow prince, but it also carried great financial implications: The inhabitants of these areas, consisting mainly of craftsmen and merchants, paid a settlement tax to the treasury of the Grand Prince of Moscow. The people living in towns belonging to the sovereign enjoyed personal freedom. At the beginning of the sixteenth century only a few small towns remained under the rule of the church and secular feudalities.

From the end of the fifteenth century separate decrees forbade trade in the *uezdi,* the purpose of which was to set up monopoly rights for the towns in the market. The primary aim of this prohibition was to create a convenient collection system of customs receipts. It did not, however, lead to the establishment of monopolies in the town markets.[58]

[57] *Sobranie gosudarstvennykh gramot i dogovorov,* Pt. II, p. 58.
[58] See P. P. Smirnov, *op. cit.,* I, 99.

With regard to towns, Ivan IV carried out a policy designed to fortify the centralized state. He limited mortgaging and strengthened the position of the settlements. Here monasteries had enjoyed a great privilege in their right to acquire mortgages. The mortgagees were mainly merchants and craftsmen of the settlements who adhered to the monastery in order to be free from the settlement tax. They were under the jurisdiction of the monastery courts, paid taxes to the monasteries, and lived in monastery settlements. Mortgaging was widespread in the sixteenth century and thus worsened the position of those remaining in the settlements, since the previous tax was levied on a smaller number of people. The Sudebnik of 1550 prohibited mortgaging by settlement inhabitants to the monasteries. By forbidding city merchants to live in the monasteries, that is, on the monastery "white" land, the Sudebnik ordered them, in effect, to live in the city." [59]

It is evident from the text of the Stoglav that even before the issue of the Stoglav Sobor Ivan IV made an important decision concerning church (metropolitan, archbishop, bishop) and monastery settlements. New church and monastery settlements were deprived of their privileges and their financial and judicial immunity: "all new settlements with city inhabitants shall be subject to all taxes and courts." [60] They were to bear the settlement tax, and they came under the jurisdiction of the viceroy's court instead of that of the monastery. This order strengthened the financial and political position of the settlement.[61]

At the Stoglav Sobor Ivan IV warned the monasteries, princes, and boyars who held settlements that the growth of new privileged settlements and of mortgaging in the old settlements would lead to the elimination of the sovereign's taxes and of the land tax. In reply to this, the Sobor adopted a new policy according to which those who left for new settlements after a census should return from these to the former town. Church and monastery authorities were permitted to retain existing settlements thereafter "on the basis of former charters." To promote the establishment of new settlements it was forbidden to increase the number of houses in old settlements, except in cases of family division. The holders of old settlements were permitted to "admit" into deserted houses village people—plowing and nonplowing—with the observance of the St. George's Day rules; to admit two persons into settlements was forbidden with the exception of nontaxpaying "cos-

---

[59] See *Sudebniki XV–XVI vekov,* p. 174; I. I. Smirnov, "Sudebnik 1550 goda," *Istoricheskie zapiski,* No. 24 (1947), p. 323.

[60] *Stoglav,* p. 412.

[61] See I. I. Smirnov, "Sudebnik 1550 goda," *Istoricheskie zapiski,* No. 24 (1947), p. 323.

sacks." At the same time the populations of church and monastery settlements were granted the right to leave freely for towns or villages provided they observed the rules of the Sudebnik regarding peasant departure.[62]

Socially and economically the population of the settlements in the middle of the sixteenth century was heterogeneous. The legislation of Ivan IV clearly shows a policy designed not only to support these people in their quarrels and clashes with the church and monastery land-owning groups, but also to elevate the wealthy part of the settlement population in relation to its poorer segment. This latter aspect is clearly expressed in the Sudebnik of 1550 (Art. 26) which defines the amount of payment "for dishonesty."

This tax raised the honor of merchants and "middle" settlement people significantly above that of the peasant and the "young black" city inhabitant. The dishonor of big merchants was set by the Sudebnik at fifty rubles, that of merchants and "middle"settlement people at five rubles, and that of peasants, plowing and nonplowing, at one ruble, with the same amount stipulated for the "black city young person." [63] Thus in terms of "honor" the middle settlement person was placed on the same level as, and even above, the nobles and petty boyars of the town, who, according to the same article of the Sudebnik, incurred a penalty for dishonor based on their position, that is, three, four, or five rubles.[64]

For social support Ivan the Terrible depended upon the nobility he elevated economically and politically. At the same time in his struggle against the princely-boyar magnates he tried to obtain the backing of the city inhabitants. This is particularly apparent in the events of the oprichnina period. After departing from Moscow for the Aleksandrovskaia *sloboda,* he proclaimed, in a charter, disgrace on the boyars, officials, and clergy. But from the sloboda in January, 1565, he sent a special charter to the guests, merchants, and "to the entire Orthodox peasantry of the city of Moscow," and declared "that they should fear nothing inasmuch as they are not subject to either anger or disgrace." [65]

The city of Moscow supported the formation of the oprichnina. A strengthened centralized state was in the interests of the town population and aided the growth of trade and handicrafts.

---

[62] *Stoglav,* pp. 413–4; P. P. Smirnov, *op. cit.,* I, 112–21; I. I. Smirnov, "Sudebnik 1550 goda," *Istoricheskie zapiski,* No. 24 (1947), pp. 323–30.

[63] See *Sudebniki XV–XVI vekov,* p. 148.

[64] See P. P. Smirnov, *op. cit.,* I, 109–10.

[65] *Russkaia istoricheskaia biblioteka* [Russian Historical Library] edited by the Archeographic Commission. (St. Petersburg: 1876), III, 249.

Ivan IV elevated the merchants to political importance. Along with the nobility, clergy, boyars, and officials, representatives of the higher merchantry were invited to the Zemskii Sobor of 1556. He employed merchants to discharge various state services, collect customs duties, and so forth.

Ivan the Terrible's financial policy was also determined by his basic political philosophy—the liquidation of the remnants of feudal disunity and the strengthening of the centralized feudal state. Inasmuch as unification of political power demanded the centralization of finances, Ivan IV continued the fiscal policies of his predecessors. As was said above, the problem of obtaining the means for the maintenance of the serving nobility was solved by the extensive establishment of the pomestie system of landowning. In addition, the Moscow princes desperately needed money for the support of the court and the state apparatus and for carrying on warfare.

Ivan IV introduced important changes in the tax system which included some new levies. As has already been said, the system of kormlenie was characteristic of the period of feudal disunity. Korm was a type of tax received by the viceroys administering various localities. Ivan III tried to limit kormlenie: he decreased the period of kormlenie and distributed separate revenue items, as, for example, customs duties, to various kormlenshchiki or Grand Princely collectors. By the ukaz of 1555 Ivan IV completely abolished the system of kormlenie. The viceroys and district officials were dismissed, while the court and the collection of taxes were transferred to the "chosen men" or "landed judges" with "sworn men" selected by the city inhabitants and black peasants.

The system of kormlenie meant the atomization and decentralization of state revenues. In place of the incomes received earlier by the kormlenshchiki definite obrok—"kormlenie ransom" was now transferred directly to the treasury by local authorities. This guaranteed the increase and the centralization of the revenues for the Tsar's treasury. Provision was made for special financial institutions, called "cheti" or "chetverti," and each performed its function in specific territories of the Russian state.

In connection with the organization of the rifle regiments, new taxes, the so-called "food money" and *emchuzhnye* (for the preparation of saltpeter for powder), were introduced. Taxes were also levied for "town and fortification matters" to strengthen the boundaries of the Russian state.

By altering the tax structure, an important change in tax levies was effected. In place of the various units applied earlier a general and, at the same time, much larger major unit for the entire country, the so-called "great Moscow sokha," involving now a definite land area, was introduced in the 1550's.

The amount of the land parcel adopted as the "great sokha" was not uniform; it differed according to the quality and ownership of the land. The better the quality of the land, the smaller the sokha and the greater the tax. Monastery lands were taxed more than those of the pomestia. In regard to the latter, "the great Moscow sokha" equalled 800 chetverts (400 desiatines) of superior land in one field, 1000 chetverts of average land, and 1200 chetverts of poor land. For monastery lands the figures were 600, 700, and 800 chetverts, respectively.[66] This reform was evidently put into effect to implement the project of a general survey of lands which Ivan IV proposed at the Stoglav Sobor (1551).

The introduction of the "great Moscow sokha" corresponded to the above-mentioned proposal of Ermolai-Erazm to extend the units of land measurement. As it was applied by the government of Ivan IV, however, this measure had broader significance. Ermolai thought it necessary to abolish all money taxes on the peasants, and he associated the increase in the units of land measurement only with the granting of land to the serving people. But the new system was introduced by the Tsar primarily for fiscal reasons.

The expansion of sources of income and the consolidation of finances were also aided by Ivan's policy of limitation and liquidation of privileges. Consider his measures in the field of private credit. His legislation sought to confirm the existence in the country of pure credit relations based on the lending of money and to prevent the transformation of these relations into that of the kabala, that is, the dependence of the debtor on the creditor.

Article 82 of the Tsar's Sudebnik states: "and whoever borrows money for interest shall not serve anyone. He shall live as before and pay only interest. If anyone should lend money and force the borrower to stay with him, and should the debtor escape, the creditor will be deprived of the kabala money." [67]

Among the economic measures issued by Ivan IV in the interests of the serving nobility, those designed to protect noble debtors are noteworthy. An ukaz of December 25, 1557, decreed that the serving people

---

[66] See Miliukov, *Spornye voprosy finansovoi istorii Moskovskogo gosudarstva,* p. 47 ff.; S. Veselovskii, *Soshnoe pismo* [Plough Letter] (Moscow: 1916), II, Chapter XIV.

[67] See *Sudebniki XV–XVI vekov,* p. 170.

who at that time had money and grain debts on the basis of oral and written kabala charters were to repay them in the course of a five year period by installments of one-fifth part each year. *Rost,* that is, interest on money loans, and *naspy* [interest] on borrowed grain, incurred in transactions completed before this ukaz were entirely abolished. New loans concluded by serving people in the course of the five year immunity period (1558–1562) and not paid off during this time had to be paid in full, but rost and naspy on grain were reduced by one half compared to the level of interest (*na piat' shestoi,* that is, 20 per cent) customary until that time.[68]

At the very beginning of Ivan IV's reign, a single monetary system, corresponding to the aims of the centralized state, was created in Russia.[69] Before his reign the so-called *Novgorodka,* comprising the basic monetary unit, and the *Moskovka,* nominally equal to half a Novgorodki, circulated in the Moscow state. During the reigns of Grand Princes Ivan III and Vasilii III the value of money dropped, primarily as a result of the fiscal policies of the Moscow princes, who tried to obtain additional income for the treasury by issuing money of less than full value.

By an ukaz in 1535, during the regency of Ivan IV's mother, Elena Glinskii, a reform in the money system was introduced. For the entire Moscow state a single monetary system was established. Whereas under Ivan III and Vasilii III, 260 Novgorodki were minted out of one *grivna* (48 *zolotniks* of silver), now 300 were minted, that is, the monetary value was lowered.

With the ukaz of 1535 the weight of the new money (0.68 gm.) basically corresponded to the actual weight of the Novgorodki. Since the old term, Novgorodka, did not convey the all-Russian significance of the unit, it was changed to *copeck,* in accordance with the representation on the new money of a rider bearing a lance.

Under Ivan IV the coinage of the Moskovki, by weight equal to half a copeck, as well as money equal to a quarter of a copeck (*polushka*), continued. These real monetary units were integrated with the calculated units—the *ruble,* poltina, grivna, and *altyn.*

The monetary reform was motivated by the government's desire to set in order the monetary circulation of the country, to free it from

---

68 See Vladimirskii-Budanov, *op. cit.,* pp. 12–5.

69 See G. B. Fedorov, "Unifikatsiia russkoi monetnoi sistemy i ukaz 1535 goda" [The Unification of the Russian Monetary System and the Decree of 1535], *Izvestiia Akademii Nauk SSSR. Seriia istorii i filosofii* [Bulletin of the Academy of Sciences of the USSR. Series of History and Philosophy], VII, No. 6 (1950), pp. 547–58.

counterfeit coinage, and from undervalued money.[70] The conversion to the new monetary system involved great sacrifices on the part of the population, for the holders of the old, undervalued coins suffered a loss through recoinage: "and they began to trade with new money, the copecks, not only in Pskov, but everywhere, and people lost much in old money," [71] states the Pskov chronicles.

This survey of Ivan the Terrible's principles of economic policy indicates that feudal Russia found in him not only an outstanding politician, but also one of the most important representatives of advanced economic thought. His economic measures were inextricably linked with his political activities in strengthening the Russian feudal centralized state. Like his political views, his economic views were determined by profound processes taking place in the economic system of his Russia. At the same time his economic policy played a great role in fortifying the foundation and political superstructure of feudal Russia.

---

[70] "That winter (1535) the Grand Prince and his mother the Grand Princess, seeing the injustice done to the people by the increase of counterfeit and mutilated money decided to remove this evil from their state. After a consultation on the matter with the boyars, the sovereign and his mother ordered the coining of new money—three rubles from one grivna. Old counterfeit and mutilated money was to be smelted, and neither counterfeit nor mutilated was to be circulated. Old, good Novgorodki and Moskovki equalled two and a third rubles and one grivna. The Grand Princes ordered to be added to the grivenka new money to prevent loss for the people from counterfeit and mutilated money. Thereafter bad money was not allowed to circulate, and counterfeiters and mutilaters were to be hunted and imprisoned." *Polnoe sobranie russkikh letopisei,* XX, 429.

[71] *Ibid.,* IV, 302.

CHAPTER 7. *The Economic Ideas of the* Domostroi

From the sixteenth century has come a literary document known as the *Domostroi,* a work which differs sharply from the literature examined above.[1] Although it was evidently written in the fifteenth century, it was finally compiled only in the middle of the sixteenth century.

Unlike other literary documents of that century, the *Domostroi* deals neither with vital questions of state policy, nor with the interrelation of various social classes and groups. It is concerned rather with the rules of family life and domestic economy. It takes the form of detailed instructions to the head of the house regarding his conduct toward the members of his family: his wife, children, servants, and others outside the household. The *Domostroi* depicts the ideal of the decorous father and householder who reveres state authority, strictly observes the moral demands of the church in his relations with people, and knows how to safeguard his domestic interests.

The basic content of the *Domostroi* sets down instructions as to how the head of the family must conduct his household economy. It follows the ideological and political trend of the period—maintenance of the idea of autocratic power and the moral ideal of the life of man as laid down by the church. In its political directives the *Domostroi* strengthened the idea of indisputable obedience to the Tsar's authority and served as one of the ideological weapons of the centralized state. Just as in the state all must submit unconditionally to the Tsar's authority, so the family must be built on stern obedience to its head. The father must firmly and unswervingly exercise his authority in the family. He is the lord in the family and responsible for it to the Tsar and God.

The relations of the householder to the people beyond the bounds of his family are depicted in full accordance with the moral teachings of the church, whose substance we gave in the first chapters and whose legal norms are reflected in such documents of old Rus as *Russkaia*

[1] See "Domostroi" [Household Management], *Chteniia v Obshchestve istorii i drevnostei rossiiskikh* [Readings in the Society of Russian History and Antiquities], Bk. 2 (1881), pp. 1–202.

Pravda and the Sudebniki. Among other examples of the "unjust living" which the Christian householder must avoid as evil are force and insult, violent seizure, and failure to return what is borrowed. It was considered sinful to impose heavy and illegal obrok upon one's village peasants or to seize the fields, woods, ponds, fisheries, and hives of others. Turning a man into a kholop by dishonest and forcible means, enrichment by deceit, and taking interest on money loans and loans of grain were also condemned.[2]

The *Domostroi* contrasts these vices with the virtues of the Christian attitude. The master, it states, must judge everyone, whether rich or poor, near or far, "known" or "unknown," justly and not hypocritically. "Whether on his own or in an official [post], a good man collects only just taxes from his peasants, and these without force, theft, or torture." If his neighbor or his peasant lacks seed, horses and cows, or anything else with which to pay the Tsar's taxes, one must help him and give him loans; even though one might have little, he must aid others." "Merchants, craftsmen, and agriculturists: trade, produce, and plow with benediction, without resort to theft, robbery, seizure, slander or other machinations. Use your own strength and blessings, and trade, produce, and plow justly." [3]

In its treatment of these questions the *Domostroi* introduces nothing which had not been said before by churchmen or written in legislative documents. It is a type of encyclopedia of domestic economy. It offers detailed counsel as to the provision and safekeeping of all necessary products, the preparation and consumption of food, and other essentials. Its subject matter is not a productive type of economy, nor a votchina or pomestie, nor the economy of the large industrial enterpriser, but the *domestic economy,* the economy of the consumer. Here production is subordinated to the immediate needs of the family, such as the kitchen garden and orchard, as well as the domestic preparation of necessities, particularly provisions for the family. All this applies especially to the domestic town economy.

In his economic considerations the compiler of the *Domostroi* occasionally stresses the objective underlying the work. A number of instructions of the *Domostroi* are addressed to all persons. They admonish that all should live in accordance with their income: "Everybody, rich and poor, great and small, should make his own self-appraisal and estimate his crafts, profits, and property." [4] The official, it continues, must live "on his government salary and the income from his

---

[2] *Ibid.,* pp. 78–80.
[3] *Ibid.,* p. 82.
[4] *Ibid.,* p. 83.

pomestie and votchina" and in accordance with this maintain his house. In another place the compiler gives advice to "every good man to whom God has granted an estate or a village or a store or a warehouse or storehouses or breweries or flour mills." [5] He also admonishes the single man who is "not rich, but has some means." [6]

In the main the author of the *Domostroi* depicts the domestic economy of a wealthy person, that of a boyar living in town, or of a well-to-do merchant. Here we find butlers, stewards, and many kholopy. Luxuries and imported goods are purchased. The master of the house is a rich man who lives off the labor of others. He is in close contact with the market, and it is thus recommended that he purchase a great variety of agricultural products and household objects. The mere enumeration of these goods takes up much space in the book. Moreover, the compiler repeats frequently that goods should be bought when they are plentiful and cheap. He stresses the need to build up a great reserve of products, even for a year or more. The idea is advanced that one must store products not only for one's own future need, but for profit as well. Should market prices rise, surplus commodities could then be sold.[7] The purchase and storage of goods from "overseas" also is recommended.

The author's verbose insistence on the purchase of goods for the domestic economy and his arguments in favor of reselling some of these for the sake of profit reflect the significant development of the market and the growth of trade in the towns of the Moscow state in the sixteenth century. At the same time, the *Domostroi* reveals that the town economy was still natural. This is exemplified by the recommendation that each household should include a carpenter, tailor, shoemaker, and other craftsmen, so that all necessities can be made at home without the necessity to turn to another household.[8] The maid-servants must know how to sew, knit, weave, and embroider. The wife herself must be able to teach the servants and must know how to superintend their work. In the house, wine, beer, and various other objects of consumption must be prepared from agricultural products purchased on the market.

Various other instructions are also given: all receipts and expenditures must be carefully registered and verified regularly: purchases must be made for cash, and not on credit; imposts, taxes, and all types of obrok as well as loans and interest on loans must be paid on time or

[5] *Ibid.,* p. 136.
[6] *Ibid.,* p. 122.
[7] *Ibid.,* pp. 109–12, 119.
[8] *Ibid.,* p. 91.

even ahead of time; all waste matter from the economy must be carefully collected and utilized. Recommendations are given as to how to treat servants and hirelings ("above all do not anger a hired man with respect to his remuneration"). The advice on how to deal with kholopy, should it be impossible to keep them, is curious. It is recommended "not to sell them, but to let them go free."

In a supplement to the *Domostroi* a final theme is developed. It appears in the "Letter and Instruction from Father to Son" of the priest of the Annunciation, Sylvester, to his son, Anfim, and relates to the latter period of the priest's life. Sylvester, tutor and counsellor of Ivan the Terrible during the first period of his rule, was also an energetic entrepreneur. He carried on an extensive trade in the products of household industry. His "Letter and Instruction" contains several new points in comparison with the basic text of the *Domostroi.* He stresses the necessity of honesty in trade. He prefers free labor. He himself set his kholopy free and used only hired labor. "I have freed and given [much] to my workers; I have purchased others and freed them. All of our workers are free and live in good homes. . . . And now they live with us by their own consent." [9]

Sylvester devotes great attention to the instruction of people in crafts and trade and to their education. He is proud of the fact that he did not resort to credit and that he lent money widely to craftsmen. He says not a word about the "sinfulness" of lending money for interest, evidently considering usury a completely lawful phenomenon.

The compiler of the *Domostroi* displays no interest in *social* economy. He is occupied exclusively with private economy, with the interests of the individual person. In its economic content the *Domostroi* reflects only one aspect of the complicated and varied economic ideology of the Russian people of the fifteenth and sixteenth centuries and this, moreover, of only one group of society, that of the rich townsmen. Attempts of some historians to interpret the economic views contained in the *Domostroi* too broadly, as if they were held by the Russian people in general in the fifteenth and sixteenth centuries are entirely baseless. The *Domostroi* is looked upon by these historians as a special phase, a stage in the development of Russian economic thought, which in the period of the *Domostroi* was purportedly very poor and miserable and which showed neither interest in social problems nor awareness of the tasks of the entire national economy.

[9] A. N. Chudinov, ed., *Domostroi Silvestrovskogo izvoda* [Silvester's Household Management] (St. Petersburg: 1902), p. 67.

A clear example of such distorted interpretation of the nature of Russian economic thought is the evaluation of the significance of the *Domostroi* by V. V. Sviatlovskii. He tries to present the restricted outlook of the *Domostroi* as a testimony of the narrowness and poverty of the economic thought of pre-Petrine Russia in general. "The limited social horizon and the intellectual servility of pre-Petrine Rus is fully expressed in the views on national economy and prosperity contained in the sententious *Domostroi*. It is the typical pattern of the Moscow autocracy and displays all the tendencies of pre-Petrine Rus and its principal aspirations toward political liberty and some form of civility." [10] And further: "The pride of the century, the celebrated *Domostroi*, is an astonishing mixture of naive and ignorant barbarity and artful humility and self-assuredness. The reader is uncertain as to what astonishes him more: the wild crudeness of our forefathers or the pitiful scantiness of their social thought. Cruelty and servility existed even at the domestic hearth; nothing could justify this gloomy egotism, this animal self-esteem." [11]

Sviatlovskii contrasts the melancholy picture of the economic thought of pre-Petrine Rus with what he considers the colorful doctrines of Western Europe in the Middle Ages, where all was incomparably better and clearer than in our land. He wrote of the ideological "poverty" of pre-Petrine Rus, of the fact that before Peter I Russian thought in general had still not accomplished the formulation of its social-economic aims and had not sharpened its economic aspirations.[12] This slanderous distortion of a bourgeois cosmopolite, this ardent attempt to debase the past of the great Russian people, crumbles in the face of the facts presented above regarding the development of Russian economic thought of the last centuries.

Other lands in the Middle Ages also had their *Domostroi*, that is, codes of rules for the domestic economy, as for example *Parisian Master* (fifteenth century), *Prisoner in Bar* (thirteenth century), and *Views on the Administration of the Family* of A. Pandolphin (fifteenth century).[13] Just as in other countries, the codes of household management in Russia did not represent a phase or stage in the development of economic thought, but reflected merely one facet of economic ideology. The *Domostroi* was by no means a high point in the development of

---

[10] Sviatlovskii, *Istoriia ekonomicheskikh idei v Rossii,* I, 28.

[11] *Ibid.,* I, 29.

[12] *Ibid.,* I, 12.

[13] See I. Nekrasov, *Opyt istoriko-literaturnogo issledovaniia o proiskhozhdenii drevnerusskogo Domostroia* [Historical-Literary Essay On the Origin of the Ancient Russian Code of Household Management] (Moscow: 1873).

Russian thought, a development which had always focused its attention on the basic social questions of the life of Russia.

We have seen that even in Kievan Rus economic thought went far beyond the bounds of the interests of the individual and private economy and achieved a high degree of development. Also in Kievan Rus, and in the subsequent stages of development of the Russian state, the economic thought of the Russian people was an important factor in the progressive movement of our motherland. Even in the early period of their history the Russian people produced a number of brilliant examples of advanced progressive thought.

Also in Kievan Rus, and in the epoch of feudal disunity, as well as in the period of the creation of the centralized state, Russian economic thought played a great and important social role in the formulation of the national tasks of the Russian people and in the struggle of the progressive forces of society against conservative and reactionary trends. The facts show that for the whole of the historical period which we have examined Russian economic thought stayed abreast of the times and the progressive economic thought of the entire world.

In the fifteenth and sixteenth centuries Russian economic thought played an enormous role in the formation and consolidation of the centralized state. In the seventeenth and eighteenth centuries it rose to a still higher level of development, reflecting the advancing economic and political movement of our motherland and was one of the mightiest weapons of the class struggle in Russia.

PART IV
THE PERIOD OF COMPLETE ENSERFMENT OF THE PEASANTRY, THE FORMATION OF AN ALL-RUSSIAN MARKET, AND THE EMERGENCE OF MANUFACTURING

CHAPTER 8. *The Basic Trends of Economic Thought in the Seventeenth Century. The Demands of the Masses During the Period of the First Peasant Wars.*

The Economic Conditions of Russia. Economic Policy

During the seventeenth century Russia entered a new period of its development. The remnants of past feudal isolation were liquidated, and the centralized Russian state was strengthened. Earlier, wrote Lenin, Russia was divided into separate "lands," oblasts, and principalities. "Only the new period of Russian history (approximately from the seventeenth century onward) is characterized by the actual merger of all such oblasti, lands and principalities into one whole." [1]

The underlying causes of this process are to be found in the economic conditions of the country. They arose from the growth of the social division of labor and from the development of trade relations among the oblasti. Lenin in particular turned his attention to this important circumstance: "This merging . . . was caused by the increase in exchange among oblasti, by the gradual growth of commodity exchange, and by the concentration of small local markets into one all-Russian market." [2]

Characteristic of this period is the birth within the feudal society of new bourgeois relations, the appearance and growth among the town

[1] Lenin, *Sochineniia,* I, 137.

[2] *Ibid.*

population of new social forces—of the merchant class, the trading bourgeoisie. Revealing the class nature of the resulting processes, V. I. Lenin wrote: "Because the leaders and masters of this process were capitalist-merchants, the creation of these national ties was none other than the creation of bourgeois ties." [3]

In contrast with such western European countries as England, France, and others, in seventeenth century Russia the appearance and development of the new bourgeois relations occurred in a setting which further strengthened the feudal-serf order. This circumstance made a unique imprint on the economic policy of the Russian government and determined the nature and direction of the economic thought of Russia of that time.

The economic processes occurring in Russia were utilized by the ruling class of feudalists. In the seventeenth century the serf economy underwent a noticeable territorial expansion and entered more completely into market relations. Changes also took place in the forms of feudal property. The differences between pomestie and votchina gradually disappeared.

In the beginning of the seventeenth century Russia was attacked by the Polish-Swedish usurpers. The foreign intervention caused heavy damage to the national economy and brought destruction to the country. The estates of the votchinniki, which were stronger economically, suffered considerably less than did those of the pomestie. In an attempt to strengthen the economic position of the nobility, the government, during the entire seventeenth century, lavishly distributed to the nobles, the court, and the free peasants the so-called "black" lands in the form of votchina and pomestie holdings. The pomestia began to be considered the property of the holders and were gradually transformed into votchini. The Code of 1649 sanctioned the right of inheritance of the pomestie under conditions of hereditary service. Influential boyars frequently seized free lands arbitrarily. As a result, the number and sizes of votchiny increased significantly. The votchini of Morozov, Sheremetev, Saltykov, Cherkasskii, and others consisted of tens of thousands of desiatiny of land.

In a drive for surplus production the votchinniki and pomeshchiki increased the exploitation of the peasantry. Seigniorial tillage (*barskaia zapashka*) grew significantly. Obrok [tax] rose, also, especially in the central regions. In the majority of cases the peasants bore not only barshchina, but were subject to numerous requisitions in kind and

[3] *Ibid.*, I, 137–8.

money. The flight of the peasants took on mass proportions. In this connection the question of manpower became particularly acute. In an attempt to meet the demands of the nobility, the government established a ten-year period for seeking fugitive peasants. By the Code of 1649 the peasantry was finally enserfed. "Fixed years" were abolished. As a consequence of the increasing exploitation and arbitrariness, the position of the peasantry deteriorated still more.

In seventeenth century Russia industry was still not clearly separated from agriculture. The economy of the feudalists, as well as the small peasant economy, continued to be basically natural. Yet production for the market grew notably. The large-scale votchiny and pomestia began increasingly to produce agricultural products for sale and to organize various types of industrial production. Thus, for example, the Morozov estates included large potash and wine production, an ironworks, a tannery, linen production, and so forth. Potash making was widespread and was practical not only on boyar and monastery votchiny, but by independent merchants as well. Large-scale salt mines also underwent considerable development—at Ustiug, along the Kama, in the Urals—as did the fur, lumber, and fish industries. The peasant economy also became more involved in market relations.

Small-scale production, both handicraft and artisan, developed. The industrial population of the towns increased significantly. In the Yaroslav suburb the industrial population constituted over two thousand households; in Nizhnii Novgorod, Viatka, Kostroma, and Vologda it numbered over one thousand (on the basis of the census of 1678).[4] Moreover, specialization of crafts was already important. In the village of Murashkin the production of sheepskin coats, gauntlets, and the like was fostered, while in the village of Pavlov ironworking was greatly developed. The specialization of regions coincided more or less clearly with the various branches of production.

But handicraft production could no longer satisfy the demands of the growing market and the needs of the state. In seventeenth century Russia large-scale enterprises began to appear—the manufactories. In the first half of the seventeenth century metallurgical and ironworking mills were constructed in Tula and Kashir. Glass factories, tanneries, and paper mills were also built.

Along with the growth of the social division of labor and exchange, large trading centers arose. The Makar'evsk and Irbit fairs, which had great significance for trade relations with Siberia, the Svinskaia fair

[4] *Tsentralnyi gosudarstvennyi arkhiv drevnikh aktov* [Central State Archive of Ancient Documents], *Dela razriadnye* [Miscellaneous Affairs] Bk. 1, No. 210, sheets 550–68. Hereinafter cited *TsGADA*.

(in the Briansk region), which played an important role in the trade with the West, and others, were established.

The foreign trade of Russia with the East and West developed rapidly. Trade relations with Asiatic countries proceeded through Astrakhan, while those with Western Europe were established overland across the western frontier. The White Sea and the port of Archangel acquired greater importance for trade with the West. However foreign trade was almost exclusively in the hands of foreigners. Russia did not have her own trading fleet, and she was cut off from the shores of the Baltic and Black Seas.

In the seventeenth century large Russian trading enterprises carried on wholesale trade in the various towns of Russia, and were active in the sphere of foreign and transit trade. Commercial capital began to broaden the sphere of trade operations. The merchant became not only a broker and moneylender, but in various cases also a manufacturer and landholder. For example, the merchants Vasilii Shorin, Sveteshnikov, Bosov, and others occupied themselves with manufacture and bought up large tracts of land. But in seventeenth century Russia, the conditions necessary for the mass transformation of commodity production into capitalistic production did not yet exist. "Commodity production," as I. V. Stalin has written, "leads to capitalism only *if* private ownership of the means of production exists, *if* the labor power appears in the market as a commodity which can be bought by the capitalist and exploited in the process of production, and *if*, consequently, the system of exploitation of wage workers by capitalists exists in the country." [5]

In the period under consideration there was still no system of free hiring of workers in Russia. The existence of crafts and manufactures was based mainly on the labor of enserfed peasants. True, there sometimes was hired labor in the crafts, manufactures, handicrafts, peasant holdings, and also on the feudal estates, but this hiring (mainly of impoverished or landless peasants, "poor" city dwellers and the "beggars") had in the majority of cases the character of enslaving agreements. The free—in the full sense of the word—hiring of the working force was only a chance or temporary manifestation.

There can be no doubt, however, that the growth of the social division of labor and the formation of a domestic national market inescapably called forth a further development of commodity production. Along with the big trade entrepreneur appeared a new figure, the broker (*skupshchik*), who, as a rule, came from among the peasants and

[5] I. V. Stalin, *Ekonomicheskie problemy sotsializma v SSSR* [Economic Problems of Socialism in the USSR] (Moscow: Gospolitizdat, 1952), pp. 14–15.

craftsmen. In earlier times the small producers themselves disposed of their commodities in local markets, but under the new conditions they lost direct connection with the market and became dependent on the broker and the large merchant.

The law of value, inherent in commodity production, found a comparatively greater scope for its action and was utilized by the emerging class of the commercial bourgeoisie. The merchants not only bought goods from small producers at low prices, but also lent them money. This turn of affairs made the small producers still more dependent. Under conditions of serfdom, however, these processes developed extremely slowly. Their results became more or less noticeable only in the eighteenth century.

In connection with the socio-economic development of the country serious changes, accompanied by stubborn class struggles, took place in the positions of the various classes. The complete victory of the feudal-serf system and the absorption of the estates of the feudalists into the commodity-money system sharply added to the oppression of the peasants. The latter were subjected to ever-increasing exploitations not only by feudalists, but by traders, brokers and moneylenders.

The populations of the suburbs found themselves in no better position, as they suffered from the predominance and arbitrariness of the rich upper classes. The general condition of the suburban inhabitants was not far removed from that of the serfs, a fact which brought the interests of the two groups closer together.

The movement of the peasantry and the urban poor exploded in numerous uprisings throughout the seventeenth century. Beginning in 1606, the uprising of the peasants and Cossacks, headed by Ivan Bolotnikov, assumed the nature of a peasant war and affected a wide area. This spontaneous uprising of the peasantry was directed against feudal oppression. Not only the petty officials and townspeople participated in the revolt, but also the nobles who were dissatisfied with Tsar Vasilii Shuiskii, the puppet of the big boyars. But the nobles could not support the antifeudal trend of Bolotnikov's uprising; they displayed indecision and at the same time weakened the rebel forces. In 1607 the revolt was put down with extraordinary cruelty.

At the end of the first half of the seventeenth century a wave of town revolts erupted. These uprisings were a spontaneous burst of protest by the toiling masses against unbearable taxation and against their cruel exploitation and enslavement by feudalists and the upper classes of the towns.

The tax policy of the government was especially hard on the majority of the townspeople. Direct taxes were extremely inequitable. The inhabitants of the sufficiently numerous "white painted" households and of the entire "white settlements," established by boyars and monasteries, as well as the petty officials and the clergy, were free from taxes and could engage in trade and crafts without hindrance. The entire burden of taxation fell upon the least secure part of the population. Particularly hard for this sector were the innumerable collections which had the character of indirect taxes; the salt tax, the immediate cause of the revolt of 1648, was one of these.

Beginning in Moscow, the uprising (the "Salt Riot") engulfed a number of towns in the north, in the south, in Siberia, and, finally, in 1650 spread to Novgorod and Pskov. The "Copper Riot," which took place in the city of Moscow in 1662, was a kind of continuation of these upheavals.

In 1666 an uprising of the Cossacks and peasants under the leadership of Vasili Us occurred. Subsequently (from 1667) began a Cossack-peasant movement led by Stepan Razin. In 1670–1671 the movement acquired enormous dimensions, sweeping the entire Volga region and many other areas of the Russian state. This popular uprising, the greatest after that of Bolotnikov, had also the character of a peasant war directed against the feudal-serf oppression in the country. The rebels burned manors and took revenge on the pomeshchiki. The main standard-bearer of the uprising, from the time of the second expedition of Razin from the Don to the Volga, was the enserfed peasantry. The peasants, the poorer Cossacks, and the town poor rallied around Razin and were joined by Chuvashes, Tartars, Mordva, and Mari. Although the uprising was cruelly put down, it nevertheless dealt a strong blow to the ruling class.

A struggle also took place within the ruling class of the feudalists. During the period of foreign intervention the boyars, making use of strained conditions in the country, elected the puppet Vasilii Shuiskii as their Tsar. In 1610 a provisional government of seven boyars from the old princely families was formed. It recognized the Polish prince Wladislaw as Tsar, under condition that he would rule together with them. Following the ousting of the interventionists by popular levies, the nobles again seized power and elected Mikhail Romanov as Tsar. Under Romanov a new boyar aristocracy emerged from among the persons nearest to the Tsar and enjoyed his graces and privileges.

The main segment of the ruling class, the nobility, achieved more active participation in the state administration and fought against the boyar aristocracy and the *mestnichestvo*. In 1682 the mestnichestvo was finally abolished.

The leadership of the clergy in its turn aspired to political independence from the Tsar's rule, and its struggle in this direction was especially clearly visible in the affair of the Patriarch Nikon. In its fight against the pretensions of the church feudalists the government found support in the pomestie nobility, whose interests clashed with the aspirations of the churchmen.

The Nikon affair was closely connected with the rise and spread of the schism. The schism took the distinctive form of the struggle of the masses against the feudal-serf oppression, inasmuch as the ruling church supported the oppressors. It must not be forgotten, however, that the schism attracted the most reactionary elements, which opposed everything new.

The merchant class also began to exert an influence on state affairs. However, it was still economically weak and was relegated to the background by the representatives of the nobility.

In the seventeenth century the state structure of Russia assumed more and more the character of an absolute monarchy, a development brought about by the economic growth of the country and the sharpening class struggle. The significance of the bureaucratic state apparatus with its system of multitudinous departments grew, and a standing army of riflemen, cavalry, and so forth, was created.

The growth of expenditures for the maintenance of the state and the army created a sharp demand on the treasury. Numerous direct and indirect taxes and collections for the state, as well as the wide application of a system of leasing, ruined the masses. In the 1650's, at the time of the war with Poland and Sweden, the financial position of Russia became particularly strained. Money circulation in the country fell into chaos. In an attempt to find a way out of its difficult position the government resorted in 1654 to the issue of copper money with a high par value and a compulsory rate of exchange. The unavoidable consequence of this measure was the rapid depreciation of the money, the rise in the price of goods, and the emergence of an *agio* (premium) on the silver ruble. The strong protest of the masses (the "Copper Riot" of 1662) forced the government to take the depreciated copper money out of circulation.

In order to increase its financial resources the government resorted to the search for gold and silver ores, to the obtaining of foreign loans, and so forth. But these attempts were unsuccessful. The growing demand of the state for money and the widening of trade relations called into existence a system of government measures designed to attract into the country the largest possible amount of precious metals in coins and ingots and to retain it there. From the middle of the seventeenth century the government aspired ever more decisively toward the achievement of an active trade balance. The policy of the state in the realm of trade was connected with the formation and development of an all-Russian market and reflected to a significant degree the interests of the merchant class.

The basic line of economic policy in the realm of trade was the removal of the privileges, [that is], "*tarkhanov*," enjoyed by foreign merchants, some groups of *gosti* merchants, and townspeople. In 1646 duty-free trade by the English, the Dutch, and other foreigners was abolished, and, following the petition from the Russian merchants in 1649, foreign merchants were forbidden to carry on trade within the country as well as transit trade with eastern countries.

The new principles of economic policy received more definite expression in the Commercial Charter of 1654 and the New Commercial Code of 1667. The former introduced a protective system of customs duties, established a uniform duty, and outlined a number of other measures aimed at controlling foreign trade. The New Commercial Code contained a detailed regulation of the trade of foreigners intended to strengthen Russian foreign trade and to attract and retain gold and silver in the country.

The government introduced a broad system of measures directed toward the development of foreign and transit trade and the search for new trade routes and new markets. Aspiring to widen trade relations with Western European and Asiatic countries, the government sent out its ambassadors to clarify conditions of trade with various countries, concluded trade treaties, and continued to seek an outlet to the Baltic Sea. In the 1660's a project was worked out for a canal which would connect the White Sea with Moscow by way of the Volga.

Russia set up close ties with the eastern countries, and took increasing possession of the transit trade of the West with the East. Attempts were made to establish trade relations with India and China and to discover the closest convenient routes to these countries. During the seventeenth century Russians penetrated farther east and annexed all of Siberia as far as the Sea of Okhotsk.

Putting into effect a complex and developed system of foreign trade, the tsarist government also inaugurated a number of separate measures directed at the development of domestic production. State metallurgical, military, and other manufacturing enterprises were built in Russia. Foreign entrepreneurs and Russian merchants were attracted to construct these factories. They were given various inducements such as the monopoly right to the production of goods, the privilege of customfree sale of the goods produced, and temporary freedom from taxes. In certain cases the entrepreneurs were given government subsidies. But these measures were still haphazard and did not represent a developed system of protective economic policy.

Although economic principles were basically progressive for the time, a policy was urgently needed not only for internal socio-economic reasons, but also for the sake of the Russian state in its foreign affairs. Throughout the seventeenth century Russia was forced to carry on a difficult and strenuous struggle for its national independence against Polish, Swedish, and Turkish usurpers. The bulwark of feudal reaction, the Vatican, striving everywhere to spread Catholicism, had long before prepared and, at the begining of the seventeenth century, organized the aggression of the feudalists of Catholic Poland against Russia. Through his representatives in Poland, the Roman Pope subsidized and supported the False Dimitri. Thanks to the heroic effort, self-denial, and patriotism of the Russian people the Polish interventionists who invaded Russia at the beginning of the seventeenth century were driven from the land. During the following exhausting wars with aristocratic Poland, Sweden, and Turkey, the Russian people foiled all attempts by the foreign aggressors to seize the primordial Russian lands and to enslave Russia.

In the seventeenth century a remarkable historical event occurred: the union of the Ukraine with Russia. The Ukrainian people, closely allied with the Russians by origin, proximity, and a common historical development, constantly strove for affiliation with the fraternal Russians. For a long time the Ukraine had suffered from oppression by the greedy and power-loving Polish nobles, the Turkish sultans, and the Tartar khans, who repeatedly plundered and ruined it. In the war of liberation of 1648–1654, which was led by the outstanding statesman and military leader Bogdan Khmel'nitskii, the Ukrainian people struggled heroically against the Polish oppression and for union with Russia. The main and decisive force in the war was the oppressed peasantry, struggling for the liberation of the Ukraine from foreign enslavment.

On January 8 (18), 1654, the Pereiaslav Council adopted a resolution for union of the Ukraine with Russia. This remarkable event had great progressive significance for the economic, political, and cultural development of the Ukrainian and Russian peoples. The union facilitated a broadening of economic and cultural ties, the growth of industry and trade, and the spread of education. The Ukrainian and Russian peoples were enabled to combine forces to defend themselves against foreign interventionists and to conduct a joint struggle against the pomeshchiki-serfowners, and later against capitalistic enslavement.

Turning to the characteristics of Russian economic thought of this period, it must be noted that various tendencies reflected the contradictions of the time and the struggle of new progressive forces against outmoded orders.

The Economic Demands of the Rebellious Peasantry

The class struggle of the peasantry against the feudalists took two basic directions. The black plowlands [free] peasantry fought against the extension of feudal landownership, the seizure of peasant lands, and the enserfment of peasants. The enserfed peasantry contended against increased exploitation, which the pomeshchiki practiced by curtailing allotted land, and against the growing seigniorial tillage. It was vitally interested in the liquidation of feudalist power over the person of the peasant and in the elimination of feudal landownership. This struggle of the peasantry against the feudalists naturally grew into one against the bases of the feudal structure.

The demands of the peasantry were most clearly expressed in the peasant wars of 1606–1607 and 1670–1671, both of which were anti-feudal and anti-enserfment in character. The aims and programs of these uprisings can be gleaned from government acts, letters, and dispatches preserved from the areas of the uprisings, from communications about the "Lists," or proclamations, of Bolotnikov, and from the "Provocative Letters" and "Decrees" of Stepan Razin. These documents provide the main sources for the study of the peasant uprisings under the leadership of Bolotnikov and Razin. Folk songs and legends, which truthfully reveal the aspirations and hopes of the toiling masses, are also valuable source material.

The economic and political demands of the peasants were as yet not clearly formulated. However the slogans under which the uprisings took place and the forms and methods of struggle adopted by the rebellious masses indicate that the objective content of the demands of the peasants was the liquidation of feudal-serf relationships. The peasantry struggled against serf oppression and exploitation. It was they and the kholopy under the leadership of Bolotnikov, who constituted the chief motivating force of the first peasant uprising. Their predominance also determined the social trend and, to a significant degree, the demands of the rebels.

The revolting peasantry was supported by the petty officials and townspeople, the lower layers of the Cossacks, and the riflemen. Various nobles with their retinues also went over to the side of the rebels, but they constituted only an insignificant part of Bolotnikov's troops and hence did not determine the objectives of the uprising, which in all its stages was of a clearly expressed anti-feudal nature. The aims of the nobles who joined the uprising were directly contrary to those of the rebelling peasants and kholopy. This explains the treachery of the nobles and their reversion to the camp of the enemy at the most critical and decisive moment in the uprising.

The appeals contained in the proclamations, the so-called "Lists" of Bolotnikov addressed to the population, indicate the objectives of the uprising. They contain an appeal to the kholopy "to kill one's own boyars . . . foreigners, and all merchants" and "to plunder their households." [6] This indicates that the uprising was primarily directed against the ruling class of feudalists. The peasantry fought also against the merchants, who ruined and plundered the population. The rebels took revenge on the hated voevody. Bolotnikov "began to seize voevody in the cities and to imprison them in dungeons." At the same time, serf dependence was eliminated. In one of the petitions of that time it is stated that among the rebels at Astrakhan "slaves were freed and were given homesteads." [7]

The historical documents testify that in the areas of the uprising the peasants and kholopy ruined and burned the estates of the feudalists and seized their property and cattle. The effectiveness and scope of the rebellion can be judged by the petitions of the nobles which were made to Tsar Vasilii Shuiskii. They complained that their estates "were ruined completely by traitors to the sovereign." [8]

The historico-political writings of the spokesmen of the boyars of the first half of the seventeenth century give a sufficiently clear picture of the revenge the rebels took against the feudalists and of the aspirations of the peasantry and kholopy to seize the feudal estates. Extremely significant in this respect are the remarks by the scribe, Ivan Timofeev. He writes in his *Annals* that the peasants and kholopy, or, as he calls them, the "rabble," "had firmly in mind some rather rash ideas and were even inclined to eliminate the leaders and choose better men, particularly ones more outstanding than they themselves; they planned to put to death by torture all of the leaders and *to take their estates for themselves.*" [9] The reaction of the boyars' spokesmen to the struggle of the revolting masses against the ruling class indicates that the activities of the rebels dealt a strong blow to the feudalist class.

---

[6] See Smirnov, *Vosstanie Bolotnikova,* p. 495.

[7] A. M. Gnevushev, *Akty vremen pravleniia tsaria Vasiliia Shuiskogo* [Documents Pertaining to the Administration of Tsar Vasilii Shuiskii] (Moscow: 1914), p. 206.

[8] *Ibid.,* pp. 255–7.

[9] *Vremennik Ivana Timofeeva* [Journal of Ivan Timofeev] (Moscow-Leningrad: AS USSR, 1951), p. 303. (Italics mine—E. Ia.)

Historical documents evidence the forcible seizure of monastery lands by the peasants. Thus, for example, in the "Acts of the Time of the Administration of Tsar Vasilii Shuiskii," documentary material refers to the dispute between the peasants and the Troitse-Sergievskii monastery. It is said that in 1607 the peasants of the black Vottskaia volost wanted to take forcible possession of the fields and grasslands seized from them by the monastery.[10]

The evidence presented by I. I. Smirnov in his book, *The Uprising of Bolotnikov,* shows that the peasants who seized the land from the monasteries destroyed all former signs of monastery ownership of such land. They plowed across boundaries, dug up boundary marks, and burned out brands on trees.[11]

The peasant movement under Razin's leadership carried, as did the earlier one, the slogan: "Exterminate the secular vampires, the boyar-traitors."[12] This battle cry characterizes the class orientation of the uprising. Razin was supported by the "bonded and disgraced" peasants, the poor Cossacks, and the lower layers of the town population, the "mob."

One of the folk songs of the Don Cossacks contained these words:

Cossacks, my brothers,
And you poor, wretched, and needy,
Come from wherever you are!
You comrades, beloved friends,
Come brothers, come brothers,
Towards freedom—real freedom![13]

The class differentiation of the forces led by Razin was more clearly defined than that in the previous uprising under Bolotnikov. The feudalists were opposed by the heterogeneous camp of the oppressed popular masses, who were united by one aim—to liberate themselves from unbearable oppression and serf dependence.

The description of the historical events, showing the relation of the rebels to the various classes of society, evokes keen interest. "And the rebellious Cossacks travel through districts and massacre those pomeshchiki and votchiniki who possess peasants, but they neither massacre nor rob black peasants [i.e. free peasants], nor boyar peoples, nor Cos-

---

[10] Gnevushev, *op. cit.,* p. 15.

[11] See Smirnov, *op. cit.,* pp. 497 and 500.

[12] See *Akty istoricheskie* [Historical Documents] (St. Petersburg: 1842), IV, 433.

[13] A. M. Listopadov, *Donskie istoricheskie pesni* [Historical Songs of the Don] (Rostov-on-the-Don: 1946), p. 21.

sacks, nor any other serving people." [14] This again testifies to the fact that the main force of the uprising was directed against the ruling class of the feudalists—the boyars and pomeshchiki—and against feudal exploitation. The Cossacks and peasants, congregating around Razin, declared: "And now we shall go after the boyars and voevody along the Volga because those boyars and voevody are starving us . . ." "Those boyars and voevody seized us, hanged us, decapitated us, and drowned us." [15]

A beggarly existence and the heavy oppression of serfdom, resulting in the righteous hatred of the popular masses, led them to settle scores with the feudalists and tsarist officials. In Astrakhan, Tsaritsyn, and in other towns seized by the rebels, the all-powerful voevody and their close associates were slain. The evidence in the case of the revolt of Stepan Razin states: "and having taken Astrakhan, they captured the boyar voevod Prince Ivan Semenovich Prozorovskii and his colleagues and those people who had not joined in the thievery; they flogged them and robbed their households." [16]

The relation of the revolting masses to the various classes and layers of society is also clearly depicted in folk songs. One of the most popular, entitled "What Took Place at the City of Saratov," describes the revenge inflicted by the rebels on the governor of Astrakhan:

They severed the governor's boisterous head,
And threw it into Mother Volga.[17]

The revenge taken on the governor was prompted by his cruel treatment of the population:

You, governor, you were toward us too severe,
You assaulted us, ruined us, and sent us into exile,
And you shot at our wives and children at the gates! [18]

The masses also turned against the rich merchants, whom they saw as allies of the ruling class, the feudalists. In a West Siberian folk song

---

[14] *TsGADA, Razriadnyi prikaz* [Office of Miscellaneous Affairs] Column No. 417, sheet 223.

[15] *Krestianskaia voina pod predvoditelstvom Stepana Razina. Sbornik dokumentov* [Peasant War Under the Leadership of Stepan Razin. Collection of Documents] (Moscow: AS USSR, 1954), I, 253.

[16] *Akty istoricheskie,* IV, 402.

[17] V. F. Miller, *Istoricheskie pesni russkogo naroda XVI–XVII vv. Sbornik otdeleniia russkogo iazyka i slovesnosti imperatorskoi Akademii nauk* [Historical Songs of the Russian People XVI–XVII Centuries. Collection of the Department of Russian Language and Literature of the Imperial Academy of Sciences] (Petrograd: 1915), XCIII, 775.

[18] *Ibid.*

it is said that the rebels plundered the merchants because they concealed the governor:

> Merchants kept secret the whereabouts of the governor;
> They hid him under their wares.[19]

The class nature and the aims of the uprising are most clearly expressed in Stepan Razin's declarations to the people: "to kill all princes and boyars, persons of high rank, and all Russian nobility; to root out all forms of hierarchy and authority and to bring about an order wherein all will be equal." [20] These words convincingly show that in the second peasant war the revolting peasantry struggled for the complete liquidation of the feudal-serf structure.

Karl Marx himself was interested in the uprising of Stepan Razin, as is shown in his synopsis of the book by N. I. Kostomarov, *The Revolt of Stenka Razin.* Marx stressed Kostomarov's view that one of the main reasons for the uprising of the popular masses under the leadership of Razin was *"the relationship between landowners and workers"* [21] and that the revolt was preceded by the sternest measures binding the peasant to the land.[22] The very system of state administration in Russia, which was formed in the seventeenth century after the ascent to power of the Romanovs, caused popular dissatisfaction and prepared the soil for the uprising. "The entire order of Russia at that time, *the relationship of the estates* [classes, adds Marx to Kostomarov's text], their rights, financial status, administration—all this gave the Cossacks stimulus in the movement of popular discontent, and *the entire mid-era of the seventeenth century* was a preparation for the epoch of Stenka Razin." [23]

The goal of Bolotnikov and Razin was complete liberation of the peasants and kholopy from serf dependence. In the areas where uprisings occurred they freed all enserfed peasants and abolished the enslaving charters. The peasants were released not only from serf subordination, but from all forms of duties and taxes. In the towns liberated by Bolotnikov we are told that "during those troubled years the peasants, who previously belonged to nobles and lesser boyars, together with us city dwellers, performed neither city nor palisade works, dug no ditches, built no towers, paid no taxes to the sovereign's treasury . . .

---

[19] *Ibid.*, XCIII, 716.

[20] K. I. Averin, "Istoricheskie materialy o Stenke Razine" [Historical Materials On Stenka Razin], *Moskvitianin* [Moscovite], IV, No. 7 (1841), p. 169.

[21] K. Marx, "Stenka Razin," *Molodaia gvardiia* [Young Guard], No. 1 (1926), p. 109.

[22] *Ibid.*, p. 107.

[23] *Ibid.*, p. 109.

transported no wagons, and neither provided nor shared supplies." [24]

On the pomestia and monastery votchiny the peasants refused to pay taxes and to fulfill their feudal obligations, barshchina and obrok. Thus, for example, according to the testimony of the petition of the Abbot of the Antoniev-Siiskii monastery, "monastery peasants have become too powerful for me to handle; they listen neither to our decrees, nor pay the tribute or obrok or the third of their produce to the monastery as do the peasants of other monasteries, and they neither work nor obey me or the brethren, and thereby cause great losses to me, the abbot." [25]

In towns taken by Stepan Razin taxes were abolished, and even the cadasters were burned. Authority in towns and villages was transferred to the Cossack "circle." Nobles and merchants forming the higher administration were executed or thrown into prison. Their property was divided among the rebels and the poorest classes of the population.

Nevertheless, the leaders of the peasant movements, Bolotnikov and Razin, had no clear idea of the future economic and political structure of society. They were unable to formulate a definite socio-economic program. Their wishes did not exceed the creation of the Cossack authority of the "circle" and the establishment of a state order headed by the "good tsar," but without boyars and pomeshchiki. Bolotnikov, for example, in his "Lists" called for "taking an oath of allegiance to Tsar Dimitry." I. V. Stalin, describing the leaders of the peasant uprisings, has stated: "speaking of Razin and Pugachev, it should never be forgotten that they were tsarists: they opposed the landlords, but stood for 'a good tsar.' Such was their slogan." [26]

This inability to formulate an economic and political program was explained by the position of the enserfed peasants. The disorganized peasantry was hampered by ignorance and lawlessness. V. I. Lenin and I. V. Stalin have shown with exhaustive comprehensiveness that the reason for the weakness and shortcomings of the peasant uprisings lies in the feudal-serfdom system. The spontaneous revolts could not succeed because in the Russia of that time there was still no working class to lead the struggle of the rebelling masses. "Separate peasant uprisings, even if they are not as 'brigand-like' and disorganized as that of Stepan Razin, cannot succeed. A peasant uprising can be vic-

---

[24] S. B. Veselovskii, ed., *Akty podmoskovnykh opolchenii i Zemskogo sobora 1611–1613 gg.* [Documents of Sub-Moscow Armed Revolts and the Zemskii Sobor of 1611–1613] (Moscow: 1911), p. 16.

[25] *Istoricheskii arkhiv,* I (1936), p. 35.

[26] Stalin, *Sochineniia,* XIII, 113.

torious only when it is combined with a workers' uprising and when the workers lead the peasants." [27]

Even though the first spontaneous uprisings of the peasants were cruelly put down, they had enormous historical significance, because they dealt a strong blow to the ruling class. Under the leadership of Bolotnikov and Razin they were the first historical attempts at a struggle of the oppressed peasant masses against feudal oppression and exploitation. The ideas and feats of Bolotnikov and Razin, as well as those of the entire rebelling peasantry, continued to live in the consciousness of the masses and had an undeniable influence on the further development of Russian social thought.

The Economic Demands of the Merchant Class

The emerging class of urban merchants presented their demands and proposed new tasks for the economic policy of the Russian state. The general tenor of economic thought of this segment of the population was clearly expressed in their petitions and in government acts and decrees. Their "speeches" before the Landed Assembly stressed the oppression by the big feudalists and described their own position: "and we, your slaves, are merchants, members of gostinnaia (merchant) and sukonnaia (textile) sotni (guilds), and we obtain our livelihood from our own crafts and have neither pomestia nor votchiny." [28]

The development of trade and the crafts, which were the mainstay of the urban population, faced many obstacles created by the feudal nature of town life. The merchants demanded the liquidation of the "white settlements" and tried to obtain monopoly rights in trade and the crafts. At the same time they insisted on the abolition of the monopolies and privileges—"tarkhanov"—which the government bestowed upon the huge monasteries, some of the richest votchinniki, and groups of "guests" and foreign merchants.

The competition and predominance of foreign merchants on the Russian market had an even more negative influence on the trade and crafts of the urban population. Strongly organized, the foreign merchants often acted in the role of brokers and seized control of the domestic market and of the transit trade. Complaints about the power of foreign merchants and demands to limit their rights and privileges are found in almost all the "speeches" and petitions of the merchants

---

[27] *Ibid.*, XIII, 112–3.

[28] *Akty otnosiashchiesia k istorii Zemskikh soborov* [Documents Relating to the History of Zemskii Sobors] (Moscow: 1909), p. 55.

of the time. "And the trades, Sovereign, among us thy slaves, in the past few years have become much worse, because all of our trades in Moscow and in all towns have been taken over by many foreigners, Germans and *"kizylbashtsy,"* [that is, merchants from Central Asia] who arrive in Moscow and other towns with all kinds of commodities and sell them. . . ." [29] Thus, for example, pleaded the merchants at the Zemskii Sobor of 1642.

In the petition of 1646, the merchants and petty merchants again posed the question of limiting the privileges of foreigners. Even more emphatic demands for the limitation of these rights were contained in the petition of 1649.[30] However the struggle of the urban merchants for the creation of favorable conditions for their commercial-industrial activities did not touch the bases of feudalism. It proceeded within the framework and on the foundation of serving feudalism with commodity production. The basic demands of the merchant class were supported by the nobility, insofar as the latter was interested in the development of commercial relationships and the strengthening of the centralized feudal state.

The economic demands of the new merchant class can be most fully seen in the Code of Law of 1649, particularly in the articles based on the petitions of the urban merchants dealing with the liquidation of the "white settlements" and the institution of mortgages. This Code classified the urban people into a special social stratus of taxpayers. The city settlements, which previously belonged to the tax-free monasteries and the boyar-votchinniki, were "transferred to the sovereign," that is, confiscated, and then passed on to the towns. The inhabitants of the "white settlements"—poor peasants, craftsmen and traders—became "taxable" along with all urban dwellers. The townspeople received monopoly rights on trade and crafts.

As a result of the recognition of the mutual interests of the upper-class city population and the tsarist power, a union was formed in the middle of the seventeenth century between the tsarist authority and the medieval burghers.[31]

The decision of the Zemskii Sobor to liquidate the "white settlements," as well as the mortgages, took the character of a reform in the city structure. In effect, the reform created the necessary conditions for the trading and industrial activities of the urban merchants and thus strengthened the merchant class. As a consequence, the number

---

[29] *Ibid.*

[30] See *Sbornik kniazia Khilkova* [Collection of Prince Khilkov] (St. Petersburg: 1879), pp. 238–40.

[31] See P. P. Smirnov, *Posadskie liudi i ikh klassovaia borba*, II, 240.

of city people engaged in trade and industry increased markedly. The change created a sharp distinction between the urban and the completely enserfed peasant population; it thereby hastened the growth of the social division of labor between the city and the village. All these developments created the prerequisites for further growth of commodity production and facilitated the expansion of markets within the country.

Undoubtedly favoring the interests of the trading bourgeoisie and the nobility, the Code of 1649 set forth detailed conditions for the use of hired labor and foresaw the possibility of free hiring. "And should peasants or the poor hire themselves out to work: Those peasants and poor are allowed to hire themselves out to work with or without record to persons of all official ranks. And those persons who hire them shall keep neither dwelling nor court records nor enslaving papers; neither shall they be enserfed; upon completion of their services these hired persons shall be released without delay." [32]

The demands of the urban merchants and "guests" for the limitation of the privileges of foreign merchants found partial expression in separate government enactments, such as the Commercial Charter of 1654 and, particularly, the New Commercial Code of 1667, which significantly strengthened and systematized the limitations on the trading activities of foreigners in Russia.

The Economic Views of the Spokesmen of the Boyars in the First Half of the Seventeenth Century

For the oppressed popular masses the first peasant war alone should have been sufficient to shake their faith in the durability and invulnerability of the existing conditions of social life. On the other side, the spokesmen of the ruling class, alarmed at the hitherto unknown force of the peasant movement, came to the defense of feudal ownership and feudal exploitation and sharply censured the antifeudal actions of the peasantry.

The apology for feudal society was clearly expressed in historical-political treaties of the first half of the seventeenth century, in the *Chronicle* of the clerk Ivan Timofeev,[33] in the *Narrations* of

[32] *Ulozheni gosudaria, tsaria i velikogo kniazia Alekseia Mikhailovicha* [The Code of Sovereign, Tsar, and Grand Prince Alexei Mikhailovich] (St. Petersburg: 1913), Chap. XI, Article 32, p. 137.

[33] V. P. Adrianova-Perets, ed., *Vremennik Ivana Timofeeva* [Journal of Ivan Timofeev] (Moscow-Leningrad: AS USSR, 1951).

Avraamii Palitsyn,[34] in the *Stories* of Prince Ivan Mikhailovich Katyrev-Rostovskii,[35] and in a number of other works.

The above-mentioned works, which describe the historical events taking place in Russia at the beginning of the seventeenth century, contain fundamentally similar social ideas and express the identical class orientation of all their authors. The initial position from which these writers begin is the idea of the eternal and unshakeable nature of the existing earthly order.

Clerk Ivan Timofeev wrote in his *Chronicle* that the division between lord and slave had always existed and that it was the natural order, set up on high. He did not distinguish between slaves and enserfed peasants. The slaves to whom he refers, and who on the basis of canon law included all persons subordinate to masters, were to resignedly submit to their lord and to the autocratic tsar in particular. In his view this had been the way of things even before the time when the Russian tsars themselves maintained the established natural orders. "For many centuries and up to now we have not contradicted them, for it is written that the slave must be obedient to his master." [36]

Timofeev sharply criticized Ivan the Terrible and Boris Godunov for violating the old customs by bringing nobles into the administration and thus creating the conditions under which the earlier single class of feudalists was divided and weakened. Pursuing his anti-noble attitude, he accuses the nobles of being inexperienced in the affairs of state; they are "worthless" people, sowing discord, caring only for their own well-being and enrichment, and thereby causing discontent and anger among the popular masses. Timofeev also criticizes those boyars, the "pillars" of feudal society, who did not display, in his view, the necessary bravery and firmness and who, steeped in "wordless silence," did not show active resistance to the policy of "the Terrible" and Godunov.

In the destruction of the old orders and the weakening of the forces and influences of the boyars Timofeev saw the main cause of the popular uprisings which occurred in the beginning of the seventeenth century. When the masters began to change the old laws and customs, he writes, then "even among the obedient slaves the natural fear of the subject for the ruler began to diminish." [37]

He criticized the rebels—the peasants and kholopy—for refusing "to

[34] See "Pamiatniki drevnei russkoi pismennosti, otnosiashchiesia k Smutnomu vremeni" [Memorials of Ancient Russian Literature Pertaining to the Time of Troubles], *Russkaia istoricheskaia biblioteka* (2nd edition), XIII.

[35] *Ibid.*

[36] Adrianova-Perets, *op. cit.*, p. 282.

[37] *Ibid.*, p. 283.

subordinate themselves and to submit to the authorities in the cities, which the Tsar had established by divine right." [38] Timofeev called the peasant uprising headed by Bolotnikov "disobedient self-rule of the slaves," which upset all laws and customs established earlier; "the small have begun to vanquish the great, the young the old, the dishonorable the honorable, and the slaves their masters." [39]

To him the strengthening of the state power headed by "a true tsar," who could restore the former power and influence of the boyars and reestablish the old laws and customs, was an important task. The essence of his ideas is to show the importance of the solidarity of the ruling class of feudalists for the defense of feudal ownership and the struggle against the exploiting peasant masses and against foreign enemies.

Avraamii Palitsyn and Katyrev-Rostovskii were also ardent defenders of boyar interests. However, the intensified class struggle made these spokesmen for the ruling class realize that excessive burdens of feudal obligations and taxes led to the ruin and impoverishment of the peasantry and caused sharp discontent and indignation among the popular masses. Thus in the above-mentioned works the aspirations of the feudalists toward excessive enrichment are censured. "This evil up to now has been plain for all to see—they want glory and wealth as fast as possible and they enrich themselves with the aid of all forms of injustice. If they attain their goal through tears and blood, they do not repent, they pay no heed. Their only interest on earth is how to obtain what they want. Though they know this to be sinful, they feel no fear or horror about it whatsoever; no one is ashamed any more before his elders, and as one they seem to try to get all their abundant treasure by dishonest means," wrote Ivan Timofeev.[40]

These motives are also questioned in the *Narrations* of Avraamii Palitsyn. The latter not only criticizes those who aspire "to possess much wealth," but he expresses himself also against increased taxes. As one of the reasons "for the hatred of all the world" toward Boris Godunov, Palitsyn pointed to the fact that the people were aroused by the innovations of Godunov, the higher taxes, the numerous distributions of leases, and so forth.

The Polish-Swedish intervention at the beginning of the seventeenth century emphasized the need to defend national independence. In contrast to the reactionary boyars, who put their narrow class interests above those of the nation and who entered into agreements with the

---

[38] *Ibid.*, pp. 302–3.
[39] *Ibid.*, p. 285.
[40] *Ibid.*, p. 297.

foreign interventionists, the most thoughtful spokesmen of the boyars began to comprehend the general national interests and sprang to the defense of the Fatherland.

The authors of the historical-political works of the first half of the seventeenth century—Timofeev, Palitsyn and Katyrev-Rostovskii—called for the mobilization of the nation's forces and stressed the people's responsibility for the fate of the Fatherland. They attempted to point the way toward the strengthening of the political and economic position of the state and its protection. In the face of class restrictions, however, these spokesmen of the boyars were unable to provide positive and unified political-economic programs. In an attempt to reduce the class struggle they called upon the feudalists to refrain from the excessive accumulation of wealth, to return to more patriarchal feudal relationships, and to lower taxes. In the political realm, Timofeev, Palitsyn, and Katyrev-Rostovskii proposed to set up a feudal monarchy based on the boyars, who could, in their view, play a leading role in the administration of the state. At a time when monetary-commodity relationships were rapidly developing and the multinational centralized state was being strengthened, such demands were reactionary and attested to the inability of their authors to recognize the new progressive tendencies in the historical development of Russia.

The Economic Views of the Spokesmen of the Nobility

After the expulsion of the interventionists, certain members of the nobility concerned themselves with economic questions relating to the improvement of their economic and political position. The new boyar aristocracy—the big votchinniki, who received great privileges and influence—seized not only the free lands, but often lands belonging to the nobles. Utilizing the "fixed years," they enticed away peasants and concealed fugitives. This caused discontent among the pomestie-nobility and worsened still further the relations between the two groups of the ruling class. Among them they struggled for land and for manpower—the enserfed peasants. The nobility aimed to strengthen its ruling position in the country. Its members expressed their views in numerous petitions, "speeches," and in decrees of the Zemskii Sobors. They complained about "powerful persons" who, having received pomestia and votchiny, oppressed the local small landholding and landless nobles. The nobles asked for the return of lands seized by the rich votchinniki or for new lands to replace them: "Sire, have mercy on us, your poor slaves, ruined and helpless, without pomestie, or deserted pomestie, or small pomestie, and endow us with a pomestie and/or a money grant." [41]

Simultaneously they demanded that the government take measures against the concealment "by strong persons" of fugitive peasants and that it abolish the "fixed years," and they insisted on universal registration and the legal binding of the peasants to the pomeshchiki and votchinniki.

At the same time the nobility strove to obtain the pomestie lands, sought a law of land inheritance, and asked for the change of the pomestia into votchiny. In "speeches" the nobles objected to the lack of justice in legal cases: " we, your slaves, are ruined, more than Turkish or Crimean Mohammedans, by the Moscovite intriguers and by injustices and by unjust courts. This we, your slaves, nobles of various towns and, lesser boyars, believe and declare." [42] They posed the question of court reforms and demanded that they be judged by the "decree of the sovereign."

The demands of the nobility were put into more definite form in the Code of Law of 1649. This historical document gives a clear picture of the direction in which the economic thought of the nobility of the seventeenth century proceeded. The Code raised first of all the question of the land ownership of the nobility. According to the Code, the distribution of land allotments for service was to be made in accordance with the services and ranks of the nobility. The amount of the land parcels was also increased. In addition, it fixed the owner's right to bequeath the pomestia under condition of continuation of the service, as well as the right to change pomestia into votchiny.

In the interests of the nobility another matter of great significance was decided—the question of man-power, or, in other words, the problem of the serf dependency of the peasants. Having abolished "fixed years," and having set a great fine for concealment of fugitive peasants, the Code at the same time recognized the inheritability of serfdom and the right of the pomeshchik to own the peasant, thus legalizing the complete enserfment of the peasantry.

The Code furthered the consolidation of the absolute monarchy, the most acceptable form of authority for the nobility. It set in order the system of state administration, and improved and altered the judicial legislation in accordance with the demands of the nobility.

The Code of 1649 was a legal superstructure based on a feudal society. This superstructure helped to curb the oppressed masses and strengthened the economic and political position of the nobility, as

[41] *Akty otnosiashchiesia k istorii Zemskikh soborov,* p. 52.

[42] *Ibid.,* p. 54.

well as the feudal right of the nobles to the land, labor, and person of the peasantry.

In the middle of the sevententh century a number of progressive statesmen incorporated the many urgent problems of Russian development into a broader plan and advanced as fundamental historic objectives the strengthening of the economic position and independence of Russia. Among this group can be included the important statesman B. I. Morozov (1590–1661). A large landholder-votchinnik, an outstanding business man, and a politician, Morozov is well known as a zealous partisan of the development of trade and industry, and as a financial expert.

He began his service in the court as a table setter and chamberlain, and later became a tutor of Tsarevich Aleksei. After the death of the first Romanov, he filled the post of chief of the *Streletskii prikaz* [Musketeer's Department], the Great Treasury, and a number of other institutions and, in fact, guided all the domestic and foreign policy of the Russian state. With the coming to power of Morozov, a boyar-noble government was created, in which a relatively great role was played by those who had come from among the urban merchants. A number of distinguished members of boyar families were forced into the background and eliminated from the administration of the country.

The new governmental organization determined to a significant degree the direction of the economic policy introduced by Morozov. An influential wholesale merchant himself, Morozov defended the interests of the nobility and, at the same time, energetically promoted those of the merchant class. Striving to satisfy the economic demands of the nobles, he promised to take measures against the flight of the peasants and to enserf "peasants and the poor" and all their kin. Even before the adoption of the Code of 1649 an ukaz was issued to register all the "servile population, peasants, and poor, and those to whom they belonged." [43]

Simultaneously, Morozov exerted no little effort in the development of industrial and trade activity among the urban people, and he energetically encouraged the formation of the urban population into a city *"tiagloe,"* that is, a taxable estate. In reply to the petitions of the deeply indebted townspeople, who complained of the oppression of the "tax free persons" and the untaxed trade, Morozov introduced "de-boyarization" in a number of towns.[44] He elaborated a plan for confiscation of the votchina rights to the city lands—the "white settlements"—and liquidated the institution of mortgages. Laws and charters

[43] P. P. Smirnov, *Posadskie liudi i ikh klassovaia borba,* II, 13.
[44] *Ibid.,* II, 124.

drawn by him and issued to the towns formed the basis for the nineteenth chapter of the Code of 1649 concerning the abolition of the "white settlements," that is, the tax-free settlements, and the elimination of mortgages.[45]

Morozov supported the demands of the urban population for the establishment of the right to use municipal lands and of the monopoly right to engage in trade and crafts. He listened attentively to the complaints of merchants about the domination of foreigners and introduced a number of measures to limit their privileges to trade in Russia. In reply to the petition of merchants in 1646, the government, in which Morozov played a main role, revoked the grant charters and privileges of the English, Dutch, and Hamburg merchants. Morozov fought no less energetically against the privileges enjoyed by separate groups of Russian "guests" [that is, big merchants] and monasteries. From all of this it is clear that Morozov actively aided in the development of trade, which he saw as one of the important sources of income for the state treasury.

This policy corresponded with his views on money. Looking at the latter as the "force of all forces," [46] Morozov felt that money should be put into circulation and bring income to its owner. From his own colossal fortune, 80,000 rubles (which translated into the gold money of 1913 amounted to 1,400,000 rubles) were lent to the government. This brought him an enormous profit.[47]

Being chief of the Great Treasury, Morozov paid much attention to the improvement of state finances and to the regulation of the money in circulation. He tried to solve this extremely important and current question by increasing the tax assessment and by rigidly economizing the monetary funds. He curtailed expenditures for the maintenance of the members of the tsar's court and administrative apparatus, particularly that of the serving people.

During the time that Morozov managed the state finances, tax assessments were greatly changed. The previous tax unit, the "plowland tax," was replaced by the "square field," which considered not only the land but the working force as well. In addition Morozov strengthened control over the collection of taxes by introducing extremely cruel measures against nonpayers.

A tax increase was effected by abolishing the privileges—"tarkhanov"

---

[45] *Ibid.*, II, 273–304.

[46] See *Khoziaistvo krupnogo feodala-krepostnika XVII v.* [The Economy of A Large Feudal-Serfowner in the XVII Century] (Leningrad: AS USSR, 1933), Pt. I, p. LXXII.

[47] *Ibid.*, p. LXXIII.

—enjoyed by the monasteries, "guests," and foreign merchants, and also by levying taxes on the population of the liquidated "white settlements." In 1646, by imposing a tax on salt, Morozov's government in effect levied high taxes on objects of prime necessity. For the most part, these taxes affected seriously the least secure portion of the population in the towns and villages.

Morozov's activity in the field of city administration turned the huge votchinniki and clergy against him, while his financial policy, particularly the high tax on salt, brought sharp protests from broad classes of the town population. These forces brought on the explosion of the class struggle in the form of the "salt riots" of 1648. As a result, Morozov was removed from state affairs in 1648 and temporarily exiled from Moscow. On his return, he continued for some time to manage the domestic and foreign policy of the government unofficially, and he took an active part in the compilation of the Code of 1649.

Notwithstanding the inefficacy of several of his financial measures, his policy stimulated the development of trade and industry and was for its time basically progressive.

Morozov's closest assistant and one of the authors of the program for indirect taxes and other government enactments was the Yaroslav merchant Nazarii Chistoi, the thoughtful clerk of the ambassadorial prikaz. Another important merchant, Vasilii Shorin, also took part in the preparation and execution of important government measures in the economic life of the country.

One of the prominent statesmen of this period was A. S. Matveev (1625–1682). Coming from the family of a clerk, he received a good education, occupied a number of responsible posts, and headed the Little Russian and ambassadorial prikazi. Matveev displayed an awareness of the changes taking place in the Russian economy and an understanding of the role and significance of monetary-trade relationships. He gained a reputation by his practical measures, especially the replacement of the existing system of supplying the Moscow army with provisions in kind by money payment, a scheme which was cheaper and more expedient for the government.

Matveev did much to set in order the work of the mint. He broadened the trading relationships with foreign countries and concluded trade treaties with foreign merchants. Well known, for example, is the agreement which he concluded with an Armenian company for supplying Persian silk on advantageous terms to the Russian treasury and the merchant class. Matveev was one of the initiators and organizers of a Russian expedition to China.

The most ardent exponent of the new direction of Russian economic thought in the seventeenth century was the outstanding statesman, politician, diplomat, and initiator of important state decrees, A. L. Ordyn-Nashchokin. With profound understanding of the fundamental tasks which faced the Russia of his time, Ordyn-Nashchokin introduced a number of far-reaching measures in the economic and political fields.[48]

As an illustration of the economic thought of this time, the works of the Croatian, Iurii Krizhanich (1617–1683), written during a prolonged stay in Russia, are of particular interest. In his fundamental work "Political Thoughts" ("Politics"), Krizhanich concerned himself with the question of how to increase the wealth in the country. Discussing the need for developing productive forces, Krizhanich made broad plans for measures in the fields of trade, finance, industry, agriculture, and state structure. Krizhanich's "Politics" remained unpublished; it was placed in the Tsar's library and was not made public until the middle of the nineteenth century.

It is important to note the critical regard with which several economic proposals by foreigners were met in Russia. An example is the well-known project for the increase of the income of the Russian state suggested in 1651 by the Frenchman, Jean de Gron.[49] Jean de Gron endeavored to interest the Russian government in a plan for quick enrichment of the treasury by means of large-scale construction of ships in Russia and their sale abroad. By his calculation, Russia could receive an enormous income—sixty barrels (*bochek*) of gold per year from the sale of the ships. This clearly projected plan, however, came to naught.

The important Danish merchant and manufacturer, Peter Marselis, having lived in Russia and with business interests there, strove for less cumbersome and actually duty-free trade for foreigners; in particular he sought the abolition of the articles of the New Commercial Code of 1667 regarding the obligatory surrender, at a compulsory rate of exchange, of gold and *efimki* brought into Russia by foreign merchants in exchange for Russian and foreign coins. In the memorandum which he submitted to the ambassadorial prikaz in 1669 Marselis insisted on the free import of gold and efimki into Russia and tried to prove that the collection of the customs duties in gold was disadvantageous to the Russians. Marselis' memorandum was submitted for consideration at a meeting of Moscow merchants. After examining his proposals, the meeting expressed its views in the following words: "And he, Peter, proposed only a relatively small gain in efimki, while in return for that

[48] See Chapter Nine.

[49] *TsGADA. Dela o vyezdakh inostrantsev v Rossiiu, 1651 g.* [Affairs Pertaining to the Entry of Foreigners into Russia in 1651], Fond 150, d. 12.

small gain he hoped to capture all trade in Moscow and in other cities. He also asked in that memorandum that foreigners be allowed to bring to Moscow as well as to other cities gold coins and efimki, sell their wares to everyone, exchange their wares duty-free, and for that money purchase various commodities in Moscow and in other cities. By means of this idea he desires, together with other foreigners, to establish a monolopy over the trade of all the Russian people." [50]

Nor was Marselis' proposal supported in the ambassadorial prikaz, headed at that time by Ordyn-Nashchokin. The latter's attitude to the proposal, which was shared by the Moscow merchants, indicates awareness among certain progressive layers of society of the pressing tasks of economic development of Russia and the necessity of defending her economic independence from the insistent machinations of foreigners striving to control the Russian market and to deprive Russia of economic and political independence.

The new ideas expressed by the foremost people of Russia met with resistance from the reactionary circles of the boyars and clergy, who insisted upon their privileges and attacked any changes in the economic and political life of the country. They opposed the spread of culture and enlightenment.

In this conflict of different trends of Russian social thought it was inevitable that the new progressive direction would be victorious. The idea of economic self-sufficiency and independence for Russia and the realization of the need for the development of her productive forces were evermore widely disseminated and acknowledged. Later these became the basis of the policies introduced by Peter I.

---

[50] *Ibid., Prikaznye dela starykh let, 1668 g.* [Administrative Affairs of Years Past, 1668], d. 434, sheets 37–40.

CHAPTER 9. *The Spokesman of the Struggle for the Economic Independence of Russia—A. L. Ordyn-Nashchokin.*

The General Characteristics of Ordyn-Nashchokin's Political-Economic Views

In the seventeenth century a new stage in the development of Russian economic thought began. What distinguishes the thinkers and economists of this phase from the majority of representatives of Russian economic thought examined above is, above all, their clear understanding and penetrating analysis of the necessity to overcome Russia's economic lag behind the other, more developed, European countries and thus to preserve and strengthen her independence. These Russian economists were endowed with a great breadth of vision and had a national approach to economic questions. Increasingly their attention focused not only on the separate branches of the Russian economy, but on the national economy as a whole. These economists perceived the interrelation among the various segments of the economy: agriculture, industry, trade, finance, and communication; and in their consideration of the problems of the country they acknowledged the inseparable bonds among these spheres.

The thinkers and statesmen of this epoch were united not only in their recognition of the need for major economic reforms, but also in a common understanding of the direction of evolving economic transformations. They saw the way toward the elimination of the country's economic backwardness and a guarantee of its independence through such economic reforms as the creation of a native heavy industry, the development of domestic and foreign trade, the creation of a native merchant fleet, the establishment of canal systems and other means of communication, the improvement of agriculture, the reorganization of the country's financial system, and other measures. An evolving program of Russia's economic transformation was worked out, the basis of which was a definite and orderly system of advanced views. These economic changes were undoubtedly of a progressive nature and answered the pressing demands of Russian society.

The economists of this period supported the feudal-serf structure of the country. They regarded it as a natural and stable basis of social life, and the economic transformations which they conceived would have preserved the compulsory labor of the enserfed peasants. In their considerations they began gradually to recognize the advantages of freely hired labor over the compulsory labor of the serfs, but nevertheless, the problem of a working force for heavy industry was attacked on the basis of feudal-serf methods. This placed the stamp of historical limitation on the economic views and programs of the thinkers and statesmen of this period.

The Russian economists of the second half of the seventeenth and first half of the eighteenth century were also characterized by a common understanding of the role of the feudal-absolutist state in the realization of the country's economic development. They assigned to the state a decisive part in these changes; they recognized the right and obligation of the feudal state to interfere actively in the economic life of the country, to establish protection, supervision, and regulation of the economic activity of its subjects. Enormous significance was accorded the patronage of trade monopolies and the bestowal of privileges, as well as other measures to encourage enterprising activity.

Perception concerning the role of the state and administration distinguished Russian economists of this era from thinkers and statesmen of preceding, and later, periods of Russian history. For the first time the question was raised in theoretical terms of the role of the state in the general economic life of the country. These writers also differed from the economists of later periods of feudal Russia, for the attitude toward the role of the state changed when the principles of competition and private initiative became widespread.

A. L. Ordyn-Nashchokin occupies an exalted place among the foremost representatives of Russian economic thought in the seventeenth century. Although he did not leave any special economic works, his statements on various political and economic problems in letters and reports to the Tsar, the projects for laws which he compiled, and, finally, all of his state activity enable one to speak of him as the outstanding policy-maker and economist of the second half of the seventeenth century.

Afanasii Lavrentevich Ordyn-Nashchokin came from the family of a Pskov landowner of moderate means (the year of his birth is not known). He received a good education and had a knowledge of Latin, German, Polish, and mathematics.

Ordyn-Nashchokin rose quickly. In his youth he brought diplomatic missions to a successful conclusion. In 1656 he was already voevoda of the town of Dru. During the Russo-Swedish war, which began in the same year, he took an active part in the military operations and was appointed chief administrator in Livonia. For his successful diplomatic endeavors following the truce of Valiesari with the Swedes in 1658, he was made a member of the *dumnye dvoriane.*[1] Yet his cautious policy in Livonia and his rapid advance caused dissatisfaction among the boyar magnates and champions of the old order.

Serious differences arose between Ordyn-Nashchokin and the Tsarist government concerning Russian relations with Poland and Sweden. In spite of his aspirations, which were directed at the continuation of the war with Sweden for the shore of the Baltic Sea, the Tsarist government submitted to the Swedes and, in the Kardis peace treaty of 1661, renounced all cities which had been acquired in Livonia.

During the years that followed Ordyn-Nashchokin was the voevoda of the city of Pskov. Here he introduced a bold reform for the organization of city self-government. Soon he was recalled from Pskov to conduct negotiations with Poland. In 1667, after prolonged and difficult negotiations, he concluded the truce of Andrusovo under conditions favorable to Russia. For his diplomatic services Ordyn-Nashchokin received a generous reward from the government. He was given the title of boyar and was appointed chief administrator of the ambassadorial office as well as head of several other institutions.

During this period Ordyn-Nashchokin initiated a number of important measures dealing with trade, industry, state administration, and so forth. Particularly noteworthy is the New Commercial Code of 1667, published by him, which defined the further direction of Russian foreign trade policy and which made a major contribution to the trade legislation of the country in the seventeenth century.

As may be imagined, there were sharp differences of opinion between him and the Tsarist government on the question of Russian foreign policy, and Ordyn-Nashchokin was relieved of his post and retired from government affairs in 1671. He died in 1680.

Ordyn-Nashchokin was a zealous partisan of absolute monarchy, the form of government most in accord with the economic and political conditions of seventeenth century Russia. The nobility and merchant class were interested in the establishment of an economically strong centralized state and supported the development of an autocratic system in Russia.

---

[1] *Dumnyi dvorianin* means younger member of the Boyar Duma.

The struggle for the creation of a strong absolute feudal state was the main aim and effort of Ordyn-Nashchokin's life. An experienced commander and expert in military affairs, he contributed in many ways to the growth of the military might of the Russian state. Moreover, he devoted an enormous amount of attention to strengthening the centralized apparatus of state administration. He fought energetically against boyar mestnichestvo, eliminated defects in the prikaz system, merged prikazy, and defined their functions more exactly.

Prompted by the great significance he attached to the organization of local administration, Ordyn-Nashchokin made an attempt to introduce municipal self-government into the western border cities of Russia. In the reforms which he introduced in the city of Pskov, he faced the task of protecting the merchant class from the arbitrariness of local authorities and of strengthening its economic position in the struggle with foreign trading capital. The Pskov reforms significantly limited the functions of the voevodas and transferred many of these functions to the *"zemskaia izba"* (local assembly), with its continually active leading body elected from among the "better" trading people. He also provided for an elected court to deal with all trade and "offense" cases. Only cases of treason, robbery, and murder remained in the hands of the voevoda. Disputes between nobles and townsmen were to be decided by a mixed court. In addition, he planned a system of measures designed for the protection of Russian merchants from the domination of the foreigners.

Ordyn-Nashchokin's Pskov measures were part of a broad program. For the prosperity of the state it was necessary, in his view, to provide for permanent support of the monarchy not only by the nobility, but also by the merchants, whose position needed improvement. In this new, progressive class he correctly saw the ally of the nobility in its struggle against the reactionary boyars.

In practice the reorganization of the city administration in Pskov went considerably farther than was foreseen in Ordyn-Nashchokin's plans. The Pskov commercial-industrial population, hostile toward the voevodas and prikaz officials, made wide use of this reform and, in fact, assumed all the power in Pskov. The elected organ of local authority, fulfilling the functions of city administration, managed all trade affairs, including the foreign trade passing through Pskov. This caused much discontent among Pskov boyar magnates and nobility alike. Complaints were also lodged by Sweden, which was displeased with the prohibition of the duty-free trade of its merchants. The Swedish government protested the arbitrary trade measures of the Pskov merchants.

The organization of a joint court, composed of town merchants and members of the nobility, clashed with the interests of the nobility. The nobles, although they formed a combined front with the merchants against the reactionary forces and supported their basic demands, nonetheless were threatened by the growing influence of the merchants of Pskov. The Pskov reform was soon abolished.

After failing to reorganize city self-government, Ordyn-Nashchokin endeavored to limit the administrative and judicial functions of the voevodas. He subsequently incorporated a series of measures aimed to improve the position of the merchant class into the New Commercial Code of 1667.

Ordyn-Nashchokin's views in the realm of foreign policy are equally interesting. The basic element in his program was the achievement of Russia's independence. In his opinion, Russia's most dangerous enemy was Sweden, with her clearly predatory policy and her persistent obstruction of a Russian outlet to the shores of the Baltic Sea. He regarded the struggle with Sweden as one of the most important problems of Russia's foreign policy.

Ordyn-Nashchokin attached great importance to the establishment of friendly relations with Slavic countries and to the creation of a united front in the common struggle against foreign encroachment. His desire for friendship among Slavic peoples was not a remote aim or a "political ideal," Kliuchevskii's assertion to the contrary notwithstanding.[2] A serious problem arose from international developments in the second half of the seventeenth century. Strained relations with Sweden and Turkey, countries openly preparing for a major war against Russia,[3] placed the Russian government in a difficult position. Repeated attempts were made to find allies among Western European states, particularly with Austria in the struggle against Turkey, but they were unsuccessful. Fully aware that the struggle of Russia and the other Slavic peoples against the predatory aspirations of Turkey and Sweden could succeed only under joint action, Ordyn-Nashchokin strove to set up peaceful relations with the Slavic states, particularly with Poland. He developed his view in detail in a memorandum to the Tsar,[4] evidently sent before 1665—in which he insisted on an alliance between Russia and Poland against Sweden. He argued that the alliance with Poland would permit Russia to establish the unity of

[2] Kliuchevskii, *Kurs russkoi istorii,* III, 370.

[3] See N. A. Smirnov, *Rossiia i Turtsiia v XVI–XVII vv.* [Russia and Turkey in the XVI–XVII Centuries]. (Moscow: Scientific Notes of Moscow University, 1946), Issue 94, Vol. I.

[4] See V. S. Ikonnikov, "Blizhnii boyarin A. L. Ordyn-Nashchokin" [The Friendly Boyar, A. L. Ordyn-Nashchokin], *Russkaia Starina* [Russian Antiquity], No. 10 (1883), pp. 44–5.

Slavic peoples. Moldavians and Wallachians, separated from Russia as a result of enmity with Poland, would have to become allies of Russia and Poland and combine efforts to liberate themselves from Turkish rule.

Later, in a speech to the Polish ambassadors after the conclusion of the Peace of Andrusovo (1667), Ordyn-Nashchokin again raised this problem and further urged the union of all Slavic peoples.

During his state service Ordyn-Nashchokin took the position that the economy of the country represented a single whole and that its various branches were closely interrelated. This view of the national economy distinguished him from many earlier Russian economists who centered their attention mainly on separate aspects and areas of the economy. His ideas of national economic objectives and of the economic role of the states are incomparably broader.

In the seventeenth century the tsarist regime looked upon the national economy first of all as a source for replenishing the state treasury and, accordingly, subordinated its economic policy to fiscal interests. Ordyn-Nashchokin opposed such a narrow concept of the economic role of the state. He considered the economic prosperity of the country to be of prime importance in state affairs. He realized that a successful struggle with nations hostile to Russia and an effective war against Western European trading capital and its aspirations to capture the Russian domestic market required measures which would overcome the economic backwardness of Russia.

As a basic economic task, Ordyn-Nashchokin promoted the development of the productive forces of the country. He projected a system of concrete measures which embraced the most important areas of the Russian economy. Urging active state intervention in the economic life of the country, he nevertheless criticized any suppression of personal endeavor. He was the first Russian economist to advocate the development of private initiative and enterprise.

At the core of his economic programs lay the great significance which he attached to the utilization of the rich experience of advanced Western European countries. "It is not shameful to copy what is good from abroad," he said. The bourgeois historians, Kliuchevskii in particular, have looked upon Ordyn-Nashchokin as a Russian westernizer.[5] Such an evaluation of one of the foremost Russian statesmen and economists of the seventeenth century does not correspond with the facts. His services to the state and his economic program testify to his

[5] Kliuchevskii, *op. cit.*, III, 364.

deep understanding of the current economic and political conditions of Russia and of the fundamental interests of his country.

Ordyn-Nashchokin was opposed to blind imitation of and servility to foreign customs and forms. He looked upon the experience of the West critically, and he often repeated: "Foreign customs are not our affair: their clothing is not for us, and ours is not for them." [6]

The economic views of Ordyn-Nashchokin were most definitively expressed in his "memoranda" decrees to the territorial elders of Pskov in 1665. These were appraised by the Pskov townsmen and then made the basis of the supplementary "articles" of city organization and trade there.[7] They were also incorporated into the Commercial Code of 1667,[8] or, as it is usually called, the New Commercial Code.

The basic sources of the New Commercial Code of 1667 were the same memoranda of 1665, the demands of the town merchants as expressed in petitions, and the proposals of the Danish merchant Marselis, who assisted in the compilation of the Code. The chief author and editor of the Code was the head of the Posol'skii prikaz, A. L. Ordyn-Nashchokin.[9] His letters to the Tsar and his statements on various economic questions are also of great importance for a correct understanding of his economic programs.

The Principles of Commercial Policy

Ordyn-Nashchokin looked upon trade as one of the main sources of state income and as one of the means of increasing national prosperity. His views on this issue are clearly expressed in the introduction to the New Commercial Code: "in all neighboring states a free and profitable trade is foremost in state affairs for the collection of taxes and for the accumulation of peaceful consumer goods, and it is protected by every means and kept free." [10]

"Free" trade, as conceived by Ordyn-Nashchokin, did not mean the non-interference of the state in the economic activity of private persons

---

[6] See S. Kollins, "Nyneshnee sostoianie Rossii" [Russia's Present Situation], *Chteniia v Obshchestve istorii i drevnostei rossiiskikh* [Readings in the Society of Russian History and Antiquities] (Moscow: 1846), Bk. I, p. 34.

[7] See *Dopolneniia k aktam istoricheskim* [Supplements to Historical Documents] (St. Petersburg: 1853), V, 1–8.

[8] *Sobranie gosudarstvennykh gramot i dogovorov* [Collection of State Charters and Agreements] (Moscow: 1828), Pt. IV, No. 55, pp. 189–204.

[9] See K. V. Bazilevich, "Novotorgovyi ustav 1667 g." [New Commercial Code of 1667] *Izvestiia Akademii nauk SSSR* [Bulletin of the Academy of Sciences of the USSR], *Otdelenie obshchestvennykh nauk* [Department of Social Studies], Series VII, No. 7 (1932), pp. 589–622.

[10] *Sobranie gosudarstvennykh gramot i dogovorov,* Pt. IV, No. 55, p. 190.

nor the absence of protective duties and compulsory regulation of trade. In seventeenth century Russia the demands for free trade expressed the protest of the merchant class against the privileges enjoyed by foreign merchants, leaseholders, "guests," and monasteries. Privileges and leases, which the tsarist government continued to award for money to replenish the state treasury, inhibited the trading activities of broad layers of the Russian merchant class and hindered their competition with foreign merchants.

The struggle against the privileges of foreign merchants and certain groups of the Russian merchant class was also energetically supported by B. I. Morozov, who strove to establish a uniform custom tariff and introduced a number of administrative decrees to further this aim. The same objective was pursued in the commercial regulatory statute of 1654. These government regulations, however, scarcely changed the situation.

Ordyn-Nashchokin considered it necessary to limit drastically the rights of foreign merchants and to repeal the privileges of certain groups of Russian merchants and monasteries. Indeed, even in the Pskov "memoranda" decrees and "articles" of city organization in 1665 there was a definite system of regulation of foreign trade in the border towns.

The pressing need for the control of foreign trade in these areas was dictated by economic conditions themselves. A large part of the foreign trade of Russia with the western countries went over land. The Russian merchants of the border towns could not oppose the machinations of foreign trading capital because they lacked the required funds. Regulation, beyond the collection of customs duties, was weak. Unhindered, foreign merchants bought up Russian goods and disposed of their own merchandise duty-free on the Russian market. In Pskov foreigners intent on capturing the market entered into agreements with the "petty" merchants and supplied them with money for the purchase of wares. Having no capital of their own, the latter became virtual agents of the foreign merchants and obtained commodities for them at unusually low prices. This situation enhanced still further the position of foreign commercial capital in Russia.

In the Pskov reforms of Ordyn-Nashchokin, measures were designed to protect Russian merchants from the aspirations of foreigners to corner the Russian market. Before these reforms were introduced, foreign merchants—especially the Swedes—freely crossing the border and trading in Russia throughout the entire year, bought up Russian goods at the most advantageous times. Ordyn-Nashchokin limited the purchase of Russian commodities by foreign merchants to definite periods. Foreigners were permitted to buy wares freely only at fairs organized twice a year. The "articles" of city organization state that: "goods shall not be sold to foreigners except during definite periods, nor shall they be transported by inhabitants of Pskov and towns surrounding Pskov." [11] Smuggling was "to be punished without mercy." [12]

Foreign merchants were also forbidden to supply money to Russian tradesmen for the purchase of goods. They were deprived of the right to live in "trading houses" during the period between fairs. And definite limitations were imposed during the fairs: foreign merchants were forbidden to trade with each other; trade could be carried on only with the townsmen of Pskov.

Ordyn-Nashchokin believed that the reason for the weakness of Russian trade was to be found in the lack of capital, in the presence of unhealthy competition among Russian merchants themselves, and in their ignorance as to how to organize themselves for a common struggle against stronger foreign capital. He proposed to unite the merchants and to eliminate the strife among them by creating trading companies on a commission basis. In his project, small and middle-sized merchants were, in effect, to become the trading agents of large merchants and were to receive a share of the profits.

To counter the domination of foreign merchants, and their purchase of Russian commodities at low prices, Ordyn-Nashchokin demanded the introduction of a "uniform price." He suggested that this "uniform price" be set in advance by elected local officials: "with the knowledge of elected native Pskovites, foreigners may purchase Russian commodities on the basis of an agreed price; they are to purchase and give an account of their transactions . . ." [13] As a consequence, foreigners would be deprived of the possibility of arbitrarily lowering prices to the disadvantage of the Russians.

It would, however, be incorrect to regard these measures as a manifestation of national isolation. While Ordyn-Nashchokin argued strongly against the subjection of the Russian market to foreign capital, at the same time he considered it necessary to attract foreign capital, but only on conditions advantageous to Russia. More specifically, and as a means to revive trade in Pskov, he proposed to introduce duty-free trade between tradesmen and foreigners twice a year at local fairs. He justified this measure by the fact that "in all states those trade fairs which are exempt from duties are famous." [14] During the rest of the year, however, foreigners would have to pay duties.

This notion of a Russian merchant class whose interests would be

---

11 *Dopolneniia k aktam istoricheskim,* V, 6.
12 *Ibid.*
13 *Ibid.,* V, 5–6.
14 *Ibid.,* V, 5.

supported and whose competitive position would be strengthened was expressed even more emphatically in the New Commercial Code of 1667. The Code limited the right of foreign merchants much more severely than did the above-mentioned Pskov reforms. It established a stronger territorial limitation on the trade of foreigners. They could trade freely only in the border towns, with exceptions made only for those foreigners who possessed special permission to trade elsewhere. Traffic with merchants coming from other towns was also forbidden. Violation of this rule was punished by confiscation of the goods: "And if any foreigners sell their goods to foreigners or to citizens coming from other towns, or if they purchase anything—no matter how large the quantities—these goods shall be confiscated for the great sovereign." [15]

In addition, the Code established other limitations on the rights of alien merchants, for example, the prohibition of duty-free trade among themselves. Tax-free mutual trade arrangements among foreign merchants resulted in losses to the treasury as well as to Russian merchants. As Russian merchants complained in their petitions, foreigners bought up Russian goods and loaded them on their ships presumably to be shipped home, but actually they "traded among themselves on shipboard in a duty-free market." The New Commercial Code forbade this kind of trade, since it caused "much loss to the great sovereign, to the treasury, and to the Russian people." [16] Violations of this decree led to the confiscation of the merchandise. Nevertheless, the New Commercial Code permitted foreigners to trade among themselves in the border towns, provided that they paid the established duties.

Finally, the New Commercial Code denied foreign merchants access to retail trade, for they had been found to engage in this activity in the interior towns of Russia in spite of earlier prohibitions. The Russian merchants wrote in their petitions that the foreigners, residing freely in Russia, were well aware of Russia's market conditions and, thanks to their good connections with foreign countries, knew how to maneuver and to lower prices on Russian goods and to raise them on foreign goods. The New Commercial Code again prohibited the transaction of retail trade with foreign merchants. "In Moscow and in towns throughout the land foreigners shall not sell any foreign goods retail, and they shall not go with their goods and money, nor shall they send their salesmen to the fairs nor to towns." [17] If foreign mer-

[15] *Sobranie gosudarstvennykh gramot i dogovorov,* Pt. IV, No. 55, p. 199.
[16] *Ibid.,* Pt. IV, No. 55, p. 200.
[17] *Ibid.,* Pt. IV, No. 55, p. 202.

chants carried on retail trade their goods and money were subject to seizure.

In the fight against foreign domination of the Russian domestic market Ordyn-Nashchokin utilized such effective means as the raising of customs duties. This was achieved above all by enforced payment of duties in gold and efimiki at a low compulsory rate of exchange. Also, the amount of duty taken from foreigners for the sale or transport of goods was increased. Thus, for example, transport duties were increased to 10 per cent, and the tax placed on the sale of goods was set at 6 per cent.

In the development of an all-Russian market and the growth of commercial relations, the progressive nature of Ordyn-Nashchokin's foreign trade policy is indisputable: It fostered the accumulation of national capital.

Since he regarded foreign trade as one of the most important sources of national income, Ordyn-Nashchokin introduced other provisions into the New Commercial Code to facilitate the development of profitable trade between Russia and the outside world. These aims were partly served by a differentiation in customs duties. The heaviest duties were placed on wine, sugar, and luxury items. The fifty-first article of the New Commercial Code states: "At Archangel higher duties are to be taken from the foreigners on wine and other liquors than on any other goods . . ." [18] With the aid of these measures the import of foreign goods was limited. At the same time, the Code encouraged the export of domestic goods. Russian merchants were permitted "to trade freely with foreigners in all goods," in all border towns, and at all fairs. Money obtained from exports could be used to buy foreign goods duty-free.

In other cases the purchase of foreign goods was subject to duty. While foreigners had to pay these in gold or efimiki, Russian merchants were permitted "at the town of Archangel and in all other border towns . . ." to pay duties in small Russian silver coins.

Ordyn-Nashchokin's measures for the regulation of the export and import of goods and for the development of an advantageous foreign trade confirm the fact that he pursued a clearly expressed policy of mercantilism.

In accordance with his belief in the development of private initiative, he developed a number of provisions to improve the position and stimulate the trade of Russian merchants. The New Commercial Code supported the commercial regulatory statute of 1654 concerning the

[18] *Ibid.*, Pt. IV, No. 55, p. 198.

replacement of small taxes: poll, household, hundredth, thirtieth, tenth, *"svalnogo,"* article, bridge, tavern, and other single taxes to the amount of ten dengi per ruble. Transit duties for Russian merchants were abolished entirely. Russian merchants buying commodities in their own town were also freed from the payment of taxes because "merchants serve the great sovereign in their trade in such cities and pay all manner of taxes." [19] Finally, the Code permitted "guests" and merchants to purchase without duty produce and items for their personal use.

A considerable number of articles of the New Commercial Code in regard to internal trade were directed toward the elimination of abuses by customs officials and local authorities. The revision of the system of taxation itself eliminated to a considerable degree the possibility of corruption on the part of the customs administration and the voevodas. Moreover, the Code contained a direct order that neither voevodas nor the customs heads should obstruct the free passage of merchants: "the voevodas in towns and the customs heads shall not detain merchants with their goods, but they shall allow them to go everywhere without hindrance . . ." [20] Merchants were also permitted to hire workers freely without securing the permission of voevodas.

The Code also planned the organization of a "department of merchant affairs." The aims and tasks of this department were clearly defined by Ordyn-Nashchokin: "Because considerable red tape prevails in all prikazy, merchants should be supervised by their own prikaz; the great sovereign can instruct his state official as to which prikaz should protect merchants in all border cities and foreign states and [which] should defend merchants in all cities against the voevodas' taxes and administration." [21] For the same department a court and justice were designed to deal with those cases in which merchants should "petition people of other ranks." The "department of merchant affairs," which was called upon to protect the interests of the merchants, would appear to be the forerunner of the office of the Burmister later established by Peter I.

Ordyn-Nashchokin's concern for the development of trade was also shown in other aspects of his activity. While still a voevoda in the Livonian towns, then in Pskov, and particularly during his subsequent diplomatic career, he sought to expand trade abroad, made trade connections with foreign states, and concluded trade agreements with foreign governments. At the signing of the Peace of Andrusovo with

---

[19] *Ibid.*, Pt. IV, No. 55, p. 194.
[20] *Ibid.*, Pt. IV, No. 55, p. 193.
[21] *Ibid.*, Pt. IV, No. 55, p. 203.

Poland in 1667, Ordyn-Nashchokin agreed that in the same year a congress of plenipotentiaries from Russia, Poland, and Sweden should be called to conclude a trade treaty, "in order that the merchants in each country will not be ruined by excessive collection of taxes, since every nation is accustomed to fill its treasury by the trade of goods." [22]

In 1667 ambassadors were sent from Russia to Spain and France with proposals to enter into trade relations. In Spain the ambassadors signed an agreement with Charles II allowing Russian merchants to carry on trade freely in all Spanish ports. The negotiations with France did not engender any concrete results. In 1668 the Russian ambassadors proposed to establish regular trade between Russia and France. The French, on their part, offered to conclude an eternal peace treaty and to permit Russian merchants to trade freely in France under condition of payment of fixed taxes for the sale and export of goods. In return for this concession, however, they demanded that French merchants in Russia be given the right of free export and free transit of goods through Russia to the eastern countries, including Persia, and requested a number of other privileges. Ordyn-Nashchokin refused to support these demands, as he saw in them an antithesis to the basic principles which guided him in foreign trade policy. As a consequence, regular trade with France was not established.

Ordyn-Nashchokin exerted no little effort toward the development of trade with eastern countries. The English and Dutch tried to acquire control of the transit trade with the East, which was carried on through Archangel and the Caspian Sea. The Moscow government itself wanted to exploit the advantages of transit commerce and was therefore anxious to control all trade with the eastern countries. It was Ordyn-Nashchokin's aim that all European trade with Asia should pass through Russia. In 1667 he concluded a contract with a Persian company that all raw silk sold abroad by Persia should be shipped to western countries through Russia and not, as previously, through Turkey.

This monopoly trade with Persia was possible only if certain advantages were accorded to Persian merchants. The latter were permitted to trade freely in Astrakhan, Moscow, Archangel, and other towns of Russia upon payment of a set duty. In addition, they were allowed to take abroad all goods not sold in Russia and to carry gold and efimki to Persia.

The prospect of controlling the eastern trade was so alluring that Ordyn-Nashchokin was ready to take this step, despite the New Com-

---

[22] See S. M. Solovev, *Istoriia Rossii s drevneishikh vremen* [History of Russia from Ancient Times] (St. Petersburg: 1894–5) XI, Bk. III, p. 183.

mercial Code so recently passed. The Russian merchantry, which profited from the trade with Persia was, however, dissatisfied with the privileges given the Persian merchants. After the retirement of Ordyn-Nashchokin from state affairs, when the Posolskii prikaz was managed by Matveev, the arrangement with the Persian company was altered.

As the struggle mounted among foreign merchants for the Russian market, Ordyn-Nashchokin strove to deny privileges—particularly trade monopolies—to the foreigners. To the request by England in 1667 for the return to English merchants of their former rights and privileges, Ordyn-Nashchokin replied: "In the Moscow state, trade is now subject to great scrutiny so that it will proceed without quarrel and abuse. The presence of former companies is undesirable, for more controversy than friendship arose from it. Evidence reveals that foreigners trade in stolen and damaged goods, make secret agreements, and burden the Russian people with many debts." [23]

The activities of Ordyn-Nashchokin, as they concerned the development of Russian trade, were accompanied by an increase in the power of the new class emerging in Russia, the merchants, a class in whom Ordyn-Nashchokin saw a force to strengthen the continued growth of the economic might of the Russian centralized state.

The Principles of Financial Policy

A. L. Ordyn-Nashchokin devoted much attention to the improvement of the financial position of Russia and made the first attempt to organize credit there. Lack of money and the absence of properly organized credit hindered the turnover of commodities and impeded the growth of trade with foreign countries. The state treasury was likewise perpetually in need of money.

The question dealing with the increase in the precious metals in the country and the money in circulation grew in importance. Ordyn-Nashchokin recognized the need for strict regulation of trade and effective control over the import and export of gold and silver. He took various measures to guarantee a net inflow of specie. As in the Pskov "memoranda" decree and the "articles" of city administration of 1665, so in the New Commercial Code of 1667 a complete system of monetary regulation, as well as an improvement in the collection of customs duties, was provided.

In order to attract precious metal into the country the Pskov articles directed Russian merchants to sell goods to foreigners only under

[23] See *ibid.*, XII, Bk. III, p. 534.

the condition that they pay a third of their value in efimki. "According to the announced Code," assert the Pskov "articles," "two thirds of the Russian goods will be exchanged for foreign goods, and, for the third, efimki were to be taken against the price agreed to by the foreigner." [24] This measure not only limited the trade of foreign merchants in Russia to a specific degree, but, more important, it brought a perpetual stream of silver into the country. These provisions served especially the interests of the treasury, which derived considerable income from the recoinage of the German Joachimsthalers.

According to Ordyn-Nashchokin's project, all Joachimsthalers obtained from the sale of goods to foreigners were to be exchanged in the "customs house" for Russian metal money of inferior value. For the recoinage of German Joachimsthalers into Russian coins construction of a mint in Pskov was proposed. "And to aid trade and accelerate purchasing among the Russian people, there should be established a mint in Pskov to collect large sums of money for the treasury. And if it should prove sufficient to pay seven rubles per pound, then the Russian people will not take the efimki into various border towns; for a good price, efimki will be brought to the mint in Pskov. Thus the pounds [of efimki] will bring considerable profit to the treasury of the great sovereign." [25]

These aspirations to solve the problem of the precious metals by the introduction of state controls over monetary circulation were more fully expressed in the New Commercial Code of 1667. Article 73 states: "And all gold and efimki, which are accepted from foreigners who come from beyond the seas to the towns of Archangel and to Novgorod and to Pskov and to all border towns, will be given to the treasury of the great sovereign, and they will be exchanged for small Russian coins, one gold coin per ruble, while the efimki of Lübek will receive one-half ruble." [26] For violation of this rule a fine of 10 per cent "of every hundred gold coins and of efimki" was imposed. Gold coins and efimki secretly brought into Moscow were subject to confiscation. This exchange of gold and efimkov for Russian money was designed to provide the government with a very significant revenue.

To encourage foreigners to import precious metals into the country, those bringing gold and efimki into Russia were accorded the right to buy and export Russian goods duty-free. In addition, the Code prohibited the export of gold and silver from Russia. This applied mainly

[24] *Dopolneniia k aktam istoricheskim,* V, 6.
[25] *Ibid.,* V, 7.
[26] *Sobranie gosudarstvennykh gramot i dogovorov,* Pt. IV, No. 55, p. 201.

to the eastern countries and in particular to the Persian merchants who had been exporting large amounts of the precious metals. Article 79 of the New Commercial Code stated: "and they shall not buy gold and efimki, and the Russian people are forbidden to sell them to the Persian merchants; and should gold and efimki be found on their persons, the specie will be confiscated for the great sovereign, because they carry out much gold and silver from the state of Moscow." [27]

Undoubtedly coincident with this aim of the New Commercial Code to prevent the export of precious metals were a number of provisions against the purchase of luxury goods, although these were formally motivated by the danger that the needless expenditures would be ruinous for the Russians. The real motive, however, lay in the fact that silver was also protected in other states. In the Code it is written: "In border towns the chiefs and certified officials shall question foreigners and search their trunks, coffers, and boxes carefully for pearls and stones, to see that . . . no precious items are hidden; and these shall neither be purchased nor exchanged for Russian goods, because other states protect silver, prohibit the purchase of useless products, and confiscate them from common, non-official people in order to prevent them from falling into poverty; also common and lower strata of society shall not wear expensive silk and wool cloth; and in this regard there is a decree of the great sovereign which imposes without mercy an additional burdensome tax in order to prevent the common people from purchasing expensive items . . ." [28]

The Code standardized a previously existing rule of inspection and registration of goods coming from Archangel through Vologda to the interior towns of Russia, including goods for export which came from various Russian towns to Archangel. It further established a system of controls over foreign ships carrying goods.

Not only the amount but also the quality of goods was controlled. Foreign merchants usually tried to dispose of inferior goods in Russia, a fact which Russian merchants constantly bemoaned in their petitions. Therefore the New Commercial Code proposed to place a stamp on all goods, thus identifying their quality. Where a commodity appeared faulty, the Code gave the order "to remove it dishonorably from the fair so that it cannot depress the price of a good commodity." [29]

Trade arrangements concluded at the fairs by Russian merchants

---

[27] *Ibid.*, Pt. IV, No. 55, p. 202.
[28] *Ibid.*, Pt. IV, No. 55, p. 204.
[29] *Ibid.*, Pt. IV, No. 55, p. 197.

with each other and with foreign merchants were subject to exact accounting.

The strict regulation of trade established by Ordyn-Nashchokin, designed to guarantee an inflow of specie, shows the similarity of this policy with that of the Western European states, a policy characteristic of the early period of mercantilism, the so-called bullion system. In the Russia of the seventeenth century this policy was dictated by the mounting money shortage and the growth of trade turnover, in addition to the growing demand by the state for money. It was also caused by the need for defense against domination of the Russian market by foreign merchants. State regulation of trade and strict control over the import and export of specie had to be used later by Peter I, as well.

The shortage of money in the country made credit expensive. The archaic form of credit in Russia—money-lender credit—could not satisfy the demand for money. The project for establishing a trading company in Pskov included an attempt at the organization of credit. In joining "petty" merchants with big merchants, Ordyn-Nashchokin was fully aware that the Russian big merchants had no free capital to enable them to provide credit to the "petty" merchants. To free the "petty" merchants from subordination to foreigners, who supplied them with money and turned them into their agents, Ordyn-Nashchokin proposed that the local assembly provide them with credit. The local assembly was thus called upon to fulfill the functions of a unique [central?] bank.

This attempt was unsuccessful. In practice it was not supported by the big merchants, who considered it more advantageous to hold the "petty" merchants in bondage.[30] Even so, Ordyn-Nashchokin did not abandon his idea. In the New Commercial Code of 1667 he again tried to give the "local assembly" those functions which by their nature would have transformed it into a form of merchants' bank. In the introductory articles of the New Commercial Code it is stated: "and domestic insufficiencies will be made up in worth from the peaceful aid of the Moscow customs and from the local town assemblies."[31]

Despite the fact that this rule became law, it was not enforced; the Russia of the seventeenth century did not yet possess the economic prerequisites for the broad development of credit. Ordyn-Nashchokin's ideas concerning the organization of credit were put into effect only in the middle of the eighteenth century.

---

[30] See *Dopolneniia k aktam istoricheskim,* V, No. 1, pp. xv–xvi.

[31] *Sobranie gosudarstvennykh gramot i dogovorov,* Pt. IV, No. 55, p. 190.

Principles of Policy in the Fields of Industry and Communication

A. L. Ordyn-Nashchokin frequently expressed the hope that Russia would eclipse the Western European countries in industrial and cultural endeavors. He insisted on the necessity of developing not only those branches of industry which produced goods for export, but also those which supplied the internal needs of the country, particularly the metallurgical and iron making industries. This viewpoint distinguishes Ordyn-Nashchokin from the western mercantilists, who fixed their attention mainly on the development of branches of the manufacturing industry producing for export.

Ordyn-Nashchokin's views on the role and significance of industry are expressed in detail in one of his orders regarding the return of metallurgical and iron-making mills to their former owner, Marselis. The Russian iron works, he wrote, should "satisfy the needs of the treasury with respect to iron, as well as those of the Moscow state; it is necessary to manufacture all kinds of items in those mills, and to that end an agreement should be concluded that will be favorable to the treasury of the great sovereign both with respect to iron and finished products . . ." [32]

He regarded the main reasons for the lag in the development of Russian industry to be the weaknesses of the system of state administration, the excessive oppression of entrepreneurial activity, and the absence of government concern for the national economy. He considered it necessary to give state aid and coöperation to entrepreneurs, while at the same time allowing them great freedom of initiative. It was with the creation of these prerequisites for the development of industrial enterprise that Ordyn-Nashchokin struggled.

The large metallurgical and metal processing enterprises created in seventeenth century Russia—large manufactories for their time—were mainly in the hands of foreigners who had received the right to work the ore on the basis of special agreements concluded with the state. When certain terms of these contracts were not fulfilled, the government could confiscate the enterprises.

In 1662 the treasury took over the biggest metallurgical and iron founding mills, which belonged to the Danish industrialist, Peter Marselis. Under the treasury's control the mill fell into ruin. Thus, in view of Marselis' ability and enterprise, Ordyn-Nashchokin decided that they should be returned to their former owner. However these

---

[32] *Dopolneniia k aktam istoricheskim*, V, 390.

mills, which were of utmost importance to the country, remained under the unremitting supervision of Ordyn-Nashchokin. He assisted their development in every way, issued loans from the Novgorod account, and strove to rescind the lower price demanded by the Moscow government for iron goods produced by the mills. He also took active part in the organization of paper production, glass, and tanneries in Russia.

Although he stubbornly insisted on the need for outlets to the Baltic Sea, Ordyn-Nashchokin also devoted great attention to the search for new routes of communication with the eastern countries. The trade with Khiva and Bukhara suffered considerably from poor communications and repeated robberies. He worked hard to eliminate these impediments. He dispatched Russian ambassadors to India and other eastern countries to seek better routes of communication.

To A. L. Ordyn-Nashchokin belongs the honor of organizing the first post in Russia. In this endeavor he was guided primarily by economic considerations. The regulation of the post was undertaken to prevent the secret dispatch of gold and other precious items. As he explained to the Tsar, it was desirable "to guard against the merchants secretly hiring and sending someone with letters, as in former years, and thus depriving your treasury of taxes, by sending precious things, stones and pearls and gold in bags and in bundles . . . via the mails." [33]

Ordyn-Nashchokin appreciated the importance of building a Russian fleet. He considered it necessary both for the Western Dvina and the Volga, and made several attempts in this direction. Equally as concerned with the dissemination of science and technical knowledge in Russia, he invited specialists and schoolmasters from abroad to teach crafts and military science. He was also the initiator of a number of other cultural innovations.

This outstanding Russian statesman, diplomat, and economist understood only too well the complicated and critical circumstances which characterised the internal life and external relations of Russia in the mid-seventeenth century. Better than any of his contemporaries, he was aware of the threat posed by strong Western European trading capital, which persistently penetrated the Russian market with efforts to subject the Russian economy to its influence. To work for the independence of Russia and to overcome her economic backward-

---

[33] See I. P. Kozlovskii, *Pervye pochty i pervye pochmeistery v Moskovskom gosudarstve* [The First Post Offices and the First Postmasters in the Moscovite State] (Warsaw: 1913), II, 8.

ness were the basic goals of his economic programs and the guiding criteria of his foreign policy.

One of the important objectives of his foreign policy was his aspiration to establish friendly mutual relations with Slavic countries and to unite all Slavic peoples in the struggle with foreign aggressors.

Ordyn-Nashchokin was not a worshipper and imitator of the West, as the bourgeois historians have asserted. He learned and borrowed from the experience of other countries, but he always kept in mind the interests of his country and his class. His economic program emerged from the specific Russian economic and political conditions and was based on contemporary reality. It clearly represented the class nature of the economic views of Ordyn-Nashchokin as a spokesman of the nobility, who in his activity reflected the interests of his class and who, from the position of that class, defended the merchant class and gave them all possible cooperation.

In Ordyn-Nashchokin's statements on various economic problems, as well as in his economic program, the ideas of mercantilism are fully discernible. It would be incorrect, however, to exaggerate the significance of this fact and to look upon Ordyn-Nashchokin as a narrow mercantilist. The ideas of mercantilism did not occupy a central place either in his economic program or in his economic policy. The policy of mercantilism promoted by Ordyn-Nashchokin sprang from the urgent necessity to solve the country's money problem. Nevertheless, the solution of this problem was only part of his program of economic development.

His economic policy was marked by the desire to liquidate the economic and cultural backwardness of Russia, to abolish the domination of foreign trading capital, to strengthen Russian commerce, and to create a native industry. This program, which corresponded to the fundamental interests of the rising class of nobles and the demands of a new class—the merchants—did not go beyond the framework of the feudal-serf structure. In effect it helped to strengthen the feudal-absolutist centralized authority of nobles and merchants. It is in his systematic and consistent struggle for this program that Ordyn-Nashchokin emerges as the direct and immediate forerunner of Peter I.

CHAPTER 10. *The Basic Traits of Economic Thought in the First Half of the Eighteenth Century. The Demands of the Peasant Masses in the Uprising of 1707-1708.*

The Condition of Russia at the Beginning of the Eighteenth Century and the Reforms of Peter I. Economic Policy in the Second Quarter of the Eighteenth Century

During the seventeenth century the economy of Russia clearly underwent important changes. The growth of the social division of labor, the development of market connections among separate districts and regions of Russia and between branches of the national economy, the merging of local markets into a national whole, and the rise of manufactures—all this heralded the opening of a new period in the history of our country. These new trends experienced significant development in the eighteenth century. The economic transformations which took place in Russia during the first quarter of the eighteenth century, connected with the activity of Peter I, were foreshadowed by all the preceding developments. The tendencies noted in the seventeenth century were most clearly defined and expressed under Peter I. In the first quarter of the eighteenth century a significant rise in the development of the productive forces of Russia took place. With the growing economic unification of the country, a concomitant process, broadening and strengthening the multinational Russian state as well as its political centralization, continued and accelerated.

Feudal-serf production relations dominated the overwhelming part of the population. According to the census records of 1678, in the state of Moscow the peasant households of the boyar and noble landholdings constituted 67 per cent of all taxable households, the church 13.3 per cent, the palace 9.3 per cent, and the landholdings of monastery peasants and townspeople 10.4 per cent. Thus 90 per cent of all peasant households were under serfdom.[1]

The predominant form of exploitation of subjected peasant labor was the barshchina. At the end of the century seignorial plowland increased significantly over peasant land. The exploitation of peasants by landlords increased, and peasant obligations to the feudal state grew.

Agriculture continued to remain basically "natural," but it was drawn increasingly into commodity trade as a result of the development of industry, the spread of monetary rent and the monastery economy, and the expansion of the peasants' monetary obligations to the state, which made it necessary for them to sell a part of their produce.

Trade and industry developed. In the villages industrial production existed in various forms, but household processing of agricultural products for the family's own needs predominated. Connected with agriculture, but yet independent of it, craft activity—goods produced on specification for the consumer and for the market—also occupied a significant place. Regional specialization evolved.

Processing of foodstuffs for the needs of the owner and for sale also existed in the votchina economy. Many votchiny and monasteries had large industries—wood, salt, and others—whose production entered the internal market and even went abroad.

The various crafts were also found in the towns and settlements. Trade capital in the country played an increasing economic role and made itself deeply felt in rural areas. The merchant ever more frequently assumed the position of entrepreneur-manufacturer.

Russia carried on substantial trade with Western Europe and with the eastern countries. This connection with the world market also facilitated the growth of domestic monetary-trade relationships. Within the feudal society new bourgeois ties and relationships spread rapidly.

Notwithstanding these economic upheavals Russia remained a backward country in comparison with many European nations. Economically, England, France, Holland, and Sweden were significantly ahead of her. Russian agriculture was characterized by poor techniques and low harvests; the state of livestock production and technical crops was weak; and many branches of a truly developed agriculture were not present at all.

Domestic industry was unable to satisfy the military needs of the state and the growing demands of the population for industrial

---

[1] See Kliuchsevkii, *Kurs russkoi istorii,* III, 250.

products. At the start of the eighteenth century Russia's annual production of cast iron amounted to no more than 150,000 puds—five times less than that of England. Better quality iron needed in the country was imported from Sweden. For many industrial products the country was dependent on others.

Russia was surrounded by Sweden, Poland, Turkey, and other hostile, aggressive nations ready to profit from the backwardness of their neighbor. Her frequent and prolonged wars with these countries in the seventeenth century revealed her military weakness and emphasized the backwardness of the Russian army in armament and organization as compared with the armies of the Western European countries.

Possessing enormous expanses of land, a numerous and industrious population, and rich natural resources, Russia at the same time was cut off from the sea. Only the White Sea, frozen for a significant part of the year and therefore unsuitable for navigation, belonged to Russia. The Baltic Sea and its southeastern shores, earlier occupied by Russia, were now at the disposal of Sweden. The Black, Azov, and Caspian Seas were in the possession of Turkey and Persia. The Crimean Tartars ravaged the borderlands of Russia with their forays. The trans-Dnepr region was under Turkish rule. The backwardness of Russia created a direct and immediate threat to her political and economic independence, a condition which put her in real danger of becoming dependent upon the more developed European countries.

As was stated above, the most far-seeing statesmen of the seventeenth century perceived this peril. The position of Russia and her consequent problems were clearly understood by Peter I, who with his unique energy set about to find a solution.

Versatile and active, Peter I endeavored to reduce Russia's lag, to improve her condition, to foster her development, and to guarantee her might and independence. Chernyshevskii lauded Peter's "highest patriotism—a terrible, boundless wish for the welfare of the country, inspiring the whole life and directing all the activity of this great man." [2]

The basic and immediate aim of his military activities was a quest for the sea. " 'Russia needs water,' these words, which he directed to Prince Kantemir, were the slogan of his whole life," wrote Marx of Peter I: [3]

---

[2] N. G. Chernyshevskii, *Polnoe sobranie sochinenii* [Complete Collection of Works] (Moscow: Gosizdat, 1947), III, 136.

[3] Marx, *Secret Diplomatic History,* p. 87.

> No great nation has existed, nor can exist, so distant from all seas as was the early empire of Peter the Great; no great nation has ever been able to stand by tranquilly while her seacoasts and river mouths were torn from her. No one can visualize a great nation wrested from the seashore. Russia could not leave in the hands of the Swedes the mouth of the Neva, which was the natural outlet for the market of the products of Northern Russia, nor could she leave the mouths of the Don, Dnepr, and Bug and the Kerch Straits in the hands of the nomadic Tartar-plunderers.[4]

Under Peter I Russia went to war with Turkey for the Azov and Black Sea and fought with Sweden for the Baltic Sea. The war for the Baltic Sea was long and hard. It left a deep impression on the entire life of the country, and in significant degree determined the course of Peter's reforms.

The war demanded the fundamental reorganization of the Russian army. Under Peter it was equipped with the most modern armaments—rifles with bayonets and artillery—and it was taught military formations. A war fleet was created. Peter said that whoever has a land army and no fleet has only one arm.

The war necessitated the organization of heavy metallurgical and other industrial enterprises, and it required the domestic production of materials for the supply and armament of the army and fleet. Peter feverishly developed a heavy industry, one which was primarily military. He subsequently introduced a system of important economic measures in various branches of the national economy.

The complicated problems posed by military affairs, as well as those in economic, administrative, cultural and other fields of life, demanded a fundamental reform of the central government apparatus and local administration of the country. The Russian state became a "regulated" police-bureaucratic country like the advanced Western European states of that time. A court reform was put through, and an attempt was made to separate the judicial organs from the state administration.

Much attention was given to the dissemination of culture, and to the development of science and education in Russia. On the initiative and under the leadership of Peter I, the first newspaper, *Vedomosti,* appeared in Russia. A new alphabet was introduced in place of the inconvenient Church Slavonic. Many books on various fields of knowledge were published. Special and general-educational schools were

---

[4] *Ibid.*

established. "Academies and schools are necessary for popular education," stated Peter. A naval academy and schools of navigation were established; engineering, artillery, medical, arithmetic, and trade schools were founded. Others, some of which provided training for big business enterprises, were also established.

Many youths were sent abroad to study. Peter decreed the opening of an Academy of Science in Russia, with a university and gymnasium. A great library was built and a start made at scientific collections.

The economic and other reforms, as well as the prolonged and difficult wars, took their toll of the peasantry, whose position continually deteriorated. In the eighteenth century the class struggle between the feudalists and the enserfed peasantry became sharper and took the form of open peasant warfare. The struggles were of peasants against the exploiter-feudalists, the city lower classes against the boyars and the moneylenders, and these were supplemented by the struggle of the oppressed nationalities. In 1705 an uprising broke out in Astrakhan as a result of the arbitrariness of the authorities and the increase of feudal oppression. In 1707–1708 a peasant-Cossack uprising on the Don, in the Slobodskaia Ukraine, and in the Volga region arose under the leadership of Bulavin. Uprisings of Bashkirs, Tartars, and Udmurts were prompted by the oppressive colonial policy of Tsarism and the arbitrariness and oppression of the "profiteers" and other officials. The agitations embraced the broad Bashkir and Tartar masses; the struggle continued until 1711. All these uprisings were crushed, and cruel punishment was inflicted on the rebels.

The enormous growth of class contradictions in the country, the strengthening of the rule of the nobility, and the growth of a new economic force, the merchantry, served as the basis for further changes in the nature of the Russian feudal state. The absolute monarchy was strengthened and the feudal state acquired all the typical traits of a police-bureaucratic state.

In the second quarter of the eighteenth century the national economy of Russia developed under an economic policy which, in general, continued the line of Peter I, albeit with departures dictated mainly by the group interests of the upper layers of the nobility and their puppets on the throne. The pomeshchik form of land ownership and the number of serfs grew, thanks to the distribution to the pomeshchiki of treasury lands and their peasants. The barshchina obligations and the amount of quit-rent increased. The peasants were forced more and more to work in the industrial enterprises organized by the pomeshchiki as a part of barshchina. "Factory barshchina" further ruined the peasant economy. The peasants protested against the increase in this feudal oppression, and their protests were expressed in the form of desertions and uprisings.

In industry the exploitation of forced labor continued to expand. At the insistence of the factory owners, legislation was enacted in 1736 which bound to the enterprises people who practiced any sort of craft and their children who learned the craft.[5] In 1744 entrepreneurs were permitted to purchase villages,[6] and there began a large registration of peasants to the factories.

The spread of serf relationships in industry was combined with the growth of capitalistic forms of exploitation. The material and legal position of the workers became worse as factories were transferred from the treasury to private entrepreneurs (nobles and merchants) and their companies. Protest against such transfers was the main motive for the series of agitations that occurred in factories in various parts of the country, especially in the Urals. With the development of the mining industry in the Urals came the requisition of forests from the Bashkirs who were driven from their lands. This in turn brought on the uprising of the Bashkir people from 1735 to 1741.

The industrial entrepreneurs sought to ensure their monopoly position. Thus private factory owners tried to undermine the industries owned by the treasury, to seize its enterprises, and to prevent interference by state organs in the activities of private enterprises. The increasing spread of monopolies and the granting of leases to industry and trade left their harsh mark on the status of the masses.

During the period under review capitalistic elements in Russian industry grew significantly, but the feudal serf-owning system of economy continued to reign unchecked. The development of commodity production served feudalism; industry depended basically on forced labor.

It is to the second quarter of the eighteenth century that we must turn for the great geographic discoveries and profound scientific inquiries of the Russian people: the first Kamchatka expedition under the leadership of V. Bering and A. I. Chirikov (1725–1729); the Orenburg expedition led by I. K. Kirilov (1734–1737); the Great Northern expedition of 1733–1743, and the second Kamchatka expedition associated with it. In 1725 the Academy of Science was established in St. Petersburg, and as early as the 1740's Russian science, as exemplified

---

[5] *Polnoe sobranie zakonov Rossiiskoi imperii s 1649 g.* [Complete Collection of the Laws of the Russian Empire from 1649], IX, No. 6858, p. 707. Hereinafter cited *PSZ.*

[6] *Ibid.,* XII, No. 9004, p. 181.

by M. V. Lomonosov, achieved enormous successes—not only of national, but of world-wide significance.

The changes in the Russian economy in the eighteenth century also caused changes in economic thought. As was stated above, the economic views and program of Ordyn-Nashchokin marked a new stage in the development of Russian economic thought: the economists' focused their attention on the national economy and began to turn their attention to the problem of eliminating the economic, military, and cultural backwardness of Russia. The advances in this trend of thought were most clearly expressed under Peter the Great.

The period of Petrine reforms, touching the most diverse aspects of Russian life, was simultaneously an epoch of significant advance in Russian economic thought. There was a substantial increase in the number of persons actively considering the problems of Russian economic development and a significant increase in the number of economic problems which generally preoccupied the thinkers and statesmen of the age. Among them, Peter I undoubtedly made the greatest contribution to the development of economic thought. His devoted activity in various areas of the national economy indicates a profound understanding of the economic problems of the country and of the methods required to resolve them. As will be shown, Peter I expressed ideas which were quite advanced and progressive for his times.

It would, of course, be incorrect to ascribe all the economic reforms of the first quarter of the eighteenth century to Peter personally. A great role was played by his closest counsellors, who took immediate leadership in these reform activities. Numerous economic memoranda and projects were sent to the Tsar at this time by authors known and unknown.

The economic views and programs of Peter I were, of course, determined by the real conditions of Russian life and by the needs for the progressive development of the country. In this period, as in any other, the original creators of history were the people, the toiling masses. At the same time it would be incorrect not to note Peter's enormous share in the reforms. In all of them, including the economic, the leading role belongs to him. The reforms were carried out amidst a stubborn and sharp struggle against all the conservative and reactionary forces of society, forces which held fast to the old way of life—the old order and customs.

The reforms received legal expression and form in frequently issued decrees and regulations. Many decrees defining important economic reforms were written by Peter in his own hand. Thus, for example, the great and very important decree of January 16, 1712, was written by Peter himself almost in its entirety. "Textile mills will be increased throughout the country so that in five years it will not be necessary to purchase uniforms abroad," states one of the points of this decree; "to establish stud farms . . . to establish a collegium for trade affairs and administration so that they will be brought to better conditions . . . ,"[7] and so forth. The very important decree of November 5, 1723: "On the establishment of factories in Russia," is written entirely in Peter's hand. In this decree were formulated the basic principles of the policy introduced by Peter I for the development of heavy industry in Russia. In many decrees, regulations, and other legal acts, Peter himself made important additions of a fundamental nature. Actually, he was the originator of many decrees, instructions, and regulations.

The distinguishing traits of Peter's economic views were their efficacy and great practical significance. They received their real embodiment in the economic policy of the feudal state. Through his vigorous economic activity, determined by the objective realities of the country, Peter I exerted great influence on his contemporaries. Around him were numerous devoted counsellors full of initiative. He received many proposals from persons wishing to contribute their share to the economic development of the country: from Fedor Saltykov, Kurbatov, Nesterov, I. T. Pososhkov, Konon Zotov, Lodygin, Filippov, and others.[8] The authors of these memoranda touched on the most timely economic questions: on the relations between pomeshchiki and enserfed peasants, on the development of trade, native industry, and agriculture; on money, taxes, and so on. Some of the authors' proposals in these memoranda were realized in Peter's subsequent legislation.

Of all the authors of economic memoranda and projects, the most interesting and the one achieving greatest historical significance was a contemporary of Peter I, I. T. Pososhkov, author of the remarkable *Book on Poverty and Wealth.* I. T. Pososhkov was an extremely colorful and interesting figure. He was an outstandingly original economic thinker who endeavored to examine thoroughly the most acute problems of contemporary life and to provide penetrating solutions to them.

---

[7] See *ibid.*, IV, No. 2467, pp. 776–9.

[8] Part of these proposals can be found in N. Pavlov-Silvanskii, *Proekty reform v zapiskakh sovremennikov Petra Velikogo. Opyt izucheniia russkikh proektov i neizdannye ikh teksty* [The Reform Projects of Contemporaries of Peter the Great. An Attempt to Study Russian Projects and their Unpublished Texts] (St. Petersburg: 1897).

A. L. Ordyn-Nashchokin, Peter I, F. Saltykov, and V. N. Tatishchev were, above all, representatives of the nobility. With the entry on the scene of I. T. Pososhkov, the new social force, the merchants, with their insistent demands, were represented. True, Pososhkov still held strongly to the feudal serf-owning order of social life; he made no infringement on this order and, indeed, attempted to enter the ranks of the landowners himself; but his works began to reveal the dissatisfaction of the merchants with the nobility's arbitrariness. His writings also display aspirations to weaken somewhat the ruling preëminence of the feudal class and to provide a very modest place to representatives of other classes of society. Without infringing on the serf laws, Pososhkov proposed a series of measures in the form of state regulation of the economic interrelations between pomeshchiki and enserfed peasants. He considered it necessary that some limitation be imposed on the arbitrariness of the landowner in his relations with labor and the product of labor.

To the first quarter of the eighteenth century belong the interesting projects of Fedor Saltykov, projects which deal primarily with economic questions. These same problems also preoccupied A. P. Volynskii and V. N. Tatishchev, whose activities belong to the first and second quarters of the eighteenth century. The 1740's saw the beginnings of the work of the great scholar M. V. Lomonosov, in whose rich heritage are found many important thoughts on the development of the productive forces of the motherland.

This period in Russia also marks the birth of a native political economy, a gradual discovery of internal ties and economic phenomena, that is, of economic laws.

As Marx said, the science of political economy arose when thinkers turned from the study of the process of circulation with which the mercantilists were preoccupied to the theoretical study of the process of production and began to understand that the value of goods is determined by labor. The beginning of this awareness is connected with the English economist William Petty (1623–1687) and the French economist P. Boisguilbert (1646–1714). They still did not understand what kind of labor creates value. In the solution of this problem a "great step forward" was made much later by A. Smith and D. Ricardo; however it was Marx who finally worked out the labor theory of value.

Marx greatly admired the first steps toward the scientific discovery of the economic law of value.[9]

It is interesting to note that in Russia at the end of the seventeenth

[9] See, Marx, *K kritike politicheskoi ekonomii;* Engels, *Anti-Diuring,* etc.

century various theoretical proposals are found which cannot be considered as anything other than the embryo of the labor theory of value. We have in mind the "Notebooks" first published several years ago of the elder Avraamii, a monk and abbot of the Andreevskii monastery near Moscow.[10] These Notebooks consist of materials compiled by the author at the end of 1696 for Peter I. In them Avraamii criticizes the disorders in various spheres of contemporary social life, exposes the corruption of judges, expresses his views as to the obligations of the Tsar for the administration of the state, and gives counsel on questions relating to church affairs, the court, finances, and other areas of life. It is not without interest to note that among the many visitors who chatted with Avraamii about contemporary affairs was the economist I. T. Pososhkov. Concerning finances, Avraamii counselled the Tsar to economize the state funds, and to that end he called for a budget for the Tsar's court: "The autocrat should determine the amount of annual expenditure of his household; he should be firm and thrifty and issue either a law or a rule about it; he should not contribute to ruin." [11] Avraamii decisively opposes the levying of sales taxes on commodities and consumer goods, taxes which lead to higher prices. Concerning this he reflects on what determines the price of goods. To produce some items much labor is lost; other items demand an average amount of labor, and still others a small amount. Contrasting things which require much labor with things which need less, Avraamii writes: "Those goods that are produced at a moderate cost should have a moderate price; those goods that are produced easily and fast should be priced low. I, sinful monk, have written how logically an autocrat should govern his subjects, what items are indispensable to anyone in his daily life, and that those items should not be made expensive by the decree of taxes." [12]

In these words is expressed the thought that the price of goods is determined by labor and the range of prices depends on the amount of labor expended on the goods. This was in essence the nucleus of the labor theory of value, the beginning step of Russian economic thought along the path of economic science.

The economic views of the toiling masses were distinctly expressed

---

10 See *Istoricheskii arkhiv*, VI (1951), pp. 143–155. See also the introductory article about these "Notebooks" by N. A. Baklanova, *ibid.*, VI (1951), pp. 131–143. On Avraamii, see also B. B. Kafengauz, *I. T. Pososhkov. Zhizn i deiatelnost* [I. T. Pososhkov. Life and Activity] (Moscow: AS USSR, 1951).

11 " 'Tetradi' startsa Avraamiia" [Notebooks of Elder Avraamii], *Istoricheskii arkhiv*, VI (1951), p. 153.

12 *Ibid.*, VI (1951), p. 155. (Italics mine—A. P.)

in the peasant uprisings of the beginning of the eighteenth century. The demands of the rebels were most clearly apparent in the appeals, the "provocative letters" of K. Bulavin and his associates.

The Demands of the Revolting Peasantry

The first quarter of the eighteenth century was a period of intensified feudal-serf exploitation of the peasantry. The oppression of the peasants by the pomeshchiki increased. Taxes and all other peasant dues and obligations to the state grew significantly. Great masses of peasants performed exhausting labor in the construction of St. Petersburg, Azov, and other towns and fortresses, on canal building, roads, warfs, and so on. The peasants bore on their shoulders the entire burden of long and difficult wars.

The number of peasants and other segments of the population drawn by the state into these labors and into the army can be judged, for example, by these telling figures: from the votchina of the Makariev-Unzhenskii monastery, which had 500 households at the beginning of the century, 67 persons were taken in 1704 for land work in the construction of St. Petersburg and for labor in Azov and other places. From the settlement of Solikamsk, where in 1678 there were 465 households, no less than 200 persons were taken into the army and to perform other works in the five years from 1703 to 1707.[13]

Under Peter I money taxes rose sharply. They were numerous and burdensome. About thirty customary taxes were collected annually, and in the Volga and Ural provinces there were still more. The following facts testify to the character of these taxes and levies: In 1710 a decree was issued concerning the collection of money from peasant households and merchants for the hire of horses and wagons, for artillery and other supplies; in the same year there were decrees concerning the collection in the Moscow *gubernia* from all revenues of one denga per ruble; in 1712, concerning the annual collection from the gubernias of 20,000 rubles for the preparation and processing of lime in St. Petersburg; in 1713, "concerning the preparation of wine, vinegar, and beer for the regiments under Field Marshal Sheremetev, and concerning the collection of money for that purpose from every household in all gubernias"; in the same year, 1713, concerning the collection of money from each household for fodder for the army regiments in the St. Petersburg gubernia; in 1714, "concerning the collection of money for

---

[13] See P. Liubomirov, "Krepostnaia Rossiia" [Enserfed Russia], *Entsiklopedicheskii slovar obshchestva Granat* [Encyclopedic Dictionary of the Granat Society], XXXVI, Pt. III, p. 536.

the construction of houses on Kotlina Island"; in 1717, concerning the collection of money for provisions in the St. Petersburg "warehouse"; in 1721, concerning the collection of money for provisions and all sorts of nautical supplies for the sea campaign of 1721; in the same year, concerning the collection of money for the construction of the Ladoga Canal, and so on.

The main burden of taxation fell on the peasantry. To find new revenues, a special post of "revenue seeker" or "inventor" was created, whose direct obligation was "to sit and bring profit to the sovereign," and who, according to the picturesque expression of Kliuchevskii, "prepared a general roundup of the inhabitants." A special tax on beards was paid by peasants on coming to town; heretics paid all taxes double. The zealous "profiteers" slyly imposed on the population of the Volga and Ural provinces a tax on eyes, with various prices on black eyes and grey eyes. It was not surprising that they earned the deep hatred of the people.

In the first quarter of the eighteenth century, the general collection of state revenue (translated into gold rubles), rose approximately threefold. The position of the town poor became worse. The colonial policy of tsarism was a heavy burden on the other nationalities of the Russian state.

The enserfed peasantry, the town poor, and the oppressed nationalities stubbornly resisted their exploiters—the boyars, the pomeshchiki, and the feudal state. This opposition was expressed in various ways—in complaints against masters and imperial officials, in frequent escapes of the enserfed peasants from their pomeshchiki, in the increase of robbery, and finally in the open, armed struggle of the revolting toiling masses against the whole feudal serf-owning system which dominated the country. One manifestation of protest by the peasantry and the town poor against the oppression of the feudal state was the growth in heresy.

The relation of the enserfed peasants to their exploiters was sharply evident in the content of several petitions. Ignorant of the deep connections and unity of interests between the chief of the feudal state on the one side, and the class of feudal landowners—the boyars and pomeshchiki—on the other, the downtrodden, oppressed peasants sometimes turned to the Tsar in naive hope of receiving protection from him. Some of their documents portray with poignant directness the deep hatred of the peasants toward their oppressors and the passionate hope for liberation from the serf yoke. In one petition to Peter the enserfed people wrote:

> We beg, pray, and kindly exclaim in hope that we will influence you regarding [our] liberation, to take us out of Sodom and Gomorrah. Our petition to you, Great Sovereign, will be blocked by your proud boyars and princes, who want to keep us in distress as in Sodom and Gomorrah; like lions they tear our flesh, like poisonous, enraged snakes they ring us, and like ferocious wolves they beat us, like merciless Pilates; Great Sovereign, have mercy, help us! [14]

Although he introduced important reforms in all fields of the economy, the policy of Peter I contributed to the still greater elevation of the nobility and the further enslavement of the peasant masses.

The flight of enserfed peasants assumed enormous proportions. The peasants secretly fled from their landlords, abandoned compulsory labor in the construction of towns and fortresses, and went south to the borders of the country, in order to discover places where no enslavement by landlords prevailed. The imperial government took decisive measures for the apprehension of the fugitives and their return to the feudal landlords. Agents went in search of the fugitives, and military units were sent to bring them back.

The peasants, the town poor, and the non-Russian nationalities revolted against the feudal-serfdom system. In the Astrakhan uprisings of 1705–1707, settlement people, riflemen, soldiers, dock workers, and "idle people" took part. Astrakhan was then a big market; many fugitive peasants and "idle people" were employed in industries (fish and salt) and in the loading and unloading of ships. The cause of the uprising was the corruption and oppression of the Astrakhan governor. The rebels wiped out the representatives of the tsarist power and divided up their property. They elected their own government—elders—from among the settlement people. The revolt spread to other towns and engulfed almost the entire southeast. It had a strong antifeudal character, the objective of the revolt being to eliminate the boyars and profiteers and to embark on a campaign up the Volga to Moscow.

During the uprising sharp class contradictions between the participants developed. A split occurred. The popular masses—the escapees, workers, "idle people," and soldiers—threatened to seize the merchants' stocks. The Astrakhan merchants, the settlement leadership, and the higher clergy quickly deserted the uprising and betrayed it. Antifeudal, also, was the peasant-Cossack uprising led by K. Bulavin, which in 1707–1708 engulfed a vast territory—the Don, Free Ukraine, and the Volga provinces, as well as adjoining districts. The large in-

[14] See Solovev, *Istoriia Rossii s drevneishikh vremen,* XVIII, 356–7.

crease in Russian serfdom at the end of the seventeenth and beginning of the eighteenth century caused a mass flight of peasants to the south and southeast of Russia, where serf law did not exist. Many fugitive peasants assembled in the towns of the Upper Don and the Free Ukraine. Together with the town poor they became beggars. These beggars were used by the wealthy Cossacks as a cheap working force. The tsarist government demanded the return of the fugitives, a request which was against the economic interests of the well-to-do Cossacks. On the other hand, the Don Cossacks feared to lose their well-known independence from Moscow.

The immediate cause of the Bulavin uprising was Peter's dispatch to the Upper Don of a military detachment led by Iu. Dolgorukii with orders to seize and return the fugitive peasants. Dolgorukii was particularly cruel toward the fugitives. The main force of the uprising consisted of the fugitive peasantry, soldiers, riflemen, petty settlement and serving people, heretics, boors, and workers assembled by the tsarist government for ship building and woodcutting. Well-to-do Cossacks also took part in the uprising.

The aims of the rebellion were proclaimed in the "provocative letters" of 1708 which were written and widely distributed by Bulavin "to the good officials, merchants and free peasants" in various towns, villages and hamlets. These letters expressed Bulavin's aspiration to unite various social elements in the uprising: the beggars and well-to-do Cossacks, the adherents of the dominant Orthodox church, the heretics, under the slogan of struggle against the boyars and profiteers, and the Don Cossacks who wished to defend their independence. These basic slogans were strengthened by an appeal to struggle for the "true Christian faith" and "for the pious Tsar." To wit:

> *An appeal from Kandratii Afonasevich Bulavin and the entire Don Army, to the leading citizens of Russian cities, villages, hamlets, and settlements, as well as to merchants and peasants:* This is to inform you that we agreed unanimously with the Don Army to defend and die for the holy churches, the Orthodox Christian faith, our most pious Tsar, and ourselves—son for father, brother for brother, friend for friend. And all you good, leading citizens, and all you free peasants should also join us. Defend with us jointly our holy churches, the Orthodox Christian faith, our most pious Tsar, and the great Don Army. You settlement inhabitants, merchants, and free peasants, do not fear any abuse from us. You should not keep silent about bad deeds of princes, boyars, profiteers, and foreigners. Neither should you allow them to lead you away from

> Orthodox Christianity to the Greek faith by many of their signs and provocative miracles. And henceforth you leading settlement people, merchants, and all free peasants should not quarrel, fight uselessly, steal and destroy.[15]

In the governors' reports to the Tsar and in other documents originating in the areas engulfed by the revolt the aim of the rebels is usually depicted as a struggle against the boyars, profiteers, tsarist administrators, and officials. Actually this was the most important aim of the beggars taking part in the uprising. One report read: "And these rebels have declared: We have a task to perform—to remove the boyars, Colonel Prince Grigoriev Ivanovich, profiteers, and petty clerks." [16] And another: "These rebels want to remove boyars, and even me, your humble slave, and profiteers and petty clerks." [17]

It was planned that after taking the center of the wealthy Don Cossack area, the town of Cherkassy, then Azov and Taganrog, the rebels would move on toward Moscow in order to free all of Russia from feudal-serf exploitation. "The rebels planned to march on Cherkassy, destroy Azov, and then march on Moscow. In Azov, Moscow, and all other cities they intended to hang boyars, profiteers, and foreigners." [18] The Bulavinites were gathering "to go to Rus to kill the boyars." [19]

After the rebels took Cherkassy, in May, 1708, there developed considerable social heterogeneity among the participants in the uprising, and class conflicts arose between the beggars and the well-to-do Cossacks.[20] The beggars wanted revenge, not only on the boyars and profiteers, but on the local exploiters and the well-to-do Cossacks. Immediately after the victory of Cherkassy the beggars demanded that Bulavin "kill all the wealthy Cherkassy Cossacks and plunder their belongings." The well-to-do Cossacks, however, wished to utilize the antifeudal movement of the beggars only to advance their own interests, that is, to defend the independence of the Don Cossack host from Moscow.

Bulavin established low prices on bread and salt. Confiscated property of crown officials and of the church was distributed among the beggars. The wealthy Cossacks soon left the uprising, weakening it significantly; its entire weight now fell on the beggars.

The hopes of the beggars are expressed in the "provocative letter"

---

15 See *Bulavinskoe vosstanie (1707–1708 gg.)* [Bulavin's Uprising, 1707–1708] (Moscow: 1935), pp. 450–1.

16 *Ibid.*, p. 166.

17 *Ibid.*, p. 174.

18 *Ibid.*, p. 187.

19 *Ibid.*, p. 365.

20 See N. S. Chaev, *Bulavinskoe vosstanie (1707–1708 gg.)* [Bulavin's Uprising (1707–1708)] (Moscow: 1934).

of Ataman N. Golyi, who led the struggle after the death of Bulavin. While Bulavin aspired to consolidate the various participating social groups without setting the wealthy against the beggars, N. Golyi wanted to depend on the beggars alone.

> *An appeal from Nikita Goloi and his entire army to court officials, governors, and administrative officials in Russian cities, and to supervisors and policemen in hamlets and villages, and to all monks:* We do not want to bother monks. We have business with boyars who cause injustice. You beggars, and everybody, leave all cities on horseback and on foot, naked and barefoot, go and be not afraid. You will receive horses, arms, clothing, and money. We rebelled in order to defend the old faith, holy churches, and all monks, so that we shall not fall into the Greek faith.[21]

The Bulavin uprising was put down with exceptional cruelty. Sending an army to the Ukraine under the command of V. V. Dolgorukii, Peter I ordered him to carry out the decree: "spare nothing to put out the fire." [22] The chief of the feudal state directed that the harshest measures be taken against the rebels. He ordered Dolgorukii to "go to those cities and villages . . . which joined the rebellion and burn them completely, beat people and put agitators on wheels and pikes, thus weaken the desire among people to join the rebellion . . . because without firmness this upheaval cannot be ended." [23] After the suppression of the Bulavin uprising, serf law was introduced on the Don, and thus the Don lost its independence.

The Bulavin uprising, like others at the beginning of the eighteenth century, was directed not against the reforms of Peter I, but against feudal-serf exploitation, the feudalists, and Tsarist official arbitrariness. This insurrection shook the foundation of the feudal-serf system and therefore had a progressive character like all other antifeudal resistance and wars.

Peter I also cruelly put down uprisings of the Bashkirs, the Tartars, and the Udmurts. Nevertheless, the peasant uprisings continued. For example, in 1713 the peasants of several landlords of Nizhegorod, Rostov, and Vereisk districts "refused . . . to obey their masters, and left them." [24] The peasants would not become reconciled to their difficult position, and whenever they could they struggled against the serf yoke.

---

[21] *Bulavinskoe vosstanie,* p. 466.
[22] *Ibid.,* p. 193.
[23] *Ibid.*
[24] See *PSZ,* No. 2668, p. 24.

CHAPTER 11. *The Economic Views and Principles of Peter I.*

The Views of Peter I on the Economic Role of the State

The main source for the study of the economic views and policies of Peter is the legislation of the first quarter of the eighteenth century, compiled in chronological order in Volumes 3 to 7 of the *Complete Collection of Laws of the Russian Empire,* published in 1830 by Speranskii. The letters and papers of Peter are another important source. To a significant degree they are connected with legislation and therefore have great relevance for the study of the laws of that epoch. In these letters, memoranda, and notes one can often see the origin and development of the basic ideas of the reforms.

The Russian state of this period was *feudal-absolutist,* that is, it represented a definite stage in the development of the feudal, nobilitary state. Peter I strengthened the absolute monarchy and brought about the victory of absolutism in Russia. The feudal state was "the organ of the nobility for suppression of the enserfed peasants . . ." [1] In the absolute monarchy the real power remained in the hands of the feudalists.

The class nature of the Russian state of this period and the character of the Petrine reforms are clearly defined by I. V. Stalin: "Peter the Great did much for the elevation of the class of pomeshchiki and the development of the rising merchant class. He contributed much to the creation and strengthening of the national state of the pomeshchiki and merchants." [2]

The far-reaching and complex task of Russia—to eliminate the backwardness of the country—was closely connected with the immediate task to gain military victory in the struggle for sea outlets. Both of these aims forced Peter to deal resolutely with the economic problems of the country. He formulated a broad program of economic transformation which included: 1) the establishment of heavy industry and

---

[1] F. Engels, *Proiskhozhdenie semi, chastnoi sobstvennosti i gosudarstva* [The Origin of Family, Private Property, and State] (Moscow: Gospolitizdat, 1953), p. 178.

[2] Stalin, *Sochineniia,* XIII, 105.

the development of handicrafts; 2) the improvement of external and internal trade; 3) the promotion of agriculture; 4) the extension of the water routes of communication; 5) the advancement of the finances of the country.

The economic functions of the Russian feudal state were narrow and one-sided. The problem of developing the productive forces of the country remained outside the interests of [central] government authority. Only in the second half of the seventeenth century did the [central] government begin to concern itself with economic tasks other than those of requisition and taxation and to adopt measures for the development of trade and industry. Ordyn-Nashchokin emphasized the development of the national economy as the immediate task of the state. The economic reforms of the first quarter of the eighteenth century marked the further progress of political thought and government activity in this direction.

Peter I's understanding of the economic tasks and functions of the state was closely connected with the very nature of absolutism and the police-bureaucratic state. The latter is characterized by the fact that the state power, based on officialdom, the police, and the army, entirely suppresses the personal rights of the lower classes of society, establishes unlimited interference in the life of the subjects, and introduces powerful regulation as well as complex enforced guardianship. This enforcement, guardianship, and supervision of the feudal-noble state also embrace the realm of economic life. As chief of a feudal-absolutist, police-bureaucratic state, Peter I utilized state power as a weapon to suppress the resistance of the toilers against their exploiters, as a weapon of supra-economic compulsion. He significantly extended the application of forced serf labor in the country, and chained the peasant to the landowner more relentlessly than before.

Under Peter, treasury needs continued to play a central, but no longer exclusive, role in the economic policies of the state. Although always concerned about revenue (indeed, his fiscal policy was unprecedented in its energy and scope) Peter devoted serious attention to the development of the productive forces of the country, the growth of technology, and the increase of the productivity of labor. This was the first time that Russia witnessed extensive state activity in these fields.

The political ideology of Peter received literary expression in a prominent treatise of the time, *The Right of Monarchial Will* by Feofan Prokopovich. The cornerstone of this philosophy was that state power has not only rights over its subjects, but also obligations to them. These obligations center in the responsibility of the state for the "general welfare," the "public good." Consequently, Peter laid a broad legislative foundation for measures of state authority. "We hereby declare that we always have a diligent interest in the spread of *general well-being* and benefits to our subject merchants and to all other arts and crafts which all other wealthy states have and foster," [3] notes the Tsar's 1718 charter to Savelov, a member of a provincial court, and to the Tomilin merchants for the establishment of a mill. The "Regulation of the Manufacturing College" also refers to the increase in Russian manufactories "for the general welfare and prosperity of the subjects . . ." [4] In his historic speech on the conclusion of peace with Sweden (October 22, 1721), Peter I said, "One must work for the general well-being."

The principle of "general welfare" is customary in the theories of absolutism and is found among all spokesmen of the absolutist variant of the theories of "national law" both in Russia and in Western Europe. Under the pretext of the "general welfare" of the subjects, absolutists and their theoreticians everywhere defended autocratic power. In Russia the contemporary of Peter I, Feofan Prokopovich, used this same idea as the basis for absolutism.

The theoreticians of absolutism and the absolutists present the principle of "general welfare" as a supra-class principle, and the state power is portrayed as an extra-class force equally concerned with the entire population. In actuality the feudal state is the political organization of the class of feudalists. In a society where some classes are exploited by others, the state defends not only the general national interests of the given country against other countries, but above all, and mainly, the interests of the ruling class against the oppressed classes of the country. The subjugation of the exploited and the suppression of their resistance represent significant functions of the feudal-absolutist state. Expanding these ideas of "general welfare" and "public good" as the basic task of unlimited monarchy, the theoreticians of absolutism and the absolutists themselves mask the two-faced class nature of the feudal state. In feudal society the "general welfare" is above all the welfare of the noble class and the merchants. Security from external foes, the growth of culture in the country, and the development of productive forces are accomplished at the expense of the toiling, oppressed masses; and the benefits of culture and of the development of technology and productive forces are utilized first of all by the ruling classes—the nobility and merchants.

At a specific historical level in the evolution of society, absolutism

[3] *PSZ,* V, No. 3180, p. 552. (Italics mine—A. P.)
[4] *Ibid.,* VII, No. 4378, p. 169. (Italics mine—A. P.)

was a political form corresponding to the progressive tendencies of the development of society, expressing itself in a struggle for the creation and establishment of a national state as opposed to feudal disunity.

Peter I attached great significance to the activity of the state in economic life. In his view the state was a force directing the economic development of the country, and state legislation was the mighty lever of this development. The issuing of corresponding law decrees, regulations, and instructions concerning economic life and the struggle for their implementation were, therefore, one of the most important aspects of Peter's state activity. He maintained that the state is an organ immediately responsible for broad economic activity. Peter energetically developed the economic activity of the state and realized, to a high degree for that time, the construction of crown industrial enterprises, canals, sheep farms, stud farms, and the development of state domestic and foreign trade.

But the economic functions of the state were interpreted by Peter I in a much broader form than the direct economic activity of the organs of the state. The state, in Peter's view, ought in all ways to call forth and encourage private initiative and private enterprise so as to teach its subjects the rules of rational husbandry and sensible economy and to show people how to be "good economists." The state should implant new forms of organization for labor and new techniques. The means of implanting the rules of good economy by the state are understood in broad terms. Here are both direct compulsion and propaganda: practical initiative of the state, aid to the people, encouragement of private enterprise, and its compulsion. Peter broadly applied these various methods of implanting new forms of economy, and they were often combined.

He considered it necessary to use propaganda widely to urge the wisdom of the economic measures being introduced by the state. The decrees not only informed the subjects of the norms obligatory for execution, but they were also utilized as a means of propaganda in favor of the measures taken. Thus, for example, the decree directing that Russian leather be made only with train oil, and not with pitch, explained the reason for the measure: leather made with pitch admits moisture and soon wears out. In a decree directing the use of the scythe and rake in harvesting grain instead of the sickle, there is the explanation that other countries work primarily with the scythe and rake. Peter attached great significance to the wide distribution of decrees and other laws among the people, and he required these to be printed and disseminated and the most important to be displayed in the churches, fairs and trading places ("to be spread by the town crier").

Guardianship, regulation, and compulsion in the implementation of new forms of economic activity are looked upon as unavoidable because of the backwardness and ignorance of the people in questions of economic life and their distrust of new ways. In one of the outstanding laws—the decree of November 5, 1723—concerning the spread of factories in Russia, admitting that few volunteers are willing to start factories, Peter writes: "because our people are like children about their learning, they will not learn the alphabet until they are forced by their master; at first they complain, but when they learn, then they are thankful, as is evident from contemporary affairs; not everything has been accomplished willingly which has brought fruits, and about many things one hears praise; in manufactories we apply not only proposals, but we also force and instruct and use machines and other measures to teach you how to be a good economist." [5]

In the same spirit a decree establishing a company for trade with Spain was issued: "because everyone knows that our people will not undertake anything without compulsion: as a result the Commerce College shall have direction like a mother over her children until they are mature and administer this new affair." [6]

In accordance with this broad understanding of the economic tasks and functions of the state, the state apparatus was also reorganized. Characteristically, of the number of state colleges created under Peter (in place of the outmoded system of departments) almost half were economic colleges: the Mining College, managing the mining industry; the Manufacturing College, taking charge of all other industries; the Commerce College, supervising foreign commerce and trade in ship building; the Finance College, handling the collection of state revenues; the State Control College, dealing with state expenditures. The Chief Magistrate supervised internal trade and handicrafts. For the management of agriculture there was no special college, but the development of agriculture was included in the functions of the Finance College.

The Principles of Industrial and Trade Policy

Most notable and fruitful was Peter's activity in the development of heavy industry in Russia. "When Peter the Great, having relations with the more developed countries in the West, feverishly

[5] *Ibid.*, VII, No. 4345, p. 150.
[6] *Ibid.*, VII, No. 4540, p. 332.

built mills and factories for the supply of the army and the strengthening of the country's defense, this was an original attempt to escape from the framework of backwardness," said I. V. Stalin.[7]

In the Peterine policy of the development of native heavy industry two periods are discernible. The first dates from the beginning of the Russian war against Turkey and Sweden until 1709–1710. This was the most difficult stage of the conflict. The long, stubborn struggle required much armament and various supplies for the army. The importation of weapons into Russia from abroad was cut off by the foreigners. Previously iron of high quality was imported from Sweden, but the war with Sweden ended this trade and threatened Russia with a shortage of iron.

Prior to and during the war for an outlet to the sea Peter forced the construction of industrial enterprises directly concerned with the supply of the armies and the fleet—metallurgical, armament, and cannon industries, saw mills, sailcloth and rope factories, and so forth. A metallurgical industry, large for that time, was established, and foundations were laid for the development of the Urals as a major metalworking center. A number of big enterprises were created there. In the north, in the Olonets region, in St. Petersburg, and also in other areas iron and armament mills were built.

The second period, following the victory at Poltava, is characterized by Peter's increased attention not only to military but also to civilian, industry. Great effort was spent to establish a native textile industry with the purpose of freeing the country from dependence on cloth from abroad for army uniforms and civilian needs. At the same time tanneries and glass factories, paper, silk, tobacco, and other industrial enterprises were set up.

During Peter I's reign about two hundred industrial enterprises were created in Russia, including fifty-two for ordinary and seventeen for fine metallurgy, fifteen for the textile industry, eight for sailcloth, nine for silk, six for writing paper, fourteen for leather, ten for glass, seventeen for powder making, twenty-three for lumber.[8] The establishment of a native heavy industry—metallurgy, the production of arms, and other things—played a great role in the increase of Russian military power and was a decisive factor in the victory of Russia over Sweden. At the end of the first quarter of the eighteenth century Russia was no longer faced with the necessity of importing iron, but even began to export it.

[7] Stalin, *op. cit.*, XI, 248–9.

[8] See E. I. Zaozerskaia, *Manufaktura pri Petre I* [Manufacture Under Peter I] (Moscow-Leningrad: AS USSR, 1947), p. 10.

Great attention was given to the discovery and extraction of ores, minerals, and other useful natural resources. In 1700 a decree was issued regarding the search for ores over all Russia. Peter, wishing to make this exploration for ores, and other minerals, a national affair, widely publicized and materially supported this endeavor. In 1700 a separate Department for Mining Affairs, and in 1719 the Mining College, a special organ managing the mining industry, were organized. "Our . . . Russian State, more than many other lands, abounds in useful metals and minerals," [9] states the decree establishing the Mining College. The decree represents an elaborate program for the development of mining in Russia.

Attention was also given to peat procurement. Peter was keenly interested in the extraction of coal and oil, and an expedition was made for coal on the Don, in the area of Bakhmut, in the Voronezh gubernia, and on the Dnepr.[10] The Ukhtinsk oil deposits in the Archangel gubernia were investigated, as well as others. The search for various dyes was also encouraged so that their importation could be eliminated.

The industrial establishments inaugurated by Peter were manufactories, but they also utilized the mechanical forces of water mills (as, for example, in the mechanical boring of cannon). Peter attached great importance to the equipping of big enterprises with water power. He paid close attention to the construction of water mills in the West, invited masters of mill operations to Russia, and forced Russians to learn this art. In the selection of a place for building new mills the possibility of utilizing water energy had decisive significance.

Techniques advanced for that time were introduced into heavy industry. The Manufacturing College was entrusted with the obligation to "be alert to any newly-invented machinery and instruments, and, should there be any, to obtain them." [11] Peter himself gave particular emphasis to the latest methods and was very well informed on western technical advancements. While abroad, he visited mills and inventors, carefully examined new machines, and tried to import the most useful to Russia. He sent people abroad on various missions and, in fact, ordered them to learn new techniques.

Throughout the country better methods for the processing of leather, using train oil instead of pitch, were introduced. A detailed study of newer techniques in making leather was undertaken, and severe pun-

---

[9] *PSZ*, V. No. 3464, p. 760.

[10] *Ibid.*, VI, No. 4129, p. 796; VII, No. 4297, p. 110; E. I. Zaozerskaia, "Poiski kamennogo uglia pri Petre I" [Coal Prospecting Under Peter I], *Izvestiia Vsesoiuznogo geograficheskogo obshchestva* [Bulletin of the All-Union Geographic Society], LXXV, Issue 2 (1943).

[11] *PSZ*, VII, No. 4381, p. 182.

ishment was prescribed for those who continued to use old procedures. New and more perfect means of preparing lumber with saws instead of axes were introduced, and the instruction of people in these improvements was organized. A decree regarding methods of salting fish was introduced in Astrakhan, and so on.

Peter gave close consideration to the problem of military technology. In a struggle with a strong and experienced enemy, such as Sweden, military technique played an important role. Much attention was paid to the equipping of the Russian army and navy with first-class weapons. When it came to tactical means of fighting and other questions of military art and technique, Peter I not only utilized the newest achievements of the Western European countries, but also encouraged the initiative and independent creations of the Russian people. Thanks to this, Petrine Russia did not fall behind the advanced countries of Western Europe and in some armament techniques outstripped them.

In Russia many people worked creatively on complicated technical problems; [12] Peter himself made several inventions in various realms of technology. Among his close co-workers were remarkable technological inventors such as Nartov, who developed original forms of stands and made many other important inventions.

Peter highly valued private enterprise and industry. Capital was still insufficient for the creation of heavy industry, so that private initiative and governmental financing acquired greater importance. The military-industrial enterprises were built at state expense. But even in the early period of the Petrine reforms, private enterpreneurs were also attracted to the creation of big industry, as, for example, Demidov and Stroganov.

In the second decade of the eighteenth century, while continuing to build enterprises at state expense, Peter took a decisive step to attract private capital. He knew that for the flourishing of industry the efforts of the state alone were not enough, and that the economically interested owners of capital would have a decisive significance in these new Russian projects. Companies were created for the organization of big industrial enterprises. The state mills were given over to private companies. It was ordered that mills should not for much longer be supported by state funds. "These manufactories and factories which have been, and those which will be, established by the treasury . . . shall be brought into good condition and be given out to private persons,

---

[12] V. V. Danilevskii, *Russkaia tekhnika* [Russian Technology] (2nd edition, Leningrad: 1948), cites many examples of the technical creativeness of the Russian people during this period.

and the College shall be responsible for them," [13] states the "Regulations of the Manufacturing College."

Peter did not hesitate to force the compulsory merger of merchants into companies, although this means of introducing trading capital into industry did not have great significance at the time. According to P. Liubomirov's argument: "Cases of creation of factories by direct compulsion by Peter are known to be comparatively few, and among a number of examples no sort of special compulsion is evident." [14] The assertion of M. N. Pokrovskii that Peter I had to bludgeon merchant capital into industry is entirely untrue. The merchants themselves showed initiative in building factories and mills. The weight of crown and private enterprise is seen in the following figures: of fifty-two industries of ordinary metallurgy formed during this time, twenty-two were state-owned and thirty private; of seventeen mills of fine metallurgy, thirteen were crown and four private; of eight cloth factories, four were crown property. In paper and leather output and in powder production the crown owned half the enterprises, and in all heavy industry established under Peter, 43 per cent belonged to the crown and 57 per cent to private owners.[15] Thus private capital was even then predominant in heavy industry.

Peter considered it necessary to guarantee the interests of the merchant class in the affairs of production and consequently gave them various privileges. The owners of industrial enterprises were freed from all government service. The companies received loans from the treasury without interest; often they were given land, state buildings, and equipment. Industries were transferred to companies in perpetuity, with the obligation to keep them "in good order," seldom for a definite period. In case of poor management the industries were returned to the crown, and, in some instances, each participant in the company was fined. The state enterprises were sold to private companies on generous terms and the latter were exempt from taxation for a definite period of time. It was decreed that in all affairs except state and criminal offenses the manufacturers were subject only to the Manufacturing College.[16]

In order to supply adequate raw materials to native enterprises it

---

[13] *PSZ*, VII, No. 4378, p. 171.

[14] P. G. Liubomirov, "Rol kazennogo, dvorianskogo i kupecheskogo kapitala v stroitelstve krupnoi promyshlennosti Rossii v XVII–XVIII vekakh" [The Role of the State, Nobility, and Merchant Capital in the Organization of Heavy Industry in Russia in the XVII–XVIII Centuries] *Istoricheskie zapiski* [Historical Notes], No. 16 (1945), p. 81; see also Zaozerskaia, *Manufaktura pri Petre I*, p. 55, 59, and 64.

[15] See *ibid.*, pp. 9–10.

[16] See *PSZ*, VII, No. 4378, p. 170.

was proposed to increase the domestic production of flax and other types of agricultural products. Tax-free importation of several types of raw materials was permitted, and, on the other hand, the export of certain raw materials (wool, for example) was limited or entirely forbidden. The state supplied industrial enterprises with a working force recruited from the serfs and from other layers of the population. Monopoly rights were granted by the government to various companies for the production of specific goods; this was of great significance.

But these privileges were not characteristic of the industrial policy of Peter. He appreciated the importance of competition for the development of industry, and as a rule he did not permit complete monopoly either by private persons or by companies. The "Regulations of the Manufacturing College" stressed one special point—"the non-exclusion of other factories." It stated: "The College should be cautious as to when and to whom a privilege to establish a factory should be extended and should not exclude others who would like to establish similar factories in the future; such a condition should not be permitted because rivalry betwen mill owners will not only lead to an increase in numbers but also in value and the goods made will sell at a moderate price, which will be beneficial to the subjects of his majesty." [17]

Competition, however, should be permitted with caution and within a narrow framework: "The College will watch whether some manufactories are organized satisfactorily; and if so, then the introduction of similar manufactories must not harm those already established, especially if they should provide poor products, even thought these be sold at a low price." [18] Peter considered it important to secure the trust of the merchants with respect to the economic policy of the state. It was prescribed, for example, that payments from merchants for state enterprises be "taken annually with moderation in order to enable them to operate without inconvenience." It was forbidden to demand that merchants provide substantial capital at once upon joining a company; instead it was recommended that they be treated "moderately and carefully . . ." [19]

Tariff policy had great significance for the development of native industry. Its basis was the protection of Russian industry from foreign competition, but Peter I did not consider it expedient to protect Russian industry completely from the importation of foreign goods. Industrial companies petitioned insistently that the government forbid the

[17] *Ibid.*, VII, No. 4378, p. 169.
[18] *Ibid.*
[19] *Ibid.*, VII, No. 4378, p. 172.

importation of goods which they produced and always received the reply that importation would be forbidden only when native production satisfied domestic demands. With this principle in mind, the importation of dyes and several other wares was forbidden. Thus competition from foreign capital was not completely eliminated, but only limited.

Peter considered customs duties sufficient protection for Russian industry from foreign competition. By a decree of November 6, 1723, import duties on listed goods were determined on the basis of the level of domestic production of these goods.[20] A new customs tariff, highly protectionist in character, was developed on this principle. The majority of imported items carried a duty of 75 per cent, 50 per cent and 25 per cent of their value in rubles.[21] Export duties were also determined by the developmental needs of native industry. They were greatly raised on several types of unprocessed skins, as well as on yarn from flax and hemp, because these raw materials were needed for domestic manufactories.

It was also a complicated matter to provide organized enterprises with a working force in general, and in particular with qualified cadres. In contrast to many countries of Western Europe (for example, England and Holland), Russia had neither a large number of workers freed from serfdom and released from their land, nor did she possess a trained, qualified cadre of craftsmen. Consequently, the problem of providing heavy industry with a working force was resolved on the basis of the forced serf labor then prevailing in the country. The manufactories which were being established, although they employed a significant amount of hired labor, in general made wide use of the labor of enserfed peasants and enserfed workers.

In the crown manufactories, masters (smiths, carpenters and other shop workers) were forcibly assembled from various gubernias by decree of the Tsar and the Senate.[22] Simple and dirty work was done by peasants assigned to the mills. Manufactories were looked upon as a place for the forced labor of the poor, the condemned, and the tax offenders; women were sent to the weaving mills.

In manufactories, as was the case throughout the entire country, an atmosphere of forced labor and serf discipline by the cudgel reigned. In the state mills a police-bureaucratic state imposed labor discipline

---

[20] *Ibid.*, VII, No. 4346, p. 151.

[21] See K. Lodyzhenskii, *Istoriia russkogo tamozhennogo tarifa* [History of Russian Custom Tariff] (St. Petersburg: 1886), p. 61.

[22] See *PSZ*, IV, Nos. 2449, 2485, 2575; V, Nos. 2736, 2806; VII, No. 4421, and others.

by serfdom's methods, and in private enterprises the worker was subject to the complete arbitrariness of the entrepreneur. Thus, for example, in an order to the superintendent of the Tula crown smiths (1706) it was decreed that drunken and lazy skilled workers would be punished not only by fines, but also by beatings, and would be confined in chains and irons for two or three days. Workers were cudgeled for disobedience to the superintendent.[23] In 1702 the imperial charter to the Demidovs included the right to punish the shiftless with cudgels and lashes. In both crown and private enterprises sticks, lashes, cudgels, and confinement in "iron" and in prison were widely used. Strong measures were adopted in order to force the poor to work. Legislation against the needy was frequent and severe. Begging was forbidden, and the poor were sternly punished: after a second offense a healthy beggar was sentenced to forced labor. Healthy beggars were forcibly sent to factories.

Nevertheless, the problem of supplying heavy industrial enterprises with an adequate working force remained acute. The entrepreneurs continually complained about the lack of workers. By a decree of January 18, 1721, Peter I gave the nobility and the merchants the right to purchase villages for the mills "in order to increase the number of such mills," "under condition that these villages will always be attached to the mills."[24] No one was allowed to sell or lease villages separately from the mills. This decree had great theoretical and practical significance. Previously merchants did not have the right to purchase serfs; this was an exclusive privilege of the nobility, although forced labor in private enterprises was actually practiced even before the decree of 1721. The decree led to a considerable increase in the practice of serf labor in Russian industry. The right to purchase villages for industries accorded a great privilege to the merchants.

While widening the application of serf labor to industrial enterprises, Peter I also aspired to introduce free hired labor into the factories, insofar as this practice did not contradict the prevailing system of serfdom. Tsarist charters establishing industrial enterprises usually stipulated that free hiring of all persons (except fugitive serfs) was permitted "with payment for their labor in appropriate amounts." Sometimes it was said that only free persons and not serfs were to be hired.[25]

While he encouraged the use of hired labor by private entrepreneurs, Peter nevertheless struggled in behalf of the nobility's interests to pre-

---

[23] See K. A. Pazhitnov, *Polozhenie rabochego klassa v Rossii* [The Condition of the Working Class in Russia] (2nd edition, Leningrad: 1925), I, 194–5.

[24] *PSZ,* VI, No. 3711, pp. 311–2.

[25] *Ibid.,* VI, No. 3543, pp. 163–4.

vent manufacturers from accepting fugitive serfs for work. The latter were unconditionally returned to their former owners, the nobles. At the end of his reign Peter found it necessary, however, to retreat from this principle in the interests of industry: by a decree of July 18, 1722, workers and apprentices—fugitive serfs—were allowed to work in the mills and factories if it were evident that their return to former owners threatened a cessation of the enterprise's work.[26] Clearly this measure was a great advantage to the entrepreneur.

Under Peter much attention was given to the preparation of qualified cadres for industry: masters to teach the Russian people were carefully selected from abroad. The industrial enterprises were obliged to take apprentices, and the sending of youths abroad for training was widely practiced. Since heavy industry in Russia was weakly developed, it did not as a rule compete with small peasant industry. The two industries produced different products and had different markets. Wherever the interests of heavy industry and small peasant production clashed, the latter was as a rule sacrificed to the former.

While aiding the growth of heavy industry, Peter at the same time adopted some measures for the development of handicraft production in the towns. On April 27, 1722, he issued a decree regarding the formation of guilds in Russian towns. Although he borrowed the form of organization of the crafts from the West, Peter did not transfer it mechanically; he adapted it in accordance with prevailing conditions in Russia. One of the characteristics of the guild organization of the Western European countries was the monopoly position of the guild in the city market. This was achieved by various measures, such as forbidding non-members to practice a craft in the town, by making it difficult to join the guild, by limiting the number of journeymen and apprentices under each master, and so on. These limitations did not exist in Russia. The right of registering in the guild was given each craftsman, and this included serfs who possessed a release paper from a landowner or steward.

By subsequent decrees of the Senate (in 1722) and instructions of the Chief Magistrate of separate guilds (in 1724), craftsmen who failed to join the guilds were forbidden to engage in their crafts. In practice, nonmembers were strictly forbidden to display signs of their trade (that is, signboards) on the street. The number of journeymen and apprentices working under a master was not limited. In other respects the guild organization introduced by Peter was similar to that of Western Europe: the division of craftsmen into masters, journeymen,

---

[26] *Ibid.*, VI, No. 4055, p. 746.

and apprentices; the obligatory apprenticeship and period of service; the taking of examinations for advancement to master; the marking of products by the masters and officials of the guild; various punishments for low quality of products made; and so forth.

It is known that the craft guild organization did not take root in Russia. In the literature on the subject, Peter's organization of guilds is evaluated in various ways. The view has been expressed that Peter borrowed forms from the West which were already obsolete even there. In the West the appearance and development of the guild system progressed differently than it did in Russia: "The need to combine against the united brigand nobility, the necessity for various markets at the time when a manufacturer was simultaneously a merchant, the increase of competition from the fugitive serfs in the growing cities, the feudal system of the entire country—all this gave rise to *guilds;* thanks to the gradual accumulation of small capital by the savings of various craftsmen and their static number in a growing population, a system of journeymen and apprentices developed, and created in the towns a hierarchy similar to that in the village population." [27]

The absolutist state authority in Russia attempted to implant the guild organization by compulsory measures and to conform to historical conditions different from those which existed in the West when guilds originated there. But even in Russia at the beginning of the eighteenth century the craft guilds were not at all novel. Even before Peter several elements of guild organization of the crafts, particularly apprenticeship, were in evidence. On the other hand, at the beginning of the eighteenth century, the craft guild organization in the West was far from moribund, although conditions had changed. The medieval monopoly of guilds in the city market was at that time significantly undermined, but not eliminated, by the development of manufactures and trading capital. The guild system continued to exist under the protection of the absolutist state, which carried on the policy of mercantilism. In France the privileges of the guilds were finally abolished at the end of the eighteenth century by the bourgeois revolution. In Germany the guild organization of crafts continued until the twentieth century. In post-Petrine Russia during the entire eighteenth century the government took measures to implant the guild system, but it met with just as little success as under Peter I.

The industrial policy of Peter was characterized by the regulation of production. It affected all forms of industry—state, private, and craft production. The degree of protection and interference by the state in

---

[27] Marx and Engels, *Nemetskaia ideologiia,* pp. 14–5.

industrial activity varied for different social forms of production. In manufactories belonging to the government all economic activity was strictly controlled by the state. The activity of enterprises which were transferred to private persons and companies was also subject to stringent rules. Private enterprises were considerably less affected by regulation. But even here the Manufacturing College had broad rights of supervision and control. Peter demanded from the Manufacturing College exact knowledge concerning the work of the industrial enterprises and their leadership. In order to maintain control over the quality of industrial products, all enterprises had to send the Manufacturing College samples of their work "so that the College can see the quality of what they produce." [28] In 1722 a decree required the testing and grading of iron and prohibited its sale without a brand.[29]

It is noteworthy that the regulation of industrial production introduced under Peter I did not have the same petty character which was evident, for example, in the measures of Colbert and his successors in France. There is no similarity between the industrial legislation of Peter I and Colbert's "Ordinance on the Production of Materials," or his "General Instruction" (317 articles), published in 1671, which regulated the dyeing of wool materials and which set down to the minutest detail and under fear of stern penalty the rules for dyeing materials. The violators of these provisions were punished by fine, confiscation, and pillory. This cult, this mania for control by a severe regime of "industrial soldiery" [30] did not exist in Russia. Peter's regulations usually had a rational character and were dictated by the conditions of technical and economic development.

Peter attached great significance to the growth of the internal and external trade of Russia. He instituted a number of measures directed toward the creation of a particular class, privileged in contrast to the peasantry and city lower classes, namely the Russian merchants. With the aim of establishing for the latter a more favorable position in the country, self-government was accorded the city populations as early as 1699. In the towns, elected organs of administration were established—*ratushi*—and merchants and settlers were removed from the supervision of governors and departments of central administration. In 1718 magistrates were created in the towns. The merchants together with the

[28] *PSZ*, VII, No. 4378, p. 171.

[29] *Ibid.*, VI, No. 3952, p. 645.

[30] See Pierre Brizon, *Istoriia truda i trudiashchikhsia* [History of Labor and of the Workingmen]. Translated from the French. (Petrograd: Gosizdat, 1921), p. 128.

industrialists and several other elements of the city population were designated as a special privilege group—the guilds. In all of their legal problems, except those of state, the merchants were subject to the magistrate. Measures were adopted to increase the number of merchants, and decrees were issued regarding the compulsory return to the towns and settlements of merchants registered there as taxpayers. Peter impelled the Commerce College to look after the merchants, "so that such treasure will not be wasted." [31]

Although he granted the merchants self-government, Peter I at the same time exacted a number of obligations: timely and complete submittal of crown duties, that is, trade duties, taxes and other obligations of the city population, and also observation of other state rules.

The Code of 1649 stipulated that only those persons registered as settlement taxpayers (*posadskoe tiaglo*) could engage in trade; peasants were forbidden to engage in trade in the towns, and they were not allowed to register as settlement taxpayers. In the towns peasants could sell the products of their farms to merchants only wholesale and in the merchants' inns, and not to consumers from stands or stores. The limitation on the number of persons with the right to enter the merchant class meant the accordance of a monopoly position to this class. Peter I maintained and enforced the ban on engaging in trade in the towns without registering there as a taxpayer. The peasant, as before, could sell his produce in towns only to merchants in the merchant inns. This measure preserved the interests of the treasury and those of the settlement merchants, for persons engaging in trade without registration in the settlement made the levy of trade taxes difficult on the one hand, while their trade increased the competition among town merchants, on the other. Nevertheless, the prohibition against peasants trading in towns was not obeyed. They traded there widely, not under their own names, but under the names of merchants, without paying trade taxes. This ban hindered the development of trade and brought losses to the treasury. Consequently Peter rescinded the previous prohibition, and in 1699 crown, monastery and nobles' peasants were allowed to register in the merchant class and to engage in trade in Moscow. In 1700 a decree dealt with the movement of peasants into the settlements, that is, peasants who lived in the towns, traded, and paid taxes. By the decrees of 1711 it was permitted that "all ranks of people may trade in any commodity anywhere under their own names, with payment of all customary taxes." [32]

Thus the rural inhabitants were enabled to settle in the towns, regis-

[31] *PSZ*, VII, No. 4453, p. 247.
[32] *Ibid.*, IV, No. 2327, p. 642; No. 2433, p. 743.

ter as merchants, and engage in trade. The transfer to settlements was proclaimed open to all peasants—"free, regardless of who they are." In reality, this was not meaningful to all peasants, but only to those who had a considerable amount of capital in trade (a turnover of not less than five hundred rubles, or, if they took goods to the port of St. Petersburg, not less than three hundred rubles.) The fugitive peasants who had lived long in the settlement were not returned to their former owners, and, if in possession of adequate capital, they were registered in the settlement. These decrees legally formulated the economic process of the origin and growth of bourgeois elements among the peasantry and aided the further growth of the merchant class and its capital.

One of the most important problems in Russian commercial policy at this time was that of state monopolies in foreign and domestic trade. During a considerable period of his reign, approximately up to 1714, Peter I increased the volume of goods which fell to state monopolies. This action was prompted by fiscal considerations and the government's acute need of revenue for military and other expenditures. The monopoly goods were Russian leather, rope, potash, pitch, tallow, fish glue, rhubarb, caviar, resin, pig bristles, masts, and sable furs. The state monopoly also extended to wine, salt, and tobacco. The right to deal in monopoly goods was either given by the government to private persons on lease or exercised by the state itself in the form of state trade. The monopoly trade in these goods provided the treasury with income, but it seriously impaired the development of trade by private entrepreneurs and hence imposed a constraint on the possible expansion of state fiscal activities.

In later years the policy of Peter I in this sphere changed drastically. For a majority of goods the state monopoly on export was discontinued. In 1719 the monopoly of export goods was abolished except for two, potash and resin, where it was retained "for conservation of the forests." Simultaneously taxes were raised on goods on which the monopoly of trade had been removed. The cessation of the state monopoly on the export of goods assisted the development of trade.

Foreign trade interested Peter I especially as a means of enriching the treasury and increasing state revenue. At the same time, he appreciated the role of foreign trade in the development of the national economy. Peter looked upon foreign trade as one of the levers of the state's foreign policy; its skillful use could foster the realization of diplomatic aims. Trade agreements between Russia and other countries often supplemented political covenants.

Peter I firmly held to the following maxim: export more, import less. The basis of his trade policy was therefore the concept of an active trade balance. He expressed it clearly in the decree to the Commerce College on November 8, 1723: "Strive by all means to sell our goods for hard currency rather than exchange them for goods." [33] The trade balance of Russia was at the time acutely passive.

The shortage of trading capital, the absence of suitable sea routes, the inexperience of Russian merchants—all brought about a considerable concentration of foreign trade in foreign hands. These were mainly Dutchmen and Englishmen, who served as intermediaries in Russian trade with other countries and reaped enormous profits.

As a result of the victory over Sweden, Russia gained several harbors on the Baltic Sea and thereby the necessary conditions for the extension of foreign trade. Peter inaugurated a number of measures to transform the recently founded city of St. Petersburg into a foreign trade center for Russia, and by administrative measures, incentives, and exemptions to merchants, Russian foreign trade was transferred from Archangel to that city.

But to expand its foreign trade Russia needed more than open seaports. Western European countries were in firm control of world trade. They stubbornly refused to give Russia a direct route to world markets and tried by every means to constrain the Russian merchants. Peter insistently strove to free Russian foreign trade from the expensive Dutch and English middlemen. He endeavored to establish direct trade with France, Spain, and other European countries, and even with America. He sent his agents to these countries with instructions to acquaint themselves there with the conditions of foreign trade, to ascertain what goods were imported from where, and to where they were exported, what were the prices, and so forth. These representatives were instructed to influence the merchants in Cadiz (Spain), in Bordeaux (France), and other big cities to trade directly with Russia and to show them the advantage of trade without intermediaries. In order to develop trade and protect the interests of Russian merchants, consulates were established in Cadiz, Bordeaux, and other cities of Western Europe.[34]

Peter also tried to build a native merchant fleet in the hope of eliminating Russia's dependence on Holland and England. "We ought to increase our commerce . . . and to transport goods to Spain and Portugal in our own ships; such commerce can bring great profit," [35] stated a decree of November 8, 1723. To encourage this policy, a favorable customs tariff was established (less than one third) on those goods

---

[33] *Ibid.*, VII, No. 4348, p. 152.
[34] *Ibid.*, VII, No. 4286, pp. 102–4; No. 4341, pp. 143–4.
[35] *Ibid.*, VII, No. 4348, p. 152.

which were exported from, or imported into, Russia in Russian merchant ships.

Great attention was paid to the development of trade with the countries of the East—Persia, China, and others. Here, too, the aim was to free the country from the intermediation of European countries, to establish direct access to make Russia an intermediary between the East and Western Europe, and to enhance transit trade. Expeditions were sent to the Eastern countries to find suitable routes and collect information on the feasibility of trade with them. In 1716, for example, an expedition was sent along the Amu-Daria and other rivers, "in order to find a water route to India"; it was instructed to "see what goods, especially spicy herbs and the like, come from India." [36]

In order to provide the necessary capital for foreign trade and to organize the Russian merchants, Peter I tried to form trading companies after the example of England and Holland. As is known, even Ordyn-Nashchokin had made efforts in this direction. In 1699 Peter I issued a decree ordering "that merchants of all ranks of the Moscovite state and cities shall trade in companies like those of other countries . . ." [37] This decree, however, remained on paper, like similar orders of a somewhat later time (1723).

In the sphere of internal trade the policy of Peter was directed at general development of local trade and fairs and also at raising the level of trade itself. Decrees were issued on the establishment of trade exchanges, on the collection and publication of data on prices of goods in various parts of Russia and in foreign markets—"so that it may be known where [goods] are cheap or expensive." [38]

The growth of heavy industry in Russia had even at that time led to the appearance of definite contradictions among industrial entrepreneurs and merchants. In cases where their interests clashed, Peter sided with the industrial entrepreneurs.[39]

Peter introduced a number of measures aimed at the regulation and supervision of trade. But this regulation was not petty and rigid. In part, prices were set only on goods which were a state monopoly—wine, salt, tobacco, sable furs, and so on. The prices on goods supplied to the state by private enterprise were set by agreement of the owners and the treasury, although, as may be judged, for example, by the decree of December 3, 1713, the treasury tried to use the competition of its sup-

---

[36] *Ibid.*, V, No. 2994, p. 198.
[37] *Ibid.*, III, No. 1706, p. 653.
[38] *Ibid.*, VII, No. 4293, p. 106.
[39] *Ibid.*, VI, No. 4057, pp. 747–8.

pliers for the lowering of prices.[40] The products of the first Russian factories were very expensive. In 1723 a decree was issued ordering the sale of goods from Russian factories "*not* at a high price . . . in order that they may be bought more quickly and not ruined by remaining a long time in the factories . . ." [41]

Measures instituted by Peter I in canal construction were characterized by farsightedness. He had in view a system of canals which would unite the Caspian, Azov, Black, Baltic, and White Seas, and the central regions of European Russia. Attempts were made to connect the Volga and the Don by two canals, one at the source of the Don (Ivan-Lake), and the other in the south between the rivers Kamyshinka and Ilovlia, tributaries of the Volga and the Don. Work on the Volga-Don canal was carried on for a long time in both places. The Northern War and then the loss of Azov (in 1711) forced the abandonment of the project. In 1708 the construction of the Vyshnevolotskaia ship transit system joining the Volga to the Neva and the Caspian Sea to the Baltic was completed. In 1718 was begun a bypass canal to avoid shipping on stormy Lake Ladoga. Investigations were conducted regarding connecting the White Sea with the Baltic. By order of Peter in 1722, a plan to build a canal joining the Moscow River with the Volga was drawn up. The Senate was ordered to watch over the preparation of the construction material for this canal, but the work was not begun.

This grandiose program for canal construction conceived by Peter was not within the realm of achievement by an autocratic and bourgeois-pomestie Russia. It took Soviet rule to execute the construction of the White Sea-Baltic canal, the canal joining the Moscow with the Volga, and the Volga-Don canal.

Peter was also interested in the possibility of opening a sea route across the Arctic Ocean to China, Japan, and India, and in 1719 he sent an expedition to Kamchatka with orders to ascertain whether America and Asia were connected.

The Principles of Financial Policy

Of all facets of the economy the field of finance attracted Peter's most continuous and systematic attention. This can be seen from the extraordinary number of decrees issued regarding taxes, duties, the monetary system, and other measures dealing with finance. This great concern with fiscal matters is understandable. The upkeep of the standing army, the long wars, the construction of large indus-

[40] *Ibid.*, V, No. 2746, p. 73.
[41] *Ibid.*, VII, No. 4368, p. 163.

trial enterprises, the support of the state apparatus—all of these demanded a great deal of money. Military expenditures were the main reason for the perpetual and acute need for money and constituted the moving force in Peter's financial reforms. "Money is the artery of war," he said repeatedly. The state budget of Russia under Peter I had a clearly defined military nature. In 1701, for example, military expenditures constituted 78.3 per cent of all budgetary expenses, and in 1724, 63 per cent. A number of historians err, however, in trying to explain most of Peter's reforms by fiscal considerations.

The idea of establishing a state budget in Russia had arisen as early as the seventeenth century.[42] A document which relates to 1680–1681 is preserved and contains a list of expenditures and revenue for all departments for the previous year and proposed figures for the next year. This had not as yet taken the form of a single state budget with the general balance of state revenues and expenditures, but was a simple compilation, a mechanical listing of the budgets of the various departments. Under Peter I budget matters for the first time became stabilized and acquired a more regulated nature.

At the end of the seventeenth century Peter entrusted a special institution, the so-called Close Chancellery, with the gathering of information on the revenue and expenditure of all departments. By a decree of March 14, 1701, all departments and town halls were obliged to supply the Close Chancellery with accounts of their income and expenditures and with various detailed monthly and annual information of a financial nature "in order that the great sovereign always be aware of such matters." The Close Chancellery for the years 1701 through 1709 listed actual revenues, expenditures and surpluses for the expiring year, presented monthly accounts of the cash at the disposal of the departments, and compiled tax books which gave data on revenues and expenditures for the current year. But these materials still did not represent a complete state inventory in the full sense of the word.

A major step in establishing the idea of a state budget was shown as an outline in Peter's decree of the so-called table of December 8, 1710.[43] "Determine 1) How much revenue is collected in the entire state from each separate category; 2) How much is spent on the army, garrisons, in all gubernias, and in the entire state, and also on the fleet—each separately as well as the overall amount; 3) What the other expenditures in the gubernias are and how much they amount to," this

[42] See L. N. Iasnopolskii, *Ocherki russkogo biudzhetnogo prava* [Outlines of Russian Budgetary Law] (Moscow: 1912), Chapter I.
[43] *Ibid.*, p. 32.

decree instructs. The tables of 1710 and 1711 represented a genuine state budget. However, their practical value was insignificant.

The idea of the state budget was further developed with the establishment of a system of centralized state administration in the form of colleges and with the reform of direct taxation. In the regulations of the State Controller College and the Finance College, correct annual compilations of expected state expenditures and revenues were formulated. Thus in the time of Peter "the concept of an annual budget was theoretically presented; but in practice it was not achieved." [44]

Peter paid much attention to attracting precious metals into the country, the demand for which increased greatly to meet the requirements of the wars and the growing national commodity markets. Russia then mined virtually none of her own precious metals. Under Peter an accelerated search for precious-metal ores was instituted, but their mining did not develop significantly.[45] The supply of gold and silver increased mainly through inflow from abroad.

Although the desire to bring money into the country was acute, this was never the sole purpose of enlarging the export of goods. Special measures were adopted to increase the inflow of specie, some of which were practiced by earlier Moscow tsars. The issuance of numerous decrees strongly supported the rule of the New Commercial Code, permitting foreign merchants to purchase goods in Russia, and Russian merchants to sell goods to foreigners, but only for efimki and gold. Foreign merchants were obliged to pay customs dues on goods imported to Russia in efimki and gold, but not those imported in Russian currency. Foreign money attracted by such means was utilized by the treasury mainly for the issuance of national money, which provided the treasury with a great monetary revenue and the national economy with additional means of circulation and payment.

As in the seventeenth century, the treasury was particularly interested in the influx of fully valued foreign silver money—for example, the Joachimsthaler (efimki), which was minted into Russian money at a significantly raised par value in comparison with its actual value, the difference constituting the money income of the treasury. The active policy for the attraction of precious metals was supplemented by, and interwoven with, an equally clear policy of forbidding the export of bullion and Russian money.[46]

---

[44] *Ibid.*, p. 57.

[45] Annual domestic procurement of silver did not exceed 15 puds 14 pounds in 1717 and in the subsequent years it was even smaller.

[46] See on this the following ukazy of Peter I: June 21, 1711, in *PSZ*, IV, No. 2383, p. 702; September 15, 1713, *ibid.*, V, No. 2713, p. 55; April 6, 1714, *ibid.*, V, No. 2793, p. 95; October 29, 1719, *ibid.*, V, No. 3441, p. 744; February 28, 1721, *ibid.*, VI, No. 3741, pp. 363–6.

Similar prohibitions had been used in the past. The novelty of the procedure undertaken by Peter centered, in the first place, on the insistence with which he sought complete cessation of the export of money, and, secondly, on the manner in which more than ever before this policy coincided with a policy of active trade balance and encouragement of native heavy industry. The prohibition on the export of money from Russia cannot be identified mechanically with the "monetary system" and the policy of "money balance" instituted in the Western European countries from the fourteenth to the seventeenth centuries, and it cannot be concluded (as is done in the literature on the subject) that this policy of Peter is a testimony to the backwardness of Russian economic thought of the time. The ban on the export of money from the country was dictated first of all by the aspiration to preserve the treasury from the loss of money income. Gold and silver as monetary metal were removed from free circulation in foreign trade. Russian merchants were obliged to hand over to the treasury, in exchange for Russian money at the established rate, all gold and silver gained by them from the sale of goods to foreign merchants. The state increasingly purchased monetary metal from the population within the country and attracted precious metals into the treasury to be transformed into money and thus provide monetary income. For these reasons, as well as to prevent the possible import of counterfeit money, Peter also forbade the importing of Russian money from abroad.

Under Peter important reforms of the monetary system were instituted. Never before (if one does not count the experiment of Aleksei Mikhailovich with copper rubles) was the issuance of money in Russia undertaken on such a large scale, and never had there been such bold plans for monetary affairs. For the period 1690–1724, 31,500,000 rubles (at par) of silver money, 706,000 of gold, and 4,354,000 of copper were issued, clearly an enormous sum for that time.[47] According to the approximate calculation of Patlaevskii, the total sum of silver money in the Russian market in 1725 amounted to about 40,200,000 rubles.[48]

Before, as well as in the first years of, Peters' reign the coinage of money took place not only in the state mint, but was also carried on by private artisans and by goldsmiths and silversmiths under government supervision. A duty had to be paid for this privilege. Peter transformed the coinage of money into a state monopoly. This change gave the

[47] See I. I. Kaufman, "Serebrianyi rubl v Rossii ot ego vozniknoveniia do kontsa XIX veka" [The Silver Ruble in Russia From Its Appearance to the End of the XIX Century], *Zapiski numizmaticheskogo otdeleniia russkogo arkhelogicheskogo obshchestva* [Notes of the Numismatic Branch of the Russian Archeological Society] (St. Petersburg: 1910), II, Issue 1–2, pp. 150–1.

[48] See I. Patlaevskii, *Denezhnyi rynok v Rossii ot 1700 do 1762 g.* [The Financial Market in Russia from 1700 to 1762] (n.p: n.d.), p. 249.

treasury a broader and more direct influence in monetary affairs and in the organization of the monetary system of Russia.

Peter viewed the study of money as one of the most important sources of war finance. When the need for money was particularly great, he did not refrain from such extreme measures as using copper church bells for the coinage of money, just as after the Russian defeat at Narva the church bells were melted down to make cannon.

The most widely circulated money in Russia at the end of the seventeenth century were small silver coins. The independent coinage of large silver denominations practically did not exist. The silver ruble was neither real money nor an official numéraire, but only an ideal private unit of account, the sum of 100 silver kopecks or 200 "deneg" (half kopecks). Since the growing market suffered from a chronic shortage of means of exchange, particularly of small money, in several places it was necessary to revert to the ancient practice of using leather money. Peter increased the issuance of silver money, introduced a number of silver coins of new values, issued silver rubles, and transformed the ruble into a real monetary unit for Russia. The technique of coining money was improved and made more significant.

The treasury's interests were served by a lowering of the metal content of coins by two alternative means—decreasing the general weight of money and decreasing the amount of precious metal used. The proportion of silver coins in circulation was one change effected in 1698 when weight was decreased by 30 per cent, and in 1718 the base of silver money was decreased from 84 to 70 per cent for large money, and to as much as 38 per cent for altynniky and copecks. These measures affected the monetary system by decreasing the purchasing value of the ruble almost by half. In reducing the amount of precious metal in the money, Peter was following a practice already widespread in countries of Western Europe and throughout Muscovite Rus.

Beginning with 1700, the coinage of copper money of small denominations was begun. Its aim was to provide revenue for the treasury and, at the same time, to supply the market with a convenient medium of exchange. The issuance of silver and copper money was carefully prepared and put into effect with caution. Gold money was also coined, and in 1718 it was incorporated into the monetary system of Russia.

By a decree of April 7, 1723 free coinage of money—silver and gold—was established to correct the diminishing revenue of silver and gold coins of the treasury. Scholars have correctly interpreted Peter's initiation of free coinage of gold and silver as an attempt to move toward a fresh understanding of monetary prerogatives, a practice which in the nineteenth century became axiomatic. These prerogatives were not dictated by the interests of the treasury; they were designed to correct the defects in the monetary system.[49] Peter's monetary reforms improved the Russian monetary system. They were a response to the demands of a growing trade and industry and of the whole national economy.

As in the past, Peter's tax system included direct and indirect taxes, usual and extraordinary. The exigencies of war brought about more and more new taxes, which placed a heavy burden on the shoulders of the toilers. The so-called rate (or assessment) taxes predominated: the state set up a general total of tax collection which had to go to the treasury, and in the taxpaying commune this sum was then distributed among the taxpayers in accordance with the amount of their property and other criteria. The lesser part of the state revenue was received in the form of nonassessed revenues whose general sum could not be established by the treasury in advance.

Before Peter, indirect taxes predominated in the state budget. In 1680 direct taxes constituted 33.7 per cent, while indirect taxes made up 44.4 per cent of the total state revenue.[50] Reviewing the tax policy of Peter during his entire reign, one cannot say definitely which taxes he preferred—direct or indirect. He widely utilized both forms. As a result of the introduction of the head tax and the increase of its amount in contrast to the sum of direct taxes which it replaced, the amount of direct taxes in the budget increased to 55.5 per cent in 1724. Henceforth direct taxes predominated in the Russian state budget for a long time.

Peter's decrees often stressed the necessity of guaranteeing the growth of state income "without putting a burden on the people." [51] He felt that the burden of taxes was determined not so much by their amount as by the injustice of their distribution and method of collection. The "Regulation of the State Finance College," which contains Peter's fundamental principles on tax policy, proclaims: "There is no state in the world which could not ease the burden of taxes if it applied justice, equality and dignity in its taxes and expenditures." [52] The "Regulation" is a very interesting document. It stresses the mutual interdependence of the tax system and the entire economy of the country

---

[49] See Kaufman, *op. cit.*, pp. 146–7.

[50] See P. Miliukov, *Gosudarstvennoe khoziaistvo Rossii v pervoi chetverti XVIII stoletiia i reforma Petra Velikogo* [Russian State Economy of the First Quarter of the XVIII Century and the Reform of Peter the Great] (2nd edition, St. Petersburg: 1905), p. 490.

[51] See *PSZ*, III, No. 1595, p. 380; IV, No. 2028, p. 287; V, No. 3080, pp. 492–3; VII, No. 4348, pp. 152–3.

[52] *Ibid.*, V, No. 3466, p. 765.

and the necessity of assessing the amount of taxes in accordance with the prosperity of the taxpayer. These financial principles were on a par with the most progressive theories of the time. Similar ideas were developed in the economic literature of the West and expressed by the most outstanding Russian thinkers of the time, as, for example, Pososhkov.

The desire to increase state revenue "without burdening the people" and to distribute taxes justly was in shameful variance with practice. The growth of state revenue from trade and industry was inadequate to cover the ever-growing needs of the state. The main burden of taxes therefore lay, as before, on the peasantry with its backward economy. Both taxes and collections were unequally distributed. Peter preserved and accentuated the division of the population into tax-paying classes and classes exempt from taxes. The serving nobility and clergy were freed from personal direct taxes, a fact which underlines the discriminatory character of Peter's tax policy. He introduced a vital change in tax units: the household levy was replaced by a head tax. In ancient Rus the taxes and collections were levied in head tax, household tax, or land tax, differently at various times and in different forms of payment. The head tax principle existed in Russia even at the time of the Tartar-Mongol yoke. The household levy under the name "chimney" and "gate" also existed in Russia in early times. In the middle of the fifteenth century the unit of tax levy was the so-called "sokha," which earlier meant a specific amount of the working force and implements of labor and later, a definite amount of plow land. In the beginning of the seventeenth century, the "sokha" began to be applied and the so-called "living quarters"—a definite number of peasants or landless peasant households.[53]

The land levy by "sokha" and "living quarters" led to a decrease in peasant planting in order to lessen the taxes; this was disadvantageous for the treasury and for the taxpayer, as the latter was obliged to pay taxes for idle land. Therefore in the seventeenth century the Moscow government changed from the landplow levy to the household levy, at first only for some collections, but from 1680 on for all direct taxes and collections. The answer of taxpayers to this reform was mass mergings of several peasant families into single households with one gate during

---

[53] See A. S. Lappo-Danilevskii, *Organizatsiia priamogo oblozheniia v Moskovskom gosudarstve so vremen smuty do epokhi preobrazovanii* [Organization of Direct Taxation in the Moscovite State from the Time of Troubles to the Period of Reforms] (St. Petersburg: 1890); Miliukov, *Spornye voprosy finansovoi istorii Moskovskogo gosudarstva* (St. Petersburg: 1892).

the household census, and sometimes permanently, so as to lower the tax burden.

In 1718 a decree ordered a census of the male population and the determination of the head tax, based on the cost of the upkeep of the army and the number of males; it also sought to determine the manner of collection of the head tax and its transfer to the regiments. The tax reform was connected with the dispersal of the armies throughout the gubernias among the peasant population and in the towns and had a definite purpose—the upkeep of the armies. The census lasted for a number of years, and the head tax was collected for the first time in 1724, replacing all other direct taxes. The peasants of the pomeshchiki were assessed at seventy-four copecks, and the city population at one ruble twenty copecks. The peasants on crown lands were also assessed with quit-rent for the treasury at forty copecks per head, as they were free from obligations to the pomeshchiki.

The aim of the head tax was to gain more taxpayers and a more equal tax distribution. The taxpayer was accessible now to the treasury regardless of his connection with land or a definite household. The reform eliminated the inequality connected with the household principle of taxation, but it introduced other disparities. The basic weakness of the head tax system was its neglect of the property position of the taxpayer. The tax was taken from each male regardless of age, ability to work, or ownership of property. But the great advantage of the head tax for the treasury was the great simplicity in financial technique. This explains the wide use of the head tax in all countries of the ancient world and the Middle Ages and its survival in later times.

The introduction of the head tax in place of the household tax was recommended to Peter by several authors of reports, as, for example, the Treasury Chief Nesterov (in 1714) and the unknown author of a "New Project of Tax Collection for the Treasury in Order to Increase State Revenue." The idea of the head tax then spread through Russia, even though it was not generally accepted. Ivan Filippov and Pososhkov, criticising the household system of taxation, proposed to replace it, not with a head tax, but with a different unit of levy.[54] The introduction of the head tax had far-reaching effects on the toilers' condition and on the whole national economy. It sharply increased the tax burden on the peasantry.

[54] See "Ivan Filippov's Reports" in N. P. Pavlov-Silvanskii, *Proekty reform v zapiskakh sovremennikov Petra Velikogo* [Reform Projects in the Memoranda of Contemporaries of Peter the Great] (St. Petersburg: 1897), pp. 61–7. On Pososhkov see below.

Peter I and Serfdom. Policy in the Realm of Agriculture

The question of Peter I's views regarding the peasantry, and the significance of the Petrine reforms for the evolution of serfdom have attracted a great deal of scholarly attention. In the literature on the importance of the social policy of Peter I and the role of his reforms in the development of serfdom in Russia, conflicting views prevail: some attribute to Peter I the chief and decisive role in establishing serfdom in Russia, while others completely reject any import to his activity in this process. Soviet historical science has done much to establish the correct understanding of the process of the origin and development of serfdom in Russia, of the role of actual practice and customs in this process, on the one hand, and of the state authority on the other, all of which makes it possible to evaluate accurately the role of Peter in this development.

But if the general influence of the state activity of Peter on serfdom in Russia has been more or less established in our literature, the same is not true of the evaluation of the significance of Peter's individual measures. Entirely unfounded is the idea, present in our literature up to now, that Peter I was an opponent of serfdom in principle and only consented to it as an unavoidable evil. Actually the question of serfdom did not create any doubts in Peter's mind. Serfdom had existed in the country long before his time, and he accepted this as a fact and made wide use of it in instituting his reforms in various spheres of life. He considered the right of the nobility to the ownership of land and peasants as a condition of the obligatory service of the nobility to the state. Nobles who did not serve had their land and peasants taken from them, and such nobles were subjected to civil punishments and even proclaimed as outlaws.[55] Such a view of serfdom differed from that which was set up later under Peter III and Catherine II, which existed until the peasant reforms—an understanding by the tsars and nobility of serfdom as an exclusive class privilege of the nobility, entirely independent of the obligation of the nobility to the state.

The reforms of Peter led to a considerable strengthening of serfdom in Russia; he did much to elevate the pomeshchiki class. The decree of March 23, 1714, which dealt with primogeniture, had great significance in this regard. It completed an earlier process of fusion of the two forms of landowning, votchina and pomestie, into one form—hereditary ownership, although some differences in the distribution of

[55] See *PSZ*, VI, No. 3874, p. 478, and others.

votchina and pomestie were actually preserved until the end of the eighteenth century.

As early as the seventeenth century the pomestie landownership closely resembled the votchina, inasmuch as the Code of 1649 established the transfer of the pomestia to the son, along with the obligation of service to the state; on the other hand, the votchinnik who inherited his estate, along with the pomeshchik, was obligated to serve the state.

The decree of 1714 does not differentiate between the pomestie and the votchina forms of ownership. The significance here is another division, that between immovable and movable property. The decree altered the existing order of inheritance of the noble ownership; such inheritance was legally formulated, and different systems of inheritance for immovable and movable property were established. The division of immovable property between heirs was abolished, and primogeniture was introduced: immovable property went to only one heir, by order of the owner himself; and if such an order was lacking, it went to the eldest son of the deceased landowner. Movable property was divided among all the heirs.

The motives for the reforms were stated in the decree. First, they aimed at the preservation of the noble families' influence and power; second, in the fiscal interests of the state, they aimed at halting the impoverishment of the peasantry resulting from division of the property of the nobles, and, third, they aimed at creating a stimulus for nobles who received no property to engage in labor useful to the state.

The decree of 1714 clearly expressed Peter's aristocratic tendencies and his concern for the fate of the nobility. He feared that dispersal and degeneration of the noble class would result from division of the estates. Such divisions, the decree notes, lead to the eventual impoverishment of the noble families and to the decline of their glory. If they were not halted, the noble families would in time become freeholders and settlers, "because there are already many such examples among the Russian people." As a result of the establishment of primogeniture, "families will not decline, and their serenity will be firmly sustained by their glorious and great houses." [56]

This new order of inheritance was contrary to the established traditions of the nobility, and it was abolished in 1730. Property again began to be divided. However the other important aspect of the reforms of 1714—the inheritance of pomestie property—was preserved, and this had great significance in the furtherance of serf oppression.

The tradition of the seventeenth century had demonstrated that in

[56] *Ibid.*, V, No. 2789, p. 91.

the votchina estates where ownership was transferred by inheritance from father to children, the personal dependence of the peasant on the owner, the lack of rights of the serf, and his abuse by the owner were greater than in the case of pomestie property, where ownership of the land and peasants was temporary and conditional. The process of approximating the pomestie estate ownership to the votchina which occurred in the eighteenth century meant a simultaneous increase in the oppression of the serfs and an actual growth of the personal power of the landowner. The owner of the estate gradually appropriated judicial and administrative control over his serfs.

The decree of 1714, which merged the pomestie with the votchina and established the inheritability of all noble, immovable property, was thus a great stride along the way of increasing serfdom, elevating the nobility, and lowering the peasantry. The increase in inheritability of noble ownership also meant the inheritability of the right of the noble to the person and labor of the serf.

In Russia serfdom took "the crudest of forms, which in no way differed from slavery." [57] The widespread trade in serfs clearly testifies to this. Serfs were sold in Russia separately from land in the seventeenth century. Under Peter I this traffic in serfs by families and by individuals grew rapidly. It was supported by the established system of supplying the army with recruits according to the number of households and by the permissibility, ruled in 1717 and 1720, of accepting purchased recruits for this service.

During his entire reign Peter carried on a stubborn struggle against the flight of the peasants and sponsored severe measures against fugitives and against persons assisting them. Fugitives who were found were severely punished, and those who sheltered them were heavily fined.

Oppression of the serf was augmented by Peter's tax reform, which replaced the household levy with a head levy. The head tax was levied on all kholopy, regardless of whether they tilled land or were in the personal service of their lords.[58] The head system of levies increased still more the personal dependence of the peasant on the noble. The transfer of the tax from the "house" to the "head" gave the landowner a still greater opportunity to utilize the land according to his own discretion.

Peter's head tax was levied equally on kholopy and on enserfed peasants; and thus the class of kholopstvo as a form of involuntary labor separate from serfdom was eliminated in Russia. The blending of these two forms of involuntary labor began in Russia long before

[57] Lenin, *Sochineniia,* XXIX, 439.
[58] See *PSZ,* VII, No. 4145, p. 10.

Peter. The tax reform of Peter only completed the process. By Peter's decree in regard to the census, the kholopy were made equal with the enserfed peasants; but this produced little change in their position, as the preceding and later development of serfdom in Russia had a tendency to transform the enserfed peasants into kholopy—that is, into slaves. Whereas earlier kholpstvo meant full, but temporary, dependence of the kholop on his master (until the death of the latter), now, being transferred to the position of the enserfed peasant, the kholop remained in perpetual servitude.

But the tax reform embodied another extremely important factor in the increase of serf oppression. It was legally joined with the fiscal function of the landlord, who was given the official assignment to collect the head tax from the peasant and to turn it over to the treasury. This strengthened still further the power of the pomeshchik over the person, property, and labor of the enserfed peasants and still further increased the possibility of abuse by the landlord.

The entire police organization of the state apparatus tended in the same direction. In 1724 a passport system was introduced as one means of preventing the flight of the serfs and their evasion of military service and taxes. The peasant could now leave the village only with a permit which had to be signed by the local administration as well as the landowner. This system added to the injustice done the peasant and prevented any likelihood of escape.

It must be said that under Peter the practical application of a number of decrees could have provided some amelioration of the position of the serfs. Thus, for example, in abolishing a point of the Code of 1649, Peter prohibited the nobles from sending peasants to court as defendants in place of themselves or from placing them as security for debts of the pomeshchiki. In 1724 Peter forbade the landowners to give their serfs and kholopy in marriage without the latter's consent.[59] In a letter to the Senate on April 15, 1721, Peter expressed dissatisfaction with the widely prevalent custom of selling serfs singly, "like cattle, as nowhere else in the world," thereby separating parents and children. He proposed to the Senate that it decide this question by examining the Code to seek means of preventing such sale of people, "and if this cannot be stopped at all, then at least they should sell families and not individual members . . ." [60] This is a revealing letter, for when it came to improving the position of the serf or defending his rights before the landowner, the all-powerful monarch, who usually issued stern decrees, became an uncertain exhorter.

---

[59] *Ibid.*, VII, No. 4406, p. 197.
[60] *Ibid.*, VI, No. 3770, p. 377.

Although his interference in the life of his subjects was broad, far-reaching, and often despotic, Peter I left the serf problem to the complete arbitrariness of the landowner. Pososhkov's proposal to define and limit by law the obligation of the peasant to the landowner was foreign to Peter. He felt compelled to intervene only in cases of extreme abuse and where relations between the landowner and his serfs were harmful. In January, 1779, Peter instructed the governors and land commissars to prevent situations wherein, as he wrote, "some useless persons . . . because of drunkenness or other unwholesome living, ruin their votchiny and force upon the peasants numerous unbearable burdens, abuses, and tortures, with the result that the peasants leave their tax burdens and flee and contribute thereby to the creation of wastelands and the decrease of revenues for the sovereign . . ." According to this decree the votchina of the bad manager could be transferred to his next of kin.[61] In this case, as in other, similar, decrees, the protection of the peasant against a bad landowner was dictated and motivated not by Peter's concern for the peasants and their life, but by the interests of the feudal state, particularly those of a fiscal character.

Moreover, a considerable part of these measures never became effective law. Peter's order forbidding the sale of people singly was not heeded; the nobles went on forcibly giving their peasants in marriage. Neither was the decree with respect to taking the estates and peasants of wastrel landholders enforced.

Under Peter, the practice of transferring crown lands with the peasants living on them to the nobles produced a significant rise in the number of serfs. In contrast to the old pomestie system of landownership, lands and peasants were no longer distributed so as to enable the nobleman to perform military service vicariously and increase the military power, but as a reward and encouragement to individual nobles and favorites. Individual magnates, particularly Menshikov, received enormous estates from the Tsar.

After the crushing of the Bulavin uprising, serfdom was extended to the upper Don. Its incidence was considerably increased by the adoption of forced peasant labor in factories.

The census of the population in connection with the introduction of the head tax was combined with a survey which divided the populace into classes and social groups. A single registration to pay the head tax meant for many a registration into serfdom; it is true that the victim received the right to petition the court about unjust registration, but the census decree forced tramps to register with serving people, and thus they fell into dependence.

61 *Ibid.*, V, No. 3294, pp. 628–9.

As I. V. Stalin has said: "the elevation of the landlord class, the encouragement of the rising merchant class, and the advancement of their status was attained at the expense of the peasant serf, who was bled white." [62]

The relatively insignificant number of decrees dealing with agriculture indicates that this branch of the national economy attracted little of Peter's attention. Peter's economic policy, however, did not possess that one-sidedness characteristic, for instance, of Colbert's program, which ignored the needs of agriculture and completely subordinated its interests to those of heavy industry.

Peter laid the foundation for a number of innovations in the agricultural economy of Russia. He was concerned mainly with those areas of agriculture which as raw material bases were immediately connected with the development of industry. He devoted attention to the introduction of sheep raising to supply the native textile industry with wool. Ewes and rams of those varieties of sheep whose wool was used in fine cloth were purchased abroad. Experienced shepherds were hired to teach Russians to care for flocks and to shear the sheep. Russians were also sent abroad to learn new methods. Sheep farms were established in Russia and peasants were taught to raise sheep "so that in the Russian state more wool will be produced and sold domestically." These peasants would then instruct "their fellow peasants in how to care for sheep and shear their wool."

Much attention was given the development of horse breeding.

Flax and hemp raising were introduced. In 1715 a decree was issued "On the Increase in all Gubernias of the Flax and Hemp Industry"; it forecast an annual increase in the amount to be sowed and envisaged the education of the peasants in the correct techniques "for the benefit of all the people and for their individual benefit." [63] Detailed instructions were issued for growing hemp and improving its quality.

In order to guarantee the supply of native silk, steps were taken to increase the plantings of mulberry trees [64] and to invite experts from abroad "to care for the operation and make silk in the Italian manner." [65]

In regard to field techniques, the decree which proposed to replace the sickle with the scythe and rake in the harvesting of grain is most interesting. Referring to the experience of other countries, Peter, by

62 Stalin, *op. cit.,* XIII, 105.
63 *PSZ,* V, No. 2966, p. 185.
64 See *ibid.,* IV, No. 1792, p. 42.
65 *Ibid.,* VII, No. 4600, p. 372.

a decree of May 11, 1721, ordered the president of the Finance College, Prince Golitsyn, to see that peasants in the grain gubernias were taught to use scythes and rakes, and also to organize the manufacture of these implements "so that in the following year everyone in the grain-growing areas will cut the grain in this manner." [66] As in the case of many other measures, this one was made compulsory. [67]

Steps were taken for the development of horticulture. Several experimental orchards were established in various parts of Russia, and horticulture was expanded in Astrakhan. Special gardens for the cultivation of medicinal herbs were planted.

The needs of shipbuilding forced Peter to look into the condition of forestry. During his reign the foundation for correct forest management was laid, and measures were introduced for the protection of forests against harmful plundering.

Attempts To Spread Academic Knowledge

The transformations in various branches of the country's economy created an acute need to prepare qualified cadres among the Russian people. Attempts were made to prepare *economic* cadres by sending young nobles and merchants abroad and by the introduction of economic education into Russia itself. Peter even intended to establish a special Academy where the youth could learn economy and law; in the interim he planned to open a "preparatory school." The President of the heraldic office, who among other duties was responsible for the economic education of the nobility, received the following order: "And because learning in civil, and especially in economic, affairs has not been firmly established, there is nothing to read. Therefore, until the completion of the Academy there shall be established a brief course; it shall provide instruction for all famous and noble families in economy and civil affairs." [68]

His plan, however, was not carried out. One of the memoranda of Peter states: "In the past, anyone who received credits was assured of

---

[66] *Ibid.*, VI, No. 3781, p. 388.

[67] "For you know that regardless of its usefulness, if it is new our people will not do it without compulsion" (in the same decree to Prince Golitsyn). Five years after this decree in the Moscow, Nizhegorod, and Kiev Gubernias and in the Pereiaslav Province, 13,000 persons were instructed, and there were produced 20,000 scythes and rakes. See N. V. Ponomarev, *Istoricheskii obzor pravitelstvennykh meropriiatii k razvitiiu selskogo khoziastva v Rossii* [Historical Review of Government Measures on the Development of Agriculture in Russia] (St. Petersburg: 1888), p. 239.

[68] *PSZ*, VI, No. 3896, p. 499.

a place where youth could go and study their economy."[69] This referred to the sending of young people abroad for economic training.

How highly Peter valued economic knowledge is evident from the fact that in the Academy of Science it was proposed that the teaching and study of economic science and other subjects be introduced. In Peter's project establishing the Academy it is said: "Economy will be taught here, because in daily life its teaching brings great benefit and usefulness."[70] In addition to the general task of developing science, the Academy was charged with a practical obligation: to further the development in Russia of productive forces and technology "so that the free arts and manufactures which have already been introduced or which will be introduced in the future will derive benefit from the said institution, which will demonstrate suitable machines and prepare instruments for their use."[71]

Peter attached importance to the publication of literature in Russian. As may be seen from available materials, he intended to publish a number of economic works. While in Holland, he engaged the learned Pole, Kopievskii of Amsterdam, to publish books in the Russian language. In 1699 he commissioned Kopievskii to write a book, which, judging from the plan, would have been a sort of encyclopedia of politics, economics, and their practical application. In the first part of the book, along with purely political questions, it was proposed to discuss questions of "state economies in all towns, what benefits they bring, and how they should be organized." The second part of the book was to discuss concrete questions of separate branches of the economy relative to definite areas of Russia: "1) the nature of household industries, 2) agricultural [products] which Riazan', North, and White Russia required; 3) forest [products], like those of the great forest of the Osetr River, the Viazma Forest, and others; 4) water [products] as those of Novgorod, the Volga, and the Don; 5) meadow [products] as those of Velikiia Luki and others; 6) town; 7) trade; 8) companies; 9) alloys; and 10) the opening of resources for village industries."[72]

This book was never written. Kopievskii, unfamiliar with Russia, could not write a book in Amsterdam which would discuss the economy and techniques of production of various Russian regions. But the commission itself shows Peter's awareness of the need for economic

---

[69] N. A. Voskresenskii, *Zakonodatelnye akty Petra I* [Legislative Documents of Peter I] (Moscow-Leningrad: AS USSR, 1945), I, 139.

[70] *PSZ*, VII, No. 4443, p. 222.

[71] *Ibid.*, VII, No. 4443, p. 221.

[72] P. Pekarskii, *Nauka i literatura v Rossii pri Petre Velikom* [Education and Literature in Russia Under Peter the Great] (St. Petersburg: 1862), I, 526.

literature and the definite and quite practical trend which he envisaged for it.

Attempts were made to find in other countries economic works which would be useful to Russia. One of Peter's memoranda reads: "On economic books, and particularly whether there are any in Sweden." [73] In 1723 Peter ordered the translation of the German edition of 1716 of the three-volume work of Hochberg, *Georgica curiosa,* which dealt with questions of agricultural and household economy, based on the experience of the European countries. Peter took a lively interest in the progress of the translation and gave instructions on how a book should be translated; and he himself edited and abridged one of the chapters.[74] As a result, he wrote an interesting commentary in the "Decree to those working on the translation of economic books": "Because the Germans are accustomed to filling their books with many superfluous stories in order to make them longer, translate only pertinent material, leave out high-flown language which does not contribute to the discussion of grain growing. I send an example with the redundant passages struck out, so that the book will be translated without excessive details which will only waste time and distract the reader's attention. Peter. In Petersburg, 16 September 1724." [75] The translation of Hochberg's book was finished in 1730, after Peter's death, and was not published in Russia.

Peter I's Place in the History of Economic Thought

An analysis of the views and principles of the economic policy of Peter I will yield the conclusion that the Russian people had in him an outstanding economist.

He addressed himself to the elimination of the economic backwardness of Russia, the creation of a native heavy industry, the development of trade, agriculture, and water transport, and the strengthening of the financial system. Peter's reforms played a major role in the historical development of our country. He relied first of all on the ruling class—the pomeshchiki. His reform helped to elevate them further, while it led to the increased enslavement of the peasantry. As a result of his policies Russian serfdom was significantly strengthened; it spread and became still more burdensome for the peasant. Reforms were carried out at the expense of the peasantry and to its further impoverishment and ruin. The attempts of the oppressed classes to rise against their exploiters, the pomeshchiki and the feudal state, were cruelly put down.

---

[73] Voskresenskii, *op. cit.,* I, 120.
[74] Pekarskii, *op. cit.,* I, 214.
[75] Voskresenskii, *op. cit.,* I, 148; see also Pekarskii, *op. cit.,* I, 214.

Peter I greatly assisted the rising class of merchants; he extended his protection to them and to the industrialists. In some instances his measures, directed toward the development of native industry, encroached on the interests of various segments of the nobility. For example, with the aim of encouraging private economic initiative in the development of mining and metallurgy, Peter extended, in 1719, to "each and every one" the right to "seek, smelt, melt, and refine all metals," not only on their own land, but also on that of others. The pomeshchiki, wrote Peter, unwilling or unable to provide the means to extract metals, "is required to permit others to seek and process ores and minerals on his land, so that the resources placed under the earth by God will not remain unused." [76]

In the interests of the development of heavy industry Peter frequently confiscated water mills from the nobility and monastaries and appropriated river banks suitable for the construction of such mills. Intent upon increasing the revenue of the treasury, he expropriated fishing areas and then leased or resold them to their former owners. The rights of landlords to the forests on their lands were significantly limited. The decree of 1721, wherein merchants were given the right to purchase villages for mills, meant a certain weakening of the monopoly of the pomeshchiki in the ownership of serfs.

But these and similar measures do not constitute a basis for characterizing Peter's social reforms as an antifeudal, antinoble, bourgeois policy directed against the class interests of the pomeshchiki. Such an erroneous interpretation was given by M. N. Pokrovskii and his followers. It is again evident in the book of B. I. Syromiatnikov on the *"Regulated" State of Peter I and His Ideology,* Part I (AN USSR, M-L, 1943), which fundamentally distorts Peter's characteristics, and reappears in the introduction by Syromiatnikov to the collection of N. A. Voskresenskii *Legislative Acts of Peter I.* Such interpretations contradict reality. The measures which encroached upon the interests of various segments of the nobility did not, and could not, undermine its predominant economic and political position. We have seen that all of Peter's policies led to the elevation of the nobility as a class. These policies manifested themselves particularly in the fact that with Peter the nobility finally emerged, under the general term *"shliakhetstvo,"* as a privileged and "noble" class with special rights, in contrast to the "low" persons; their coats of arms and titles were legalized.[77]

In Russia as in the West, absolute power during its rise and early

[76] *PSZ,* V, No. 3464, p. 761.

[77] See A. Romanovich-Slavatinskii, *Dvorianstvo v Rossii ot nachala XVIII veka do otmeny krepostnogo prava* [Nobility in Russia from the Beginning of the XVIII Century to the Abolition of Serfdom] (Kiev: 1912), Chapter I.

period assisted the development of trade and industry, as well as the growth of the new bourgeois class. Merchants and industrialists in their turn supported for a long time the absolute monarchy which aspired toward economic and political centralization, toward the development of productive power, and the strengthening and expansion of the economic and political might of the national state. "Earlier [the absolute monarchy] protected trade and industry and, consequently, the emergence of the bourgeoisie, in which it saw the necessary prerequisites for both the national might and its own splendor . . ." [78]

Of course, the growth of trade and industry in Russia created forces whose further development inescapably helped to undermine the feudal-serf structure and in the end led to its collapse. But under Peter I, as well as after him, absolutism faithfully served the interests of the nobility and strengthened feudal relationships in the country rather than weakening them. In effect, absolutism greatly intensified serfdom. Aid to the merchants was not granted at the expense of the nobility. The weight of the reforms fell on the peasant masses and on the city poor.

The feudal-serf economy of Russia with its comparatively narrow base made it difficult for the country to emerge from backwardness and to catch up with the more developed countries of Western Europe. As a result of Peter's reforms, to a significant degree Russia approached the industrial standards of the foremost countries of Europe, but the historic task of liquidating its backwardness continued to be unsolved. Writing on Peter's reform activities, I. V. Stalin said:

> Not one of the old classes, neither the feudal aristocracy, nor the bourgeoisie, could accomplish the liquidation of the backwardness of our country. More than that, not only were these classes incapable of solving this problem, they were even unable to delineate the task in any satisfactory way. The century-long backwardness of our country could be liquidated only on the basis of successful socialistic construction. Only the proletariat could liquidate it, by building a dictatorship and holding in its hands the leadership of the country.[79]

while retaining serfdom Russia could not overtake the countries which were already on the road of capitalist development.

Peter put forth reforms with rude and severe measures which, however, were in the spirit of the time. His decrees, wrote Pushkin, "*were*

---

[78] Marx and Engels, *Sochineniia,* V, 214.

[79] Stalin, *op. cit.,* XI, 249.

often cruel, capricious, and seemingly written with the knout." [80] Judged by the measures of his administration, Peter I was a genuine despot, but through his despotic activities he aspired to a high aim—to civilize Russia. "Peter the Great triumphed through barbarism over Russian barbarism . . ." wrote Marx.[81] Lenin also stressed that "Peter accelerated the westernization of barbarian Rus, without stopping at barbarian means in his struggle against barbarism." [82]

The place of Peter and his reforms in Russian social thought has varied during subsequent centuries. There have been two sharply distinct trends: the progressive, which valued highly the significance of Peter's reforms, and the reactionary and backward view, which saw Peter as a crude violator of the century-old ways of old Russia. The progressive thinkers of the eighteenth and nineteenth centuries—Lomonosov, Radishchev, the Decembrists, Herzen, Belinskii, Chernyshevskii, and Dobroliubov—valued Peter's services to our country highly. Marx and Engels considered Peter I a great man. Lenin and Stalin repeatedly mentioned the enormous importance of Peter's activity for the life of Russia and stressed at the same time the historical limits of this activity and the deteriorated position of the toilers caused by it.

The economic views of Peter I and the principles of his economic policy were shaped by the concrete Russian economic and political conditions of the time. An examination of these ideas illustrates their direct connection with the economic views of the progressive thinkers and statesmen of Russia in the second half of the seventeenth century. Ordyn-Nashchokin presents an excellent example. Moreover, comparison of the seventeenth and the first quarter of the eighteenth century testifies to the great advance of progressive Russian economic thought. Peter's economic views and his program of reforms represented a clearer, more complete, and more mature expression and realization of advanced seventeenth century thought.

Entirely unfounded are attempts to explain Peter's reform activities, not in terms of extant Russian conditions, nor by the demands of the material life of our country during the seventeenth and eighteenth centuries, but by the supposedly direct influence on Peter of the economic views and economic policies prevailing in the advanced countries of Western Europe, that is, as "imitations" of foreign ways. Although Peter's economic policy has much in common with mercantil-

---

[80] A. S. Pushkin, *Polnoe sobranie sochinenii* [Complete Collection of Works] (Moscow-Leningrad: AS USSR, 1951), IX, 413.

[81] Marx and Engels, *op. cit.*, XIII, Pt. I, 29.

[82] Lenin, *op. cit.*, XXVII, 307.

ism, which prevailed in the most developed countries of Western Europe, he cannot be accused of imitating Western European mercantilism or of importing or "assimilating" the ideas of Colbertism.

Concern about the flow of money into the country and about the development of trade and industry was dictated not by the influence of Western European ideas, but by the manifested and vital economic demands of the country. Progressive Russian thought turned to the development of trade and industry as the only means of guaranteeing the independence of Russia, of making the motherland mighty and rich, and of winning for her an honored place among the countries of the world. Wrote S. M. Solovev:

> This movement . . . [was] natural and necessary. There can be no thought of borrowing or imitation: France with Colbert at the helm and Russia with Peter the Great acted from the same motivation as two different persons, one in Europe and the other in Asia, who go into the sun to get a suntan, and when sunburned seek the shade. Ivan IV, fighting with all his strength to establish himself on the shores of the seas, could not imitate Colbert. But when Russia entered into close relations with Western Europe, it was important that she found the same movement here, which she did, as seemed certainly justifiable.[83]

In their historical development the various peoples of Europe not only created technology and established economic organizations, but in one degree or another borrowed from the experience of other countries. Holland, at the dawn of its bourgeois development, drew heavily upon the economic experience of Spain and Italy, England learned from Holland,[84] and France adapted the experience of England and Holland. At the end of the seventeenth century, Russia, in its movement forward, could learn not from one or two but from a number of economically developed countries of Western Europe, a situation which Peter was quick to recognize.

But the usefulness of the economic experience of the Western European countries by no means meant the dependence of progressive Russian economic thought on that of Western Europe; it did not mean the "import" into Russia of prepared ideas. As before Peter, so during his time, progressive Russian economic thought represented an in-

[83] S. M. Solovev, *Publichnye chteniia o Petre Velikom* [Public Lectures on Peter the Great] (Moscow: 1872), p. 22.

[84] In the XVII century English mercantilists envied the naval might of Holland and its enrichment from trade and called upon the Englishmen to learn from the Dutch.

dependent ideological reflection of the conditions and needs of the life of the country.

Peter I opened wide the doors of Russian trade to foreigners; he knew how to utilize them and how to protect the interests of his country. This ability to gain from the experience of the countries of the West was not to be found in Peter's successors and their associates. It was from the time of Peter I on that the servility of the Russian nobility to the culture of the West commenced and became a characteristic trait of this class. This obeisance of the nobility to everything foreign continued throughout this period of class rule and did enormous harm to the Russian people and to the development of their national culture.

Are the economic ideas and policies of Peter the Great mercantilistic? This question has been the subject of dispute for a long time. Recognition of Peter's independence is in no way synonymous with the conclusion that his ideas were basically different from the prevailing mercantilistic views and policies in the West.

Mercantilism is a system of ideas and policies the most important trait of which is the view that only gold and silver—that is, money—represent wealth; and the main task of the economic policy of a state is considered to be the guarantee of the flow of money into the country by means of foreign trade. An inseparable and extremely important characteristic of this system is the recognition of the right and obligation of the feudal-absolutist state to interfere in the economic activity of the population, to regulate it, and to establish guardianship and supervision over it. Mercantilism presupposes the absence or the strong suppression of free competition and the predominance of privileges and of trade and other monopolies.

In the Western European countries there were two phases in the development of this system, both of which differed as to the methods and means of guaranteeing the flow of money into a country. The adherents of the earlier, or so-called monetary, system, considered it necessary, and possible, to guarantee the inflow of money by means of increasing the export of goods, by decreasing merchandise imports from other countries, and by direct administrative prohibition of the export of money and precious metals.

The representatives of the later system of mercantilism, which became known as "the system of the trade balance," argued that abundant flow of money into their country could be guaranteed by a balanced development of the export of goods (which should exceed imports); and that the export of money from their country was useful inasmuch as the money sent abroad would return again and in greater quantity. In accordance with this concept the spokesmen of the system of the trade balance stressed the need for balanced development of those branches of industry which produced goods for export, but of those industries which could free the country from the import of goods. The developed mercantilism, or the trade balance system, thus presupposes the encouragement of the growth of manufactures. Marx, therefore, called this system the *manufacturing* or commercial system.[85] It requires the encouragement not only of trade, but of industrial production as well. Marx pointed out:

> The so-called monetary system is simply the expression of the irrational form D-T-D', movement flowing exclusively within the sphere of circulation . . . In contrast, D-T . . . P . . . T'-D', being fixed in the quality of exclusive form, lies at the foundation of the developed mercantile system, whose necessary element is not only commodity circulation, but commodity production.[86]

It is therefore incorrect to identify mercantilism with the economic policy of trade capital and to consider it as an ideology of the period of trade capital. Such an analysis appears, for example, in the work of D. Rozenberg.[87] It is incorrect in the first place because there was in general no special "period of trade capital"; and, secondly, developed mercantilism was an economic policy beneficial not only to trade, but also to industrial capital in the early stage of its development. The protection of manufactories and their establishment by an absolutist government are characteristic traits of developed mercantilism. As Marx states, "manufacturing in general could not be accomplished without protection . . ." [88]

A. Smith, in his criticism of mercantilist policy, particularly stressed that this policy was advantageous only to merchants and manufacturers: "In mercantilist decrees . . . the interests of our manufacturers were taken into consideration most of all . . ." [89] Considering the question historically, Marx revealed both the substance and the significance of the practical policies of mercantilism as well as the theoretical es-

---

[85] Marx, *K kritike politicheskoi ekonomii,* p. 217.

[86] Marx, *Kapital,* II, 58.

[87] See D. Rozenberg, *Istoriia politicheskoi ekonomii* [History of Political Economy] (Moscow: 1934), Pt. I, pp. 24, 33.

[88] Marx and Engels, *Nemetskaia ideologiia,* p. 49.

[89] A. Smith, *Issledovanie o prirode i prichinakh bogatstva narodov* [Inquiry into the Nature and Causes of the Wealth of Nations] (Moscow-Leningrad: Sotsekgiz, 1935), II, 209.

sence of the statements by mercantilists on wealth and ways of increasing it.

The spokesmen of mercantilism stressed the national character of their system and expressed concern for the interests of the state. Actually, this was a hypocritical defense of the interests of the capitalist class and its desire to place the feudal-absolutist state at the service of these goals. Marx maintained that:

> the national character of the mercantile system in the words of its defenders . . . is not a simple phrase. Under the pretext of occupying themselves only with the wealth of nations and the resources of the state, they actually espouse the interests and enrichment of the capitalist class as the final aim of the government and proclaim bourgeois society in contrast to the old Utopian state. But at the same time it was acknowledged that the development of capitalism, the class of capitalists, and of capitalist production were the basis of national power and predominance in contemporary society.[90]

Analysing the theoretical teachings of the mercantilists and defining their role in the development of political economy, Marx showed that the mercantile system presented the first theoretical treatment of the capitalist means of production; it corresponded to the "infantile period" of bourgeois society, when these means of production were still within the bosom of feudal society. In Marx's conception the system represents not a naive delusion of human thought, as A. Smith and other bourgeois economists—defenders of free competition—asserted, but the first theoretical analysis of bourgeois production; what appeared to later economists as mercantilist peculiarity and naivete were actually the budding characteristics of capitalist economics in its earliest stages.

Mercantilism can historically claim the first theoretical concept of bourgeois wealth and labor, and thereby its creation: The mercantilists "distinguished world trade and various segments of national labor directly connected with world trade as the sole and genuine sources of wealth or money . . ." [91] This view of the problem Marx attributed to the lack of development of "goods production" and to the fact that "the proper bourgeois economic sphere was at that time the sphere of goods circulation." [92] Identification of wealth with money by the mercantilists, Marx wrote, is none other than the disclosure of the secrets

---

90 Marx, *Kapital,* III, 798.
91 Marx, *K kritike politicheskoi ekonomii,* p. 158.
92 *Ibid.,* p. 159.

of bourgeois production—its full subordination to exchange value. Marx shows that in criticizing the mercantile system, bourgeois political economy errs, because it attacks the system as a simple illusion and a false theory and does not recognize it as simply a barbaric form of its own basic positions.[93]

Marx stresses that the mercantile system preserves not only historical right, but also "full civil right," even within the very developed bourgeois economics. Under the bourgeois means of production, exchange value naturally assumes the form of money, and wealth always returns for one moment into money form; specific functions of gold and silver as money, in distinction from their functions as a means of circulation and in contrast to all other goods, do not disappear, but are only limited. [94]

Thus the mercantile system was for its time the most advanced and progressive system. Its policies played an enormous role in the creation of capitalist means of production; and the theoretical views of the mercantilists were the precursors of the theoretical analysis of bourgeois production. At the same time, within the bounds of the mercantile system a definite forward movement in the understanding of wealth and its sources appeared. Marx observes that if "the monetary system" still regarded wealth quite objectively, as a thing outside itself, in money, then "the manufacturing, or commercial system" transferred the source of wealth from the objective to the subjective activity and is still understood in the limited form, especially as a money producer." [95] Further progress consisted in the fact that the physiocrats understood by wealth not money, but the general product resulting from labor, although they viewed it as the product of the land. Of great importance was the conception of A. Smith that wealth-creating labor is labor as such: neither manufacturing, nor commercial, nor agricultural labor, but any labor. By wealth, A. Smith understood the product of labor in general, of past, material labor: "After agriculture, manufacturing, shipping, trade, and so one, were in turn declared the true sources of wealth, Adam Smith pronounced labor in general, and especially in its socio-communal aspect in the form of *division of labor,* as the only source of material wealth, or costs." [96]

In the field of economic policy progress was made when the physiocrats and A. Smith, believing in objective, "natural" economic laws of society, proclaimed as unnecessary and harmful the interference of the

[93] *Ibid.*
[94] *Ibid.*
[95] *Ibid.*, p. 217.
[96] *Ibid.*, p. 48.

state in economic activity and relegated the state to the position of a "night watchman" of bourgeois property. While the bourgeoisie, by means of mercantilist policy, had earlier utilized the state in its interests, it now began to use the state for conducting another policy, that of free trade, which was at this stage more advantageous to it. War was declared on medieval privileges and monopolies; the principle of petty guardianship and regulation of economic activity by the state gave way to the new principle of free competition.

We have here intentionally presented general, characteristic, basic traits of mercantilism; for in examining the question of whether Russian economists of the seventeenth century and the first half of the eighteenth century can be called mercantilists, the very concept of mercantilism is often extremely narrow and treated as a very backward trend of economic thought. In reality mercantilism was for its time, that is, from the sixteenth through the first half of the eighteenth century, a very advanced system of economic theory and of progressive economic policy; it played an enormous role in the West in the creation and strengthening of a new capitalist means of production, in the transition from the old feudal to the new bourgeois society.

One must also remember that although mercantilism was theoretically surpassed in several works of Western European economists as early as the end of the seventeenth and the beginning of the eighteenth century (W. Petty, Locke, North, Hume, and others), the practice of mercantilism as a definite economic policy remained predominant in the western European countries throughout the first half and even into the second half of the eighteenth century. The physiocrats and A. Smith carried on a struggle with existing mercantilism.

In its practical manifestations mercantilism was a complicated and multiform policy, difficult to fit into the narrow formulas of the monetary or trade balance systems. In Holland, England, and France, late mercantilism really implied concern about the flow of money into the country, increased protection of native trade, shipping and manufacturing industry, protection by a system of tariffs (industrial protectionism), regulation of trade and industry, measures for the development of those areas of agriculture which supply raw materials for home industry, the drive of one country to dominate the world market, and the struggle of other countries to preserve their economic independence.

The concrete policies of mercantilism were so much broader and more complex than that system's theoretically formulated general principle in relation to inflow of specie (seeking to guarantee it by the increase of exports and decrease of imports) that some scholars attempted on this ground to label Cromwell and Colbert mercantilists, although qualifying this by admitting that the state activity of these statesmen was much wider than the formulas generally subscribed to by mercantilists. In reality, these two were undoubtedly typical mercantilists, in spite of the scholars.

Mercantilism was not a peculiarity of any particular country, but was inherent in all European countries at a particular stage of their economic development. While it was usually a combination of the above mentioned basic traits and characteristics, mercantilism at the same time varied greatly from country to country. One cannot name two western European nations of the sixteenth through the eighteenth centuries where the policy of mercantilism was realized in exactly the same way. One can speak of the various types of mercantilist policies. In some countries, for example in England, it operated without serfdom; in others, such as Prussia and Austria, it functioned with serfdom. Whether countries did or did not carry on an extensive transit trade also played an important role.

As regards the problem as to whether the economic views and policies of Peter I can be ascribed to the mercantilistic trend, one must note the inadmissibility of solving this question by singling out certain traits and certain periods of Peter's policies and activities and thus neglecting to view them in their entirety. Nevertheless this problem is often solved in just this way.

One must first of all reject the attempts of a number of scholars to narrow Peter's multisided economic activity to his concern over the influx of specie and to interpret this concern as the main motivating force of his reforms. Peter I did not identify wealth with money. As was said above, to a certain degree he understood the positive role of competition. Regulation and guardianship by the state of manufacturing industry and trade were looked upon as a temporary phenomenon caused by their novelty in Russia. It is possible to state, therefore, that Peter's rejection of the basic principle of mercantilism, namely that wealth is only money and that the main task of the state's economic policy should be the attraction of money into the country, and his awareness of the importance of other aspects of economic policy illustrate his ability to rise above the ideas then dominant in the West.

At the same time it would be incorrect to separate Peter I entirely from the mercantilists of the West and to look on his economic views and policy as belonging to the next higher phase in the development of world economic thought. It would be erroneous to compare Peter's ideas to those which arose in Russia only in the second half of the eighteenth century and which were developed in the West by the physiocrats and A. Smith. Such a procedure contradicts historical reality.

Although Peter I's interest in the flow of specie into the country was not the main motive for his economic reforms, this concern nevertheless played a significant role in his policy, especially since much money was needed to wage wars and its availability was one of the most important conditions for the implementation of all of his reforms. These reforms were costly; they were designed for the precise purpose of guaranteeing the flow of money into the country and of keeping it there. Peter's broad and many-sided reforms in the field of military affairs, economics, culture, and so on, were closely and directly linked to his continuous and extremely acute concern for the inflow of money. One must not underestimate the enormous significance of his measures for the attraction of money, nor contrast Peter in this regard to Cromwell, Colbert and other statesmen of mercantilist leanings for whom, strictly speaking, and in contrast to Thomas Mun and other spokesmen of the bourgeoisie, money was not the sole end either, but only the means by which broad national policies were decided.

It is important to stress that the methods which Peter I used to increase the money in the country were the usual mercantilistic ones: prohibition of the export of money and of precious metals from the country; attempts to increase the export of goods and to guarantee an active trade balance; the development of native heavy industry; the creation of a national merchant fleet, and other measures. These, however, were not simple "imitations" of the West, but the result of Peter's deep awareness of the tasks of the motherland and the needs of its development. At the same time, Peter's policy of increasing money in the country, though similar in many respects to that of the countries of Western Europe, differed in essence from the policies pursued then, for example, by England.

In England two successive stages were evident—the monetary system, dominant in the beginning, was later replaced by the trade balance system. The latter meant the rejection of the prohibition of the export of money. Thomas Mun convincingly proved that for a country like England, which carried on a large transit trade, the export of money was a necessary condition for its subsequent abundant import. Mun picturesquely compared money sent abroad by English merchants and spent, for example, in India, on goods subsequently resold not only in their own, but in other countries with seeds sowed for yielding a harvest.

Peter's policy was different. The development of foreign trade, the guarantee of an active trade balance, and the development of heavy industry were combined in Russia with the prohibition of the export of money and of precious metals.

In general one must remember that even in Western Europe the ban on the export of money was not dictated by a "delusion" of the government, nor by abstract identification of wealth with money, nor by the aspiration of kings to increase money as a form of wealth, but by extremely concrete and practical considerations. "At first an insignificant amount of gold and silver in circulation caused a prohibition on the export of these metals, "wrote Marx and Engels in "German Ideology." [97] "The appearance in the European market of American gold and silver, the gradual development of industry, the swift rise of trade and the resultant flourishing of the non-guild bourgeoisie and money—all this gave these measures another significance. The state, which could function less and less satisfactorily without money, preserved the embargo on the export of gold and silver for fiscal considerations; the bourgeoisie, to whom an increased amount of money on the market became the main object of desire, were fully satisfied with this; the former privileges became the source of revenue for the government and were sold for money . . ." [98]

The lifting of the prohibition of the export of gold and silver occurred later, in the second period of the development of mercantilism, which began in the middle of the seventeenth and continued almost to the end of the eighteenth century, when trade and shipping quickly expanded and manufacturing grew. "The eighteenth century was a century of trade." [99] The necessity of removing the prohibition was dictated by this development of trade, and in particular that of transit trade.

"Fiscal considerations" which dictated the prohibition were connected with monetary value; the treasury received monetary income as the difference between the nominal and real value of not fully valued money released in the country. The adulteration of money drove good money out of the country, while bad money remained. This circumstance not only decreased the amount of metal necessary for circulation, but curtailed the possibility of the government receiving monetary income from the subsequent alteration of money. The permission to export adulterated money led to the necessity for its ultimate return to the country, which again lowered the chances of revenue for the treasury. Forbidding the export of money usually was combined with the prohibition of import of all, including its own, money at less than

[97] Marx and Engels, *Nemetskaia ideologiia,* p. 47.
[98] *Ibid.,* p. 48.
[99] *Ibid.,* p. 49.

full value. Some governments therefore forbade the export not only of monetary metal, gold and silver in ingots, and fully valued money, but also of money of less than full value; others limited themselves to embargoes only of precious metal in ingots and fully valued money, while allowing the export of adulterated money.

Paper money did not exist at that time. The income of the government from the adulteration of money in the Middle Ages corresponded to revenue from the issuance of paper money at a later date. In those countries where the adulteration was carried on to an insignificant degree, as in England before the sixteenth century, the prohibition of the export of gold and silver was directed not only at preserving money in the country, but also at providing revenue for the treasury by permitting for a fee the export of metal from the country.

Moreover, in a number of western European countries the difference between the two stages of development—the monetary system, on the one hand, and the mercantile-manufacturing-commercial system, on the other—both with respect to the theoretical views of the economists and to economic policies, was seldom as sharp and complete as was the case in England. Even during the dominance of the monetary system strong voices were heard insistently expounding the inadvisability of prohibiting the export of gold and silver from the country (Serra in Italy, Bodin in France).

On the other hand, among the countries of Western Europe the prohibition existed even during the period of developed mercantilism. Colbert, for example, prohibited the export of money. In the eighteenth century the export of monetary metal was forbidden not only in Russia, but also in France, in the German states, in Austria, and in other countries.

The economic policy of Peter I was similar to the mercantilist policies of the Western European countries. Like the latter, Peter established a policy of industrial protectionism.

Extremely important and inextricable traits of mercantilism were the supervision, guardianship, and regulation of the economic activity of the population by policy-bureaucratic methods. Peter's policy in this regard resembled fully that of the Western European states, although it had its own peculiarities, which are mentioned above. With his economic policy, Peter strengthened the position of the nobility. But he also contributed a great deal to the development of a new class—the merchants and industrial enterpreneurs. He did much for the promotion of capitalistic elements in the national economy.

The economic views and policies of Peter I were significantly broader than the theoretical views formulated by the spokesmen of Western

European mercantilism in respect to the nature of wealth and the basic method of its increase. At the same time his practical economic policies were, in their basic traits, similar to those of most developed countries of Western Europe from the sixteenth to the nineteenth centuries, namely mercantilist. But there were extremely important differences, determined by the peculiarities of Russia. For their time, Peter's economic views and policies were advanced and progressive. They helped the development of the productive forces of Russia.

CHAPTER 12. *The Spokesman of the Merchant Class I. T. Pososhkov and His Book on Poverty and Wealth.*

The General Characteristics of the Economic Program of Pososhkov

The basic source of information on the life of Ivan Tikhonovich Pososhkov (1652–1726) is the autobiographical data which Pososhkov included in his works. In addition, some official documents concerning his life and activity have been found in the archives.[1]

Pososhkov's parents were landless obrok peasants in the crown village of Pokrovskoe, which later was incorporated into the city of Moscow. The village was administered by the Armaments Office. Pososhkov came from a family of craftsmen; both his grandfather and father were silversmiths and jewelers.

He himself was an extremely versatile artisan. Among his pursuits were coin making, the fashioning of arms, icon painting, engraving, drawing, carpentry, and wine making. In 1694, on order from Avraamii, the abbot of the Andreevsk monastery in Moscow, he made a model of a coin-stamping machine for presentation to the Tsar. In 1697 he invented a special catapult for the Russian artillery, which he submitted to the Tsar. At the end of the seventeenth and in the first years of the eighteenth centuries, Pososhkov worked as a coinmaster in the Armaments Office. Subsequently he served the crown as a master distiller in Moscow until 1708, and in Novgorod from 1709 or 1710.

At the same time Pososhkov entered into considerable private enterprise and became a merchant-manufacturer. It is believed that even earlier—at the end of the 1680's—he and his brother owned a winery in the Likhvin district. In 1704, together with two companions, he tried to open a playing card factory. In Novgorod, Pososhkov engaged in trade, in addition to his state service. In 1719 he built his own winery in the Novgorod district, and there he also held a lease on

[1] For a detailed biography of Pososhkov see B. B. Kafengauz, *I. T. Pososhkov. Zhizn i deiatelnost* [I. T. Pososhkov. Life and Activity] (Moscow-Leningrad: AS USSR, 1950). A second edition appeared in Moscow in 1951.

the customs collection and on the sale of wine and beer. At the end of his life Pososhkov owned a house in St. Petersburg and two houses in Novgorod, 258 desiatiny of land and eighty-one serfs. In official documents he called himself a merchant.

Pososhkov is known not only as an energetic practical businessman, but also as an active literary figure of his day. In his own words he was "very zealous" and irreconcilably opposed to everything that seemed unjust and harmful. He compiled reports for influential persons which pointed out various "injustices" and outlined measures for their elimination. He also wrote tracts on religion, morals, economics, and allied subjects. At the end of the seventeenth century he sent the government his "Letter on Monetary Problems," in which he counselled the issuance of money of "small denomination." This "Letter" has not been preserved. In 1701, soon after the defeat of the Russian army at Narva, Pososhkov presented the boyar Golovin with a report "On Military Organization," in which he criticized the existing military order and proposed concrete reforms. In the period 1703–1710 Pososhkov sent the Metropolitan Stefan Iavorskii three memoranda in which he proposed certain steps against heretics in order to strengthen orthodoxy among the Russian people and the clergy. In 1708 he completed a major work (of over seven hundred printed pages), *A Mirror, or An Obvious and Known Testimony Regarding the Sophism of Heretics,* in which he attacked the heretics and the Lutherans. In 1718 he tried to provide Peter I, through cabinet-secretary Makarov, with a report on new currency. In 1719 Pososhkov finished *The Testament of a Father to His Son* (330 printed pages). And finally, in 1724 he completed his *Book on Poverty and Wealth,* together with a special "Report" to Peter.

It is unknown whether Pososhkov succeeded in presenting his *Book* to Peter I. It was published for the first time more than a hundred years after it was written (in 1842) by a collector of old Russian manuscripts, the historian Pogodin, when it accidentally fell into his hands.[2]

The Book on Poverty and Wealth was Pososhkov's last work, written in his eighties. In the summer of 1725 he came to [St.] Petersburg to obtain permission to open a textile factory in Novgorod, and here he was arrested and confined in Petropavlovsk prison. This occurred seven months after the death of Peter I. The cause of Pososhkov's arrest is not known. In the "extract" of his case prepared for the Empress Catherine I it was stated that "he was detained for reasons of a vital

[2] *Kniga o skudosti i bogatstve* [A Book on Poverty and Wealth] was published a second time in 1911. In 1937 the Soviet edition of the book appeared, and in 1951 the Academy of Sciences of the USSR published a new edition.

state secret." Materials in the archives suggest that his arrest was connected with his *Book on Poverty and Wealth.*[3] Pososhkov remained in Petropavlovsk prison for five months, and there he died (February 1, 1726) and was interred in the cemetery where other prisoners of the Secret Chancellery were buried.

Pososhkov did not receive a systematic education; he was self-taught. His knowledge of life was versatile and encyclopedic in nature. With profound insight he considered military and church affairs, judicial and economic problems, the art of icon painting, the principles of land surveying, education, the shortcomings of Russian grammar, and so forth. Possessed of an astute mind, Pososhkov experienced a long and useful life. He traveled widely in Russia, met many people, observed his surroundings avidly, and noted and evaluated everything within his range.

His world outlook is expressed most fully in his religious-moral work, *The Testament of a Father to his Son, with Moral Teachings Based on the Holy Scriptures.* Here Pososhkov appears as an extremely reactionary, conservative person. He was not only a deep believer, but also a stern zealot of the old faith, a fervent defender of the church, and an ardent representative of militant orthodoxy. He believed that such barbaric rites as the burning of stubborn heretics were permissible. He struggled passionately against Lutheranism, which he viewed as a direct road to atheism. From Luther, wrote Pososhkov, decended both atheism and the system of Copernicus. He repeatedly defamed "Copernicus as God's opponent," who by his teaching repudiated the biblical version of the creation of the earth.[4]

The *Father's Testament* is fundamentally inferior to *Domostroi.* Pososhkov's ideal was the devout Christian whose highest aim was the attainment of the heavenly kingdom and who subordinated his entire earthly life to this purpose. He preached the biblical commandment of nonresistance to evil ("and whoever strikes your cheek, turn the other to him . . ."); he lauded patience and humility, demanded an ascetic way of life, and sharply criticized music, dancing, and gaiety. Pososhkov considered it necessary to raise children in perpetual fear, with the use of the most extreme means of punishment.

Alongside of such views, which at the beginning of the eighteenth century had been rejected by progressive people, we also find ideas in Pososhkov which were bold and even advanced for his time. For example, he held education in great esteem, warmly preached the

---

[3] See Kafengauz, *op. cit.,* pp. 138–42.

[4] See I. T. Pososhkov, *Zaveshchanie otecheskoe* [Father's Testament] (St. Petersburg: 1893), p. 129.

benefit of popular education, and proposed universal education of children, including those of peasants. He considered it necessary to educate not only Russians, but the children of other nationalities in Russia. Pososhkov advised his son to marry for love, to conduct himself with honor toward his wife, and to confide in her.

In his political views he was a confirmed and ardent partisan of unlimited autocracy. On the other hand, he did not unconditionally defend the Russian order and administrative system, but subjected both to severe and sharp criticism, since he saw in them a basic obstacle to the elimination of poverty and to the increase of the country's wealth. He was indignant at the lack of an elementary legal order in Russia; he deplored the fact that strong persons went unpunished, and he opposed their arbitrary conduct in relation to the weak and poor. He wrote of the obsolescence of the administrative and legal system. "Until we establish here in Rus a direct court system and allow it to develop fully we cannot increase the wealth of our dwellings, as compared to other lands, regardless of what measures we adopt. Likewise we cannot attain any fame while harm and insecurity are caused by unhealthy judgment and unsupervised administration." [5] Injustice, he believed, had taken strong root among the people, and he says distressfully: "Anyone who can, oppresses others; the evil-minded ruin the weak; judges, though they see that the strong and the slanderers attack without cause, dare not stop them." [6]

This injustice—this arbitrariness, bribery, and chicanery—Pososhkov identified with the dominance of the nobles in the administration and the courts and with the solidarity of the nobility and its immunity to punishment. He was highly antagonistic toward the upper, hereditary nobility and hostile toward the lower nobility.

Pososhkov maintained that "all ancient codes have decayed and become distorted," that it was necessary to "replace the old order," to examine the "law book." By "ancient codes" he meant the Code of 1649. In order to examine the state laws and the Code [of Ivan the Terrible] Pososhkov advised the Tsar to create a commission to be composed of two or three elected representatives of each class and rank, including that of the peasantry. After the commission had completed its work, it would be necessary for the project to be "examined by all people freely and not under duress, so that this new declaration will contain no provision harmful or oppressive to anyone, whether they

[5] I. T. Pososhkov, *Kniga o skudosti i bogatstve i drugie sochineniia* [A Book on Poverty and Wealth and other Works] (Moscow: AS USSR, 1951), pp. 91–2.

[6] *Ibid.*, p. 92.

be high-born or low-born, rich or poor, high ranking or low ranking officials or agriculturists; nor should ignorance of their place [in society] be a detriment." [7] By "free examination" Pososhkov referred to the broad acquaintance of the whole population with the project and the submission of written declarations by anyone who might be in disagreement with any part of it. After examination by a "popular Council" the project would be submitted for the Tsar's endorsement.

This proposal is quite bold and original. Its significance has been diversely evaluated by scholars. Plekhanov, for example, saw it as a reactionary aspiration to revive the outmoded practice of the Land Assemblies.[8] Others, Brikner for example, have interpreted it as an attempt "to organize something in the way of a legislative assembly." [9]

Neither view can be considered correct. Pososhkov's project had nothing in common either with the practice of the Land Assemblies of the sixteenth and seventeenth centuries, nor with the parliamentary practices of other countries. Undoubtedly his proposal has democratic aspects. He appears here as a perceptive political thinker, far ahead of his time in his views on the role of the masses in the formulation of laws. In the reality of the absolutist state his scheme was utopian. He wanted to adapt the irreconcilable absolutism of the Tsar to the participation of the masses in the law-making process, albeit the role of the people would be consultative only.

At the same time Pososhkov cannot be looked upon as a sponsor and defender of democratic principles and ideas. While the radical measure which he proposed undoubtedly may have had progressive significance, it had an entirely different connotation for him and was directly opposed to democracy.

Pososhkov was an ardent spokesman for the police state. He wanted each aspect of the individual's life to be completely subordinate to the surveillance of the feudal-absolutist state. Indeed, his desire to regulate the entire life of an individual and to determine everything by the Tsar's decree, that is by a norm, was unlimited. In his view the peasants were to be under the constant control and supervision of the pomeshchik. He demanded that the Tsar issue a decree obligating the pomeshchiki to see that their peasants worked ceaselessly.

Of all the social classes, Pososhkov was most sympathetic toward the merchants. He was both their spokesman and representative. This role corresponded directly with his actual position in Russia during the first quarter of the eighteenth century, when his works were written.

---

[7] *Ibid.*, p. 82.

[8] See G. V. Plekhanov, *Sochineniia* [Works] (n.p: n.d.) XXI, 129–30.

[9] A. Brikner, *Ivan Pososhkov* (St. Petersburg: 1876), Pt. I, p. 5.

At the beginning of the eighteenth century, the existence of an economy which was an integral part of the national market and the leading role of the merchants in formulating these ties between various regions and areas made it possible for Pososhkov to understand broad state tasks and the interests of the entire economy within the framework of the system of serfdom. While he expressed and protected the interests of the merchant class, Pososhkov considered it his right and obligation to examine other classes, and to act as a kind of social arbiter in the relationships of other classes and social groups, which included those between the nobility and the peasantry, between each of these classes and the state, between the clergy and the state, and so forth. The position of the merchant in Russian society and economics and his role in the development of new bourgeois relationships enabled Pososhkov to defend not only the interests of his class, but also the national interests of Russia and the progressive character of many points in his political and economic program.

In reading the works of Pososhkov, one is struck by his deep and vigorous patriotism. His continuous concern for the well-being of his country, his extreme impatience with what seems to him unjust, and his vigilant search for "truth," were dictated by a profound devotion to his people. He was intensely disturbed by the lofty, contemptuous attitude of foreigners toward the Russians. He wanted to devote his energy to the strengthening of the military, economic, cultural, and moral status of his people. His vast love for them and his faith in their great future permeate Pososhkov's "reports" and treatises.

The writing of the *Report on Correction of All Injustices,* begun by Pososhkov at the end of the 1690's or in the first years of the eighteenth century, occupied him for more than two decades. The *Book on Poverty and Wealth* is also the result of prolonged reflection.

The aim of the *Book on Poverty and Wealth* is described in the subtitle: "An explanation of what causes useless poverty and why abundant wealth increases." The elimination of poverty and the increase of wealth form the basis of the *Book.* But even this massive and extremely complex theme does not exhaust the content of the *Book* or the aims set by the author. From the "foreword" alone it is evident that the author intended to propose to the Tsar methods to eliminate injustice and negligence, and "to create friendship and a secure life for the people." [10]

The grandiose nature of this task and the exceptional boldness of

---

[10] Pososhkov, *Kniga o skudosti i bogatstve,* p. 8.

the scheme are striking. Pososhkov presented the Tsar with a concrete set of reforms which would transform Russia into a rich, cultured, and mighty power. He assures the Tsar that if what he proposes is put into effect, then "all of our Russia will revive both spiritually and secularly, and not only will the Tsar's treasury be filled, but all the inhabitants of Russia will be enriched and glorified. And with improved military affairs [our country] will not only be famous, but all of our neighbors will be afraid of us." [11] Pososhkov hopes further that enmity and insult will disappear within the country, and that the haughty nobility will be changed into gentle sheep who will love the common people. The treasury will be filled to overflowing and all the people will be enriched, he promised.[12]

We can now see that Pososhkov's scheme was utopian; the problems were far greater than the proposals by which he hoped to solve them. Pososhkov stood firmly behind the social relationships of his time. He left them unchanged even in the projects set forth in the *Book,* wanting to achieve his great aims within the framework of noble, serf-owning Russia.

The form of the *Book* is original. It contains nine chapters: "On spirituality," "On Military Affairs," "On Justice," "On the Merchant Class," "On Art," "On Brigandage," "On the Peasantry," "On Agricultural Affairs," and "On the Tsar's Interest." The chapter headings and their arrangement are understandable if we consider the task which Pososhkov set for himself. The *Book* is more than an economic treatise. It is a sort of encyclopedia of the shortcomings of Russia and of practical formulas for their elimination. The purely economic chapters deal with the following: trade ("On the Merchant Class"), industry ("On Art"), agriculture (two chapters: "On the Peasantry" and "On Agricultural Affairs"), and finances ("On the Tsar's Interest").

The *Book* offers revealing criticism of the state of the country's affairs as well as basic proposals as to how to improve this situation. The critical portion forms its most valuable aspect. Clearly, with his peculiar mastery of the situation and with the passion of the accuser, Pososhkov has sketched a picture of "injustices." This phase of his work is independent of the other, the positive side; moreover, the presentation of the facts has great significance for the correct understanding of the actual conditions in Russia at the beginning of the eighteenth century.

In the economic part of the *Book,* Pososhkov discusses the broad area of economic policy. At the same time his book contains theoretical

[11] *Ibid.,* p. 243.
[12] *Ibid.,* pp. 8, 20.

discussions on economic questions. The roots of his economic views must be sought in the reality which he perceived and evaluated in accordance with his general concepts and ideals. Naturally the formulation of Pososhkov's concepts were influenced by the ideas which were embodied in the works of the outstanding economists of the seventeenth century and which were obviously related to the intense economic activity of Peter I. Pososhkov was unfamiliar with the economic literature of the West and knew little of the economic practices of other countries. This lack of knowledge significantly narrowed his scope and led to certain views of a backward character. Consequently, the forceful originality of his mind is most evident in those fields which he approached as an innovator and bold reformer.

The formation of his economic ideas was undoubtedly effected by the reforms of Peter I. They stirred his inquisitive mind, posed a multitude of new questions, and demanded definite answers. In this regard and in his awareness of basic economic problems, Pososhkov must be considered Peter's pupil. But he possessed a mind too great and independent that he can be looked upon as merely Peter's mouthpiece. His ideas were entirely original and often contradicted those of his teacher.

Under Peter numerous individuals conceived a variety of programs, many of which dealt with economic problems (Fedor Saltykov, Ivan Filippov, Lodygin, and others). The evaluations of the position of the country and the reforms projected by these men have much in common with Pososhkov's views. However, a similarity does not in itself indicate either the impact of these men or other "projectors" on Pososhkov or his influence upon them. Pososhkov advocates many economic measures which are not found anywhere else in the Petrine period. The similarity between a number of his proposals and those of other "reporters" attests to the vitality and the deep practical sense of Pososhkov's plans. Neither the breadth of thought nor the depth of treatment in the *Book on Poverty and Wealth* can be found in other projects of that period, which are fragmentary in nature and are usually devoted to only a few problems.

Pososhkov distinguishes betwen material and non-material wealth, but he does not define wealth itself. This division is the result of his religious nature and of the idealistic character of his world view. A similar classification of wealth is known to have characterized the thinkers of the Middle Ages. Under material wealth Pososhkov considers the wealth of the state (the treasury) and that of the people. He writes that the wealth of the people means "that all the people be rich on the basis of their own domestic resources . . ." [13]

[13] *Ibid.*, pp. 13–4.

Under nonmaterial wealth he understands "righteousness," that is, competent administration of the country, good laws, and just courts. We cannot, of course, directly classify this factor as wealth; but one cannot deny that good administration and just laws are very important conditions for the growth of real material wealth. Such was Pososhkov's own understanding of the matter. He writes of "righteousness" as a necessary prerequisite for eliminating poverty and increasing wealth in the country: "without extermination of abusers, thieves, brigands, and all overt and covert plunderers no measures will help in improving the conditions of the people." [14]

Although Pososhkov belonged to the propertied class, he often experienced the arbitrariness of high officials, the heartless formalism of judges, and so on. His views on nonmaterial wealth were embodied in his demands for court and administrative reforms and in his project for the preparation of laws; they therefore had a progressive character and were directed against arbitrariness, embezzlement, and bribery, all of which prevailed in the country.

Pososhkov shows great interest in the relationship between state (treasury) wealth and the wealth of the people: "in a Tsardom where people are rich, the Tsardom is rich; and in a Tsardom where people are poor, this Tsardom cannot be rich." [15] Pososhkov thus distinguishes between the state, on the one hand, and the national economy, on the other, and he recognized contradictions in their respective material interests. He tries to eliminate these divergencies by focusing the attention of the state on the development of the national economy. In principle, Pososhkov believes in the possibility of eliminating the conflicts of interest between the feudal-absolute state and the nobility, merchant class, entrepreneurs, peasantry, and craftsmen. He perceives the existing contradictions as the result of the erroneous policy of the state authority, which concerned itself only with the interests of the treasury, to the detriment of the national economy. This testifies to the historical limitation of his understanding of the nature and role of the contemporary Russian state, which appeared to him as a supra-class organization in which the interests of all classes and groups were harmonized. Pososhkov naively believed in the possibility of a wealthy people living within the feudal-serf system.

This illusion, that in a society founded on the exploitation of one group by another the people can be wealthy, was also widely held by the economists of Western Europe. "In the eighteenth century it was not so clear as in the nineteenth century that national wealth was

[14] *Ibid.*, p. 15.
[15] *Ibid.*, p. 77.

identified with national poverty," [16] wrote K. Marx. In another place Marx noted: "The very concept of national wealth was accepted by the economists of the seventeenth century in the sense that wealth is created only for the state and that the might of the state depends on this wealth, an interpretation which was partially preserved among the economists of the eighteenth century as well. The unconsciously hypocritical belief was that wealth and its production were the aim of the contemporary state and that the state was regarded only as a means for the production of wealth." [17]

Pososhkov's thesis, that a wealthy treasury could exist only in a state where the people were wealthy, was designed to preserve the interests of the people against the fiscal enthusiasm of the government. Growth of national wealth, he maintained, was advantageous both to the people and to the state. Other thinkers of Western Europe before Pososhkov expressed this relation between the wealth of the state and that of the people and urged the necessity of giving attention to the development of national wealth. Among them were Montchrétien, Boisguilbert and others. Pososhkov arrived at this idea independently, however. His views on the relation between national wealth and state revenues and the practical orientation of these views make him a major and original economist. His ideas did not lose their sharpness and significance during the entire period of feudal-noble and bourgeois-noble Russia.

Pososhkov proposed a number of steps to eliminate poverty in the country and to increase its wealth. Let us examine first the general measures touching on the economy as a whole. His conception of the role of the state in economic life was based firmly on the notion of the police state and its principles of interference, guardianship, and regulation. Moreover, he never questioned their validity. His proposals were usually accompanied by corresponding decrees to be issued by the Tsar. He considered decrees a mighty weapon for various reforms.

Of the general measures proposed by Pososhkov, the greatest significance is attached to the following two: 1) to require all people to work diligently and productively and to eliminate idleness in all its forms; 2) to struggle decisively against unproductive expenditures, to establish the severest economy in everything, and to oppose luxury and superfluities in the lives of the people.

Pososhkov was firmly against idleness. He wanted to force all people to work, to eliminate all inactivity—all free or forced idleness. Nobody had the right to live without working or to eat bread without earning

---

[16] Marx, *Kapital,* I, 729–30.

[17] Marx, *K kritike politicheskoi ekonomii,* p. 222.

it. Every person should produce by labor the necessities for his existence and, in addition, contribute a "surplus."

Although Pososhkov does not state it explicitly, his ideas indicate that labor, irrespective of its physical and social characteristics, is to be considered the source of wealth. Unlike the representative "classical" mercantilists of Western Europe, he did not identify wealth with money alone. By wealth, he understands goods, material welfare, and money.

Pososhkov established quite clearly the connection between the growth of wealth, on the one hand, and the level of productivity of labor, on the other. As an obligatory principle he demanded not only labor from everyone, but also labor with a "surplus" in excess of what was needed for existence. In the terminology of Marxist political economy this is the surplus product. Judges and clerks should be concerned "that no person remain idle or eat bread without purpose day in and day out. God did not give us bread that we should eat it like worms and transform it into rot. Instead, it is necessary, while consuming bread, to bring gain to God, Tsar, friends, and oneself, so as not to resemble the useless worms who transform everything into rot and bring not help but harm to people." [18] From these views it is evident that he had a definite conception of productive labor as labor creating a product with a "surplus."

Pososhkov's demand that everyone be forced to work was dictated by the existing difficulties of providing heavy industry with a sufficient laboring force and by the lack of sources for its replenishment, both caused by serfdom, which bound the worker to the land. As noted above, Peter was also motivated to reduce poverty, as is shown by his utilization of prison labor and his attempts to have monks and nuns trained for industry.

Pososhkov's thoughts flowed in the same direction. In order to develop industrial enterprises he proposes their taking healthy paupers from the street and teaching them trades such as spinning, weaving, and finishing. He suggests the construction, at treasury expense, of special "craft houses" where these "idle parasites" would be forced to work. Moreover, the pomeshchiki should see that the peasants do not loaf and that they are always—during summer and winter, except for Sundays and holidays—occupied with work, either on the farm or for hire. The peasant, who would "loaf," he believes, should be punished severely.[19]

Thus extra-economic compulsion appears to be the normal form of

---

[18] Pososhkov, *Kniga o skudosti i bogatstve*, p. 107. (Italics mine—A. P.)
[19] *Ibid.*, pp. 106–7, 146–7, and 166.

labor discipline. At the same time Pososhkov attached great importance to providing material work incentives. This is evident by his approval of higher wages in state enterprises, of piecework, and overtime pay for hired labor, and for the serf a definition by law of the extent of his obligation to the pomeshchik.

His second important general measure designed to eliminate poverty and increase wealth is the reduction of unnecessary expenditures, superfluities, and luxury, both from public and private spheres of the economy. The need for frugality is stressed throughout Pososhkov's *Book.*

He proceeds from considerations of general national-economic interests to attacks on the thoughtless, rapacious attitude of the population toward natural wealth, the destruction of young forests and fish, the collection of green nuts, and so forth. He presents what he deems very expedient principles for the utilization of natural wealth, which are intended to lead to its conservation and growth.

Pososhkov demands from officials and judges an honest approach to their obligations and a strict observance of the interests of the national economy; he condemns niggardliness and that formal concern for state interests which are a cover for personal greed. Thus he criticises the judges who often for the sake of mere copecks tear the peasants from their work and who, under the cloak of defending state interests, inflict great harm on the national economy. He further deplores the miserly pay received by workers in state industries (five copecks per day). "Thus their intention to bring gain to the great sovereign by not feeding the workers only contributes to his loss. Our administrators everywhere wince whenever a crumb is wasted, but do nothing when thousands of rubles are lost; by their denial of food they cut short the inclination of the Russian people towards craftsmanship and prevent the development of good crafts." [20]

Pososhkov felt that one of the most important tasks is the creation of a rational economy. He persistently stressed the significance of economizing in small things, for this would yield great results on a national scale. "A bee is a very small creature and collects its honey not in large quantities but in very small drops and thus collects many thousands of puds. The accumulation of state wealth operates similarly; if all people live carefully, waste nothing and try to save everything from ruin, then the state will also prosper." [21]

Pososhkov shows the need of importing only good wares, even though they may be more expensive. A number of commodities should not be

---

[20] *Ibid.,* p. 144.
[21] *Ibid.,* pp. 89–90.

imported at all in order not to waste money. Foreigners will never teach us to live thriftily and not to waste things foolishly; they praise that commodity which brings them, and not us, more profit." [22] Economizing is necessary not only on imported goods, but also on goods produced within the country. He insists upon moderation in eating, dress, and the satisfaction of other needs.

Opposed to the spoilage of materials collected for the government, such as furs, due to the negligence of officials, Pososhkov stresses the great significance of careful and wise conservation. "Good friend, protect the collection, for where there is no protection a collector will have a hard time to collect." [23]

Such were Pososhkov's methods of eliminating poverty and increasing wealth. As in the experience of Western Europe, so in Russia, the pressing need for the accumulation [of wealth] in that historic period determined the character of his principles of economy and thrift. He placed these practical principles of the rising bourgeoisie among the first of national and state tasks. Let us now examine Pososhkov's economic program more specifically as it applied to various sectors and spheres of the national economy.

On Trade and Industry

Of all the aspects of economic activity Pososhkov ascribes the most significance to trade, and of all the social classes he stresses the importance of the merchant class. "Trade is a great business! . . . through merchants a Tsardom enriches itself, and without merchants no state, not even the smallest, can exist," [24] he writes. "Trade and the military are friends; the military fight and trade aids them and prepares for them all types of necessities . . . As the soul cannot exist without a body, so the military cannot exist without trade . . . The Tsardom has increased [because of] the military and has been beautified by trade . . . No social group can survive in the world without [the services of] the merchant." [25]

Pososhkov wanted to imbue trade and the merchant class with the serious concern of the Tsar, the officials, and the courts. He was dissatisfied with the existing status of the merchant class in Russia; in other countries, he writes, "many people are protected, above all the merchants; and as a result the latter are wealthy." [26] He feels that

[22] *Ibid.*, p. 127.
[23] *Ibid.*, p. 200.
[24] *Ibid.*, p. 17.
[25] *Ibid.*, p. 113.
[26] *Ibid.*, p. 77.

the Russian merchant class needs "free trade." However, he defines the term in a peculiar fashion. He sees free trade as the right of Russian merchants to be delivered from the competition of "foreigners," as well as from that of the other classes and ranks in Russia. Now, he complains, everyone is engaged in trade—boyars, nobles, officers, soldiers, government officials, and peasants, and, since their trade is not taxed, the merchant class and the treasury suffer. Such a situation is unjust. Every "rank" should occupy itself with its own affairs; "it should not enter other spheres." He insists that everyone outside the merchant class be forbidden to engage in trade.

At the same time Pososhkov would not limit the right of persons of other occupations from entering into the merchant class; the condition for entry is relinquishment of the previous occupation and, as he sees it, the possession of a certain minimum of capital. Those outside the merchant class who engage in trade should be heavily fined. In this way he hopes to eliminate competition and to guarantee a high profit to the merchant. This aspiration toward monopoly was dictated above all by the narrow interests of the merchant class. Other planners, such as Filippov, pointed out to Peter the necessity of forbidding nobles and peasants to engage in trade.

Pososhkov also advocated uniform fixed prices on domestic goods, "so that they would be the same in adjacent shops," [27] the "set price" to be guaranteed by the strict supervision of merchants. Pososhkov's measures designed to regulate the prices and quality of goods have a clearly bureaucratic character. From them blows the wind of the distant past. To the extent that his proposals were meant to root out deception and injustice in trade, they had a worthy goal; if adopted, however, the bureaucratic restrictions which they imposed would have been a great hindrance to the development of trade. Schemes which had some meaning and justification in the medieval towns of Western Europe could not be applied under conditions of growing trade capital in the Russia of the eighteenth century. As in a number of other cases, Pososhkov clearly carried to excess his desire to regulate and supervise everything.

His proposal to reorganize the internal taxation of goods deserves attention. He shows the undesirability of multiple small taxes. In place of the taxes established by the New Commercial Code and the many small imposts, he proposed a single tax, somewhat lower than the total of the existing ones.[28] If this measure had been put into effect it would actually have aided the development of internal trade.

---

[27] *Ibid.,* p. 120.
[28] *Ibid.,* p. 210.

Pososhkov is sharply critical of the crown monopoly on the salt trade, because it resulted in a high price for the commodity and thus caused many villagers to go without it and to suffer and die of scurvy. The trade in salt was to be made free, since this would be beneficial to the people, to merchants, and to the treasury.[29] *The Book* also contains many arguments concerning the crown trade in wine.

Pososhkov further devotes much attention to foreign trade. He proposes an organization of foreign commerce which, in his view, could guarantee the Russian merchant a dominant position. He recommends the formation of merchant companies with monopoly rights to trade with other countries. While Pososhkov was writing his *Book*, Peter I decreed the establishment of such companies, but they remained on paper only.

Pososhkov believed that the sale of commodities to foreign merchants should be permitted by a merchant "commandant" and at prices set by the companies. The members of the trading companies would share in the foreign sale on the basis of their capital, "gaining according to the amount of their trade, so that neither rich nor poor will suffer loss." This same principle was to be applied to the purchase of imports; the goods imported were to be divided in accordance with the amount of goods sold by the merchants.

Pososhkov saw the necessity to attract into these companies not only rich merchants, but also middle and petty merchants. He wanted to eliminate enmity among them and to reach the stage where they would "help each other and would not allow anyone to be ruined." The imperial treasury and the town hall were to lend them money at interest for trading purposes.

He proposed the following trade policy: utilizing their monopoly position, the companies were to dictate to the foreign merchants prices and other conditions for the sale of Russian goods and for the purchase of foreign commodities by Russians. The price of the Russian goods would be fixed by the companies on the basis of their interests: "And should the price of a commodity be determined by a general council, then the foreigners might not take it at that price.[30] If the foreign merchants refused to buy goods at that price, then native goods should not be sold to them, and goods they had brought into Russia should not be purchased. If the foreign merchants should return the following year, for their obstinacy the prices of Russian goods must be raised, so that [Russian] merchants would not suffer and money invested in a com-

[29] *Ibid.*, pp. 212–3.
[30] *Ibid.*, p. 121.

modity would not be lost." If two years elapse before their return, the price must be doubled, if three years, tripled, and so on.

Pososhkov was convinced that as soon as foreign merchants knew that Russian merchants intended to raise prices, alien traders would cease their obstinacy and would purchase annually, because Russia could get along without their goods, but without Russian goods they "could not last for ten years." "We should stand quite firmly on this point in order to break their pride and to bring them to their senses so that they will follow us." [31]

Scholars usually note only the crudeness of Pososhkov's recommendations for the struggle with foreign merchants. One must remember, however, that the principle of trade wars with other countries, which lies at the base of these proposals, by no means indicates that his views are backward. This technique was widely used and was propagated by the mercantilists. Other views on trade, such as those of W. Petty, North and other prophets of free trade, remained mere good intentions; in practice international trade was built on the principle of monopoly and the exploitation of economically weak countries by the trading bourgeoisie of the more developed nations. This custom was also applicable to Russia in this period. Only the means used by others were more ingenious and subtle than those proposed by Pososhkov.

Pososhkov was concerned with the preservation and increase of money in the country. He considered it necessary to import only those indispensable things which could not be produced in Russia. He was strongly against the import of wines, glassware, and luxury articles, since he considered them a waste of money. In order to prevent the import of these articles and to keep money in the country, he recommended the creation of corresponding industries in Russia.

Although he does not deal directly with the trade balance, all of his thoughts on foreign trade and industry indicate that he proceeded from the trade balance concept: import less, export more. Moreover, the export of silver and copper money was to be prohibited. He proposed to permit only the export of ducats, since they were not used for money in Russia. In his opposition to the export of silver and copper money Pososhkov agreed with Peter I.

Pososhkov also concurred with Peter's belief that heavy industry must be developed. Peter recognized the need to create a native military industry, to replace the import of industrial goods by domestic production, to satisfy the wants of the population and to foster the ex-

[31] *Ibid.*, p. 137.

port of industrial goods. Pososhkov, however, took a more distinctly mercantilistic approach to this question. He viewed the establishment of heavy industry primarily as a means of preserving and increasing the money supply of the country; he recommended the development of native industry in order to avoid the loss of money in the purchase of foreign goods and in order to export goods abroad.

Pososhkov strongly favored the export of finished products from Russia, but not that of raw materials. He was alarmed by the fact that Russia imported cloth made from raw materials purchased from her: "instead of selling flax and hemp it is better for us to sell prepared cloth for sails, ropes, and calico and to take for that cloth efimki and other things we need." [32]

Pososhkov endorsed the general principle that "It is vital that the materials be processed where they are found." [33] This would lead to cheaper goods and to the enrichment of the Russian people. He felt that glassware could be produced in Russia in quantities large enough to satisfy the need of the country and to cover the demand of all Europe. In the same way "we could satisfy the European need for cloth . . ." We could produce enough tobacco to permit its export. And in general, "rather than allow others to get rich from our materials, we the Russians should eat our food and gain wealth from it." [34]

Pososhkov counselled people not to worry about the fact that at first Russian goods would be more expensive than foreign products and that the project would not be profitable. For as soon as the Russians gained experience the plan would pay for itself completely.

"In order to enrich the Tsardom," Pososhkov recommended that Peter I build industrial enterprises at the state's expense "in those towns where bread and food are inexpensive" and that he lease them out for quit-rent "so that the people will be enriched and the Tsar's treasury will be increased." [35] He advocated financial aid to merchants for the construction of mills, as well as commercial loans from the town hall at a small interest.

Pososhkov also envisaged an adequate labor force for industrial establishments. He held that enserfed peasants should work in factories during the winter and recommended that peasant children be taught weaving and other crafts. As already mentioned, he urged that the healthy poor be detained, taught trades, forced to work, and controlled by the masters of the enterprises. Thus his treatment of the

---

[32] *Ibid.*, p. 147.
[33] *Ibid.*, p. 146.
[34] *Ibid.*, p. 148.
[35] *Ibid.*

question of a labor force for industry has a clearly defined serf character. He bypassed the use of hired labor in industry, a subject which, as we have seen, interested Peter I.

Pososhkov paid much attention to the training of workers. He recommended the importation of good craftsmen from aboard to instruct Russians. He stressed the importance of substantial remuneration for artisans. Pososhkov was troubled by the improper relation of "Russian supervisors" to the working people. The employers, he wrote, "do not value the worth of the Russian individual and do not wish to feed him sufficiently, so that he will be content and without need." Here one sees the difficult position of workers in the state enterprises.

Pososhkov's views on piece payment are interesting. He considered it greatly superior to time payment and proposed that the existing obligatory three months work for peasants in St. Petersburg and in other places be changed to the piece payment system. Now, he writes, "they view their work sadly, because they are driven from dawn to dusk and do not finish it." [36] If they are able to perform their obligation, even within one month, the peasants should be considered as having fulfilled their duty. Pososhkov also proposed the adoption of the piecework system for state enterprises: "it would be desirable to introduce everywhere a piecework system. Monthly pay would be discontinued and each worker would be paid on the basis of his performance. This change would facilitate production." [37]

In order to foster the development of industry, Pososhkov believed that inventiveness should be encouraged and protected. He recommended, on the basis of the experience of other countries "that a civil code be prepared to safeguard each new invention in the crafts or industry, so that no one can infringe on it as long as the inventor lives," [38] that is, patents should be issued. England and France were the only European countries having patent laws at that time.

Pososhkov devoted much attention to the problem of obtaining natural dyes and other materials useful to industry. He hoped to stimulate the search for such resources by offering good pay and by attracting foreigners who were familiar with such things. During his travels in Russia, Pososhkov himself found sulphur, naphtha, and ochre.

The subject of handicrafts occupies a prominent place in Pososhkov's discourses on industry. He wished to create in Russia a handicraft guild organization like that in other countries. He attributed all the shortcomings of Russian handicrafts to lack of control and government

---

[36] *Ibid.*, p. 206.
[37] *Ibid.*, p. 207.
[38] *Ibid.*, p. 140.

supervision, and proposed measures for improving handicraft production in the country.

Pososhkov attached the greatest importance to the reorganization of apprenticeship and to strict control over the quality of production. As he saw it, the chief reason for the success of handicrafts in the West was good apprentice training. He recommended the establishment of a rigid term of apprenticeship, within which period the pupils, under threat of military service, would be categorically forbidden to leave their masters. Supervisors for each master, as well as a chief director who would oversee all masters and supervisors, were to be provided. In order to assure a high quality of handicraft goods, Pososhkov suggested obligatory stamping of products by masters and supervisors and the imposition of high fines for the sale of items of inferior quality.

The creation of such a handicraft guild organization would raise the quality of handicraft production, on the one hand, and decrease competition among artisans, on the other. As one might judge from his discourses, Pososhkov made membership in the organization mandatary for employment in a handicraft. A guild system, according to Pososhkov, would enable Russian artisans not only to catch up with, but also to surpass, foreigners. "And should craftsmen be prohibited from working as they please without supervision or civil administration, then all good artisans would enrich themselves and be as renowned as foreigners. Foreigners are no better than we, but they have a strict civil code and are good masters; if we establish such a code, our craftsmen can surpass them." [39]

While Pososhkov was writing his *Book,* Peter I had taken steps to create a handicraft guild organization. Pososhkov's discourses show that the idea of using guilds as a means of improving handicraft production was not unique to Peter.

Such were Pososhkov's views on matters of trade and industry. Basically their purpose was identical to that of Peter, namely the establishment of heavy industry and the development of handicrafts and trade. But the range of problems which interested Peter and those which concerned Pososhkov does not coincide. Peter dealt with a number of questions which remained outside Pososhkov's field of inquiry, as, for example, the relation between monopoly and competition in industry and the purchase of peasants by the merchantry as a solution to the problem of a source of labor for industry. On the other hand, Pososhkov raised questions which did not exist for Peter, such as the advantage of piecework payment, overtime payment, and the protection of inventions.

---

[39] *Ibid.*, p. 143.

Pososhkov's views on trade and industry show the mercantile influence on his economic philosophy and policy recommendations. He demonstrates the necessity of developing trade and industry by means of state regulation and protection. His discourses on the importance of the merchant class and trade, the formation of companies for foreign trade, the curtailment of imports, the inadmissibility of exporting raw materials from the country, and the necessity of developing home industry in order to export goods all have a mercantilist flavor.

Similar ideas were expressed by the mercantilists of Western Europe before Pososhkov: Stafford and Raleigh in England, Colbert in France, Peter de la Cur in Holland, and others. But this circumstance in no way diminishes Pososhkov's originality and the importance of his program. It is not so much that he developed his ideas without the slightest influence from West European mercantilists, but rather that he took a precise theoretical position and developed a definite program in conformity with the interests of his country. Pososhkov's great service lies in this concrete formulation of the problems of the economic development of Russia.

Pososhkov's Attitude Toward Serfdom

We have seen that Peter I paid great attention to the creation and development of new segments of agriculture, especially those connected with industry. Pososhkov makes no suggestions of this kind, except to advise cultivation of tobacco in Russia so as to eliminate its importation and to make possible its export. This proposal was not new, however, to Peter, who attached great significance to the development of tobacco cultivation in Russia. Speaking of its great possibilities, Pososhkov prepared a thorough survey of future tobacco cultivation.

Pososhkov devoted himself to questions concerning the rational management of forests and fisheries. He gave detailed directions for the protection of existing forests and the planting of new ones and for the conservation and improvement of Russian fishery resources. It is noted in the literature that his ideas on forests and fisheries are in many respects similar to those conclusions which science reached much later.[40]

Although the development of productive forces in agriculture occupies a comparatively small place in Pososhkov's work, he devotes great attention to the interrelation of pomeshchiki and peasants. His strong

[40] See Brikner, *op. cit.*, pp. 131 and 147–51.

preoccupation with the situation of the peasant masses differentiates him considerably from the majority of earlier or contemporary West European economists. Questions of agriculture and the relation between pomeshchiki and peasants are considered in two chapters of the *Book:* "On The Peasantry" and "On Agriculture." The first deals with the peasant economy and the second with the pomestie economy, but there is no strict demarcation between the two chapters. The two economies were closely linked, and therefore their treatment is interwoven.

Pososhkov is greatly interested in the peasant economy, and in his discourses on agriculture he gives it primary attention. There is not a word in the *Book* on the elimination of the "poverty" of the nobles or their enrichment, although a number of Pososhkov's proposed measures concerning the struggle against the escape of peasant serfs, the surveying of land, and so on, are intended to protect the interests of the nobles.

Pososhkov's *Book* gives a clear picture of the very difficult position of the peasantry at the time of Peter I. It is a most valuable historical document, written by an intelligent living witness who was in general kindly disposed toward the peasantry. Pososhkov shows the poverty of the peasants, who often lacked the means to buy salt and who died of scurvy, who were weighed down by the heavy yoke of obligations to the pomeshchiki and the state, and whose illiteracy was often exploited by officials for their personal profit. His accurate portrayal of the impoverished situation of the Russian peasants is somewhat similar to the pictures drawn in Radishchev's *Journey from Petersburg to Moscow,* but the class orientations and interests of the authors are entirely different. Pososhkov frequently characterizes the condition of the Russian peasantry as "poverty-stricken." He tries stubbornly to understand the causes for this poverty and to find a method for eliminating it. As in other economic areas, his program on the peasant question is distinguished by its breadth of concept, its courage, and by its duality; clearly expressed views on serfdom are interwoven with a number of demands undoubtedly progressive and advanced for the time.

Pososhkov neither justifies nor criticizes serfdom as such. His proposals touch only on the practice of serfdom and the relationship of nobles and peasants. His efforts to charge the pomeshchiki with unremitting surveillance over the peasants in order to combat the "laziness" of the latter, his suggestion of measures to prevent the flight of peasants from pomeshchiki, and his proposals concerning the introduction of a passport system of supervision over the peasants were directed toward a still greater enslavement of the peasantry. But his proposals to define by law the scope of the peasants' obligation to the pomeshchiki, to bring these obligations within the power of the peasants, and to establish obligatory training in reading and writing for the children of peasants were extremely radical and progressive for his time.

Pososhkov's advanced views are also evident in his awareness of the causes of peasant poverty. "Peasants live in poverty primarily as a result of their laziness; but neglect by administrators, abuses by the pomeshchiki, and inadequate protection aggravate their misery." [41] Thus begins Pososhkov's chapter on "The Peasantry." The peasant would never be impoverished if Tsarist taxes were collected according to the amount of land which he cultivated for himself and at a time convenient for the peasant; if pomeshchiki would impose work and taxes according to the allotment of land and would not require extra work and taxes; and if they would see that their peasants were never idle and always at work, except on Sundays and holidays. Such, in very general terms, are his recommendations regarding the peasant question.

Thus Pososhkov considers laziness one of the basic causes of peasant poverty. It was the usual thing for all the spokesmen of the ruling class—the nobility, which influenced the views of other classes—to accuse the peasants of "laziness." The notion that forced labor cannot interest the worker and cannot be productive gradually penetrated the consciousness of the spokesmen, until finally it was clearly expressed.

Although Pososhkov makes no direct statements about the connection between "laziness" and the social form of peasant labor, his presentation differs from that of the spokesmen of the nobility. His analysis discloses his concern for the peasants themselves and for their well-being. Moreover, he proposes a radical measure to protect the interests of the peasant serfs: limitation by law of their obligations to the pomeshchiki. In contrast to the spokesmen of the nobility, Pososhkov does not consider "laziness" to be the only, or the chief, reason for the poverty of peasant life.

Among the causes, Pososhkov attaches great, if not the greatest, significance to the arbitrary rule of the pomeshchiki over the peasants. He paints a picture of the pitiless exploitation of the peasantry and its complete ruin by its masters. "The pomeshchiki," he writes, "impose upon their peasants unbearable burdens and there are inhuman nobles who do not allow their peasants one day off during the work period so that they can work for themselves. They spend all their time

[41] Pososhkov, *Kniga o skudosti i bogatstve*, p. 166.

on the nobles' estates during spring and harvest time, and when some peasants pay the quit-rent or food supplies, then in addition to the required portions the nobles demand extra collections. By these excesses they force peasants into ruin, and should a peasant improve his condition they increase his taxes. Under such a system the peasant can never become rich. Indeed many nobles say: 'Do not allow the peasant to acquire anything, but shave him naked like a sheep.' In so doing, they create emptiness, since many peasants do not even have a goat left; because of these miseries many peasants leave their homes and escape to the lower regions, some go to the Ukraine, and still others flee beyond the frontiers . . ." [42]

Pososhkov urged the Tsar to take the peasantry under his protection, to guard them against the arbitrary rule of the pomeshchiki. He gave a most curious explanation of the cruelty of the pomeshchiki: "The pomeshchiki do not control the peasants in perpetuity; hence they do not protect them; whereas the direct master is the all-Russian autocrat, they own [the peasants] only temporarily. Therefore the pomeschiki should not ruin them; rather [the peasants] should be protected by the Tsar's decree, so that they may be upright instead of poor, especially since the peasant wealth is the Tsar's wealth." [43]

Pososhkov expressed more than once this idea of the temporary right of the pomeshchiki to the peasants. In the same chapter ("On The Peasantry") he writes, "In my opinion, the Tsar, rather than the pomeshchiki, should protect the peasantry, for the pomeshchiki have only temporary ownership, while that of the Tsar lasts forever, and the peasant wealth is the Tsar's wealth, and the peasant poverty is the Tsar's poverty. Therefore the Tsar should protect equally the high-born and the military, as well as the merchants and the peasantry, so that no one falls into poverty, but all are wealthy in accordance with their own means." [44] He placed the merchantry and the peasantry in the same category, in opposition to the nobility, and demanded from the Tsar the kind of concern for these classes as those enjoyed by the "high-born"—the nobility.

In the chapter on "The Tsar's Interests," Pososhkov also wrote about the temporary nature of the pomeshchiki possession of the land. Convinced that the wine trade should be a state monopoly, Pososhkov was indignant that the nobles often violated this monopoly. The nobles have forgotten "that the very land which they use does not belong to them, but to the great sovereign, that they themselves are

[42] *Ibid.*, p. 177.
[43] *Ibid.*, p. 178.
[44] *Ibid.*, pp. 182–3.

not free, but are his majesty's subjects and that they are greatly afraid of him. Various obstacles are placed in the way of the petty pomeshchiki, to say nothing about influential people. They cannot, without the Tsar's permission, step on the land which is under their temporary ownership."[45] He believed that the pomeshchiki should pay the state for that land.

Pososhkov's views on the temporary nature of the pomeshchiki rights over the peasants has stirred much interest among scholars and produced great differences of opinion about their true meaning. Some interpreted Pososhkov's words as foreseeing the liberation of the peasantry. For instance, Romanovich-Slavatinskii wrote that Pososhkov envisaged the emancipation of the peasants.[46] Semevskii thought that Pososhkov anticipated the possibility of freeing the peasants in the future, but, for the time, limited himself to demanding a definition of the requisitions and obligations owed to the pomeshchiki.[47] Pavlov-Silvanskii saw in Pososhkov's words "a statement of the eventual freedom of the peasants."[48] Kliuchevskii interpreted them in the same way.[49]

Others—Karnovich,[50] Tsarevskii,[51] Kliuchkov[52]—argued that Pososhkov did not have in mind the future liberation of the peasants. In the Soviet literature this point of view is defended by B. B. Kafengauz.[53] To our way of thinking, the latter interpretation is the correct one. There is no basis in his works for asserting that Pososhkov foresaw the emancipation of the peasants.

---

45 *Ibid.*, pp. 221–2.

46 See Romanovich-Slavatinskii, *Dvorianstvo v Rossii*, p. 330.

47 See V. I. Semevskii, *Krestianskii vopros v Rossii v XVIII i pervoi polovine XIX veka* [The Peasant Problem in Russia in the XVIII and in the First Half of the XIX Century] (St. Petersburg: 1888), I, 5–7.

48 N. P. Pavlov-Silvanskii, *Ocherki po russkoi istorii XVIII–XIX vv.* [Outlines of Russian History of the XVIII and XIX Centuries] (St. Petersburg: 1910), II, 69.

49 See Kliuchevskii, *Kurs russkoi istorii,* IV, 106.

50 See E. Karnovich, "Krestiane i pomeshchiki po ideiam Ivana Pososhkova, russkogo myslitelia v nachale XVIII veka" [Peasants and the pomeshchiki as Viewed by Ivan Pososhkov, Russian Thinker in the Beginning of the XVIII Century], *Sovremennik* [Contemporary], No. 10 (1858), Pt. 4, p. 42.

51 See A. Tsarevskii, *Pososhkov i ego sochineniia. Obzor sochinenii Pososhkova so storony ikh religioznogo kharaktera i istoriko literaturnogo znacheniia* [Pososhkov and His Works. A Review of Pososhkov's Works On the Basis of Their Religious Nature and Historical-Literary Significance] (Moscow: 1883).

52 See M. V. Kliuchkov, "Pososhkov o krestianakh" [Pososhkov's Views on Peasants], *Velikaia reforma 19 fevralia 1861* [The Great Reform of February 19, 1861] (Moscow: 1911), I, 72.

53 See his introductory chapter to Pososhkov's *Book* (1937 edition) and his article in *Problemy ekonomiki,* No. 2 (1936), p. 155, and also his *I. T. Pososhkov. Zhizn i deiatelnost,* Chapter VII.

As with other socio-political problems examined by Pososhkov, his position on the peasant question is inconsistent. The inconsistency is marked by predominating motives: in the constant struggle between the pomeshchik and the serf over the division of the production of the peasantry, Pososhkov's sympathies are clearly on the side of the peasantry. He defends the peasantry's interests against the unbridled arbitrariness of the pomeshchiki.

His attitude toward serfdom cannot justly be understood and evaluated by asking whether or not he foresaw the liberation of the peasants. More important is his practical position towards the then existing and burning questions of peasant life. In order to comprehend his basic attitude toward serfdom it is essential to understand that he connects the right of the pomeshchik over the peasant and the land with the obligation of the pomeshchik to serve his state. According to Pososhkov, this right was not holy, absolute, or inalienable, but conditional and temporary, and resulted from the pomeshchik's obligation to the state. Herein lies the true meaning of Pososhkov's discourses on the temporary nature of the pomeshchik's rights to the peasant and the land.

The senseless wrangling over whether Pososhkov did or did not "foresee" the possibility of freeing the peasants has caused historians to overlook the real significance of his suggested measures for improving the peasants' present and future condition. In his discussion of the nature of the pomeshchik's rights to the land and to the peasant, Pososhkov fought for several very genuine and important principles: 1) that the nobility serve the state honorably, 2) that they pay the state for the land they occupy, 3) that their exploitation of the peasant be limited.

He exposed those nobles who used various tricks to escape serving the state. Nobles who "gain position by trickery," or who are appointed as "judges or commissars or to any other position, or who stay at home without appointment and own peasants without performing a service to the great sovereign, should all be deprived of their people; their peasants should be transferred to those who serve their Tsarist majesty." [54]

Pososhkov proposed a limitation upon the pomeshchik's right to serf labor and the products of that labor. He advised the Tsar "to issue an order to the pomeshchiki establishing the amount of quit-rent they can collect from peasants and defining the extent of other obligations they can impose and the number of days a week a peasant should

---

[54] Pososhkov, *Kniga o skudosti i bogatstve,* p. 98.

work for pomeshchiki and perform other tasks. All this is necessary in order to ease the burden of tax payments to the sovereign and to the pomeshchik, as well as to allow the peasants to provide a living for themselves." [55]

According to Pososhkov, the scope of these obligations should be decided by a special assembly of nobles called for this purpose, and later ratified by the Tsar. He did not consider the participation of the peasants in this endeavor, but he emphasized that these obligations should be so determined "that the peasants would not be unduly burdened." The pomeshchiki should be strictly forbidden to demand more from the peasants than the Tsar's decree allowed, and the courts should see that the decree was enforced. In addition, Pososhkov suggested rewards of freedom and money (fifty rubles) to the peasant who reported to the court that the pomeshchik exacted more than the legal amount; if the peasant failed to do this, he should be punished by the whip. Should a pomeshchik demand more than the decree provided, he would be deprived of both land and peasants. "Even the most evil pomeshchik will think twice and will not ruin the peasants." [56]

Pososhkov proposed to determine the scope of the peasant's obligation in accordance with the amount of land and crops in question. The more land the peasant cultivates for himself, the greater should be his obligations to the pomeshchik. As the unit of measurement he suggested the consideration of "the entire farmstead" as the definite amount of land and crops, or as much land as the peasant needs to harvest four quarters of rye and eight quarters of spring corn in one year, that is, six desiatinas of arable land, twenty haystacks, and 600–720 square sazhens of farmland. A peasant could have a whole, half, fourth, or eighth part of a farmstead, or more than one farmstead. According to the amount of land and crops, he would have to fulfill a corresponding obligation to the pomeshchik.

Pososhkov did not propose an obligatory norm for alloting the peasants land. He only insisted that the peasants' obligations correspond strictly to the amount of land which they worked for themselves. The allotment would be set according to the will of the pomeshchik and with the consent of the peasant. Pososhkov also considered this principle necessary to determine the scope of the peasant's obligation to the state.

He advised a considerable reduction in the taxes of the peasants and proposed a tax on the lands of nobles. In this connection he recommended a very important measure to Peter: to separate completely

[55] *Ibid.*, p. 178.
[56] *Ibid.*, p. 183.

the peasants' land from the pomeshchiki land, so that the former would not be considered as belonging to the pomeshchiki. "On the basis of the size of that land, which will be added to the peasant's farmstead, the peasant will pay a tax . . . and therefore that land should not be considered as belonging to the pomeshchiki." [57]

This idea of separation arises as a result of the assertion that the real owner of the land is the Tsar, that is, the state, and not the pomeshchik. Putting this scheme into actual practice would have meant transforming the peasants into [people] obligated only personally. Since he considered the land to be the property of the state, Pososhkov admitted that the peasants had a right to own state land just like the pomeshchiki; however, he did not consider the peasants' landownership to be temporary. He recognized the (temporary) right of the pomeshchiki to own the land and the peasants which "they had," but completely rejected the pomeshchiki right to that land which the peasants worked for themselves.

It is remarkable that Pososhkov, who considered it necessary to require the pomeshchiki to make certain that the peasants would not "be lazy," did not say a word about the pomeshchiki responsibility to see that their serfs paid taxes. According to his plan, peasants should pay taxes on their land directly to the state, and [likewise] the pomeshchiki on the land temporarily given to them by the Tsar on condition of their bearing military and state service. Essentially, Pososhkov proposed to reduce the relation of peasant and pomeshchik in Russia to that incomplete form of bondage which existed in some countries of Western Europe. The realization of Pososhkov's views would have created a state of affairs in which the peasant was not forced to buy his land from the pomeshchik.

Viewing the question in historical perspective, one must admit the courage and originality of Pososhkov's program concerning the peasant problem. Of all of Peter's contemporaries, Pososhkov was the only man who spoke out against the unlimited arbitrariness of the pomeshchiki.

Among his plans to improve the peasants' condition we also find his proposal to educate their children, even if this required forceful measures (fines for the parents who did not send their children to school). Significantly, Pososhkov based the need to educate the peasant children on the interests of the peasantry: when dealing with literate peasants, the Tsar's officials were to be limited in their use of arbitrary rule in the village.[58]

---

[57] *Ibid.*, p. 193. (Italics mine—A. P.)
[58] *Ibid.*, pp. 171–2.

For an evaluation of Pososhkov's views on the peasant question, his attitude toward their flight has considerable importance. He discusses this problem at length. As the reason for the mass flight from the pomeshchiki, Pososhkov correctly saw the extremely severe circumstances under which the peasants lived and their subjection to merciless exploitation by the greedy pomeshchiki. In other words, he put the chief blame for the flights on the pomeshchiki themselves.

It should be noted that in calling for the struggle against the flight of peasants, Pososhkov was motivated not so much by the interests of the pomeshchik class (of which he says almost nothing) as by the interests of the state (the stability of the taxed population) and the merchant class. He maintains that if his plan were put into practice, "in one year all the empty villages will fill up, and other uninhabited areas will be settled. With this development the interests of the Tsarist majesty will increase, and when the land becomes more populated, then the merchants' markets will spread." [59] Among other measures designed to eliminate poverty among the peasantry and to increase its wealth are his views on the prevention of fires in villages and his awareness of the urgent need of a general land survey. Bickering over property lines was a cause of constant quarrels, sometimes resulting in murder.

Pososhkov suggested that for tax purposes the survey should include the nature of the lands, designating them as hay fields, meadows, gardens, orchards, and so forth. In effect, he developed the idea of a cadastral survey. Although an attempt was made to launch a general land survey in the 1680's, it was not successful. During the reign of Peter I, in 1713, Fedor Saltykov mentioned the need for such a survey. A general land survey, of twenty-three gubernias was not, however, undertaken until the end of the eighteenth century; twelve additional gubernias were only surveyed as late as the first half of the nineteenth century.

In the chapter, "On Justice," Pososhkov recommended a number of administrative measures to deal with peasant flight. Although Pososhkov did not oppose the foundations of serfdom as a system and was not a spokesman of the oppressed peasantry, the measures he suggested would nevertheless have considerably weakened the oppression of the peasants by the pomeshchiki, as well as the tax burden imposed by the state.

During Peter's time the growing merchant class sought the consideration and support of the Tsar. While it did not attempt to un-

[59] *Ibid.*, pp. 103–4.

dermine the political and economic domination of the nobility, it endeavoured to weaken its rights and power by strengthening itself.

Pososhkov's program regarding the peasant problem was progressive for its time. Plekhanov's *History of Russian Social Thought* did not give full due to Pososhkov's progressive demand to limit the scope of peasant obligations. Plekhanov erroneously identified this demand with the alleged "concern" for the peasants of Moscovite Tsars, which expressed itself in issuing grant-charters to boyars and the nobility. In fact, the Moscovite Tsars' concern was for the state of the Treasury, hence they cautioned the boyars not to ruin their peasants.[60]

On Finances

Financial measures taken by the state conflicted with the interests of the population, particularly those of the toiling masses. Pososhkov reacted forcefully to such inequities and devoted much attention to the problems of money and finance. His *Book* contains lengthy passages on the value of money. He thought that in Russia, the Tsar might use his own discretion in establishing the purchasing power of money, regardless of its metallic content. In Western European countries where there was no autocratic power the value of money had to depend on the amount of metal it contained. In Russia, wrote Pososhkov, copper money should be minted "not according to foreign ways, that is, in terms of the value of copper, but according to the will of His Imperial Majesty . . . We are not foreigners, we do not cherish the value of copper; we esteem the name of our Tsar. It is His Imperial name that is dear to us, not copper; and hence we do not value the coins by their weight, but by the Tsar's image engraved thereon." [61] Moreover: "in our country it is not the weight of coins, but the Tsar's will that has power. Foreign rulers do not possess as much power as their people. These rulers cannot govern arbitrarily, for their subjects are independent; even the merchants share in this independence. Indeed, the merchants determine the value of goods and money in terms of one another and stamp the royal image on the money as a symbol of its worth in terms of goods and that it should be exchanged for that amount. To our simple understanding this would not contribute to the honor, but to the dishonor, of our ruler: that money be valued not according to his name but according to a price set by a merchant." [62]

---

[60] Plekhanov, *op. cit.,* XXI, 111–2.
[61] Pososhkov, *Kniga o skudosti i bogatstve,* p. 238.
[62] *Ibid.,* p. 239.

We need not accept foreign advice and add silver to copper money in order to make our money "equal in material value to its worth. It seems to me that such advice is completely inapplicable to us because our monarch is an autocrat, not an aristocrat or a democrat. Because of this we value neither silver nor copper but respect the name of His Imperial Majesty.

"The word of His Illustrious Highness is so powerful in our country that if he were to decree that a symbol of the ruble be placed on a copper coin, that coin would be accepted as a ruble and would be used as such in trade for eternity." [63] Thus Pososhkov's views on the source of the value of money are coupled completely with his views on the nature of state authority and the economic role of the state.

In an autocratic country the value of money is determined by fiat. Thus with respect to Russia Pososhkov appears to be a clear-cut nominalist. So far as Western European countries were concerned, whose rulers enjoyed less authority, Pososhkov believed in a commodity-metallic explanation of the value of money. Pososhkov's nominalist position as regards Russia should not be considered an indication of the backwardness of his views, nor a reflection of backwardness in Russia. Witness, for example, D. I. Rozenberg's erroneous statement: "The imprint of Russia's backwardness is also evident in Pososhkov's ideas on the theory of money . . . In backward Russia the exaggerated view of the all-powerful autocracy and of the autocrat reached truly fantastic proportions." [64]

This view is historically inaccurate. The nominalist conception of money appeared long before Pososhkov. It served as a justification for the widespread practice of debasing money by rulers of the Middle Ages. During Pososhkov's time, a different view of the value of money prevailed in the West. It was associated with the names of Stafford, Mun, Petty, North, and others. These economists emphasized that metallic content determined the value of money. But the metallic-commodity theory of money does not appear to be scientific.

By emphasizing the prime importance of metal in evaluating money, this theory concerns itself with only some of the functions of money (for example, measure of value, world currency) and ignores its other functions (for example, means of circulation). Critics of the commodity-metallic theory, by de-emphasizing the role of metal in the valuation of money, ignore its functions as a measure of value and as a world currency and generalize only the practical service of money as a means of circulation. The one-sidedness of the metallic-commodity

---

63 *Ibid.*

64 Rozenberg, *Istoriia politicheskoi ekonomii,* I, 60–1.

theory provoked a reaction in Western Europe in the latter seventeenth century and in the eighteenth.

The development of industry as the main source of wealth led people to stop considering foreign trade important. Economists criticising mercantilism turned their attention to the function of money as a means of circulation and concluded that money had no inherent value. In France as early as the end of the seventeenth century Vauban and Boisguilbert rejected the mercantilist notion that money is the essence of national wealth and attacked the fetish of gold. Boisguilbert thought that a simple piece of paper could fulfill the function of money. The well-known experiment by John Law represented a rejection of the metallic explanation of value. Physiocrats in the middle of the eighteenth century regarded money as a counting-symbol-denomination. Quesnay suggested that paper could replace coin.

In 1690 Nicholas Barbon, a critic of mercantilism in England, argued that "money is value created by law." Barbon maintained then, as Pososhkov did later, that a stamp on money does not represent proof of weight, but government control over value. He rejected the significance of gold and silver in the determination of the value of money, for money, he said, was a creation of the state. Barbon went much farther in his nominalism than Pososhkov, stating that it was not the value of the precious metals that determines the value of money, but the value of money that determines the value of the precious metals. No one, however, has tried to explain "the backwardness of England" by pointing to Barbon's nominalist theory of money.

As we know, the state theory of money lived on in succeeding centuries in countries of different levels of economic development and with different political systems. In the twentieth century it reappeared in the theories of Knapp, Bendiksen, and other nominalists. The reasons for this constant recurrence of the nominalist theory must be sought not in the "backwardness" of one country or another, but in phenomena of a different nature.

In Russia the nominalist concept was expounded by a number of spokesmen even after Pososhkov. Karamazin and Sharapov were nominalists in the nineteenth century. Their theorizing had a clear noble-class orientation and was directed against the growing Russian bourgeoisie. Karamazin's argument against the projects of Speranskii and Sharapov's opposition to the monetary reforms of Witte have much in common with Pososhkov's discourses. In their denial of the significance of metal for the value of money, they and other nominalists were motivated by their view of the power of the Russian sovereign. They represented the reactionary opposition to the growing

Russian capitalism.[65] Pososhkov's nominalism is connected with the mercantilist principle of the development of trade and industry.

How did Pososhkov understand the nature of money in its function as world money? He thought that the value of money as established by the Tsar was effective only within the state, while beyond the frontiers Russian money was valued by foreign merchants. He was in favor of prohibiting the export of silver and copper money. But he cannot be identified with the proponents of a monetary system. His views belong to an advanced stage of development, linked to the growth of native industry.

Pososhkov's discourses on the value of money have strong practical significance. With his nominalistic theory he essentially justifies the financial policies of Peter I, who resorted widely to coining depreciated money for the finance of wars.

In his practical proposals on the issuance of money Pososhkov suggested two important measures: observance of the purity of metal in all money and a further decrease of the metal content of money. As we have seen, a decrease in the pure metal content of money took place in two ways—during Peter's reign by reduction of assay and by alteration of the money's content. The reduction of the assay of silver money, which Peter carried out in 1718, drew sharp criticism from Pososhkov. He came out decisively against the decrease of the assay of silver and gold money.

Pososhkov urged the Tsar to coin gold, silver, and copper money only from pure metal. He proposed the use of pure gold for the *chervontsy*. He also objected to adding silver to copper money in order to give the latter a silver appearance. Copper money should be made of pure copper. He based his demand for the purity of metal in money on motives of an ideal-political character, as well as on practical considerations. This purity is dictated by the purity of the Christian faith and the fact that the Tsar's name is on the money. Pososhkov's practical objection to "false" money, that is, money made of an alloy of various metals, is the ease of counterfeit and the mass appearance of "thieves" money. His criticism of the monetary operation of 1718 was largely directed against the issuance of silver altyns and copecks of low assay.

At first glance Pososhkov's proposal for coining money only from pure metal seems contradictory to his nominalistic theories. Once the

[65] See A. B. Eidelnant, *Noveishii nominalizm i ego predshestvenniki. Ocherki iz istorii denezhnykh teorii* [New Nominalism and Its Predecessors. Outlines from the History of Monetary Theories] (2nd edition, Moscow: Gosfinizdat, 1948), Chapter XI.

value of the metal has no meaning for money, what sense, one may ask, has the demand for purity? According to Pososhkov, purity is necessary to guard the state against counterfeiters. In striving for purity, he was not fighting for the full value of money. The relation of nominal value to real value, that is, to the value of the monetary material, depends not only on the degree of purity, that is, on the assay of the metal, but on the overall weight of the money. While sharply critical of the mixture of various metals in money, he calmly passes over Peter I's frequent devaluation of money by lowering its overall weight.

Moreover, while categorically opposed to mixing silver with copper in "silver" copecks and altyns, Pososhkov proposed just as decisively a decrease in the weight of copper money in order to replenish the Tsar's treasury. In his project the nominal value of the money differs sharply from the real value. The issue of altyns and copecks in 1718 gave the treasury eighty-five rubles of profit on the pud, and the copper five-copeck pieces issued in 1723 produced thirty-two rubles. Pososhkov's project promised about 140 rubles on a pud of copecks, 220 on a pud of altyns, and 370 rubles on a pud of grivnias. His plan envisaged a gap between the nominal and the real value of money, similar to that which existed under Aleksei Mikhailovich. Pososhkov evidently did not know the consequences of the latter's experiment with the issue of copper rubles.

If we proceed from the present day practice of money circulation, then Pososhkov's effort to prove to the Tsar his right to mint small silver and copper coins of a real value lower than their nominal value, does not make sense. One must keep in mind, however, that at that time these coins were not exchangeable, as they are today. There was no limit to their acceptance; but they did not have a fixed relation to the silver ruble.

In his *Book* Pososhkov devotes much attention to taxes. As has been said, his basic idea concerning wealth consists of combining effectively the interests of the state with those of the people. "It is a small and easy problem to increase the Tsar's wealth, for he is like a god, and what he desires he can do. But it is a great and difficult task to bring prosperity to all the people . . ." [66]

Pososhkov also applies this principle in his practical treatment of taxation. His proposals are derived from the following basic ideas: 1) all classes of society except the clergy should pay taxes; 2) taxes should not harm the national economy or ruin the people; 3) land

[66] Pososhkov, *Kniga o skudosti i bogatstve,* p. 15.

should be the basis of taxation, and the tax should correspond to the amount of land held.

Pososhkov thinks it unjust that the nobility does not pay taxes to the state and suggests that they too be taxed. He is aware that this proposal will meet sharp resistance from the nobles: "I think that powerful people will oppose this with all their means, for they are used to living as they wish and do not like to give nearly as much as they like to take." [67]

He recommends to Peter I that he be careful in his policy of taxation and in his relation to the taxpayers. "Continuous requisitions mean, not collection, but certain ruin to peasants as well as merchants and are a clear drain on the Tsardom. The Tsar's collections will not be exhausted and will always bring satisfaction if they are not imposed in excess; excessive collection is not collection but ruin." [68] He speaks angrily of the offenders and robber-officials who ruin the people for their personal enrichment.

Pososhkov rejects the principle of the head tax, as well as that of the household tax, which had been used up to that time. He reproaches the "nobles" because they "own peasants, but do not know their names, do not understand the value of the peasant household and count only gates or enclosures; some even count smoke from the chimney. And as smoke disappears in the air, so does their calculation —it disappears into nothing." [69] The soul tax, established by Peter, is severely criticized by Pososhkov in a very curious argument: "I do not believe that there is any benefit in soul counting, because the soul is an intangible thing, incomprehensible to the mind and priceless. One should price only material things." [70] Pososhkov sees the failure of the head tax system in the fact that it ignores differences in the material position of the taxpayers.

The only just system of direct taxation he declares to be the land tax—calculating the amount of tax "according to the possession of land and the yield from it." [71] In contrast to the intangible "soul" and the undefined peasant "household," the land is a firm, constant and unchanging basis for taxation. "Land is the greatest gift of our great monarch, and it can never be changed." [72] According to Pososhkov, nobles, peasants, merchants, and all other people, such as town dwell-

---

[67] *Ibid.,* p. 194. "They like to ride piggy-back," writes Pososhkov about "influential persons," *ibid.,* p. 103.

[68] *Ibid.,* p. 78.

[69] *Ibid.,* p. 179.

[70] *Ibid.*

[71] *Ibid.,* p. 180.

[72] *Ibid.,* p. 20.

ers, state servants, and judges, should pay land taxes, "so that no one would live free on his Tsarist Majesty's land." [73]

As a basis for the land tax to be imposed on the peasants, Pososhkov suggests the adoption of the same tax unit—the "household," "farm"—which was used to determine the amount of the peasant's obligation to the landowner. The tax on nobles' lands should be a considerably smaller amount than that on the peasants' lands.

Pososhkov suggested different rates of tax on nobles' lands depending on their designation and also differential taxation of city and suburban land. He indicates, for example, the necessity for considerably higher rates on suburban and garden lands on which herds are kept or vegetables grown.

Pososhkov showed great courage and originality when he proposed the substitution of the land-based system of direct taxation for the head tax and when he urged the Tsar to coerce the nobles to carry tax obligations. His tax unit is a combination of the two methods used in Russia prior to Peter's tax reforms: land and household. It would have assured a tax load more proportional to the material conditions of the taxpayers than plowland taxation (with its auxiliary units—the "land strip" and the "living quarters") or the household taxation established in Russia at the end of the seventeenth century.

In spite of the obvious simplicity of the tax unit suggested by Pososhkov, there would have been many difficulties to putting his plan into practice. For the taxpayer the head tax was burdensome and inconvenient, but for the treasury it had one important advantage over all others—the simplicity of the technique, a fact which forced Peter to give preference to this system.

The unsound nature of the head tax is one of the undisputable truths of financial science. In England Petty indicated its negative features. In Russia Radishchev, at the end of the eighteenth century, and N. Turgenev, almost a hundred years after Pososhkov, sharply criticized the head tax. As we see, Pososhkov was far ahead of his time on this question.

Among other proposals in the field of taxation, Pososhkov insistently urged Peter I to introduce tithes for the church—a tenth part of all the products used. This proposal reeks of antiquity.

Pososhkov also examined the question of taxes on trade. He did not object to a tax on internal trade. He evidently considered it fully expedient, but he thought the existing means of taxing trade unfair and the amount of the tax too high. He spoke out sharply

[73] *Ibid.*, p. 196.

against multiform taxation. He declared that of the decreed taxes, which generally amount to 15 per cent of the price of the goods turnover, the state often receives nothing, since many people do not buy at the markets, but at home or on the side. It was, according to Pososhkov, these multiform taxes on trade and the manner of collecting them which made it possible to escape them. "They try to get two or three skins from one ox, but actually they cannot get one whole skin; no matter what they do, they just skin off shreds. This is harmful to the Tsar's interests; the attempt to collect additional taxes causes a total loss." [74] Multiform taxation requires for each collection special bailiffs, sworn officials, and messengers, all of whom live off the state. "As a result there are neither collections nor disputes, but all people lose." In place of all the old and new taxes on trade, Pososhkov suggests the establishment of a single collection of 10 per cent of the price; the collection must be made only once, regardless of the place of sale of the goods or whether there is a resale.

Taxes on internal trade certainly were one of the barriers to the devolpment of trade within the country. Anxious to improve on this matter, Pososhkov brought up the important question of trade policy. Approximately thirty years after Pososhkov wrote his proposals to the Tsar, internal trade taxes were completely abolished in Russia.

Among other issues relating to state revenues, Pososhkov gives much attention to the state's wine and salt trade. As already mentioned, he suggested that the Tsar abolish the state monopoly of the salt trade and convert it into free trade, levying only one tax on it "at the source, from which it will then be distributed." We spoke above of Pososhkov's motives for this proposal (the rise in salt prices led to mass illness among the peasants). He also notes the great waste of funds in supporting all the different bailiffs, sworn officials, administrators, and other employees and supervisors of the state salt trade: "and all of them gnaw away at the salt like worms, and from this salt make their living." [75]

After Peter's death the government abolished the state salt trade (in 1727); but in 1731 it was restored for financial reasons. Pososhkov's idea of the free sale of salt was realized only in the second half of the nineteenth century.

---

[74] *Ibid.*, p. 208.
[75] *Ibid.*, p. 213.

I. T. Pososhkov's Historical Place and Role in the Development of Economic Thought

Pososhkov and his role in the development of Russian social thought have been subject to contradictory evaluations. To a significant degree this was the result of the class position and social outlook of the scholars themselves. The combination in Pososhkov's views of the most contradictory positions—progressive and conservative—led to various interpretations of his views and programs. Thus, for instance, to the historian Pogodin, Pososhkov was "a genius of the Russian national state, with a shrewd, calm, penetrating mind, a man devoted to church, state, and nation." [76]

A high evaluation of Pososhkov's significance in the development of Russian social thought was presented by the militant organ of Russian revolutionary democracy—*Contemporary*. The October, 1858, issue of this magazine contained an article by E. Karnovich, "Peasantry and Pomeshchiki According to the Ideas of Ivan Pososhkov, Russian Thinker of the Beginning of the Eighteenth Century." The article is distinguished by the truly historical approach of the author and the editorial board of *Contemporary* toward Pososhkov's views. Pososhkov's ideas on the peasantry and pomeshchiki are examined and evaluated in connection with the real conditions of Russia in the first quarter of the eighteenth century. The negative aspects of his ideology and program are noted in detail; yet these traits are not used to indict him, but are explained by the spirit of the times. On the whole, Pososhkov is characterized here as a man progressive for his time, in many respects ahead of his century, more farsighted than his contemporaries. "In spite of some errors characteristic of the age in which he lived, he expressed many ideas which were basically true and which applied to the life of the peasantry." [77]

The bourgeois historians—A. Brikner, N. Pavlov-Silvanskii, and others—devoted great effort to Pososhkov's works. Although they were not in a position to give a fully correct interpretation or to determine his place in the development of economic thought, these historians nevertheless valued Pososhkov's works highly. "Pososhkov," writes A. Brikner, "can be considered in a certain sense a representative of the literature of enlightenment in the eighteenth century. In some ways he deserves the name of encyclopedist, since his works touch on

---

[76] *Sochineniia Ivana Pososhkova* [Ivan Pososhkov's Works] (Moscow: 1863), II, 11.

[77] Karnovich, *op. cit.*, p. 62.

many sciences and in places include many interesting generalizations and theses, like the works of the noted publicists of the West." [78]

N. Pavlov-Silvanskii, indicating the duality and contradiction of Pososhkov's views, writes that "without the slightest influence from the economic science rising in the West at that time he explains independently some of the main characteristics of the national economy." [79]

While they consider justly that Pososhkov's works, especially as judged by their content and originality, should be placed on a level with the most important works of world thought of the seventeenth and eighteenth centuries, these historians nevertheless stand on false methodological grounds: the main, and in fact only, criterion for their evaluation of Pososhkov's importance is a mechanical comparison with the thinkers of other countries acting in other historical conditions.

The bourgeois historians isolate Pososhkov from the real conditions in Russia at the beginning of the eighteenth century and therefore show that they are not in a position to determine correctly Pososhkov's real role in the development of Russian and world social, especially economic, thought. Without clarifying Pososhkov's class position, Brikner discovers in him such generally human traits as "humanity," "truth," and "morality," which he takes as the basis for comparing Pososhkov to the advanced thinkers of the eighteenth century.

Such an approach is vicious. It has served as the basis for the fundamental misinterpretation of Pososhkov's place in the development of social thought by a number of scholars. Thus, for instance, Bezobrazov, bowing before the bourgeois economic science of the West, absolutely refused to ascribe to Pososhkov's works any significance in the history of science, either world or national.[80]

In his famous work on the history of Russian social thought, Plekhanov did not give a correct analysis of Pososhkov's proposals. While emphasizing the conservative side of Pososhkov's views, Plekhanov underestimated the progressiveness of a number of these ideas and failed to indicate adequately those elements in his argument, which distinguished Pososhkov from his forerunners and contemporaries.[81]

We have examined Pososhkov's views on various questions and have indicated the significance of these ideas. We have seen the complexity and, in many respects, the contradictions in his petitions. His pro-

---

[78] Brikner, *op. cit.*, p. 3.

[79] Pavlov-Silvanskii, *Ocherki po russkoi istorii*, II, 67.

[80] *Zapiski imperatorskoi Akademii nauk* [Notes of the Imperial Academy of Sciences] (St. Petersburg: 1879), XXXIII, 763.

[81] Plekhanov, *op. cit.*, XXI, 117, 135, 136, and others.

posals do not include anything revolutionary. At the same time, the basic line of Pososhkov's economic program is definitely advanced and progressive for the time. This line is the universal development of Russia's productive power, the growth of native trade, industry, and agriculture, and the strengthening of Russia's economic power, as well as her independence from other, more developed countries.

As a whole Pososhkov's progressive economic program bears the severe stamp of historical limitation. In all his discourses he stood firmly on the ground of serfdom. Like Peter I he saw in serfdom the most important means for the achievement of the broad aims he proposed.

However, Pososhkov's service to the Russian people consists in the fact that, within the limits of his period, he understood correctly Russia's basic tasks and fought selflessly, with all the means at his disposal, for their realization. His economic program was worked out independently; it derived from a profound appreciation of Russia's position and the reforms of Peter I.

The valid argument by Plekhanov and a few other scholars that many of Pososhkov's correct ideas were first expressed by mercantilists of other countries in no way decreased either the originality of his views or the scope of his services to his country. That Pososhkov was unfamiliar with economists of the West is not open to question. This limitation is not a merit, but an insufficiency caused by all the conditions of his life. The simple truths that it is necessary to develop a native industry and to export not raw materials but finished industrial products, that education is necessary for the people, and so forth, were proclaimed and demonstrated by Pososhkov not "in general" terms, but specifically for his own country. Pososhkov's originality and merit can be correctly evaluated not so much by comparing his views with those of Stafford, Montchrétien, Serra, Mun, and other mercantilists of the West, as by contrasting his economic program with the views developed in Russia before and during his time.

Independently of the West European economists, and as a result of his understanding of reality, Pososhkov founded a relatively well-constructed program of economic development for Russia. He did not borrow his ideas from other countries; indeed, on some questions he was more independent than many antecedent and contemporary mercantilists of the West. This can justly be said, for example, of his views on the relation between the wealth of the treasury and that of the people. While he arrived independently at these ideas, which were being defended in other countries by the representatives of a mercantilistic and progressive economic thought, Pososhkov was a stranger to the one-sided concept of a trade balance advocated by the majority of his contemporaries in the West; and on a number of questions of primary importance he managed to rise above contemporary mercantilists. He was a stranger, for instance, to the disdain for agriculture which was characteristic of the majority of mercantilists of the West.

The reactionary elements of the revolution of 1905 tried to use Pososhkov's name in order to woo the peasants to their side. "The Society Named for the Peasant I. T. Pososhkov" was founded in Petersburg in 1905.[82] Its formation was a step forward toward the creation of a new party, the "Imperial People's Party," which was formed by its organizers as a kulak party based on Stolypin's land legislation and was characterized by a strong spirit of chauvinism and power nationalism. Fundamentally, its program was different from that of the progressives, which represented in Lenin's words *"a cross of the Octobrists with the Cadets."* [83]

The program of the Russian "progressives" of the twentieth century, rather than being progressive, was actually a system of counterrevolutionary liberalism, while Pososhkov's scheme was courageous and original for the beginning of the eighteenth century. It was truly progressive for its time.

Pososhkov can be considered one of the first Russian *writer*-economists to produce a developed, constructive, and workable system of economic views. He is at the same time one of the most distinguished and original representatives of the school of world economic thought of the sixteenth to eighteenth centuries known as mercantilism. His works show that Russian economic thought was, during his lifetime, truly on a level with the most advanced economic thought of that time.

---

[82] Among the founders of this society and members of its administration were seven members of the State Duma. The president of the society was M. A. Karaulov—a deputy in the Second and Fourth State Dumas from Terek oblast, a landowner, sub-captain, and author of works on the history of the Terek Cossacks. Karaulov's politics are well known. In the Second Duma he acted like a rightist Cossack and defended Stolypin; in the Fourth Duma he joined the progressives and then joined the "independent group." During the October socialist revolution Karaulov was one of the leaders of counterrevolution in the Terek oblast.

[83] Lenin, *Sochineniia,* XVIII, 469.

CHAPTER 13. *The Spokesmen of the Nobility of the First Half of the Eighteenth Century, F. S. Saltykov, A. P. Volynskii, and V. N. Tatishchev*

This chapter will be concerned with the economic views of prominent spokesmen of the nobility who took an active part in executing the reforms and economic policies of Peter I. In spite of the many economic problems which interested these men and which they eleborated, they are all united by their desire to strengthen the preëminent position of the nobility and by their common attitude toward serfdom. Furthermore, they were all concerned with the development of the productive powers of Russia.

The Projects for Economic Reform in the Notes of F. S. Saltykov

Fedor Stepanovich Saltykov came from an old boyar family.[1] His father was for some time governor of Velikii Ustiug; from 1690 to 1696 he was governor of the city of Tobol'sk, and from 1698 to 1700 governor of newly conquered Azov.

In 1697 along with other young people, Saltykov was sent abroad to study seamanship and the art of ship-building. On his return he was assigned to the Guards; in 1700 he participated in the battle of Narva as a captain. Early in 1703 he left the military service and received the honorary office of ship master. He worked at the Olonets and then at the Petersburg and Novoladoga shipyards, where vessels for the Baltic fleet were built.

In June 1711 Peter I sent Saltykov abroad on a special assignment: to buy ships to strengthen the Baltic fleet. On this mission he visited Copenhagen, Amsterdam, Hamburg, and other cities of Western Europe. From March, 1712, until his death (August 2, 1715) he lived

1 For biographical data on F. S. Saltykov see the foreword to P. N. Tikhanov, *Pamiatniki drevnei pismennosti* [Memorials of Ancient Literature] (St. Petersburg: 1892), pp. i–xxvii; see also Pavlov-Silvanskii, *Proekty reform,* pp. 11–20.

in England and visited Amsterdam and the Hague from time to time.

F. Saltykov observed the life of other peoples so that Russia could profit by their experience. During the first year of his stay abroad, he prepared proposals which, in his opinion, needed to be put into effect in Russia. The basic aim of these measures and the motives which guided him in preparing this project are evident from the following communication to Peter I. "I hereby report to your Majesty that, while fulfilling your orders, I have during my spare time tried diligently to extract [ideas] from the prevailing decrees in England as well as in those countries of Europe where only autocracies and not republics or parliaments prevail, ideas which, if dutifully introduced, would benefit the state greatly both externally and internally; many of these concepts are unknown in our country and their implementation would not burden the people. Moreover, universal education in all the sciences and arts could be undertaken, so that in a short time we could equal the best European states . . ." [2]

Saltykov asked the Tsar to accept his views on these questions. The letter was written on December 1, 1712. In April, 1713, soon after he received Peter I's permission to acquaint him with his work, F. Saltykov forwarded his memorandum. Entitled "Propositions of Feodor Saltykov," it was published in 1892.[3] On August 1, 1714, Saltykov sent his second and more complete memorandum; and on November 5 of the same year, he forwarded a duplicate with the addition of one new chapter. This memorandum was published in 1897 under the title "Views Beneficial to the State." [4]

Fedor Saltykov was an educated man. The scope of the problems which he presented to the Tsar was quite broad and his reforms were distinguished by their versatility. For example, he recommended to the Tsar that the history of the Russian state, and especially that of Peter I's rule, be written and then translated into other languages and that it be sent to the European states in order to expose the falsehoods spread by foreign historians about the Russian state and to acquaint everyone with the bravery and wisdom of the Tsar and the

---

[2] See Berkh, *Sobranie pisem imperatora Petra I k raznym litsam s otvetami na onyia* [Collection of Letters of Emperor Peter I to Various Individuals and Their Replies] (St. Petersburg: 1829), Pt. II, pp. 172–3.

[3] Tikhanov, *op. cit.*, Tikhanov selected the term "propositions," i.e., proposals.

[4] Pavlov-Silvanskii, *Proekty reform*, Pt. II, pp. 1–46. This title has been supplied by Pavlov-Silvanskii. In a letter to Peter I, Saltykov, in asking permission to forward to the Tsar the second memorandum, stated that he had several "proposals which could be of use to the state and beneficial to You [the Tsar]." *Ibid.*, Pt. I, p. 19.

"military courage of the Russian people." [5] He advised the Tsar to issue, for the information of his people and other states, a manifesto showing the historical basis of the right of Russia to certain parts of Lifland and to Ingria and Karelia, which Peter I had won from the Swedes and which had belonged to Russia in the past.[6]

Saltykov attached great significance to the expansion of education in Russia. He recommended that the Tsar establish in each gubernia one or two academies in which would be gathered the children of nobles, merchants, and others for a period of seventeen years—from the age of six to twenty-three. He proposed that schools be created in monasteries, and that they be maintained by monastery incomes. In his opinion, students should be taught foreign languages, grammar, geography, philosophy, history, mathematics, mechanics, navigation, artillery, and other sciences and arts. The academies were to have their own printing presses and libraries. "And thus in all natural sciences we will equal the best European states, for without natural sciences and good crafts a state cannot have a solid system of education; instead, it will always depend on the services and help of the educated states." [7] He also advised the establishment in all gubernias of women's schools to teach the "women's crafts," so that our women will equal those of the European states." [8]

A large part of F. Saltykov's proposals related to the economic sphere. He recommended that Peter set up a comprehensive system of measures for the development of industry, agriculture, trade, and finance. His proposals were of a strictly practical nature. They contain no theoretical views on economic themes. The general and central idea, as seen from his letter to Peter I cited above, is the attempt to lead Russia out of economic and cultural backwardness and to place her "in a short time" on a level equal "with the best European states." This task runs like a red thread through both of Saltykov's memoranda, linking his many, and often randomly selected, proposals.

Another important task, but separate and secondary to the basic one, is the practical aim to increase the revenue of the Russian state and to discover new sources of income "not yet known in our country." This motive invariably accompanies the majority of Saltykov's recommendations.

While stressing the financial significance of his proposals for the direct "gains" to the state, F. Saltykov nevertheless approaches the

---

[5] Tikhanov, *op. cit.*, p. 24; Pavlov-Silvanskii, *op. cit.*, Pt. II, pp. 14–6.
[6] See *ibid.*, Pt. II, pp. 1–6.
[7] Tikhanov, *op. cit.*, p. 24
[8] *Ibid.*, p. 25.

problem more broadly than the many "profit seekers" of that time, who were specifically concerned with new sources of revenue for the treasury without regard for the development of the entire national economy. In this respect F. Saltykov resembles his contemporary I. T. Pososhkov.

F. Saltykov also resembles Peter I, Pososhkov, and other Russian economists of his time in appreciating the function of the state in any economic reforms of the country. Assigning to the state the decisive role in the realization of economic reforms, he advises Peter I to establish a special "state adviser." Among the duties of the latter would be the examination and recommendation to the Senate of measures which would assure the growth of state revenues, the increase of manufactories and of mining and smelting enterprises, the improvement of their work, and the organization of merchant companies.[9]

As is evident from the many remarks he made on the margins of the memoranda, Peter I seriously considered Saltykov's proposals. He sent some of Saltykov's recommendations to the Senate, and others were given special attention.[10] However, the office of state adviser was not established. As has been observed, Peter I created, considerably later, a number of special economic colleges whose functions resembled those assigned by Saltykov to the state's adviser, but Peter had defined those functions more broadly and concretely.

F. Saltykov's memoranda clearly reflect the class orientation of the author, an exponent and defender of the interests of the nobility and the feudal-absolute state. He completely avoided problems which concerned the bulk of the population of feudal Russia—the enserfed peasantry. In this regard, his proposals differ sharply from the reform projects of I. Pososhkov.

The recommendations which F. Saltykov presented to the Tsar aimed at the further strengthening of the nobility; for example he proposed that special titles for nobles be introduced into Russia comparable to those of European states: landgraves, marquises, counts, barons, and so forth, which would be awarded according to the number of peasant households the noble possessed and which would carry a corresponding coat of arms.

He also advised that Russian cities be turned into principalities, marquisates, and counties, on the example of England, where the city bears the noble's name without his owning or controlling it.[11] The

---

[9] See Pavlov-Silvanskii, *op. cit.*, Pt. II, pp. 36–7.

[10] See Miliukov, *Gosudarstvennoe khoziaistvo Rossii*, p. 399; Pavlov-Silvanskii, *op. cit.*, Pt. I, p. 35.

[11] See Tikhanov, *op. cit.*, pp. 11–2.

votchiny of monasteries and churches were also to be turned into "ranks" and be given special coats of arms.[12] It is interesting to note that Saltykov justified this measure, which aimed at the elevation of the feudal aristocracy, by the interests of the treasury; he proposed the introduction of a registration fee on coats of arms—the higher the noble's title, the higher the fee.

Saltykov thought that the nobility should remain a privileged class and retain a monopoly on landownership. He spoke out against the nobility engaging in trade or industry and against the granting of noble titles to people coming from other classes. "The nobles should not own business establishments or retail stores, nor should they participate in trade and industry, except in cases especially granted by your decrees, because these areas belong to merchants." [13] He proposed to tax nobles who were engaged in trade or industry one and a half times as much as the others; as an alternative, they could withdraw from the nobility and register with the merchants. "And should anyone coming from a simple rank or a city rank or from the service personnel acquire wealth, he shall not be allowed to purchase a title of nobility or estates, for these belong to the nobles." [14]

The author of the "Propositions" advised Peter I to introduce a system of primogeniture in Russia. He believed that the immovable property of "lords and nobles" should be inherited by the eldest son, while the younger sons would have to be satisfied with their share of the movable property.[15] This proposition he justified by the fact that under primogeniture the older sons, having many peasant households, would pay the state more taxes and would be enriched by acquiring "large gains," while the younger sons, deprived of immovable property, would be more useful in the state services and in the sciences.[16]

F. Saltykov's justification for the need of primogeniture in Russia coincides in part with that given by Peter I in his decree on primogeniture of 1714. There is, however, no basis for attributing to these propositions any great influence on Peter's legislation. Peter conceived the idea of primogeniture long before Saltykov's memorandum. The decree itself differed from the later's propositions in a number of important ways. Saltykov proposed primogeniture in the fullest sense of the word, that is, guaranteeing the interests of the eldest son. Peter's order required the transfer of immovable property to one of the sons

[12] *Ibid.*, pp. 2–4.
[13] *Ibid.*, p. 6.
[14] *Ibid.*
[15] *Ibid.*, p. 4.
[16] *Ibid.*, pp. 4–5.

regardless of precedence. Saltykov had in view only the property of "lords and nobles," while the decree of 1714 established a new order of inheritance for all classes. It is possible, however, that Saltykov's proposition hastened the issuance of Peter's decree. Saltykov's aspiration to preserve land ownership as a class privilege of the nobles and yet actually to deprive the nobles of the possibility to engage in trade or industry did not coincide with Peter's policy on these matters.

Distorting the class nature of the feudal Russian state and the class character of Peter's policy, the bourgeois historian N. Pavlov-Silvanskii contrasts F. Saltykov with the aristocratic tendency of his proposition to Peter I, as if he were representative of a democratic social policy.[17] The futility of contrasting two spokesmen of one and the same class of feudalists and of a feudal absolutist state is obvious. Both Peter I and Saltykov served the interests of the Russian national state of pomeshchiki and merchants, elevated the ruling class—the nobility—and aided the development of the merchant class. F. Saltykov, while calling for measures directed toward further promotion of "lords and nobles," at the same time assigned the merchant class a large role in overcoming the economic backwardness of the country. "The merchant class," he wrote "is essential to the wealth of all states, as is evidenced by England and Holland." [18]

He considered it expedient to abolish the "old merchant ranks"—members of the merchants and textile hundreds—and, following the example of other countries, to establish special titles for the merchant class—baronets, patricians, burgraves—with the right to corresponding coats of arms.[19]

F. Saltykov's program in the field of industry took the same direction as the economic policy of Peter I. The former considered it necessary to build enterprises for the production of silk brocades, woolen cloth, paper, glass, needles, and pins and factories for white iron, cheese, and butter.[20] He was firmly convinced that the Russian people were fully capable of creating their own native industry. "The Russian people have the same feelings and convictions as any other people; all they need is guidance in these matters." [21]

F. Saltykov also discussed the location of industrial enterprises. He attached great importance to the proximity of sources of raw materials.

---

[17] See Pavlov-Silvanskii, *op. cit.*, Pt. I, p. 26.
[18] Tikhanov, *op. cit.*, p. 16.
[19] *Ibid.*, pp. 17–8.
[20] Pavlov-Silvanskii, *op. cit.*, Pt. II, pp. 23–41.
[21] *Ibid.*, Pt. II, p. 24.

Thus he recommended building the factories for silk brocades in Astrakhan and Siberia, that is, in places close to Persia and China, where silk could be bought. Woolen cloth factories were to be built in the Ukraine and Astrakhan to process the wool of the local breeds of sheep. Wind and water mills for sawing wood, as well as resin factories, were to be built in the Archangel gubernia, on the Pechora river and its tributaries. Factories for the production of glass, white iron, needles, and paper he considered necessary for each gubernia.

According to Saltykov, factories should be multiplied in Russia in order to satisfy the needs of the country with native goods, in order to free the state from the expenditure of money for the purchase of foreign goods, and in order to increase the state's revenues from taxes on industrial products. "And if such factories are introduced, a considerable amount of money will be kept in the Russian state . . . and this will contribute to the enrichment, not of foreigners, but of Russian people from their own state." [22]

At the same time, he did not limit the tasks of native industry merely to satisfying the needs of the internal market. He thought that industrial goods should be produced in quantities large enough to stop foreign imports and to allow for exports as well. "And should the above-mentioned manufactories be increased and developed to perfection, then their products could be sold to other countries; this will benefit Russia, just as England developed and improved her crafts, and now goods are exported, a fact which greatly benefits England, both its people and its customs revenues." [23]

Factories should be built both at the expense of the treasury and with merchants' funds. Some factories—for silk brocades, paper, glass, and needles—were to be constructed only with the funds of merchants, who were to be organized into a company for this purpose, "since this will bring them gain, and the sale of the products of these industries will yield tax revenues." [24] The merchants were to share in the company in accordance with their means and receive profits in proportion to the amount of their share, "for thus they will be diligent and careful about their gains." [25]

F. Saltykov advised Peter I to organize the search for various minerals all over the country and to set up monetary rewards to provide incentives.[26]

---

[22] *Ibid.*, Pt. II, p. 27.
[23] *Ibid.*, Pt. II, p. 11.
[24] *Ibid.*, Pt. II, p. 24.
[25] *Ibid.*, Pt. II, p. 27.
[26] *Ibid.*, Pt. II, p. 29.

Of his other propositions relating to the development of native industry, one must mention his plan to provide trained workers. He thought that everyone engaged in crafts and industry in Russian towns and those wishing to learn crafts by apprenticeship should register in the town halls. The period of apprenticeship was to last seven years, at the end of which time the trainee would have to take a master's examination. Persons not registered in the town halls and unable to show proficiency would not be allowed to enter the crafts. He devoted great attention to the introduction of such a system, as he visualized in it a way to perfect the crafts and industries. He set England as an example, where crafts and industry "have arrived at the highest refinement." Although Saltykov did not speak directly about guilds, this was essentially what he meant when he referred to the need for a craft guild or at least the important elements of this organization.

He suggested a number of measures to deal with poverty in the country. In particular, he recommended the obligatory training of orphans and poor people in "manufacturing or handicrafts." In his opinion, orphans and the poor of both sexes up to twenty years of age should be taught to read and write in church establishments and should then be sent to the "main shops" of the monastery to learn crafts and industry useful to society. Those who learned how to work in manufacturing ought to be set free: "And following such training, the Russian state will save much money on those manufactures upon which the country now depends on foreign 'States.'"[27] Maintenance and training of orphans and the the poor in church establishments should be at the expense of the church, while training in crafts in the shops should be financed by the monasteries. The churches should support the sick and aged poor; healthy orphans and poor over twenty years of age should be sent into the navy, army, and "other kinds of work."[28] The social significance of these measures, during times of a growing need for personnel, was discussed in the chapters on Peter I and on Pososhkov.

Saltykov made few proposals relating to agriculture. He recommended land surveys to avoid disputes over boundaries. Maintaining that hemp and flax were important products, the sale of which was profitable to the population, the merchants, and the state, Saltykov insistently favored their increasing cultivation. He advised strict prohibtion of the export of hemp and flax seeds to England and Holland in order to prevent increased production of linen and hemp in other countries and the consequent fall in their prices. He favored the

[27] *Ibid.*, Pt. II, p. 11.
[28] *Ibid.*, Pt. II, p. 8.

cultivation of vineyards and of the mulberry tree for silk production, as well as increased tobacco cultivation. He also emphasized the importance of stud farms for the needs of the cavalry.

As was pointed out above, Saltykov assigned to trade and the merchant class a vital role in overcoming Russia's economic backwardness. He writes of the necessity of developing Russia's trade with Holland, England, Persia, China, Bukhara, and other countries. In all gubernias merchant companies were to be set up to conduct trade with those states nearest to them. The profits and losses of these companies were to be distributed among the participants in proportion to the shares of each, while the treasury would reimburse these companies for one-fourth of their capital. In the states with which the Russian companies would trade, trade consulates were to be established to protect the interests of the Russian merchants and the Russian state. Saltykov also proposed to send the children of merchants to study trade affairs, bookkeeping, and trade correspondence in Holland and England.

In the interests of developing internal trade, F. Saltykov wished to establish fairs and markets throughout the country in towns, monasteries, and in large villages. Concern about the development of Russian trade led him to make an interesting proposal about the organization of a Northern sea route to China and India. In his first memorandum to Peter I he advised the building of ships at the mouths of the Yenisei and other Siberian rivers. Expeditions would then be sent around the Siberian coast in order to determine whether any islands existed which Russia might acquire. "And should there be no such islands, it would perhaps be possible to develop a sea trade with China or to ship lumber, masts, planks, tar, and pitch from China to Europe, for forests are abundant in China, whereas in Europe the acute shortage of these things makes them extremely expensive; thus the state would profit greatly from this trade," [29] Saltykov returned to this theme in his second memorandum. It contains a special chapter entitled "On the Search for a Free Sea Route from the River Dvina to the Mouth of the Amur and even to China." [30] He proposed an expedition to map the seashore, river mouths, bays, and islands, as well as to report on the nature, climate, and population of these places. Saltykov attached great economic significance to a Northern Sea route. He believed that there was a strait between Asia and America. "And should it be established that the straits to the Chinese and Japanese coasts be open, your state will benefit greatly, since all countries, in-

[29] Tikhanov, *op. cit.*, pp. 28–9.
[30] Pavlov-Silvanskii, *op. cit.*, Pt. II, pp. 32–4.

cluding England and Holland, send ships to the East Indies. They must cross the equator twice in each direction; many people die of heat and of the lack of food. Should it be established, they would want to use that strait." [31]

"You would then be able to enter the East India trade, which would produce many benefits and great wealth, especially since your state is closer to that trade area than any other country." [32] He recommended the construction of fortresses in definite places along the Northern Sea route.

Although the idea of a sea route from Russia to China by way of the Arctic Ocean was known to Peter I before Saltykov's memoranda, it must be noted that the latter's proposals preceded Peter's practical efforts to discover whether such a strait did exist. It was for this reason that he sent a special expedition to Kamchatka. The existence of such a route had already been discovered in the seventeenth century, when in 1648 Fedot Alekseev (Popov) and Semeon Dezhnev passed through the strait later named after Bering; but in the beginning of the eighteenth century no one knew much about it, and the question demanded special clarification.

In the field of finance Fedor Saltykov's memoranda are characterized by his great concern for increasing state revenue. His proposals, which touched upon various facets of life, usually stressed the contribution they would make toward this end. Of his many suggestions, we shall here deal only with those which had more or less basic significance.

While he did not touch on the problem of taxing "lords and nobles," Saltykov emphasized the inexpediency of the prevailing system, under which rich and poor nobles paid the state equal amounts from their estates. Indeed, he proposed to establish a varying levy depending on the titles which should be bestowed upon "lords and nobles." [33]

Saltykov's memoranda reveal the wish to impose taxation on churches and monasteries. He recommended an additional levy on churches "to help pay for soldiers, since they defend churches and the faith from enemies, and the priests have sufficient revenue from their faithful and from other sources . . ." [34] As was noted, he wanted to impose upon the church the responsibility of maintaining and educating orphans and poor children until they reached twenty years of age and of caring for the sick; monasteries were also to contribute to the

---

[31] *Ibid.*, Pt. II, p. 33.
[32] *Ibid.*
[33] Tikhanov, *op. cit.*, pp. 9 ff.
[34] *Ibid.*, pp. 3–4.

upkeep of academies, libraries, and schools for women and to finance the training of orphans and the poor "in manufacturing and craft trades." Estates of "the clergy" were to be taxed one and a half times as much as those of the nobles.

Saltykov's memorandum contains the idea of a soul tax in Russia, but this applies to only one segment of the population, the city inhabitants. One of his proposals states: "All city inhabitants should pay a soul tax in the amount of a half ruble." [35]

He also proposed the appointment of a "state regent," among whose duties would have been the concern for economy in state expenditure and the responsibility to insure that the salaries of military and civilian officials did not exceed their "rank" and that the number of civil officials in gubernias was not higher than necessary. He was to receive annual reports from all gubernias on revenues and expenditures and to attempt to increase gubernia revenues.

Saltykov thought it expedient to study the experiences of other countries in the field of finance. For this reason three or four men "from among the lords," experienced men who knew the condition of the Russian state, were to be sent to England, Holland, and France. There "they were to examine land and other tax revenues, the use of money, and the revenues from industries, from customs dues, taverns, and other sources . . ." [36]

Of his various proposals one should note his original and detailed project which dealt with the construction of stone buildings in Russia.[37] He proposed a program of grandiose scale to be put into effect throughout the country, both in towns and villages, to convert the wooden dwellings, with all their outbuildings, into stone structures. According to Saltykov, this would include the homes of nobles, lords, pomeshchiki, and merchants, as well as those of artisans and peasants.

To realize this measure Saltykov thought it necessary to establish Stone Offices in all gubernias. The necessary money would be collected in the form of an annual household tax corresponding to rank and "standard of living": "from lords and big merchants two rubles a year per household, from nobles and merchant guild members one ruble, from pomeshchiki and settlement people a half ruble, from master craftsmen and peasants eight copecks." [38] By the Tsar's decree architects, stonemasons, bricklayers, tilelayers, joiners, smiths, and other masters were to be assembled for the preparation of building material

---

[35] *Ibid.*, p. 18.
[36] Pavlov-Silvanskii, *op. cit.*, Pt. II, pp. 38–9.
[37] *Ibid.*, Pt. II, pp. 42–6.
[38] *Ibid.*, Pt. II, p. 46.

and for the construction of buildings. Architects were to work out sketches and plans of buildings of various kinds for nobles, pomeshchiki, and merchants, and also houses for craftsmen and peasants.

Saltykov proposed that the preparation of materials and the construction of buildings be undertaken not individually, but in organized form with the means and resources of the Stone Office. For, in the absence of collective effort, the lords and the rich would raise the wages of workers to a level otherwise unattainable by poor people. With the participation of the Stone Office, "workers will benefit by the hire, events will proceed correctly and gradually and without losses, and thus everything will be built with great ease in a few short years." [39]

By decree of the Tsar quarries would be opened in appropriate places to cut white stone for buildings and to provide lime, brick, and tile; at these establishments masters and workers would work for a definite salary under the supervision of overseers from the Stone Office.

In the villages the peasants were to make bricks and tile during the winter months; in places which possessed no clay and few forests, houses would be made from native stone. Peasant houses would contain two stories, the second story being for summer living only. According to Saltykov, they would be built in a row along wide roads, and streets and courtyards would be paved with native stone. Stone construction would save the peasants from ruin by fire, and the country from destruction of the forests; "and these peasant households should be built not in the old, but in more suitable, places, near rivers or mountains, by ponds or lakes, or in grounds which belong to the pomeshchiki." [40] The streets of the cities would be paved with stone, and sidewalks would be laid around the houses. And in cities and villages no wooden bridges would be erected, but only stone ones, so as to assure convenience and beauty for travelers.

In his letter to Peter I of June 22, 1713, Saltykov estimated the approximate time needed for the realization of his plan at about 15 years. Stone construction, he wrote, "can be accomplished in less than 15 years without losses; it could be adopted with great ease, as the experience of England proves." [41]

This project was utopian. Within the feudal-serfowning system and during a time when national energies were directed toward conducting the long and difficult war over an outlet to the Baltic Sea, the plan could not have been realized; it would have required great supple-

---

[39] *Ibid.*, Pt. II, p. 43.
[40] *Ibid.*, Pt. II., p. 45.
[41] *Ibid.*, Pt. II, p. 73.

mentary expenditures of labor and funds by a people already overburdened by the yoke of feudal exploitation. Peter I paid no attention to Saltykov's fantastic project.

Other proposals by Saltykov were also impractical; although they were constructive in general, they were conceived on a scale clearly beyond the possibilities of the Russia of that time. An example is his above-mentioned recommendation to establish academies, foreign trade companies, and silk and needle factories in all gubernias of Russia.

As a whole the reforms proposed by Saltykov were undoubtedly progressive in character. They were directed toward overcoming the economic and cultural backwardness of Russia. As in the case of Peter I's program, so his own suffered from historical limitation, inasmuch as he proposed to conduct the intended reforms within the framework of a feudal serf-owning society. His economic views and program are basically the same as those of Peter I. However the practical significance of Saltykov's proposals, in the sense of their direct influence on the activities of Peter I, varied. Some came too late, since the measures recommended, as for instance the production of silk cloth, glass, and cotton goods and the cultivation of vineyards, tobacco, and so on, had already been realized to some degree. Saltykov was evidently unaware of this. Other proposals received no recognition at all in Peter's policy because of their inapplicability to existing conditions. Still others, such as those dealing with the expansion of flax and hemp production, the prohibition of the export of the seeds of these crops, and the visits of Russians to foreign countries to learn trades, were, judging by his legislation, immediately put into effect by Peter I. And, finally, many of Saltykov's proposals coincide to some degree with the policies which Peter I realized or tried to realize during the years following Saltykov's memoranda. It is possible that in putting these schemes into practice, Peter I was influenced to a greater or lesser degree by these memoranda.

To sum up, F. Saltykov's economic views portrayed, on the one hand, traits typical of all progressive Russian economic thought of the first quarter of the eighteenth century, and, on the other, they depicted certain variations caused by the fact that he belonged to the feudal aristocracy and had lived abroad for a long period of time. Particularly characteristic is his servility to the West and his desire to transfer from England, quite mechanically, certain methods which were unsuited to the real conditions of Russia.

Saltykov's economic views, while not representative of any special movement or trend of social thought, nevertheless deserve serious attention, inasmuch as they add to the general picture of the condition of Russian economic thought in the first quarter of the eighteenth century.

The "Instructions" of A. P. Volynskii as an Image of the Ideology of the Period

Among the records which reveal the character of the ideology of the nobility of the period are the "Instructions," the practical guides for the management of property compiled by the landowners for their stewards. Extant are such short "Memoranda" and "Orders," as for instance, those of A. I. Bezobrazov,[42] B. I. Morozov,[43] and other figures of the seventeenth century. In the eighteenth century these "Orders" took the form of developed instructions in which the feudal master gave a detailed outline of the rules governing property and regulating life on the estates. In these documents the present-day reader finds precise and extensive information on the state of Russian agriculture in the eighteenth century, the technique of agricultural production, the level of agricultural knowledge, the economy of the pomestie and peasant establishments, peasant obligations, and so forth. For the historian of economic thought they are especially important, since these instructions clearly express the feudal, serf-owning ideology of the landowners and their views on feudal rights and on the obligations of the peasants.

Characteristic of the first quarter of the eighteenth century are the "Instructions to the Steward Ivan Nemchinov Regarding the Administration of the House and Villages,"[44] written in 1724 by A. P. Volynskii, a notable personage of the reign of Peter and of Anna Ivanovna. A. P. Volynskii (1689–1740) came from an ancient noble family. In 1704 he entered the military service. In 1715 he became

---

42 Published as an appendix in A. A. Novoselskii, *Votchinnik i ego khoziaistvo v XVII v.* [A Votchinnik and His Estate in the XVII Century] (Moscow-Leningrad: 1929), pp. 184–9.

43 See E. I. Zabelin, "Bolshoi boiarin v svoem votchinnom khoziaistve (XVII vek)" [A Big Boyar on His Hereditary Estate in the XVII Century], *Vestnik Evropy* [European Herald], I (1871), pp. 16–22.

44 Published by Pogodin for the first time in *Moskvitianin,* I–II, Pt. IV (1854), pp. 11–32, and III–IV, Pt. IV, pp. 33–42. Pogodin's publication was incomplete. It did not include a part of the *Instruction* entitled *Regulation About Horses.* In 1881 a complete edition appeared entitled *Instruksiia dvoretskomu Ivanu Nemchinovu o upravlenii domu i dereven i regula ob loshadiakh, kak soderzhat i pritom prilezhno smotret nadlezhat, chtob v dobrom zdorovi byli* [An Instruction to House Steward Ivan Nemchinov On House Management and Village Administration and Regulation of Horses, and How They Should be Cared For and Maintained So That They Stay Healthy], *Pamiatniki drevnei pismennosti* (St. Petersburg: 1881).

ambassador to Persia and in 1719 governor in the new Astrakhan gubernia. Catherine I appointed Volynskii governor of Kazan', where he remained, except for a brief absence, until the end of 1730. Upon the ascendance of Anna he was appointed military inspector under the direction of Münnich, and in 1736 he was made Imperial Huntmaster. In 1738 Volynskii was appointed cabinet minister. In this high post he was very active, but soon clashed with the German swindlers, headed by Biron, who surrounded Anna and who tried to eliminate Russians from the direction of state affairs. Volynskii led the opposition against the German party in the palace. The intrigues of Biron, however, resulted in Volynskii's arrest in 1740. He was accused of bribery, concealment of treasury funds, and planning a coup in favor of Elizabeth; he was executed in the same year.

Volynskii strongly defended the interests of the nobility and supported the further extension of the rights of the ruling class. During Anna's reign he formulated a broad project entitled "General Discourse on the Direction of Internal State Affairs," in which he outlined comprehensive measures touching on various aspects of life, including the problems of trade and finance. He destroyed the project before his arrest, and its content is known only from indications left by others indicted with Volynskii.

The "Instructions" of A. P. Volynskii epitomized the views of the nobles on their rights regarding peasants and on the proper organization of the pomestie. It described the economy of the pomestie and the organization of the noble's estate in the first quarter of the eighteenth century, but it contained no theoretical discourses. Its purpose was intensely practical—to give the steward directions and guidance for administering the pomestie and the serfs. The "Instructions" provided a kind of "house rule." It is all the more interesting in that it was composed not by an ordinary man, but by an outstanding pomeshchik with a broad outlook and vast administrative experience. He was also an expert on agriculture. His "Instructions" reflected the legislative activities of Peter I in connection with peasantry and agriculture. The economic argument centered in the basic socio-economic relation of the time—the relation of the pomeshchik to the serfs.

For the history of Russian economic thought the most important parts of the "Instructions" are those which deal directly with the obligations, work, and life of the serfs. Here the present-day reader is given a clear view of the nobles' complete domination over the serfs and the unceremonial violation of the serfs' rights and personal freedom. The "Instructions" shows how deeply rooted had become the idea of complete domination of the peasant and the right to interfere and control every one of his actions. Through the "Instructions" the spirit of the police surveillance of the pomeshchik over the peasant runs like a red thread. In order to hold the serf under constant supervision, Volynskii ordered the steward to select one out of every ten men in the villages, who would be obliged to watch constantly over the other nine. Stewards, orderlies, elders, and the "tenth men" were to see that the peasants were always at work, not absent unnecessarily, and so on.

The extent to which Volynskii wished to transform villages into strict barracks is seen from the following directives: A peasant who needed to travel to another town or beyond a radius of fifty verst from his village, had to obtain permission from the steward; he was forced to acquire a passport signed by the steward and priest indicating the route, destination, and duration of his voyage, as well as the nature of his business. Within a range of ten to thirty verst the peasant was allowed to travel for commercial or other purposes upon only the steward's authorization and with the obligatory accompaniment of an elder and elected person. The peasant desiring to go to market no farther than ten versts from his home was to notify his "tenth man" a day ahead and indicate precisely what he wished to sell. The "tenth man" was then to notify the steward. Even at the market the peasant was always to be under the vigilant surveillance of one of the "tenth men" of his village, "so as to prevent him from buying or selling without permission or from eating and drinking excessively." On returning from market the peasant was to present himself to the "tenth man," describe what he had bought and sold, and show the money.[45] Moreover, "every morning and evening the "tenth man" was to check the households under his supervision, ascertain whether everyone spent the night in his own home, see whether there were any newcomers . . ." [46]

During Peter's reign the passport system was introduced throughout Russia in order to check the peasant flight from the pomeshchiki, the evasion of military service, and widespread robbery. By forbidding his peasants to go fifty verst without a passport, Volynskii reiterated Peter's decree of 1724. But in his police-like tracking of the peasants Volynskii went much farther than this decree; his orders reveal his initiative and zeal.

Thus the "Instructions" discloses a pomeshchik who exercised as complete a power over his serfs as an autocratic monarch displays to-

[45] *Moskvitianin,* I, Pt. IV (1854), p. 16.

[46] *Ibid.* A similar point was also included in D. A. Shepelev's "Instruction" to orderly Ivan Balashev. See *Istoricheskii arkhiv,* VIII (1953), p. 237.

ward the entire toiling mass of the country. It depicted the strength of the pomeshchik and the lack of peasants' rights in Peter's Russia.

The "Instructions" contemplated ideological influence on the peasants through religion and the official church and directed that the peasants be kept within "the law and Christian obligation." Consequently, the distribution of "newly printed books about God's Ten Commandments, about the symbols of faith, and about heavenly bliss" was suggested; stewards were ordered to see that the peasants go to church and that they confess once a year. Violators of this order would be subject to punishment. Peter I decreed church training for all Russia, and Volynskii merely reiterated the idea. Volynskii further ordered that every village contain several literate men, and this not for the benefit of the peasant. Literacy, he explained, was necessary to provide scribes for the stewards.

As can be judged from this document, Volynskii's exploitation of serf labor existed exclusively in the form of a barshchina. The obrok system is not mentioned.

The "Instructions" proposed to eliminate any misunderstanding regarding "taxes" and to set up a uniform system for all villages. Two men over twenty years of age and two married women were to constitute one tax unit. Moreover, the amount of land which was to be worked for the pomeshchik by each tax unit was clearly defined. "And every full tax unit should till two desiatina of my land, where a desiatina is eighty siazhen long and forty siazhen wide. The land should be set aside for produce: wheat, peas, hemp, poppy, millet, turnips, and flax—these should be tilled and harvested individually, aside from the imposed desiatina tillage." [47]

The "Instructions" also defines the amount of land to be allotted to each tax unit for the needs of the peasants themselves: "when a tax unit tills two desiatinay of my land, then it is proper that its own land equal twice the size of the tax unit, which, of course, should not be left fallow, but each peasant should till and plant all his own land . . ." [48] Cultivation of a definite quantity of land for himself was the peasant's duty. Stewards and orderlies were to see that his land "did not lie idle." Furthermore, each tax unit was to possess no less than two horses.

In addition, Volynskii gave the following order: "from each tax unit collect in the month of December one pud of pork, three pounds of butter, and one young male sheep. In June collect three pounds of wool and five arshins of linen cloth. In addition, collect from the

[47] *Moskvitianin*, I, Pt. IV (1854), p. 23.
[48] *Ibid.*

Vasiliev and Nikolskii peasants one pound of dried morels and one pound of dried berries from each tax unit, and from the Bytiev peasants, two pounds of dried mushrooms, instead of morels and berries. And when I am in Moscow or Petersburg collect from each tax unit one goose, one Russian hen, one suckling pig and twenty eggs." [49] Thus the barshchina was combined with rent in produce.

It should be mentioned that in the "Instructions" nothing was said about the sale of the pomeshchik's grain and cattle. As is evident, Volynskii's estate displayed a strong natural economy character. The "Instructions" stresses the need for self-cultivation of certain products and allowed the purchase of only a few manufactured goods, such as soap, candles, and other household needs.

Volynskii ordered harsh measures for the maintenance of labor discipline. The document described the peasants as lazy, negligent, and inclined to drunkenness, theft, and other sins. The words "laziness" and "lazy" are often repeated. Stewards and elders were commanded to ensure that the peasants worked constantly and carefully and that severe punishment be invoked against laziness and negligence.

The "Instructions" outlined in detail the method of collecting taxes from the peasants. Volynskii decided to levy not by souls, but by the tax unit; a count of persons was to be used only for determining the overall sum of taxes owed by the village. He based his order on the conviction that levying taxes by souls would lead to the quick and complete ruin of poor families with a large number of males.[50] Like all pomeshchiki, he failed to interpret the Tsar's decree literally, but made essential corrections in it, repudiating the principle of soul levying.

The steward was ordered to see that the aged and orphaned did not wander about; they were all to be registered; and the able were to be selected and given to the peasants to work in exchange for food and clothing. Peasants were strictly forbidden to hire outside workers, but were urged to take help from the same village. Healthy people who wandered about as poor were "to be forced to work." This corresponded to Peter's decrees. Forbidding poverty in Russia, Peter I imposed on the pomeshchiki the duty to see that their peasants did not remain idle. The pomeshchik was fined for poverty-striken peasants.

Volynskii posed as an enterprising master who wished to improve agriculture. Thus he instructed the steward to clean the ponds and fill them with fish, to build gardens on every property, and to install apiaries; he also ordered birds and livestock for every property. The

[49] *Ibid.*, III–IV, Pt. IV (1854), p. 35.
[50] *Ibid.*, I, Pt. IV (1854), p. 29.

means by which Volynskii intended to improve animal husbandry on his properties is interesting. He proposed to buy calves, lambs, young pigs, and chicks and to supply "nurse maids" to raise them. In order to provide material incentives for the good care of his animals, he devised the following rule: the number of expected offspring from the animals and birds was to be established, and the peasant who, by his own efforts, raised more than this minimum would be allowed to retain the extra offspring. But those whose animals and birds died as a result of carelessness had to pay the pomeshchik for them.

Earlier we said that Peter made the pomeshchiki responsible for the increase of peasant production and for the more rational cultivation of the land. This policy was also reflected in Volynskii's "Instructions." The steward was ordered to see that the production of grain was increased, for which purpose he was to expand acreage, buy good seeds to be exchanged with the peasants for bad, and insure that the peasants sow and reap at the proper time.

One of the reasons for low crop yields, noted Volynskii, was the prevailing practice of scattering seeds sparsely. He proposed an experiment: to sow on one desiatina twice as much seed and on another one and one-half times as much as was usually done. He also paid great attention to the necessity of improved fertilization. The usual fertilization by manure, he wrote, did not help sufficiently. At the same time, he pointed out that "some householders have discovered the means whereby the land grows grain as if it were new"; he ordered the steward to experiment on three desiatiny: in the autumn prepare brushwood, cut it up, take it to the field, and spread the branches evenly on the mown land; collect tree leaves and pine needles, and mix them in manure, and in the spring, when the snow melts, burn the brushwood in the fields. The steward was ordered to see that the land was plowed deeply, then shallowly, and then harrowed.[51]

Volynskii insisted that in January of each year the steward register all peasants of their households, indicating the size of their families, the livestock they possessed, the amount of tribute paid, the size of the tax, the amount of land cultivated for the pomeshchik and for themselves, their occupation with handicrafts, their transportation, and so on. A systematic and full accounting of the economic situation of the

---

[51] In his instruction to stewards and elders of his sub-Moscow votchiny [hereditary estates] A. A. Vinius, among others, recommended the following method of preparing seeds for planting: "It would be beneficial if seeds were put into sacks, placed in a tub, and soaked in manure diluted with water for one day. The sacks should be tied properly to enable the seeds to get moist without damaging them; then they should be taken out, aired slightly, and planted in God's name." *Istoricheskii arkhiv,* VIII (1953), 274.

serfs in hands of the pomeshchiki was to facilitate total control and regulation of the peasant economy for the most rational exploitation of the peasants. At the same time the registration gave the pomeshchiki control over the activities of the administrative orderlies.

Special attention was devoted to practical measures in the struggle against robbers, thieves, and also against fires. In the appendix to the "Instructions," entitled "Rules about Horses," detailed instructions were provided for their care.

Comparing Volynskii's "Instructions" with the "House Rule" and Pososhkov's *Book on Poverty and Wealth,* Professor Leshkov saw in the "Instructions" a kind of guide for the well-being of agricultural society, in contrast to the "House Rule," which considered the well-being of all the people and the nation as a whole. According to Leshkov, "Volynskii wrote the rules for the well-being of agricultural society and was justly convinced that he contributed to the social good by intelligently and legally building his own personal welfare." [52] Actually, there is no ground to speak of "social good" here. The direct and basic aim of the "Instructions" was to develop the welfare of the pomeshchik through the brutal exploitation of the serfs.

The "Instructions" interpreted economic matters differently than did the "House Rule" in the sixteenth century. However, the "House Rule" of the sixteenth and the pomestie "house rule" of the eighteenth century were similar in that both mentioned the benefit, or the good of the individual establishment and of the national economy as a whole, of the state.

The importance of labor exploitation in a feudal society and the inseparable tie between the pomestie and the serf economy forced Volynskii to take into consideration the condition of the peasants. But he was interested in them only in so far as the pomeshchik's well-being depended on the state of the peasant economy. At the same time, the "Instructions" showed how the pomeshchiki serf owners interpreted and put into practice Peter's decrees: they even further increased the exploitation of the serfs and their own power, while the people were accorded still fewer rights.

Volynskii's experiments in the sowing of grain and the burning of brushwood in the fields in order to raise the crop yield showed the progressive movement of Russian agro-technical thought. Subsequent authors go much more thoroughly into the question of agriculture than did Volynskii. They utilize and develop more widely the progressive experiments in agro-techniques in pomestie estates and the experience of other countries.

---

[52] *V vospominanie 12 ianvaria 1855 g.*, p. 5.

The "Instructions" of Volynskii clearly expressed the class position of the author as a pomeshchik exploiting serf labor. The fact that the "Instructions" was written not as a literary work destined for publication, but as a purely practical means of organizing the administration of an estate gave it the appearance of complete documentation and at the same time considerable directness. The "Instructions" represented a frank business-like conversation between a pomeshchik and the administrator of his estates. This clear view of class orientation is not always seen in the subsequent authors who wrote "Instructions" for a broader circle of readers. This particularity of Volynskii's "Instructions" makes it an especially valuable source, expressing well the ideology of the pomeshchik serf owner of Peter's time. Herein lies the historical significance of the "Instructions."

Expressing certain traits characteristic of its author, in basic content the "Instructions" is also typical of the ideology of all the feudalists of the time. In the "Instructions" of Stroganov, for instance, the peasants were forbidden, under threat of severe punishment, to come directly to him with a complaint against the orderly,[53] and in the "Instruction to Administrators of Crown Villages" (1731), issued by a great landowner—the all-Russian Empress—it was ordered that peasants who did not work well in the crown fields "should be punished mercilessly."[54]

The ideology of serfdom is clearly shown in other documents of this kind. Instructions to the administrators of estates were written also in the second half of the eighteenth century, and some of these were published ("Instructions to the Administrator or Orderly" by Rychkov, "Instructions for the Village Administrator" by Bolotov, "Economic Notes" by Chulkov).

The Economic Views of V. N. Tatishchev

Vasilii Nikitich Tatishchev (1686–1750) came from a once well-known, but in his day impoverished, noble family. It is believed that he was educated in the Moscow school for the artillery and engineers. He read much and was one of the most learned persons of his time. At the age of eighteen Tatishchev entered military service and participated in the campaigns of Peter I. Peter noticed the educated officer and repeatedly (from 1713 through 1719) sent him abroad on diplomatic and other missions.

In 1719, on Peter's order, Tatishchev began work on a geographical description of Russia and almost simultaneously on a Russian history.

[53] *Istoricheskii arkhiv,* IV (1949), 165.
[54] *Ibid.,* VI (1951), 175.

At that time no Russian had as yet compiled a national geography or history; the works of foreigners, as Tatishchev correctly noted, contained many factual errors, lies, and slander.[55]

In 1720 Tatishchev was sent to the Urals where he supervised the operation of factories and the building of new ones, organized a search for useful minerals, and established schools for training masters of metallurgy. Under his direction construction was begun in the town of Ekaterinburg (now Sverdlovsk), which became the center of metallurgy in the Urals. He was again sent to the Urals in 1734 as chief director of metallurgy in the Siberian and Kazan gubernias. His activity caused great dissatisfaction on the part of the mining tycoons, Demidov and Stroganov. His continued administration of mining affairs was also attacked by Biron, Shemberg, and other foreign swindlers, who sought to transfer the treasury's factories in the Urals into private hands. As a result, in 1737 Tatishchev was recalled from Ekaterinburg and sent to Orenburg territory as chief of the Orenburg expedition.

In 1741 Tatishchev was appointed governor of the Astrakhan gubernia. He formulated plans to settle the Astrakhan steppes and to build cities, encouraged the development of fishing on the lower Volga, and aided the growth of internal and foreign trade. At the same time he fought the English trade company (headed by the adventurer Elton), whose activities infringed on Russian interests. He ended his Astrakhan governorship in 1745 with yet another disgrace and was, in fact, taken to court. The last years of his life Tatishchev spent on his Moscow estate, Boldino, where he devoted his time to the sciences. It was here that he completed the first great national *Russian History;* he also summarized his works and ideas on economic problems in the memorandum "On Merchants and Crafts" (1748).[56]

A spokesman of the nobility and a partisan of feudal absolutism, Tatishchev tried to justify the need for social inequality on the basis of the existing "natural inequality" among people. He regarded the class division of society as a product of natural law. The nobility was called upon to administer the state and to provide leadership for its defense, and in return it received monopoly rights to own land and

---

[55] See A. I. Andreev, "Perepiska V. N. Tatishcheva za 1746–1750 gg." [V. N. Tatishchev's Correspondence for the Years 1746–1750], *ibid.*, VI (1951), 252.

[56] See *ibid.*, VII (1951), pp. 410–26; see also P. K. Alefirenko, "Ekonomicheskie vzgliady V. N. Tatishcheva" [Economic Views of V. N. Tatishchev], *Voprosy istorii* [Problems of History], No. 12 (1948), pp. 89–97. Some documents to which this article makes references have been utilized in Chapter XIII.

peasants. The merchant class was to concern itself with trade and industry, and the peasants were either to work hard or to be the object of exploitation.

In his works Tatishchev defended serfdom. To justify its existence he used the so-called theory of the social contract. In *A Discourse on the Benefit of Education and Schools* (1773) he argued that serfdom arose as a contract under which the pomeshchiki undertook to feed the peasants, who in return gave up their freedom. Elsewhere, in notes on *"Russkaia Pravda and Laws of the Tsar and the Grand Prince Ivan Vasilevich"* (1738), Tatishchev considered freedom for peasants inappropriate for Russia, although he recognized its general usefulness. In his opinion, such freedom "is incompatible with our form of monarchial government, and it is dangerous to change the deep-rooted habit of serfdom." [57]

Tatishchev criticized Peter's successors, whose policies contradicted Peter's principles of political economy. He spoke with "great disgust" of what had happened in the Russian economy—especially under the young Peter II, when "the magistrate was undermined, the Mining and Manufacturing Colleges were made into insignificant compartments of the Commerce College, sheep and other stock farms were completely destroyed, and new schools were not built, but existing ones abandoned; in effect, many useful decrees and institutions of His Majesty were either repealed or altered." [58] At the same time Tatishchev approved the policy of Elizabeth Petrovna, who revived Peter's decrees and reinstated the organs for the administration of trade and industry established by Peter I, which had also been destroyed by his immediate successors.

Tatishchev maintained that the economic policy of the state should be improved in accordance with the new conditions. He advised Elizabeth to retain the foundations of Peter's economic policy and at the same time to "correct, supplement and alter some things in it . . ." [59] The changes he recommended were directed both toward strengthening the class position of the nobility—at a time of growing bourgeois

---

[57] *Prodolzhenie Drevnei rossiskoi vifliofiki. Chast 1. Soderzhashchaia Pravdu russkuiu i sudebnik tsaria i velikogo kniazia Ivana Vasilevicha s primechaniiami g. tainogo sovetnika Vasilia Nikiticha Tatishcheva* [Continuation of Ancient Russian Library. Part 1. Containing Russkaia Pravda and the Code of Tsar and Grand Prince Ivan Vasilevich with Notes of the State Secret Counsellor Vasilii Nikitich Tatishchev] (St. Petersburg: 1786), p. 175.

[58] V. N. Tatishchev, "Naprimer predstavlenie o kupechestve i remeslakh" [For Example the Proposal on Trade and Crafts], *Istoricheskii arkhiv,* VII (1951), p. 415. Hereinafter cited *O kupechestve i remeslakh.*

[59] *Ibid.,* VII (1951), pp. 415–6.

connections in a feudal society—and toward enhancing the role of the merchant class in the economy of the country.

According to Tatishchev, trade (which he called, in the Russian terminology of the time, "merchantry"), particularly foreign trade, was the chief source of wealth and the prime cause of its expansion. He considered trade as important to the Russian economy as is the heart to the human organism. The role of industry in the creation of wealth, he said, consists of processing raw materials and making articles available to merchants who, in turn, "distribute them everywhere, sell them to those who want to buy, exchange them for surpluses, and satisfy everyone." [60] The source of all state revenue, according to Tatishchev, is trade: for it "is the root and basis of all wealth." [61] He concludes that "all state revenue, whatever its kind, comes solely from trade." [62]

Tatishchev attributed to foreign trade an especially important role in the creation and growth of a nation's wealth: "Foreign trade brings about the greatest wealth and welfare." [63] For proof he turned to history. Although England and Holland had no indigenous sources of gold and silver, they "accumulated great wealth and power through crafts and trade alone"; Spain, on the other hand, had much gold and silver, but was forced by its underdeveloped industry and trade—especially foreign trade—"to transfer its wealth to others." [64]

It is important to note that Tatishchev argued for the development of trade not only on the basis of Western European experience, but he also spoke in detail of native experience. He recalled that in the tenth century Russian rulers, beginning with Oleg, assiduously promoted the development of trade. He wrote of the great role played in the development of Russia's trade with England and Holland by Ivan the Terrible (and Aleksei Mikhailovich) during whose reign the Commercial Code was issued, in 1667, and various manufactories were created. Thus Tatishchev established for the first time the connection between the economic meaures of Aleksei Mikhailovich, whom he considered "a great economist," [65] and the reforms of Peter I. Tati-

[60] *Ibid.*, VII (1951), p. 410.

[61] N. Popov, *V. N. Tatishchev i ego vremia* [V. N. Tatishchev and His Time] (Moscow: 1861), Appendix XVI, p. 719.

[62] Tatishchev, *O kupechestve i remeslakh*, p. 411.

[63] *Ibid.*, p. 418.

[64] *Ibid.*, p. 411.

[65] V. N. Tatishchev, *Leksikon Rossiiskoi istoricheskoi, geograficheskoi politicheskoi i grazhdanskoi* [Russian Historical, Geographical, Political, and Civil Lexicon] (St. Petersburg: 1793), Pt. III, p. 4.

shchev emphasized especially Peter's role in the development of Russian trade and in the creation of organs for its administration.

Insisting on the development of exports and the curtailment of imports, Tatishchev appeared as a defender of an active balance of trade. He emphasized the importance of exporting products of native manufacture: exporting more of the latter than of raw materials would activate the trade balance of the country.

Tatishchev proposed to develop trade not only with the countries of Western Europe, but also with China, Persia, Bukhara, and Turkey. Striving to activate Russia's trade, he considered it necessary to change the existing tariffs and to introduce special duties for various ports and cities. Thus in 1744 he presented to the College of Commerce a tariff plan entitled "Discourse on Goods Imported and Exported Through the Astrakhan Port." In this "Discourse," Tatishchev proposed to levy "a light tax" on the export of "all Russian articles"; on surplus industrial raw materials and on food (in good harvest years), "a medium tax"; and on all raw materials and on food (in poor harvest years), "a heavy tax." Instead of the export of raw materials destined for industry, the export of finished products was to be increased.

As for precious metals, Tatishchev advised against the export of gold and silver in the form of bars, money, or simple objects; but he favored the export of gold and silver products of which the value added by workmanship was not less than half the price: "permitting these [to be exported] would not be harmful." [66] He proposed the removal of duties on the import of gold and silver in the form of bars, money, or objects: such a measure would lead to the increase of precious metals in the country. According to Tatishchev it would be necessary to remove duties on imports of raw and secondary materials which were unavailable or scarce in Russia, "in order to aid thereby the growth of Russian factories."

He also thought that "one should ease" the transit trade of Russian merchants. He proposed that the tax on "all goods transported across Russia," be smaller for Russian merchants than for foreigners. Small and medium taxes should be levied on the import of goods which "are not absolutely necessary, but useful, and which are not produced in Russia," while the import of goods which "could be better produced

---

[66] *Arkhiv* AS USSR, Fund 95, Description 5, No. 30. *Rassuzhdenie o tovarakh privoznykh i otvoznykh Astrakhanskogo porta so mneniem tainogo sovetnika i astrakhanskogo gubernatora Tatishcheva* [An Appraisal of Goods Which are Exported and Imported Through the Astrakhan Harbor With the View of Secret Councellor and Governor of Astrakhan, Tatishchev], Sheets 10, 11, 12, and 17. Hereinafter cited *Rassuzhdenie o tovarakh.*

in Russia" should be subject to a high tax. The latter imports would be detrimental to native industry; such foreign goods "would interfere with Russian manufactories." [67]

In defending the limitation of imports of manufactured products and goods which could be made in Russia, Tatishchev objected especially to the import of luxury goods. In his report to the Commerce College written while he was governor of Astrakhan, he insisted on the prohibition of the sale in Russia and in the Ukraine of brocade and sash cloth with gold and silver inlays which were brought from Persia to Astrakhan. He thought that Russian merchants transporting these goods should sell them abroad and that the Persian merchants should take them back to Persia.[68]

In his efforts to protect Russian merchants from foreign competition Tatishchev proposed, in the reissued New Commercial Code of 1667, that Persian merchants be prohibited from carrying on retail trade ("in no city should they be allowed to carry on retail trade") and that they be confined to wholesale dealings in goods ("of no less than 300 rubles") which they brought in from Persia or the countries of Western Europe.[69]

The trade balance system, characteristic of developed mercantilism, was the basis of Tatishchev's economic views. Like Peter I, he did not hold the conviction, customary with the majority of West European mercantilists, that wealth consisted only of money and specie—gold and silver. At the same time, Tatishchev assigned great importance to the inflow of money and precious metals for the increase of the country's wealth.

As has been stated earlier, in the interests of finance Peter I lowered both the value of the then most widely used silver money in Russia, and the silver assay.[70] As a result of this, Tatishchev claimed, the export of gold money was increased considerably, to the detriment of trade. "Because silver money (which has been made in Russia up to now) contains a low assay [of silver] and much copper and because of its unstandardized mixing and depreciation when compared with gold money, the latter leaves the country and brings the state great loss, causes great difficulties in accounting, is the chief factor responsible for the export of gold from the state, and is, I believe, detrimental to trade." [71]

---

[67] *Ibid.*, Fund 95, Description 5, No. 30, sheets 7 and 9.
[68] *Ibid.*, Sheets 1 and 2.
[69] *Ibid.*, Sheet 5.
[70] See Chapter XI.
[71] *Rassuzhdenie o tovarakh,* Fund 95, Description 5, No. 51, Sheet 1.

The Senate turned its attention to the increased outflow of the precious metals, for it was interested in the underlying causes of this phenomenon. Answering the Senate's inquiry, Tatishchev emphasized that the reasons lay not only in the lowering of the value of the silver ruble, but also in the worsening of the trade balance of the country.

To foster the development of the national economy and the growth of the nation's wealth he proposed to raise the value of the silver ruble by increasing its metallic content and by improving the assay of silver. Such a "recoining of silver money" would have beneficial results for trade and the treasury: "by improving money the treasury will not lose, but gain, and people will profit even if the treasury does not; it would be enough to have a better and more systematized medium of currency, which would benefit trade as well as the state." [72]

Tatishchev attacked the use of paper money. Aware of the sad experience of France, where in 1716–1720 paper money was issued for the first time in history by the bank of John Law, Tatishchev opposed its use and generally did not recognize paper money as money: "they give paper instead of money." [73] He rightly considered the weaknesses and abuses of credit an obstacle to the development of trade. Noting that in foreign trade normal credit circulation was already established, he deemed the existing credit as unsuitable for internal trade and called for its regulation. The development of "improved and orderly trade," [74] he said, required a satisfactory organization of credit for the merchant class. The merchant cannot have continuous liquid funds, since his capital is invested in goods; however the nobility and clergy usually have free funds which they are afraid to lend directly to the merchants. The problem of finding funds and making them available to the merchants and craftsmen in the form of credit could and should be solved in Russia, as it was solved in other European states, with the establishment of banks. It is important to note that Tatishchev insisted on the need for banks not for the nobles—*pomeshchiki*—but for industry and mainly for trade, the development of which (under the existing domestic duties) would have greatly increased state revenues. The banks which Tatishchev conceived had a feudal imprint, since their liabilities were to be based not on the capital of merchants (as was the case in the commercial banks of the countries of Western Europe), but on the funds of the pomeshchiki and clergy.

Tatishchev thought it necessary to develop trade fairs for the domes-

[72] *Ibid.*, Sheet 2.
[73] Tatishchev, *O kupechestve i remeslakh,* p. 411.
[74] *Ibid.*, p. 422.

tic market. Fairs were a trade institution appropriate for the level of Russia's economic development. The predominantly agricultural population, scattered in villages and living chiefly within a natural economy, precluded a widely developed permanent trade, and this gave special importance to such temporary arrangements as the fair. Tatishchev made a number of related proposals in this regard: the creation of canals for transporting goods and the development of postal services for improving communication and information. He emphasized the importance of the post not only for internal and foreign trade, but also for the development of the people and the state. In addition to favoring a positive trade balance, in Marxian terminology, Tatishchev was also a representative of the "manufacturing system." He stressed the importance of producing goods for export as well as importing substitutes. Thus, while he was governor of Astrakhan, he wrote: "I strongly favor the cultivation of silk and cotton here and in Kizliar, as well as the increase of silk and cotton mills and the curtailment of the import of useless goods from Persia; and, if it were within my power, I could demonstrate the feasibility of such measures not only here, but also in factories in Siberia." [75]

While insisting on the growth of manufactories which would produce goods for export and end the necessity of importing them, Tatishchev fought energetically for the development of the mining industry, metallurgy, and smelting. These enterprises would satisfy, above all, the military and other needs of the feudal-absolutist state in its attempts to assure the economic independence of Russia. A central point in his scheme was the development of Russia's mining indusrty, especially in its chief region—the Urals. Here he aimed to raise the production of the state and private factories to a level which would meet not only the requirements of the state and of the internal market, but which would also produce an exportable surplus.

Striving to increase the output of factories and mines Tatishchev fought for the introduction of machines. In his report to Catherine I (1726), he wrote from Sweden that in spite of the greater depth of Swedish mines, double pay to workers, and double cost for fuel metals extracted from ore of almost the same quality are "not more expensive than ours, and are even cheaper than those found close to Moscow." The reasons were the use of "various machines run by water, in which one wheel does the work of several hundred men." Tatishchev emphasized the significance of machines not only in metallurgy but also in

[75] V. N. Tatishchev, "Na pamiat o delakh astrakhanskikh" [Recollections About Astrakhan Affairs], *Istoricheskii arkhiv*, VII, 403.

all segments of industry. "In other factories machines also greatly facilitate the work." [76]

His views on the development of mining and metallurgy, as well as his ideas on industrial policy, were expressed in three projects: the Mining Code, the Factory Code,[77] and Instructions to the Shaft Master.[78] In these writings he strongly defended the development of a state mining industry and the strict regulation and interference in private mining industries by the absolute state. He thought the state should assist the latter, provide them with laborers, technical aid, and financial support. State agents, particularly special officials of the enterprises—shaft masters—should watch carefully over private enterprises. The work of the supervisor should range from technical control over production and the quality of products to assurance that the products be sold according to established state prices.

The entrepreneurs gladly accepted the assistance of the state, especially its financial aid and the various exemptions and privileges; but they objected to government supervision and interference in their affairs. They protested against Tatishchev's requirement of strict accountability, regulation of the worker's pay, the construction of schools, control of sales, and the like. Resenting the deprivation of "all their freedom," the mining industrialists of the Urals, headed by Demidov, demanded that "in his own industry each be allowed to use his own capital as he thinks best." [79] Having grown economically strong, they were dissatisfied with state guardianship; their protests, which were upheld by the Commerce College,[80] succeeded in preventing Tatishchev's projects from being adopted. The codes and the instruction prepared by Tatishchev, however, were used to a limited extent in private establishments and to a considerable degree in the state industry of the Urals.

Tatishchev considered it necessary to develop not only heavy industrial production—"large factories" which, in his opinion, "comprise a

---

[76] TsGADA, Fund of the Former State Archive of the Russian Empire, Section IX, Bk. 81, Sheet 35.

[77] Published in *Gornyi zhurnal* [Mining Journal] (1831), Bks. 1–3 and 5–10.

[78] See N. I. Pavelenko, " 'Nakaz shikhtmeisteru' V. N. Tatischeva" [V. N. Tatishchev's Instruction to a Foreman in a Mine] *Istoricheskii arkhiv,* VI (1951), pp. 199–209. The Text of the Instruction is in *ibid.,* pp. 210–28.

[79] "Proshenie uralskikh promyshlennikov imperatritse Anne Ivanovne po povodu vvedeniia Tatishchevym instituta shikhtmeisterov" [A Petition of Ural Industrialists to Empress Anna Ivanovna as a Result of Tatishchev's Introduction of an Institute for Mine Foremen], *ibid.,* VI, 230.

[80] " 'Rassuzhdenie' Kommerts-kollegii kabinetu ministrov 'O nakaze shikhtmeisteru' " [An Argument of the Commerce College to the Cabinet of Ministers Regarding the Instruction to a Mine Foreman], *ibid.,* VI, 235–40.

great number of people and works"—but also small production by craftsmen who "work only in their own homes and with their own hands." [81] The development of both needed the aid and guidance of the state. While he argued that the growth of crafts required special attention and care, Tatishchev proposed to remove craftsmen from administering the Manufacturing College, to organize them into guilds, and to transfer the administration of the College to local city magistrates. At the same time he thought it absolutely mandatory to introduce quality controls over the goods produced in the factories and by craftsmen, particularly before they were exported.

Fully aware that crafts and factories needed qualified workers, Tatishchev spoke of establishing schools for them. In fact, he himself organized the first mining school in the Urals.[82] He suggested the training of craftsmen and technicians in city vocational schools, to be supported by the magistrates. Tatishchev insistently pleaded for an Academy of Crafts in Russia. Instruction in the Academy should serve "the good of factories and crafts." [83] This idea was realized after his death, but in a somewhat different form. In 1757 the "Academy of Three Important Arts" was founded in Petersburg; it was transformed in 1764 into the Russian Imperial Academy of Arts.

Like Peter I, Tatishchev wanted to protect native trade, industry, and agriculture. The state should provide privileges and encouragement to thrifty persons, but, at the same time, it should supervise and regulate their economic activities.

As if in contradiction to the protectionism which was characteristic of the economic views of the mercantilists, Tatishchev asserted that the chief condition for the development of internal and foreign trade was "freedom of trade." [84] It must be remembered that Tatishchev defined "freedom of trade" peculiarly and very narrowly as being combined with state interference and regulation; he thought that the state should provide "inducements and assistance to crafts, industries, trades,

---

[81] V. N. Tatishchev, "Predlozhenie o razmnozhenii fabrik [A Proposal on the Increase of Factories], *ibid.*, VII, 408.

[82] See N. F. Demidova, ed., "Instruktsiia V. N. Tatishcheva o prepodavanii v shkolakh pri uralskikh zavodakh, 1736 g. noiabria 9" [V. N. Tatishchev's Instruction of November 9, 1736, on Teaching in Schools Attached to Ural Factories], *ibid.*, V, 166–78.

[83] TsGADA, Fund of the State Archive, Section XVII, No. 54, "Zapiska V. N. Tatishcheva ob uchashchikhsia i raskhodakh na prosveshchenie v Rossii . . . " [V. N. Tatishchev's Memorandum About Those Who Study and Expenditures on Education in Russia . . .], Sheet 1.

[84] Popov, *op. cit.*, p. 719.

and agriculture." [85] Moreover, the government could and should assure freedom to merchants, especially by "protecting them from excessive taxation." [86]

Tatishchev proposed to exempt the merchants from military quartering and to stop the arbitrary rule of local authorities, which only impeded the merchants. The middle and small merchants should also be safeguarded from oppression by the big merchants. In this connection his advice as to the method of selecting city magistrates is interesting. In accordance with Peter's Regulations of the Chief Magistrate of 1721, the presidents of the city magistracy were to come from the local merchant class.[87] Tatishchev objected to this situation, which, he thought, presented opportunities for those presidents, usually big merchants, to engulf their competitors. He insisted that the presidents be nobles, not merchants. In reality this meant strengthening the influence of the local nobility in the development of trade and industry.

Tatishchev was strongly opposed to farming out the collection of treasury revenues and to the system of contractors supplying the state. He thought that tax farmers and contractors not only hampered the trade of other merchants, but also brought significant material loss to the state; the contract system of supplying the army and navy resulted in a reduction of their supplies. His proposal supported the development of trade and the interests of the middle and petty merchants. It was soon reiterated by the merchant deputies in the Code Commission meeting in 1754. They asked for cessation of all monopolies, "so that neither one person nor one company obtains [a monopoly] in trade from which many should benefit." [88] This demand was satisfied, though not completely, in the economic policy beginning with the 1760's.

Although he favored a strong merchantry, Tatishchev guarded jealously the monopoly of the nobility in the exploitation of forced labor. Citing France, England, and Holland (where heavy industry was developed by hired labor and the merchants did not have the right to exploit forced labor), Tatishchev sought to abolish the right, given to the merchants under Peter I, of buying villages for their enterprises.

---

[85] *Izbrannye trudy po geografii Rossii* [Selected Works on Russian Geography] (Moscow: 1950), p. 202.

[86] Popov, *op. cit.,* p. 729.

[87] *PSZ,* VI, No. 3708.

[88] See N. L. Rubinshtein, "Ulozhennaia komissiia 1754–1766 gg. i ee proekt novogo ulozheniia 'O sostoianii poddanykh voobshche' " [The Code Commission of 1754–1766 and Its Project for a New Code "On the Condition of Subjects in General"], *Istoricheskie zapiski* [Historical Notes], No. 38 (1951), p. 248.

While he fought for the improvement of trade and industry, Tatishchev also attached great importance to agriculture, which supplied raw materials, food, and forage for the internal and foreign market.

The development of industry and trade fostered the growth both of agricultural production and markets. Tatishchev thought that the nobles, the pomeshchiki, should use this progress to increase the revenues from their estates. He discussed the means for doing so in his article, "Short Economic Notes Relating to the Village" (1742).[89] This work consists of twenty-two chapters. It treats of systems of agriculture, animal and poultry husbandry, horticulture, and apiculture; it deals with artificial irrigation and water conservation, domestic peasant industries, and storehouses and repositories for the agricultural inventory.

While rejecting the administration of pomestie estates by a steward or other trusted person, Tatishchev recommended the barshchina system only where the village was near the pomeshchik's residence, "so that he can oversee the entire estate himself"; distant villages should be on quit-rent. In those cases where the landowner lived in the city, Tatishchev advised the quit-rent system, with the land distributed to the peasants in tracts; for this was "more useful than maintaining a steward or elder." [90] If, after allotment of land for barshchina work, a peasant and his wife were not assured of at least one desiatina of land, that is, no less than three desiatiny of quit-rent allotment, then Tatishchev opposed the barshchina system and favored quit-rent. Finally, even if all the necessary conditions existed for the introduction of a barshchina economy, the peasants should bear the barshchina obligations and pay quit-rent, for which it was necessary to allot them land. Thus he paid attention not only to the pomestie economy, but also to the peasant economy as a source of quit-rent for the pomeshchik.

With the interests of the pomeshchik in mind, he argued for the development of a high norm of peasant land usage by providing peasants with cattle and poultry, improving the quality of livestock, laying out more gardens, extending agriculture, and so on. Tatishchev favored the wide development of domestic industries among the peasants, "so that no one is without hand work, especially in winter . . ."

---

89 "Kratkie ekonomicheskie do derevni sleduiushchie zapiski . . ." [Brief Economic Notes About the Village . . .] in *Vremennik imperatorskogo Moskovskogo obshchestva istorii i drevnostei rossiiskikh* [A Chronicle of the Imperial Moscow Society of History and Russian Antiquities], Bk. XII (1852), p. 20.

90 *Ibid.*, p. 29.

Aware of the fact that to improve the peasant economy the peasants must be trained, he proposed that peasant children aged from five to ten years be taught reading and writing. It is important to note that Tatishchev applied this proposal to "both sexes." Children aged from ten to fifteen years should study "various arts," that is, crafts.

A convinced believer in serf ownership, Tatishchev helped to spread the notion among pomeshchiki that the peasants were naturally lazy. He did not believe that they could improve their economy independently and did not consider it possible to give "them freedom to do so"; he thus ordered the stewards and elders to supervise the work of the peasants not only in the pomestie estate, but even in the peasant establishment. Tatishchev recommended that harsh measures, including imprisonment, be used in dealing with "lazy" peasants.

We should note especially his proposal regarding those peasants who could not provide the pomeshchik with a high quit-rent. He recommended that they be given "as indigent farm hands" to other peasants who would "pay their taxes, own their land, and supervise them until they improved." [91]

Tatishchev wanted to separate the peasant economy from the market in order to bind it even more firmly to the pomeshchik. "The peasant should sell surplus grain, cattle, and poultry exclusively in his own village, and where there are no merchants the pomeshchik should buy them at a satisfactory price; only when the pomeshchik does not want to buy, should the peasant sell to an outsider." [92] Tatishchev's aim was clear—to guarantee the pomeshchik additional income by selling the products of the peasant economy at the difference between the market and the "satisfactory," price, the latter being quite arbitrary, and established by the pomeshchik.

During poor harvest years Tatishchev proposed to prohibit peasants from selling grain. The steward was to dispose of all the peasants' grain, and seek "various means of supplying" the village population. For "unforeseen circumstances," chiefly natural disasters, Tatishchev recommended that each peasant create a reserve by setting aside annually one fifth of the harvest. For this purpose the pomeshchik was to maintain a "storehouse," which would also hold the agricultural inventory; "then if a peasant needs to buy something he will not lose much time during the working period." [93]

Because he understood that for the development of agriculture (as

---

[91] *Ibid.*, p. 28.
[92] *Ibid.*, p. 21.
[93] *Ibid.*, p. 20.

well as for industry at that time) many workers were needed, Tatishchev was quite disturbed by the flight of peasants, which had assumed dangerous proportions. It is important to note that Tatishchev, in contrast to contemporary statesmen, wanted to combat the chief reasons for the flights not by repression but by elimination of the underlying causes. He spoke again of the desirability of larger peasant allotments, more livestock for the peasant, and other measures designed to improve the condition of the peasantry within the framework of serfdom, as means to strengthen this system. His concern for the peasant economy reflects a pomeshchik, a nobleman who knew, as Plekhanov noted, "the value of the 'baptized property' and who was capable of utilizing labor." [94]

Tatishchev is noted for his desire to give scientific foundation to his economic views, projects, and practical proposals. Thus, planning the distribution of factories in the Urals and the means of transporting raw materials, fuel, and finished articles, he collected information on the nature of the area as well as statistical data on its economy.

First to describe the geography of Russia,[95] Tatishchev was interested in the social life, especially in the economy, of the people. Therefore he set aside a special part in the geography—political geography—which was closely linked to history. Political geography, in Tatishchev's definition, should describe in detail "large and small villages, as well as cities and harbors, civil and ecclesiastical governments, and so on. It should deal with the population's abilities, its industriousness, and with the state of the arts, as well as with the people's habits and living conditions, since these factors change with time." [96] Thus political geography includes economic geography. In this sense Tatishchev must be looked upon as a forerunner of the founder of Russian economic geography—M. V. Lomonosov.[97]

To verify his theoretical ideas on political geography, its aims, and methods, Tatishchev encountered inadequate factual material and an

---

[94] Plekhanov, *Sochineniia,* XXI, 73.

[95] V. N. Tatishchev, *Obshchee geograficheskoe opisanie vseia Sibiri* (1726) [General Geographic Description of All of Siberia]; *Russia ili, kak nyne zovut, Rossia* [Russia, or as They Call it Now, Rossia] (1739); *Vvedenie k istoricheskomu i geograficheskomu opisaniiu rossiiskoi imperii* [An Introduction to Historical and Geographic Description of the Russian Empire] (1744) in *Izbrannye trudy po geografii Rossii.*

[96] *Ibid.,* p. 211.

[97] On Tatishchev as economic geographer, see N. P. Nikitin, "Zarozhdenie ekonomicheskoi geografii v Rossii. Obzor materialov XVIII v." [The Origin of Economic Geography in Russia. A Review of Sources of the XVIII Century], *Voprosy geografii* [Problems of Geography], Collection 17 (1950), pp. 49–52.

almost complete absence of statistical data.[98] To obtain these data he resorted to questionnaires. In 1734 he made up a statistical-geographic questionnaire comprising ninety-two questions. It was sent to the Siberian and Kazan gubernias and to the provincial offices; but he received very few satisfactory answers. In 1737 he presented to the Academy of Sciences his "Proposal for Preparing the History and Geography of Russia," [99] which was a new questionnaire containing 198 questions, comprehending trade, industry, means of commnuication, and so forth. The new questionnaire had not only more questions, but the queries were also developed in greater detail. It was sent to the cities of Siberia in the second half of 1737. Tatishchev was thus the author of the first scientifically developed statistical questionnaire in Russia, and it served as a model for subsequent researches of the eighteenth century, including the famous questionnaire of M. V. Lomonosov. Thus it is necessary to consider Tatishchev Lomonosov's forerunner, who laid the foundation for Russian statistical science.

As a spokesman of the nobility and protector of the feudal order, Tatishchev defended economic development within the framework of feudalism. His economic works relate to the second quarter of the eighteenth century, when the productive forces of Russia still had scope for development within the limits of a feudal economy. Therefore, as a whole, his economic program was progressive for the time, in spite of the author's views on serfdom.

His practical proposals and plans and his resulting theoretical positions were basically mercantilistic. His economic works, especially, for example, the "Proposal on Trade and Crafts" and the "Discourse on Goods Imported and Exported Through the Astrakhan Port," were written from the viewpoint of the "trade balance" and the "manufacturing systems." Tatishchev was an outstanding representative of an economic ideology which was progressive for the Russia of his time.

---

[98] On Tatishchev as geographer and statistician see L. E. Iofa, *Sovremenniki Lomonosova: I. K. Kirilov, i V. N. Tatishchev. Geografy pervoi poloviny XVIII v.* [Lomonosov's Contemporaries: I. K. Kirilov and V. N. Tatishchev. Geographers of the First Half of the XVIII Century]. (Moscow: Geografgiz, 1949), pp. 38–87; A. I. Andreev's "Introduction" to V. N. Tatishchev, *Izbrannye trudy po geografii Rossii* [Selected Works on Russian Geography] (Moscow: 1950), pp. 3–35; M. Ptukha, *Ocherki po istorii statistiki XVII–XVIII vekov* [Outlines of the History of Statistics of the XVII–XVIII Centuries] (Moscow: Gospolitizdat, 1945), pp. 278–80.

[99] Published in Popov, *op. cit.*, pp. 663–96.

CHAPTER 14. *M. V. Lomonosov and the Struggle to Develop the Productive Forces of Russia*

Mikhail Vasilevich Lomonosov was born in 1711 in the village of Mishanin Kurostrov volost (located on one of the islands of the Northern Dvina, opposite Kholmogory) of Dvina nezd, Archangel gubernia, into the family of a state peasant engaged in agriculture, fishing, and hunting sea animals. From the age of ten he accompanied his father in voyages on the Northern Dvina and on the White and Barents Seas. At nineteen Lomonosov went to Moscow on foot and in January, 1731, entered the Slavonia-Greek-Latin Academy. In December, 1735, he was sent to the Petersburg Academy of Sciences to continue his education; the following September he was sent abroad to study mining.

In June, 1741, M. V. Lomonosov returned to the Petersburg Academy of Sciences. During the first half of the 1740's, he worked on atomic-molecular studies, the mechanical theory of heat, and the action of chemical solvents. In 1745 he was appointed professor (academician) of chemistry, and in 1748 (in a letter to the mathematician L. Euler) Lomonosov formulated "a general law of nature" which he had discovered—the conservation of matter (substance) and motion (energy). He developed the kinetic theory of gases, organized the first scientific chemical laboratory in Russia, and completed his *Rhetoric*. In 1749 Lomonosov came out against the "Norman theory" of the origin of Rus.

In the first half of the 1750's, he wrote "A Discourse on the Use of Chemistry," compiled the "Course of True Physical Chemistry," and founded a "factory for making varicolored glass and beads" in Ust'-Ruditsa. Lomonosov not only suggested the founding of, but developed the plan for, Moscow University, which was opened in 1755 and which now bears his name. In the same year he completed the compilation of a "Russian Grammar."

In 1758 Lomonosov headed the Department of Geography in the Academy of Sciences. In 1759 he invented and constructed instruments for seagoing vessels and wrote the "Discourse on a More Exact Sea Route." In 1760 he published "Discourse on Fluids and Solids," which set forth in print for the first time his law of the conservation of substance and energy. In 1761 the letter "On the Preservation and Increase of the Russian people" was written; the book *First Principles of Metallurgy or Mining Affairs* appeared in 1763; and the same year he presented "A Brief Description of Various Voyages on the Northern Seas and the Evidence of a Possible Passage from the Arctic Ocean to the East Indies." He died on April 15 (4), 1765.[1]

The ingenious works of Mikhail Vasilevich Lomonosov in Russia represent the apex of world science at this time. The basis of Lomonosov's brilliant scientific achievements was his materialism. With the idea of the evolution and change of nature as a foundation, he clarified geological and biological phenomena: the origin of mountains, minerals, plants and other living organisms, and so forth. As one of the founders of Russian naturalism, Lomonosov has worldwide significance as a classicist of natural science. As the father of Russian materialistic philosophy, he is one of the greatest philosopher-materialists of the pre-Marxist period. The materialism of Lomonosov, like that of the eighteenth century, was basically of a mechanistic character with metaphysical traits. By his generalizations and discoveries, however, and his defense of the idea of the evolution and changeability of nature, Lomonosov went beyond metaphysical materialism.

His scientific activity caused displeasure to and attacks by the clergy, whose influence had greatly increased during the reign of Elizabeth Petrovna.

In his creativity Lomonosov was exceptionally varied; his scientific interests were strikingly versatile. As Pushkin put it: Lomonosov not only "created the first university; he himself was our first university." [2] Along with his immortal services in the natural sciences, he also rendered important services to Russian literature, to the development of the Russian literary language, to historical science, statistics, and the development of Russian economic thought. His role in the development of economic thought certainly has been underestimated. Foreign historians of political economy (Ingram, Kosse, Gide, Rist, Onken, among others) do not mention Lomonosov. In pre-revolutionary Russian literature the idea prevailed that the only economic notion developed by Lomonsov was that relating to population (I. K. Sukhopliuev,

[1] The most complete biography of Lomonosov is that by A. Morozov, *Mikhail Vasilevich Lomonosov, 1711–1765* (Leningrad: 1952); see also B. N. Menshutkin, *Zhizneopisanie Mikhaila Vasilevicha Lomonosova* [A Biography of Michael Vasilevich Lomonosov]. (3rd edition with supplements by P. N. Berkov, S. I. Vavilov, and L. B. Modzalevskii, Moscow-Leningrad: AS USSR, 1947).

[2] Pushkin, *Polnoe sobranie sochinenii,* VII, 277.

I. A. Tikhomirov). A similar view appeared even in the literature of the Soviet period. Thus Sviatlovskii, in his work devoted especially to the history of Russian economic thought, declared that, except for the letter to Shuvalo of November 1, 1761, about preserving and increasing the Russian people, "no other economic works of Lomonosov have been preserved," and his views on other "economic problems are unknown to us." [3] Such assertions are untrue. The economic views of Lomonosov can be determined on the basis of a number of his works and statements and have great significance for the history of Russian economic thought.

Lomonosov thought that economic problems and the proposals concerning them were very important: they require "deep understanding and prolonged experience in state affairs to render them intelligible and prudence to make them a reality." [4] He was, indeed, interested in Russian economic thought. By his orders a copy was made of the manuscript of Pososhkov's *Book on Poverty and Wealth,* as evidenced by note on the volume now preserved in the manuscript section of the library of the Academy of Sciences of the USSR: "Copied in 1752, and the request for copying was received from counsellor Mikhail Vasilevich Lomonosov."

The creativity of Lomonosov answered the growing problems of Russian development. His scientific works (on the natural sciences, technology, geography, and so forth) were primarily concerned with their practical application. "Lomonosov passionately loved science," wrote Chernyshevskii, "but he thought and cared only for the good of his country. He wanted to serve not just pure science, but the fatherland as well." [5] Lomonosov called upon science to penetrate "into the the very farthest places" and to investigate "the land, desert, steppe, and deep forest." [6] To him science was directly linked with experience and practice and with the development of the productive forces and culture of his native land, into whose feudal economy bourgeois relationships had already made inroads.

The basic aim of state policy should be, according to Lomonosov, "the welfare, glory, and flourishing condition" of his beloved country; he understood, above all, the political and economic independence of Russia, the development of her productive forces, the improvement of the material situation of her people, and the raising of the cultural

---

[3] Sviatlovskii, *Istoriia ekonomicheskikh idei v Rossii,* I, 74.

[4] M. V. Lomonosov, *Polnoe sobranie sochinenii* [Complete Collection of Works] (Moscow-Leningrad: AS USSR, 1952), VI, 383–4.

[5] N. G. Chernyshevskii, *Polnoe sobranie sochinenii* [Complete Collection of Works] (Moscow: 1947), III, 137.

[6] M. V. Lomonosov, *Sochineniia* [Works] (St. Petersburg: 1891), I, 218.

level of the country. Considering Peter I as the initiator and director of such a policy, Lomonosov felt that the aim of his life, the basis of his activity, was "to defend the work of Peter the Great." Lomonosov idealized Peter, who in reality effected his reforms at the expense of the serfs, and he called upon the successors of Peter to follow his policy.

Lomonosov's activity developed under conditions of a bitter and tense struggle. He led an unending fight against foreigners, most often pseudo scientists, who, while living in Russia, harmed her, and hindered the development of her economy, science, and culture. Plekhanov says that "these pseudo-scientists looked down upon the Russian people and tried to dominate them and to monopolize their education. Lomonosov saw, as did Pososhkov, the exploiting designs of foreign merchants and, like Pososhkov, tried to save Russia from the domination of foreigners." [7] He came out sharply against such foreigners, "who were malevolent towards Russian scientists." [8] He demanded removal of the German, Schumacher, and his clique, who then had considerable influence in the administration of the Russian Academy of Sciences. Lomonosov fought the attempts of foreigners to distort and demean the history of the great Russian people.

Supporting those foreigners who as true scholars worked honorably for the good of Russia, Lomonosov saw the future of Russian science in the rearing of Russian scientists "whom the nation awaits from within its bosom." Lomonosov himself nurtured a number of Russian scholars. He was also strongly opposed to those Russians who dragged Russia backward. His sharp polemic against the spokesman of the nobility, A. P. Sumarokov, is interesting in this regard.[9] The noble and bourgeois literary historians have interpreted the enmity between Lomonosov and Sumarokov as a personal conflict. Actually it was a battle of opinions with definite political and economic origins. Lomonosov passionately fought Sumarokov and other reactionary and conservative spokesmen who strove to hamper the industrial development of the country.

On the Industrial Development of Russia

Lomonosov's guiding economic idea was the guarantee of Russian independence, which could be insured by the many-sided develop-

---

[7] Plekhanov, *Sochineniia*, XXI, 153.

[8] See Biliarskii, *Materialy dlia biografii Lomonosova* [Materials for Lomonosov's Biography] (St. Petersburg: 1865), p. 99.

[9] See Chapter XVI.

ment of her productive forces. The great Russian scientist conceived the growth of productive forces as a chief factor in the industrial development of the country. In this development the production of metals was of primary importance. "Metals," wrote Lomonosov, "add strength and beauty to important things required in society . . . with them we defend ourselves from enemy attack; they strengthen ships and enable them to sail safely in stormy seas. Metals prepare the soil for cultivation; metals serve us in catching land and sea animals for our food." Metals make possible trade in money rather than direct barter of goods, which is so inconvenient. All branches of society's production, concludes Lomonosov, require the use of metals: "In short, not one art [10] and not one simple craft can avoid the use of metals." [11]

Lomonosov emphasized the decisive role of metal production in assuring the economic independence of Russia, in the development of her war industry, and in the growth of the country's military might. "Military affairs, trade, navigation, and other vital state institutions need metals, which prior to the enlightenment introduced by Peter's works were almost all obtained from neighboring peoples, so that military arms sometimes had to be bought from the enemies themselves through intermediaries and at a high price." [12]

Lomonosov considered metallurgy, by which he understood all mining production, including the extraction of ores, the basis for the growth of national wealth. He defined metallurgy as "the conductor of all internal wealth." [13] The Russian mining industry, which enjoyed first place in the world at that time, not only in volume of production and export of ferrous metals, but also in quality, was always the center of Lomonosov's attention.

Vigorously protesting against the absurd opinion propagated by foreigners that Russia was poor in useful minerals, Lomonosov pointed out that the resources of Russia were unusually rich but little explored. The causes for this lack of exploration Lomonosov divided into two groups. The first group included "natural" causes and the second, "political." "Natural" causes, according to Lomonosov, consisted of the depth at which minerals are found, covered by a thick layer of earth or sand. "Political," that is, social, conditions were the main reason for the insufficient exploration of Russian resources. First, he

---

[10] At that time *khudozhestvo* referred to various branches of industrial production.

[11] Lomonosov, *Polnoe sobranie sochinenii, II,* 359–60.

[12] M. V. Lomonosov, *Sochineniia* [Works] (Leningrad: 1934), VII, 15.

[13] *Ibid.,* VII, 17.

said, mineralogy and geology as sciences were little developed at that time, and mineralogical and geological knowledge was not widespread. Another social condition hampering the exploration of resources and the search for minerals was the "sparse population" of Siberia, the Urals, and other areas rich in minerals.

Lomonosov correctly suggested that the rich mineral wealth of Russia required scientific and technical research and the application of the labor of the miners for its development. Deeply convinced that "immense and rich Russia needs only zealousness and work to search out metals," [14] he advocated the broad development of geological research and the exploration for minerals. He called on "lovers of mining" to seek everywhere for "minerals needed in society, the development of which might bring much profit." [15]

Lomonosov's investigations led to his conclusion that northern Russia was rich in useful minerals. "I conclude on the basis of much evidence that there is also abundance in the north and that nature governs," but "no one searches for those resources." He added, "But metals and minerals do not come home by themselves; they require eyes and hands to seek them out." [16]

The pomeshchiki and capitalists had left the natural resources in the north almost untouched. Industrial development there had to await the Soviet period. Referring to Lomonosov's words on the need of industrial development of the resources of northern Russia, Sergei Mironovich Kirov remarked to the Leningrad Bolsheviks: "Even in his time Lomonosov called for a look at the north, which is being done now . . . I think that all our educational organizations, beginning with the Academy of Sciences, and all practical workers should follow the advice of Lomonosov and actually feel with eyes and hands everything in that rich and extensive region." [17]

Lomonosov foresaw the substitution of peat and coal for wood fuel, the use of which denuded the forests. Recognizing the great significance to the national economy of the displacement of wood fuel, Lomonosov disclosed that great uninvestigated reserves of coal and peat existed in Russia; he called peat the underground economic treasure.[18]

Lomonosov's discoveries and inventions had far-reaching practical and economic implications. He unswervingly and insistently strove for

---

[14] Lomonosov, *Polnoe sobranie sochinenii,* II, 361–2.

[15] Lomonosov, *Sochineniia* (1934), VII, 261.

[16] *Ibid.*

[17] S. M. Kirov, *Izbrannye stati i rechi, 1912–1934* [Selected Articles and Speeches, 1912–1934] (Moscow: Gospolitizdat, 1939), p. 475.

[18] Lomonosov, *Sochineniia* (1934), VII, 245.

wide industrial use of the results of his theoretical findings and laboratory work. In formulating his plans and discoveries, Lomonosov gave them an economic basis. He valued technical inventions for their labor-saving potential. Thus the competition offered in 1763 by the Academy of Sciences at Lomonosov's suggestion had for its purposes the saving of time and the prevention of losses in metallurgical production. The question was: "Is there no way to separate metal from its ore that is faster and less expensive . . . ?" [19]

Lomonosov was interested not only in the efficiency of technical constructions, but also in replacing people by machines in heavy and dangerous pursuits. He was especially concerned with safeguarding the health of children, whose labor was mercilessly exploited in existing factories. Recalling his visit to the mines of Saxony, Lomonosov was angered by the brutal exploitation of the labor of children who were forced to crush and grind ore, "despite today's enlightenment . . . [and] grinding mills." It would be possible to eliminate these conditions by using mills "for speeding up work and saving young children, whose health is ruined by heavy work and poisonous dust, and who are thus maimed for life." [20]

In the manufacturing period when in general little concern was displayed for labor safeguards, Lomonosov proposed putting smelting furnaces at set distances, "so smelters will not be harmed by the heat of the work," and supplying workers with special protective boots ("thick leather or birch bark boots").[21] He was also interested in the improvement of conditions of production.

Lomonosov promoted the economic ideas of Peter I which broadly protected industrial entrepreneurs, including the merchant class. Such an economic policy would have aided the industrial development of the country.

On Agriculture

As a defender of the industrial development of the country, Lomonosov was also concerned with the advancement of agriculture. One of his great services is found in the area of Russian agricultural science. His works of natural science were the basis of materialistic biology in Russia. Developing Lomonosov's beliefs, the Academician I. I. Lepekhin supported the thesis of the mutability of plants and

---

[19] See P. Pekarskii, *Istoriia imperatorskoi Akademii nauk v Peterburge* [History of the Imperial Academy of Sciences in Petersburg] (St. Petersburg: 1873), II, 751.

[20] Lomonosov, *Sochineniia* (1934), VII, 21.

[21] See *ibid.*, VII, 119.

animals under the influence of environment. With his work "On the Layers of the Earth," and other publications, Lomonosov prepared the way for scientific agriculture in Russia.

He translated from the German the book of Hubertus, *Stratagema Oeconomicum, oder Akker-Student,* which appeared in Riga in 1688 in the third edition [22] and which was a manual on the organization of a pomestie estate. This treatise was widely circulated in various manuscript translations among the nobility. Lomonosov called it "Lifland Economy." [23]

The author of "Lifland Economy" defends "at least" the three-field system of agriculture, which provides room "where cattle may graze," [24] that is, which makes it possible to combine animal husbandry with agriculture. Interesting are his recommendations to expand crop land by draining swamps: "If only the water could be drained off or transverse canals built . . . fields would be possible there. The Dutch and the Frieslanders have made fertile fields out of the swamps." [25] The directions emphasize the importance and necessity of regulation and seasonal performance of agricultural work: "A skillful agriculturist should, according to the conditions of his household, lay out his work month by month . . . It is very urgent that everything be done at the proper time . . ." [26]

Lomonosov is responsible for a plan to create a central scientific establishment which would study the agriculture of Russia and devise methods to advance agricultural production. His plan (formulated, evidently, in 1763) he called "An Opinion on Establishing a State College of Agriculture." The tasks of the College, according to Lomonosov, should not be limited to agriculture. It should also concern itself with forests, roads, and canals, with the study and development of

---

[22] See P. N. Berkov, "Lomonosov i 'Lifliandskaia ekonomiia' " [Lomonosov and the Lifland Economy] in *Lomonosov. Sbornik statei i materialov* [Lomonosov. A Collection of Articles and Materials], edited by A. I. Andreev and L. B. Modzalevskii, (Moscow-Leningrad: AS USSR, 1946), pp. 271–6.

[23] *Lifliandskaia ekonomiia. Perevedena s nemetskogo na rossiiskii khimii professorom Mikhailom Lomonosovym, v Sanktpeterburge 1747 goda. S podlinnoi spisana v 1760 godu. Iz domu gospod baronov Cherkasovykh.* [Lifland Economy. Translated from German into Russian by Michael Lomonosov, Professor of Chemistry, in St. Petersburg, 1747. Copied from the Original in 1760. From the House of Baron Cherkaskii.]

This copy contains 117 sheets (234 pp.) and is preserved in the Manuscript Division of the State Library of the USSR, Museum Collection, No. 2649. The copy of 1747 has not been preserved.

[24] Manuscript Division of the State Library of the USSR, *Museum Collection,* No. 2649, Sheet 19.

[25] *Ibid.,* Sheet 28.

[26] *Ibid.,* Sheet 4.

"village crafts," and with the discovery of export resources. To accomplish its objectives, the College should attract people engaged in agriculture, invite their proposals, and sponsor competitive "tasks with rewards."

Lomonosov saw the College as a scientific establishment with a solid experimental base. For the purpose of testing different proposals and plans and for independent experiments, he proposed alloting the College a section containing diversified soils, "where there would be various places, mountainous and dry, and swamps, clay, and meadows." [27]

He thought the "College of Agriculture" should be a state scientific establishment, independent of the Academy of Sciences. His plan reflected the growing need for such an organization to study Russian agriculture and aid its development.

In 1763 "a class of agriculture, or land management was set up in the Academy of Sciences." This new scientific establishment, which, contrary to Lomonosov's proposals, was part of the Academy of Sciences, did not play a significant role. In 1765, the year of Lomonosov's death, Catherine II approved the plan and charter of "The Free Economic Society for the Encouragement of Agriculture and Household Management in Russia." Being independent of the Academy of Sciences, the Society was in fact an organization to protect the narrow class interests of the nobles–pomeshchiki. This was the realization of Lomonosov's idea in a limited and distorted form.

On Trade

While devoting most of his attention to production, Lomonosov at the same time constantly stressed the great economic importance of trade and the necessity of its development. Speaking of "merchantry" (by which Lomonosov, like his contemporaries, understood trade) he gave special emphasis to foreign trade. Among the themes which he outlines for his works is one entitled "On Merchantry, Especially with Foreign Peoples." [28]

Lomonosov considered foreign trade one of the factors contributing most to the wealth and prosperity of a country. "The well-being and glory of the state stem from three sources," wrote Lomonosov, citing above all the importance of "internal peace, safety, and satisfaction of its subjects." He correlated the satisfaction of the subjects with the satisfaction of the needs and well-being of the entire population, achievements which were contingent upon the "victorious action

[27] Lomonosov, *Polnoe sobranie sochinenii,* VI, 412.

[28] *Ibid.,* VI, 379.

against the enemy, with the conclusion of successful and glorious peace." He emphasized also the importance of the "mutual exchange of domestic surpluses with distant peoples through trade" [29] as one of the main sources of the wealth and prosperity of the entire state.

Lomonosov believed that the growth of native production affects both internal and foreign trade. A surplus of products of native production over the domestic needs of the country makes possible the appearance and development of export trade: "How many necessary things which were once brought into Russia from distant lands with difficulty and at a high price are now produced within the state and not only satisfy us, but supply other lands with our surplus." [30] Seeking such surplus resources for export, Lomonosov wished to encourage the development of those branches of production which have decisive importance for the industrial growth of the country. He also called for the promotion of certain industries secondary to the national economy but with export value, in order to activate the country's trade balance. His letter regarding the production of colored glass is an example of this point of view. In the Senate decree of 1752 "Re: Permitting Professor Lomonosov to Establish a Factory for Making Varicolored Glass, Beads, Bugles, and Other Objects of Jewelry," in Ust' Ruditsa (drawn up at Lomonosov's request) it is indicated that as a result of building a factory a considerable amount of revenue would be saved: "the sums which the Russian people now spend for such imports leave the state, but henceforth will remain here in Russia." After the satisfaction of domestic needs, the further production of colored glass can be exported. Lomonosov thought that if this factory were established it could produce sufficient quantities of goods for the internal and the foreign market.[31] After several years (1763) of developing the production of colored glass Lomonosov wrote that he soon would "request that its import be forbidden." [32]

To aid the development of both internal and external trade Lomonosov thought that internal trade should be free. "Freedom of internal trade" (Lomonosov's words), which Elizabeth Petrovna established by abolishing internal customs, was seen by him as one of the greatest acts of her reign.[33]

For the advancement of foreign trade he believed that the state must encourage exports and limit and forbid imports. Speaking of the

---

[29] *Ibid.*, VI, 421.
[30] Lomonosov, *Sochineniia* (1898), IV, 368–9.
[31] *PSZ*, XIII, No. 10057.
[32] *Lomonosov. Sbornik statei i materialov,* p. 162.
[33] Lomonosov, *Sochineniia* (1902), V, 90.

services of Peter I in developing foreign trade, Lomonosov mentioned tariff regulation, along with such measures as connecting rivers by canals, building new ports, and concluding trade agreements with foreign states.[34] The customs tariff introduced under Peter had a clearly protectionist nature.

Discussing the foreign trade of Russia, Lomonosov stressed especially that "the Russian empire equals in its domestic abundance and in its great victories the best European states and surpasses many"; but, although the Russians at the beginning of the eighteenth century had attained important successes in the development of foreign trade, they still remained behind the most advanced states of Europe. Lomonosov presents a historical explanation of this lag. The economically developed countries of Western Europe, having access to the sea, created their fleets and developed foreign trade on the basis of sea commerce. Russia, deprived of such ports before Peter I, was forced to limit itself to "internal navigation"—internal trade based on river traffic. In addition, says Lomonosov, "after Peter opened many seaports and introduced the knowledge of sailing and shipbuilding, the former inconveniences disappeared and now the movement of Russian naval and merchant ships is growing noticeably." The necessary conditions were created for Russia to occupy a prominent place among the commercial powers of the world. Russia was in a position "to assert itself both in European trade ports and in Japan, China, and India, and to reach the western shores of America." [35]

The idea of suitable sea communication with the chief countries of Asia and America was propagated from the forties on in solemn speeches and odes by Lomonosov. The collective image of the "Russian Columbus" pushing on through the ice toward the East reflected the real figures of the renowned Russian sailors of the far north and eastern coasts of Asia and the Pacific—Malygin, Chelyuskin, the Laptevs, Chirikov, and Bering—who opened the way for Russia's foreign trade.

The Project for a Northern Sea Route

In 1755 Lomonosov wrote of the necessity of establishing a trade route from Archangel to the East Indies via the Arctic and Pacific Oceans ("Letter on a northern passage to the East Indies via the Siberian Ocean"). This idea he later developed fully, especially in "A Brief Description of Various Voyages in the Arctic and the Evi-

[34] *Ibid.*, IV, 381.
[35] Lomonosov, *Polnoe sobranie sochinenii,* VI, 422.

dence of a Possible Passage from the Arctic Ocean to the East Indies" (1763)—a valuable contribution to Russian and world science. Lomonosov proceeded from a deep understanding of the economic needs and political tasks of contemporary Russia in regard to the international political and economic situation.

He pointed out the advantages of a northeast passage (along the northern coast of Siberia) for communication with the countries of the east, as opposed to the northwest passage (along the northern coasts of America), which "is narrow, difficult, unprofitable, useless, and always dangerous." [36] And his judgment was correct. In spite of the fact that England, Holland, Denmark, and later the USA tried to master the northwest passage, the latter has no practical importance even in our own time.

Noting the great importance of the northern sea route for the development of trade with eastern nations,[37] Lomonosov showed that, thanks to "the tireless efforts of our people," the movement of trade eastward went by the northern route. His work was the first summary in the world of all the previous attempts in the struggle to go east via the Arctic Ocean. He gave a theoretical basis to the navigability of the Arctic Ocean in the indicated direction.[38]

According to Lomonosov, opening the northern sea route would complete the transformation of Russia from a continental to a maritime nation. Traffic on this route would elevate Russia into a power prominent along world trade routes; Russia "in time can equal not only other sea powers, but can also surpass them." [39] The opening of a northern sea route would greatly promote the foreign trade of Russia. He thought that with its mastery the brave and active Russian people would settle and live on the barren coasts and islands of the Arctic Ocean and the northern basin of the Pacific. Trade ports, manufacturing settlements, and towns would rise on the banks of the mainland and islands, especially in the mouths of rivers. Agriculture, animal husbandry, various processing industries, and the extraction of iron ore would develop in the interior regions distant from the coast, which would supply the settlers on the coast "with grain, cattle, and fish, ship building, timber, hemp, tar, and, happily, iron, for this ore

---

[36] *Ibid.*, VI, 440.

[37] Fedor Saltykov already had written about a sea route from Russia to China via the Arctic Ocean. See Chapter XIII.

[38] See V. A. Perevalov, *Lomonosov i Arktika. Iz istorii geograficheskoi nauki i geograficheskikh otkrytii* [Lomonosov and the Arctic. From the History of Geographic Science and Geographic Discoveries] (Moscow-Leningrad: Glavsevmorput, 1949).

[39] Lomonosov, *Polnoe sobranie sochinenii,* VI, 422.

is found in many places." [40] Thus Lomonosov especially emphasized the importance of the northern sea route in obtaining and processing useful minerals "in the northern regions" [41] and the East, both of which are full of "incredible wealth and powers.[42] The great scientist stressed the urgency to develop the northern sea route "in order not to be forestalled by others in such a great and glorious undertaking." [43]

Lomonosov indicated the necessity of encouraging settlement in the North and Far East by providing various privileges and exemptions especially in internal and foreign trade: "To settle those places . . . undoubtedly many volunteers will want to go, if they are promised excellent privileges and freedoms, especially in trading among themselves and with neighboring peoples." Along with voluntary settlement of the north and northeast coasts of Asia, Lomonosov recommended forced colonization—"annually, send people there of both sexes, people who loaf here in Russia or are to be exiled for crimes." These resettled loafers and criminals would perform useful work in the new regions. "A new place and new circumstances will change their habits, and the need for food will make them seek to learn useful work." [44]

The northern sea route, according to Lomonosov, should aid the development not only of the economic, but also of the cultural ties of Russia with the eastern countries and the growth of her defensive strength and political might. "Thus the road and hope are cut off for others, and Russian power will grow through Siberia and the Arctic Ocean." [45]

The formulation of the idea of a northern sea route shows the grandiosity of his thinking and his brilliant foresight. The validity of his basic plan was confirmed by later study of the Arctic and by the practice of polar navigation. However, the solution of the problem of the northern sea route was not within the resources of tsarist Russia. Moreover, Alaska, united to Russia by the heroic toil of the Russian people, was sold in 1867 to the USA by the tsarist government for the paltry sum of 7.2 million dollars. In 1912 there was even a plan for surrender of the northern sea route to English and American capitalists as a concession.[46]

The problem of the northern sea route in all its breadth was posed and solved only under the Soviets. Several months after the establish-

[40] *Ibid.*, VI, 494.
[41] Lomonosov, *Sochineniia* (1934), VII, 261.
[42] Lomonosov, *Sochineniia* (1902), V, 90.
[43] Lomonosov, *Polnoe sobranie sochinenii,* VI, 425.
[44] *Ibid.*, VI, 494–5.
[45] *Ibid.*, VI, 498.
[46] *Lomonosov. Sbornik statei i materialov*, pp. 284–5.

ment of Soviet power, on July 2, 1918, Lenin signed a decree organizing an expedition to investigate a northern sea route. In 1932 the icebreaker *Sibiryakov* sailed on the first nonstop voyage in history from Archangel to the Pacific by the northern sea route. Thanks to the great toil and heroism of the Soviet people, the northern sea route became a normal integrated part of Soviet socialist economy. The realization in the USSR of the idea of a northern sea route on a scale immeasurably broader than that planned by Lomonosov only emphasizes the genius of his idea. Only in the Soviet period was the great economic, political, and cultural importance of the northern sea route fully realized.

Economic-Geographical and Statistical Works

For the further development of the national economy of Russia, a study of her economic and geographic structure was necessary. Development of basic branches of Russian industry—mining, metallurgy, metal-processing, and textiles—required research into their locations, study of raw material and fuel bases, knowledge of routes of supply of raw materials, fuel, auxiliary materials, and transport of finished products.

Agriculture, producing food for the population, including the increasing non-agricultural part, and raw materials for industry as well, especially for the textile and leather industries, became more and more a commodity agriculture. With the growth of commodity agriculture the need for a study of the flora and fauna of the country, its soil, fertility, and crops, its markets and means of transportation became more pressing. The growth of industry and commodity agriculture, the development of all-Russian and local markets, the increase of exports, the agricultural and industrial colonization of outlying areas, and the search for new land and sea routes, all spurred the quest for economic and geographical knowledge of the country, its regions, and its lines of communication.

The great work of preparing a number of geographical maps, to be combined in an atlas, was assigned to the Department of Geography of the Academy of Sciences, which from March, 1758, was headed by Lomonosov. The "Russian Atlas" published by the Academy of Sciences in 1745 did not satisfy the great scholar.[47] He viewed the preparation of an atlas of Russia as no mere geographic task. He thought that it should show the economy of a country, "so that the internal state

[47] See Biliarskii, *op. cit.*, p. 396.

economy would benefit." [48] Lomonosov was the first to advance the idea and to develop a plan for an economic and geographic atlas of Russia. The work, including cartographic and textual material, was to be in reality an economic geography of Russia. It was to include not only extensive cartographic material, but also a political and economic description of Russia, compiled by statistical methods. Lomonosov viewed the preparation of the atlas primarily as a great project in the study of the national economy.

To obtain the necessary data Lomonosov in 1759 prepared a statistical questionnaire ("form of inquiry," as he called it) containing a number of inquiries regarding trade, crafts, "factories," and so on. It contained thirteen points, most of which were economic in nature:

"1. Is the town surrounded with stone or wooden walls, earthen ramparts or moats?

2. Are there many entrances to the city; which churches are stone and which wood; how many *verst* wide is the city?

3. On what river or lake is the town situated, and on which side of the river or lake by the compass?

4. On those rivers, what vessels sail in spring and in midsummer?

5. When are markets held, and from where and with what goods do the majority of [people] come, and on which day of the trade week?

6. What is grown in the vicinity of the town, and what are its industries?

7. In which crafts do the people chiefly engage?

8. What and where are the plants in the city or village, such as silver, gold, copper, or ore; likewise factories?

9. If there are ancient manuscripts in the city, send in an authenticated copy for the compilation of a history of Russia.

10. How many people are in the village or hamlet, according to the census?

11. How many chimneys?

12. Are there shops and fairs?

13. Where are water mills, saw or grain?" [49]

In the finished text, sent to localities, points ten and eleven were not included, evidently because of the approaching third census (1764), which would provide more accurate data. The majority of points were developed and new ones added. The number of "inquiry points"

---

[48] *Ibid.*, p. 604.

[49] See V. F. Gnucheva, *Geograficheskii, departament Akademii nauk XVIII veka* [The Department of Geography of the Academy of Sciences in the XVIII Century] (Moscow-Leningrad: AS USSR, 1946), p. 73; see also *Lomonosov. Sbornik statei i materialov*, pp. 257–9.

increased to thirty and were mainly concerned with economic questions: for example, on sowing, harvests, livestock, trade wharfs.

The printed questionnaire was finally sent out only in the beginning of 1761, and in January, 1763, Lomonosov reported that "four volumes of answers have been collected, and we already have a circumstantial topography of half the state." [50] Answers to the questionnaire continued to be received for almost an entire decade. Only after several years following Lomonosov's death were they processed and (supplemented by materials of the Nobility Corps of the Land Forces) partly published under the title *Topographical Materials Serving as a Complete Geographical Description of the Russian Empire.* The four parts of the first volume, which were published in 1771–1774, described the provinces of the huge Moscow gubernia and part of the Novgorod gubernia.

To obtain materials for the preparation of maps, statistical tables, and the text of the atlas, Lomonosov proposed in 1746 to use the help of the census (a census of the population subject to head tax). The inseparable connection between Lomonosov's economic and geographic researches and the application of the statistical method also found expression in his proposal to re-issue the atlas with corrections every twenty years, that is, corresponding to the periods of the census. He attached special importance to geographical expeditions to obtain source material. The results of the expedition of the Academy of Sciences between 1768–74 showed how correct he was in this regard.

This atlas of Russia, judged by the plan and progress of the work, should have considerably surpassed the atlas of 1745. In addition to greater accuracy and wealth of content, the basic advantage of Lomonosov's project should have been its economic-geographical character. The opposition of his enemies interfered with his program, and his departure from the Department of Geography, caused by their intrigues, completely halted his work on the new atlas.

To complete the cartographic work, Lomonosov felt it especially necessary to compile "an appropriate description . . . of Russian products." He requested a variety of economic-statistical data from colleges and government offices. This information covered an economic-statistical survey of the entire country and included data on native materials for ship building and arms production. The program also anticipated receipt of data on equipping the army. A number of questions dealt with foreign trade, clarifying "what kind of domestic goods was sent abroad via Russian ports or overland." Finally, several

[50] Biliarskii, *op. cit.*, p. 582.

points of the program posed questions on the nature and location of industrial enterprises.

The results of this preparatory work for a Russian atlas should have been presented, according to Lomonosov, in the form of an "Economic Lexicon of Russian Products with an Indication of their Internal and Foreign Destination, with an Appropriate Map." Lomonosov tried to collect the "names of all Russian goods" produced in agriculture ("naturally") and in industry ("artificially"). Each product was to include data on quality, price, place and volume of production, markets, and supply routes.[51] This comprehensive study was begun in the second half of 1763. Lomonosov personally accomplished the first stage of the work: he compiled "an alphabetical register of Russian products, natural and handmade." [52] Death interrupted his work on the "Economic Lexicon."

The economic tenor of the geographic works of Lomonosov is emphasized by the terms he introduced into scientific use: "economic geography" and "economic map." In his opinion, geography, as well as cartography, should be "combined with the knowledge of state economy." [53] In 1763 he proposed a plan for publishing the political and economic geography of Russia. He must rightfully be acknowledged as the founder of Russian economic geography.

Lomonosov also envisaged the publication of a special Russian economic newspaper: in 1759 he proposed the *Domestic Russian News.* This newspaper would satisfy the desire for economic information of all state organizations ("in all offices of the state") and of private individuals ("private persons"). He emphasized the special need for such information for trade. The newspaper would provide information on surpluses and shortages of grain, on harvests, on the export and import of goods, and so on. To assure current information in the *News,* the Senate would issue an order "for supplying the required news from gubernias and cities" on the basis of a plan prepared by the Academy of Sciences. In addition to economic information, Lomonosov proposed to print news of a general nature, as in a regular newspaper ("print everything which is printed as news in the usual papers"). Lomonosov proposed that the publication of the *Domestic Russian News* be entrusted to the Academy of Sciences.[54] This cor-

[51] *Ibid.,* pp. 611–3.

[52] Added in Appendix No. 19 in a collection of materials selected by A. Budilovich, *M. V. Lomonosov kak naturalist i filolog* [M. V. Lomonosov as Naturalist and Philologist] (1869), pp. 23–5.

[53] Biliarskii, *op. cit.,* p. 609.

[54] *Ibid.,* pp. 392–3.

responded to his conviction of the practical mission of science and that the Academy of Sciences should aid the economic development of the country.

The plan for a Russian economic newspaper was not realized during Lomonosov's life, nor in the years immediately following his death. It is uncertain whether the decree signed by Catherine II (1764)—"for the benefit of trade, the Commerce College is to introduce hereafter printed lists of prices of goods, called price lists . . ." [55]—prepared under the influence of Lomonosov, for its content shows that Catherine's decree realized only a small part of Lomonosov's plan. This again indicates the misunderstanding by the government of the feudal empire of Lomonosov's economic ideas, which reflected the need to develop trade.

Lomonosov also wanted to establish a Russian scientific economic journal. Not long before his death, he proposed that the Academy of Sciences, in place of its periodical *Monthly Works and News of Scientific Matters,* publish a special economic and natural science journal —*Economic and Physical Works.*" [56] This plan, also unrealized, once again points to his high evaluation of economic knowledge and his demand for a study of the economy of Russia.

"On the Preservation and Increase of the Russian People"

Lomonosov intended to outline his economic views in a systematic form. In a letter to I. I. Shuvalov on November 1, 1761, he wrote, "all the ideas noted separately at various times could be classified, it seems to me, under the following headings: 1) On the Increase and Preservation of the Russian People. 2) On the Elimination of Idleness. 3) On the Improvement of Customs and the Increased Enlightenment of the People. 4) On the Improvement of Agriculture. 5) On the Improvement and Increase of Crafts and Arts. 6) On the Improved Utilization of Trade. 7) On the Improvement of State Economy. 8) On Preserving Military Arts During a Prolonged Period of Peace." [57]

Thus in his plan of outlining his economic views Lomonosov proceeds with questions of policy concerning the population and the productive use of its labor; then he passes on to what should be done in the branches of the national economy (agriculture, industry, trade)

[55] *PSZ,* XVI, No. 12009, p. 491.
[56] See Biliarskii, *op. cit.,* p. 737.
[57] Lomonosov, *Polnoe sobranie sochinenii,* VI, 383.

and in the national economy as a whole ("On the Improvement of State Economy"); and finally he emphasizes the need for continuous concern for the armed forces of the state in peacetime.

A plan of Lomonosov's works on socio-political and economic questions appears also in a holographic manuscript (undated).[58] It includes the same eight themes, the titles of which were made more precise and concrete in Lomonosov's letter of November 1, 1761. The manuscript is probably an earlier version of that on socio-political and economic questions. In the manuscript the first-named subject is the same as in the letter of November 1, 1761. In the former Lomonosov entitles this theme "On the Preservation and Increase of the People" while in the latter, worded more precisely, he emphasizes that it is not abstract and about people in general, but about "the Russian people." The manuscript contains additional themes, which evolve from the basic ones. For the economic historian special interest is found in the theme, "Orientation Academy" (referring to heading five, "On Trade, Especially with Foreign Peoples) and the themes, "Economic Geography," "Economic Maps," "On Forests," (referring to heading seven, "On State Economy").

In addition to the first "chapter" on population policy, Lomonosov's "Notes" on the obligations of the clergy have come down to us.[59] The content of the "Notes" represents part of the proposed heading, "On the Improvement of Customs and Increased Enlightenment of the People." [60] In the "Notes" Lomonosov sharply criticizes the priests and their parasitic life and activity and suggests that churchmen be compelled to occupy themselves with the enlightenment of the people.

In the letter of November 1, 1761 Lomonosov fully developed the first of the proposed basic socio-economic themes, and in the "Notes" he partially completed the third theme. In regard to the rest of the headings, no information exists to indicate whether they were written by Lomonosov and then lost to posterity,[61] or whether they remained only as titles of proposed works. The letter to Shuvalov, mentioned

---

[58] See L. B. Modzalevskii, ed., *Rukopisi Lomonosova v Akademii nauk SSSR. Nauchnoe opisanie* [Lomonosov's Manuscripts in the Academy of Sciences of the USSR. Scientific Description] (Moscow-Leningrad: 1937), p. 13; Lomonosov, *Polnoe sobranie sochinenii,* VI, 379.

[59] *Ibid.,* VI, 405–8.

[60] *Ibid.,* VI, 600.

[61] Literally on the second day after Lomonosov's death Count Orlov, on Catherine II's orders, sealed his [Lomonosov's] office. Taubert, who informed Miller about this, noted that "there is no doubt that it contains papers which they do not wish to fall into alien hands." (See P. Pekarskii, *Dopolnitelnye izvestiia dlia biografii Lomonosova* [Supplementary Information for Lomonosov's Biography] (St. Petersburg: 1865), pp. 88–9.

above, contains the outline of only the first heading—"On the Preservation and Increase of the Russian People." [62] Lomonosov thought this a "most important problem" because "the greatness, might, and wealth of every state" consist not of vast, sparsely populated territory, but of a large and industrious population.

The problem of population posed by Lomonosov in this letter attracted the attention of statesmen and writers of the eighteenth century not only in Russia, but in Western Europe. The development of commercial agriculture and manufacturing required many workers. Losses of a considerable part of the population as a result of wars, religious persecutions, famine, epidemics, illness, and high infant mortality caused great difficulties. In Western Europe scientific treatises proposed various measures for preserving and increasing the population, including monetary rewards for large families, authorization of extra-marital relations, and even polygamy.

Politicians and writers on population in Western Europe were

---

[62] Lomonosov's letter to I. I. Shuvalov remained for more than a half century unknown not only to a broad strata of society, but even to scholars—specialists. In 1819 this letter, with important omissions, was published by V. Olin in his *Journal of Ancient and New Literature* (Vol. 5 (March), No. 6), and simultaneously he published it in a separate brochure called *Letter of the Late Mikhail Vasilevich Lomonosov to Ivan Ivanovich Shuvalov* (St. Petersburg: 1819). The Tsarist government was displeased by the appearance of the letter in print; censor Yatsenkov almost lost his post for allowing its publication.

In 1842 Lomonosov's letter was published by M. P. Pogodin in *Moskovitianin* (No. 1, *Materials for a History of Russian History in General, and of Russian Literature*), from which it was reprinted in the works of Lomonosov edited by A. Smirdin (Vol. 1). In both editions there were even more omissions than in Olin's.

Lomonosov's letter was first published in full in the third issue of *Conversations in the Society of Lovers of Russian Literature at the Imperial Moscow University* in 1871, i.e., 110 years after its writing, according to the copy of N. S. Tikhonravov.

Two years later the letter was again published in full in *Russkaia Starina* [Russian Antiquity] (October, 1873), following a copy presented to the editors by the Academician P. P. Pekarskii.

Lomonosov's letter to Shuvalov, not having, naturally, a title, upon publication in various editions was usually headed by the name of the first chapter (indicated in the manuscript and letter), "The Preservation and Increase of the Russian People."

In the indicated full publications of the letter there are varied uses of words and phrases.

Publication of the letter was made from copies, since the original no longer exists. Proof that the letter is Lomonosov's is his (above mentioned) handwritten manuscript. The original manuscript is not preserved. A lithographed facsimile is in the Archive of the Academy of Sciences of the USSR, Collection 20, Inventory 4, No. 10, Sheet 3. In the manuscript Lomonosov enumerates the themes of his works, among which the theme of the letter is first.

divided into two groups: those who favored the growth of population and those who feared overpopulation. The physiocrats belonged to the latter group. They thought that "progressive increase of the products of the land should precede progressive increase in population" (Mercier de la Rivière). The mercantilists were in the first group. They defended the necessity of the growth of population as a reservoir of military power for conquering new markets, as a means of increasing the volume of production and the export of goods, as a source of fiscal revenues, and so forth. Marshal Vauban in his "Plan for a Royal Tithe" (1707) showed that growth of "that part of the population which achieves the means of existence by the labor of its own hands" is the basic essence and development of the state. Voltaire, Montesquieu, and Rousseau were also of the first group.

In Russia at that time the problem of population had traits characteristic of a country with a feudal economy, but the development of bourgeois, capitalist relations had already begun. The problem of population was linked with the question of the economic and legal positions of a population whose majority was enserfed. Objectively the problem of population in Russia was thus inseparably linked with that of serfdom.

Approaching the issue of population, Lomonosov thought that the economic and political growth of the country depended on a large industrious population whose growth was a necessary condition for progressive development. His suggestions, directed at the preservation of the Russian people and the increase of their numbers, were based on the principle of the attainment of general happiness and the natural right of each man to happiness. He spoke of his ideas on this question as "striving toward the growth of the general good." [63] He thought the state should realize these objectives by using governmental measures whose importance and effect he exaggerated. Lomonosov did not consider the question of serfdom as the main obstacle to the realization of the measures he proposed. Hence the internal contradiction of his discourse on the preservation and increase of the Russian people.

He was opposed to everything that "is harmful to the growth of population" and leads to its decrease. He demanded prohibition of the "unequal marriage" then practiced in the villages, where "young boys incapable of marital obligations are married to grown women" or when "a very old man marries a very young girl." Lomonosov also

---

[63] Lomonosov, *Polnoe sobranie sochinenii,* VI, 383.

demanded prohibition of forced marriages, "for when there is no love there is no hope of children." [64]

Under serfdom such proposals were unrealistic. Unequal and especially forced marriages were inseparably linked to serfdom, under which a pomeshchik had the right to arrange the marriages of peasants. It is necessary to emphasize, however, that Lomonosov's declarations against unequal and forced marriages were made just before new privileges were extended to the nobles under Peter III and Catherine II and were contrary to the interests of the nobility.

Lomonosov also demanded that men under fifty years of age and women under forty-five be forbidden to enter monasteries. The proposal "to forbid cowls" before a certain age was reached was, indeed, bold, especially if we take into consideration the negative attitude of the then influential clergy toward Lomonosov.

Having considered the obstacles to population growth, Lomonosov turned to what is harmful to the preservation of the Russian people. He first recommended measures to lower infant mortality. He dwelt on the fate of illegitimate children and developed the idea expressed in the decrees of Peter I of opening "foundling homes." These decrees were not put into practice. Lomonosov wrote of the necessity of "establishing charity homes" where "children of shame" would study "crafts" and "arts." Thus, according to Lomonosov, in these homes illegitimate children would be raised and educated so as to be qualified workers, who were then needed in Russian industry. Such homes were soon established in Moscow (1764) and Petersburg (1765).

Lomonosov spoke with deep sorrow of the inadequate medical aid, organized according "to rules dictated by medical science." Lack of medical care leads to a situation in which "many who might have received treatment die of neglect." [65] Lomonosov indicated the necessity of providing the population and army with an adequate supply of doctors and a network of pharmacies. A considerable number of Russians should be sent abroad immediately to receive medical training, and foreign doctors and pharmacists should be employed in Russia to teach Russians. Lomonosov desired strongly the development of native medical education and the preparation of native doctors, medical assistants, and pharmacists. Considering the almost total lack of doctors in Russia at that time, Lomonosov insisted that medical knowledge be spread among the people. He proposed the publication of popular medical literature, "so that priests and literate people can inform

[64] *Ibid.*, VI, 384–5.
[65] *Ibid.*, VI, 397.

themselves and help others." In 1763 pharmacies were opened in several cities, the title of doctor of medicine was established, and the Medical Office was reorganized into the Medical College.

Lomonosov dwelt also on the influence of food on the increase and health of the people. He compared the Lapps, who ate fish almost exclusively, with the "Samoyeds," who consumed mainly meat. Lomonosov said the Lapps are short in stature, "and it is very rare that they can be used as soldiers." Contrasting the Samoyeds with the Lapps, he noted their differences in height and stockiness. While the Lapps were limited in number, the Samoyeds represented numerically a considerable mass of the population; their land was more thickly settled than that of the Lapps. Lomonosov concluded that "those Russian areas are more populous where more livestock flourishes." [66]

Lomonosov opposed self-starvation during fasts and gluttony during the Easter and carnival seasons. The Commandments require men to love "God with all their heart (not with their stomach)." Lomonosov recommended, therefore, in the interest of preserving the health of the people, that changes be made in holidays and fasts.

He pointed out the baneful effects of "plagues, fires, floods, and frosts," on the population, but did not mention famine, which was then one of the main causes for the high death rate of the peasantry. Lomonosov did not link this high mortality rate to serfdom.

Investigating the prevalence of fights and robbery, which depleted the population, he saw the absence of a definite survey of the land as a contributing factor. Actually, murders over disputed territory were then so widespread that in 1752 a special decree, "On Ceasing Fights and Quarrels over Disputed Lands," was issued.[67] Many statesmen of that time, and especially Peter Ivanovich Shuvalov, insisted on a "general survey." But an effort made in 1752 [68] met rigid opposition from the pomeshchiki. Many law suits arose between pomeshchiki, and the survey was halted. Supporting a general land survey again in 1761 as a means to reduce violence and bloodshed, Lomonosov proposed a palliative and timely measure. Catherine II in 1765 issued a decree establishing a Commission on state surveying "for the peace of the state and people." [69] But even the accomplishment of a general survey could not wholly eliminate conflicts and slaughter. Under serf con-

[66] *Ibid.*, VI, 394.

[67] *PSZ*, XIII, No. 9932.

[68] *Ibid.*, XIII, No. 9948.

[69] *Ibid.*, XVII, No. 12347; see also No. 12570.

ditions every survey, always carried out to the detriment of the peasant masses, unavoidably brought new quarrels accompanied by more loss of life.

The decrease in population also resulted from flight—the immemorial form of class struggle of the serfs. Escapes were especially rife in the Baltic region, where the German nobility ruled and the yoke of serfdom was even heavier than in other places in the Russian empire. "We know," wrote Catherine II, "that the number of escapes from Lifland is so great that many places have been ruined." [70] Flights from other places in the empire also increased considerably. Escapees often headed for Poland. Through their agents, Polish nobles promised the fugitives every exemption, only later to enslave and subject them to even greater exploitation than before. Lomonosov spoke of the great proportions these flights had assumed in the first third of the eighteenth century.

The government took only repressive measures against the escaping peasants. The measures then proposed in the various plans of Russian statesmen were also of this nature (P. I. Shuvalov, P. I. Panin, Ia. I. Sivers, and others). Lomonosov, however, cognizant of the reasons for flight, placed the responsibility "mostly on pomeshchiki oppressions and on military drafts." It was wrong to combat escapes exclusively by punitive acts. He stated that "it is better to act with gentleness." Instead of repression, he recommended the reduction of taxes for the people living on the Polish border and removal of the military draft," and these reforms should be spread over the whole state." [71]

Lomonosov correctly attributed the causes for flight to the social phenomena intrinsically linked to serfdom; but the steps he proposed to counteract this situation did not touch the base of serfdom. It is necessary to repeat, however, that Lomonosov wanted to initiate reforms of an economic and political nature to ease the situation of the peasants.

Lomonosov also advised encouragement of immigration to settle the wastelands, since immense Russia is "in a position to accommodate whole nations within its safe heartland and to provide all the necessary things of life which require only increased labor for their useful production." [72] Immigration to Russia at that time was fairly exten-

[70] *Osmnadtsatyi vek. Istoricheskii sbornik* [Eighteenth Century. A Historical Collection] (Moscow: 1869), Bk. III, p. 188.

[71] Lomonosov, *Polnoe sobranie sochinenii,* VI, 401–2.

[72] *Ibid.,* VI, 402.

sive. In the 1760's Serbs, Bulgarians, Macedonians, and others had settled in the Ukraine. The government took measures for the voluntary return of escapees from Poland.[73] We have no data to confirm that these steps were due to the direct influence of Lomonosov. The adoption of these measures, however, soon after Lomonosov wrote his letter on the preservation and increase of the Russian population, confirms that he touched on a timely question and that he offered a practical solution. He thought that the realization of his proposals would mean not only an increase in the birthrate, but also a decrease in the death rate, curtailment of escapes abroad, return of escapees, and immigration into Russia, all of which would lead to an enlargement of the population.

In this particular letter, Lomonosov's motives were directed at improving the situation of the peasantry. Although he desired to improve the well-being of the masses, he did not comprehend that these proposals were unattainable under the conditions of serfdom, nor did he raise an angry voice of protest against the system.

The discourse on preservation and increase of the Russian people is the first Russian treatise on population policy. In prerevolutionary literature efforts were made to present his original works as an imitation of West European ideas.[74] It is impossible to deny that Lomonosov was acquainted with the foreign literature on this subject. His personal library included the work of the German populationist, Bell,[75] but it was not Lomonosov's acquaintance with West European literature which caused his interest in this problem. By observing Russian life, reflecting on it, reading Russian (for example, Pososhkov) and foreign authors, Lomonosov developed his own original thesis for "correcting the faults" of Russian reality.

His measures were concerned with separate phenomena of serfdom. He tried to eliminate these without affecting the foundations of serfdom—the main obstacle to the preservation and increase of the Russian people. As a result of such internal contradictions, such measures could not be considered radical and realistic. They had only a pallia-

---

[73] See *PSZ,* XVI, No. 11815.

[74] See I. K. Sukhopliuev, "Vzgliady Lomonosova na politiku narodonaseleniia" [Lomonosov's Views on the Population Policy], *Lomonosovskii sbornik* [Lomonosov's Collection] (St. Petersburg: 1911); I. A. Tikhomirov, "O trudakh M. V. Lomonosova po politicheskoi ekonomii" [Lomonosov's Works on Political Economy], *Zhurnal Ministerstva narodnogo prosveshcheniia,* [Journal of the Ministry of Public Education], New Series, Pt. 49 (February, 1914).

[75] See a list of books of Lomonosov's personal library which is included in a collection edited by A. Budilovich, *Lomonosov kak pisatel* [Lomonosov As Author] (St. Petersburg: 1871), p. 268.

tive nature, although they were directed toward the progressive economic development of the country.

Lomonosov's great creativity was aimed at the solution of the problems resulting from the development of his native land. To assure Russia's economic and political independence, he emphasized the development of native production, particularly of industry. In the development of industry he attached primary importance to those branches connected with the production and processing of nonferrous metals: mining, metallurgy, and metal processing.

While he defended the necessity of industrial advancement, he was also concerned about agriculture. He constantly emphasized the great economic importance of trade and its development, recognizing that the growth of native production would lead to the development of internal and foreign trade. Since he considered the latter such an important factor in the wealth of nations, Lomonosov saw the need for state aid in order to promote the trade balance of Russia. He was deeply convinced that Russia, endowed with great export possibilities and with sea exits on international trade routes, could and should become the foremost commercial power of the world.

Lomonosov believed that the state should be the guiding power in economic development. Like the preceding Russian thinkers and statesmen (Pososhkov, Fedor Saltykov, Tatishchev, and others), he advocated active government interference in economic life. He charted a broad program of development for Russia's productive forces and her markets, but disregarded the problem of serfdom, which had already begun to be a brake on such development. Such is the contradiction of the economic views of Lomonosov, who tried to act in behalf of the progressive economic development of his country.

His ideas contained some mercantile elements: an exaggerated presentation of the role of the feudal-absolute state in the development of production and markets, of the function of foreign trade, of the importance of an active foreign trade policy, and so forth. But, on the whole, his economic views were not mercantilistic.

According to the mercantilists, the wealth of the country centered in precious metals, while for Lomonosov it centered in the abundance "of things necessary for life." The mercantilists considered the aim of economic policy to be the accumulation of precious metals and money in the country; for Lomonosov it was the "satisfaction of the subjects," that is, primarily the satisfaction of the material needs of the population.

The mercantilists defended mainly the development of the export branches of the processing industry; in this regard Colbert's protection of the development of the textile industry is characteristic. For Lomonosov the development of the mining industry and metallurgy were of prime importance. Ferrous metal had an important place in Russian exports at the time. Lomonosov, however, called for development of metal production, not for its export. The aim of increased production of metal, according to Lomonosov, was above all to satisfy the internal needs of the country.

Finally, according to the mercantilists, the source of profits and wealth of the country is foreign trade, and therefore it is necessary to export as much as possible of the products of native industry, especially those of the processing industry. But according to Lomonosov, exports should develop only when "domestic surplus" exists, that is, when the personal needs of the population and the production needs of the state economy are satisfied.

In regard to the basic productive force of the economy of Russia at that time—the peasantry—Lomonosov proposed measures to improve the situation within the limits of serfdom, which in itself was the decisive reason for the terrible situation of the peasantry. This view reveals the historically conditioned limitation of the socio-political philosophy of the great Russian scientist, thinker, and statesman, who was in all other ways immeasurably ahead of his contemporaries.[76]

---

[76] All great thinkers of the XVIII Century were historically limited. "Great thinkers of the XVIII Century—as well as the thinkers of all preceeding centuries—were unable to move beyond the limits which were placed around them by their epochs." Marx and Engels, *Sochineniia,* XIV, 358.

PART V
THE BEGINNING OF THE DECAY OF THE FEUDAL SERF ORDER AND THE EMERGENCE OF CAPITALISM

CHAPTER 15. *Basic Economic Problems and the Course of Economic Thought from the 1760's to the 1790's.*

The Economy of Russia in the Second Half of the Eighteenth Century. Class Struggle

The development of the productive forces of feudal-serf Russia in the second half of the eighteenth century led to the growth of the social division of labor, not only between town and village, but also to a considerable degree between the regions of the vast country. This progress increased the commodity economy and developed the internal market.

The production of the main branch of the feudal economy—agriculture—grew, and the volume of agricultural products increased immensely. The growth of agricultural production was achieved by the expansion of the cultivated areas in the old settlements and by colonization of the borderlands, especially in the south and southeast of European Russia. In the old agricultural regions, where the nonblack soil gubernias predominated (Moscow, Vladimir, Smolensk, Tver, Yaroslav), the three-field system obtained. Productivity under this fallow field method of farming remained low as a result of the prevalence of serfdom.

In the development of agricultural production the serf economy played a decisive role, both in the obrok, and in the barshchina system of serf exploitation. The lord's land, like the peasant's allotment, was cultivated by peasants, who were oppressed by need and humiliated by personal dependence. The crudest and simplest techniques were used in production.

Low crop productivity resulted in intolerable conditions. Pomeshchiki began to talk about "agricultural impoverishment," and they increased exploitation of the serfs by raising the rate of the obrok, augmenting the number of barshchina, and transferring the work of the peasants to a monthly basis.

The black land regions, which had a grain surplus but lacked suitable means of transportation, were forced to be satisfied with the limited local market. Therefore the processing of grain (mainly into alcohol) in the area of its production took on great importance. This processing spread not only in the black land areas, but in the nonblack soil region as well.

In the nonblack soil districts agriculture alone could not provide the peasants with sufficient means of subsistence, much less the revenue to pay feudal rent to the pomeshchik and taxes to the state. As a result, in the peasant economy of these regions nonagricultural occupations developed, and many peasants took flight. The bulk of the small industrial producers of the country was located in the village. For them industry was either a side line (supplementary to agriculture) or a basic occupation.

The production of small goods necessarily presupposes the existence of trade capital and the activity of the speculator. Accordingly, entrepreneurs emerged from among the craftsmen and the village well-to-do. Small producers, who were personally dependent upon the pomeshchik or the feudal-absolute state, became also economically enslaved by trade capital. The trade capitalists, gradually transforming small producers into hired workers at home or in the shop, developed into industrial capitalists and manufacturers. Manufacturing furthered the productive specialization of entire regions.

In industry the most advanced branches were metallurgy, metalprocessing and textile production. By the middle of the eighteenth century the Central and Southern Urals were "a productive region, grandiose for the time not only on a Russian, but on a world scale." [1] From the beginning of the second quarter of the eighteenth century until its end, Russia held first place in the world in the production of ferrous metals. This was not only quantitative superiority. Russian iron surpassed English iron in quality, and iron was exported in increasing quantities, mainly to England. "In the eighteenth century," notes Lenin, "iron was one of the principal articles of Russian ex-

---

[1] P. G. Liubomirov, *Ocherki po isotrii russkoi promyshlennosti, XVII, XVIII, i nachalo XIX veka* [Outlines of the History of Russian Industry, XVII, XVIII, and the Beginning of the XIX Centuries] (Moscow: Gospolitizdat, 1947), p. 382.

port . . ." [2] The brand then put on the iron of the Urals, "Old Fox," was well known in Western Europe, especially in England.

The state and some private factories in the Urals supplied primarily the needs of the government, especially in arms and ammunition. A majority of the private factories in the Urals worked mainly for export; only a few produced for the internal market. The metallurgical and metal-processing factories outside the Urals, while continuing to provide for state needs, turned more and more to the internal market as an outlet for their iron, cast-iron pots, and other iron goods.

Light industry, particularly textiles, developed in various places. Its chief center was Moscow, with its vast adjacent region of peasant industries. Petersburg industry grew in importance. Other great areas of textile production were the Ivanovo-Voznesensk (linen and, at the end of the eighteenth century, cotton), the Kineshmo-Kostroma, and the Yaroslav regions (linen production). Cloth factories increased in the Kazan, Voronezh and Tambov locales. Numerous leather, tallow, and candle factories operated in the central Volga territory.

The struggle between heavy and light industry and between capitalist and serf forms of industry produced further development. Serf industry was represented primarily by votchina enterprises—"manorial factories"; they were based on exploitation of serf labor in the votchiny and used raw materials produced on the votchina itself. Possessional factories also used forced labor. Their owners were mainly merchants (not landlords, who owned the serfs as personal property).[3] The factories belonging to the merchants and peasants and operating with hired labor were capitalistic. V. I. Lenin notes that the transformation of manpower into goods, and the exploitation of hired labor are basic in capitalistic relations: "in the development of capitalism the degree of the spread of hired labor is of the utmost importance." [4]

The conditions of serfdom left a deep impression on the capitalist relations developing within it and invested them with a feudal form. The entrepreneur who was a peasant was not legally a free owner of captial. Being a serf, he could not obtain an enterprise in his own name and was not its legal owner. A worker who hired himself to the factory and who was usually a quit-rent peasant of a feudal-serf state or of a pomeshchik was not the owner of his own labor. The quit-rent

[2] Lenin, *Sochineniia,* III, 424.

[3] Under pressure from the nobles, on March 12, 1752, a decree limited the acquisition of people by the factories (*PSZ,* XIII, No. 9954) and on March 29, 1762, and August 8, 1762, decrees abolished possessional law, *ibid.,* XV, No. 11490; XVI, No. 11638. Under the possessional law only those factories which purchased people before 1762 remained.

[4] Lenin, *op. cit.,* III, 509.

peasant sold his labor with the permission of the person to whom he belonged. But in relation to the employer, the owner of the factory, the quit-rent peasant acted like a hired laborer.

Among the classes of feudal society, the struggle for different forms of industry was motivated by their various interests. The nobility defended the development of the votchina industry and upheld the establishment of peasant industries and factories which increased the quit-rent income of the pomeshchiki. At the same time the nobility opposed merchant factories, whether based on hired labor, that is, capitalistic, or based on serfdom, that is, possessional. On the other hand, the merchants supported the development of merchant factories —both capitalist and serf (possessional). The merchants also fought the votchina industry and peasant manufactures, because they feared their competition.

The importance of serf and capitalist manufactures and the struggle between them differed in various stages of historical development. In the eighteenth century serfdom helped the Urals to attain great heights. "In those days serfdom was at the basis of the flourishing Urals and contributed greatly to its domination not only in Russia, but also in Europe." [5]

At the beginning of the eighteenth century during the early stages of heavy industry in Russia, serf manufacturing did not as yet have a conservative aspect. Later, in the struggle with capitalist manufacturing, as bourgeois relations developed within the serf economy and its deterioration increased, serf manufacturing turned into a conservative, and then a reactionary, force.

The progressive role of capitalist manufacture was enhanced as serf industry and the institution of serfdom declined. The growth of commodity agriculture and the development of industrial production, especially of manufactures, intensified the social division of labor between regions and between cities and villages. This increased specialization led to stronger ties in the sphere of circulation. The internal market became nationwide, as well as regional.

The growth of the all-Russian market was expressly evident in the ever increasing trade turnover in such centers as Moscow, Petersburg, Nizhnii-Novgorod, Tula, Kaluga, Yaroslav, Kazan, Astrakhan, Archangel, and other great Russian cities. This progress was also indicated by the growing volumes handled at the Makarev, Troitsk, Irbit, Irkutsk, Kiakhta, Kiev, Archangel, and other great fairs, which served not only adjoining, but also distant regions.

---

[5] *Ibid.*, III, 424.

Foreign trade prospered and eventually surpassed internal trade in volume of turnover. Annual exports increased from 4.2 million rubles in 1726 to 12 million in 1763–65. Toward the end of the century it reached 67.7 million rubles (1796). Agricultural products such as hemp, flax, their seeds and oils, fats, raw leather, and furs were the chief exports. The export of grain was still not very large, primarily because good means of transportation were lacking between grain-producing regions and ports. Of industrial products, iron and linen cloth, which were sent especially to England, played the main role in foreign trade.[6]

Imports into Russia consisted chiefly of objects for the personal use of the nobles–pomeshchiki and the upper merchant class. They included such items as sugar, wine, coffee, cloth, brocade, and silk. Of goods for industrial use, a great part of the imports were dyes and raw silk for the textile industry. Other goods for industrial needs occupied a relatively insignificant place. In the second half of the eighteenth century the development of Russian industry was based more and more on native raw materials. The internal market for metals and technical agriculture crops expanded.

In the foreign trade of Russia with Western Europe, exports (especially of raw materials) exceeded imports (primarily of finished goods). In trade with Eastern countries, however, Russia, importing raw materials (mainly for the textile industry) and exporting finished goods, had a passive trade balance. The active trade balance with Western Europe, exports plus imports comprising at that time up to 85 per cent of Russian foreign trade, made possible the general level of foreign trade activity, as well as the negative trade balance of Russia with the East. Central Asia constituted the main market in the trade of Russia with the East. It provided the necessary cotton for the Rus-

---

[6] See Semenov, *Izuchenie istoricheskikh svedenii o rossisskoi vneshnei torgovle i promyshlennosti s poloviny XVII stoletiia po 1858 god.* [A Study of Historical Data on Russian Foreign Trade and Industry from the Middle of the XVII Century to 1858] (St. Petersburg: 1859), Pt. III, Appendices 1–4; V. I. Pokrovskii, ed., *Sbornik svedenii po istorii i statistike vneshnei torgovli Rossii* [A Collection of Data on the History and Statistics of Russia's Foreign Trade] (St. Petersburg: 1902), I, xxi–xxviii.

The increasing domestic demand for iron (as a result of the increased production of metal items of wide consumption, weapons production, ship building, etc.) limited the volume of its export. At the turn of the XVIII and the XIX centuries another reason cut down the export of iron from Russia, namely the introduction in England of new methods in the production of pig iron (use of hard coal), which led to an increase of the volume of production and a considerable decrease in prices for English iron as compared with the Russian, which continued to be produced by wooden fuel.

sian textile industries which were emerging at the end of the eighteenth century.

The growth of the social division of labor and of markets during the second half of the eighteenth century was aided by the extension of Russian territory, the colonization of borderlands, the acquisition of new sea oulets, and the increase of the population (from 15 million in the 1740's to 27–28 million in the 1780's).

The Russian empire included a portion of the southern steppe, part of Finland, and, in the last third of the eighteenth century (under Catherine II), the Crimea, the Sea of Azov region, cis-Caucasus, the right bank of the (Dnepr) Ukraine, Polesie, Belorussia, and Kurland. Colonization of the Urals and Siberia continued. Acquisition of Azov, Kerch, and the coastal strip at the mouth of the Dniestr gave access to the Azov and Black Seas. The Russians merchant fleet obtained not only the right of free navigation on the Black Sea, but passage through the Dardanelles and Bosphorus. Southern exits to the international trade routes were opened for Russia. The country grew both in territory and in its extended coastline. The Russian state, notes Marx, was transformed "from a purely continental country into a power surrounded by seas." [7]

Expeditions of the second half of the eighteenth century, among which those of the Academy (1768–74) were the most important, continued the glorious work of the Russian geographers, travellers, and sailors of the first half of the century. These expeditions explored the territory and natural wealth of Russia, her roads, and her sea and river routes.

At the end of the eighteenth century Russian colonization of the west coast of North America developed under the leadership of the merchant Grigorii Ivanovich Shelikhov. Russian fishing and sealing spread to the northern basin of the Pacific Ocean. Russian colonies in Alaska and California established trade relations with the cities of Siberia and European Russia and became linked with the all-Russian market.

The growth of commodity production in agriculture and the development of trade and industry required credit, especially for the merchants. The interests of the latter dictated the development of exchange and of commercial banks. The basic task of these banks under feudalism was to free the merchants from the power of usurers.

Trying above all to relieve the nobility from the grip of the usurers, the feudal absolute monarchy created banks for the nobles. All Russian

---

[7] Marx, *Secret Diplomatic History*, p. 87.

credit establishments in the second half of the eighteenth century, other than the recently created Merchants' Bank, were placed at the service of the nobility. What N. G. Chernyshevskii said of banks of prereform Russia in general is applicable to the Russian banks of the second half of the eighteenth century: They "gave loans often used only for spending by the pomeshchiki." [8] Having squandered the money, the pomeshchiki usually did not repay these loans; they became enforced subsidies. Giving credit to the nobility, which diverted millions of rubles by preserving the monopoly of usury in trade and industry, threatened the growth of capitalist organization in the serf economy.

Industrial and city construction, the building of roads and canals, credit for the nobility, the preparation for war, and wars themselves, during the reign of Catherine II, caused an uninterrupted expansion of the state budget. In an effort to utilize the issue of currency as a supplementary financial resource, the government began to print paper money—assignats. In 1767 Petersburg and Moscow saw the establishment of the first exchange banks "for the exchange of assignats," [9] which were merged into the State Bank of Assignats in 1786.

Toward the end of the century more than 150 million rubles in assignats were in circulation. This sum roughly doubled the average yearly state budget. When the exchange of assignats for metal money was discontinued (in 1786 for silver and in the middle of the 1790's for copper money) a surplus of assignats emerged. The value of the assignats began to fall and prices of goods to increase, and an exchange rate unfavorable to Russia developed in the foreign market. State revenues could not cover budget expenses. The deficit of the state budget became chronic. For the first time in the history of Russia there occurred a state debt—foreign and domestic—which, toward the end of the eighteenth century, exceeded 200 million rubles.[10]

The economic development of Russia in the second half of the eighteenth century was characterized by an increasing incompatibility

[8] N. G. Chernyshevskii, *Izbrannye ekonomicheskie proizvedeniia* [Selected Economic Works] (Moscow: Gospolitizdat, 1948), II, 530.

[9] PSZ, XVIII, No. 13219.

[10] See N. D. Chechulin, *Ocherki po istorii russkikh finansov v tsarstvovanie Ekateriny II* [Outlines of the History of Russian Finances During the Reign of Catherine II] (St. Petersburg: 1906), p. 378; A. S. Lappo-Danilevskii, *Ocherki vnutrennei politiki imp. Ekateriny II* [Outlines of Domestic Policy of Empress Catherine II] (St. Petersburg: 1898), pp. 56–7; A. Kulomzin, "Gosudarstvennye dokhody i raskhody v tsarstvovanie Ekateriny II" [State Revenues and Expenditures During the Reign of Catherine II], *Russkii vestnik* [Russian Herald], No. 84 (1869), pp. 108–51.

between the ruling feudal productive [institutional] relations and the nature of the growing productive [technological] forces.

Thanks to the growth of the latter, new bourgeois productive relations arose and developed. The law of compulsory conformity between productive relations and the nature of productive forces itself favored capitalism in the struggle between new capitalist productive relations and the prevailing feudal serf system. Capitalist productive relations, becoming ever more widespread, were formed into a bourgeois organization.

The development of capitalist organization was expressed in the participation of many merchants in industrial enterprise,[11] in the growth of merchant and peasant factories based on hired labor, in greater numbers of hired "workers," and in expanding markets and the appearance of a new commodity–manpower.[12]

The growth of a capitalist bourgeois organization sharpened the inconsistencies which developed in the feudal-serf economy. This contradiction increased between the ruling feudal class and the productive forces, whose growth introduced new capitalist productive relations. Serfdom deterred the development of productive forces and of the market. It impeded the industrial development of resources held as the personal monopoly of the noble-pomeshchiki or their state, and it discouraged the processing industry. Serfdom hampered practical application of the great scientific discoveries and inventions of M. V. Lomonosov, I. I. Polzunov, K. D. Frolov, I. P. Kilibin, and many other talented Russians; the creative forces of the great people were suppressed. Serfdom strangled Russian technical thought and retarded the introduction of machines into manufacturing. It kept agriculture on a low technical level and impeded the development of markets for its produce.

The growth of capitalism, expressed especially in the exploitation of hired labor, also caused an increase in serf exploitation. While adapting to the new conditions and trying within the framework of a developing money economy to increase the income from their votchini, the pomeshchiki persisted in exploiting serf labor. The noble-pome-

---

[11] See V. N. Iakovtsevskii, *Kupecheskii kapital v feodalno-krepostnicheskoi Rossii* [Commercial Capital in Feudal-Serf Russia] (Moscow: AS USSR, 1953).

[12] New data on the number of workers in Russian manufactories and on the formation of a working force market in Russia in the second half of the XVIII century are given and illuminated by S. G. Strumilin, "Rabochie russkoi manufaktury k kontsu XVIII v." [Workers of Russian Manufactories at the End of the XVIII Century], *Voprosy ekonomiki,* No. 9 (1953); N. L. Rubinshtein, "Nekotorye voprosy formirovaniia rynka rabochei sily v Rossii XVIII veka" [Some Problems of the Formation of the Working Force Market in Russia in the XVIII Century], *Voprosy istorii,* No. 2 (1952).

shchiki raised the obrok rates, increased the barshchina, and placed the peasant's contribution on a monthy basis. In effect, the serf became a slave. Factory barshchina spread, and the exploitation of the peasants assigned to the factory increased. Under the influence of capitalism this growing serf exploitation ruined the peasant economy and undermined its base.

Flights and revolts of the peasants resulted. The labor situation for agriculture and the developing industry became acute. Labor in industry was at that time even more difficult than in agriculture. From the 1750's, uprisings among the pomestie and factory peasants were common occurrences. The scope and force of these uprisings led to the calling of troops and artillery to suppress them, and armed clashes took place. In her "Notes," Catherine II says that on her accession to the throne (1762) uprisings occurred not only among pomestie peasants, but also among factory peasants who "were almost all clearly disobedient to the authorities." [13]

Land seizure, theft, and heavy oppression of "natives" in the borderlands, especially in Bashkiriia, a new mining area, also caused uprisings. During 1735–1740 and 1775 rebellions broke out among the Bashkirs. In the decade (1762–1772) immediately before the peasant war at least forty major peasant uprisings in the Tver, Novgorod, Viatka, Kazan, and Smolensk localities were put down by armed force with cruel repression. The "working people" and assigned peasants in the Urals also revolted, especially in the factories of the large Ural mine owners, the Demidovs.

The growth of the bourgeois organization not only increased the antagonism between peasants and noble-pomeshchiki, but also the class struggle between noble-pomeshchiki and merchants and between merchants and peasantry. In addition, conflicts developed within each of these classes.

Thanks to the development of peasant industries, trade, and unequal utilization of land, groups with various interests appeared within the peasantry. To meet tax payments and obrok, prosperous villagers "helped" the poor and those with little land by providing enslaving and usurious loans of money and goods, under conditions of reciprocal bond. Lands were seized for payment of debts. The landless peasant was forced either to work for the rich, often on property formerly his own, or to depart, with the landlord's permission. Those who left hired out as farm hands, worked as craftsmen, became factory workers, or served in transport.

---

[13] *Zapiski imperatritsy Ekateriny II* [Notes of Empress Catherine II] (St. Petersburg: 1907), p. 538.

Far more unjust than conditions among the pomeshchiki peasants was the land problem of the state peasants, who had had some legal possibilities of buying land.[14] Usury led to land turnover among state peasants. According to a contemporary testimony, "the poor remain eternal debtors to the rich or become their workers and . . . are forced to give up their cultivated lands to creditors, depriving themselves of the means of subsistence." [15] Under conditions of serfdom, however, where it was difficult for peasants to rent land and the sale of property was forbidden, inequality of land use could not develop to any considerable extent. Even more than in agriculture, peasant industry and trade created divisions among various groups within the peasantry.

The existence of capitalists, the first class, the intermediates, those with little land, and the landless among the peasants was evidence of the disintegration of the peasantry. The prevalence of serfdom slowed down this process, but could not stop it. In feudal serfdom all peasant groups were united by common interests. "In serfdom," says V. I. Lenin, "the entire mass of the peasantry fought their oppressors, the pomeshchiki class, which the Tsarist government guarded, defended, and upheld." [16]

In 1773–74 a spontaneous peasant war occurred. Spreading over a vast area, it rocked the state "from Siberia to Moscow and from the Kuban to the Murom forest." [17] The suppression of the war increased the dictatorship of the nobility, as was reflected in government acts. Examples were the "Regulation for Governing the Provinces of the Russian Empire" (1775), which put power in the hands of the local nobility, and the "Charter of the Nobility" (1785), which legally formulated and systematized the rights and privileges obtained earlier by the nobles. In spite of the rebels' defeat, the peasant war, led by Pugachev, was very important; it undermined the foundations of serfdom as it was beginning to disintegrate.

After the peasant war of 1773–74, peasant uprisings erupted in separate places. In 1778, after the revolt of Count Apraksin's peasants

---

[14] See N. M. Druzhinin, *Gosudarstvennye krestiane i reforma P. D. Kisileva* [State Peasants and P. D. Kisilev's Reform] (Moscow-Leningrad: AS USSR, 1946), I, 69–78.

[15] Manuscript Division of the State Library of the USSR, Museum Collection, No. 2930. *Istoricheskie primechaniia o drevnostiakh Olonetskogo kraia i o narodakh tam obytavshikh; topograficheskoe opisanie o gorodakh i uezdakh Olonetskogo namestnichestva* [Historical Notes on Villages of the Olonets Land and the People Who Inhabit It; A Topographic Description of Cities and Counties of the Olonets Administration], Sheets 53–4. Written after 1784.

[16] Lenin, *Sochineniia*, VI, 384.

[17] Pushkin, *Polnoe sobranie sochinenii,* VIII, 268.

was crushed, the Novgorod governor Sivers wrote Catherine: "If order is not restored as soon as possible the matter will have disastrous results. In a country with a despotic form of government the embryo of uprising is ready to grow at any suitable moment. Therefore it is mandatory to be on the alert." [18] At the end of the century many uprisings occurred. During three years of the rule of Paul I, 278 peasant uprisings in thirty-two gubernias were registered.[19] The peasant struggle was directed against the feudal order, which was already starting to disintegrate, but oppression increased even more with the growth of capitalism within the existing regime.

Principles of Economic Policy. The Struggle of the Schools of Economic Thought

The struggle of classes and of groups within them was displayed in various legislative commissions, such as that of 1754, and especially in the Commission called in 1767 to prepare a new Code. The deputies to the latter were chosen from central state institutions (one from each institution), from among the nobles (one from each uezd), the city population (one from each city), the free peasants, the freeholders, the Cossacks, the tribute-paying people, the settled people, the soldiers engaged in agriculture, and the officials of old services (one from each province). The clergy was represented by only one deputy from the synod. The pomestie and "economic" (that is, former monastery) possessional and assigned peasants had no representation. Of the 564 deputies who convened in Moscow in July, 1767, twenty-eight represented government institutions, 161 the nobility, 208 the cities,[20] fifty came from the Cossacks, seventy-nine from among state peasants, and thirty-four from settled peoples.

The Commission of 1767 had at its disposal much material, the legacy of the legislative commission of 1754 and the instructions brought by the deputies. These instructions reflected the position, opinions, hopes, and demands of the various components of the population.

The nobility, controlling the land and exploiting forced labor, demanded for itself the monopoly of industrial resources and of the

---

[18] See V. I. Semevskii, *Krestiane v tsarstvovanie imperatritsy Ekateriny II* [Peasants During the Reign of Empress Catherine II] (St. Petersburg: 1881), I, 388.

[19] Liashchenko, *Istoriia narodnogo khoziaistva SSSR,* I, 425.

[20] Among town deputies, merchants predominated, but there were also many nobles because every house owner of the town participated in the election.

processing of agricultural products, especially distilling.[21] The nobility also solicited monopolies on trade (wholesale and export) in farm products, and on leases of wine, beer, mead, and so forth. These demands were meant to restrain merchant and, in part, peasant enterprises.

As a result of exploitation by the nobles of serf labor, merchants and rich peasant entrepreneurs developed production chiefly with hired labor. In aiding the growth of capitalism and the breakdown of serfdom, the demands of the merchants assumed an ambiguous, contradictory position. On the one side, it fought the monopolies and privileges of the nobility, the feudal limitations on merchant self-government and courts, and the various restrictions on trade. On the other, the merchants demanded prohibitions to prevent the nobility and, especially, the peasants from engaging in industry and trade and sought a monopoly of trade and industrial activity *in toto,* or at least in some branches. The merchants also petitioned for restoration of their right to buy peasants for factories, a right which had been abrogated in 1762. Although they represented a considerable economic force in industry and trade, the merchants had no serious political influence with which to obtain their ends.

Peasants who were not enserfed by the pomeshchiki, as well as the nationalities of the Volga region, the Urals, and Siberia, complained of their lack of rights and spoke of the heavy tax burdens and state obligations, the despotism of civil servants, and the seizure of land by pomeshchiki and factory owners.

The speeches of the representatives of the state peasants, of the merchants and of progressive deputies of the nobility met with sharp opposition from the nobility, who violently defended their political and economic monopolies. Displeased with these bitter quarrels, Catherine, in December, 1768, dissolved the "main meeting" of the Commission and retained "special commissions" only.

The attitude of the pomestie serfs—who numbered more than half of all the peasants—toward their lack of representation in the Commission is revealed in the "Cry of the Kholopy," the work of an unknown poet, by all indications a serf:

"To their own advantage they alter the law,
And choose not serfs as deputies;

[21] Over the nobility's monopoly on distilling, approved by the Code of 1765, there developed anew the struggle between the nobility and the merchants in the Code Commission. The nobility continued to maintain its monopoly on distilling.

What can the serfs there say?
They are given the freedom to oppress us 'til death." [22]

The spontaneous protest of the peasants against serfdom was shown in complaints, suicides, escapes, and murders of pomeshchiki and their stewards, officials, and officers. Their demands resulted in disturbances and uprisings and in the battles of the peasant war of 1773–74.[23] The peasantry demanded freedom and land. Yet while it spontaneously opposed feudalism, the peasantry in effect fought for the victory of capitalism.

The economic policy of the feudal-absolutist empire supported the interests of the pomeshchiki-noble class. For the latter's benefit the state broadened the sphere of serfdom. It legalized serfdom in the Ukraine, registered the people by census, and distributed to the pomeshchiki crown land with state peasants, transforming these peasants into serfs of the pomeshchiki. The state of the nobility strengthened serfdom; the pomeshchiki were given the right to send their serfs to Siberia for settlement or hard labor; and the serfs were forbidden to complain against the pomeshchiki.

At the same time the empire of the nobles had to consider the merchants, who played an important role in trade and industry and without whose growth the further development of the national economy and the strengthening of state finances were impossible. But whenever the interests of the merchants sharply conflicted with those of the nobles, the feudal-absolutist state protected the nobility to the detriment of the merchants.

The economic development of the country caused some change in the trade and industrial policy of the absolutist monarchy. Internal tariffs and road taxes, which impeded the development of an all-Russian market, were abolished in 1754.[24] It is interesting to note that internal tariffs and road taxes had not as yet been abolished in France, nor in feudally disunited Germany. Their abolition in Russia was a progressive measure.

A number of plans expressed the negative attitude of broad layers of the nobility and merchants toward leases and monopolies. In 1760 a

---

22 "Pochin" [Beginning], *Sbornik Obshchestva liubitelei rossiiskoi slovesnosti* [A Collection of the Society of Lovers of Russian Literature] (Moscow: 1895), p. 12.

23 On economic demands of the peasantry during that war see Chapter XX.

24 *PSZ,* XIII, No. 10164.

plan was drawn up for a Senate decree abolishing a number of lease monopolies "which are harmful to the extension of trade." [25]

Of the plans of 1760 the most interesting is a letter of Conference secretary D. V. Volkov to Count I. G. Chernyshev. Volkov proposed [that] "all goods of native production which have been forbidden to be imported in any form and as a result have disappeared from trade and will not soon reappear should be permitted entry duty-free, or at least with a duty so small as to be inconsequential." The letter emphasized the advantage of an active trade balance, even if it meant a decrease in tariff revenue: "if the treasury lost, for instance, 200,000 rubles, but the state gained a million, I think this loss could be considered a great gain." [26] Volkov emphasized the interests of the national economy over the fiscal interests of the treasury. His ideas coincided with the fundamental provisions of the famous decree of Peter III (March 28, 1762) in which it was ordered that "all trade be free." [27]

Continuing the line of trade-industry policy noted earlier, Catherine's government abolished by a series of legal acts the majority of leases and monopolies and, by a decree of March 17, 1775, allowed "everyone to introduce freely all sorts of mills and crafts without requiring any permission from higher or lower authorities." [28]

The gradual liquidation of the system of industrial privileges accomplished under Catherine II reduced the need for the Manufacturing College established by Peter I for administering this system, and in 1779 it was abolished.[29] It must be kept in mind, however, that the "limitless freedom" declared by Catherine's government for trade and industry hardly resembled, or could resemble, freedom as it was understood by the English free traders. Catherine's legislation abolished only the system of *exclusive* privileges, but preserved the general limitations, prohibitions, and encouragements, including protective foreign trade tariffs. The moderately protective tariffs of 1766 and 1782 had a positive influence on the development of Russian industry, which no longer needed exclusive privileges, but *still* demanded general protective measures.

The new tariffs aided the activation of the trade balance of the country and the growth of state revenues. A more or less high tariff

[25] See *Istoriia Pravitelstvuiushchego Senata za dvesti let 1711–1911* [A History of the Governing Senate for the Past 200 Years, 1711–1911] (St. Petersburg: 1911), II, 303,

[26] *Arkhiv kn. Vorontsova* [Prince Vorontsov's Archive] (Moscow: 1880), Bk. 24, pp. 123–4.

[27] *PSZ*, XV, No. 11489.

[28] *Ibid.*, XX, No. 14275.

[29] *Ibid.*, XX, No. 14947.

on imports remained the dominant idea of government foreign trade policy, as well as that of the majority of Russian political figures and thinkers of the eighteenth century.

After the abolition of exclusive privileges and detailed regulation, Russian industry grew considerably. According to Burnashev, of the number of active manufactories in 1796 (excluding mining and metallurgy), more than two-thirds were established during the reign of Catherine II,[30] when a number of leases and monopolies were abolished.

In pre-revolutionary Russian science the idea prevailed that this change in trade and industrial policy from full to partial protectionism took place under Catherine II and under the influence of notable successes in Russian industrial development (Kliuchevskii, Bilbasov, and others). In our time this opinion was shared by the late academician Iu. V. Got'e, who maintained that the abolition of monopolies began with Catherine II. Many bourgeois historians and economists (for example, Korsak, Lodyzhenskii, Vitchevskii, Verner) added that this change occurred under the influence of Western European economic ideas, to which Catherine II was attracted. Actually, as noted above, such changes in trade and industrial policy began earlier, at the end of the reign of Elizabeth and under Peter III. Thus are removed the interrelated questions of the role of Catherine II, who was not the creator of any new course in Russian economic policy, and of the influence of Western European economic ideas, which did not play a decisive role in the abandonment of the policy of exclusive protectionism by the Russian government. Rather, these changes in economic policy were the result of internal causes the development of feudal economy, the growth of capitalism within it, and the course of class struggle in Russia.

The growth of capitalism, which aggravated the contradictions developing within serfdom and renewed the intensification of class struggle, again posed for contemporaries old economic problems and called forth new ones. Plans to limit serfdom and to expand the possibilities of developing the economic activity of the peasants in agriculture, industry, and trade appeared. Realization of these plans would have

---

30 See V. Burnashev, *Ocherk istorii manufaktur v Rossii* [An Outline of the History of Manufactories in Russia] (St. Petersburg: 1833), pp. 16–18 and 26–9. Burnashev's figures exaggerate the numerical strength of manufactories inasmuch as they include a number of small enterprises. This, however, does not alter the correctly noted tendency of the development of industry in Russia of that time.

aided the growth of the bourgeoisie and the formation of capitalism.

At the end of eighteenth century the growth of capitalism and the contradictions within the serf economy reached such a degree of aggravation that the question of the revolutionary liquidation of serfdom and autocracy was raised for the first time. Such a demand was aimed at the victory of capitalism, for "destruction of feudalism, expressed positively, means the establishment of the bourgeoisie." [31]

The moment of demarcation of the tendencies of Russian economic thought in the second half of the eighteenth century is found in the attitude toward those elements and forms of the economy whose development aided the growth of the bourgeoisie and therefore was directed against serfdom and led to its decay. In the second half of the eighteenth century Russian economic thought was more and more concerned with problems of commodity production in agriculture and the growth of industry, especially heavy industry, the development of trade—internal and foreign—the activization of trade and improvement of the balance of payments, and the search for new sources of state revenue. Problems of prices of goods, exchange rates, circulation of paper money, organization of credit, and other economic matters arose. The question of population became more acute. Labor had to be provided for industry and agriculture. The need to increase state revenue and to master the huge unsettled expanses of Russia with their natural resources required solution.

Because of their economic content these questions were considerably more complicated than those which had arisen in the preceding period. The Free Economic Society called this era "the economic century." [32] The struggle over economic ideas concerned itself with the question of the direction of Russian economic development. Progressive thinkers, among them students and followers of the great Lomonosov, fought to transform Russia into a country which would have a well-developed agriculture and a mighty industry. This progressive movement was opposed by the apologists of a one-sided agrarian economy, who fought the development of heavy industry (A. P. Sumarokov and others).

The promotion of heavy industry and markets induced the nobility to take advantage of this growth for their own purposes. In the 1760's, therefore, the program of another publicist and political figure, a deputy from the Yaroslav nobility to the Commission on the Code of 1767, M. M. Shcherbatov, acquired greater influence among the no-

---

[31] Engels, *Krestianskaia voina v Germanii,* p. 14.

[32] *Trudy volnogo ekonomicheskogo obshchestva* [Works of the Free Economic Society], I (1765), Announcement p. 1.

bility than the views of Sumarokov.[33] Shcherbatov called on the nobility to develop both agriculture and industry on the basis of forced labor, to the detriment of the merchants and capitalist enterprises. In 1765 the "Free Economic Society for encouraging agriculture and household management in Russia" was founded. This was a purely social organization of the nobility, dedicated to serve the economic interests of the ruling class. The Society was called "free" to signify that it was under no department, standing only "under the protection of the Empress." From the very beginning of its activity the Society was forced to deal with the question of the position of the main productive force in agriculture—the peasantry.

In 1766, on the initiative of Catherine II, a competition was announced to determine "which is more useful for society, that the peasant have his own land or only movable property and how far his right to this or other property should extend." Thus the participants in the competition were to consider the question of the expediency of giving the peasants ownership of only movable property, or of land also, and of defining the nature of the ownership of this property. One hundred sixty entries, both native and foreign, were submitted. Among the reactionary answers the letter of A. P. Sumarokov must be mentioned.[34] Of the progressive solutions the most interesting is that of A. Ia. Polenov.[35] The competition, however, had no noticeable effect on economic policy and the position of the peasantry.

The interest of the Society was concentrated not on the question of the peasantry or of serfdom, but on pomestie economy, the study of its development, and the problem of raising the income of the pomestie estates.

In 1765 an agricultural questionnaire containing 65 "economic questions" was compiled. The best answers, printed in the "Works of the Free Economic Society," are still invaluable material for the history of agriculture and Russian economic history in general. The questionnaire of 1790 is also very interesting.

Soon after its establishment, the Free Economic Society discussed the question of what crops were most profitable. Wheat was ranked first. The Society called on its members to cultivate potatoes also, to expand production of flax and hemp, to develop animal husbandry, and to conserve and plant forests. It was interested in methods of fertilization, drainage of swamps, eradication of farm pests, and in the development of gardening and horticulture. The means of initial

33 See Chapter XVI.
34 See Chapter XVI.
35 See Chapter XIX.

processing of agricultural products also attracted their attention. The Society was also concerned with those phases of the processing industry which were directly linked to farm production and which were a part of the votchina economy; this was votchina industry. In addition, the Society held competitions on the management of the votchina economy. An interesting competition was announced in 1768 on the subject of "Instruction for the Administrator in the Absence of the Lord."

All the activity of the Free Economic Society in this period was devoted to solving the economic problems of the votchina and increasing its production and income within the serf structure. Noted members of the Free Economic Society, among whom were A. T. Bolotov, P. I. Rychkov, I. M. Komov, and others, tried to rationalize serf agriculture by agronomical and "zootechnical" improvements. Imbued with the point of view of the pomeshchiki, they sought better organization of serf labor, having as its purpose their exploitation in order to raise the income of the votchina.

Andrei Timofeevich Bolotov (1738–1833), the first Russian agronomist, developed concrete proposals for improving agriculture. Emphasizing the need for basic improvements in agriculture, he insisted on combining agriculture with animal husbandry as a necessary condition for the successful development of each of these basic branches of Russian agriculture. Among his many published works appearing between 1766 and 1789, the one entitled "On the Allotment of Fields" is especially important.[36]

The early Russian agronomists based their proposals on studies of native agricultural conditions and on generalizations of centuries-old productive experiences of the Russian peasantry. They fought automatic transfer of foreign experience into Russia and stressed the necessity of critical analysis of this experience as applied to Russian conditions. Bolotov, Rychkov, Komov,[37] and their pupils served the cause of Russian agricultural science. Being confirmed serf owners, however, they did not understand, and did not want to understand,

---

[36] See *Trudy Volnogo ekonomicheskogo obshchestva,* Pt. XVII and XVIII (1771). See also Manuscript Division of the State Library of the USSR, Museum Collection, No. 4314. *Ekonomicheskii magazein, ili sobranie vsiakikh zapisok, primechanii i otvetov, kasaiushchikhsia zemledeliia i domostroitelstva is vsei ekonomii. 1766 g.* [Economic Magazine, or a Collection of Various Notes, Remarks and Answers Related to Agriculture and Household Management and the Entire Economy.] with A. T. Bolotov's signature. See also A. T. Bolotov, *Izbrannye sochineniia po agronomii plodovodstvu, lesovodstvu, botanike* [Selected Works on Agronomy, Productivity, Forestry, Botany] (Moscow: 1952).

[37] See V. P. Gurianov, *Ivan Mikhailovich Komov, ego zhizn i deiatelnost* [Ivan Mikhailovich Komov, His Life and Activity] (Moscow: 1953).

the impossibility of realizing their scientific conclusions within serfdom. Any considerable elevation of and basic improvement in agriculture were hopeless under conditions of serfdom.

Many nobles, including such conservatives and reactionaries as M. M. Shcherbatov and a number of other members of the Free Economic Society, recognized certain negative aspects in serfdom and advised their elimination. One of their recommendations was to forbid the sale of individual peasants separate from their families and without land. Some suggested other measures, even the publication by the government of a general code of peasant obligations (P. I. Panin and others). All these proposals, however, did not strike at the root of serfdom.

This conservative approach included also those who spoke of the desirability of the abolition of serfdom, but only after prolonged education and peasant enlightenment (for example, I. N. Boltin, E. R. Dashkova). Thus these spokesmen wanted to postpone any real limitation on serfdom for an indefinite period. They did not, and did not want to, understand that education of the peasantry was possible only with the abolition of serfdom.

The conservative views of Boltin on peasant education emphasized also his erroneous conviction that the Russian peasants, having use of the land under serfdom, lived better than the free peasants of Western Europe. In Western European states, "theoretically free" farmers, wrote Boltin, "are as oppressed as ours who are called slaves." Instead of reaching the only just deduction, that the peasant should be given land and freedom, serf-owner Boltin concluded that in general the peasants did not need personal freedom—"this empty and imaginary freedom, so much preached and praised . . ." [38] Such an apology for serfdom was typical of the conservative and reactionary spokesmen of the nobility, including Catherine II. The political and economic views of Catherine II were expressed in her "Instructions" to the Code Commission which convened in 1767.[39]

The "Instructions," in its aim, task, and content, was a defense of serfdom and autocracy. Catherine wanted this "Instructions" to be the main basis for preparing a new Code. The debates in the Commission, however, revolved around questions directly concerned with class interests, and it turned into an arena of bitter quarrels. This develop-

---

[38] I. Boltin, *Primechaniia na istoriiu drevnyia i nyneshnyia Rossii g. Le. Klerka* [Remarks About the History of Ancient and Contemporary Russia by Mr. Le Clerc] (1788), II, 234.

[39] See Chapter XVI.

ment displeased Catherine, who hurriedly dissolved the "main meeting" of the Commission.

At the beginning of 1769 Catherine, through her secretary G. V. Kozitskii, began to publish the journal *All Variety of Things* and contributed to it herself. Catherine wished to detract attention from the sharp political and economic controversies and prevent revelations of the evils and contradictions of serfdom. She tried to direct the attention of society to the criticism of certain human weaknesses which are not sins and which always have existed and always will. The journal recommended that its contributors be not negative, but positive. The purpose of this journal, like the "Instructions," was that of an apologia for serfdom and autocracy.

In the same year, 1769, a number of satirical journals began to appear.[40] Judging by their articles, the majority of these journals were conservative. Some of them, like the completely colorless publication, *Neither This Nor That* of V. G. Ruban, cannot even be considered satirical.

A different position was taken by the *Drone,* published in 1769–1770 by Nikolai Ivanovich Novikov (1744–1818).[41] Novikov tried not to lead his readers away from the controversial questions in the Code Commission of 1767, but to continue their social discussion. His evaluation of the social role of the peasantry and the parasitism of the nobility was reflected in the very name of the journal, *Drone,* and in its epigraph: "They work, and you eat their labor." While Novikov did not criticize serfdom directly, he dealt with "criticism of individuals:" he castigated landlords who used their power for evil and officials who took bribes. Novikov spoke of the actual social importance of the unfortunate, powerless peasant, the "feeder of Russia." In *Drone* Novikov and his coworkers opposed the journal *All Variety of Things* and called it "All Sorts of Nonsense." This led to the suppression of the *Drone,* which informed its readers that it was dying "against its will."

Many Russian satirical journals continued the work of the closed *Drone,* among them Novikov's *Painter* and *Purse.*[42] In the second half

---

[40] See P. N. Berkov, *Istoriia russkoi zhurnalistiki XVIII veka* [History of Russian Journalism of the XVIII Century] (Moscow-Leningrad: AS USSR, 1952).

[41] Novikov's literary activity is presented in detail by G. Makogonenko, *Nikolai Novikov i russkoe prosveshchenie XVIII veka* [Nikolai Novikov and Russian Enlightment of the XVIII Century] (Moscow-Leningrad: Gosizdat, 1951).

[42] In the second half of the XVIII century many periodicals were published in Russia. In the 1750's 5 new journals appeared, in the 1760's 18, in the

of the eighteenth century many advanced Russian propagators of enlightenment appeared. Denis Ivanovich Fonvizin, Ivan Andreevich Krylov, and the founder of Russian jurisprudence, Semen Efimovich Desnitskii, were examples.[43] Novikov criticized not only Catherine's *All Variety of Things,* but other journals, including M. D. Chulkov's *This and That.*

Unlike the conservative and reactionary proponents of the nobility, the spokesman of the merchants, Mikhail Dmitrievich Chulkov,[44] in his articles and the voluminous work *Historical Description of Russian Commerce,* did not apologize for serfdom, but, on the other hand, he did not oppose it. In his numerous writings Chulkov tried to show the merchant class how it could, and should, get the most profit from its activities under conditions of serfdom. The ideology of Chulkov reflected the contradictions and duality of the class position of the merchantry under the Russian serf economy of the second half of the eighteenth century.

Chulkov demanded the elimination of feudal limitations on merchant enterprise and the creation of the most favorable foundations for the development of heavy industry and trade within serfdom. Realization of this demand would aid the growth of capitalism. Such a progressive demand Chulkov combined with conservative efforts to incorporate parts of the merchant class into the structure of serfdom (by giving titles to certain important merchants).

The rise of criticism of serfdom was the most important aspect of the development of Russian economic thought of the period under examination. In this criticism, which revealed the contradictions in serfdom and the beginning of its breakdown, two tendencies are evident. The first was presented, beginning in the 1760's, by Dmitrii Alekseevich Golitsyn.[45] He proposed reforms which, in his opinion, would strengthen the rule of noble pomeshchiki. He proposed the abolition of personal dependence of the peasant on a large redemption payment, which only a few of the richest peasants could manage. Golitsyn thought the peasant who bought his freedom should be given the right to movable property only. This reform would turn him into a capitalist renter of land exploiting the hired labor of his neighbors and other peasants who were serfs of the pomeshchiki. The land, ac-

---

1770's 22, in the 1780's 39, and in the 1790's 32. Of the 9,500 books (excluding those with religious content) which were published in Russia in the XVIII century, 90 per cent appeared in the second half of the XVIII century.

[43] See Chapter XIX.

[44] See Chapter XVIII.

[45] See Chapter XIX.

cording to Golitsyn, should remain in the hands of noble-pomeshchiki in order to assure their economic and political domination.

Golitsyn gave a noble-pomeshchik criticism of serfdom, which was expressed in certain proposed reforms. But even such a criticism was progressive for the 1760's: his propositions, independent of his wishes and even contrary to them, would have led to the growth of bourgeois relationships in feudal society. These reforms, however, would actually have extended to only a few rich peasants, while serfdom for the masses would have been retained for a long time.

The second tendency of the prevalent criticism was presented by Polenov, the philosopher Kozelskii, another Kozelskii (a deputy to the Code Commission), Desnitskii, and Tretyakov.[46] Criticizing serfdom in theory, these spokesmen did not draw, however, the corresponding practical and political conclusions from such criticism. Their limited political program was determined by economic conditions and the class struggle. The development of capitalism and the attendant breakdown of serfdom were only beginning in the 1760's. The struggle of ideas did not yet envisage the abolition of serfdom and the triumph of capitalism. Various reforms would effect the growth of bourgeois elements in the feudal economy, but they did not go beyond the limits of feudalism in their practical application. Their essentially antifeudal demands were often presented in feudal form, which lessened the progressiveness of their content.

Considering the basic, normal, and economically reasonable right of the producer to the means of production, these spokesmen proposed to give to the Russian peasant not the bourgeois right of personal property, but a characteristic feudal right: the possession of movable property, the separation of peasant land from that of the pomeshchiki, and hereditary lease of these lands. Directing their proposals to the noble pomeshchiki, these thinkers tried to prove that both the peasants and the noble pomeshchiki would benefit. Nevertheless they went further than D. A. Golitsyn in their theoretical criticism of serfdom and in their practical proposals. Their suggested reforms would have changed not only the position of the upper strata, but also of the peasant masses. Unlike Golitsyn, they endeavored to weaken and limit the serf's dependence on the pomeshchik. In contrast to Golitsyn's program, they opened a great expanse of the growth of bourgeois relations.

Polenov and Kozelskii called on the ruling class to do everything possible to avoid popular uprisings. In his "Philosophical Proposals"

---

[46] See Chapter XIX.

Kozelskii considered rebellions undesirable but justified when caused by the cruel exploitation of landlord nobles and the intransigence of the nobility.

As capitalism grew within serfdom, as serfdom began to disintegrate, and as the class struggle increased, the contradictions in Russian social thought were aggravated. The peasant war of 1773–74 exercised great influence on the basic trends in Russian political and economic thought. The struggle of ideas in Russia in the last quarter of the eighteenth century was also intensified by the economic processes, political events, and philosophies then developing abroad.

In England, the industrial revolution of the last third of the eighteenth century finally confirmed the domination of the bourgeoisie, and its role in the political life of the country was decisively strengthened. The ideological reflection of this process was the development of the English classical bourgeois political economy.

The fast growth of capitalism in the English colonies of North America brought about their struggle for independence. The Declaration of Independence of the USA, adopted in 1776 by a congress of the colonial representatives during a war of national liberation, proclaimed the right of the people to revolt against a government violating its rights.

The demand of the law of compulsory conformity of productive relations to the nature of productive forces led France to bourgeois revolution at the end of the eighteenth century. The ideological preparation for the revolution was expressed in the philosophy of French Enlightment and in the economic teachings of the physiocrats. The first bourgeois revolution in France caused an upheaval in the life of society, its base, and superstructure. "The victory of the bourgeoisie then meant the victory of a new social structure, the victory of bourgeois over feudal ownership . . . enlightenment over superstition . . . bourgeois law over medieval privileges." [47] Complete triumph of the bourgeoisie in England, the war of independence in North America in 1775–1783, and especially the French bourgeois revolution of 1789–1794 frightened the Russian nobility and at the same time inspired the foes of serfdom and tsarism. Liberal representatives of the Russian nobility joined its conservative reactionary core. The various noble spokesmen united before the threatening danger to feudalism.

On the other hand, the antiserfdom trend in Russian socio-economic thought, which defended the development of bourgeois relations, was given impetus in the struggle with conservative and reactionary forces.

---

[47] Marx and Engels, *Sochineniia,* VII, pp. 54–55.

Beginning with the criticism of serfdom and the timid, moderate demands of the 1760's, this trend made a qualitative advance by the end of the eighteenth century.

The development of Russian *revolutionary*, antiserf, socio-economic thought begins with Radishchev. Unlike the earlier critics, Radishchev gave a profound analysis of the defects of serfdom and of tsarism; he called for replacement of the monarchy by a republic. As he developed the idea of revolution, Radishchev fought for the political freedom of the masses, as well as their freedom from constraint in their economic activity. His struggle for the revolutionary destruction of serfdom led to the victory of capitalism.

In reality, Aleksandr Nikolaevich Radishchev developed the most important economic theory and policy of his time. Elaborating advanced solutions to a number of economic problems, he deserves to be called one of the most progressive thinkers in world economic literature of the eighteenth century and the originator of the revolutionary direction of Russian economic thought, which had universal historical importance.

CHAPTER 16. *Reactionary and Conservative Spokesmen of the Nobility.*

Apology for Serfdom in the "Nakaz" of Catherine II.

A characteristic feature of the policy and literary activity of Catherine II (1729–1796) was the effort to convince everyone that for Russia the most appropriate, and the only expedient, social structure was serfdom, and the only political regime, autocracy. Using the theory of "enlightened absolutism," Catherine II set herself up as a wise lawmaker, leading Russia toward "general well-being." Catherine II, that "Tartufe in skirts and crown," in the words of A. S. Pushkin, adorned even her cruelest laws against the peasants with fancy phrases about being filled with "motherly concern" for the "welfare of her subjects," "and/or all of the people."

One of the main literary reflections of the "enlightened despotism" of Catherine II was her "Nakaz" of 1767 to the Code Commission. The "Nakaz" contains above all an apology for Russian autocracy. According to Catherine, the need for autocracy in Russia stemmed from the wide extent of the country: "No other . . . authority can operate properly within the expanse of such a great state." [1]

In the first manuscript of her "Nakaz" Catherine put the question of serfdom in the declarative form: "Laws can create something useful for the personal property of the slaves and place them in such a position that they can buy their own freedom." She wanted "civil laws to state firmly that slaves must pay their lord for freedom." [2] But she found some faults here. It appears that "in some states" it was impossible to free the agriculturists, since this would have led to their flight. As a result, the land was to remain "untilled." For those states "it is possible to find some means to bind these same agriculturists to the land." For this, it was necessary to leave "to them their land, and

---

[1] N. D. Chechulin, ed., *Nakaz imperatritsy Ekateriny II, dannyi Komissii o sochinenii proekta novogo Ulozheniia* [The Instruction of Empress Catherine II Given to the Commission Charged With the Preparation of a New Code] (St. Petersburg: 1907), Chapt. II, No. 9.

[2] *Ibid.*, p. xxxviii.

to their children, for as long a time as they will work it according to the agreement concluded with them, for a price or tribute corresponding to the fruits of that land." [3]

Thus, even in the manuscript of the "Nakaz," Catherine narrowed the problem of serfdom in Russia from one of freedom (for a price) to that of the allotment of land to the serfs. The question of serfdom was, then, for Catherine only a method of pacifying the peasants while preserving serfdom and stimulating their work.

Later Catherine removed from the original manuscript of the "Nakaz" everything considered liberal by her advisors (P. I. and N. I. Panin, I. P. Elagin, G. G. Orlov, Bishop Gavriil, A. P. Sumarokov, and others). "More than half of my work was struck out, destroyed, and burnt," [4] she wrote to D'Alembert. The greatest deletion and alteration were found in Chapter 11, concerning the problem of interrelations of pomeshchiki and peasants. The only thing that remained was a general meaningless declaration that "laws could create something useful for the personal property of the slaves." Thus in the printed text of the "Nakaz" Catherine did not mention the freedom of the peasants even in vague terms. She recommended the limitation of excessive abuse of serfdom by pomeshchiki and the stimulation of peasant work under conditions of serfdom. For successful economic activity, according to Catherine, it was necessary that "everyone be firmly convinced that he is striving to improve his own personal good." [5] She thought "agriculture could not flourish where one had nothing of his own." [6] In summary, these views, without binding anyone, led to a general, diffused wish to grant the peasants a limited right of ownership of movable property only.[7]

While assigning a decisive role to agriculture as the basis for the growth of population and the development of industry in the towns,[8] Catherine considered "freedom of commerce" [9] a requisite to developing industry and trade; she opposed leases and monopolies. This "limitless freedom," however, did not resemble freedom as understood by the physiocrats and representatives of classical bourgeois political economy in England. In her "Nakaz" Catherine argued that "social or state

[3] *Ibid.*, p. xxxix.

[4] *Sbornik Russkogo istoricheskogo obshchestva* [A Collection of the Russian Historical Society] (St. Petersburg: 1872), X, 167.

[5] Chechulin, *op. cit.*, Chapter VI, No. 43.

[6] *Ibid.*, Chapter XIII, No. 295.

[7] *Ibid.*, Chapter XI, No. 261.

[8] *Ibid.*, Chapter XXII, No. 606, and Chapter XIII, Nos. 294, 297, and 313.

[9] *Ibid.*, Chapter XIII, No. 321.

freedom is not the right to do anything one likes," [10] but only the right to "do everything the law allows." [11]

Some scholars (V. Burnashev, A. Lappo-Danilevskii, A. Korsak, K. Lodyzhenskii, and others) considered Catherine a physiocrat on the Russian throne. This view is entirely false, for physiocracy was essentially antifeudal. This is evident in the sharply negative references to the "Nakaz" and to Catherine's policy in general by the French physiocrats and by their sympathisers, the philosophes (Mercier de la Rivière, Diderot, and so on). In addition, Catherine cannot be classified as a physiocrat, because her understanding of "free commerce" was completely different from that of the physiocrats. She favored very moderate economic liberalism, remarkably combined with numerous "general prohibitions" for limiting and encouraging economic activity. Moreover, Catherine never considered herself a physiocrat, but referred negatively to the physiocrats, whom she called a "sect harmful to the state." [12]

Catherine remained faithful to this view all her life. Not long before her death she characterized the physiocrats as "devils" and "loudmouths wanting to lecture" her.[13] She also referred positively to the opponents of the physiocrats, citing sympathetically Montesquieu, Voltaire, Galiani, Necker, and Beccaria. She used only those ideas of the physiocrats which she found convenient. She even borrowed some expressions from Rousseau, whom she hated, when they seemed to strengthen her position.

The Struggle Against the Development of Manufactures in Russia—A. P. Sumarokov

Aleksandr Petrovich Sumarokov (1718–1777) came from a famous family. His father was an influential official; however, he himself preferred literature to public service. Even when he was engaged in military and civil service, in the latter as a theatre director, his main interest was literary. Sumarokov was the first Russian noble to become a professional writer. He was a dramatist, poet, critic, literary theoretician, and historian. He acted as a publicist through articles on various socio-economic and political questions written from his own

---

[10] *Ibid.*, Chapter V, No. 36.

[11] *Ibid.*, Chapter V, No. 38.

[12] *Sbornik Russkogo istoricheskogo obshchestva*, XXIII, 44. Catherine's letter of February 28, 1776.

[13] *Ibid.*, XXIII, 674. Catherine's letter of May 11, 1796.

noble-pomestie point of view. Recognizing him as a spokesman popular in noble circles, Catherine II turned to Sumarokov for advice.

In considering the economic development of Russia, Sumarokov insisted on the preservation of the agrarian character of the country's economy and opposed the development of heavy industry and manufacturing. Maintaining that "Russia must place its hopes on agriculture," [14] Sumarokov asked: "Cloth factories are popular now; but are they useful for agriculture?", and answered sharply in the negative. Here he referred to the opinion of "various French examiners" as he called the French physiocrats. Believing that "an agriculturist supports all officials and sciences," Sumarokov said that "the cloth factories of the nobles, and the silk ones of Lyons, according to various French examiners, bring fewer riches than agriculture." He thought heavy industry should develop only where land was scarce: "Factories are useful where there is little land and many peasants exist." Russia, on the other hand, "having extensive but insufficiently populated fields," does not need heavy industry. Sumarokov opposed the development of merchant industry and the nobility's votchina industry, which he called "an invention of the pomeshchiki." He suggested that in Russia heavy industry should exist only "in certain places." [15]

Despite his approval of the physiocrats, Sumarokov cannot be considered a physiocrat. While referring to the physiocrats' essentially bourgeois economic teachings, which had a feudal aspect,[16] Sumarokov pursued other aims. While the physiocrats cleared the way for the growth of capitalism, Sumarokov defended the inviolability of serfdom, the strengthening of the feudal absolute state, the preservation of the agrarian economy, the rejection of the development of industry and the elimination of competition. He used various statements of the physiocrats only to bolster his conservative and reactionary ideas and proposals. Sumarokov was against competition, since he aimed at the realization of the feudal principle of stable prices on the internal market.[17] He wanted only such trade as would not violate the feudal order, but would strengthen it economically.

In this regard his advice to develop foreign trade with the "savages" (and not with the West European countries) is typical, that is, a plundering trade based on unequivalent exchange. He tried to justify the

[14] A. P. Sumarokov, *Polnoe sobranie sochinenii* [Complete Collection of Works] (Moscow: 1787), Pt. X, p. 161.

[15] *Ibid.*

[16] Marx, *Kapital,* IV, Pt. I, pp. 16–20.

[17] See A. P. Sumarokov, "O vsegdashnei ravnosti v prodazhe tovarov" [On Constant Equality in the Sale of Goods], *I to i sio* [This and That], February, 1769.

expediency of maintaining serfdom unaltered, his views being expressed in his letter to the Free Economic Society, in the article "On Household Management" and in his "Views" of Catherine's "Nakaz."

In reply to the competition announced by the Free Economic Society, he sent an exasperated letter.[18] He declared that on the question whether "the peasants should be free or serfs" one should be guided by the interests of all society: "It should first be asked: is freedom necessary to the general good of the serfs?"

He acknowledged that the interests of the peasants and nobles were different. "Regarding this I would ask whether the canary which amuses me requires freedom or the cage, and is a chain required for a dog guarding my house? A canary is better without a cage and a dog without a chain. However, the one will fly away, and the other will bite people; thus one thing is required for the peasant and another for the noble." Therefore, the deciding point is "what is required for the general well-being": "freedom" or "serfdom"?

Sumarokov believed that freedom for the peasant was "bad," since it was contrary to the interests of society, which Sumarokov identifies with those of the nobility. But the strengthening of "serfdom" was "bad" because it violated the interests of the peasantry. He was certain that "every member of society, even its slaves (that is, serfs), will admit that of the two evils it is better for the peasants not to own land."

Furthermore, Sumarokov tried to prove that the peasants could not possess land and should be serfs of the pomeshchiki, because "all lands are the noble's property." To him, feudal land ownership was inviolable, the unconditional and exclusive right of the Russian nobility: "Ought the nobles to give up to the peasants the purchased, granted, inherited, and other lands when they do not want to, and can serfs own land in Russia? This is the right of the nobles." Sumarokov cannot even imagine a different situation: "What will the noble be when the peasants and land are not his: what will be left for him?" He concluded that Russia would be lost without serfdom: "freedom of the peasant is not only harmful to society, but it is also disastrous." He thought this conclusion unarguable: "and why [it is] disastrous need not be discussed."

Thus, accepting the "general welfare" as a guiding criterion, Sumarokov identified the interests of society with those of the nobles and

---

[18] Sumarokov's letter, which was received by the Free Economic Society on November 28, 1766, is included in A. I. Khodnev, *Istoriia imperatorskogo Volnogo ekonomicheskogo obshchestva s 1765 do 1865* [A History of the Imperial Free Economic Society from 1765 to 1865] (St. Petersburg: 1865), pp. 24–5.

defended the inviolable, exclusive rights of the nobility. Noble society should be protected from the "freedom" of the peasants.

In his notes on Catherine's "Nakaz," [19] Sumarokov was as categorically opposed to "freedom" as he was in favor of "serfdom." He adds new arguments in support of his opinion, for the "Nakaz" seemed liberal to him. He firmly declared that "it is impossible to free the Russian serfs." On the one hand, he held that "our lowly people do not yet save any sort of noble feelings." On the other, he spoke for the interests of the entire noble class, including even the "poorest" of nobles. He asserted that if "the Russian peasants are freed" then the "poor [noble] people will have neither cook, coachman, nor lackey, unless they flatter their servants and overlook many of their failures, lest they have no servants or obedient peasants . . ." And he asked, where would one get servants when the peasants were freed? Certainly as soon as the peasant is taught something "he will depart to a famous master, who will pay him better . . . and one will have lost money training him."

Thus all nobles, even the "poor," need "servants" and "obedient peasants." But, since the "lowly people have not yet any sort of noble feelings," then only in serfdom can its obedience be assured. Otherwise, "terrible disagreement between pomeshchiki and peasants will develop, and it will take many troops to suppress them and continuous civil warfare in the state will ensue. . . ." As for the nobles, "their votchiny would be turned into a place dangerous for them to live, for they would depend on the peasants, and not the peasants on them."

In defense of the interests of the nobility Sumarokov went so far as to contrast the "horrors" after freeing the peasants with the "love" between pomeshchiki and peasants which theoretically exists under serfdom. "I have not lived long in villages, but [it seems to me] that all nobles and perhaps the peasants themselves would not be satisfied with such freedom, for diligence would decrease on both sides. And it is noted that the pomeshchiki love the peasants very much, and the peasants love them." Sumarokov stated that therefore the "pomeshchiki now live peacefully in their votchiny."

He was against any kind of government interference in the relations between pomeshchiki and peasants (called "servants" in the "Nakaz"). Agreeing that "servants must have food and clothes" as the "Nakaz" requires, Sumarokov declared that all peasants have food and clothes, "but the lords cannot be ordered as to what kind of food and clothes."

---

[19] *Sbornik Russkogo istoricheskogo obshchestva,* X, 82–7.

He thought that the justice over the serfs should be the "consciences of the lords," who should be "good lords," not "tyrants."

While insisting on the preservation of serfdom without any changes, Sumarokov at the same time opposed the apparent evils of serfdom. He was troubled that people were sold "like cattle." Obviously Sumarokov favored stopping the sale of the peasant away from his family and his land. Even the most ardent defenders of serfdom were in favor of such a limitation on the power of the lords. Sumarokov condemned cruel pomeshchiki, to whom he refused the honorary name of "household managers," calling them instead "household destroyers." The latter did not understand that they must take care of their peasants. For if a nobleman represented a "head" and the peasant a "little toe," one must remember that the body cannot be without a head; however even the little toe is also part of the body." [20] These attacks did not go beyond the limits of the usual attacks by spokesmen of the nobility of the time against the sins of their class.

The fact that Sumarokov was a firm supporter of serfdom does not contradict his sharp criticism of the evil uses of serfdom and his humanitarian attitude toward the "lowly people," the serfs. "Honest spokesmen of any given social order based on submission of one class to another were always against abuse of the exclusive rights enjoyed by the ruling class. And the more sincerely they were convinced that the existence of these rights was necessary for the general welfare, the more energetically they opposed their abuse." Therefore Sumarokov "could, without contradicting himself, insist on serfdom and at the same time condemn inhuman pomeshchiki." [21]

Opposing the development of heavy industry and manufacturing already under way in Russia and seeking to retain the exclusively agrarian nature of the country's economy and the inviolability of serfdom, Sumarokov belonged to the conservative and reactionary economic faction.

The Extremist Serf-owner, M. M. Shcherbatov

The economic views of Shcherbatov most clearly expressed the reactionary ideology of the ruling class, against which the best people of the time fought. In this struggle against reactionary ideology, progressive Russian economic thought developed and became revolution-

---

[20] Sumarokov, *Polnoe sobranie sochinenii,* Pt. X, p. 160.
[21] Plekhanov, *Sochineniia,* XXI, 224.

ary. A. N. Radishchev and M. M. Shcherbatov represented opposite sides in Russian socio-economic thought at the end of the eighteenth century. "Prince Shcherbatov and A. Radishchev," says Herzen, "symbolize the two extremes of thought during the time of Catherine. The sad sentinels of two different doors, they, like Janus, look in opposite directions." [22]

Prince Mikhail Michailovich Shcherbatov (1733–1790) was a frank defender of serfdom and a violent enemy not only of the hopes of freedom of the peasantry, but also of the most cautious liberal tendencies of certain nobles. The most interesting of Shcherbatov's economic works are "Statistics in the Judgment of Russia," "Thoughts on the Damage to Trade Caused by the Entrance of a large Number of Merchants into the Nobility and Officer Corps," "The Condition of Russia in Terms of Money and Bread at the Beginning of 1788 Before the Turkish War," "Justification of Encouragement of Sobriety by Law." The Utopia of Shcherbatov, the "Journey to the Land of Ophir of Mr. S . . . , a Swedish Noble" also provides material for judging his economic views.[23]

A justification of serf production, typical of the views of the spokesmen for the ruling feudal class, was given by Shcherbatov in his notes, in his speeches as a deputy for the Yaroslav nobility to Catherine's Commission on a new Code of 1767, and also in his specially written work of 1785, "Thoughts on the Inconvenience for Russia of Freeing the Peasants and Servants or Letting Them Own Land." [24]

Shcherbatov favored a monarchy limited by the counsel of "wise" hereditary nobles. Here he continued the reactionary line of the "leaders" of 1730. In the utopian "Journey to the Land of Ophir" he presented his ideal of a police-noble serf state which relegated the peasant to eternal slavery devoid of rights. The Utopia is permeated with the idea of the necessity of strengthening feudal serfdom. Man is born for society, but the union of people in a society is impossible without leaders; therefore all power should be considered established by God.

Shcherbatov was dissatisfied with the autocratic policy of Catherine II and criticized it from the viewpoint of a reactionary noble seeking to promote his domination of the political and economic life of

---

[22] A. I. Hertsen, *Sochineniia* [Works] (Moscow: 1919), IX, 270.

[23] See M. M. Shcherbatov, *Sochineniia* [Works] (St. Petersburg: 1896–8), 2 vols.; see also his *Neizdannye sochineniia* [Unpublished Works] (Moscow: Sotsekgiz, 1935).

[24] Published in *Chteniia v Obshchestve istorii i drevnostei rossiiskikh* [Readings in the Society of Russian History and Antiquities], Bk. 3, Pt. V (1861), pp. 98–134.

Russia. In spite of the fact that serfdom and the privileges of the pomeshchiki had been expanded to the limit in the second half of the eighteenth century and that serfdom differed little from slavery, Shcherbatov demanded their further extension. He thought that the rights and demands of the hereditary nobility were insufficiently satisfied by the policy of Catherine II and considered this neglect the basic reason for the retarded economic development of the country. Shcherbatov's criticism of autocracy was *criticism of the right;* it aimed at strengthening the power of the reactionary aristocratic circles.

Shcherbatov was an educated man. In his speeches and literary works he demagogically used radical phraseology, which led to the confusion of some scholars who saw in Shcherbatov a virtual propagandist for the teachings of the French encyclopedists. Some contemporary authors erroneously include Shcherbatov among the leaders of progressive ideas in Russia.[25] This faulty evaluation of Shcherbatov's positions was not new. Even in the nineteenth century, A. Brikner argued that in the Commission on a new Code, Shcherbatov "favored some liberal beginnings, was a defender of humanism, a noble thinker, and a philanthropist." [26] In comparing Shcherbatov to Mirabeau, Brikner ignores the historical truth that Mirabeau defended the interests of the third estate against the nobility, whereas Shcherbatov tried to strengthen and expand the rights and privileges of the nobility. Plekhanov also incorrectly judged Shcherbatov as a noble-thinking man, who *in his own way* espoused the good of the people.[27]

Actually, Prince Shcherbatov was a representative of the reactionary aristocratic element in Russian economic thought during the heyday of serfdom and the beginning of its decomposition. The chief aim of his economic works was the preservation and consolidation of serfdom. He led a fierce struggle against representatives of Russian progressive economic thought. Shcherbatov was the most frank exponent of the economic demands of his class. They were directed against the liberation of the peasants, against the aims of the merchant, and also against the actions of certain liberal members of the nobility.

In his works Shcherbatov showed the advantage of separating the "various layers of people living in the state, so that each, knowing its

[25] See G. Vasetskii and M. Iovchuk, *Ocherki po istorii russkogo materializma XVIII i XIX vv.* [Outlines of the History of Russian Materialism of the XVIII and of the XIX Centuries] (Moscow: Gospolitizdat, 1942), pp. 43–4.

[26] A. Brikner, "Kniaz M. M. Shcherbatov kak chlen Bolshoi Komissii 1767 g." [Prince M. M. Shcherbatov as a Member of the Great Commission of 1767], *Istoricheskii vestnik,* VI (October, 1881), p. 245.

[27] Plekhanov, *op. cit.,* XXII, 217.

rights and limits, would not interfere with the calling of the other." [28] This idea expressed the desire to perpetuate feudalism and attempted to prove the "naturalness" of stratified society, the legality of the nobles' privileges, and the peasants' complete lack of rights.

Shcherbatov interpreted the teachings of enlightened men of the eighteenth century on natural law in the most reactionary manner. He stated that people were different by nature and nature itself destined some to be leaders and others to be slaves. He claimed that it was not a social system, but eternal nature which once and for all theoretically determined "some to be leaders, others to be willing accomplices, and still a third [class] to be blind obeyers." [29]

The belief that it was the "destiny" of the peasants to give unquestioned obedience is clearly shown in his reactionary utopian "Journey to the Land of Ophir." In this utopian state all land belonged to the pomeshchiki, who were members of the state and military service. Soldiers live in military settlements and, like peasants, have some land and perform barshchina. The officers' land "must be worked by the soldiers and their children." The cruelest serflike exploitation prevails in the military settlements. Shcherbatov contended that such a system in the army would induce officers to "increase the number of their subordinates." He thought that the advantage of a military settlement was that the soldiers would place their sons in the army and thus free the pomeshchiki from supplying recruits. In addition, the military settlements were to serve as outposts against peasant uprisings. "In case of any internal danger, the enemy of the state finds fortifications everywhere." [30]

Shcherbatov accorded the state complete responsibility for the maintenance of officials and officers according to their social position so that the nobles could use their income from large estates "to improve their households and buildings in their villages."

In the ideal state, according to Shcherbatov, it is determined for all time that each class is to live within its income, and the ambition to live better is even considered dishonest. Such ideas showed the efforts of the spokesmen of the ruling class to cut off every effort of the oppressed toiling masses to improve their situation. Shcherbatov struggled most actively and insistently to stem the movement to free the peasants. Opposing the peasants' efforts to attain equality, he set himself the task of "showing the chimera of equality in the views of

---

[28] Shcherbatov, *Sochineniia,* I, 114.
[29] *Ibid.,* I, 222.
[30] *Ibid.,* I, 914.

the enlightened philosophers," [31] that is, the unreality of their teachings on natural human equality and the necessity of social equality.

Shcherbatov tried to prove the futility of the general striving for wealth. In the article "On the Benefits of Insufficiency" he spoke of the relative value of wealth and the necessity for each class to be once and for all satisfied with its place and level of life; he hypocritically praised the saving power of "insufficiency" and wrote of the ruin borne by corrupting wealth. Shcherbatov especially showed his reactionary aims in his discourse on the *rights of ownership*. He well understood that the nobles' monopoly of land ownership was the basis of their economic and political rule. He constantly stressed that only the nobility, "the first rank of the state," and the "famous corps of the wellborn" could have exclusive right to own land with villages of serfs and all the "land products" and natural resources. The nobles should have the right to process agricultural raw materials and to exploit the natural resources. Shcherbatov even said that the nobles "show restraint and do not usurp the rights of others." [32]

He advised a purely feudal measure to counteract the impoverishment of ancient noble families—to preserve the difference in the right of disposing of hereditary and acquired estates. The nobles ought to keep not only all the land they have but obtain state and former church lands with the peasants settled thereon.

For "improving" agriculture he proposed *"selling all state and economic villages to the nobles."* [33] Such sale should be made at reduced prices in order that money would not be taken from the nobles, and the sold villages should be declared permanently endowed. Actually this meant free distribution of all state lands with peasants to the pomeshchiki. This plan clearly shows his leanings toward serfdom. Shcherbatov welcomed the enserfment of the Ukrainian peasants and suggested giving the free unsettled Ukrainian lands as a gift to the Russian nobles.

The progressive demands of the deputies Korobin and Kozelskii to limit the arbitrariness of the pomeshchiki in disposing of peasant property evoked violent objections from Shcherbatov. He did not even want to hear of giving the peasant the right of ownership not only of land, but also of movable property. Contradicting reality, he asserted that serfs "have complete ownership . . . of all their movable property," [34] and the pomeshchiki lend them everything necessary for con-

[31] *Ibid.*, I, 221.
[32] *Ibid.*, I, 95.
[33] *Ibid.*, I, 667.
[34] *Ibid.*, I, 184.

ducting their establishments. He declared that he was "terror-stricken" by the very proposal of taking even a portion of the pomestie land for use by the peasants. Giving the peasant the right to own land was harmful both to the landlord and to the peasant himself. It would cause increased mobilization of all land, including pomeshchiki, and make part of the peasantry landless. This opinion was typical of feudal spokesmen. Contradictions in the bourgeois development were used as one of the means of defending the feudal system of exploitation and justifying its existence. The old ruling class was ideologically opposed to the development of new forms of ownership and productive relations.

Shcherbatov was decisively against freedom for the peasants. Trying to present the nobles' exploitation of the serfs as some kind of "union" of these classes, he stressed that "this union and interdependence should be strengthened, not broken down." [35]

In his ardent defense of the class privileges of the noble-exploiters Shcherbatov unashamedly and demagogically exploited even the high patriotism of the Russian people. Adroitly juggling words concerning patriotism, he constantly emphasized that an individual who loves his fatherland "cannot have disturbing thoughts," [36] among which he listed not only ideas of liberating the peasants, but even the most timid demands for partial weakening of the pressure of serfdom and limiting the arbitrariness of the pomeshchiki. In the Commission on preparing a new Code, Shcherbatov as a leader of the extreme right wing deputy-serf owners stimulated reactionary agitation against any and all efforts to improve the situation of the peasants. In the discussions on the "plan of nobles' rights" he sharply opposed giving pomeshchiki the right to free certain villages from serfdom if they so desired.

Shcherbatov thought the peasants were incapable of conducting their establishments independently. Without pomeshchiki supervision, the peasant would "give himself up to laziness," discard farming and trade, and would not go to work in the factories where the pomeshchiki sent him during the winter, to "increase their profits." Shcherbatov tried demagogically to present the narrow mercenary interests of the nobles as the general national interests; he threatened the state with every evil if the government should consent to the demands of some of the deputies for lightening the peasant burden.

Shcherbatov, like all serf owners, feared peasant uprisings. The extreme class prejudice of this spokesman of the nobility is clearly expressed in his hope of averting peasant uprisings by further increas-

[35] *Ibid.*, I, 197.
[36] *Ibid.*, II, 268.

ing the yoke of serfdom and the exploitation of the peasantry. Frightened by the peasant war led by Pugachev, Shcherbatov strove even more ardently to strengthen "the ancient power of the pomeshchik over the peasant"; he defamed the working people in every way and considered them unworthy of freedom and ownership of land.

Trying to becloud the deep material basis of the peasant war, Shcherbatov saw its cause in the speeches of the deputies defending peasant interests in the Commission on drafting a new Code which met in 1767. In "Thoughts on the Inconvenience of Freeing the Peasants and Servants in Russia or Letting Them Own Land" he argued that "the carelessly proposed views of the deputies, and especially those of Korobin, implanted this disease into the hearts of the lowly people, present here as deputies . . . and entrenched itself in coarse and thoughtless souls. A spirit of insubordination and depravity has resulted from various false rumors and the idle talk of peasants, freeholders, old servants, and other deputies of low ranks who, after their departure, spread these bad seeds into the distant regions of Russia . . ." [37] "And after the dismissal of the deputies," he continued, "great evil developed, when almost all the peasants united for the slightest cause with the enemies of the fatherland . . ." Calling Emelyan Pugachev "an enemy of the fatherland," Shcherbatov could not help but note that the "spirit of revolt" was present not only among those peasants who directly participated in the armed rebellion, "but also among almost all the other peasants, who were awaiting a chance to commit a crime." [38]

The activities of the noble, serf-owning, reactionary spokesmen, frightened by the peasant war of 1773–1774, were increased still more by the fear that the ideas of the bourgeois French Revolution of 1789 would spread in Russia.

Constantly defending serfdom, Shcherbatov threatened the revolt of the nobles if the government tried to free the peasants. Advancing various arguments against giving the peasants freedom and ownership of land, he concluded: "In spite of what natural law says, it is best to leave Russian peasants in the condition in which they have remained for several centuries." [39] He asserted that France could not be a model for Russia. In France the peasants were dissatisfied with their dependence. In Russia, he claimed, the peasants were content with their pomeshchiki, they did not feel that the land was not their own. As for

---

[37] *Chteniia v Obshchestve istorii i drevnostei rossiiskikh,* Bk. 3, Pt. V (1861), p. 98.

[38] *Chteniia v Obshchestve istorii i drevnostei rossiiskikh,* Bk. 3, Pt. V, p. 99.

[39] Shcherbatov, *Neizdanye sochineniia,* p. 8.

the pomeshchiki, they were not interested in freeing the peasants, because "the payment that could be obtained from the peasants for those lands which they received would never equal the income the pomeshchik gets from his peasants . . . What has worked out beautifully in France would be unfeasible in Russia." [40]

Opposing the liberation of the peasants, Shcherbatov thus freely admitted that the pomeshchiki extorted incomparably more surplus product from the serfs than they could get from free renters of their land. He praised the Baltic pomeshchiki who, by the cruelest exploitation of the peasants, made poor land productive and profitable.

According to Shcherbatov, the decline of Russian agriculture in the second half of the eighteenth century "comes from the wastefulness of peasants and pomeshchiki and the lack of people to oversee this necessary work for the State." [41] Shcherbatov attributed the partial crop failure and terrible famine of 1787–1788 to the movement of the village population to non-agricultural work as a result of the spread of the obrok system, to the increased idleness of monastery lands after their secularization, to the export of grain, and to the lack of experienced managers on the pomestie estates. Another reason for the famine, according to Shcherbatov, was the rapid growth of population. Thus he carefully avoided the principal cause of peasant poverty and hunger, the merciless exploitation of the serfs.

Shcherbatov conceded as just the demand to alleviate the situation of the peasants under "bad" pomeshchiki, but this should be accomplished "without interfering with ancient state institutions," [42] that is, in no case should serfdom be infringed upon. He categorically opposed the sale of peasants without land. This belief was not dictated by any defense of peasant interests, but by an effort to preserve the free labor for the pomeshchiki and to halt the "impoverishment" of noble estates. Such a desire accounted for his plan for "military settlements," directed against recruitment from pomeshchiki estates.

Shcherbatov's works reflect the bitter competition between capitalist and votchina-serf manufacturing. He emphasized the necessity of the nobility's ownership of industry, which he believed would be one of the factors in strengthening the economic dominance of the noble class.

Processing Russian raw materials in pomestie factories he consid-

---

[40] *Ibid.*, p. 12. Shcherbatov wrote "A Memorandum on the Peasant Problem" in 1768 in answer to Bearde de l'Abbaye's essay which won Catherine's prize in 1766.

[41] Shcherbatov, *Sochineniia,* I, 635.

[42] *Ibid.*, I, 198.

ered a chief task and economic duty of the nobility. He maintained that the votchina factory was very important in raising the income of the pomeshchik. The chief advantage of a votchina factory over that of the merchant was in the union of industry and agriculture. This would stimulate production of agricultural raw materials and encourage "love of work" in the peasants, that is, force them to work full time summer and winter for the pomeshchik and liquidate the seasonal use of serf labor on the estate. Shcherbatov's views on the economic role of the votchina factory expressed the adaptation of the nobility to conditions of rising capitalism.

The right to own land, Shcherbatov emphasized, includes the right to own everything on and within the land. He defended the exclusive right of the nobles to own "factories processing flax and hemp and other land and economic products." [43] Along with distilling enterprises, factories processing agricultural raw materials should belong only to nobles. Shcherbatov ardently resisted the granting of titles and privileges to merchants. In the Commission on drafting a new Code he sharply opposed the deputy from the city of Serpe'sk, Rodion Glinkov,[44] who defended the merchants from oppression by the nobility. The nobles—the owners of land, raw materials, and serfs—must have preference over merchants, who possessed none of these assets.

Shcherbatov justified his belief in the nobility's exclusive right of ownership by its service to the state, although the obligatory services of the nobility had been abolished earlier by Peter III. He persistently denied the right of the merchants to own serfs. Peasants and merchants, said this jealous defender of the privileges of the nobility, have an identical "low" origin; and it should not be "that an equal owns an equal." Shcherbatov thought that merchants should use only hired labor in their enterprises and that this labor should be recruited exclusively from quit-rent peasants. Once again his main purpose was to augment the pomeshchiki income from quit-rent peasants.

Shcherbatov used other arguments to hide his real reasons for opposing the merchants. Buying serfs was ruinous to the merchants and harmful to the state, since a large number of people are thus taken away from agriculture. Every agriculturist in Russia produced bread for five [classes of] people (officials, nobles, merchants, workers, and soldiers). The purchase of serfs by merchants and industrialists would

---

[43] *Ibid.*, I, 17.

[44] Rodion Glinkov was an outstanding pioneer in technology. In 1760 Glinkov constructed a mechanical water-frame. In England Arkwright's mechanical water-frame did not appear until 1771. See V. V. Danilevskii, *Russkaia tekhnika* [Russian Technology] (2nd edition, Leningrad: 1948), p. 162.

remove them from agriculture, which would inevitably result in famine.

Shcherbatov opposed the purchase of serfs by merchants, not because he preferred freely hired labor to forced serf labor, but because he intended to retain the exclusive right of serf exploitation for the nobility. He emphasized that buying villages for factories was necessary only under Peter, for then it was impossible to hire people at any price. Now conditions had changed, and peasants were willing to work in factories for hire. As another argument in support of his position he pointed out the difficult position of the serfs in merchant factories, where they worked "under very bad conditions both in regard to their maintenance and their morals," and where skilled workers "in order not to reveal their mastery to outsiders are treated almost like slaves." [45] He contrasted this state of affairs to the allegedly "fatherly" attitude of the pomeshchiki toward serfs in factories on their estates. Shcherbatov showed the necessity and advantage of maintaining serf labor as the basis not only of agriculture, but also of the developing industry.

In his work "Statistics in the Judgment of Russia" he described the great natural wealth of the country, especially that in the Orenburg gubernia, all of which must be utilized. To develop industry successfully, it is necessary first of all to have a clear knowledge of the location of useful minerals and the means of extracting and processing them. Lack of statistical information resulted from the incompetence of officials and from the stubbornness of factory owners, who hid their wealth. These statements were aimed at arousing the nobility to take all industry into their hands and to eliminate the competition of the merchant factory owners. He emphasized that in organizing industry merchants heeded only their own selfish interests, while the nobles were capable of assuring the interests of the state first and then their own. Thus he exaggerated the economic role of the nobility.

Shcherbatov admitted the historical necessity of the economic policy of Peter I, which endeavored to overcome the backwardness of Russia. In his "Calculation" of how many years it would have taken Russia without Peter I to attain the level of development which it had reached at the end of the eighteenth century, he concluded that 210 years would have been required. Peter, by his insistent and powerful policy, stimulated the study of the experience of the leading countries, without which Russia would have had to invent everything already

---

[45] Shcherbatov, *Sochineniia,* I, 98–9.

known in other lands, which would have taken "many thousands of years." [46] The government should not begrudge money to investigate the technical methods of production of the most highly developed industrial countries and to transfer this experience to Russia; he recommended particularly the study of the fine linen produced in Europe from Russian flax. He suggested that premiums be granted to those Russian factory owners who first learned to make this material.

Although he admitted the correctness of the economic policy of Peter I at the beginning of the century, Shcherbatov was strongly against any measures which would elevate the merchant. He defended the policy protective of noble enterprises pursued by the successors of Peter I—a policy designed to hamper and limit the rights of the merchant. Competition of capitalist production in industry had disrupted the economic position of the nobility. Therefore its spokesman, Shcherbatov, gave much attention to the problems of industry and trade. He defended noble interests against the merchant, urged the nobility to own factories, and demanded from the government every sort of limitation on the merchant. This was the ideology of the adaptation of the old ruling class, the nobility, to the new trends of economic development. In order to strengthen the economic domination of the nobility and increase its income from quit-rent peasants, Shcherbatov insistently defended the freedom of peasant industries and trade against attempts by the merchant to limit peasant enterprise.

He sharply disagreed with the guild limitation and the requirement that all peasant craftsmen be obligatorily registered in guilds and that all peasant tradesmen be placed in the merchant class. These demands of the merchant class were disadvantageous to the noble serf owners, who had craftsmen working not only for them, but also for the market. Registration of these craftsmen in a guild would deprive the pomeshchik of the free work of the home craftsman and of a source of considerable money income. Shcherbatov insisted on the freedom of peasant industries, but, at the same time, regarded the removal of peasants from agriculture for work in industry, building, and trade as a "basic evil in Russia."

Fighting any gradual removal of workers from agriculture, Shcherbatov tried to reveal the economic basis for the development of crafts among the peasantry. The chief cause of this process he considered to be the imposition on the peasant of taxes, first by the state, and then by the pomeshchiki. As a result, peasants left agriculture and took up

---

[46] *Ibid.*, II, 13–22.

other work, and agriculture began to decline. Shcherbatov preferred the barshchina form of exploitation to obrok—natural over money rent—that is, he defended the more backward forms of economy.

The second cause of the decline of agriculture Shcherbatov saw in the insufficient land held by many peasants. For example, in the Moscow gubernia, according to Shcherbatov, the peasants had so little land that they were forced to take up crafts in order to eat. While paying attention to peasant lack of land, Shcherbatov was silent about the great pomestie latifundia, which were the real reason why peasants had so little land.

The third reason for the development of industry and crafts he placed with the efforts of peasants to find work easier than that of pomestie serfs. They desired to escape even temporarily from the surveillance of the pomeshchik. Their ambition to obtain a better life reflected "a love for luxury which has filled all the state ranks, even that of the peasants,"[47] according to Shcherbatov. He was concerned with the development of noble trade in agricultural products. In his demand that merchants be prevented from buying grain from peasants in the villages, he sought to monopolize the grain trade for the pomeshchiki. In his opinion, trade was the link between agriculturist and craftsman. Through trade they fulfilled their "obligations to one another" and labored for one another while each worked for his own good.

Russia needed especially a well developed domestic trade because of her sparse population, few towns, and great distances. Shcherbatov proposed the creation throughout Russia of trade fairs to serve the cities and surrounding areas within a radius of twenty verst and to serve villages and surrounding areas within a radius of twelve verst, "so that one does not undermine the other." At these fairs peasants and craftsmen would sell, at retail and free-market prices, their goods to the local population or to merchants, and not at predetermined "moderate prices," as the merchants demanded.

Shcherbatov's proposal to limit the area of trade fairs was to effect a convenient control by the local noble organizations and pomeshchiki over peasant trade in order to increase their obrok. Shcherbatov's reasoning on free trade was pervaded by the interests of the nobility against the persistent demands of the merchant that all trading nobles and peasants be registered as merchants.

Showing the nobility all the advantages of controlling industry and trade and demanding for them privileges and exclusive rights, Shcher-

[47] *Ibid.*, I, 631.

batov sharply opposed the imposition on the trading nobles of the various duties and taxes levied on the merchant. Shcherbatov was strongly against merchant efforts to equal the nobility "in luxury and ostentation" and at the same time tried to justify the parasitic need of the nobility, the fabulous luxury of the "wellborn."

In "Thoughts on the Nobility" Shcherbatov wrote that "a nobleman who has extra income should either spend it or lend it at interest, and not hoard it in the cellar." [48] By spending his income, the noble "encourages art, crafts, and trade," and by lending it, he "satisfies another's need to his profit." Shcherbatov tried to make the parasitic need of the nobles a factor in the economic development of the country. On the other hand, according to Shcherbatov, merchants should observe "moderation in everything";[49] they should be moderate in their personal needs, should not pursue luxury, and should invest their money in trade and industry.

In the article "On the Ruin of Morals in Russia," Shcherbatov asserted that when merchants stop wanting to be officers and nobles, then trade will increase and arts and crafts flourish "to make the necessary things for the elegance and splendor of a certain number of people in Russia." [50] This justification of the luxury of noble life and the condemnation of the attempts of others to raise their standard of living Shcherbatov also espoused in "Statistics in the Judgment of Russia." Opposing popular education, which leads to "a spirit of insubordination," Shcherbatov feared that "if lowly people are educated and compare their heavy taxes with the elegance of the rulers and nobles, yet unaware both of the needs of the state and the uses of that elegance, will they not rebel at the taxes and finally rise in mutiny?" [51] This is the frank class presentation by a serf-owner reactionary of the problem of accumulation and demand.

Stinginess and thrift, typical traits of the bourgeoisie in the period of early accumulation, were foreign to Shcherbatov. Frugality and abstention from waste were the lot of the merchant and not of the nobility, according to this apologist of feudalism. Upholding the parasitic luxury of the nobility, Shcherbatov anticipated the English parson Malthus, who, as Marx shows, "at the beginning of the 1820's defended a particular division of labor where saving was the affair of the capitalist actually concerned with production, and spending was that of the other participants in the distribution of surplus value:

[48] *Ibid.*, I, 252.
[49] *Ibid.*, I, 254.
[50] *Ibid.*, II, 246.
[51] *Ibid.*, I, 618.

landed aristocracy, people supported by the state, clergy, and so forth." [52]

The arrogant nobles found themselves increasingly at the mercy of merchant-usurers. For luxurious life in the capital, in other cities, and on estates, the nobility had to spend a considerably greater amount of money than their income provided, in spite of the merciless exploitation of the serfs. Estates were mortgaged and remortgaged, but even this was insufficient. Usurers charged high interest for loans. Shcherbatov sharply opposed the proposals of some economists to allow money lenders "to set the price on their money as they liked." Since usurers ruined the nobles by high interest rates, Shcherbatov thought it just that the government should limit the interest rate by law. In case of violation of this law he recommended punishment not by imprisonment, but by "that which is his soul, conscience, and whole being, that is, money." [53] As a whole, Shcherbatov's conclusions against usurious interest rates were less economic than ethical in nature.

Prince M. M. Shcherbatov was the central figure of the reactionary direction of economic thought of the second half of the eighteenth century. His economic works are a frank defense of existing serfdom. He saw a further increase of the noble dictatorship and of oppression of the peasants as the only means to prevent the peasantry from rising to fight for its freedom.

Shcherbatov could not ignore the development of capitalism and its disruptive influence on serfdom. To preserve the economic domination of his class he persistently recommended that the nobility own industry and trade. With this aim he always exaggerated the advantages of votchina manufacturing over capitalist manufacturing, and even defended peasant industry and trade against the claims of the merchant, not realizing that development of peasant trade and industry was the broadest base of growth of the new capitalist order on its way to relieve serfdom.

Shcherbatov's concern for the ever stronger domination of the hereditary nobility permeated all his works on economic questions—on land ownership, the freedom of internal trade and peasant industry, the development of industry, and the utilization of natural wealth. Through his program Shcherbatov did not call Russia forward on the path of economic and political progress, but dragged her back to pre-Petrine Rus.

This spokesman of the pomeshchiki regarded serf agriculture as the firm economic base for the existence of the Russian state. He saw the

[52] Marx, *Kapital,* I, 600–1.

[53] Shcherbatov, *Neizdanye sochineniia,* p. 134.

cause for the "impoverishment" of agriculture and the downfall of the pomestie economy in the development of trade and industry. To "improve" the pomestie, he demanded the cessation of the flow of peasants to the towns. He saw the development of votchina factories, closely linked to agriculture, as an important but incidental source of pomeshchiki income and as a means of adjusting the nobility to the newly arising market conditions. This reactionary spokesman would have destined Russia to eternal vegetation as an agrarian country.

CHAPTER 17. *P. I. Rychkov, Inquirer into the Economy of Russia. His Economic-Geographic Works.*

Peter Ivanovich Rychkov (1712–1777) was born into the family of a merchant-exporter. While still a boy, he entered the service of a merchant company of linen manufacturers and learned "to keep books and accounts by the European bookkeeping rules." [1] He was one of the first Russians to master the theory and practice of double entry and the balance sheet.[2]

Having worked some time in the administration of treasury factories and in the Petersburg port customs, Rychkov at twenty-two years of age was signed on as "expert bookkeeper" for the Orenburg expedition. Later he became principal aide to I. K. Kirilov, and then to V. N. Tatishchev, successive chiefs of the Orenburg territory. Kirilov and Tatishchev [3] directed his attention to the study of Bashkiriia and the exploration of the southern Urals. He devoted his scientific and practical activity to an investigation of this territory—as economist, historian, geographer, and agronomist.

Rychkov was associated with many of the famous figures of Russian science and culture of his time. M. V. Lomonosov, who valued Rychkov and his work highly, was instrumental in having the Academy of Sciences confer the title of corresponding member on him.[4] In addition

[1] See "Zapiski P. I. Rychkova" [P. I. Rychkov's Notes], *Russkii arkhiv,* III (1905), pp. 298–300.

[2] For a general description of discount development in Russia in the XVIII century see V. F. Shirokii, "Voprosy torgovogo ucheta v zakonodatelnykh aktakh i literature Rossii XVIII veka" [Problems of Commercial Discount in Legal Documents and Literature of Russia in the XVIII Century], *Trudy Leningradskogo instituta sovetskoi torgovli* [Works of the Leningrad Institute of Soviet Trade], Issue III (1940), pp. 51–87.

[3] See Chapter XIII.

[4] See *Protokoly zasedanii Konferentsii imperatorskoi Akademii nauk s 1725 po 1803 gg.* [Minutes of the Meetings of Conferences of the Imperial Academy of Sciences from 1725 to 1803] (St. Petersburg: 1899), II, 420; Modzalevskii, *Rukopisi Lomonosova v Akademii nauk SSSR,* pp. 327–31. Rychkov's relations with the Academy of Sciences are adequately treated by Pekarskii, *Snosheniia P. I. Rychkova s Akademiei nauk v XVIII stoletii* [P. I Rychkov's Relations With the Academy of Sciences in the XVIII Century] (St. Petersburg: 1866).

to being the first corresponding member of the Petersburg Academy of Sciences, he was also a member of the Free Economic Society [5] and of the Free Russian Society at the University of Moscow.

The most important of Rychkov's works (in the 1740's) was the *History of Orenburg After the Founding of the Orenburg Gubernia.* In 1755 Rychkov finished the first part of his major work, *Orenburg's Topography or a Detailed Description of Orenburg Gubernia,*[6] and sent it to Lomonosov. The appearance of the manuscript of the first part of the *Topography* was an event in the development of Russian science and culture and in the struggle with foreign, especially German, domination.

In the printed organ of the Academy of Sciences, *Monthly Works,* appeared an editorial with the deeply significant title "A Proposal on How to Correct the Errors of Foreign Authors Writing on the Russian State." Publication of this editorial showed that Russian scientists recognized their independence and strength. It showed that "every attentive reader of foreign books on Russia who has some knowledge of Russian history and geography has to admit that these books are full of errors." From this followed the conclusion that Russian scientists must themselves prepare the true history and geography of the Russian state. But such a task could not be undertaken so long as the separate parts of the country were unknown. It would be possible only if "there were a man in each gubernia like Rychkov in the Orenburg gubernia, who last year sent the Academy of Sciences a description of that gubernia with accompanying maps." [7] The struggle for independent study of native history, geography, and economy runs through all of Rychkov's scientific activity.

When the first part of the *Topography . . . of the Orenburg Gubernia* was nearing completion, *Monthly Works* in 1755 published the "Correspondence Between Two Friends on Commerce," which consisted of several letters. In this work Rychkov expressed the economic ideas which he held at that time. He finished the second part of *Topography . . . of the Orenburg Gubernia* in 1760 [8] and published

---

[5] TsGADA, Fund 199, No. 385, Pt. I, copy 14, Sheet 16. A diploma given to P. I. Rychkov by the Free Economic Society in St. Petersburg in 1766 (copy).

[6] Published first in *Sochineniia i perevody k polze i uveseleniiu sluzhashchie* [Works and Translations, Serving Useful and Enjoyable Ends] (January–June, 1762).

[7] *Ezhemesiachnye sochineniia, k polze i uveseleniiu sluzhashchie* [Monthly Works, Serving Useful and Enjoyable Ends] (March, 1757), pp. 224 and 227–8.

[8] State Library of the USSR, Department of Manuscripts, Museum Collection, No. 6792. *"Topografiia ili opisanie Orenburgskoi gubernii"* [Topog-

both parts in 1762. Among the first works on the economic geography of our country, *Topography . . . of the Orenburg Gubernia* is famous as a detailed historical, geographical, and economic description, with the inclusion of statistical data.[9]

In his later years Rychkov wrote a continuation of his *History of Orenburg* [10] and compiled "historical extracts" on the Bashkir [11] and Kirgiz-Kaisak [12] people. Several months before his death he finished the description of Orenburg gubernia, arranged not geographically (like the *Topography*), but alphabetically: this was the two-volume *Lexicon, or Topographic Dictionary of the Orenburg Gubernia."* [13]

While describing its nature and economy, Rychkov indicated the great possibilities of the new region for mining, its prospects for the further development of agriculture, animal husbandry, hunting, and fishing, and he insisted on the conservation of the forests. He spoke of the necessity of strengthening the commercial ties of this broad region with the central regions of Russia and indicated the great importance to the southeast regions of Russia of foreign trade with the Central Asian Khanates, India, and China.

For Rychkov the basis of economic development was the division of labor, which he understood as the social division of labor. This awareness, however, he combined with an erroneous explanation of the causes for the social division of labor (the growth of population) and with naive historical ideas. Thus he began the social division of labor

---

raphy, or the Description of the Orenburg Gubernia], Part II (1760). First published in *Sochineniia i perevody* (July–November, 1762).

9 Rychkov's major work became known in Russia and abroad. It appeared in German translation in Hesse in 1771, and in Halle, Riga, in 1772. Schlözer published a review of this work in *Göttingischer Anzeigen von gelehrten Sachen* in 1766.

10 State Library of the USSR, Department of Manuscripts, *Sobranie arkhiva Paninykh* [Collection of Panin's Archive], VIII, 2. "Pisma ot statskogo sovetnika Petra Rychkova, kasaiushchiesia Orenburgskoi gubernii o inovercheskikh i drugikh ord proisshestviakh, takzhe i po bashkirskim delam" [Letters from the State Counsellor Peter Rychkov Related to the Orenburg Gubernia, About the Events Among the Dissenting and Other Hordes and also About the Bashkir Affairs], 1774 and 1775.

11 *Ibid.,* XII, Sheets 3–26, "Ekstrakt istoricheskoi o bashkirskom narode" [A Historical Treatise About the Bashkir People].

12 *Ibid.,* XI, Sheets 10–139 "Ekstrakt istoricheskoi o kirgiz-kaisatskom narode" [A Historical Treatise About the Kirghiz-Kaisak People], and *ibid.,* XII, Pt. 2, Sheets 83–94, and Pt. 3, Sheets 105–139.

13 State Library of the USSR, Department of Manuscripts, Museum Collection No. 2931. *Leksikon ili slovar topograficheskoi Orenburgskoi gubernii . . .* [Lexicon or a Topographic Dictionary of the Orenburg Gubernia], I–II (1776–7).

literally with the two biblical sons of Adam, the farmer, Cain, and the herder, Abel. Rychkov correctly viewed the social division of labor as the cause of the rise and development of barter. But the false premise of the eternal existence of a social division of labor gave rise to the idea that barter had always existed. As proof he cites forefather Noah, who, while building the Ark, supposedly employed barter. "Even in earliest times trade existed and, to a lesser degree, reciprocity of a form similar to contemporary commerce." [14] Rychkov saw the development of barter as having two stages: direct exchange ("reciprocity") and exchange through the medium of merchants ("trade"), that is, professional trade.

He was the first Russian author to present an outline of the "history of commerce," showing how the market developed on the basis of the social division of labor. This led him to conclude that "it is not now possible to limit further development in this direction." [15]

Of special interest in Rychkov's historical outline is the first short study of the development of "Russian commerce." Historical data led him to certain conclusions regarding the great economic possibilities of Russia: within her vast territory were centered a variety of natural resources like those of no other land. Therefore Russia, depending only on her natural resources, could develop her economy without the aid of foreign countries. At the same time, the "most glorious nations," by which Rychkov meant Holland and England, could not get along without Russian goods, whose production exceeded internal needs. Russia also occupied a favorable commercial-geographical position in the world: "the natural location of Russia for commerce is considered the best in the world." [16]

Rychkov thought the task of commerce was the creation of wealth. Defending the trade balance system, he viewed the origin of the wealth of Russia from this position. He wrote that Russia was acquiring precious metals like the great trade powers of the time. England and Holland never extracted valuable ores in their own territory, but secured and hoarded more gold and silver from foreign trade than the Spanish and Portuguese, who mined them in their American colonies. "As for silver and gold," wrote Rychkov in 1755, "which today means not only wealth, but also great power . . . these metals came to Russia, as far as I know, mainly through commerce, just as today Englishmen,

---

[14] P. I. Rychkov, "Perepiska mezhdu dvumia priiateliami o komertsii" [Correspondence Between Two Friends About Commerce], *Ezhemesiachnye sochineniia* (February, 1755), p. 107.

[15] *Ibid.* (February, 1755), p. 114.

[16] *Ibid.* (December, 1755), p. 494.

Dutchmen, and other commercial peoples who possess no mines nevertheless obtained through commerce a great amount of these metals. They, in fact, have more than other nations including those which extract these precious things." [17]

He maintained that Russia had always retained the precious metals which she received for goods, since the population was satisfied with domestic output; the insignificant import of foreign products was paid for in native goods, not in gold or silver. Hence Rychkov attacked the "luxury and well-being of the nobility under the successors of Peter." In contrast to M. M. Shcherbatov [18] who thought the extravagance of the nobility aided the development of the market and industry, Rychkov assailed the excesses of the nobility. In their demand for foreign goods the nobility caused an outflow of money; their excesses, in his opinion, also expanded internal consumption and cut down the export resources of the country. He spoke with disgust of nobles who surrounded themselves with numerous household retinues and thus withdrew labor from productive uses.

Dividing goods into raw products ("material" and "natural") and processed products ("manufactures"), Rychkov felt that only the latter should be exported. Only those raw materials which could not be processed within the country because of a surplus or a lack of qualified craftsmen and workers should be exported.[19]

Rychkov thought industry played a great role in the creation of wealth. "By the increase of manufactories, states always enrich themselves; it is not the regions which abound in agricultural goods that are prosperous and sound, but those in which manufactories and useful crafts are numerous and flourish." [20] Contrasting agricultural to industrial areas, he clearly preferred the latter. He thought the guiding principle in economic life and policy should be the "general idea of commerce." He included in the term "commerce" not only internal and foreign trade, but also industry. The chief and basic task of economic policy was to "increase all kinds of factories, manufactories, and industry; to establish companies and [conclude] treaties." [21] Thus Rychkov's economic views, presented in his works of the 1750's, pointed in the same direction as those of Peter I, Pososhkov, and Tatishchev.

At the end of the 1750's and the beginning of the 1760's pomestie

[17] *Ibid.* (April, 1755), pp. 326–8.

[18] See Chapter XVI.

[19] Rychkov, "Perepiska mezhdu dvumia priiateliami o komertsii," *Ezhemesiachnye sochineniia* (December, 1755), p. 509.

[20] *Ibid.*

[21] *Ibid.* (February, 1755), p. 121.

circles and the government became more interested in developing commodity agriculture, and the "Free Economic Society for the encouragement of agriculture and household management in Russia" was founded. At this time, Rychkov wrote two of his first works on agriculture: "A Letter on the Practice of Village Life" (1757) and "A Letter on Agriculture in the Kazan' and Orenburg Gubernias" (1758). In his later works he emphasized the basic importance of agriculture: "for the entire society no industry or craft can be so useful and profitable as agriculture." [22]

While giving decisive importance to the development of agriculture in respect to the agricultural population, Rychkov thought that the growth of industry which was taking place through the flow of population from the villages was expedient, but that the further promotion of industry should not be at the expense of agriculture. Thus, speaking of the development of factories for processing cotton and camel hair, he noted that "the state would benefit more if it employed masters and workers who had no previous connection with agriculture; for in the present state of our agriculture I consider it not only senseless but harmful to take these people for such or similar new employment." [23]

Rychkov was particularly opposed to removing workers from agriculture and using them in town crafts or small town trade. He admitted that sometimes "taking away peasants" was profitable both to peasants and pomeshchiki, but regarded it as a deeply negative phenomenon, for "the good which comes to society from agriculture is not had from them, and they feed on the bread sown by their brothers' hands." [24]

The same opinion was expressed a year later in Catherine's Commission on drafting a project for a new Code. An *ad hoc* commission organized from its membership to study the increase of population, agriculture, household management, colonization, crafts, and arts pointed out that it was harmful for the peasants to engage in "industry and trade," especially peddling and carting, which reduce the

---

[22] P. I. Rychkov, "Nakaz dlia upravitelia ili prikashchika o poriadochnom soderzhanii i upravlenii dereven v otsutstve gospodina" [An Instruction for the Administrator or a Steward About the Orderly Maintenance and Administration of Villages in the Lord's Absence], *Trudy Volnogo ekonomicheskogo obshchestva,* Pt. XVI (1770), p. 35.

[23] P. I. Rychkov, "O manufakturakh iz khlopchatoi bumagy i iz verbliuzhei shersti" [About Manufactures from Cotton and Camel's Hair], *ibid.,* Pt. II (1766), p. 101.

[24] P. I. Rychkov, "O sposobakh k umnozheniiu zemledeliia v Orenburgskoi gubernii" [About Methods to Increase Agriculture in the Orenburg Gubernia], *ibid.,* Pt. VII (1767), p. 20.

number in agriculture, since others must grow bread and deliver it for all these people."[25]

In Rychkov's works of the period 1765–75 the idea of the impossibility of any further growth of the Russian economy, except for agricultural progress, appears. Development of industry could not be achieved, in his opinion, without strengthening agriculture. Since he believed that agriculture was the basis of the country's economy, he insisted that it be given equal emphasis, yet he thought of progress in agriculture only within the framework of serfdom, especially along the lines of a barshchina economy. Preferring barshchina to obrok, Rychkov permitted the latter only where little arable land was available.

In the "Instructions for the Administrator or Steward," written for the competition of the Free Economic Society (1770), Rychkov, seeking various means of organizing barshchina labor in order to decrease its exploitation, proposed "intelligent" limits to exploitation, in order to assure the continued existence of serfdom. He thought it most expedient that the peasant work three days a week for the pomeshchik, an equal number for himself, and that he rest on Sunday.[26] He recommended that the pomeshchik be made responsible for "an intentional grain reserve" for the peasants, created by additional work at the end of the sowing and harvest period on the barshchina land.

According to Rychkov, the peasants themselves did not know their own interests and therefore worked their own establishments "poorly and little." He recommended supervision over the manner in which each peasant managed his farm; they were to be encouraged to plant vegetables and fruit gardens. But if all this "enlightenment" did not help Rychkov proposed that the landlords take repressive measures against recalcitrant peasants: send them to colonies, into the army, and so on.

The importance which Rychkov attributed to trade and industry

---

[25] State Library of the USSR, Department of Manuscripts, Museum Collection 2394/1. "Dela po Komissii sochineniia proekta novogo Ulozheniia" [Affairs of the Legislative Commission], II, Sheet 126.

[26] It is interesting to note that almost 30 years later (1797) Paul I, fearing a second "Pugachevshchina" following a new rise of peasant unrest, issued a manifesto on not forcing the peasants to work on Sunday. The manifesto decreed "that no one in any form should force peasants to work on Sundays, the more so since for agricultural work there are six days in the week, and these should be divided equally, for peasants and for pomeshchiki; by good administration these can be satisfactory to every economic need." (PSZ, Vol. 24, No. 17909). Limiting the barshchina to three days is not ordered, but only suggested, to the pomeshchiki. Thus the manifesto recommended the limitation on the barshchina, which Rychkov suggested in his "Instruction."

determined his high evaluation of the role of the merchant.[27] Accordingly the merchant should be the carrier of commerce. The chief merchants should be ennobled, while the leading nobles who were turning bourgeois should become a "trading nobility." Herein lies partly the difference between Rychkov's views and those of Pososhkov, who opposed nobles entering trade. Pososhkov thought that a noble who wanted to engage in trade should relinquish his title and enter the merchant class. Here, too, Rychkov differs from those spokesmen of the nobility, especially Shcherbatov, who, representing narrow class interests, demanded a noble monopoly on industry.

Rychkov fought for the enlightenment of the merchantry. Merchants should know commodities and markets, study law, and master bookkeeping. Insisting on the adoption of Italian bookkeeping, he said it should be adjusted to Russian conditions: "to adapt it to the condition of our trade and the nature of our merchants . . ." He proposed the compilation of a manual of all this information, "a merchants' lexicon" based on those published abroad, but excelling foreign models.

Supporting the advancement of productive forces and the market, Rychkov thought this development should not be spontaneous. He was opposed to competition, which he called cunning: rival merchants were guided only by their personal interests, often to the detriment of merchant trade interests and of the national economy as a whole. Thus he favored the elimination of competition and suggested that craft and merchant guilds were the agencies to accomplish this end. He also argued that these agencies should be used for active interference in economic life by the feudal-absolute state.

Rychkov insisted on the exclusive political domination of the nobility. After publication of the manifesto on the emancipation of the nobility (1762), he triumphantly declared that Peter III deserved not a golden, but a diamond, statue on a pearl pedestal. While he emphasized the guiding role of the nobility in agriculture and the desirability of attracting nobles into trade and industrial circles, he spoke of the great importance of the merchant in the development of the market and of industrial production. In order to strengthen the feudal-serf order and autocracy, Rychkov fought for the improvement and increased productivity of agriculture, for industrial growth, and for the extension of the market. His works, especially those on economics and

---

[27] Speaking of the merchantry, it is necessary to keep in mind that in Russia of the eighteenth century and a large part of the nineteenth, not only representatives of commercial capital, but those of industrial capital, were called merchants.

geography, were directed toward aiding the increase of productive forces and the market of the country. Therefore, with all his conservative political convictions, Rychkov's works on concrete economic questions had a progressive significance in the historical conditions of Russia at the time.

CHAPTER 18. *Spokesman of the Merchantry, M. D. Chulkov.*

A Short Survey of His Works.

Mikhail Dmitrievich Chulkov (1743–1793) was a famous spokesman of the merchantry during the period of rising capitalism. Chulkov stemmed from commoners. He studied at the gymnasium in Moscow University. In 1772 he was appointed a secretary to the Commerce College, where A. N. Radishchev served from 1777. Extant documents testify to the joint work of Radishchev and Chulkov in the Commerce College. In his later years Chulkov was a Senate secretary. During his youth he was poor, lived on a meager salary, and worked studiously to improve his education by reading books on various subjects. After attaining the position of a court counsellor and being granted a rank in the nobility, Chulkov bought a small estate in the village of Dmitrov in Moscow gubernia.[1]

Chulkov was famous as a publisher of satirical journals, and he was the first eminent collector of Russian tales and songs. In 1776 he published *The Mocker, or Glorious Tales,* in 1767, the *Short Mythological Dictionary,* in 1769–1770, *This and That* and *The Parnassian Mercer.* In 1770–1774 he published the *Collection of Various Songs,* in 1781–1788, the *Historical Description of Russian Commerce,* in 1788, *Economic Notes,* in 1789–1790, *Country Doctor,* and in 1792, the *Legal Dictionary.* Clearly his interests were very broad. The majority of Chulkov's works were published by N. I. Novikov under the imprint of the Moscow University Press.

In his satirical journals Chulkov ridiculed the evils of feudal society, without, however, criticizing its bases. He attacked the servility of the nobility toward foreigners and their scorn of Russian culture, and he tried to instill a feeling of national pride in his readers. Chulkov was opposed to burdening the Russian language with foreign words: "Why use the unnecessary to speak truthfully? This creates more harm and does not lead to elegant speech." [2]

---

[1] See V. Shklovskii, *Chulkov i Levshin* [Chulkov and Levshin] (Leningrad: 1933).

[2] M. D. Chulkov, "Peresmeshnik ili slavenskie skazki" [Mocker, or Famous Stories], *Russkaia proza XVIII veka* [Russian Prose of the XVIII Century] (Moscow-Leningrad: 1950), I, 90.

It must be confessed that Chulkov's economic views have scarcely been studied in our literature. His chief economic work, the *Historical Description of Russian Commerce at Ports and Borders from Ancient Times to the Present, and All Existing Laws Regarding It of the Sovereign Emperor Peter the Great and the Present Reigning Sovereign Empress Catherine the Great,* in seven volumes (twenty-one books), contained detailed documents, discussions, descriptions, decrees, information on mills, factories, and manufactories, on water and "land" routes, on internal and foreign trade, on money, and so on. Chulkov's work has much rich factual material.

The author presents his views in the prefaces and "forewords" to each book, in comments on various documents, and often by exposition of the ideas of various writers with whose views he agrees. References to literary sources are often inaccurate or completely absent, and the original words of the cited authors are rarely quoted, so that it is sometimes difficult to distinguish Chulkov's ideas from those of others. These methods were usual in eighteenth century literature.

This *Historical Description of Russian Commerce* was published in 1781–1788, first by the Academy of Sciences in Petersburg and then by Novikov's university press in Moscow. From this great work, Chulkov made extracts: the *Short History of Russian Trade* (1788); the *Dictionary of Established Markets in Russia, Published for the Use of Those Engaging in Trade* (1788); and also a special manual on bookkeeping, *Regulations Necessary for Russian Merchants, Primarily Young People, Containing Bookkeeping Rules* (1788).

While attached to the Commerce College, Chulkov set himself the task of filling the gap in Russian economic literature and creating a work which would supply merchants with special knowledge in the realm of trade and industry. He asserted that many foreign and Russian writers had dealt with Russian trade only in passing and in connection with other questions. Theirs were only "piecemeal" treatments, rather than the work of specialists, and therefore "up to now, we have not seen a complete system, nor a sufficient history of it."

Chulkov knew and used Rychkov's work, "Correspondence between two Friends on Commerce," but he considered it unsystematic and not complete enough. Rychkov's work had great influence on Chulkov, who adhered to the same broad interpretation of commerce and continued work on certain problems posed by his forerunners.

Progressive Russian merchants attached great importance to Chulkov's work. The merchants Golikov sent the first book of the first volume at their own expense "to every magistrate and town hall in Russia except capitals and towns settled by big merchants."

The fundamental work of Chulkov aimed at giving a general systematic history of Russian trade and industry and clarified many economic problems from the point of view of the interests of a merchant entering into entrepreneurial activity. This new, higher stage of the task of economic knowledge distinguishes Chulkov from his predecessors, the other spokesmen of the merchant class.

He tried to prove the importance of the development of industry and trade for increasing the power and economic independence of the state. As if arguing with Shcherbatov, he showed that in a country like Russia agriculture could be raised to a higher level only through the development of industry in the form of manufacturing, that is, of heavy industry.

In the "foreword" to the first book of the first volume of the *Historical Description of Russian Commerce* the plan of the whole work is outlined. As Chulkov himself emphasized, his work is not a simple history of trade, but a history of *commerce,* which included a survey of the development of industry, trade, transport and communications, credit, and monetary circulation. In this broad conception Chulkov declared commerce "the most useful occupation of mankind." Commerce discovers minerals and "extracts from them for our use products, the use, agreeability, and beauty of which we would never dream of if we did not see them." Commerce collects from the whole universe goods which a man, living in one land, can have at his disposal from a variety of other natural zones and countries. Contrasting production and wide market communication to natural economy, Chulkov even exaggerated the role of commerce, by calling it "that knot which alone is strong enough to sustain the well-being of human society." [3]

He aimed to perform the following tasks: to show what comprised the wealth of Russia, and whence it came; to give a history of the rise of industry and heavy industry and calculate the volume of production of factories; to discuss the social composition of enterprise owners and the forms of labor—serf and hired—used in industry; to examine domestic and foreign trade, with special attention to export and import goods; to explain the economic ties between Russia and other states, the nature of those ties, and determine the possibilities of the many-sided, independent economic development of his country; and, finally, to "add to this history" all regulations, instructions, and decrees. The author elucidates these problems by means of a study and a description of the physical and economic geography of Russia "in as true a form as possible." Here are described the boundaries of the country, its

[3] M. D. Chulkov, *Istoricheskoe opisanie rossiiskoi kommertsii* [Historical Description of Russian Commerce] (St. Petersburg: 1785), II, Bk. 1, p. 2.

lakes, rivers, ports, and land routes; also "in which parts of Russia and wherein lies her abundance; which products are produced and where and how "good are they." Chulkov was convinced that Russian merchants, having this "plan of Great Russian commerce" would be able "to distribute ideally the use of its capital." [4]

The material in his multi-volume work is arranged in the following order:

Volume 1, Books 1–2. A geographical description of Russia and information on the peoples inhabiting it. The trade of the Black, Caspian, White and Baltic Seas. Trade in the Archangel and Kol ports and the maritime industries;

Volume 2, Books 1–3. Trade via the Black Sea with Constantinople, Venice, Italy, the Levant, and also by land routes with Turkey, Poland, Danzig, Prussia, Breslau, and Leipzig; trade via Astrakhan with Persia, Bukhara, and Khiva; trade via Orenburg with Bukhara, India, and the steppe peoples;

Volume 3, Books 1–2. Siberian markets with Chinese, Kalmuks, and Mongolians. Trade between Kamchatka and the Eastern Archipelago;

Volume 4, Books 1–6. Trade in the St. Petersburg and Kronstadt ports;

Volume 5, Books 1–2. Trade in Riga, Revel', Narva, Vyborg, and other ports;

Volume 6, Books 1–3. Internal Russian trade, transport, industry, Russian towns, money, and postal service throughout the empire;

Volume 7, Books 1–3. Merchant lexicon, or general state of all goods in Russian trade; treaties on trade, various instructions to directors, consuls, brokers, sorters of goods, skippers, notaries, auctioneers, and so on.

From these basic divisions of Chulkov's ambitious work can be seen the wealth and variety of the economic problems treated and the amount of factual data used. In compiling the *Historical Description of Russian Commerce* Chulkov used chronicles, the works of Tatishchev, Lomonosov, Rychkov, Shcherbatov, Pallas, and other Russian scholars—geographers, naturalists, economists, and historians—as well as extensive archival material of various departments, decrees of the Tsar and Senate, petitions, and so forth.

In formulating his opinions, Chulkov also consulted the works of foreign economists and noted that, although these authors write "about matters relating to their countries," their views nevertheless contain "much that can be of use not only to the English and French,

---

[4] *Ibid.*, I, Bk. 1, pp. 16–8.

but to other people engaged in trade."[5] Thus Chulkov recognized above all the national tasks of economic literature, as did other Russian economists. Utilizing the works of foreign economists, he constantly centered his attention on questions and needs of the economic development of Russia.

Chulkov had a critical attitude toward the materials used and accompanied them with wise comments. He carefully checked foreign literary accounts of Russia with Russian data. Analyzing various official documents, he tried to uncover not only the reasons for the internal, but also the foreign, policy and certain economic measures of the Tsar's government. For example, he noted the stormy reaction of Russian ruling circles to the English bourgeois revolution of the seventeenth century.

Chulkov's *Historical Description of Russian Commerce* was a significant step forward from Rychkov's work on the same question. It encompassed the most important branches of the national economy—industry, trade, transport, credit, the circulation of money, and their interrelations. The rich material collected and prepared by him was widely used by succeeding generations of historians covering the Russian economy; even today it has not lost its importance in the characterization of various aspects of the history of the economic development of feudal Russia.

On the Significance and Necessity of Development of Industry in Russia

Chulkov did not recognize that the development of heavy industry leads unavoidably to the rise of a new social system which replaces serfdom. He did not see that serfdom was the main hindrance to the development of Russian industry. With all the limitation of his views, however, his ideas on the necessity of full development of industry and on the great transforming role of industry were original and progressive for his time. His works exposed the reactionary ideology of the serf-owners who were trying to preserve the backward, agrarian nature of the economy of Russia and thus destine her to eternal dependence on the industrially developed countries.

Chulkov thought the basis of economic power and the means to guarantee improved agriculture was the development of industry and the wide internal circulation of goods. In expressing his progressive views on the economic development of Russia, the protagonist of the

[5] *Ibid.*, VI, Bk. 4, p. 7.

merchant was bound to clash with those of the ruling class of pomeshchiki on vital economic issues: on the right to land and exploitation of its resources, on the origin of public wealth, on the role and place of industry and trade in the economy of the country, on money and its circulation, on the sources of manpower, on production and demand, and on the means to further economic development.

Chulkov insisted that industry plays a decisive role in assuring the economic independence and military and political might of the state. He gave a pioneering economic treatment of the necessity of close ties between industry and agriculture, of the principles of industry location, the size of industrial enterprises and the ways to accelerate their construction so as to speed production of goods, the training of qualified workers, as well as numerous other problems.

Concerning the sources of public wealth, Chulkov expressed the interesting idea that wealth is created chiefly by "agriculture" and "crafts" and that all other wealth represents a deduction from a product created in production; this deduction limits the possibility of expanding production. Considering merchants as organizers of industry, he wrote: "A powerless state comes to power by nothing so much as by agriculture and merchantry, to which crafts belong: all wealth accruing from other than these two sources . . . can be considered a kind of tax which, though allegedly taken from commerce and agriculture, remains with them in close application and work." [6] Elsewhere Chulkov said "factories . . . give a livelihood to many more people than does commerce." [7]

Although he expressed the thesis that material production in industry and agriculture is the source of social wealth, Chulkov did not understand that the origin of the wealth of industrialists, merchants, and landowners lay in exploitation. Like the Western European bourgeois spokesmen during the growth of capitalism, Chulkov praised the "love of work" and the thrift of capitalists and contrasted the "do-gooders" of the bourgeoisie of the first generation to the impudence and hardheartedness of usurers.

In contrast to the mercantilists, Chulkov asserted that a state even without foreign trade "can flourish and be powerful and rich if only its own manufactories and factories are flourishing." Inhabitants of such a state "can be satisfied by their own manufactures and by the distribution of goods from one province to another." [8]

Chulkov treated theoretically the problem of the economic inde-

[6] *Ibid.*, VI, Bk. 4, pp. 18–9.
[7] *Ibid.*, VI, Bk. 3, pp. 39–40.
[8] *Ibid.*, VI, Bk. 3, pp. 32–3.

pendence of Russia. He insistently urged the necessity of increasing every kind of industrial construction in Russia and showed that the development of industry would affect all other branches of production and trade and bring about the growth of cities and population. Without the development of industry, and at the same time without trade, the economy remains natural; the pomeshchiki "will allot agriculture on the basis of their needs and those with large surpluses will maintain many useless servants for the sake of splendor." [9] In those countries where a natural economy prevails a peasant is forced to do everything for his family himself: whatever "he produces on the land he consumes." Completely different are the level of demand and the economic situation of the various layers of society in a country with a well-developed trade and industry.

Chulkov linked the development of industry with the need to satisfy the material wants of the people, especially those of "the working people," who produce goods for the market and live by the products of the labor of other people. His views on this problem are materialistic and show a high degree of awareness concerning socio-economic phenomena. "It is not difficult to understand the great increase of people caused by factories," wrote Chulkov, "as well as the fact that many workers derive their living from this: these workers need numerous things for their sustenance, and so all kinds of crafts and industries appear; when craftsmen help in the consumption of manufactured and other goods, population increases. This will contribute to a growth in agriculture and the land will be able to feed more people. The prospect of more sale of land products at a profit will make the agriculturist care more ardently for agriculture." [10]

These views reflect the new economic conditions of development in Russia—the formation of capitalism. They highlight the contradiction between new productive forces and the old feudal-serf economic relations which were based on feudal land ownership and agriculture as the chief branch of social production.

As if objecting to Shcherbatov, who repeatedly asserted that development of factories and crafts ruins agriculture because it takes agriculturists into industry, Chulkov showed that the opposite was true; he emphasized the interdependence, the direct link between industry and agriculture, between production and demand. Agriculture provides industry with both food for the workers and materials for processing. The greater the development in industry, the greater will be the demand for agricultural products, and thus the interest of the agricul-

[9] *Ibid.*, VI, Bk. 3, p. 35.
[10] *Ibid.*, VI, Bk. 3, pp. 37–8.

turist in increasing his production and the productivity of labor will rise. In turn, this will lead to cheaper food and raw materials, improve conditions for industrial development, and lower the price of manufactured goods.

Chulkov's theories on the relationship between production and demand and industry and agriculture are quite mature considering the level of eighteenth century economic thought, as is evidenced in the following quotation. "Manufactories and factories are closely associated with the village economy. The latter not only supplies food for workers [in industry—E.P.] but provides also the factories with the required materials. When workers can be cheaply maintained and materials cheaply bought, factories and manufactories are successful; this results in reducing the price of manufactured goods, which promotes large exports to other countries and consumption within the country. The village economy contributes both to the flourishing of factories and manufactories and to its own growth. From the increase of workers in manufactories and factories comes a greater and speedier sale of all agricultural products; therefore the agriculturist will strive to improve the land and augment its products; and the increase in products will lead to a lower price. Thus the impact of manufactures on the economy and of the economy on manufactures ensues." [11]

Chulkov criticized the Shcherbatov-like contrast of agriculture and industry and showed the necessity of full economic development of the country; to accomplish this Russia had all the natural conditions. But to guarantee such development the government must provide encouragement for industry. "The state should subsidize manufactories and factories until the quality of their goods equals that of imports sold at the same price." [12] He thought it would be better and more convenient for the population temporarily to pay additional taxes for the aid of industry than always to overpay for expensive foreign goods and to be economically dependent on other countries. He felt that the development of industry would raise the well-being of everyone, since manufactures "will increase profits to the highest degree not only for merchants and the treasury, but also for all peoples.[13]

According to Chulkov, the development of industry depends not only on the protective policy of the government, but also on science and its practical application. He noted that if factories fail to show the results expected of them, then the blame is to be placed on "the scientists who do not work on what is really beneficial, but are more

---

[11] *Ibid.*, VI, Bk. 3, pp. 63–5.
[12] *Ibid.*, VI, Bk. 3, p. 75.
[13] *Ibid.*, I, Bk. 1, pp. 46–7.

preoccupied with theories than with practice." [14] Chulkov also wanted religious freedom and other conditions which were, in his opinion, necessary to raise the rate of economic development. Although his demands for state action in the development of science and the realization of numerous bourgeois freedoms were progressive for his time, he erroneously supposed that all these conditions could be secured under autocracy. Citing the positive results of the policy of Peter I, he believed that autocracy was the form of power best able to speed this development.

Chulkov was not limited by a narrow national outlook. He gave great attention to the state of industry in other countries. In his opinion two things hampered the development of industry in France: 1) overburdening the peasantry with "high taxes" and forbidding them to engage in industry and crafts; 2) the guild system in cities and the high taxes on guild workers and their goods. Chulkov contrasted prerevolutionary France of the eighteenth century with England, where feudalism had been destroyed earlier and where a parliamentary monarchy, a bourgeois form of government, aided "commerce." In England, he writes, "the people themselves (or better, those whom they elect to parliament) look after their own interests." [15] Thus, by preferring bourgeois England to feudal France, he revealed himself to be the supporter of a bourgeois system.

He argued that a country starting later than others on the road to industrial development could quickly achieve perfection, since nations can borrow methods of production from each other. Naturally, he wrote, Englishmen, Dutchmen, and Frenchmen have progressed so far industrially that in the beginning it is hard for a nation to equal or even overtake them. "However, this difficulty can be overcome." France, for instance, began industrial development later than England but quickly attained great success. Thus Chulkov disclosed the necessity and possibility of rapid industrial development for Russia, which could take advantage of the experiences of industrial advanced countries.

The potential of great natural wealth in Russia, widely studied in the eighteenth century, showed, according to Chulkov, the feasibility of an independent native industry. "This vast empire enjoys within its frontiers almost all those benefits which are spread over Europe, and it is, indeed, in a position to satisfy itself and enjoy its abundance, borrowing very little or not at all from other peoples." [16]

[14] *Ibid.*, VI, Bk. 3, p. 63.
[15] *Ibid.*, VI, Bk. 4, p. 32.
[16] *Ibid.*, I, Bk. 1, p. 9.

To the industrially young state Chulkov recommended that it abstain from undertaking all branches of manufacturing at once, but that it follow a familiar gradualness. It should begin with the most needed "from which more people can earn a living," and which would free the country from importing foreign goods.

Chulkov tried to analyze the various phenomena which would aid the speedy industrialization of Russia and assure its economic independence. In this study he considered both technology and social conditions, which he approached from the point of view of the merchants and of the entrepreneurs. One of the acute problems in the eighteenth century was a lack of qualified workers and masters caused by the prevalence of serfdom. New branches should hire foreign masters at the beginning, but decisive measures should be taken to train Russian masters and workmen. As stated above, although Chulkov did not question the dominance of serfdom, on the question of assuring manpower to industry he recognized the necessity of creating factories not with serf and forced labor, but with hired labor. Workers should be obtained wherever a supply of free manpower was available.

In order to foster more advanced methods of industrial production Chulkov recommended the founding of a "House of Manufacturing" where anyone desiring to study any industrial specialty could do so without cost. This valuable proposal to create a kind of polytechnical school of industrial learning was not realized, since the nobility opposed any innovation of this kind.

Chulkov had original ideas on the location of industry. His statements on this problem clearly reveal the ideology of the entrepreneurs. In his opinion factories should be built where "the most profits" could be obtained with the least losses, that is, near the source of raw materials and cheap labor. He recommended that enterprises be built "where the most workers can be found and maintained at the least cost."

As one of the conditions of rapid industrial development, Chulkov proposed economizing on wages. He felt that factories should not be established in capital cities, because "there, unlike elsewhere, housing and food are more expensive. Accordingly, higher salaries and prices greatly hinder the growth of these industries." [17] As these statements show, workers' wages should assure them food, housing, and so on, that is, the necessary means of existence, but should not be high, since

[17] *Ibid.*, VI, Bk. 3, p. 106.

that raises the price of goods and makes their production difficult.

Chulkov thought the most important condition of rapid industrial development was low cost construction and rapid activation of new enterprises. He advised entrepreneurs not to build "splendid" factories. He wrote, "It is absolutely necessary that as little money as possible be used in construction."[18] Thus, in the interests of the entrepreneur, the small, dark and smoky factories of the time were justified.

The size of factories should not be very large. Smaller factories are more quickly built and activated. Chulkov favored those factories which provide a livelihood for a great number of people. "For the state and for all industries, it is more useful when a hundred families live well and have enough, than when they are poor and only one family profits from their work . . ."[19] Here is expressed the idea of thrift, a negation of the excessive luxury of the privileged group of aristocrats—an idea peculiar to the personal ideology of the merchantry during its transition from pure trade operations to entrepreneurial activities.

Chulkov thought it expedient to build small private factories with the funds of only one entrepreneur and to build large ones through companies of a small number of participants. In his opinion, state enterprises were necessary only as initial steps. In the future, all enterprises except military ones should be privately owned. In this respect, Chulkov followed the policy of Peter I.

The purpose of building Russian factories was to process native raw materials. Chulkov insistently advanced the necessity of organizing the industrial processing of raw materials at their source throughout the country, including the most distant provinces. This was one of his weightiest arguments in favor of protectionism. "In a word, this rule is indisputable, that people who are the most powerful require no help from others; therefore each ruler should try to find the means to have everything necessary on his own soil in order to depend on other peoples as little as possible."[20] The development of factories was a hopeful sign, auguring the economic independence of Russia. This was an advanced, progressive position. Thus Chulkov treated the problem of the economic independence of Russia more fully and deeply than his predecessors. His thoughts concerning the necessity of industrial development expressed the country's growing material needs.

---

[18] *Ibid.*, VI, Bk. 3, p. 103.
[19] *Ibid.*, VI, Bk. 3, pp. 122–3.
[20] *Ibid.*, VI, Bk. 3, p. 67.

On the Importance of Trade and the Role of the Merchantry

Chulkov gave great importance to trade in the national economy. To him it was a link between different producers, between cities and villages, between industry and agriculture, between separate internal markets, and between various countries.

He divided all goods into two categories: raw and manufactured. The latter included all goods "produced masterfully for better convenience and use." He admitted that in Russia it was not manufactured goods which predominated in trade, but agricultural raw materials. He fully justified the production of luxury items. Such goods became "necessary for the needs of the state, although actually it was possible to live without them." Should the government forbid use of luxury items, it "would kill the industriousness of its subjects," for the greatest stimulant of human labor, according to Chulkov, is striving to "obtain wealth."

Emphasizing the tie between production and circulation, Chulkov showed, with sufficient clarity for his time, the deciding role of production in the economic life of the country. Industry and trade influence each other and cannot be viewed separately. The government would greatly damage the economy if it began to change something in trade or industry, "without examining how the one would relate to the other." [21] In this unity of production and circulation, production is basic and determining, according to Chulkov. "The number and happiness of the merchants depend on the number and happiness of craftsmen," he wrote.[22] Trade brings great advantage to the state, but sound trade can exist only where "flourishing factories lay a foundation for it." [23]

Thus as a spokesman of the merchants Chulkov arrived at a higher level of understanding of economic ties than I. T. Pososhkov, a spokesman of the merchant at the beginning of the eighteenth century. Unlike Pososhkov, Chulkov did not view trade from the mercantilist position, nor from the point of view of serving feudal production, but from the point of view of the economic development of Russia, of safeguarding her economic independence, and of subordinating trade to the interests of production. In his works, Chulkov reflected a new phase in the economic development of Russia, the rise of capitalism

[21] *Ibid.*, VI, Bk. 3, p. 70.
[22] *Ibid.*, VI, Bk. 4, p. 12.
[23] *Ibid.*, VI, Bk. 3, p. 44.

and the passing of the merchant into business enterprise and into the ownership of production.

In his opinion trade played an important part in industry and agriculture. He showed that trade undermines the nature of the feudal economy and aids extension of production beyond the limits of use within a given economy. Trade, according to Chulkov, is also an economic bond between different peoples.

He favored complete freedom of internal trade and believed that any hampering of trade within the country was harmful to factories and their development. He thought that the policy of Catherine II did not sufficiently assure freedom of domestic trade.

Chulkov advanced competition, that is, the principle of bourgeois economy, as the first stimulant of economic activity. In acknowledging the advantages of free competition within the country, he depended on the ideas of "the best contemporary calculators in commerce and politics," although, it is true, without mentioning their names and works, as was usual in the literature of the time. He was certain that trade and industry developed most fully when "each seeks his own interests, adapts always to his own situation, accounts to no one, and determines everything according to his own will." [24]

Chulkov, however, did not countenance freedom of foreign trade for Russia. He upheld generally the prevalent Russian policy of state interference, supervision, and regulation, but without the slightest restraints. The mercantilist view that foreign trade was the sole, or chief, means of enriching the country was not embraced by Chulkov. By this time in Russia and in the West mercantilism had already outlived its usefulness. "However profitable foreign trade is for the state, it is not absolutely necessary," wrote Chulkov.[25] This view of foreign trade was in full harmony with his conviction that only complete development of native production would make possible the satisfaction of the needs of the population and the state and assure Russia's economic independence from outside forces.

Import duties, argued Chulkov, form a sizable part, but they are not the chief source, of state revenue. It would be more profitable to forbid foreign goods and thus "encourage the activity of its subjects" and stimulate native production. Therein lies the chief "means of gaining wealth," said Chulkov. In contrast to the mercantilists, he thought that consumer goods, not money, constituted public wealth. "Neither gold nor silver represents the chief wealth of mankind: those people

[24] *Ibid.,* I, Bk. 1, p. 29.
[25] *Ibid.,* I, Bk. 3, p. 32.

who believe all their well-being lies in these metals are mistaken." [26]

Chulkov based his criticism of mercantilism not on the theoretical positions of the newest economic science of the West, which fought for freedom of international trade, but on the needs of his country, where, at the time, the merchants and brokers were moving intensively toward enterprise, especially after the promulgation of the famous decree of Catherine II which authorized everyone to introduce various "mills" and "crafts."

The state with a developed industry and an internal trade can get by entirely without foreign trade, said Chulkov. Naturally, not everything can be produced so cheaply in one's own country as in others, and much has to be imported. Export of one's goods is very profitable. But despite all this, native production must be encouraged.

Although he upheld the progressive tendency of industrial development in Russia, he opposed the principles of the bourgeois economists of the West of noninterference of the state in economic activity. Rather, he insisted on a protective policy toward industry and regulation of foreign trade in order to stimulate native production.

Chulkov's works reflect the struggle of the merchant with peasant trade. He shows how the peasants, who did not have the right to carry on foreign trade transactions, circumvented the law. They combined their small capitals into an artel, registered themselves in the name of some big merchant, and carried on not only small and vending operations, but large scale trade with foreign merchants, without being subjected to any of the obligations and payments levied on the merchant class. Big merchants used trading peasants as their agents in retail trade. At the same time, the merchants demanded obligatory registration of trading peasants into the merchant class with a much higher rate of declared capital than that required for guild membership for the merchants.

The purpose of this demand of the merchants was to protect merchant capital from competition by trading peasants and to subjugate the latter to the big merchant capitalists. Demands were expressed which, twenty years before Chulkov's work, had been put forth by the merchant deputies in the Commission on drafting a project for a new Code. Catherine II did not satisfy these demands either during the sitting of the Commission or later. Chulkov opposed merchant mo-

---

[26] *Ibid.*, VI, Bk. 4, pp. 30–1. In his comparison of English, French, and Russian trade Chulkov utilized two works: Josiah Tucker, *Opyt o kommertsii* [A Treatise on Commerce] (London: 1753); Jean Nicols, *Primechaniia o pribitkakh i ubytkakh Frantsii i Velikoi Britanii* [Notes on Revenues and Expenditures of France and Great Britain] (Leyden: 1754).

nopoly companies because they hampered free competition and because "a few are enriched at the expense of others; a merchant having a large amount of capital invested in a company will not stop intimidating the one with little capital." In the markets, "capital" merchants "swindle" and finally ruin "medium and small capital" merchants and constantly turn peasants into slaves through usurious loans.

The contradictions between merchants and nobles were described by Chulkov. He shows in many places in his work that in Russian heavy industry and trade of the eighteenth century the merchantry held the controlling position, not the nobility, although the nobility ruled the country. "Merchants are scorned by the nobility, their children are considered inferior, and, just as others, they are drafted into the army; therefore they are ashamed of their position and seek honorable ranks, a situation which is harmful both to them and to society." [27] The Russian bourgeoisie of the eighteenth century were still forced to strengthen their economic position by means of old feudal methods; they sought rank and noble titles in order to receive the personal right to buy villages and exploit serf labor.

Chulkov opposed giving the merchants exclusive right to conduct industry and trade. Indeed, he thought that it was foolish for nobles to abstain from commerce because they considered it demeaning and unsuitable to their status. Citing the enlightened literature of the West, Chulkov wrote that "the most famous philosophers and legislators did not scorne trade." Chulkov thought that commerce should be encouraged by "allowing all subjects . . . the possibility of entering any rank, except that of the lowest class engaged in commerce and petty retail trade." [28]

All these ideas distinctly show that the growing Russian bourgeoisie at the end of the eighteenth century did not yet present itself to the nobility as a new economic class and as a representative of a new order, but instead tried to adapt itself to the prevailing system. Thus Chulkov's works exemplify the struggle between the new and old, between the growing, but still far from dominant, new capitalist system and the old ruling system which was beginning to disintegrate. Also reflected in his works is the struggle of various class interests for industry and trade.

Chulkov approached the problems of the development of internal and foreign trade with an abiding patriotism, concerned with the endeavor by progressive Russians to attain the economic independence of their motherland. This love of and pride in their country are clearly

[27] Chulkov, *Istoricheskoe opisanie rossiiskoi kommertsii,* VI, Bk. 4, p. 13.
[28] *Ibid.,* VI, Bk. 4, p. 373.

epitomized in the instructions of the Commerce College to the Russian consul, jointly signed by Radishchev and Chulkov in March 1778, now in the Vladimir oblast archives.[29]

On Money Circulation and Credit

Chulkov's works dealt with certain theories on the nature, role, and value of money; on the meaning of credit and interest; on money circulation and the methods to strengthen it. His views on money and credit are permeated with the desire to prove that a sound and active monetary system are necessary prerequisites to the development of commodity production, especially in manufacturing. Chulkov picturesquely stated that "All distrust impedes money circulation, just as fear stops the blood in the body." [30]

He traced the origin of money to the inconvenience of natural barter. But he admitted that "money in itself is nothing but another commodity about which so many respectable treatises have been published and printed." [31] Consequently, on the nature of money he adopted the position of the commodity-metallic theory. In some instances Chulkov still identified coins with money. "A coin is only a known measure of all goods; it is given in exchange or can be sold; and it was invented as a standard of value to avoid difficulties when goods cannot be exchanged for goods." [32] Thus he showed that money fulfills the functions of a measure of value and a means of circulation.

According to Chulkov, a coin has a twofold value: "The first refers to the inherent value, the material itself, its value and quantity; the other, to the exterior, that is, the stamp and price which are ordinarily assigned to it." [33] He made an effort to separate money as a bearer of value from coins as a scale of relative prices. Although the price of a coin is arbitrarily set by the state, in world trade its monetary value "is considered no higher than its metal content," that is, its value by weight. Chulkov said that the value of precious metals depends on the "effort required to extract them from the earth." This statement still falls short of a clear definition of the value of money in terms of the labor lost to obtain the metal, for "effort" can also mean production expenses. Nevertheless, his views are important by virtue of their very

---

[29] See A. Shmakov, "Neizvestnye sluzhebnye bumagi A. N. Radishcheva" [Unknown Service Papers of A. N. Radishchev], *Iuzhnyi Ural* [Southern Urals], No. 11 (1954), pp. 140–5.

[30] Chulkov, *Istoricheskoe opisanie rossiiskoi kommertsii,* VI, Bk. 3, p. 89.

[31] *Ibid.,* III, Bk. 2, p. 23.

[32] *Ibid.,* VI, Bk. 4, p. 334.

[33] *Ibid.,* VI, Bk. 4, p. 336.

realistic approach toward the problem of the value of money. On this question Chulkov stands considerably above Pososhkov, who took an idealistic position in the matter.

Chulkov noted the influence of changes in the value of gold and silver on the circulation of money. If the price of gold rises, then silver is added to, and gold is withdrawn from, circulation and vice versa. Like his contemporaries, he saw danger in the devaluation of money. Recognizing the enormous importance of stable money circulation for the entire national economy, Chulkov asked: "What kind of relationships exist among money matters, manufacturing, and factories?" Comparing money with the life blood of an organism, he gave a picturesque and clear answer to the question. "For the blood to flow properly in the veins it must be healthy. In the same fashion, growth of factories, manufactories, or other industries cannot be hoped for from bad money. Lively circulation of money depends on the ability to exchange money for the same price at which it was obtained. With bad coins this does not happen." [34]

All prices rise when money is devalued by debasing the coinage, and fewer goods are bought for a given amount of money; even foreign goods are more expensive. As a result, the price of foreign coins in native money rises correspondingly. This opinion described the actual state of money circulation at the end of the eighteenth century not only in Russia, but also in several Western European countries, particularly France. Therefore Chulkov, like Radishchev later on, saw the main reason for the drop in exchange rates in the devaluation of money within the country. Radishchev, however, linked the fall of the exchange rate with the growth of military expenditures and an increased issue of assignats. Chulkov, on the other hand, directly defined the exchange rate as "the price of the money of foreign states," [35] which depends chiefly upon the condition of exports and imports. The more exports, the higher the rate, and vice versa. Exchange rates, he said, are the barometer for the state of foreign trade. Chulkov thought that government policy should be directed toward "increased circulation of money among the people." Here he noted that rich people always have a considerable part of the money outside of circulation in the form of treasure, but with "poor people . . . money has great power of increase through constant circulation." [36] While he fought for the development of commodity production, Chulkov thought that the state derives great benefit from increased money circulation among the

[34] *Ibid.*, VI, Bk. 3, p. 88.
[35] *Ibid.*, VI, Bk. 4, p. 338.
[36] *Ibid.*, VI, Bk. 4, p. 366.

peasants. "Money is like blood in the body politic, and the government is its heart. Through taxes blood flows to the heart, and through wise state expenditures it spreads through all the veins. Industriousness can be considered as the heat which promotes circulation." [37]

On the tax question Chulkov adhered to the policy that taxes should not be levied on persons but on "the property and income of each subject." Pososhkov was the first in Russian literature to favor replacing the feudal head tax by the more progressive land tax. This idea was developed more fully by Radishchev and later by M. M. Speranskii and the Decembrists. Chulkov proposed both a property and an income tax. This proposed reform reflected the progressive tendency of the bourgeois development in Russia. Chulkov argued that a change in the tax policy would strengthen money circulation and would aid Russian industrial development.

He regarded the introduction of paper money as very useful, but, like the western economists of the eighteenth century, he failed to discover the nature of paper money as a token of gold. He thought of paper money as "written obligations which have the same power in the market as money"; its introduction was explained by the fact that not every state had as much full-valued money as it needed for circulation. He advised the government to "maintain these obligations in perfect credit in order to make useful to the state and industry this thing which in itself brings no advantage." [38] He warned that paper money, with an enforced rate of exchange, must be used very "cautiously; otherwise it can have harmful effects."

Chulkov distinguished trade in goods from that in money, which is "giving money for a legalized or prevailing interest." [39] Trade in money, that is, the lending of capital, he recognized as normal and necessary for the merchantry and industrialists, but he strongly opposed usury. This spokesman of the merchant had to give attention to the fact that high interest rates made goods expensive and hampered the growth of production, but he did not see that the rate of interest depends on the general level of economic development of a country.

He emphasized the necessity of credit: "In trade credit is a weapon which quite often causes an increase in trade, and which, if absent, prevents one from making a bold move at the appropriate time." [40] This description corresponds to the actual picture, but it does not reveal the theoretical nature of credit. According to Chulkov, the con-

---

[37] *Ibid.*, VI, Bk. 3, p. 87.
[38] *Ibid.*, VI, Bk. 3, pp. 90–1.
[39] *Ibid.*, I, Bk. 1, p. 24.
[40] *Ibid.*, I, Bk. 1, p. 39.

dition for a stable credit is dependent upon the stability of money itself and of money circulation. Although he did not directly mention the superfluous issuance of assignats, he hinted at it clearly enough.

In his discussions of the problems concerning the theory of money, Chulkov was ahead of some of his Western contemporaries. Thus he recognizes money as a commodity, but also viewed it as that which expresses the value of all goods. He differentiates between the functions of money as a measure of value and as a means of circulation, while the classical bourgeois school of the eighteenth century considered money a means of circulation and did not distinguish money from coins.

On Agriculture. The Problem of Organizing Serf Labor

Chulkov's understanding of the significance of agriculture in the national economy and his views on the organization of pomestie and the serf economy were set forth in a special volume, *Economic Notes for Constant Use in Villages by Stewards and Responsible Economists, Which if Used Properly, Will Without Doubt Enrich an Insufficient Pomeshchik. Selections by Mikhail Chulkov From His Dictionary of Agriculture, Husbandry, and Household Management.* This work was first published in 1788 and was followed by a second edition in 1790. Here Chulkov gives an administrator instructions as to how to manage an estate in the absence of the pomeshchik. This treatise is actually a guide book to organize serf exploitation on small estates.

The "Foreword" stated that this work was originally intended "for a steward in my own small villages" but Chulkov decided to publish it, on the insistence of many nobles, to aid "those small pomeshchiki like myself,"[41] who always live in town because of service duties and are deprived of the possibility of personally administering their own estates. *Economic Notes* was compiled in dictionary form: various instructions and points of information on agriculture and household management are given in alphabetical order. Chulkov also included general thoughts on the significance of agriculture. Noting that agriculture and husbandry are "the direct source of well-being of all peoples," Chulkov argued that they "deserve to be the most worthy object of discussion and attention of high-placed people and intelligent minds."

---

[41] M. D. Chulkov, *Ekonomicheskie zapiski* [Economic Notes] (Moscow: 1788), p. 3.

He called on the "infant economy" to pay more attention to agriculture.

During the various periods of his activity, Chulkov defined differently the role and place of agriculture in the national economy. In the 1760's, when his views as a spokesman of the merchants were not yet formed, he placed agriculture in first place in the state. "A peasant, a plowman, an agriculturist—all three were according to ancient writers, and modern men agree, the main providers for the nation in peace and in war strong defenders; they affirm that the state without an agriculturist, like a man without a head, cannot live." [42] His writings in the 1760's pointed to the poverty, hard labor, want, and hunger of the peasant masses. Without specifying the main cause for the ruin of the peasants—pomestie serf exploitation—Chulkov attributes their poverty only to the rapacious activity of usurers from the village upper class.

In a story, "The Bitter Share," published during the period of Catherine's Commission on drafting a new Code (in the collection *The Mocker, or Glorious Tales*), Chulkov was the first in Russian literature to portray realistically the village kulak. He wrote: "Such village inhabitants are called cannibals; having the fate of other peasants in their hands, they get rich at their expense by lending them money and harnessing them to their work like oxen to a plow; where there are one or two of these, the whole village is poor and only one among them rich. His sowing, harvest, and threshing are done first by his debtors, whose own fields must wait. And when sowing is done too late there is nothing to harvest, and thus they remain eternally indebted to the cannibal who profits, since the whole village comes to him, as to a lord, for work." [43] While correctly depicting kulak-usurer bondage, Chulkov did not think that serf exploitation and unbearable feudal taxes drove "the chief feeder of the nation" into this servitude.

Admitting that "nothing in the world is constant . . . and philosophers alter their systems," Chulkov changed his own mind in respect to the role and place of agriculture in social production. In the 1780's he had already assigned first place to industry and to merchant industrialists, and not to agriculture and to agriculturists. Nevertheless, even then he called upon representatives of science to give greater attention to agriculture and, at the same time, defended the barshchina

---

[42] *Russkaia proza XVIII veka,* I, 145.

[43] *Ibid.,* I, 146. By its economic content Chulkov's *"seduga"* [Glutton] expresses the same meaning as *"zhivoglot"* [glutton] did in literature of the end of the XIX century.

system as the basic method of managing the small estate of a pomeshchik, to which class he belonged.

According to Chulkov, the ideal pomeshchik "lives within his means, without debt, all his life, retains his honor, is satisfied with his fate, scorns luxury, and allows no waste in the house." [44] This ideal reflected the economic position of the petty Russian pomeshchik who was ennobled and, for mentorious service, given the right to buy "villages." In *Instructions to My Young Son Upon His Entry Into the Service,* written in 1785, Chulkov argued that debt is the worst evil, that it can destroy the spiritual peace of even the best man. As a result he advised his son to "refrain as much as you can from borrowing money or things." If borrowing cannot be avoided, then borrow "in proportion to your condition, and keep your credit sacred." [45]

Chulkov recognized the disrupting influence of commodity-money relations on the basically natural pomestie-serf economy, but could offer nothing but moralizations to pomeshchiki, whom he advised to live "in proportion to their condition." He understood the importance of credit for the development of industry and trade, but at the same time saw that the pomeshchiki used credit parasitically. Therefore he wrote of the dangers of debts and loans.

Chulkov wrote that a pomeshchik engaged in agriculture brings benfit to the state, but the peasant-agriculturist, who works the pomestie and his own alloted field and toils for the general welfare, is worthy of the true respect and concern of all those whom service, inheritance, and luck have made higher and more prosperous than he." [46] While respecting agricultural labor, Chulkov did not doubt or hide the forced nature of serf labor in Russia.

Chulkov determined work standards of the peasant for the pomeshchik not by barshchina days, but by amounts of acreage per tax unit. "Each tax unit should work for the pomeshchik one and a half desiatiny per field." [47] This norm was evidently common for the middle belt of Russia (Chulkov's estate was in the village of Dmitrov in the Moscow gubernia). In the "Instructions" of Volynskii the pattern was two desiatiny per field. Radishchev, in the "Description of My Property" gave almost the same arrangement—four and two-thirds desiatiny per horse, that is, one tax unit per three fields.[48] Along with

---

[44] Chulkov, *Ekonomicheskie zapiski,* p. 53.

[45] *Ibid.,* p. 85.

[46] *Ibid.,* p. 6.

[47] *Ibid.,* p. 68.

[48] See A. N. Radishchev, *Sochineniia* [Works] (Moscow-Leningrad: AS USSR, 1941), II, 179.

this high norm of barshchina labor, the peasant had to perform additional jobs for the pomeshchik, as the following "philosophical" statement by Chulkov indicates: "People should be masters of the land, not the land master of the people; therefore the peasant should work as much land for the pomeshchik as his strength and capabilities will allow." [49] Here any curtailment of peasant obligations is rejected, and the pomeshchik is given unlimited power of exploitation over his serfs.

For the peasants who were unable to pay state taxes or even feed themselves, Chulkov recommended compulsory land labor. A poor peasant "should be given, along with his home and land, as an agricultural laborer to another peasant who will feed him and his family and pay his taxes; if the peasant is not willing, then he should be taken into the pomestie household." [50] This measure to combat peasant poverty was not an original proposal. It was foreseen much earlier in A. P. Volynskii's "Instructions" to his steward and also in Tatishchev's "Short Economic Notes Pertaining to the Village."

Chulkov's work expressed the idea of combining agriculture with home industry under feudalism and the desire of the pomeshchiki to utilize serf labor more fully throughout the year. His *Economic Notes* contains many articles devoted to peasant industry and the teaching of crafts to the peasants, especially those who had little land. He proposed that peasant children from seven to ten years of age should learn how to read and write and that those from ten to twenty years of age should be taught various crafts.

For the more successful development of crafts, Chulkov was in favor of establishing in the village a tailor shop, a factory for processing leather and sheepskin, and a store for the sale of peasant goods. Barshchina serfs, however, were not to be free to dispose of their own goods. Chulkov specified that "No peasant is to *sell* anything without the consent of the pomeshchik." Obviously this limitation was to guarantee pomeshchik supervision over all sources of peasant income in order to raise pomestie collections and quit-rents. In general, Chulkov advised controlling every step of the serf, especially his work both on the land and in industry, for the pomeshchik and for his personal needs. Such supervision was the necessary concomitant of the barshchina system of economy. A steward was to see to it that each peasant had a garden, that every household had *kvass,* that "barns had roofs," that in place of corn kilns, barns be built "which are quite safe from fire," that there be "two cattle for every plowed desiatina,"

---

[49] Chulkov, *Ekonomicheskie zapiski,* p. 34.
[50] *Ibid.,* p. 52.

and, finally, that "he try with all his power to instill cooperation and mutual aid among the peasants." [51]

Like all other serf owners, Chulkov attributed the poverty of the peasant to his own laziness, and not to serfdom itself. It must be noted, however, that his *Economic Notes* did not contain as many cruel measures for subduing the peasants as did Rychkov's "Instructions to the Administrator of An Estate," and Volynskii's "Instructions." Chulkov accepted serfdom as a matter of course; nowhere did he especially insist on it, but nowhere did he refute it. He never truly understood the negative influence of serfdom on the whole national economy, particularly on industry, for the development of which he so convincingly and eloquently fought. His views on serfdom fully reflected the early stage of capitalism and showed the limitation and political backwardness of the Russian merchant and the industrial bourgeoisie in the second half of the eighteenth century. Chulkov saw the necessity of developing industry and commodity-money relations, but he did not realize that this would lead to the breakdown of serfdom as new forces would irresistibly arise to effect its destruction. Chulkov did not comprehend this dilemma.

Contradictions in Russian economic development gave rise to inconsistencies in Chulkov's views and their historical limitation. Although he failed to denounce serfdom, his principal economic interests as a spokesman of the merchantry lay in plane different from those of the ruling class of noble-pomeshchiki. The latter believed that the growth of industry and trade "impoverished" agriculture and doomed Russia to eternal vegetation as an agrarian country. Chulkov considered the broad development of the manufacturing industry and domestic circulation of goods as the basis of national economic power and a guarantee to the promotion of productive forces.

Chulkov made important theoretical generalizations on a number of problems. He stressed the leading role of industry in the economic development of the country, in assuring its independence from other countries, and in strengthening its military might, and he fought for the liquidation of Russia's backwardness. He showed that Russia, rich

---

[51] *Ibid.*, pp. 60, 66–7. It must be remembered that Chulkov's attitude towards the serfs differed from that of his contemporary as well as spokesman of the merchantry, I. I. Golikov.

Chulkov thought it necessary to teach all peasants literacy and trades. Golikov thought it dangerous to educate peasants because once educated the peasants will not be "as obedient." Golikov considered harmful even the discussion of peasant freedom. See I. I. Golikov, *Deianiia Petra Velikogo* [Activities of Peter the Great] (2nd edition, Moscow: 1840), XIII, p. 309.

in natural resources, had all the prerequisites for an all-round, independent economy. He posed certain problems relating to the theory of money. In his works we see how economic thought gradually rose to the level of scientific generalization.

In his treatment of industry, trade, money, and credit, Chulkov supported the essentially bourgeois means of production, although the Russian bourgeoisie had not yet solidified as a class and was not strong enough to oppose the nobility.

Chulkov did not rise against serfdom and autocracy, but felt it necessary to uphold the efforts of merchants and industrialists to obtain titles, which opened the door for them to own land and serf labor. At the same time, he recognized the necessity and progressiveness of organizing manufactories on the basis of hired labor. In the realm of agriculture he adhered fully to serfdom and defended the barshchina system which, as a rule, was followed by petty pomeshchiki. Chulkov failed to understand that to further progressive Russian growth serfdom had to be liquidated. Herein lies the great historical limitation of his views.

The contradiction of Chulkov's views—progressive on questions of development of industry and trade, the theory of money, and money circulation, and conservative on serfdom and the organization of agricultural production—was a reflection of the accentuated inconsistencies of the feudal economy during the formation of capitalism.

CHAPTER 19. *Early Criticism of Serfdom.*

Beginning in the 1760's the most significant phenomenon in the development of Russian economic thought was the criticism of serfdom. This was an ideological reflection of the incipient breakdown of serfdom and the germination of the bourgeoisie. The first critics of serfdom were recruited from the aristocracy (D. A. Golitsyn); from the middle serving nobility, the military (A. Ia. Polenov, the brothers Kozelskii, and I. A. Tretiakov), and the petty bourgeois (S. E. Desnitskii). The nature of the criticism revealed their various social origins.

The Economic Contributions of D. A. Golitsyn

A scientist and author of many books and articles on natural science (on electricity, mineralogy, physical geography, and so on), philosophy, and political economy, Prince Dmitrii Alekseevich Golitsyn (1734–1803) spent a great portion of his creative life abroad as a diplomat.[1] At the age of twenty he was sent to the Russian Embassy in Paris, and in 1762 he was appointed ambassador to France. Golitsyn was more than the customary ambassador. He became an honorary member of the Petersburg Academy of Sciences and of the Academies of Brussels, Stockholm, and Berlin, as well as the Free Economic Society in Petersburg. Friend of Voltaire, Diderot, and Mercier de la Rivière, frequent guest in Paris salons, participant in meetings of physiocrats at Mirabeau's, Golitsyn was a companion of the "princes of philosophy" from the first years of the reign of Catherine II and was her link with them. In 1768 he was recalled from Paris[2] and

---

[1] See N. N. Golitsyn, *Rodoslovnaia rospis potomstva Gedimina* [Genealogical Table of Gedimin's Descendants] (St. Petersburg: 1899), p. 44.

[2] The recall of D. A. Golitsyn from Paris if one were to judge by Catherine II's remarks on his letters to Vice Chancellor A. M. Golitsyn and by her correspondence with Falconet (*Sbornik russkogo istoricheskogo obshchestva,* XVII, 21–3 and 26–30) was apparently brought about by her dissatisfaction

assigned to The Hague, where he represented the Russian empire for thirty years.

His letters to Vice-Chancellor A. M. Golitsyn, sent two or three times a week for almost a quarter of a century (1760–1784),[3] unfold a picture of the socio-political life of France and Holland; they illuminate the intellectual life of Western Europe. Giving special attention to economic policy and theory, Golitsyn declared himself a supporter of the prevailing French "school of economists"—the physiocrats. He offered advice on Russian economic policy to the Vice-Chancellor and to the Empress. Catherine II read the letters he sent to the Vice-Chancellor and made notes on the margins.[4]

In 1796 Golitsyn published his book, *On the Spirit of Economists, or the Economists Exculpated from Blame of Having Laid the Basis of the French Revolution by Their Principles.*[5] Although his views on the peasant problem, as stated in his letters to Vice-Chancellor A. M. Golitsyn, were thoroughly examined by V. I. Semevskii,[6] it is this book alone which is remembered in the literature. Onken limits himself to a notation that it is "the only book with physiocratic content written by a Russian."[7] Semevskii also refers to the book.[8] Higgs, enumerating the main pupils of the physiocrats in various countries, mentions Golitsyn in Russia,[9] without, however, pausing to analyze his

---

with D. A. Golitsyn's views and proposals on the peasant problem and his role in inviting to St. Petersburg physiocrat Mercier de La Rivière, who disappointed the Empress' expectations. See V. A. Bilbasov, *Nikita Panin i Mercier de La Rivière. Istoricheskie monografii* [Nikita Panin and Mercier de La Rivière. Historical Monographs] (St. Petersburg: 1901), IV, 1–83.

3 TsGADA, Golitsyn's Fund, Affairs 1111–1125.

4 Rachinskii, who published five letters of Prince D. A. Golitsyn, expressed a view that marginal remarks were made not only by Catherine II, but also by A. M. Golitsyn and N. I. Panin (*Sbornik Moskovskogo glavnogo arkhiva Ministerstva inostrannykh del* [A Collection of the Moscow Main Archive of the Ministry for Foreign Affairs], Issue II [Moscow: 1881], p. 104). However V. I. Semevskii maintains that all marginal remarks are Catherine II's (V. I. Semevskii, *Krestianskii vopros v Rossii v XVIII i pervoi polovine XIX veka* [The Peasant Problem in Russia in the XVIII and the First Half of the XIX Century] [St. Petersburg: 1888], I, 23).

5 *De l'esprit des économistes ou les économistes justifiés d'avoir posé par leurs principles les bases de la Révolution Françoise, par le prince D . . . de G . . .* (Brunsvick: 1796). A German translation appeared in 1798 entitled *Vom Geiste der Oekonomisten.*

6 Semevskii, *op. cit.*, I, 23–7 and 160–8.

7 A. Onken, *Istoriia politicheskoi ekonomii do Adama Smita* [History of Political Economy Before Adam Smith]. Translated from the German. (St. Petersburg: 1908), p. 428.

8 Semevskii, *op. cit.*, I, 168–9.

9 Henry Higgs, *Fiziokraty. Frantsuzkie ekonomisty XVIII veka* [Physiocrats. French Economists of the XVIII Century] (St. Petersburg: 1899), pp. 72–3.

views, V. V. Sviatlovskii went no farther than Higgs, simply characterizing Golitsyn as the sole "native theoretician" of physiocracy.[10]

In his economic views Golitsyn proceeded from the idea that labor, "the mother of well-being," and land are the main sources of the wealth of a country and the growth of its economy and culture. Labor and the land with its inexhaustible gifts always reward the industrious man with a surplus. Therefore the agriculturists, constituting the greatest part of the inhabitants of the state, assure its existence and development. From this, according to Golitsyn, stems the decisive significance of the productivity of agricultural labor for the development of the economy and culture.

The conditions for high productivity of labor, according to Golitsyn, were the personal freedom of the producer and his right to possess property. Personal freedom and private ownership make possible the exchange of surpluses which the producers accumulate. And constant assurance of the possibility of exchange of surpluses is a factor in their creation. "Freedom to dispose of surpluses, or wealth, is the real cause of the productivity of lands, the development of resources, the appearance of inventions, discoveries, and everything that can make a nation flourish." [11]

Golitsyn believed that serfdom is never advantageous to a state. It can benefit only the pomeshchiki; but in the final analysis it contradicts even their interests. Under serfdom land is poorly worked or not worked at all. Peasants are poor, and as a result nobles do not get rich and the state suffers a loss. Golitsyn assured pomeshchiki it would be better for them to rent the land to rich peasants. Then their income would be four times as large as under serfdom. Nevertheless, he felt that the decision to abolish serfdom and to introduce agrarian reforms had to be undertaken with intelligence and temperance.

Golitsyn opposed small land ownership by peasants. Above all, it was necessary to determine whether the peasants had the "know-how" to manage a farm. It would be much more beneficial to society and even to the peasant if the lord retained the right to own land. Peasants who owned movable property and increased it by receiving income from it would have funds to rent land. Well-to-do peasants would become renters with enough resources to manage the farm properly. One should not send the poor to colonize the wastelands. Similarly, a free peasant unable to make the necessary expenditures would be in a bad way, for he would have to neglect his new property and would con-

[10] Sviatlovskii, *Istoriia ekonomicheskikh idei v Rossii*, I, 94–5.
[11] *De l'esprit des économistes*, Chapter XXVII.

sequently be more discontent than under serfdom. Granting peasants personal freedom and the right to buy land would require much time. By supporting the idea of renting land to rich peasants who had the means for the necessary expenditures, including that of hiring workers, Golitsyn visualized farmer-capitalist land rentals for which conditions were not suitable in Russia at the time.

While defending the economic policy of protecting agriculture, Golitsyn nevertheless condemned the laws which forbade peasants to enter urban classes. He thought such prohibitive measures could not stem the flow from the villages of the poor who hoped for a better life in the town. In his opinion, the growth of rural population could take place only upon the creation of favorable agricultural conditions. But even under such conditions a surplus population in the villages would prevail. He held that transfer of part of the village population to the city is a positive phenomenon.

People who own only movable property and engage in industry and trade, writes Golitsyn, represent a class called the third estate, and they can very easily depart from their homes and go where they like. "They are less citizens of the state than members of universal society." [12] In contrast to the third estate, land owners are closely bound to the state within whose limits their property lies. They have neither the urge nor the possibility to leave. Even more important, they have a direct share in the fortune or misfortune of the state to which they belong. Only land owners, he continues, comprise a nation which flourishes when its proprietors are happy. Their privileges, which center in direct participation in the administration of the state, cannot in the slightest degree harm those who do not take part in the administration, if the latter is based on just laws. "On the other hand, land owners will awaken in everyone the desire to obtain land, and many owners of movable property will place their funds in land." [13] The administration of the state should be based on an understanding of the importance of agriculture and the desire that it flourish. Golitsyn exalts land ownership and defends the interests of the noble-pomeshchik class.

He wanted to link these ideas, expressed in his letters of the 1760's and 1770's and in *On the Spirit of Economists,* with physiocracy and to proceed from its basic principles. Golitsyn was one of the nobles who was influential in spreading the physiocratic system, in which exaltation of land ownership leaps to its economic repudiation and to the consolidation of capitalist production.

[12] *Ibid.*
[13] *Ibid.*

The physiocrats viewed land owners as a class "paying the way" (according to the terminology of the founder of physiocracy, Quesnay) of those engaged in all other branches of the economy except agriculture, that is, in industry, trade, and so on. In this latter group Quesnay included capitalists and workers. The physiocrats believed that the net product is created only in agriculture, especially under conditions of "large scale cultivation" and that it accrues to the land owner in the form of land rent. As a result, the physiocrats proposed the replacement of many taxes by a single uniform tax on land rent. Under such exclusive taxation of land ownership, says Marx, "the tax burden is removed from industry, which is thus freed from any kind of state interference. This supposedly is done for the good of land ownership, not in the interests of industry." As a result of the transfer of the entire tax burden to land rent "land ownership undergoes partial confiscation . . ." [14]

Golitsyn, like Mirabeau the elder in France and many other feudalists, was attracted by the exaltation of land ownership by the physiocrats and by the feudal veneer of the system which was essentially an an expression of "a new capitalist society, paving a path within the framework of feudal society." [15]

Golitsyn showed the sharply negative influence of forced peasant labor on the development of the Russian economy and culture. "Since the peasant is forced to give a great part of his time to cruel masters, unfair and always unkind, laziness, waste, and even deception are the natural companions of his work." [16] Inability to own property weakened the peasants' stimulus to work. "Why should the peasant work, when the fruits of his labor go to another? Should he become rich he will be tormented even more." [17] Golitsyn noted that Russian agriculture yielded a crop which hardly provided the peasants with the necessary means for subsistence and payment of taxes. Conditions under which the peasant "rarely had grain left over to sell" hindered, in Golitsyn's view, the development of internal trade and money circulation, especially under "insufficient road and water communications and the prohibition against exporting grain . . ." [18] According to

[14] Marx, *Kapital,* IV, 19.

[15] *Ibid.,* IV, 16.

[16] TsGADA, Golitsyn's Fund, Affair 1114, Letter of March 16, 1766.

[17] *Ibid.,* Affair 1120, Letter of July 19, 1771.

[18] *Ibid.,* Affair 1114, Letter of March 16, 1766. Catherine was irritated by D. A. Golitsyn's views, which correctly linked low crop yield and the peasants' lack of grain to sell with serfdom. She noted on the margin of Golitsyn's letter regarding his statement of the lack of grain: "This is not true, since they, or to put it more accurately, their masters, make vodka and supply all stores: they will export grain also when that is allowed, but that must be done

Golitsyn, the development of industry and science in Russia was also impeded by the absence of a middle class. Formation of a middle class was hampered because the large nobility satisfied its needs by natural production based on the forced labor of serf masters. "Such a custom is the rule and basis of our economy . . . ," testified Golitsyn. A direct result of this situation was, in his opinion, the extreme limitation of demand in cities and even in capitals. "If one excluded important nobles from the population of Moscow, and even Petersburg, how many people would be left for whom the free artisan could produce?" [19] In Golitsyn's view, barriers to the growth of a middle class resulted from the very nature of the peasants, which had been molded under serfdom. "The prolonged slavery under which our peasantry has stagnated created their true character, and presently very few among them strive for the kind of work or industry which would enrich them." [20]

Golitsyn demanded the abolition of serfdom in the interests of his class, the nobility, as well as those of the state: "Each of us will gain from this change, for as long as serfdom exists the Russian empire and our nobility, which are destined to be the richest in Europe, will remain poor. And how are we otherwise to form a third estate, without which we cannot hope to create art, science, trade, and so forth?" [21]

Regarding serfdom as the chief obstacle to the development of the economy and culture of Russia, Golitsyn foresaw the solution of this problem in extending to the peasants the right of "ownership and corresponding freedom." He spoke of the historical lesson of France, England, and Holland: "History provides examples and experience confirms that arts and crafts developed and morals improved only in countries where the peasants were free and possessed the right of ownership." He believed that the right to own land was "the true basis and stable foundation of a state's well-being; without it, arts and science will never flourish." [22]

He soon retreated, however, from this view after having received Vice-Chancellor A. M. Golitsyn's opinion that "general and universal introduction of such a system into a state as vast as Russia might be

gradually, not suddenly. We never bought even a chetverik [of grain] abroad . . ." Referring to the abundance of grain in Russia, Catherine tried to show that serfdom did not reduce crop yield and agricultural productivity.

19 *Ibid.* Letter of January 12, 1766; see also *Izbrannye proizvedeniia russkikh myslitelei vtoroi poloviny XVIII veka* [Selected Works of Russian Thinkers of the Second Half of the XVIII Century] (Moscow: Gospolitizdat, 1952), II, 37 (hereinafter cited as *Izbrannye proizvedeniia russkikh myslitelei*).

20 TsGADA, Golitsyn's Fund, Affair 1114, Letter of January 12, 1766.

21 *Ibid.* Letter of November 13, 1770.

22 *Ibid.*, Affair 1113, Letter of September 6, 1765.

inappropriate, and a gradual change would be better." D. A. Golitsyn conceded that a gradual development is necessary in order to make it take root firmly, and it should be introduced not by "decrees," but be adopted by "the people themselves." [23] It appears further, that by "the people themselves" Golitsyn meant only his own class, the nobles-pomeshchiki, on whose consent he let the solution to the problem of the peasants depend.

He advised Catherine II to set an example by changing the status of the court peasants. The pomeshchiki would emulate such a course, both for their own advantage and the desire to please the Empress; others would follow. Catherine was not at all inclined to accept this advice. Moreover, she ridiculed his belief in the power of her example to lead the pomeshchiki to act contrary to their own material interests. On the margin of Golitsyn's letter Catherine II wrote: "It is doubtful whether an example would make our fellow countrymen wise and attract them to it; it is even improbable. Also, such an order could imperil the security of the pomeshchiki and others." Further, Catherine noted: "There are few who want to sacrifice great advantages for the lovely feeling of patriotism." [24]

Guided by the somewhat better condition of village peasants who were on monetary obrok, Golitsyn proposed the substitution of money obrok for product obrok (including, naturally, the barshchina system). It is not clear, however, what would be the basis of money payment of obrok if the land became the property of the peasants. Golitsyn, defending noble interests, later removed this contradiction by opposing peasant ownership of land.

He recognized that, "in the absence of authority to protect the peasant from the tryranny of the Russian pomeshchik, peasant ownership would remain illusory, and the slightest progress in agriculture, arts, crafts, money circulation, or internal trade would be impossible." Hence he proposed to create "circuit courts" in crown villages (two judges per province) and "chambers" in each oblast town." The duties of these institutions were to include allotment of land, surveying and taxing of sectors, and settlement of all quarrels over land ownership and agriculture. The "circuit courts" and "chambers," having jurisdiction over agricultural matters, should "assure each the free use of his own land."

It must be admitted that Catherine II appraised the nobility more realistically than Golitsyn. At the end of his letter she notes: "Sincere

[23] *Ibid.* Letter of October 30, 1765; see also *Izbrannye proizvedeniia russkikh myslitelei,* II, 33.

[24] *Ibid.*, II, 33–4.

love of mankind, sympathy, and good will are not enough to realize great proposals. For Golitsyn and his ilk it is easy and inexpensive to be magnanimous. It costs them nothing to give their peasants the right to own land, but rich landowners who have many thousands of peasants will think and speak otherwise." [25] This was true not only of large land owners, but, as we shall see later, of Golitsyn himself, when it came to his own interests as a land owner.

Later Golitsyn spoke even more firmly of the necessity of the *gradual* abolition of serfdom, since "there is nothing more dangerous and even ruinous than to go from one extreme to the other." And slaves with sudden freedom "would not use it to improve their well-being; rather a large portion of them would become idle."

At the same time, Golitsyn retracted his first statements concerning peasant land ownership. According to his new plan, the peasants should be freed and receive only the right to the movable property which they owned. "Thus it is the right to own movable property which is necessary at the present time"; the Empress herself "will well understand when the time is ripe to grant them full ownership." Even this measure was to apply only "to the peasants on the estates of the Empress." [26] However, V. I. Semevskii is correct in pointing out that the crown peasants, for whom the barshchina system had everywhere been replaced by obrok to the same degree as for state peasants, with their large land allotments and the possibility of expropriation and inheritance of movable property, did not need Golitsyn's proposed reform.[27]

Golitsyn was certain that the pomeshchiki would not delay in following the example of Catherine II, and the "rest would take care of themselves under the influence of those benefits and good results which each would feel." [28] After Vice-Chancellor A. M. Golitsyn suggested that D. A. Golitsyn abolish serfdom on his own estate, the latter denied that he had at any time desired to cede to the peasants "those lands which they now work." He declared that "such an absurdity never entered my mind," that the "land belongs to us," and that therefore it would be "completely unjust" to take land from the pomeshchiki. Further, Golitsyn explained that what he had proposed was: "1) freedom, that is, the right to their own person, without which all other forms of ownership are unthinkable; 2) the right to own movable

---

[25] *Ibid.*, II, 36.

[26] TsGADA, Golitsyn's Fund, Affair 1114, Letters of January 12 and March 16, 1766.

[27] See Semevskii, *op. cit.*, I, 28.

[28] TsGADA, Golitsyn's Fund, Affair 1114, Letter of March 16, 1766.

property, that is, belongings; and 3) permission to those who have the means to buy land . . ." [29]

Thus Golitsyn came to a final conclusion to which he remained faithful for the remainder of his life: peasants should have personal freedom and the right to own movable property. Land, however, should remain under noble-pomestie ownership. Prosperous peasants could rent land, and the richest could buy it.

Herein Golitsyn foresaw a transition most profitable for the pomeshchiki and most burdensome for the peasantry. Adhering to the opinion of his uncle Prince Gagarin, he proposed a high price for the personal freedom of peasants: two hundred rubles per head to the pomeshchik and fifty to the state, and these were not to be payable in installments. Golitsyn realized clearly the advantages of his plan to the nobility and the treasury of a feudal-absolute state. "Now the peasants pay the pomeshchik an average of two rubles per head; at the price of two hundred rubles, the lord will have, at five per cent, ten rubles income, and he will still retain his land . . ." This scheme "was beneficial also to the treasury, which will receive two and a half rubles instead of seventy-five copecks." [30]

Thus Golitsyn proposed freedom at an impossibly high price. The pomeshchik would acquire the sum paid by the peasant and yet retain the land. And the peasant, landless and in debt from purchasing his freedom, would be forced to rent the pomestie land. Hence the pomeshchik would receive both the price of the peasant's freedom and assure himself a steady income from rent.

At the same time Golitsyn foresaw that peasants would acquire land by buying it from the pomeshchik. He speaks of allowing "those who have the means to buy land in their own name and to own it as do the lords." [31] Thus he envisaged a separation of the peasants, or rather, of those peasants who had bought freedom, into renters and landowners. He understood that rich peasants who were capable of buying their freedom would use the labor of their villages. And he even posed the question: would not the situation of these laborers be worse than that of those who work for a pomeshchik? To that query he answered in the negative. For, he said, work for rich peasants is based on the free employment of their "former brothers" who are "at liberty to work

---

[29] *Ibid.*, Affair 1118, Letter of September 30, 1770; see also *Izbrannye proizvedeniia russkikh myslitelei*, II, 42–5.

[30] TsGADA, Golitsyn's Fund, Affair 1120, Letter of July 19, 1771.

[31] *Ibid.*, Affair 1118, Letter of September 30, 1770; the same thought is expressed in Affair 1120, Letter of July 19, 1771; *Izbrannye proizvedeniia russkikh myslitelei*, II, 44.

or not to work for them; if they are harsh toward their workers, the latter can go elsewhere." [32] Golitsyn understood that rent and landed peasants would inevitably increase the use of hired labor in the villages. And this would mean the stratification of the peasantry and the growth of capitalism in agriculture. However, he did not look upon rent and the acquisition of land by a small number of peasants as a threat to the prevalence of pomestie ownership. Rather, he thought that the extension of these relations would strengthen the economic and political dominance of the noble-pomestie class.

The aim of Golitsyn's work, *On the Spirit of Economists,* was to prove that physiocratic ideas, of which he declared himself to be an adherent, did not inspire the economic policy of the French bourgeois revolution, but defended and supported the feudal order. Sovereigns of Europe should struggle against "the disorder and anarchy" which had engulfed France, where "a stupid people . . . intoxicated and infuriated" adopted "the most repulsive and barbaric code." Annihilation of this code means "preserving the crowns on your heads." And these crowns, he adds, "are already shaking." [33]

It is impossible to avert revolution, asserts Golitsyn, without a just economic policy, based on true economic theory. Such economic policy was presented, he thinks, in the works of the first physiocrats: Quesnay, Mirabeau the elder, Mercier de la Rivière, and the "founder of physiocracy," Turgot, but not in those of their pupils, whose literary and socio-political activity took place during the revolution 1789–1794. The latter "appropriated the jargon of the first economists, but not their honor and conduct." [34] He criticized the physiocrats of the revolutionary period for their assertion that the principles of the "system of the economists" formed the basis of the economic policy of the bourgeois revolution.

Golitsyn set himself the task of showing that the economic theory and policy of physiocracy supported the existing feudal order and presented the surest defense against revolution. He viewed this system as a defense of feudalism, by which he understood "altar, throne, ownership—in short, the wisest perceptible principles." During the revolution, he said, these ideas "were exchanged for chimeras and extremes, such as unlimited freedom, complete and absolute equality." [35] Ac-

[32] TsGADA, Golitsyn's Fund, Affair 1120, Letter of July 19, 1771.
[33] *De l'esprit des économistes,* p. 21.
[34] *Ibid.,* p. 8.
[35] *Ibid.,* pp. 20–1.

cording to Golitsyn, it was not the founders of physiocracy, but their disciples,[36] who were responsible for this debacle." [37]

The writers and statesmen of the French bourgeois revolution, Dupont de Nemours in particular, were physiocrats in name only, Golitsyn asserted. They formulated revolutionary conclusions beyond the tenets of the founders. This development was recognized by their reactionary and conservative contemporaries, including Catherine II, who considered the physiocrats a "sect harmful to the state," and called them devils and bawlers after the Revolution.

After the bourgeois revolution in France, Golitsyn, who steadfastly had declared himself to be a physiocrat, felt the necessity to justify physiocracy. At the same time, he repudiated the accusation that the economic policy of the French revolution was linked to the ideas of the physiocrats. This was the essence of his declarations on the French bourgeois revolution and its economic ideology.

Golitsyn's economic views differed considerably from those of Sumarokov and Shcherbatov, conservative and reactionary representatives of Russian economic thought in the second half of the eighteenth century. In contrast to the latter, Golitsyn sponsored proposals which would have directly aided the development of the bourgeois system. He favored certain concessions to the peasantry in the interests of his noble-pomestie class, and the preservation of its political and economic domination. His position was noble-liberal.

His plan to abolish serfdom and to give the peasants the right to own property apparently influenced Catherine. In 1766 she announced a prize through the newly founded Free Economic Society in Petersburg, for an essay on the theme, "What is more useful for society: that the peasants have the right to own land or only movable property, and how far should the right to one or the other be extended?" Golitsyn's alternate proposal to free the peasants without land appeared also in the "plan for the rights of nobles" prepared by a special commission of the Code Commission of 1767, but the degree of his influence is not known.

Golitsyn's economic views contained a number of contradictions. He sought in physiocracy the theoretical basis of what in his opinion was

---

36 Among physiocrats belonged such writers and statesmen of the bourgeois revolution in France at the end of the XVIII century as Condorcet, Mirabeau (Jr.), and Dupont de Nemours. Apparently Golitsyn had them in mind when he spoke of students and epigones "of the first economists."

37 *Ibid.*, p. 7.

the key to development—the land rented by rich peasants from the pomeshchiki. He defended a capitalist type of rent. When the article by l'Abbé de Bearde[38] received first prize in the competition of the Free Economic Society in 1767, Golitsyn found that the latter's views coincided with his own.

Béarde de l'Abbé (1704–1771), French economist and agronomist, however, opposed the ideas of Quesnay and Turgot. In contrast to the development of farming, that is, capitalist agriculture, which the physiocrats defended, he praised the advantages of giving freedom and "small ownership" to agriculturists (for a high price). This reform would have found the peasant who had bought his freedom to a strip of land insufficient to feed him and his family and would, therefore, have made him economically dependent on the pomeshchik. Under such conditions peasants would have been forced to rent a small section of pomestie land for a ruinously high price. "They will never consider flight, as soon as they possess some small property," wrote l'Abbé de Bearde: "the rich, untroubled by constant surveillance, will receive their income fairly and regularly. Pleasure can be derived from seeing a faithful dog follow his master, but can this be similar to the labor of leading a bear?"[39]

In this frankly cynical way, so admired by some Russian aristocrat-bosses of the Free Economic Society, l'Abbé de Bearde propagated his economic and political ideas—small peasant ownership of land and enslaving rent, both of which could gradually ensue over many generations. And of this opponent of physiocracy, Golitsyn wrote that "his ideas coincide perfectly with mine."[40]

Golitsyn, as we have seen, did not fully understand the meaning of "uniform tax," its role in the partial removal of land rent, and, therefore, in the partial confiscation of feudally owned land. His effort to interpret physiocracy as the support of altar, throne, and ownership and to deny the link between the economic and political ideology of the bourgeois revolution and the ideas of physiocracy shows his inconsistency and inherent contradiction. These errors are explained by the fact that while he appreciated the development of bourgeois relationships within the framework of the feudal-serfdom order, he strove to direct this development toward the interests of his pomestie class. But such a contradictory analysis of physiocracy was represented in Russia only by D. A. Golitsyn.

---

38 The translation of this work is in *Trudy Volnogo ekonomicheskogo obshchestva,* Pt. VIII (1768), pp. 1–59.

39 *Ibid.,* Pt. VIII (1768), pp. 51–2.

40 TsGADA, Golitsyn's Fund, Affair 1116, Letter of July 30, 1768.

Physiocracy did not exist in Russia as a trend of economic thought, for there were no prerequisites for its development. As contrasted to eighteenth century France, where farming and the phenomenon of capitalist rent were emerging, the dominance of feudal serfdom in Russian agriculture precluded physiocracy as a trend in Russian economic thought. Golitsyn's economic ideas were directed against serfdom and toward a limited development of the bourgeoisie. Therefore, although his projects reflected the interests of the noble-pomeshchiki, his economic views were to a significant degree progressive.

A. Ia. Polenov on Conditions of Russian Serfdom

Aleksei Iakovlevich Polenov (1738–1816) was born into a noble Moscow family; he was the son of a military man.[41] After finishing his studies at the gymnasium of the Academy of Sciences in Petersburg, he entered Petersburg University, which was at that time part of the Academy. In 1762 the Academy sent him abroad to study jurisprudence at Strasbourg University.

On his return to Petersburg in 1767, Polenov was appointed a translator in the Academy. In the same year, in response to the competition of the Free Economic Society, he wrote an article on the conditions of serfdom in Russia. As a result, Polenov, an educated jurist, was not employed by the Commission to participate in the drafting of a new Code, but remained merely a translator.

In 1768 Polenov (with Bashilov) published the second part of *The Chronicle of Nikon*. Since he found translation irksome, he requested that he be "allowed to seek a position where matters of jurisprudence are dealt with." [42] In 1771 he was sent to work for the Senate, where he subsequently advanced to the post of chief secretary. In 1793 he left the Senate and became a counsellor to the Loan Bank. Three years later he became a member of the Commission on Compiling the Laws of the Russian Empire. He retired in 1800.

Serfdom, upheld by tsarist legislation, bothered the student Polenov. He began to realize that the existing Russian laws not only failed to

[41] The most complete biography of A. Ia. Polenov is that by his grandson, the famous historian and jurist, D. V. Polenov, "A. Ia. Polenov–russkii zakonoved XVIII veka" [A. Ia. Polenov–Russian Legal Pioneer of the XVIII Century], *Russkii arkhiv* (1865), pp. 445–70 and 704–36.

[42] Archive of the AS USSR, Fund 3, No. 14. "V uchrezhdennuiu pri imperatorskoi Akademii nauk Komissiiu pokorneishee proshenie perevodchika Alekseia Polenova ot 6 aprelia 1771" [A Humble Petition of Interpreter Aleksei Polenov to a Commission at the Imperial Academy of Sciences of April 6, 1771].

aid the economic, political, and cultural progress of the country, but also hindered its development. He became convinced that Russian laws needed amendment. "I examine the decrees and codes, and, except for disorder, interference, want, and injustice, I find almost nothing. I discovered such great defects in our laws that they can sometimes greatly harm both the sovereign and the people; however, in spite of these shortcomings, work and intelligence can overcome them." [43]

To resolve the socio-political questions which bothered him, Polenov turned to philosophy, jurisprudence, and political economy.[44] Defining the basic task of science, Polenov, like all men of the enlightenment of the eighteenth century, stressed the significance of science for social practice and the well-being of the people. "Science in general searches for a direct road to obtain continuous well-being." [45]

Polenov returned from abroad not only with a law degree, but also with a broad philosophical, historical, and economic background, which was influenced by philosophical materialism, natural law, and the physiocratic school of political economy.

His socio-political aspirations reflected the contradictions in the social life of Russia and the need for their solution. His reaction is shown in his entry in the competition of the Free Economic Society in 1766. While Catherine II and the Free Economic Society limited the question to *property rights* of peasants,[46] Polenov spoke of their status in general and of *serfdom* in particular.

In his composition [47] Polenov asked the following questions: 1) "Do the peasants belong to the state, crown, or lord?" 2) "Are they in personal serf dependency or not?" and 3) "Are they landed or landless?" He contended that the status of all Russian peasants had one general characteristic–slavery. "The condition of our peasants . . . is standard, and they are, in their person and thier property, generally not free." [48] Polenov studied the influence of serfdom on ownership. He examined the question whether "the slavery to which our peasants are subject is harmful or useful in regard to property." He began his research by pointing out the natural "advantages of ownership." This approach

---

[43] *Russkii arkhiv* (1865), pp. 467–8. Polenov's letter of September 13, 1765.

[44] Archive of the AS USSR, Fund 3, No. 14. Polenov's letter of April 20, 1764.

[45] Polenov's foreword to this translation of *Razsuzhdenie o prichinakh ustanovleniia ili unichtozheniia zakonov* [A Discussion of the Causes of Introduction or Destruction of Laws] (St. Petersburg: 1769).

[46] See Chapters XV and XVI.

[47] Polenov's reply was published for the first time in *Russkii arkhiv,* (1865), pp. 287–316 entitled "O krepostnom sostoianii krestian v rossii" [On Peasant Serf Conditions in Russia].

[48] *Izbrannye proizvedeniia russkikh myslitelei,* II, 7–8.

was typical of a progressive spokesman of the eighteenth century. Bourgeois development in that century proclaimed that one of the most essential rights of man was ownership.[49]

According to Polenov, the right to own property would permit the peasant to use and dispose of it for his own benefit. Then the peasant would be concerned with his health, the increase of his family, and suitable education of his children. As a result, the pomeshchik would regularly receive obrok. The town population would also flourish, since peasant industriousness would add to the food supply and raw materials for industry and their price would decline. All this would contribute to the growth of national well-being and to increased state revenues. "From the peasant ownership of property, the whole state will feel a great relief: its revenues will grow immeasurably." [50]

To the peasant who possessed the right to ownership Polenov contrasted a "sad object"—the peasant, deprived of the right of ownership, representing "nothing more than a living image of laziness, carelessness, distrust, and fear . . ." Such a condition is unavoidable, because, deprived of ownership, a peasant knows in advance that he will receive nothing from his work but danger, torture, and coercion.[51]

Finally, Polenov called on the self-preservation of the ruling classes. Indeed, this argument was advanced almost a hundred years later in connection with the reforms of 1861. Polenov indicated the political danger to the state when the masses are without ownership. A man without advantages has no incentive to preserve a society in which he represents little and only suffers; he knows that, no matter what change may ensue, he has nothing to lose.[52] Those people who see no end to their poverty despair and resort to extremes dangerous to society. He recommended the avoidance of excesses such as uprisings and revolutions and favored concessions to the peasants.

In trying to determine the benefits of ownership, Polenov posed the question of how the majority of people are deprived of these advantages. A special chapter was devoted to "The Origin of Slavery." Rejecting the idealistic theory of Rousseau's "social contract," Polenov agreed with Turgot, who believed that slave and, generally, dependent relationships were the outgrowth of force and the "product of wars." [53] "War . . . is the cause of the poverty under which so many of our peo-

[49] Engels, *Anti-Düring*, p. 17.
[50] *Izbrannye proizvedeniia russkikh myslitelei*, II, 9.
[51] *Ibid.*, II, 10.
[52] *Ibid.*, II, 11.
[53] A. R. Turgot, "Rassuzhdenie o vseobshchei istorii" [A View On Universal History], *Izbrannye filosofskie proizvedeniia* [Selected Philosophical Works] (Moscow: Sotsekgiz, 1937), p. 85.

ple suffer." [54] Another factor was voluntary enslavement, that is, selling oneself into slavery. He saw, however, no economic causes of enslavement.

Peasant serfdom, according to Polenov, contradicts natural law. "Natural law . . . does not include the reasons for such decisions; that people would willingly agree and submit to such a cruel fate is unbelievable, considering a man's innate tendency to obtain well-being and his irresistible striving for freedom." [55]

Noting the way out of such a situation, Polenov stated that, above all, it is necessary to improve the peasants themselves by education and to observe a number of precautions. In the eighteenth century, thinkers such as Voltaire and Rousseau, Montesquieu and Morelli, Holbach and Helvetius stressed the great importance of education. They felt that education is a necessary prerequisite of social reform.

The materialistic wing of eighteenth century French philosophy believed that man was the "product of his environment." With the exception of Montesquieu, the materialists viewed environment not only as a geographic, but also as a social, phenomenon. "Not on nature, but on the differences in state organization, depend the love or indifference of various people toward benefactors." [56] Therefore, Helvetius understood by education the influence of social environment on man. For Helvetius, said Marx, it was "not only education in the usual sense of the word, but the totality of all the conditions of life of the individual." [57]

On this important theoretical problem Polenov took the more correct position, which approximated the materialist thinking of Helvetius, that it was the social, rather than Montesquieu's geographical, environment which molded man. In the foreword to his translation of the work of Montesquieu, although giving Montesquieu his due, Polenov was critical. He praised Helvetius for his "disapproval of Montesquieu's teachings on the different positions of countries and on the resultant differences in the political beliefs and customs of peoples." [58]

The French materialists thought that if changes of laws have the prerequisite of education, then laws in their turn determine the customs of people. "If laws are good, customs are good; if laws are bad,

---

[54] *Izbrannye proizvedeniia russkikh myslitelei,* II, 12.
[55] *Ibid.,* II, 11.
[56] K. A. Helvetius, *Ob ume* [On Reason] (Moscow: Sotsekgiz, 1938), p. 215.
[57] Marx and Engels, *Sochineniia,* III, 162.
[58] *Razmyshleniia o prichinakh velichestva rimskogo naroda i ego upadka* [Thoughts on the Causes of the Greatness and the Decadence of the Romans]. Translated from the French by Aleksei Polenov. (St. Petersburg: Academy of Sciences, 1769), translator's foreword.

customs are bad," [59] wrote Diderot without noticing the vicious circle of his argument. The thesis that "man is the product of environment" took this form: man's views are the product of his environment, which is itself the product of man's views.[60] To recapitulate, the French philosophical thought of the eighteenth century came to the conclusion that ideas direct social life.[61] Polenov also fell into this vicious circle in developing his socio-political views. Like the French materialists of the time he considered ideas the ruling factor of social development.

Polenov attributed decisive significance to education in the correction of national customs and in the national well-being. "It seems almost unbelievable," he said, "how much education aids the welfare of every society; thus it should have priority here." [62] He thought that the "common people" are usually prone to great vices, such as ignorance, superstition, intemperance, laziness, and thoughtlessness. With the aid of education, however, it is possible to reform any man, regardless of his previous condition. He recommended that schools be established in every village and that doctors, who would also operate pharmacies, be stationed in large villages.

He realized, however, that in improving the position of the peasant, education and enlightenment cannot play an important role so long as the peasant is deprived of "human rights." Therefore the decisive step is to grant human rights. A peasant will be transformed only when his power is returned to him.[63]

Thus Polenov contradicted his motto that "good customs are better than good laws." But in his discussion he came to the conclusion that "good customs" are impossible without good laws. Therefore, in spite of, and contrary to, his motto, he gave primary attention to the right of peasant ownership. Like the French materialists, Polenov included in the right of ownership all the "natural rights" of man. The right of ownership, according to Helvetius, embraces everything: "my person, my thoughts, my life, my freedom, my property." [64]

---

[59] D. Diderot, *Sobranie sochinenii* [Collection of Works] (Moscow-Leningrad: 1935), II, 74.

[60] See *Istoriia filosofii* [A History of Philosophy] (Moscow: Gospolitizdat, 1941), II, 74.

[61] While giving materialistic explanations to natural phenomena, French materialists of the XVIII century were idealists in their explanations of social life.

[62] *Izbrannye proizvedeniia russkikh myslitelei,* II, 17.

[63] *Ibid.,* II, 15.

[64] K. A. Helvetius, *O cheloveke, ego umstvennykh sposobnostiakh i ego vospitanii* [On Man, His Reasoning Capabilities, and His Education] (Moscow: Sotsekgiz, 1938), p. 414.

Above all, Polenov speaks of the need for an independent solution of this Russian problem, inasmuch as the examples of others need not be followed for sound decisions and the rules of humanity. Special attention must be given to the conditions of each country; each state has its peculiar character, failings and superiorities; consequently, it rarely happens that the laws and institutions of one state can be usefully applied to another.[65]

In the chapter, "On Ownership of Immovable Property," Polenov recognized the necessity to consider not only the peasant's own advantage but all others involved in such a change, that is, the advantages to the pomeshchiki must also be examined. The peasant will freely enjoy the advantages allowed him, while the nobility, after limitation on its arbitrariness, will suffer no harm.[66] At first glance it may seem that such a concession by the nobles would undermine the lawful foundations of their domination. But this is an error, since the nobles will retain a number of rights, including the ownership of places for hunting, fishing, forests, and so forth.

To evaluate correctly this declaration, we must keep in mind that the thinkers of the eighteenth century said, and said sincerely, that their "projects" corresponded to the interests of all classes of society—of society as a whole. They turned to the ruling classes to support their projects and therefore had to appeal to the interests of these groups. Polenov looked to the Free Economic Society, an organization of noble-pomeshchiki, and tried to convince them that his project did not infringe on the interests of the nobility.

Polenov's impelling motive was the improvement of peasant life, as exemplified in his solution to the problem of land allotment. Each peasant was to have enough land to sow grain and to pasture cattle, and he was to own it on a hereditary basis so that the pomeshchik would have very little power to oppress him or completely to appropriate his holdings.[67] He defended the forces which weakened the peasant's economic dependence on the pomeshchiki. Nevertheless, he wrote within the framework of feudal law, and consequently many of his demands were influenced by feudal norms. He did not go as far as to give the peasants the bourgeois right of land ownership, but spoke only of "land ownership with the necessary limitation," that is, feudal ownership. The peasant is not permitted to sell, give away, or mortgage land, but it re mains his property with the right of inheritance so long as he properly fulfills all his obligations; otherwise the

[65] *Izbrannye proizvedeniia russkikh myslitelei,* II, 22.
[66] *Ibid.,* II, 26.
[67] *Ibid.,* II, 22.

pomeshchik can take the allotment from the guilty peasant as punishment and give it to someone else.

Polenov, however, tried to protect the peasant from pomeshchik arbitrariness by demanding court action in cases of controversy. Before the pomeshchik could revoke the allotment, the matter would have to be examined by the proper court.[68] Polenov naively supposed that "peasant courts" under pomeshchiki supervision could be fair. He did not understand that under feudalism any judicial organization not only fails to assure the legality and defense of peasant interests, but is directed against them.

In addition to defending "immovable property" as a hereditary possession for the peasants, Polenov favored granting the peasant the right to ownership of movable property. He thought, however, that for the latter "concession" some kind of redemption payments, comprising a considerable sum, should be set up. Under such conditions, he felt that the pomeshchiki should willingly concede the peasants the right to own movable property. Polenov noted that it is enough if the peasant, as a sign of his gratitude, pays annually to his lord a set sum which will eventually be infinitely greater than the value of that which was given to him.[69] While defending the peasants' right to own movable property, he maintained that they should pay the pomeshchik a redemption price comparatively greater than the value of the property. In addition, Polenov approved some limited kind of work obligations: "The service required of the peasant for the lord could be set up so that the former would work one day a week for the lord and the rest for himself." [70] Such an arrangement would lead to the development of agricultural production and peasant industries.

The peasant establishment should be taxed only on its basic agricultural production. Proposing a tax of "a tenth or some other share of all agricultural products," [71] Polenov tried to lighten the tax burden of the peasantry. At the same time, taxing agricultural production only would aid the development of peasant industries, which were then, even more than agriculture, the basis for the development of capitalism in the village.

Polenov was very much concerned with the gravitation of the farm population to the cities and with the flow of workers from agriculture, which he, like the physiocrats, considered to be "the most necessary and profitable wealth for any society." On the other hand, he noted

[68] *Ibid.*
[69] *Ibid.*, II, 25.
[70] *Ibid.*, II, 26.
[71] *Ibid.*

that "we have no middle class [that is, no free city population, no bourgeoisie—I. B.] and that great losses can develop from sending peasants into cities." [72] Polenov's formula was to regulate the flow of the rural poplation to the city. He recommended that rich peasants be allowed to enter the bourgeoisie, not easily, but on the basis of some agreements which would prevent the complete desolation of the villages.[73]

The content of Polenov's plan was fairly modest. Like the other progressive thinkers of his time, he was afraid not only of revolution, but also of sudden change. He therefore called for gradual realization of his plan as the best method to protect both peasant and pomeshchiki interests. Polenov thought that the noble-pomeshchiki should not be forced to introduce these reforms. He believed that the nobles themselves would voluntarily introduce social reforms once they were convinced that their advantages would overshadow any losses.

Polenov proposed to inaugurate his plan first with crown and state peasants, of whom only the good and productive peasants should be awarded these advantages, while the lazy and ill-natured should be excluded. This would serve as a significant example to the nobility, who would become convinced by logical proof and practical demonstration.

In Polenov's views two aspects should be distinguished: the force and passion of his criticism of the prevailing socio-economic order and his exposure of the harm and evil of serfdom; and, at the same time, the weakness and timidity of his plan. But, in spite of these shortcomings, his proposals would have aided the development of bourgeois relations. Their purpose was to ameliorate the legal status and to improve the economic position of the peasantry, which comprised the greatest part of the Russian population.

Obviously the Free Economic Society recognized its merits, as Polenov's essay was awarded a prize. The Society, however, decided not to publish it because of its strong measures and improper expressions in view of the immediate situation; [74] in other words, serfdom was criticized.

Plekhanov observed that Polenov largely abandoned the noble point of view, and the development of his ideas could have easily caused the whole social order of the time to begin to crack.[75] Obviously for this reason, his work was not published by the Free Economic Society

[72] *Ibid.*, II, 23.
[73] *Ibid.*, II, 29.
[74] *Russkii arkhiv,* (1865), p. 730.
[75] Plekhanov, *Sochineniia,* XXI, 262.

and came to light only after almost a hundred years had passed. We see in Polenov one of the first representatives of that trend of Russian economic thought which was critical of serfdom and which defended the creation of conditions which would make possible the development of bourgeois relations within the feudal economy. His practical measures, however, were considerably more moderate and timid than his bold criticism of serfdom.

Economic Views of the Philosopher Ia. P. Kozelskii

In prerevolutionary and Soviet scholarly literature the view predominated that the philosopher Iakov Pavlovich Kozelskii and the deputy to the Code Commission Iakov Pavlovich Kozelskii were one and the same person.[76] The opposite view, first expressed in prerevolutionary literature, has recently been confirmed.[77] A comparison of the signatures of Kozelskii, the philosopher, and Kozelskii, the deputy (made by the author of this chapter), is absolute proof that they were different individuals.[78]

Iakov Pavlovich Kozelskii—famous thinker, philosopher, scientist-encyclopedist, and writer—was born about 1728 [79] into the family of a Ukrainian noble, a lieutenant of the Poltava regiment. Kozelskii studied in the Gymnasium and University at the Academy of Sciences in Petersburg, and lectured in the "Artillery and Engineering Noble Cadet Corps for Young Noblemen." In 1764 he published *Arithmetical Propositions* and *Mechanical Propositions.* These original scientific researches were, at the same time, intended for teaching purposes.

The center of Kozelskii's interests, however, were social questions. He was troubled by the political and economic oppression which pre-

---

76 In the past the author of this chapter also entertained this view.

77 See V. L. Modzalevskii, *Malorossiiskii rodoslovnik* [Little Russian (Ukrainian) Genealogical Table] (Kiev: 1910), Pt. II, pp. 390–2; Iu. Ia. Kogan, "Svobodomyslie Ia. P. Kozelskogo" [Free Thinking of Ia. P. Kozelskii], *Voprosy istorii religii i ateizma* [Problems of the History of Religion and Atheism] (Moscow: AS USSR, 1950), pp. 167–9.

78 See the signature of Ia. P. Kozelskii, the philosopher, on a "sworn promise" of the Senate officials to Catherine II in 1770 (located in the Central State Archive of Ancient Documents, Senate's Fund 268, Folder 3858, Sheet 263) and that of Ia. P. Kozelskii, the delegate to the Legislative Commission of 1767 (in the Central State Historical Archive of the USSR in Leningrad, Fund 1258, Folder 110, Pt. 1, Sheet 161).

79 There is still another birthday date of Ia. P. Kozelskii—1735 (Modzalevskii, *Malorossiiskii rodoslovnik,* II, 390; *Novyi entsiklopedicheskii slovar* [New Encyclopedic Dictionary], XXII, 98). In his *Philosophical Proposals,* which appeared in 1768, Kozelskii stated that he was "close to 40 years old," i.e., he was born about 1728.

vailed in feudal-absolute Russia and by the burdensome material position and lack of rights of the masses of the people, whose creative forces were chained and dulled by serfdom. To find a solution he turned to literature, history, and philosophy.

In 1764, he translated the tragedy of Otway, *Venice Preserved,* which describes sympathetically the revolt of freedom-loving Venetians against the Senate. In 1765 Kozelskii translated Shofin's *History of Famous Rulers and Great Generals, with a Discussion of their Actions and Affairs.* In his foreword to the translation he said that those matters are not always great which "are called great by historians." Kozelskii considered great those acts which contributed to the general well-being. From this point of view, he contrasted Alexander the Great, whom he considered "unjustly called great as he declared himself the enemy of the whole world," with Peter I, who was really great, for he was not satisfied with increasing the external strength of his state, that is, by wars, but tried to give Russia internal strength and power.

In 1765–1766 Kozelskii published an abridged translation of Holberg's two-volume *History of Denmark.* He annotated his translation. These notes, giving a political evaluation of historical figures and events, resembled the notes of Radishchev to his translation of Mabli's *Thoughts on Greek History,* eight years later. Kozelskii criticized Holberg's distortion of historical facts and their incorrect interpretation. He gave a number of devastating characterizations of tyrants and monarchs who were not concerned with the welfare of their subjects, but thought only of wars.

In 1766 Kozelskii left the military service,[80] abandoned the cadet corps, and joined the Senate as Secretary of the Third Department (under whose jurisdiction were the Academy of Sciences and Moscow University).

In 1768, *Philosophical Propositions,* Kozelskii's principal work, was published.[81] This book, written and published during the deliberations of the Code Commission, reflected the tense socio-political situation of the time. Various strata of Russian society awaited the satisfaction of their demands and desires. The activities of progressive Russians increased. In his foreword Kozelskii appealed to those "whose

---

[80] In the Military College report to Catherine II (1766) about Kozelskii's release from the military service it is stated that he "does not have peasants." TsGADA, Fund, 262, Folder 6007, Sheet 96.

[81] *Filosoficheskie predlozheniia, sochinennye nadvornym sovetnikom i Pravitelstvuiushchego Senata sekretarem Iakovom Kozelskim* [Philosophic Proposals, Prepared by Court Counsellor and Secretary of the Governing Senate, Iakov Kozelskii] (St. Petersburg: 1768).

minds love truth and agree with the views of the author." Calling on "comrade Russians" to exert every effort to seek direct good and wisdom, he said that "an abundant harvest of important questions has arisen for you; now is the time to expedite your well-being." [82] He indicated the great socio-political importance of philisophy, which "guides the rising and boiling passion in youth to general good and strengthens the courage for constant good deeds . . ." [83]

In 1770 Kozelskii translated a collection of selected articles from the famous *Encyclopedia* of Diderot and d'Alembert. The first part of the collection included philosophical articles,[84] and the second, a number of papers on jurisprudence, ethics, and politics.[85] Kozelskii's translations appeared after the publication of *Translations from the Encyclopedia,* prepared by Kheraskov by order of Catherine II in 1767. Kheraskov's three-volume translation contained purely factual articles on various subjects—medicine, technology, economics, and so on; it did not cover philosophy nor politics. The collection of Kozelskii's translations, obviously issued in answer to Kheraskov's edition, included these subjects which were directed against despotism and were essentially antifeudal in character.[86]

The tenor of Kozelskii's thoughts did not please the Senate administration. In 1770 it was decided to transfer Kozelskii to other pursuits where he would be more useful,[87] that is, to discharge him from the Senate. In the same year, finding himself without a position, he was appointed to the Little Russian College in Glukhov.[88] On his return to Petersburg in 1788 he joined the Commission on Drafting a new Code. About this time (1788) *Discussions of Two Indians, Kalan and Ibrahim, on Human Knowledge* was published, the first volume of a

---

[82] *Ibid.,* Appeal to "a kind reader."

[83] *Izbrannye proizvedeniia russkikh myslitelei,* I, 426.

[84] *Stati o filosofii i chastiakh ee iz Entsiklopedii, perevedennye nadvornym sovetnikom Iakovom Kozelskim* [Articles On Philosophy and Its Divisions From the Encyclopedia, Translated by Court Counsellor Iakov Kozelskii] (St. Petersburg: Academy of Sciences, 1770), Pt. I.

[85] *Stati o nravouchitelnoi filosofii i chastiakh ee iz Entsiklopedii, perevel kollezhskii sovetnik Iakov Kozelskii* [Articles on Moral Philosophy and Its Divisions from the Encyclopedia, Translated by College Counsellor, Iakov Kozelskii] (St. Petersburg: Academy of Sciences, 1770), Pt. II.

[86] Almost simultaneously with the appearance of Kozelskii's collection, Ivan Tumanskii, an interpreter in the Governing Senate, published a collection of these political articles from the "Encyclopedia" which praised "enlightened absolutism." This official collection was published by the Academy of Sciences in 1770 and was entitled *O gosudarstvennom pravlenii i raznykh rodakh onogo iz Entsiklopedii* [On Varied Forms of State Administration from the Encyclopedia].

[87] TsGADA, Senate Fund 268, Folder 3858, Sheet 261.

[88] *Ibid.,* Folder 6297, Sheets 36 and 50.

projected popular encyclopedia of sciences, written in dialogue form.

The last mention of Kozelskii's service is in 1793.[89] The year of his death is unknown.

Kozelskii was an original thinker. He took an independent position on philosophical questions and critically evaluated and reformulated the views of the major scholars of his time. He examined various theories and teachings from the point of view of their practical importance for attaining the common welfare.

In his *Philosophical Propositions* he divided philosophy into the theoretical and the practical. The theoretical part, which Kozelskii further divided into logic and metaphysics, was basically the philosophy of nature. Defending materialism, he was progressive for his time in explaining nature.

Moral philosophy, which he considered the practical aspect of philosophy, was separated into jurisprudence and politics. He stressed this part as it decides the most important philosophical question—the well-being of the people: Philosophy deserves special respect not so much because it is basic to all other sciences, but for its rules for seeking the well-being of the people.[90] In contrast to the official understanding of jurisprudence as the knowledge of laws, Kozelskii defined it as the knowledge of rights. The task of practical philosophy, he maintained, is to change the laws to correspond to the natural rights of man.

In her Nakaz, Catherine II incorporated some ideas of Voltaire, who considered social inequality a law of life, and of Montesquieu, who said that for a territorially large state the usual form of government was despotism. Catherine hated Rousseau, the only leader of the French Enlightenment who refused any relations with her. Kozelskii, on the other hand, enumerating those who "wrote fundamentally" on questions of practical philosophy, did not name Voltaire. He considered Rousseau the leader of the democratic wing of French Enlightenment, who, "like an eagle, surpassed all previous philosophers." [91] But even here Kozelskii did not simply adopt Rousseau's position.

In *Philosophical Propositions,* Kozelskii set forth his ideal social order and the means of attaining it. He agreed with Rousseau that man was happy only in a "natural state," when men lived separately

---

89 See *Mesiatsoslov s rospisiu chinovnykh osob v gosudarstve na leto . . . 1793* [Almanac with a List of Officials in State's Service for the Year 1793] (St. Petersburg: Academy of Sciences, 1793), pp. 63 and 110.

90 *Izbrannye proizvedeniia russkikh myslitelei,* I, 412.

91 *Ibid.,* I, 418.

and outside society, when private property did not exist, and when "science and art" had not yet appeared.[92] He also shared Rousseau's historical explanation that social inequality which resulted from the development of private property.

Like Rousseau, Kozelskii developed the idea of the contractual origin of the state. This theory, historically false and idealistic to the core, served as a basis for revolutionary consequences. Kozelskii himself, although foreseeing the possibility of popular uprisings, was afraid of them and, like Rousseau, preferred peaceful means to decide social questions.

The social philosophy of Kozelskii differs from that of Rousseau in such important points as the role of science and industry in social development and their influence on the condition of the people. While Rousseau believed that science and industrial production ruin morals and make people unhappy, Kozelskii recognized their progressive role in the process of social development. He concluded that the good or evil of science and arts, that is, of industry, depends on who controls them. "Evil use" of science and industry takes place where there is social inequality, which is linked to the existence of private property.

In search of happiness, the people can no longer, according to Kozelskii, return to a "natural state," give up life in society, and reject science. This would be possible only if all mankind were in a state of natural simplicity. Now, however, if one group of people thought of going back, "other learned peoples would in a short time and with great appetite consume it." The former "would doubtless be convinced by such enlightened wolves of the evil of its simplicity." [93] Kozelskii erroneously saw the "golden age" as lying in the past. Nevertheless, unlike Rousseau, he considered a return to this "golden age" not only dangerous, but also an evil.

Rousseau's philosophy was individualistic. It contrasted the injustice of the feudal order and the "sensitive personality," the perfection of which is the task of every man. Despite its antifeudalism, this philosophy, rising from the social struggle for self-perfection, did not call for social reform. G. V. Plekhanov observed that the conviction that the progress of *social morality* presupposes the perfection of *social order* disposes people to *social reform*. On the other hand, the belief that goodness consists of purity of heart and depends on sanctity of religion makes them indifferent to such reforms.[94]

The antifeudal direction of Rousseau's philosophy predetermined

[92] In those days "arts" referred to various branches of industrial production.
[93] *Ibid.,* I, 414.
[94] Plekhanov, *Sochineniia,* XXII, 258.

its future transition into a progressive ideological weapon: from his philosophy revolutionary deductions were made; it served as the ideological weapon of the first bourgeois French revolution.

At the same time Rousseau's individualistic spirit tended toward sentimentalism, which contrasted the "life of the heart" to society, and individual morals to politics. This passive, conservative side of Rousseau's teaching was accepted by the Russian nobility, who used it, especially after the Peasant War of 1773–1774, as the ideal weapon in the struggle to preserve serfdom.[95]

Spokesmen of the nobility, together with Catherine II (in her Nakaz and some of her other works), asserted that the liberation of the peasants should be preceded by their personal improvement through education; education first, then reform. Boltin, repeating the words of Rousseau, wrote that first one should free the souls of slaves, then their bodies.[96] Béarde de l'Abbé advised against making the peasant his own master until he learns to be worthy of it.[97] Finally, Catherine declared in her Nakaz that a great number of slaves ought not to be enfranchised suddenly by general law.[98]

In contrast to this conservatism Kozelskii defended the position that change of the social order should precede education of the peasants, for their education is impossible without an earlier change in society. Attributing great importance to education as a means of introducing good customs,[99] Kozelskii at the same time thought that it was impossible to refine people without lightening their burden.[100] He concluded that improvement of economic status determines the possibility of education. Thus his thesis embraced the necessity of struggle to change social conditions.

Kozelskii believed that the source of leisure-class wealth was the labor of others, independent of the kind of work, be it "agriculture, arts, or other useful occupations." [101] His views concerning the sources of wealth differed from those of the mercantilists, who emphasized foreign trade, that is, in the sphere of circulation; while the physiocrats stressed agriculture. Rather than picking out this or that form of actual labor, he viewed labor in general as the source of wealth. To

---

[95] See G. Makogonenko, *Nikolai Novikov i russkoe prosveshchenie XVIII veka* [Nikolai Novikov and Russian Enlightenment of the XVIII Century] (Moscow-Leningrad: 1951), pp. 290–5.

[96] Boltin, *Primechaniia na istoriiu,* II, 236.

[97] *Trudy Volnogo ekonomicheskogo obshchestva,* VIII (1768), p. 42.

[98] *Nakaz,* Chapter X, Article 260.

[99] *Izbrannye proizvedeniia russkikh myslitelei,* I, 532.

[100] *Ibid.,* I, 536.

[101] *Ibid.,* I, 639.

the extent that he maintained that neither gold nor silver, but industriousness, comprises the wealth of nations,[102] he approached the ideas of Adam Smith.

Kozelskii's criticism was directed against feudalism and its various forms of oppression and limitation. He defended freedom of speech and the press, for science dies without freedom.[103] Political questions should be decided by all the citizens. He opposed mechanical imitations of other nations and favored the independent development of each people, while assimilating the best things attained by others.

What was Kozelskii's social ideal? He proposed a new social contract. Man should renounce his innate right to "natural freedom" and to everything that tempts him. Instead, through the social contract he acquires civil freedom and property ownership. Thus men, being by nature unequal in strength and intelligence, are made equal by agreement and right.[104] While he correctly viewed the rise and development of private property as the source of social inequality, Kozelskii, at the same time, considered personal property the basis of the ideal social order. This is one of the main contradictions in his teachings regarding society.

According to Kozelskii, the well-being of the ideal state consists of its good conventions and industriousness. The law of social life should be one of moderation: there should be neither poverty nor luxury. Then people will not be dependent on one another. He idealistically supposed that such a condition could be attained by legislation—"one should not allow any form of borrowing other than that based on the principle of equivalence." [105]

In this ideal society everyone must labor. Work is the duty of each citizen. Kozelskii thought it possible and useful to force people to work if necessary. But work should not be a heavy burden, which can shorten a man's life. Excessive work is less productive than moderate work. An eight hour work day is enough for a man, the second eight hours being used for eating and diversion, and the third eight, for sleep. Attacking both luxury and excessive labor, Kozelskii did not think man's work should satisfy only his current needs; it is necessary to create a reserve for the future.[106]

---

102 *Ibid.*, I, 537.

103 *Razsuzhdeniia dvukh indiitsov Kalana i Ibragima o chelovecheskom poznanii, sochineny statskim sovetnikom Iakovom Kozelskim* [Views on Human Understanding by Two Indians, Kalan and Ibrahim, Prepared by State Counsellor Iakov Kozelskii] (St. Petersburg: 1788), p. 37.

104 *Izbrannye proizvedeniia russkikh myslitelei*, I, 525.

105 *Ibid.*, I, 535.

106 *Ibid.*, I, 536–7.

Advanced for his day are Kozelskii's statements that the security and power of a country are determined by its internal prosperity. He believed in economic and political independence, so that it could rely as little as possible on other societies. Kozelskii, however, did not equate independence with isolationism, for he realized that it is almost impossible for a society to be without some kind of dependence.[107]

Kozelskii naively supposed that mankind could realize its social ideal by peaceful means, by concluding a social contract. At the same time, he justified the revolt of the oppressed "who, when greatly abused by their superiors," become at an appropriate moment very cruel. Their revenge is greater after prolonged suffering. Comparing the anger of the oppressed to a roaring river long held back by a dam, Kozelskii said that in case of a revolt it is possible, in all fairness, to consider them almost innocent.[108] Kozelskii penned these thoughts during the meeting of Catherine's Code Commission and during a period of growing agitation, five years before the Peasant War of 1773–1774.

Criticizing and rejecting feudalism, Ia. P. Kozelskii called for the creation of an ideal society which would be essentially a society of free producers of goods—of private owners. Such a society would provide a broad base for the development of capitalism.

Speeches of Ia. P. Kozelskii, the Deputy to the Code Commission

Of Iakov Pavlovich Kozelskii, deputy to the Code Commission of 1767 it is known only that he came, in his own words, from pomeshchiki in the Ukraine,[109] that he was the son of a lieutenant of the Poltava regiment, that he was the namesake of the philosopher Ia. P. Kozelskii,[110] and that he entered military service in 1735.[111] In 1767 Major Kozelskii was elected to the Code Commission by the owners

---

107 *Ibid.*, I, 540–1.

108 *Ibid.*, I, 512.

109 See "V. Komissiiu o sochinenii proekta novogo Ulozheniia ot deputata Ekaterinskoi provintsii ot shliakhetstva Iakova Kozelskogo primechanie" [A Memorandum to the Code Commission by Iakov Kozelskii, a Delegate from the Nobles of the Ekaterinoslav Province], *Sbornik Russkogo istoricheskogo obshchestva*, XXXII, 496.

110 See Modzalevskii, *Malorossiiskii rodoslovnik*, II, 390–2.

111 See *Spisok voinskomu departamentu . . . na 1771 god* [A List of the Military Department . . . for the Year 1771], p. 119.

and the nobility of Ekaterinoslav province and by the Dniepr Lancer Regiment.[112]

He spoke in the Commission against the exclusive privileges of the hereditary nobility, proposed extending noble titles to persons of the lower classes for service, and demanded legal separation of children from parents who mistreated them. None of the deputies was so outspokenly in favor of the peasantry as Kozelskii: he demanded extending to the peasants not only the right to own movable property, but also the right to the hereditary ownership of land. Hence it is underable why the leader of the serf owners, Prince M. M. Shcherbatov, opposed Kozelskii, why other deputy-nobles were against him, and why, finally, in 1768 he was among the deputies who were released from their obligations with the excuse of the "present wartime" and sent into the army.[113]

When the Commission discussed laws concerning the nobility, Kozelskii opposed M. M. Shcherbatov, who declared that Russia owed her development to the hereditary nobility, which therefore should possess exclusive rights and should not be enlarged by people coming from other classes. Kozelskii countered that all groups served the state and that it was chiefly the peasantry who fed Russia and created her wealth by its labor. He reminded the nobles that their ancestors had received their dignity as a reward for their faithful and virtuous services, and not through accident of birth. Kozelskii firmly disliked the nobles' use of the word "scoundrels" in reference to other classes. He declared that, in the true, moral sense of the word, more scoundrels could be found among the rich, including the nobles. He opposed evaluating people by their clothes, inasmuch as poverty, if moral, is not contrary to honesty and dignity.

Kozelskii declared that the custom of recognizing services to Russia as belonging only to the hereditary nobility was antisocial and antistate. If only the old nobility is so honored, then the service which all society has performed is for the glorification of the nobles alone, and not for the benefit of the fatherland or for the preservation of the unity of the state. He viewed hindrances in entering the ranks of the nobility as harmful, causing disruption in state service, for the other, nonnoble classes, seeing themselves unequal to the nobility in

---

112 "Nakaz shliakhetstva Dneprovskogo pikinernogo polka" [Instruction of the Nobles of the Dniepr Lancer Regiment], *Sbornik Russkogo istoricheskogo obshchestva,* XCIII, 22.

113 "Bolshogo Sobraniia dnevnye zapiski 1768–69 godov" [Daily Notes of the Main Session for the Years 1768–9], *ibid.,* XXXVI, 148.

rewards for service, will serve unwillingly, without zeal or love for the fatherland.[114] Kozelskii's speech was directed against the feudal principle of the exclusive rights of the nobility.

Another of Kozelskii's most interesting and important speeches was his reply to the remarks of the noble deputy Grigorii Stepanovich Korobin, who proposed an amendment to the laws regarding run-away people and peasants. Korobin found such harmful results in the unlimited power of the pomeshchik over the property of his peasant that he called for legal regulation of peasant-pomeshchik relations and legal limitation of peasant obligations.

Korobin's demands were quite cloudy and vague. Like Polenov, he did not encroach on the personal dependence of the peasants on the pomeshchiki. He stated that in his project the power of the pomeshchiki over peasants would remain complete, as it then was. His project coincided with the wishes of the "good owner" and did not hinder him from improving the condition of his peasants by his wisdom. At the same time, his plan would have cut off the power of bad pomeshchiki to ruin their peasants.[115]

In Korobin's scheme, the protection of property rights was combined with the retention of the peasant's personal dependence on the pomeshchik. The defenders of the nobility saw this inconsistency. Shcherbatov expressed surprise that Korobin bothered about peasant property while retaining serf dependence: once power over the peasant's "body" is preserved, then his "property" is actually within the power of the owner of his body. Shcherbatov's comment was entirely true, wrote Plekhanov, nevertheless Korobin's inconsistent plan caused much excitement among the noble deputies: he touched upon what, in their conviction, no one should mention.[116]

Speaking after Korobin, Kozelskii remarked that not only peasant property but pomestie wealth was created by peasant labor. He opposed the declarations of the noble deputy that pomeshchiki were peasant benefactors, lending them grain, cattle, and so on, in case of need; rather, he said, the pomeshchik had earlier obtained all this from these very peasants. This idea coincided with the theses of a number of articles in Novikov's journals of the time.[117]

The peasant, argued Kozelskii, reacts strongly to the fact that even

---

[114] "Deputata Dneprovskogo pikinerskogo polka Iakova Kozelskogo . . . primechanie" [A Memorandum by Iakov Kozelskii, a Delegate from the Dniepr Lancer Regiment], *Ibid.*, IV, 187–9.

[115] "Deputata Kozelskogo dvorianstva . . . primechanie" [A Memorandum by Kozlovskii, a delegate from the Nobility], *ibid.*, XXXII, 406–10.

[116] Plekhanov, *Sochineniia*, XXI, 269.

[117] Makogonenko, *op. cit.*

his property belongs to the pomeshchik. "The peasant is a sensitive man; he understands and knows beforehand that everything belongs to the pomeshchik." The peasants, dependent on the pomeshchik's changing and arbitrary will, find their condition to be an extreme burden. Peasants, oppressed by the pomeshchik even while they enrich him, cannot be accused of laziness, drunkenness, and extravagance, since they are deprived of ownership and kept in a state of serf dependence. "It seems better, from a humane standpoint, to try to awaken the people to the advantages of free labor; then they will tirelessly work longer.[118]

It would seem that Kozelskii should have realized the necessity of immediate abolition of serfdom and of allotment of land to peasants. He did not, however, draw this conclusion. It is very possible that he simply decided not to suggest this in the Commission. He may have thought that the demand for the abolition of serfdom was then too unpopular and that such a proposal would only irritate the nobility.

Kozelskii sought state interference in pomeshchiki-peasant relations, while the nobility opposed it. The nobles usually insisted that those who abused their peasants be made responsible and be placed under pomeshchiki guardianship. Kozelskii, however, thought that it was better to seek ways of preventing such maltreatment and violations. He felt that such preventive measures, very important for "free peoples," were especially needed in Russia, where one ought to preserve the numerous peasant population from further ruin and to alleviate their unhappy lot.[119]

Kozelskii wisely showed that such preventive interference could satisfy all pomeshchiki, both "oppressors" and "humanitarians." He also emphasized that the number of pomeshchiki who mistreated peasants was large and increasing. He rejected pomeshchiki protests against state interference as a whim to control their subjects limitlessly and a violation of the right of state power. While Polenov left his plan to the consideration and willingness of the pomeshchiki, Kozelskii insisted on the adoption of laws which would regulate peasant-pomeshchik relations, independent of the desires of the latter. Korobin held the same position. Kozelskii's demands, however, were much more definite and decisive. Such views, for all of their utopian character (for a serf state always acts in the interests of the pomeshchiki), were nonetheless progressive.

---

[118] "Deputata . . . Iakova Kozelskogo primechanie" [A Memorandum of Delegate Iakov Kozelskii], *Sbornik Russkogo istoricheskogo obshchestva*, XXXII, 500.

[119] *Ibid.*, XXXII, 499.

Kozelskii proposed that the peasants work two days a week to pay government taxes, two days on barshchina, two days for themselves, and devote one day, Sunday, to prayer. The adoption of this system, he thought, would considerably alleviate the situation of the peasants. Kozelskii also suggested that obrok, like barshchina, be taken at the value of two days of peasant work. Then, he thought, the obligation of barshchina and obrok peasants would be equal. The choice between barshchina and obrok could therefore be made on the basis of variation in climate, fertility of land, and other circumstances, and in each case at the discretion of the pomeshchiki and peasant. While the state collected a head tax, the peasants were to pay obrok to the pomeshchik or contribute their work not per capita, but per household. Then the obligations to the pomeshchik, generally more burdensome than state taxes, would not cause the peasants to have fewer children, but would make possible the quantitative growth of the peasantry. As a result, state revenues from the head tax would rise.

On the peasant right of ownership, Kozelskii's position was also more decisive and consistent than that of Polenov and Korobin. Kozelskii demanded not only granting to peasants the right to ownership of movable property, but like Polenov, the right to hereditary land ownership, with the condition that they could not, without pomeshchik permission, sell immovable property or mortgage it, but that they own it hereditarily, without pomeshchik participation. This was not yet the bourgeois right of land ownership where the peasant has the right of freely disposing of the land, but it was nevertheless the peasant right to own land hereditarily, without pomeshchik interference.

Like Pososhkov earlier, Kozelskii insisted on separation of peasant lands from the pomestie, so that peasants, considering those lands their personal property, could better care for them and live on them permanently.[120]

Kozelskii thought that his proposals "will make the peasants more assiduous in farming"; childbirth would increase and begging decrease. Many peasants who had left to work in cities would return to agriculture, making possible lower prices for bread in the cities and growth of village populations; finally, escapees would return from abroad, and peasant flight would generally stop in the future.

Kozelskii's proposed separation of peasant and pomestie lands could only partially protect the peasant economy from pomeshchik arbitrariness, which was unavoidable if the personal dependence of peasant on pomeshchik was retained. Personal dependence of peasants on pomesh-

---

[120] *Ibid.*, XXXII, 500.

chik, as Plekhanov correctly stated, was that threshold over which stumbled the ideas of even the most progressive and sympathetic of noble deputies.[121] Giving the peasants, however, the right of hereditary land ownership would inevitably shatter their personal dependence on the pomeshchiki.

Even in such moderate form Kozelskii's proposal, like his other recommendations, incited the noble deputies against him. This was evident in the balloting after his first speech on the question of the nobility. This group also solidly voted against his election to various committees. The results of the voting not only emphasize the nobles' attempt to isolate one of the most progressive deputies, but also indicate that Kozelskii gained support of a rather stable group on the Commission drawn primarily from the representatives of the state peasants, the city population, and the merchants.

I. A. Tretiakov on the Causes of the Enrichment of States

Ivan Andreevich Tretiakov was born in Tver into a military family.[122] His birth date is unknown. Judging from other data, such as fear of entering the University, he was born at the end of the 1730's or the beginning of the 1740's. After finishing the Tver Theological Seminary, he entered Moscow University in 1761. The same year he went to Scotland and matriculated at Glasgow University, one of the best universities of the time, among whose professors were Adam Smith, Hume, and Blackstone. At Glasgow he was awarded the degree of Master of Free (that is, humanistic) Sciences, and then in 1767, after defending his dissertation, that of Doctor of Civil and Canon Law.

On his return to Russia in 1767 Tretiakov joined the faculty of Moscow University. This was a period of bitter struggle for a progressive world outlook, for advanced science, and for lecturing in one's native language. The students and followers of Lomonosov—N. N.

---

121 Plekhanov, *Sochineniia*, XXI, 269.

122 In literature, beginning with the *Biograficheskii slovar professorov i predpodavatelei Moskovskogo universiteta* [A Biographic Dictionary of Professors and Lecturers of Moscow University] (Moscow: 1855), Pt. II, p. 505, it is asserted that I. A. Tretiakov stemmed "from the clergy." This assertion is not supported by documentary evidence, and it probably originated from the fact that Tretiakov studied in the Tver Theological Seminary. However other students than sons of churchmen also studied at theological seminaries.

Different evidence on Tretiakov's social origin is found in the register of those admitted to the University of Glasgow for the year 1761. Tretiakov stated that he was the son of an officer (*filius centurionis*) in Tver. (See *A Roll of the Graduates of the University of Glasgow . . .* [Glasgow: 1898], p. 616).

Popovskii, D. S. Anichkov, S. G. Zybelin, and others—were creatively developing and applying the ideas of their gifted teacher in various fields of endeavor. They promoted Russian science with its materialistic tradition, originating with Lomonosov. In 1768 Tretiakov was one of the professors who began to lecture in Russian (instead of Latin). He allied himself with those progressive Russian scholars who developed and strengthened, in research and teaching, Russian scientific terminology; they wrote the first Russian language monographs and textbooks in various branches of science.

This enlightened group encountered blunt and severe opposition from the conservative-reactionary camp. To the latter belonged not only almost all the foreign professors, but also the University administrators (Adodurov, Kheraskov, and others), a fact which strengthened their position. The defenders of reactionary views, theories, and ideas in science believed in the inviolability of serfdom, grovelled before Western European civilization, and were supercilious and skeptical of Russian national culture. The progressive professors were subjected to surveillance and repression.

Tretiakov was an established scientist-materialist and an enemy of idealism when he occupied the chair of jurisprudence. He immediately joined the progressive Russian scientists. In research and teaching he followed the comparative-historical method, a method, advanced for the time, of studying social life. He was the first to teach Roman law in comparison to Russian law; he developed Russian scientific terminology and included in his lectures analyses of the laws and judicial practice of Russia. His philosophical, socio-political, judicial, and economic views were expressed in his "arguments" and "comments" at the formal University gatherings.

The situation at the University was so difficult for him that in 1773 he requested the Senate to award him a rank and assign him to state service.[123] He died in 1776.

In his study of human society Tretiakov proceeded from an economic basis and the historical satisfaction of man's needs. If animals are satisfied with what nature produces, man by his labor improves the products of nature, adapts them to his needs, and creates new ones. Thus Tretiakov understood the difference between the world of nature and human society, whose characteristic traits are production, economic activity, and development. One of the foundations of economic development was to him the division of labor in a society,[124]

[123] TsGADA, Senate Fund 261, Folder 5565, Sheets 347a–348.
[124] *Izbrannye proizvedeniia russkikh myslitelei,* I, 337.

that is, the social division of labor.

His analysis differed from that of his Russian predecessor, P. I. Rychkov, who viewed the division of labor as an eternal, unchanging phenomenon.[125] He also departed from the beliefs of his teacher in the University of Glasgow, Adam Smith. Maintaining that man has a natural inclination toward exchange, Smith concluded that the division of labor resulted from exchange.[126] Tretiakov, however, correctly inferred that exchange resulted from the division of labor and, in contrast to Rychkov, properly saw the latter as a historical phenomenon which arose at a definite stage of social development.

Explaining historically the origin of the division of labor, Tretiakov said that the primitive tools of labor and the few simple occupations in the initial stages of society's development were known to each of its members. "Their inventions and techniques were extremely simple and few and therefore could not help but be known to, and comprehended by, all of society." [127] The absence of division of labor at this time was responsible, in Tretiakov's opinion, for the inferior productivity of labor, the insignificant volume of production, and the imperfection of the products of labor. This lack accounts for the extremely low level of peoples' needs and the insufficient satisfaction of these in the early stages of social development. In this primitive state, people could scarcely provide for their own subsistence. A long time had to pass before man's labor created a surplus of goods, which was a necessary prerequisite to the division of labor. Before labor could be divided, there had to be a surplus of goods.[128]

This scholar, therefore, considered a surplus of goods—the formation of a reserve of products—as a consequence and, at the same time, a prerequisite to the increase of the productivity of society's labor, both in agriculture and in industry. Contrasting human society in its initial stage with a more highly developed one, Tretiakov wrote that even daily food was procured with relative difficulty in the earlier period. People who did not plan ahead were barely able to maintain their subsistence from year to year by the fruits of their labors. He blamed the low productivity of labor for the poverty of the people and for their obduration in an impoverished state.[129]

With the growth in the number and complexity of economic occu-

---

[125] See Chapter XVII.

[126] See Adam Smith, *Issledovanie o prirode i prichinakh bogatstva narodov,* I, Chapter II.

[127] *Izbrannye proizvedeniia russkikh myslitelei,* I, 336.

[128] *Ibid.,* I, 357.

[129] *Ibid.,* I, 358.

pations it became clear that not everyone in society was skilled and competent to understand all things.[130] Moreover, people began to realize that when the expenditure of labor-time is small the cost is less, and that things are produced better by "skilled people," by "skilled masters," that is, by specialists. Their products, in turn, are exchanged for those made by people of various other specialties. The division of labor in society enriched the artisan who specialized in a particular trade: if no division in human labors prevailed, an artisan would not be able to get rich by his own labor, nor even earn his living.[131]

The division of labor was not only the basis of the wealth of the artisan-specialist, but also a device to separate people into social groups, that is, into owners and workers.[132]

Tretiakov linked the rise of these social groups, which represent in embryonic form the classes of capitalistic society, with the development of "arts" (industrial production) and with the "artistic conditions" of people. By "artistic conditions" Tretiakov meant industrial growth, in essence, the development of capitalistic manufactures under feudalism.

Forced by economic exigencies to hire themselves out, the workers willingly took upon themselves the burden of labor, released their masters (that is, the capitalists) from it, and submitted themselves to their command. Working people had to seek their livelihood from their masters, who were left with the overseeing of labor.[133] Like his contemporary Western European economists (Turgot, A. Smith), Tretiakov did not see contradictions between workers and capitalists.

The division of labor and the development of industry, in Tretiakov's opinion, enriched not only the artisans and the manufacturing entrepreneurs ("factory owners"), but also the whole state.[134]

In contrast to the mercantilists, who considered foreign trade the major source of wealth, and the physiocrats, who considered it to be agriculture, Tretiakov, like Adam Smith, considered labor in general, independent of its area of application, as the source of wealth. Like Smith, Tretiakov proposed that the sole source of material wealth was labor in its social-aggregate aspect, in the form of division of labor.[135]

Along with the materialistic realization that the social division of labor, which increased its productivity, generated exchange and created

[130] *Ibid.*, I, 337.
[131] *Ibid.*, I, 354–5.
[132] *Ibid.*, I, 337.
[133] *Ibid.*
[134] *Ibid.*, I, 355.
[135] See Marx, *K kritike politicheskoi ekonomii*, p. 48.

wealth, Tretiakov drew another conclusion: the growth of production stimulated the needs of the people. These were better satisfied, and new and greater ones appeared. Thus gradual improvement of social conditions impelled men to strive even more diligently to live even better and more appropriately to their elevated status.[136]

Viewing the social division of labor and the increase of its productivity as the foundation for a surplus of goods and the enrichment of the state, Tretiakov, by the very title of one of his speeches, "Inquiry Into the Causes of Abundance and the Slow Enrichment of States" (1772), emphasized the gradualness and the evolutionary character of this process.

Cheapness and abundance of things are necessary facets of a nation's wealth.[137] Attempting to explain why this or that commodity is abundant and is cheaply attained in society, he concluded that the reason is the division of labor. Through division of labor into various hands a multitude of things is completed in one day and becomes cheaper for society.[138]

Having set forth this proposition, Tretiakov, without developing it, proceeds to an analysis of the phenomena connected with the problem of price. He makes price dependent on the quantity of labor applied in the production of a given commodity: the greater the labor and, therefore, the larger amount of the given commodity, the cheaper will be each unit. A different question relates to the factors determining the amount of social labor which is applied in each sphere. Tretiakov makes this quantity dependent on the amount of labor expended per unit of the product. In essence Tretiakov thus makes value depend on the amount of labor used per unit of the product. One must, however, bear in mind that Tretiakov did not differentiate price from value. The object of his immediate inquiry was price.

From these theoretical positions he analyzed the determination of price in two different areas of production—agriculture and the mining of precious metals. He stated that grain and similar crops can always be found in greater abundance than gold, silver, and precious stones, for the former are more easily attainable through human industriousness than the latter. Almost any part of the earth's surface can be made arable, but gold lies hidden in the bosom of the earth, and the acquisition of even a small amount of it requires much time, labor, and expense.[139]

---

136 *Izbrannye proizvedeniia russkikh myslitelei,* I, 337.
137 *Ibid.,* I, 353.
138 *Ibid.,* I, 355.
139 *Ibid.,* I, 356.

Concerning the "price" of money (by which he meant, in essence, its value), Tretiakov maintained that the "price" of money (that is, metal) became lower when more labor was applied to the production of monetary materials, that is, gold and silver. He believed that the greater the aggregate amount of labor involved in producing a commodity, the smaller would be the amount of labor used per unit of production, that is, the productivity of labor increases.

Tretiakov explained the high productivity of labor in agriculture and industry by the influx of much labor and the consequent output of a large number of commodities in these spheres of material production. On the other hand, the low productivity of labor in mining precious metals determined labor's insignificant application in this branch of endeavor and hence explains the output of only a small amount of precious metals, of money material. "For these reasons," he concluded, "money will never be found in such abundance as certain other things."[140] The insignificant quantity of money is the cause of its high value, which he called the price of money.

As national development takes place, however, and a given country reaches a certain level of scientific knowledge and increases the application of labor to mining precious metals, the people will be able to extract more ores which can be converted into money. With the increase of precious metals, the quantity of money increases and its value decreases: the price of money falls.[141]

Tretiakov believed that with specialization labor would become more productive, and its use per unit of a commodity would diminish. As the amount of labor increases in each sphere of activity, the volume of the commodity expands and its price declines.[142] Tretiakov considered cheapness and abundance of goods as basic factors in national wealth.

He pointed out the fallacies of many political writers,[143] particularly the mercantilists, who held that the wealth of a state consisted of a surplus of precious metals. Refuting this thesis, Tretiakov contended that the amount of money in a country does not reflect its wealth,

---

140 *Ibid.*

141 *Ibid.*

142 Adam Smith identified the quantitative explanation of the price of a commodity with the origins of the labor theory of value in his lectures at Glasgow University, which Tretiakov attended in 1763. *Lectures on Justice, Police, Revenue, and Arms, delivered in the University of Glasgow by Adam Smith in 1763* (Oxford: 1896). Labor theory of value is the essence of Smith's major work *Inquiry into the Nature and Causes of the Wealth of Nations,* published in 1776, i.e., thirteen years after his university lectures.

143 *Izbrannye proizvedeniia russkikh myslitelei,* I, 355.

which is composed of many things: "money is not indicative of the prosperity of an entire state." [144]

Tretiakov viewed money solely as a means of circulation. Money outside of circulation is not wealth; it is a dead treasure, hidden in the ground.[145] The view that money is merely a means of circulation developed in the polemic with the mercantilists and was at the time widespread in economic literature. It obtained its ultimate expression in Adam Smith's major work, *Inquiry into the Nature and Causes of the Wealth of Nations* (1776).

Characterizing money as a means of circulation, Tretiakov considered the issuance of paper money expedient. Although the value of paper money, of assignats, is immeasurably lower than that of metallic money, the assignats can fulfill the role of a means of circulation as easily as hard coin.

On the basis of this analysis of money, Tretiakov concluded that it is not wise to prohibit its export from a country. Furthermore, forbidding the export of money leads to a country's impoverishment. He cited the experience of Spain, which received, after its conquest of Mexico and her mineral wealth, a large quantity of valuable metals, the export of which was banned by the government. As a result, foreigners (the English and the Dutch) forced the Spaniards to purchase goods not being produced in their own country at double and triple prices. Subsequently, the country's economy sharply declined, and Spain became impoverished.

Tretiakov protested against the belief that foreign trade in itself could cause the impoverishment of a state. The poverty of a country never arises from trade with foreigners. The reason is not foreign trade as such, but the excess of demand over the homeland's production. In a country where more is consumed than is produced by native labor and is purchased externally, poverty inevitably results.[146] If a surplus exists in the homeland's production beyond domestic demand and it is exported, foreign trade becomes a means of the country's enrichment.

Tretiakov's theories on money, particularly paper money, and his evaluation of the importance of trade, particularly foreign trade, led to his endorsement of credit and banking. Having emphasized how advantageous was the founding of banks to commerce, which also enriches every state,[147] he decisively opposed a monopoly in banking.

[144] *Ibid.*
[145] *Ibid.*, I, 357.
[146] *Ibid.*
[147] *Ibid.*, I, 355.

It would cause bad consequences for money circulation, especially for paper money. The only way to avert such a situation was the creation of numerous banks, the increase of which should be encouraged as much as possible.[148] Theoretically, the demand to organize credit for merchants was directed towards aiding the development of capitalism within serfdom.

In his political-economic views Tretiakov has much in common with Adam Smith, who was influential in England on the eve of the industrial revolution. But on questions of the role of the state in the development of the national economy, the Moscow professor took an independent position. "The great ideologist of the bourgeois revolution" (as V. I. Lenin calls Smith) reflected the interests of the English bourgeoisie, entrenched in its economic position, no longer in need of the support of the state, and burdened by government supervision. Hence Smith opposed the state's interference in economic life.

Tretiakov's position was different. Trade and especially industry in Russia still needed state aid, and merchants constantly sought the support of the government. Therefore, Tretiakov recognized that the state plays an important positive role in the growth of the national economy, and he demanded a policy which would aid the economic development of the country.[149]

If the wealth of the people is a pillar of the state, then the state in turn influences the growth of national wealth. Among the causes which hinder the rapid enrichment of states,[150] Tretiakov above all emphasized various political conditions,[151] among which he included mutual relations between various states, between the people and the state, and between separate classes. Undeveloped and weak governments in ancient times could not stimulate the development of agricultural and artisan labor, a fact which contributed, as was the case in Rome, to a great rejection of industriousness [152] and to the growth of parasitism in society. An aggressive foreign policy and aggressive wars also have a negative influence on the development of national labor, because they ruin the people. Tretiakov noted the decline of agricul-

---

148 *Ibid.*

149 It is quite evident how incorrect was the author of the article on I. A. Tretiakov in *Biograficheskii slovar professorov i prepodavatelei imperatorskogo Moskovskogo universiteta,* Pt. II, p. 507, and even more so N. M. Korkunov, *Istoriia filosofii prava* [History of the Philosophy of Law] (4th edition, St. Petersburg: 1908), and other writers who maintained that Tretiakov simply repeated Adam Smith's ideas.

150 *Izbrannye proizvedeniia russkikh myslitelei,* I, 360.

151 *Ibid.,* I, 357.

152 *Ibid.,* I, 359.

ture and trade among the Romans, who were above all engrossed in military affairs.

But more destructive than wars is domestic disorder, which frequently arises from internal indignation toward the government. States are more often destroyed by internal strife than by enemy attack.[153] State policy must be directed toward the greatest stimulation of national labor; toward the protection and commendation of agricultural and artisan labor, which create the wealth of the country.

Tretiakov emphasized that not war and pillage, but only the labor of the common people, is the means which brings wealth to the state.[154] Only that state which rests upon the development of national labor can be stable. From attempts to stimulate the labor of the masses should emerge a negative attitude towards serfdom. In his speeches in the public meetings of the Imperial Moscow University, Professor Tretiakov did not directly explain his attitude towards serfdom. A document which has been preserved, however, attests to his position on this question.

The minutes of the conference of Moscow University for March 22, 1768 recorded that Doctor Tretiakov decided to select one of four themes for his public speech. One of these is formulated in interrogatory form: "Does the greatest benefit to the state proceed from slaves or from people of free status and from the abolition of slavery?"[155] The very form of the question leaves no doubt as to the nature of the author's answer.[156]

Tretiakov protested vigorously against the view then held by spokesmen of the nobility, especially A. P. Sumarokov and M. M. Shcherbatov,[157] that each man and his descendants always belong to the same class. In contrast to this, Tretiakov considered it possible to transfer from a lower social status to a higher one, mainly through education. He condemned the attempts of the ruling class and the state to legislate against such a "natural course," that is, a natural develop-

---

[153] I. Tretiakov, *Slovo o rimskom pravlenii i o raznykh onogo peremenakh* [A Treatise on Roman Administration and Its Varied Changes] (Moscow: 1769), p. 3.

[154] *Ibid.*, p. 24.

[155] *Protokoly Universitetskoi konferentsii . . . 1768 goda* [Protocols of the University Conference . . . of 1768], XII, 29. Manuscript of the Scientific Library of Moscow University.

[156] It is obvious that the University Conference, whose membership was overwhelmingly conservative-reactionary, rejected this theme and recommended another from among those he suggested, namely, on the origins and development of universities in Europe. He delivered a public lecture on this topic at a meeting of Moscow University on April 22, 1768, which was subsequently published.

[157] See Chapter XVI.

ment of society. Restrictions of this type could not be enforced in reality because they completely contradict human nature.

Tretiakov's views on science had a clearly anticlerical nature. He opposed religious education and condemned the interference of churchmen in the area of science and enlightenment. Emphasizing the social significance of science and its role in elevating the material and moral status of mankind and in establishing law and order, Tretiakov espoused the development of experimental science connected with practice.

Differing from the idealistic outlook on the origin of science then prevalent, especially in Germany, Tretiakov supported a true, essentially materialistic position that the development of production and industry, which are the foundation for science, precede its development: "Arts in the past and in the present day always exist before science." [158]

Opposed to metaphysical idealism in philosophy, Tretiakov believed that the teaching of social life rests upon historical experience. He rejected the method of the social-science idealists, who "only prepared human hearts to accept the tolerable governments which they visualized." He warmly defended the empirical, historical-comparative method in jurisprudence and economic thought. Scholars who followed the latter point of view and drew their outlook from experience demonstrated to the world the clear drawbacks and advantages which appear in various governments and in their actual courses of action.[159] These ideas confirm the fact that the Russian scholar attempted to draw the study of society close to that of nature and to make the method of social science approach that of natural science.

Critical of serfdom, Tretiakov viewed labor as the sole source of national wealth. He developed the theory that the social division of labor and its increased productivity were the basis of economic development and the enrichment of both the people and the state.

Relating the price of goods to their quantity and linking the quantity of a commodity with the division of social labor among various productive spheres, Tretiakov considered the productivity of labor in each sphere to be the most important factor in this division. He arrived at a definition of price not only by the quantity factor (the amount of the commodity), but also by the labor expended in the production of the commodity.

In his theoretical position and his criticism of mercantilism, Tretiakov promoted and set forth practical economic-political proposals (for example, on banking, foreign trade) objectively directed towards the

158 *Izbrannye proizvedeniia russkikh myslitelei,* I, 339.
159 Tretiakov, *Slovo o rimskom pravlenii,* p. 4.

development of bourgeois elements and relationships in the economy of feudal Russia.

The Sociological Views and Economic Proposals of S. E. Desnitskii

S. E. Desnitskii and I. A. Tretiakov shared a common conception of the world. Both criticized outworn social forms and relations, struggled against priesthood, metaphysics, idealism, and fought for progressive social relations, free science, and materialism.

Semem Efimovich Desnitskii came from a burgher family of the Ukrainian city of Nezhin.[160] The exact date of his birth is unknown, but the time of his entrance into the university would place his birth at the end of the 1730's or the beginning of the 1740's.

After graduating from the Troitsk-Laurentian Ecclesiastical Seminary, Desnitskii studied at the gymnasium in Moscow University and in 1759 enrolled as a university student. In 1760 he was sent to the Petersburg Academy of Sciences, where he studied physics, philosophy, and public speaking. In 1761, together with I. A. Tretiakov, he was sent to Glasgow University. Six years later he defended his dissertation and was awarded the scholarly degree of doctor of laws. Upon his return to Russia, Desnitskii began to lecture at Moscow University, where he and Tretiakov joined the group of progressive Russian scholars and began giving lectures in Russian.

Desnitskii was the first professor to specialize in Russian law, in the development of which he played an important part.[161] His lectures had tremendous influence. He is the founder of Russian legal science and of his own school of jurisprudence, which attracted many students and followers.

His sociological, economic, and legal views are reflected not only in his public pronouncements, but also in the project for the legislation and organization of state authority in Russia which he presented to Catherine's Legislative Commission shortly after his return from abroad in February, 1768, and in the prefaces to and comments on books which he translated into Russian.

An excellent stylist and orator, Desnitskii was elected to the member-

---

[160] This is supported by the register of those who were accepted to Glasgow University in 1761 and by a "Story, Given to the Heraldic Office About Professor Desnitskii" (TsGADA, Funds of the Former State Archive of the Russian Empire, Part XVI, No. 168, part 14, Sheet 540).

[161] *Ibid.*, Senate Fund 261, Folder 5565, Sheet 418.

ship of the Russian Academy (Russian language and literature) in 1783.

The university administration obstructed in every way the activities of this distinguished Russian scholar and the circulation of his works. It forbade the translation of Desnitskii's public speeches into Latin for distribution abroad (in exchange for foreign books),[162] although they were an outstanding contribution not only to Russian, but also to world science. In 1787 he left Moscow University. He died in 1789.

Rejecting the prevailing religious-idealistic concepts of social life, Desnitskii viewed human society as being in a state of flux and development. He criticized Puffendorf's teachings on natural law, then called natural jurisprudence, which were predominant in the universities, especially in Germany. Puffendorf wrote about the so-called "natural state" of people, not about actual existing conditions. Desnitskii considered Puffendorf's work quite superfluous, as he wrote about fictitious conditions of the human race without showing how property, possessions, inheritance, and so on arose and were distributed among the people. Puffendorf presented a problem which did not correspond with its intention and end. While Desnitskii maintained that "presently almost everywhere moralistic philosophy does not lead anywhere" and condemned scholastic "internecine polemics," he thought highly of Hume and Smith, who published their works "to the great gratification of the scholarly world." [163]

In criticizing Puffendorf, Desnitskii adhered to a positive program for studying society. One must look into the origin and development of ownership, property, inheritance, and other social institutions. Adopting the historical-comparative method, Desnitskii asserted that communal conditions of economic life inevitably produce among various peoples in different countries the same social institutions. He considered property the most important of these and gauged the development of society at a particular stage by the level of its property structure. This important social institution, like other institutions, he regarded not as constant and always existing. Property emerged at a definite stage of social development, and its forms changed according to economic conditions. Its emergence and the development of its forms determined the nature even of state administrations.[164] Believing that social development evolved gradually, Desnitskii felt that

[162] *Protokoly universitetskoi konferentsii . . . 1768 g.*, XIV, 123. Manuscript of the Scientific Library of Moscow State University.

[163] *Izbrannye proizvedeniia russkikh myslitelei*, I, 200 and 202, 204.

[164] *Ibid.*, I, 285.

society had passed legally through four phases, which he called conditions [*sostoianiia*]. The first stage is the condition of peoples living by *hunting* animals *and subsisting on the native products* of the land; the second is the pastoral state, in which people gain their livelihood by husbandry; the third is the *agricultural* stage; and the fourth, and last, the commercial.[165]

Affirming that these conditions were determined by economic occupations, Desnitskii did not concern himself with the causes of society's transition from one stage to the next. He merely noted these shifts in society.

The most important and original of Desnitskii's concepts of social progress, and his greatest scientific achievement, was expressed in the proposition that "on the basis of these four conditions of peoples, we should deduce their history, government, laws, and customs and measure their varied successes in the arts and sciences." [166]

In discussing the evolution of society Desnitskii explained first of all the emergence and development of estates and property and the historical change in their forms. He demonstrated that people's labor lies at the base of the emergence and development of property. Living in "a primitive condition," people were nourished by the products of the earth and by hunting wild animals. Not knowing how to preserve food, they did not accumulate the products they received. In Desnitskii's opinion, man at this time lost little labor in acquiring the necessities of life and therefore perceived only weakly the injustice of having them stolen, since consumption corresponded to communal ownership. If people did not have separate ownership of things, the distinction between *yours* and *mine* would have been very little understood.[167]

Under such conditions the right of ownership of a thing was inseparably linked with possession of it.[168] Moreover, an insufficient supply of subsistence obtained from harvesting and hunting prevented any basis for exchange, the development of which required the establishment and recognition of ownership of bartered objects. Thus in a primitive, hunting society, where people used only movable things, the right of ownership did not exist. Pastoral peoples having herds of various animals possessed a significantly greater number of things and were considerably more able to satisfy their needs. Even in a nomadic pastorial society, however, the institution of property could not develop. A pastoral society provided a common pasture for livestock, but

[165] *Ibid.*, I, 270.
[166] *Ibid.*, I, 271.
[167] *Ibid.*, I, 274–5.
[168] *Ibid.*, I, 275.

it had no permanent settlement. Therefore temporary use of land did not constitute property. A durable and full right of ownership, in Desnitskii's opinion, could not develop on the basis of ownership of movables.

As a bourgeois spokesman, Desnitskii identified the emergence of private property with the development of agriculture, which produced more products than the occupations of earlier periods. The transition to agriculture introduces the concept of permanent settlement. In agriculture the use of fertilizers raises the productivity of the soil and improves the pasture. Cultivation of land demanded a far greater outlay of labor than cattle raising and hunting. Working the soil stimulated the farmer to secure for himself the rights to his harvest and the possession of the cultivated plot. "In such an agricultural condition every man tills the soil adjoining his abode and naturally wishes to have exclusive and eternal right to its ownership." [169]

The right of private property, which developed on the basis of ownership of an immovable (that is, land), broadened to include movables, although historically the ownership of movables preceded that of immovables. In the agricultural society ownership of movables and immovables is separate from possession of them. On this basis arose and developed the right of property, as private property. "Such a realization of the right of property proceeded from the introduction of agriculture, and in that condition property is understood to be completely separate and different from possession." [170]

Desnitskii believed that an incomparably more perfected concept of the right of ownership [171] was established in society when it attained the stage of the "commercial condition." Along with agriculture, industry developed, and subsequently various branches of production became differentiated. The growing division of labor in society made possible the development of exchange. An exchange of the products of labor was a concomitant of private property. Desnitskii felt that only in the fourth stage of development could people attain the most perfect right of ownership; he conjectured that a society which has the most perfected right of ownership is ideal and represents the final stage in man's growth. In this conclusion the bourgeois nature of Desnitskii's sociological conceptions, as well as his bourgeois limitation, is revealed.

Property occupied the central place in Desnitskii's sociological, economic, and legal views. He identified the origin of the state with

169 *Ibid.*, I, 282.
170 *Ibid.*, I, 284.
171 *Ibid.*

the development of property and the change of its forms. He felt that the rise of the state stemmed from land ownership. Feudal ownership of land caused the emergence of feudal states, by which Desnitskii understood only feudally disunited states. The beginning of property in the advanced condition of peoples is linked with the immediate origin of state governments, and from the introduction of ownership in land the ancient European baronial and margrave authorities developed. In a word, from this beginning feudal government arose in all the original European states . . .[172]

It should be especially noted that Desnitskii viewed the emergence of the feudal political system on the basis of feudal ownership of land as a process common to all peoples, but each, nevertheless, having special characteristics of development.[173]

Desnitskii emphasized not only the similarity of the Russian historical process to that of Western European, but also its peculiarities. He urged the study of both the European feudal ownership and the Russian landed property which existed in ancient times.[174] Desnitskii was the first to recognize the existence of feudalism in Russia and linked the political system of Russian feudalism (which he erroneously limited to the period of feudal disunity) with feudal land ownership as its foundation.

Desnitskii critically characterized the government of feudally-disunited states as essentially aristocratic, based on direct force. Drawing the general conclusion that a state cannot maintain itself by force alone, because it inevitably falls into ruin (as did the states of Attila, Genghis Khan, and Tamerlane), Desnitskii believed that the development of the economy—"great reciprocal commerce"— [175] was the lasting foundation of the state. He assigned special importance to the development of trade—"merchantry," in the then prevailing terminology. "More peoples are strengthened and united through trade," he wrote, "than by any other means." [176]

Desnitskii regarded the development of the economy and the increase of the wealth of the people as the chief sources of Russia's might. He refuted Voltaire, who said that the battle of Poltava was the cause of the creation of the Russian empire, and asserted that the development of the country's economy and the growth of its wealth were responsible for the creation of the powerful Petrine empire.

[172] *Ibid.*, I, 285.
[173] *Ibid.*
[174] *Ibid.*, note.
[175] *Ibid.*, I, 191.
[176] *Ibid.*, note.

As for science, Desnitskii pointed out the material basis of its development. He said that everywhere, in the past and in the present, arts precede the sciences,[177] that is, the growth of industry precedes that of science. Desnitskii emphasized that both industry and science require proper conditions for their development, especially the freedom of citizens. By freedom he understood above all the absence of restrictions on the activity of economic institutions, that is, the removal of fetters on the development of a bourgeois economy. Desnitskii observed that only in an advanced stage of commercial growth can such a legal system be established, a stage in which the institution of private property has attained a high degree of development.

In order to evaluate the importance of Desnitskii's sociological teachings, one must know how the idea of the conformity of social life to established law [*zakonomernost'*] arose and developed. This idea was advanced by the Italian, Vico. In his treatise, *Bases of the New Science of the General Nature of Nations* (1725; Russian translation, Leningrad, 1940), he spoke about a law of development common to all nations. Despite all the rationality of the question as posed, Vico's sociological doctrine was basically idealistic and narrowed down to the so-called theory of rotation.

After Vico, but obviously not acquainted with his *Bases of the New Science . . .*, Montesquieu came forth with his major work *On the Spirit of Laws* (1748; Russian translation, St. Petersburg, 1900). Linking the political structure, legislation, and political views of society with geographical surroundings through peoples' psyche, Montesquieu also took an idealistic position.

To a certain degree, Diderot also recognized the influence of geographic conditions on the views and aspirations of people, although not directly through their psyche, but by means of the social milieu. Criticizing Montesquieu, Diderot emphasized that only a changeable factor, such as the social milieu, can have an influence in changing the popular customs and beliefs.

Helvetius, in the treatise, *On Man, His Intellectual Abilities and His Education,* decisively rejected Montesquieu's theory on the conclusive influence of geographic conditions on social development. Like Diderot, Helvetius felt that only a variable factor can change people. Thus his formula: man is a product of his environment. Setting forth this thesis, Diderot and Helvetius meant by "environment" the politi-

[177] Bouden, *Nastavnik zemledelcheskii, ili kratkoe aglinskogo khlebopashestva pokazanie* [Agricultural Teacher, or a Brief Description of English Agriculture] (Moscow: 1780). "Introduction to Translation" by S. E. Desnitskii.

cal structure, the state, its institutions, and laws created by people in accordance with their views. Thus they concluded that the development of society is explained in the long run by the opinions of people and by their ideas. Although materialists in their understanding of nature, Diderot and Helvetius in the final analysis explained society and its development idealistically.

Turgot, proceeding from the development of society according to established law, believed that the influence of the geographic environment on social life resulted not from man's psyche (as Montesquieu affirmed) or the state with its legislation (Diderot), but from the economic activity of people, on the basis of changes in the forms of economy. Turgot affirmed the dependence of progress in science and art on changes in the various economic conditions of people (hunting, pastoral, agricultural).

In his speech at the Sorbonne, December 11, 1750, on "The Logical Progress of the Human Mind," Turgot advanced and proved the idea of social development according to established laws but failed to go so far as to speculate on its temporal, material basis. He made his speculations of a materialistic nature in another work, *Discourse on General History*.[178] This book was apparently begun in 1751, but it remained incomplete and was first published after Turgot's death in 1808 and was, therefore, unknown to Desnitskii.

Desnitskii, without saying anything about the influence of geographic environment on the history of society or on changes occurring in it, considered the economic status of people to be the determining factor of social development. The influence of changing forms of economy on social development (the forms of family, state, and so on) springs from the main and basic social institutions of possession and property. Changes in the forms of possession and property result from the change in the economic occupations of people. Thus Desnitskii's sociological teaching surmounted to a considerable degree the idealistic conceptions of social development. To a greater degree than all previous and contemporary thinkers, he strove to explain social life materialistically. And in this point of view, despite all the shortcomings of his sociological schemes from our modern point of view, lies his most valuable contribution to the development of Russian and world science.

Recognizing the "commercial structure," that is, the bourgeois structure, to be a high level of social development and the ideal society, Desnitskii condemned the commercial monopolies which were under-

---

[178] Turgot, *Izbrannye filosofskie proizvedeniia*, pp. 75–142.

going considerable growth in contemporary England as institutions very harmful to the country's economy. He opposed "that very dangerous form of commerce when it falls into the hands of a few rich people, who, through their enormous incomes, eliminate all others and hold a monopoly in everything . . ." [179] He felt that the expansion of commercial monopolies in England resulted from an enormous and badly regulated commerce.[180] Thus Desnitskii, like Tretiakov, defended state interference in the economic activity of its citizens.

He found it necessary for the state to halt the development of undesirable phenomena and processes in the country's economy and to encourage positive ones. In this respect Desnitskii's conclusions were different from those of Adam Smith, who sharply opposed state interference in economic life. Desnitskii, however, believed that government policy should foster the introduction and encouragement of manufactories, the protection of commerce, and the necessary introduction of banks and money for the benefit of commerce. In addition, the government should concern itself with the best methods to improve agriculture.[181] Thus Desnitskii, like Tretiakov, took a position different from that of Smith on one of the most important economic questions—the role of the state in the country's economic development. He based his position on his own country's experience: the economic policy of the state under Peter I.

In 1768 Desnitskii presented a number of proposals to the Legislative Commission summoned by Catherine II in 1767. These were entitled "Proposals on Founding a Legislative, Judicial and Executive Authority in the Russian Empire" and expressed both his legal and basic socio-political and economic views.

Of fundamental importance was his attitude towards the feudal-serf structure of Russia and the development within it of bourgeois relationships. His ideological position contained some contradictions which reflected those of a feudal society in whose midst bourgeois relations were emerging. The feudal stamp still lay on the defenders of the incipient bourgeois-capitalistic organization. Ideas and proposals, bourgeois in essence, often had a feudal veneer which minimized their progressiveness and thus decreased their significance.

Desnitskii had a negative attitude toward slave-owning and feu-

---

[179] W. Blackstone, *Istolkovaniia aglinskikh zakonov* [Interpretations of English Laws] (Moscow: 1781), Bk. II, 137–8. Comments to the translation by S. E. Desnitskii.

[180] *Ibid.*

[181] *Izbrannye proizvedeniia russkikh myslitelei,* I, 206–7.

dalism. He believed that the task of education is to reveal "the introduction of slavery and enserfment of peoples in states, what the effect of slavery is on the judgment of the whole country, and how and why it is abolished in some states and remains in others." [182] This statement reveals clearly the author's viewpoint. He spoke of the negative influence of slavery on the entire life of the country and characterized its retention as obduration. Desnitskii deplored slavery in North America, where Europeans in trade, "treated people just like cattle and commodities." [183]

Turning to conditions for economic progress, Desnitskii pointed out that for the development of agriculture and the growth of its production, as well as for industry, trade, and science, there should be "no political impediments." [184] Personal freedom for citizens and complete private ownership of all means of production, including land, are necessary. One should not deny ownership of land to those who cultivate it. Depriving the agriculturist of land or requisitioning the fruits of his labor on the land is an inhuman and intolerable action.[185] Desnitskii, however, also advocated another measure, incompatible with the first—freedom of exchange of land: it should be "universally available in trade so that anyone who wishes may own it without hindrance," [186] he wrote.

The Russian professor viewed the system of serfdom as a hindrance to the growth of all productive branches of the economy, especially of agriculture, the main and basic branch, and as an impediment to the expansion of the market and of trade and to the development of science. He spoke with indignation of the enserfed peasants' plight. This fundamental, and largest part, of the peasantry is deprived of all benefits, and therefore cannot own even the smallest bit of property.[187] When selling peasants, the pomeshchiki often separate them from their families or sell whole families without land. It is a shameful spectacle, he observed, to see citizens roaming over the face of their country, obliged always to settle in new and unknown villages, and, finally, to see them being separated from their families.[188] Concerning the "oppression of the peasantry and agriculture" resulting from the recruitment of household serfs from among the peasants, Desnitskii said that

---

182 *Ibid.*, I, 205.
183 *Ibid.*, I, 229.
184 See Desnitskii's "Introduction" to Bouden, *Nastavnik zemledelcheskii.*
185 *Izbrannye proizvedeniia russkikh myslitelei,* I, 282.
186 See Desnitskii's "Introduction" to Bouden, *Nastavnik zemledelcheskii.*
187 *Izbrannye proizvedeniia russkikh myslitelei,* I, 318.
188 *Ibid.*, I, 320–1.

it was impossible to enumerate in detail the many forms of distress and misery.[189]

Desnitskii pointed out that the enserfed peasantry was deprived of all rights in social life and of conditions necessary to develop its economic activity. Laying special emphasis on the negative role of the absence of property among the serfs, Desnitskii considered the "commercial society" to be the ideal, by which he meant a bourgeois system.

It would seem that from Desnitskii's criticism of serfdom and his recognition of the terrible situation a demand for its liquidation would arise. Desnitskii, however, did not draw this conclusion. While assuming, as a critic of feudalism and a partisan of the bourgeois system, an anti-serfdom position in theory, he obviously feared the opposition of the economically powerful and politically dominant nobility. For this reason he felt that it was impossible to abolish serfdom immediately without disturbing "the tranquility of the state." [190] He merely proposed some measures for improving the situation of the pomestie peasants and for suppressing the gross abuses by the pomeshchiki. In suggesting these changes, Desnitskii had in mind, as he himself declared, not only the pomestie, but also the crown peasants, belonging to the Tsar, and the economic ones (formerly church-monastery peasants who were transformed into state peasants and placed under the jurisdiction of the Economic College).

Desnitskii demanded the immediate end, without consent of the pomeshchiki, of certain abuses in the treatment of the peasantry.[191] He proposed a ban on the sale of peasants alone, without family, or even with their families when without land. Desnitskii believed also that the conscription of peasants as household servants must be stopped by law.[192] A pomeshchik himself should recruit household servants from among the peasantry, and not act through his stewards. Legislation should define the age and family situation under which peasants could be made into household servants and should provide compensation for their families. Such a method of recruiting peasants into households would satisfy the pomeshchiki without oppressing the peasantry and depressing agriculture.[193]

These measures, which Desnitskii believed should have been introduced by means of legislation, independent of the pomeshchiki's consent, were extremely limited and insignificant in content. The

---

189 *Ibid.*, I, 321.
190 *Ibid.*, I, 319.
191 *Ibid.*, I, 320.
192 *Ibid.*, I, 321.
193 *Ibid.*, I, 321–2.

prohibition of the sale of serfs singly and without land was being demanded even by defenders and spokesmen of serfdom (Shcherbatov, Sumarokov, and others).

More essential and progressive was his legislative proposal to prohibit re-enserfing peasants set free by the pomeshchiki. This measure would end one of the methods of increasing the size of the enserfed peasantry.

Desnitskii proposed also, but this time with the consent of the pomeshchiki, "a scheme whereby certain advantages and property would be granted to the peasants, a scheme which would operate to the interest of the pomeshchik himself, for it would increase the industriousness of his peasants, and he would have the authority as to their remuneration.[194] This legislation, by its vague and diffused content, was obviously concerned only with establishing property for peasants in movables and in general did not obligate the pomeshchiki in any way.

Desnitskii, like a number of other representatives of Russian sociopolitical and economic thought of this period, combined theoretical criticism of serfdom with very moderate practical proposals. He attempted not to infringe upon the interests of the pomeshchiki and to secure their consent in executing measures for improving the position of the peasants. This restrained approach is typical of the first critics of feudalism in Russia and in Western Europe.

It is enough simply to recall the very moderate practical proposals concerning the enserfed peasantry made by Voltaire (in his reply to the competition announced by the Free Economic Society in 1766 on the question of peasant ownership),[195] and by the leader of the democratic wing of the French Enlightenment, Rousseau (in his project for a Polish constitution).[196] Voltaire advised the Russian feudalists to allot to the enserfed peasants small parcels of land on condition of their payment of obrok. Rousseau called for the gradual liberation of the peasants from serfdom, but only of those who distinguished themselves by good behavior (obviously in the pomeshchik's opinion) and who assiduously cultivated the land. Thus Voltaire and even Rousseau emphasized the necessity of carrying out the reforms they proposed with the consent of the pomeshchiki and in such a way as to be beneficial to the pomeshchiki. Like Desnitskii, Voltaire and Rousseau strove to persuade the pomeshchiki to initiate these reforms.

---

194 *Ibid.,* I, 320.

195 See Semevskii, *Krestianskii vopros v Rossii,* I, 61–3.

196 See J. J. Rousseau, *Considérations sur le gouvernement de Pologne et sur sa réformation projetée* (London: 1782).

Much more decisive than those dealing with the peasantry were Desnitskii's proposals to secure participation of the merchants and artisans in legislation and to give them a decisive role in "civic government" and in the economic administration of each city. Desnitskii tried to reconcile absolute monarchy and "enlightened despotism" with representation of bourgeois interests.

The desire to aid the development of bourgeois elements in the feudal economy and to improve the material condition of the popular masses permeates the project on financial policy and financial legislation entitled "On Financial Laws," which Desnitskii included in his *Proposal on Establishing . . . Government in the Russian Empire.* Attaching great significance to a proper financial policy expressed in legislation, Desnitskii said that in financial dealings even the tiniest mistake can lead to great losses to the sovereign and the impoverishment of the people.[197]

In Russia in the 1760's the financial section of the central administration was very poorly organized. Several organs—colleges—had charge of finances. Often the measures of one college contradicted the fiscal activity of another. Central control of finances actually did not exist. Audits, carried out by the Auditing College, were made at random and had an episodic character. Desnitskii considered such a situation completely abnormal and proposed the establishment of a single central organ. All branches of finances were to be under a single office, which would have no other duties. Insisting, thus, on the unification of the financial administration and limiting the work of the central financial organ to finances, Desnitskii recognized the extraordinary complexity of this matter, so important for the state. The central financial organization should "always view finances as a whole, as well as in minute detail, so that it can judiciously consider any particular affair and its consequences." [198] This single central organ should be a commission on finances or state revenues with a "complement," an Auditing College, to provide the control and audit of revenues and expenditures both nationally and locally.

The concentration of the administration of finances in a single central organ, recommended by Desnitskii as early as 1768, was realized much later. In 1802 ministries were formed in Russia, among them the Ministry of Finance,[199] which existed both under the feudal-serfdom structure and throughout the capitalist period. The proposal to centralize the administration of financial control and audits in a special

---

197 *Izbrannye proizvedeniia russkikh myslitelei,* I, 332.

198 *Ibid.*

199 See *PSZ,* XXVII, No. 20406.

office, suggested by Desnitskii also in 1768, was accomplished even later, in 1811, with the creation of the Chief Administration of Audit of State Accounts.[200]

Desnitskii set forth his financial program on this basis: expenditures of the state budget must determine needed revenue. Important and increasing expenditures connected with the administrative, economic, and defense activities of the state and with the maintenance of the Tsar's court demanded ever-increasing sums from state revenues. Desnitskii considered a basic source for state revenue to be taxes which corresponded to conditions of the feudal economy and to the relations between the feudal base and its political superstructure—the state. He recognized the necessity of temporarily continuing the head tax in view of its important contribution to the revenue of the state. But, along with this, he emphasized that the rate of the head tax should be moderate. A head tax at moderate rates, in his opinion, would not overburden the peasantry or harm agriculture. In future calculations of state revenues, however, he recommended a change from the head tax, which fell most heavily upon peasants and city dwellers, to indirect taxes, which "in general would include more of the whole population of the state." [201]

In regard to indirect taxes, Desnitskii, who desired to improve the condition of the masses, insisted on the abolition of taxes on such objects of prime necessity as bread, the reduction of taxes on salt, and the imposition of high taxes on luxury items, including tobacco and wine.

He insisted on the abolition of monopolies of private individuals and companies, as well as those of the state, and he condemned the state monopoly on wine, proposing "to end this evil once and for all." [202]

With the interests of the popular masses at heart, Desnitskii opposed the farming out of taxes, a widespread practice at the time: "The voice of the people in all countries cries out that farming of taxes is a heavy burden for them . . ." [203] The tax-farmers [*otkupshchiki*] garner enormous profits. These sums would remain among the people if the state did not resort to collecting its revenues by this means. Desnitskii spoke also of the abuses irrevocably linked with the tax-farming system, of the obstacles to the development of industry and trade, and of the restrictions on the economic activity of the popular masses.

---

200 *Ibid.*, XXXI, No. 24502.
201 *Izbrannye proizvedeniia russkikh myslitelei*, I, 329–30.
202 *Ibid.*, I, 331.
203 *Ibid.*, I, 330.

In 1754 Desnitskii approved the abolition of domestic customs collections and dues, practices which remained in use abroad (in France, Germany, and other states). He favored the use of tariffs and collections in foreign trade, however. Indeed, he even supported their increase, as this would increase prices on imported goods and would assist the sale of domestic goods competing with foreign goods on the domestic market. In this Desnitskii naively supposed that one could, by legislative enactment, shift these dues from the merchant-importer to the Russian purchaser. The most noteworthy part of his financial program was the suggested progressive tax on immovable property. He proceeded from the relative differences in wealth then prevailing in Russian society, devoting particular attention to estates. By estates he meant "only immovable property,[204] above all land. Intelligence and justice demand that, if possible, assessments be determined in accordance with this "status of inequality," and, if one may so express it, that they be set in geometric progression.[205] Desnitskii's demand amounts to general taxation of immovables on a progressive basis, increasing with the amount of immovable property.

The transformation of feudal land property into an object of progressive taxation had an antifeudal nature. Marx viewed the proposal made by the French economists, the physiocrats, to transform all taxes into land rent as a partial confiscation of land property.[206] Desnitskii's proposal in 1768 to tax immovables resulted, in the final analysis, to the same thing.

This antifeudal, in essence bourgeois-democratic, proposal of Desnitskii was not adopted in feudal-serf Russia.[207] Nor was it effected later in bourgeois Russia, given the feudal conditions or preservation of remnants of feudalism and the strong influence of the noble-pomeshchiki on the Tsarist economic policy.

In his understanding of nature Desnitskii strove to explain the development of society materialistically. This conception of social development as a lawful process to a considerable degree surmounted the idealistic-metaphysical schemes prevailing at the time. He viewed

---

204 *Ibid.*, I, 328.

205 *Ibid.*, I, 330.

206 Marx, *Kapital,* IV, Pt. I, pp. 18–9.

207 For more than twenty years the idea of progressive taxation of agricultural property was advocated in France. In 1789 Bernard de St. Pierre proposed the introduction of a tax on agricultural property which, by its increase in arithmetic progression (1, 2, 3, 4, etc.), was to grow in geometric progression (1, 2, 4, 8, etc.). French feudalists, who understood the antifeudal nature of the taxation of agricultural property on the principle of progression, called this tax progressive robbery.

the predominant type of economic occupation of people at each level of social development as the foundation of the emergence and change in forms of property. Desnitskii affirmed that each form of property corresponded to forms of relations between people—forms of family, state, and so on. No one before Desnitskii had made so many materialistic conjectures in explaining the development of society. It is in this view, above all, that Desnitskii contributed to Russian and world philosophy.

In his sociological conception, however, Desnitskii merely stated the change in people's economic occupations but failed to reveal their causes. He regarded the "commercial condition" of society, by which he meant the bourgeois structure, as the ideal, as the most perfect period, crowning the development of humanity and the evolution of society.

The Russian scholar emphasized that the development of production and science in each state are not determined basically by geographic environment (as Montesquieu believed). An advanced political structure and corresponding social relations contribute decisively to the progress of production and science.

Desnitskii took an antifeudal position. He pointed out its negative, hindering role in the development of the national economy and in the growth of the country's wealth. He exposed the role of the feudal-serf system in the development of agriculture and spoke of the difficult, unjust position of the enserfed peasantry which shackled its economic activity.

Viewing bourgeois society as the ideal social system, Desnitskii defended the interests of the bearers of bourgeois relationships—the merchants. He strove to strengthen the role of the merchants in the economy and their influence on the economic policy of the feudal-absolute state and to secure for the merchants a decisive position in city administration.

On the question of serfdom in Russia, Desnitskii's position was contradictory. While criticizing serfdom and pointing to the difficult position of the enserfed peasantry, he yet failed to raise the question of abolishing serfdom.

In his ideology, as in the ideology of all previous critics of serfdom, lay a deep contradiction between the theoretical criticism of serfdom and the narrowness of his proposed measures of economic policy.

CHAPTER 20. *The Economic Demands of the Popular Masses in the Peasant War of 1773-1774.*

The Causes of the Peasant War. Its Participants.

The peasant war of 1773–1774 was preceded by peasant disturbances in various parts of the country. These were caused by the intensified exploitation of serfs, by the distribution of state peasants to nobles, by the unlimited growth of the power of the pomeshchik over the peasants, and by the increase of pomeshchik arbitrariness. The disturbances also encompassed the "working people" in manufacturing and the peasants attached to factories, and so broke out in cities as well as the country. The cause for the so-called "plague riot" in Moscow in 1771 was not only the epidemic; the town poor were protesting against heavy exploitation and injustice. These disturbances, so ominous for feudalism, were suppressed by the feudal-absolute state with the aid of the military and by the use of massive, cruel repressions.

An intense struggle developed in the eastern gubernias, where exploitation of the popular masses had assumed a form horrible even under conditions of serfdom. In the Urals—then a major mining-metallurgical industrial region of the world—the exploitation of enserfed peasants in agriculture was interlaced with heavy exploitation of the "working people" and the peasants attached to the factories.

The instructions to the deputies to the Commission on Drafting a Project for a new Code of Laws, called in 1767, speak of the dreadful conditions among the peasants attached to factories. Peasants in the Avziano-Petrov ironworks of Demidov wrote in their instructions that they could not subsist by agriculture and horticulture, because "we can never leave these factory works," and, as a result, "we are reduced to poverty and misery and burdened by unpaid debts." [1]

The peasants in the Kama ironworks of Count P. I. Shuvalov stated the same thing in their Nakaz. The attached peasant, says the in-

[1] "Nakaz Ufimskoi provintsii ot pripisnykh pereselennykh krestian" [An Instruction from the Assigned Transferred Peasants of the Ufa Province], *Sbornik Russkogo istoricheskogo obshchestva,* CXV, 303.

structions, "not only cannot feed the horse he keeps, but cannot even feed himself . . . because for all this work he receives very little pay . . ." Those connected to the Shuvalov factories complained that they were "not permitted to carry on their peasant agricultural work," and therefore they "fell into complete ruin and poverty." [2]

Even such a defender of the interests of the pomeshchiki and factory owners as Nikolai Rychkov (the son of the famed economist P. I. Rychkov), referring to the situation of those attached to the factory of the merchant Pokhodiashin, was obliged to acknowledge that they "do not have sufficient time to carry on their agricultural pursuits: for at the time when the agriculturist should cultivate his lands . . . he is forced to go to the factory . . . located five hundred verst from the villages which are bound to it, and sometimes in such places that it can be reached on foot only with great difficulty . . . Thus these attached peasants must spend a great deal of time in factory work or on the road . . ." [3] Captain-Lieutenant S. Mavrin, a member of the committee of inquiry into the Pugachev uprising, testified to the same condition.

The disturbances and uprisings of the attached peasants and the "working people" of the Urals became ever more frequent on the eve of the peasant war. The government, concerned about the strength and scale of these outbreaks, entrusted their suppression to General-Prosecutor Prince A. A. Viazemskii, who moved military detachments and even artillery to the Ural locales and wreaked cruel vengeance on the rebels.

The mine owners seized lands and water and forest areas for charcoal burning and thus deprived the village population of the possibility of tilling the soil, pasturing cattle, hunting and fishing, and using the forests. The deputies of the Russian state peasants, of the Bashkirs, Tartars and other nationalities of the Ural and the Volga regions, complained bitterly in the Legislative Commission.

These nationalities suffered from oppression by "their own" feudal lords in addition to the tsarist colonial oppression. Lands, forests, and waters were seized from the Bashkirs not only for use by metal works, whether active or under construction, but also in connection with the formation of the Orenburg Cossack Army as well as for distribution

[2] "Nakaz Kazanskogo uezda . . . byvshikh iasashnykh krestian" [An Instruction . . . of Former Iasak [tribute] Paying Peasants of the Kazan Uezd], *ibid.*, CXV, 260–4.

[3] *Prodolzhenie zhurnala ili dnevnykh zapisok puteshestviia kapitana Rychkova po raznym provintsiiam Rossiiskogo gosudarstva 1770 godu* [Journal or Daily Notes from the Journey of Captain Rychkov Across Various Provinces of the Russian State in 1770] (St. Petersburg: 1772), pp. 103–4.

to Russian nobles and officials. The Bashkirs were forced to serve in local military detachments, to perform various labors for the factories, and to transport people and freight; their horses were requisitioned for the cavalry, their cattle were taken, and so on. They were forbidden to mine salt, and their taxes were increased. The answer of the Bashkir people to the ever-increasing oppression was the uprisings of 1735–1740 and 1755 and continuous disturbances even after these revolts had been crushed. During the suppression Bashkir villages were destroyed and lands distributed to pomeshchiki, factory owners, and officials. Such acts set off new disturbances among the Bashkirs.[4]

The Tartars of Kungur uezd complained in their instructions that for Count I. G. Chernyshev's Ashinsk copper smelting factory "a considerable number of forests are being cut down; also a significant number of hay meadows have been seized . . ."[5] The instructions of the Mordvins,[6] Udmurts,[7] Chuvash,[8] and Tartars,[9] whose indignation was continually increasing, speak also of the deprivation of the nationalities of the Ural and the Volga of the means of production which had belonged to them from time immemorial.

Unrest prevailed also among the Yaik Cossacks (renamed the Ural Cossacks after the peasant war). In the Yaik Cossack forces, the officer corps, composed of well-to-do Cossacks, took the organs of Cossack regimental self-government into its own hands and oppressed the rank-and-file Cossacks. The head of the Cossack officer corps—the ataman—designated Cossacks for service, controlled the military treasury, together with the "military office," collected taxes from the Cossacks, and paid their salaries. The army officers appropriated from the Cossacks the lease money paid to the government for revenue from the fishing industry, as well as liquor and customs collections. Abusing its power, the officer corps exploited the Cossack masses; they robbed and ruined the rank-and-file Cossacks and seized their land. In the struggle between the officer corps and the mass of rank-and-file Cossacks the government intervened with the purpose of subordinating the Yaik Cossacks. It supported the officer corps and rendered it military aid. The armed skirmishes of the government forces and the Cossack officer

---

[4] See A. P. Chuloshnikov, *Vosstanie 1755 g. v Bashkirii* [Uprising of 1755 in Bashkiria] (Moscow: AS USSR, 1940).

[5] *Sbornik Russkogo istoricheskogo obshchestva,* CXV, 363.

[6] *Ibid.,* CXV, 421–4.

[7] *Ibid.,* CXV, 368–71.

[8] *Ibid.,* CXV, 379–81.

[9] *Ibid.,* CXV, 393–403; see also *Istoriia Tatarii v materiialakh i dokumentakh* [A History of the Tartars in Materials and Documents] (Moscow: Sotsekgiz, 1937), pp. 242–6.

corps with the masses of rank-and-file Cossacks which took place during the widespread peasant disturbances and revolts were the beginning of the peasant war.

Erupting in September, 1773, among the Yaik Cossacks, the insurrection spread to the trans-Volga with its sparse agricultural population and pastoral nationalities and tribes. The war encompassed the southern Ural, which contained a great number of peasants assigned to factories, a mass of "working people," and a large Bashkir population. In July, 1774, the peasant war spread to the right bank of the Volga—to an area inhabited by peasants of the pomeshchiki. Here in the course of less than two months of war the support of the great mass of the population doubled, and the nobility and its state suffered immeasurably greater losses than in the preceding ten months of war. It was on the right bank of the Volga in the last months of the war that the social essence of the revolt, its class character as a *peasant* war, was revealed with greatest clarity.

A. S. Pushkin, who made use of manuscripts, traditions, and the testimony of witnesses who were still living, correctly noted that "all the common people supported Pugachev." [10] The most important participant in this war was the peasantry. The pomeshchik and state peasants followed Pugachev. Documents of the time testify that "peasants of all types" were "very ardent" in their support of Pugachev.[11] The aroused peasantry was joined by Cossacks, by "working people" of the Ural factories, by the lower strata of the urban population—artisans, unskilled workers, stevedores, small tradesmen, and others, and by the oppressed masses of the nationalities of the Ural and Volga (particularly the Bashkirs).

Although the Cossacks participated in this war and their leader was the Don Cossack, Pugachev, one cannot consider it a Cossack war, as G. V. Plekhanov suggested.[12] Erroneous also is the view that the participation in the war of 1773–1774 of the "working people," who had not yet emerged as a class, made it a worker-peasant war, as M. N. Pokrovskii believed.[13] The participation of Cossacks, workers, and oppressed nationalities did not change its character as a peasant war, but did place a definite imprint upon it. Among the various social and national elements of the Pugachev forces contradictions and conflicts occurred. The workers brought a certain element of organization

[10] Pushkin, *Polnoe sobranie sochinenii,* VIII, 357.
[11] See *Istoricheskii arkhiv,* VIII, 293.
[12] Plekhanov, *Sochineniia,* XXI, 284–5.
[13] *Pugachevshchina* [Pugachev's Rebellion] (Moscow-Leningrad: 1926), I, 13. Pokrovskii's foreword.

into the peasant movement. The presence of other social strata and groups along with the peasantry in the Pugachev armies led to an incorporation of their interests and hopes in the documents of the peasant leader.

The Manifestoes and Decrees of Pugachev

The economic demands of the rebels were proclaimed in the the manifestoes and decrees of Emelian Ivanovich Pugachev and his close associates. The political documents of the peasant war were not composed by Pugachev alone. They were the fruit of collective creativeness. This was stated in the decree of September 17, 1773, signed by Pugachev with the name of the sovereign emperor Peter Fedorovich. As Pugachev himself later testified at the investigation in the Secret Chancellery, this decree was written at the time of his journey to the Tolkachev estates, where it was proposed at a *stanitsa* [Cossack village] meeting to proclaim the beginning of the insurrection. Besides Pugachev, Chika-Zarubin (one of the first and most active of Pugachev's associates),[14] the Kozhevnikovs, Konovalov, and other Yaik Cossacks took part in preparing the decree; it was written by the young Cossack, Ivan Iakovlevich Pochitalin, the clerk [*"dumnyi diak"*] of his Military College, later Pugachev's first secretary.[15]

In his first manifesto Pugachev, appealing to the Cossacks and the oppressed nationalities of the Ural, promised them free use of lands and waters. He granted those living along the river Yaik (subsequently renamed Ural) "the river from its source to its mouth, and the land and the grass fields, and a monetary grant, and lead, and gunpowder, and grain provisions." [16]

This "first seditious [that is, inciting to rebellion-I.B.] appeal of Pugachev to the Yaik Cossacks," A. S. Pushkin characterized as "an amazing example of popular eloquence . . ." and contrasted it to the declarations of the Orenburg governor, the German I. A. Reinsdorp, which "were written so lifelessly and correctly, with prolonged ambiguities, and with verbs at the end of sentences." [17] Pushkin's literary evaluation of Pugachev's first decree applied as well to his later decrees and manifestoes. They were examples of popular eloquence, the fruit of collective creativeness, and reflected the thoughts and hopes of the popular masses.

---

[14] *Ibid.*, II, 128–36.
[15] *Ibid.*, II, 107.
[16] *Ibid.*, I, 25.
[17] Pushkin, *op. cit.*, VIII, 351.

Besides Ivan Chika-Zarubin, a part was taken in composing the political documents of the peasant war by Afanasii Sokolov—nicknamed Khlopusha—former serf of the Tver bishop, then a worker in the metal factory of Shuvalov in the Urals. He had been repeatedly subjected to imprisonment and torture. Later Khlopusha became one of the most outstanding associates of Pugachev, chiefly in organizing the work of the Ural arsenal for the peasant forces ("commander of the factory peasants") and supplying it with bread and other products." [18]

Another important collaborator was Ivan Naumovich Beloborodov—the son of a Ural factory peasant who had worked in the copper smelting factory and who had been in military service in the Vyborg artillery garrison and the Okhtinsk gunpowder factory. Proving himself a talented organizer of factory peasants, Beloborodov became one of the closest associates of Pugachev, who called him "chief ataman and campaign leader." [19]

One should especially mention in this connection Salavat Iulaev, one of the most important advisers of Pugachev and leader of the Bashkir people in the peasant war, a talented organizer and agitator and an outstanding Bashkir poet-improvisor.[20]

In addition to their aid to Pugachev, who, as Pushkin remarks, "did not undertake anything without their consent . . . ," [21] these men also published decrees and orders under their own names.

The names have reached us of several other persons who not only participated in the composition of the manifestoes, decrees, and orders of Pugachev and his associates, but who also wrote them. These (except for I. Ia. Pochitalin, whom we have already mentioned) were the secretaries, the scribes, and clerks of Pugachev—the son of a Misena merchant Aleksei Dubrovskii (I. S. Trofimov), who had worked in Ural factories, the Iletsk Cossack, Maksim Gorshkov, Nikita Ziablikov, Petr Gusev, and others. Another was Timofei Ivanovich Padurov, Captain of the Orenburg Cossack army and its deputy to the Legislative Commission of 1767, "colonel of the peasant army," and one of Pugachev's closest advisers. According to A. S. Pushkin, Padurov "was in charge of literary matters" for Pugachev.[22]

---

[18] *Pugachevshchina,* II, 111; *Krasnyi arkhiv* [Red Archive] LXVIII, 162–71.

[19] *Pugachevshchina,* II, 325–35; see also M. Martynov, "Pugachevskii ataman Ivan Beloborodov na Urale" [Ivan Beloborodov, Pugachev's Ataman in the Urals], *Istoricheskii zhurnal,* Nos. 5–6 (1943), pp. 33–40.

[20] See A. Nikolaenko, "Vozhd bashkirskogo naroda, pugachevskii brigadir Salavat Iulaev" [Leader of the Bashkir People, Pugachev's Brigadier, Salavat Iulaev], *ibid.,* No. 11 (1940), pp. 77–88.

[21] Pushkin, *op. cit.,* VIII, 180.

[22] *Ibid.,* VIII, 181.

At Pugachev's headquarters were representatives of various nationalities, who wrote his manifestoes and decrees to the Bashkirs, Tartars, Kazakhs, and other peoples. These "scribes" translated from the Russian (mostly into Tartar) the political documents of the peasant war. The names of several of them were: Imanov Ismail, Iskanderov Rakhmankul, Apatov Abubakir, Alaev Resiu, and others. They were not only translators of Pugachev's decrees, but also took an active part in preparing them. The scribe-translator strove to reflect in the manifestoes and decrees the hopes and aspirations of his own oppressed people.

Many decrees of Pugachev were copied and distributed locally. Thus nameless translators frequently made certain changes in the text in accordance with the conditions and needs of the local population and its demands.

Pugachev's manifestoes were addressed to the broad popular masses of the villages and towns, "to the people in cities and in provinces, also in the steppe and in the fields . . ." The appeal went to "my people with their wives, their children, their daughters . . ." He ordered that his manifestoes be distributed everywhere. "These, my decrees, should be made known everywhere, to those living in the villages, to travellers on the road and in the villages, extending along every street, and spread everywhere . . ." [23] In one of his decrees Pugachev wrote that he would publish it "in all of Russia." [24]

Emphasizing that he stood for the simple and poor people and for the improvement of their situation, Pugachev called himself in one of his first decrees (1773) "the enricher of the poor." [25] In another decree (also 1773) appealing to the Cossacks, he solemnly proclaimed: "And whatever you may desire in all benefits and wages will not be refused you . . ." [26]

Pugachev promised after the victory of the insurgents to fulfill the hopes of the popular masses. He referred to the fact that among the various social and national groups there were common, as well as special, hopes and desires, stemming from conditions of their lives and connected with liberation from the oppression forced upon them.

He promised liberty and freedom to all. In one of his last decrees, written in August 1774, looking back on the course of the peasant war, Pugachev wrote that the "wicked nobles" had placed "all of Russia under their subjection," and therefore he resolved to free the people

---

[23] *Pugachevshchina,* I, 27.
[24] *Ibid.,* I, 38.
[25] *Ibid.,* I, 26.
[26] *Ibid.*

"from their wicked tyranny and to establish freedom in all of Russia." [27]

The most important aim of the peasant war was the liberation of the peasants from feudal dependence. Pugachev granted freedom "to all who were previously peasants and under the pomeshchik's subjugation" and called for the annihilation of the latter. The peasants liberated from taxes and obligations to pomeshchiki and state would become, as Pugachev indicated, Cossacks and would be able "to experience tranquillity and to lead a peaceful life, which will continue forever." [28] The factory peasants and "working people" were granted "every freedom." [29] To the Cossacks and to "people of all estates" was granted "eternal freedom." [30]

Among the peasants, workers, and Cossacks of the Ural and Volga there were many Old Believers, dissenters, who had been subjected to persecution by the government. Penalties had been enforced for wearing beards and for adhering to the old form of the cross. Proclaiming freedom of worship, Pugachev granted the dissenters "the cross and the beard," [31] the "ancient cross and prayer." [32]

In a decree written in the Arabian, Persian, Turkish, and Tartar languages, Pugachev, appealing to the peoples of the Ural area, promised them liberation not only from tsarist, but from any kind of authority. "And you who live like animals of the steppe . . . I liberate all of you dwelling on the earth and grant freedom to your children and grandchildren forever." [33]

In a decree to the Bashkirs, Kalmyks, and other nationalities, Pugachev demanded the liberation of the people from prisons and from enserfed dependence on local feudalists. He ordered that "prisoners or people held in enslavement to other masters, all without exception are set free this very month and day." [34]

The leader of the peasant war appealed to the Bashkirs, Tartars, and other peoples subjected to religious persecution and to conversion by force. Proclaiming complete religious toleration, Pugachev solemnly announced to these peoples that he granted them "your faith and law." [35]

---

[27] *Ibid.*, I, 41–2.
[28] *Ibid.*, I, 41.
[29] *Ibid.*, I, 33.
[30] *Ibid.*, I, 32.
[31] *Ibid.*
[32] *Ibid.*, I, 40.
[33] *Ibid.*, I, 30.
[34] *Ibid.*, I, 31.
[35] *Ibid.*, I, 28.

The manifestoes of the peasant war proclaimed not only freedom to all peoples of Russia, but also granted the means of production to the toilers. In Pugachev's decrees it was stated that the lands should be taken from the pomeshchiki. All land should be given for use to agriculturists and livestock breeders. Such a solemn promise was made to the Russian peasants, to the "working people," to the Cossacks, the Bashkirs, and to all other nationalities without clarification as to how the land would be distributed among them.

Pugachev also promised everybody freedom of hunting and of felling forests, unlimited use of waters (rivers, lakes, and seas), freedom of fishing, and of mining salt. In this, as in regard to land, it was not specified on what basis this general utilization would proceed or how the distribution of means of production would be secured. The Cossacks, the factory peasants, the Bashkirs, and the Tartars were also promised a continuous supply of gunpowder, lead, and all provisions, above all, grain. The Cossacks were also to receive a monetary payment. It remained completely unclear where all these things would be procured if, after the victory, all taxes and obligations to the state, comprising at that time the basic source of state revenues, were to be abolished.

The social class nature of the revolt of 1773–1774 as a *peasant* war was most clearly revealed in Pugachev's decrees issued in the first half of July, 1774, after the uprising had spread to the right bank of the Volga, into old pomeshchiki regions populated by enserfed peasants. These manifestoes were addressed to the enserfed peasantry of Russia. They represented, in essence, various editions of a decree written, probably, by the secretary of Pugachev's college, A. I. Dubrovskii (I. S. Trofimov). First published on July 18, 1774, on the second day after the landing of the peasant armies on the right bank of the Volga, this decree was subsequently issued several times, with certain changes, and was widely distributed in the Volga region. We print the entire text of this famous decree (in the edition of July 31).

> By the grace of God We, Peter the Third, Emperor and Autocrat of all Russia, etc., etc., etc.
>
> Be it known to everyone.
>
> By Our monarchial and paternal grace by this decree we grant that all previous peasants and those subjugated to the pomeshchiki are faithful slaves of Our own crown, and We reward them with the ancient cross and prayer, and beards, and with liberty and freedom, and make them Cossacks for eternity,

without demanding conscription, or the head tax or any other taxes in money; and [reward them] with ownership of lands, forests, hay fields, fishing rights, and salt lakes, without purchase and without obrok; and We free all those previously treated abusively by the nobles and the venal city judges who imposed taxes and burdens on the peasants and all people. And We wish you salvation of your souls and a peaceful life in this world, for the sake of which We have tasted and suffered from evil nobles and from great poverty. And as now Our name flourishes in Russia We order by this decree: whoever was a nobleman in his pomestie or votchina, those opposers of our authority and disturbers of the empire and ruiners of the peasantry are to be hunted, imprisoned, to be hanged, and to be treated in the same manner as they, who had no Christianity within themselves, treated you, the peasants. Upon the downfall of these enemies and evil nobles, everyone can live quietly and in peace, which will last for eternity.

Given on the 31st day of July, 1774. Peter." [36]

In this decree the demands of the popular masses in the peasant war are most completely expressed: the abolition of personal dependence of the peasants, liquidation of pomeshchik ownership of land, forests, and waters; confiscation of the movable and immovable property of the noble pomeshchiki and struggle with them to the point of their physical annihilation; liberation of the peasants from taxes and obligations, including the most burdensome ones—conscription and the head tax; and gratuitous division of the land among the peasantry.

The Economic Measures of Pugachev's Military College

Complete freedom, liberation of the population from taxes and from all obligations to the state, release of land, forests, and waters for general usage—such were the proposals of the leaders of the peasant war for the future social structure. Pugachev's manifestoes promised all this after victory.

A different situation prevailed during the war. The great, intensive struggle against the feudal-serf structure and the state apparatus of

[36] *Ibid.*, I, 40–1.

the feudal-absolute empire presented its own demands. It was necessary to imbue the peasant armies with discipline, to secure war materiel and provisions, and to organize local authority. Various forms of force were necessary, not only within the peasant army itself but in regard to the population.

The participation in this war of the "working people" of the Urals brought certain elements of organization to the peasant movement. One should, however, note that the "working people," as well as the peasants and the oppressed non-Russian nationalities of the Ural and Volga, were under the influence of local conditions. They usually strove to start a movement only in their own factory or in their area and did not want to move beyond these limits.

Pushkin, who wrote that "stern order and obedience" were introduced among the Pugachevists,[37] without doubt was grossly exaggerating. But it is impossible to deny the fact that organization, discipline, and coercion reached a higher stage in this war than in previous peasant wars. The peasant war of 1773–1774, as spontaneous as previous peasant wars, still differed from all of them in its organization.

The existence of Pugachev's remarkable "Military College" serves as an illustration of this. The Military College and the organs of military and civil authority created by it had certain external features reminiscent of feudal-absolute power. If Pugachev called himself Peter III, then Chika-Zarubin called himself Count Chernyshev and signed his decrees and orders in this name. To give prestige to their authority, the Pugachevists tried to imitate tsarist military leaders and officials. But these were only external characteristics; this was only an external imprint. By their nature and actions the organs created by the peasant war were different.

The Military College was the highest organ of power. From Pugachev and the members of the Military College came the command to establish military discipline in the ranks of the peasant army. "By this order I strongly urge you," wrote Beloborodov to the Russian, Bashkir, and Cheremiss battalion commanders, "to maintain all strictness over the Russian and Tartar military forces under your command and to be obeyed by them and watch over them carefully . . . And if anyone of the Cossacks in your command shows himself to be self-willed and disobedient, you . . . may punish him by the lash without mercy . . . If anyone shows himself to be most excessively stubborn then send him to me for suppression." [38] In another docu-

[37] Pushkin, *op. cit.,* VIII, 181.
[38] *Pugachevshchina,* I, 81–2.

ment Beloborodov orders the Cossack captain Chigvintsov not to allow the "development of excessive drunkenness." [39]

The "admonition" directed to the administrators of the town of Kungur by another fellow-champion of Pugachev—"the chief Russian military leader," Ivan Stepanovich Kuznetsov—is permeated with an attempt to protect the interests of the toiling population and not to allow any kind of injury to them. He emphasizes Pugachev's demand "that in capturing towns . . . no persecution, destruction, affronts, taxes, and unnecessary bloodshed will be imposed on the inhabitants." [40] Then follows the enumeration of punishments for such actions. "And if anyone is found in such dealings and similar corruptions, he will not escape . . . death, which I now establish throughout the army with firmness." [41]

This "admonition" affirmed national equality in responsibility for crimes. "And both Russian and non-Russian are treated equally: upon perpetration of a crime the investigation of guilt is to be treated with all strictness." [42] All this indicates the desire of the leaders of the peasant army to establish order and discipline, but in reality these attempts had insignificant success. It was impossible to fetter the spontaneity of the peasant war with the chains of order and discipline.

Wherever the peasant army went, elected organs of authority—the "land offices" [*zemskie izby*]—were founded. Local inhabitants elected people "by peaceful general agreement, in order to have a command over us, as previously under the commandants, and not to tolerate willfulness, pillage, or disobedience, and to be obedient to them in everything . . ." [43] The Pugachevists tried to make the "land offices" responsible for the conscription of people into the peasant army and for the acquisition of horses, provisions, fodder, and money.

The preservation of the passport system expressed the desire of the leaders of the peasant war to maintain order among the population. "Tickets" were issued on discharge from military service,[44] for residence while conducting trade,[45] and for departure from the village or the city. Moreover the Pugachevists recognized the old passports and in case of their loss issued special documents.[46] In territories encompassed by the rebellion, the postal service was continued.[47]

[39] *Ibid.*, I, 83.
[40] *Ibid.*, I, 76.
[41] *Ibid.*, I, 76–7.
[42] *Ibid.*, I, 77.
[43] *Ibid.*, I, 184–5.
[44] *Ibid.*, I, 70.
[45] *Ibid.*, I, 66.
[46] *Ibid.*, I, 202.
[47] *Ibid.*, I, 101.

Pugachev and his Military College understood well the enormous importance of the Ural factories for providing weapons to the peasant army. The majority of the factories in territories involved in the rebellion had ceased operation, however. In the course of the first months of the war (the end of 1773) work stopped at the mining factories in the southern Urals. In the beginning of 1774 the factories of the Central Urals shut down. In February, 1774, ninety-two metallurgical factories, comprising about three-fourths of the mining might of the Urals, were inactive.[48]

The workers of some remaining factories attempted, with the agreement and approval of the Pugachevists, to renew production of ready supplies of ore and fuel. Thus in a Votkin factory the workers elected a management which received an "instruction" from the Pugachev ataman, Andrei Noskov. In accordance with this "instruction" the functions of the management included settling disagreements among the masters, the "working people," and the peasants and deciding disputes "with justice" and organizing the defense of the factory "should it be invaded by Tartars, Bashkirs, Votiaks, and Cossacks," who "are not to be permitted to commit even the slightest pillage and destruction."

One of the contradictions of the peasant war is reflected in this demand. Part of the rebelling Russian peasants, Cossacks, and people of non-Russian origin and separate groups of "working people" attempted to pillage, ruin, and even destroy the factories they hated. A majority of the workers and many peasants and Cossacks strove to preserve the factories. The armed clashes which arose from this conflict weakened the strength of the insurrectionists.

Calling upon the factory management elected by the workers "not to permit insults and impositions upon yourselves or those under your direction from anyone," ataman Noskov established the procedure of issuing provisions for masters and "working people" from government stores. He proposed to distribute provisions "according to family," that is, according to the number of members of the family and, in the case of women with young children (whose fathers had gone into the peasant army), to give provisions to each person.[49]

In examining similar attempts of workers to renew the activity of their factories, one should take into account the contradictory aims of various groups of workers. Part of the mining population—the "working people" and those assigned to factories—hated these factories

---

[48] See D. Kashintsev, *Istoriia metaliurgii Urala* [History of Metallurgy in the Urals] (Moscow-Leningrad: 1939), I, 149–50.

[49] See *Pugachevshchina,* I, 179.

and considered them the cause of their heavy burden. This part of the mining population attempted to return to purely agricultural occupations.

The attempts of the workers themselves to begin production and to turn the factories into forges for weapons for the people's army had no results. An example is the experience of the converted Rozhdestvenskii factory in the Prikama. Its workers, after resuming production, received neither provisions, money, nor cast iron (from other factories) for forging, and as a result they stopped work.[50] Pugachev and his associates tried to organize work in several factories. They tried to convert the Izhev factory to serve the cavalry and the Voskresenie factory of Tversyshev and Avziano-Petrovsk to provide for the artillery.

Pugachev, Beloborodov, and Khlopusha demanded from the factories a supply of war materials and those types of production which were supplied previously to the feudal-absolute state; sometimes they even wanted military-technical innovations. Thus the masters of the Voskresenie factory sent Pugachev a "secret howitzer," and they "again announced two mortars," [51] "a prepared model of the casting of another secret howitzer," [52] and so on.

The factories which worked for a time for the peasant army were not, however, its productive, technical base (as M. N. Pokrovskii believed). Their output was insignificant compared to the quantity of weapons which were gathered from factory arsenals and forts and seized from enemies. Despite all the hopes of Pugachev's Military College, it was impossible to secure even a small amount of raw materials, fuel, and provisions for the above-mentioned factories. But Pugachev's seizure of the factories deprived Catherine's government of the possibility of using them for its own military-technical base. Therein lay the significance of Pugachev's seizure of the Ural factories, and not in the unrealistic attempt to convert them, even partially, into a productive base for the popular army.[53]

Sublieutenant Mikhailo Shvanovich, a noble who joined Pugachev (and who probably served as the real-life model for Pushkin's Shvabrin in *The Captain's Daughter*), testified before the investigating commission that Pugachev took guns and war materiel which he found in forts and factories seized by his troops. According to Shvanovich's testimony, Pugachev "received artillery from the forts and from the

[50] See Kashintsev, *op. cit.*, I, 150.
[51] *Pugachevshchina,* I, 59.
[52] *Ibid.*, I, 61.
[53] See A. V. Prussak, "Zavody rabotavshie na Pugacheva" [Factories Working for Pugachev], *Istoricheskie zapiski,* No. 8 (1940), pp. 174–207.

factories, also powder and lead; provisions and fodder they obtained in quantity from surrounding villages." [54] All this came to Pugachev's camp either by means of requisitions or by voluntary contributions. In addition Pugachev's Military College strove to introduce certain other measures for supplying the peasant troops.

In this connection one should note the "Decree . . . of the State Military College to ataman Ilia Arapov," dated December 16, 1773, signed by Ivan Tvorogov, clerk Ivan Pochitalin, and secretary Maksim Gorshkov: "You are hereby authorized to requisition in surrounding villages grain of any kind; who has unthreshed grain shall thresh it and the threshed shall be ground and the ground shall be sent to this army by horses and carts belonging to those and other inhabitants; and money from the treasury will be given to them for transporting it; and how much grain will be dispatched from you is to be reported here. And, as it is necessary to execute this commission rapidly, you are permitted to select agents and to send them into these habitations with an appropriate escort with your orders to send to the army all the ground grain; also whatever oats can be found shall be sent. And you shall make certain that agents sent by you do not dare to inflict any offense upon the peasants . . ." [55]

In this document are four points worthy of attention: utilization of grain gathered on the seigniorial fields for the needs of the peasant war, organization of the threshing of this grain and its delivery, money payment for delivery, and, finally, the demand not to permit any offense to the peasants in executing this order. The latter demand is repeated in a number of decrees and orders of Pugachev and the Military College.

The Military College ordered (January 25, 1774) that the grain on the pomeshchiki estates be estimated and the Military College be informed of the amount of grain requisitioned. "And the boyar pasture and property, although that boyar may have fled, shall be given, regardless of how much there remains, to a trusted person, and it shall be reported here." And the decree further stipulated that if this grain is pillaged, "then that will not remain unpunished." [56] From this, of course, it does not follow that the Military College took the pomeshchiki' grain, saved it from destruction, and organized its grinding and delivery. In general this plan was not successfully attained. Even the Military College itself sometimes suffered from lack of provisions. The discussion pertains only to certain organizational attempts.

---

[54] *Pugachevshchina,* III, 214.
[55] *Ibid.,* I, 43–4.
[56] *Ibid.,* I, 47.

Of the economic measures in the sphere of distribution, one must first mention the utilization of grain and food "warehouses" attached to factories for distribution of supplies to the "working people," their families, and the families of those who had joined the peasant army. Although it was not realized to any significant degree, this measure demonstrated the Pugachevists' concern about the appropriate distribution of products.

A number of decrees and orders issued by the Military College and the organs of peasant authority in local areas demanded money payment "according to the usual price for products received from the peasants." [57]

The financial expenditures, connected with buying products from peasants and with other needs, required receipt of revenues in natural and money form. Revenues were obtained not only by means of confiscation and requisition of possessions of the noble-pomeshchiki and the feudal-absolutist state, but also in part through taxation of the proprietary part of the population. Especially interesting is the collection of revenues from taxes on the sale of salt and grain alcohol. An "order" of December 24, 1773 by the Pugachev army captains to the elder of the Osin crown volost and to the land scribe commanded them "to supervise both government beverages and the sale of salt. And to proceed in sales according to earlier orders and to take the money into safekeeping, writing into a receipt and account book everything without concealment . . ." [58]

With these revenues Pugachev's treasury paid the peasants for their products and remunerated the workers. A curious document which was signed by Chika-Zarubin under the name of Count Ivan Chernyshev on February 14, 1774, has been preserved. In this document it is said that the workers of the Rozhdestvenskii factory earned "from the previous boyar" 1500 rubles, but did not receive anything from him. Therefore Chika-Zarubin proposed "to give them the 1500 rubles from revenues received from salt and drink sources, so that they would not fall into extreme destitution." [59] But along with the selling of grain alcohol and salt Pugachev's treasury distributed salt free of charge; moreover, Pugachev had declared himself in general favor of abolishing the government salt monopoly. Having taken Penza, Pugachev said to the merchants: "Well, lord merchants, now you and all the city's inhabitants will be called my Cossacks. I shall take neither your head taxes nor recruits from you, and I have ordered the government's

---

[57] *Ibid.*, I, 111.
[58] *Ibid.*, I, 92.
[59] *Ibid.*, I, 187.

salt to be distributed free—three pounds per person—and from now on whoever wishes may sell it and engage in anything for himself." [60]

As Plekhanov correctly remarks, "It is impossible to say that this was a very definite 'economic policy.' " [61] But, nevertheless, these were measures which, like others, were conceived with the interests of the toiling masses in mind. As such they were distinct from the acts of economic policy of the feudal-absolute government, which protected the interests of the nobility.

The fact that Pugachev and his advisers planned individual measures and that, on certain occasions, these were partially carried out did not change the general nature of the peasant war as a spontaneous and unorganized movement. These measures cannot be viewed as a system of economic policy, as a defined revolutionary economic program, as was done by M. N. Pokrovskii.[62] A program is a consciously developed political document about the goals, tasks, and basic positions of an organization. The spontaneous peasant movement did not have a developed, clear socio-political program. One can speak only of the rather extensive reflection in its documents of the demands of the popular masses. The peasant war of 1773–1774 was directed against the feudal-serf relationships and therefore upset the feudal-serf structure as a whole. At the same time, one should bear in mind that the leaders of the peasant war were tsarists.

Pugachev, as is known, used the name of Tsar Peter III to enhance his prestige, and his associates called themselves by the names of prominent officials of the Empire. For the mass of participants in the war—peasants, those assigned to factories, "working people," Cossacks, oppressed nationalities—the peasant war was restricted to the boundaries of their own areas. Spontaneously aroused with the approach of Pugachev's forces, they were avenging themselves on "their" pomeshchiki and "their" stewards, "their" factory owners, and "their" local officials. Neither the masses who participated in the peasant war nor its leaders understood feudal relations as a system, as a structure, which could not be destroyed merely through revenge on the part of individual representatives in local areas, but only by the overthrow of the feudal political power in the entire state.

---

[60] See N. Dubrovin, *Pugachev i ego soobshchiniki. Po neizdannym istochnikam* [Pugachev and His Accomplices. On the Basis of Unpublished Sources] (St. Petersburg: 1884), III, 165–6.

[61] Plekhanov, *op. cit.*, XXI, 290.

[62] See M. Nechkina, "Krestianskie vosstaniia Razina i Pugacheva v kontseptsii M. N. Pokrovskogo" [Peasant Uprisings of Razin and Pugachev in M. N. Pokrovskii's Concept], *Protiv istoricheskoi kontseptsii M. N. Pokrovskogo* [Against the Historical Concept of M. N. Pokrovskii]. A Collection of Articles (Moscow-Leningrad: AS USSR, 1939), Pt. I.

CHAPTER 21. *The Emergence of the Revolutionary Theory of the Abolition of Serfdom—A. N. Radishchev.*

The General Characteristics of A. N. Radishchev's Writings.

Alexander Nikolaevich Radishchev originated a new, revolutionary antiserfdom theory in the socio-economic thought of Russia. This theory was called forth by economic and political conditions which were connected with the beginning of the decline of the feudal-serf system and with the sharp aggravation of the class struggle as expressed in the Peasant War of 1773–1774.

Radishchev was the first person in the history of Russian economic thought to give a legal base to the revolutionary liquidation of serfdom. He appealed to the toiling people, whom he called upon to use their own strength through revolution to liberate themselves from serfdom and autocracy. He viewed revolution as a force capable of destroying the outdated feudal structure and creating a society of independent producers free from forced labor.

In all contemporary world literature no author until Radishchev had presented such a broad program and such lofty aims of revolutionary reform in the political, economic, and cultural life of society. The Utopian Socialists—Thomas More, Morelli, Mably, and others—originated theories condemning the exploitative system, but they were not revolutionary; they invoked only reason and compassion, not revolutionary action. The great, enlightened French philosophers of the eighteenth century, Voltaire, Rousseau, and others, subjected feudalism to various criticisms, but they did not incite the popular masses to overthrow it by force. They were rationalists and hoped for the peaceful triumph of reason over "delusions."

The revolutionary ideas in the "Testament" of Jean Mallet were not published in the eighteenth century and could not have influenced the formulation of Radishchev's views. Jean Mallet's "Testament" was not completely printed until 1864. During Mallet's lifetime, as he himself wrote, he resolved not to issue an appeal to overthrow the existing order by revolutionary means. As a matter of fact, Radishchev was the first openly to urge the masses to seize political power, to realize popular sovereignty, and to place production in the hands of free producers.

Lenin emphasized that Radishchev was one of the first fighters for the liberation of the toilers in the struggle of the Russian people against the coercion of the exploiters. In his article, "On the National Pride of the Great Russians," which traced the basic trends of liberation movements historically succeeding one another, Radishchev was singled out as the first representative of revolutionary Russia, the predecessor of the Decembrists, the revolutionary intelligentsia, and others. Lenin wrote: "It is painful for us to see and feel the extent of the coercion, oppression, and mockery to which the tsarist hangmen, the nobles, and the capitalists subjected our beautiful country. We are proud of the fact that these coercions met rebuff from within, from the midst of the Great Russians, that this environment produced Radishchev, the Decembrists, and the revolutionary intelligentsia of the 1870's, that the Great Russian working class in 1905 created a powerful revolutionary party of the masses, that the great muzhik at that same time began to become a democrat and to cast off the yoke of the priest and the pomeshchik." [1]

When Stalin named the most distinguished workers of revolutionary Russia of the pre-Marxist period, he placed Radishchev by the side of Chernyshevskii and emphasized thereby the enormous historical significance of Radishchev's revolutionary accomplishment. In a letter to Dem'ian Bednii, Stalin condemned the slanderous distortions of the Russian past and the neglect of the great historical contributions of the Russian revolutionaries. Stalin wrote that "beside reactionary Russia, a revolutionary Russia eixsted—the Russia of the Radishchevs and Chernyshevskiis, the Zheliabovs and the Ulianovs, the Khalturins and the Alekseevs." [2] The leader of the Russian proletarian revolution, Lenin, and his student and coworker, Stalin, did not by accident place Radishchev first in the list of revolutionaries who created the remarkable revolutionary tradition of the Russian working class, a tradition which constitutes our revolutionary national pride.

The originality of Radishchev had a tremendously fertile influence on the development of the liberation movement in Russia. To Radishchev descended the remarkable historical traditions of the century-long struggle of the toilers of our country to free themselves from the pomeshchik and capitalist yoke. The stage was set for him by the con-

---

1 Lenin, *Sochineniia,* XXI, 85.
2 Stalin, *Sochineniia,* XIII, 25.

tradictions in Russia's social development, by those changes in the economy which were reflected in the ideological conflict during the second half of the eighteenth century. Radishchev's ideas symbolized the beginning of the decay of the base of feudal-serf society, the inconsistency between the growing productive powers and the outmoded serf productive relationships, and the class struggle, the struggle of peasants against pomeshchiki.

In the ideological sense, the decisive role in preparing for Radishchev's appearance was played by the economic demands of the peasantry, expressed in the documents of the Peasant War of 1773–1774. He was encouraged by the antifeudal opposition in western and Russian enlightened literature and also by criticisms of various aspects of serfdom in Russian satirical journals of that time.[3]

This satirical literature, however, differed greatly from the creative genius of Radishchev. N. A. Dobroliubov pointed this out as early as 1859 in his remarkably profound analysis in the critical article "Russian Satire in the Age of Catherine," published in *Sovremennik*. Dobroliubov noted that in the journals of the second half of the eighteenth century the question of the relationship of peasants and pomeshchiki was sharply posed, that the injustice and poverty of peasant existence were presented, that the hardhearted pomeshchiki, the embezzlement of public property, bribery, extravagance, judicial and financial abuses, the backwardness and inertia of the nobility, its obsequiousness before anything foreign and its disdain of anything Russian were unmasked. The satirical journals revealed many evils in contemporary society, but nevertheless, wrote Dobroliubov, this satire "does not disclose it so . . ."[4] Instead of viewing all the individual abuses and shortcomings as inevitable consequences of the whole feudal social structure, instead of attempting to seek out the basic causes of the evil, the satirists considered these dark phenomena of Russian life to be only deplorable exceptions. As Dobroliubov justly remarked, despite the fact that the satire was sometimes very sharp, "it was weak in that it did not really want to see the fundamental worthlessness of the system which it was trying to improve."[5]

This revolutionary democrat critic, Dobroliubov, recognized a new trend in Radishchev's appearance. "Radishchev's book," he remarked, in referring to the *Journey from Petersburg to Moscow*, "was almost

[3] See Makogonenko, *Nikolai Novikov i russkoe prosveshchenie*.

[4] N. A. Dobroliubov, *Izbrannye sochineniia* [Selected Works] (Moscow-Leningrad: Gosizdat, 1947), p. 171. In his study of Novikov Makogonenko bypasses sharp and correct appraisal of the Russian satire of the XVIII century offered by Dobroliubov.

[5] *Ibid.*, p. 190.

the only exception in a number of literary works of that time . . . ," [6] because it summoned the people to follow the author to "his end results," that is, to the revolutionary liquidation of serfdom.

Radishchev took a gigantic step forward in the development of Russian social thought in contrast to the other writers and statesmen of the second half of the eighteenth century (Polenov, Kozelskii, and others), who had already come to understand the negative influence of serfdom, but were still far from demanding its immediate abolition. He put on the agenda of social thought the revolutionary liquidation of the feudal-serf system as a whole, in all its forms—economic, political, and ideological. His approach represented a dialectic stride forward in the development of Russian socio-economic thought.

The revolutionary ideas of Radishchev played an enormous mobilizing role in the struggle of succeeding generations against serfdom and autocracy. The Russian enlighteners, Ivan Pnin, Vasilii Popugaev, and other "Radishchevists" of the last decade of the eighteenth and the beginning of the nineteenth century, shared his beliefs.[7] The Decembrists wrote and spoke of the beneficial influence of Radishchev's idea; Pushkin, following Radishchev, glorified freedom; the revolutionary democrats of the nineteenth century looked upon Radishchev as the founder of liberating revolutionary ideas in Russia.

The great Russian poet Pushkin, appreciating Radishchev's influence, saw in him a man "with unusual spirit . . . acting with astonishing selflessness and with a sort of chivalrous conscientiousness." [8] Chernyshevskii, the leader of Russian revolutionary democracy, regarded Radishchev's ideas with the greatest respect and felt that "Radishchev, more perhaps than any other man, had what we now call conviction or his own frame of mind." [9]

Radishchev's book had a great influence also on the formulation of the *Weltanschauung* of representatives of the proletarian movement. The leader of the famous Morozov strike, Petr Anistimovich Moiseenko, read it in prison.[10] The *Journey from Petersburg to Moscow* was studied also in the first Marxist circles. In a leaflet of the Petersburg Committee of the RSDRP of January 3, 1903, Radishchev's book

---

[6] *Ibid.*, p. 178.

[7] See Vl. Orlov, *Russkie prosvetiteli 1790–1800-kh godov* [Russian Men of Enlightenment of 1790–1800] (2nd edition, Moscow: Gosizdat, 1953).

[8] Pushkin, *Polnoe sobranie sochinenii*, VII, 355.

[9] N. G. Chernyshevskii, *Polnoe sobranie sochinenii* [Complete Collection of Works] (n.p.: 1906), VI, 353.

[10] See S. P. Shesternin, *Perezhitoe. Iz istorii rabochego i revoliutsionnogo dvizheniia 1880–1900* [Experiences. From the History of the Working and Revolutionary Movement 1880–1900] (Ivanovo: 1940), p. 215.

was described as "the first revolutionary attempt to seize by force that freedom of speech which the tsarist autocracy had taken from the Russian people." [11]

Although Radishchev's appearance was a result of the previous development of socio-political life and socio-economic thought in Russia, it is nevertheless necessary to emphasize a qualitatively different degree and a basically new trend which Radishchev created in the struggle against serfdom. He did not put his hopes on education and reforms. He insistently set forth the idea that not criticism of different aspects and discords, not the pronouncements of individual progressive people, but the toiling people themselves, by revolutionary means, would free the Russian people from slavery. Therein lies his greatest, immortal service to the toilers of our country.

Alexander Nikolaevich Radishchev was born on August 20, 1749, into the family of a fairly large-scale pomeshchik of Saratov gubernia. The estate of his father, Verkhnei Abliazov, in the third census numbered 120 male and 109 female servants; in all there were about 3500 serfs of both sexes.[12] Radishchev himself wrote: "At an early age I entered service as a court page." In 1766 he was sent with twelve young nobles "at the government's expense" to Leipzig University "to study jurisprudence and other related sciences." [13]

Radishchev awaited with impatience his return to Russia; he was full of a desire to work and firmly resolved if necessary "to sacrifice even life for the benefit of the fatherland." Immediately upon his return in the autumn of 1771, he was appointed recorder in the Senate, where a great volume of peasant problems passed through his hands. From 1773 to 1775 Radishchev worked as chief auditor on the staff of the Eighth Finland Division. Service as a military procurator gave Radishchev the opportunity to become better acquainted with the materials on the Peasant War and its causes. After the tsarist government's suppression of the peasant uprising led by Pugachev, Radishchev resigned in 1775, but in 1777 he returned to government service. He entered the office of assessor in the Commerce College under Count

---

[11] *Listovki peterburgskikh bolshevikov, 1902–1917* [Leaflets of the Petrograd Bolsheviks, 1902–1917] (Moscow: Gospolitizdat, 1939), I, 16–17.

[12] See P. G. Liubomirov, "Rod Radishcheva" [Radishchev's Family], *A. N. Radishchev. Materialy i issledovaniia* [A. N. Radishchev. Materials and Studies] (Moscow-Leningrad: AS USSR, 1936).

[13] A. N. Radishchev, *Polnoe sobranie sochinenii* [Complete Collection of Works] (Moscow-Leningrad: AS USSR, 1938), I, 157. Unless otherwise noted all subsequent references to volume I are taken from this edition.

A. R. Vorontsov, with whom he soon developed a friendship which lasted until Radishchev's death.[14]

In 1780 Radishchev was assigned to the Petersburg Customs "to aid State Counsellor Dahl," and, after the latter's death in the autumn of 1790, be became "Customs Counsellor," that is, its director.[15]

On June 30, 1790, he was arrested and imprisoned in the Petropavlovsk Fortress. The accusation against him was written by Catherine II herself, after she finished reading his book *Journey from Petersburg to Moscow.*

In a directive to the Petersburg Commandant, Count Bruce, following Radishchev's trial and the examination of his case by the Chamber of the Criminal Court, Catherine wrote that his book was filled with the "most harmful opinions, jeopardizing social peace, undermining due respect to the authorities, striving to create indignation among the people against their administrators and administration, and permeated with insulting statements against royal dignity and authority." [16]

In the Petropavlovsk Fortress, Radishchev was subjected to degrading inquisition and questioning "with persuasion" on the part of the councellor of the Secret Expedition, Sheshkovskii, who earlier in 1775 had interrogated and tortured Emelyan Pugachev. Radishchev's interrogation proceeded according to the "points of question" set forth in detail by Catherine II. Under the most difficult conditions of solitary confinement, Radishchev courageously and daringly adhered to his revolutionary views. "My desire was to take all peasants from their

---

[14] In a letter dated July 3, 1780, A. R. Vorontsov wrote to his father, R. L. Vorontsov: "In your trip to the Penza gubernia, should you see there our neighbor Nikolai Afanesevich Radishchev, I beg you kindly to visit with him. I am very fond of his son, who was with me for two years in the Commerce College and now is with Customs, assistant to the College Counsellor Dahl. I recommended him to the Empress as an excellent man who, in time, can be very useful in the service. Moreover, he is a man of most discreet and honest conduct. Nikolai Afanesevich can be proud of his son."

Ten years later, 12 September 1790, the same A. R. Vorontsov wrote to the Tver governor, G. M. Osipov: "Prior to his misfortune, Radishchev had for a long time not only been an acquaintance of mine, but I liked him . . . Supply him with all things necessary for his journey, using the enclosed money to do so." (*Arkhiv kn. Vorontsova* (Moscow: 1872), Pt. 1, Bk. 5, pp. 394, 397–398.) To the end of Radishchev's life Vorontsov gave him material aid.

[15] D. S. Babkin, *Protsess Radishcheva* [Radishchev's Trial] (Moscow: AS USSR, 1952), p. 217: "Service List of College Counsellor Alexander Radishchev."

[16] *Ibid.*, p. 196.

pomeshchiki and make them free . . . ,"[17] wrote Radishchev in his testimony.

On August 8 the Senate confirmed the decision of the Chamber of the Criminal Court of July 24, 1790: for "such harmful, violent, and insulting writings . . . to deprive him of ranks, of the title of nobility, to exclude him from the cavaliers of the order of Saint Vladimir, and to execute him, that is . . . to behead him." Only on September 4 by a special decree of Catherine was the death sentence commuted to a ten-year exile in Siberia, in the Ilimsk *ostrog.*

Imprisonment in the Petropavlovsk Fortress, the prolonged expectation of execution, and the decree of a ten-year exile to desolate Ilimsk did not demoralize Radishchev. He courageously endured all these ordeals. The cruel punishment of the tsarist regime did not change the convictions of the first writer-revolutionary. He maintained his faith in the creative forces of the people. His opposition to autocracy and slavery did not weaken, and his belief in the inevitability of revolution grew stronger. He wrote more than once that his beliefs had not altered, that he "is the same as he was." On the road to Ilimsk he expressed his feelings in the verses:

> You wish to know: who and what am I, where do I go?
> I am the same as I was and shall ever so remain:
> Not cattle, wood nor slave, but man!
> To break the road where there was no trail
> For swift daredevils, both in prose and verse,
> To sensitive hearts and truth—
> I go in peril to the Ilimsk ostrog.[18]

Even Siberia did not pervert Radishchev. In 1792 he wrote A. R. Vorontsov from Ilimsk: "Let my voice not change, let my neck never be severed and let me hold my head proudly . . ." [19] On the road to Ilimsk, in Ilimsk itself, and also on the way back from Siberia, Radishchev came into close contact with the common people and tried with all the means within his grasp to serve and help them. He nursed the sick, vaccinated for smallpox, taught children how to read, and propa-

---

[17] *Ibid.,* pp. 179–80.

[18] Radishchev, *op. cit.,* I, 123.

[19] *Ibid.,* II, 26. Here Radishchev wrote that he would acknowledge the weakness of his views if he were convinced "by evidence better than that used here. But as to the one attempted on me, as an author I could say nothing except what I recall Galileo said when pressed by the Inquisition and asked to reject his views on the immobility of the sun contrary to sound reason; he exclaimed: 'The sun rotates!'" *Ibid.,* II, 5.

gandized for new agricultural techniques.[20] Radishchev was more convinced than ever that his ideas pointed a new way, a new "road" of development for the country, for all "daredevils" entering the struggle with slavery.

A decree of Paul of November 23, 1796, allowed Radishchev to return from Siberia with permission to live in his village of Nemtsovo, Kaluga gubernia, under police surveillance. He was barred from government service and an active social life for eleven years, and only in 1801 was he called to work on the Commission on Preparing Laws. A member of this Commission, M. M. Speranskii, wrote: "Radishchev can prepare the history of laws with complete success; he has the necessary creativity, the knowledge of the country, and he can throw much light on the darkness in which we find ourselves. It would be a good idea to suggest to him that in preparing this history he give special attention to the means by which the customs of the peasantry have become fixed into law and to the situation in which this group of people has found itself in Russia during its various transformations." [21]

As a member of Alexander I's Commission on Preparing Laws, Radishchev openly advocated from the start the protection of the human rights of the peasantry before the law. At that time the Senate was considering the insertion of an amendment into the law establishing the rate for losses to the pomeshchik from serfs accidentally killed. From the promulgation of the Code of 1649 this rate had been gradually raised, but it did not satisfy the appetites of the serf owners. The Commission had prepared for the Senate a "Resolution" which proposed to pay the pomeshchik for the inadvertent death of a peasant the sum of 360 rubles for a man and 100 rubles for a woman. "In cases of the unpremeditated death of a household man or a household woman or girl who, because of artistic work, skill, handicraft, and labor, are often worth more than a good peasant man or peasant woman, then . . . such household men, women, and girls are to be paid for according to the nature of their work and the income which each of them, through his talent, handiwork, and labor, brought to his owner." [22]

To the Commission's "Resolution" Radishchev added his own view—a memo, "On the Prices for Slain Persons." In this memo, as in his

---

20 See A. Shmakov, *Radishchev v Sibiri* [Radishchev in Siberia] (Irkutsk: 1952).

21 *Arkhiv N. Turgeneva* [N. Turgenev's Archive], Folder 1006, Sheet 12, Manuscript Division of the Institute of Russian Literature of the AS USSR.

22 M. K. Sukhomlinov, *Issledovaniia i stati po russkoi literature i prosveshcheniiu* [Studies and Articles on Russian Literature and Education] (St. Petersburg: 1889), I, 626–7.

other works, Radishchev ardently opposed turning enserfed persons into a commodity; he was against their sale with families or individually, against capitalizing on income received from them in case of their death. "We cannot consider such prices, which are determined by the pomeshchiki for the death of people belonging to them; *the value of human blood cannot be determined by money,"* Radishchev emphasized.[23] During his entire life he remained an enemy of slavery and "autocracy," a convinced exponent of freedom which, in his own expression, he "first foretold" to us.

And even by his death he defied autocracy and the serf owners. "The nature of his convictions he proved upon his return from exile. Called to work by Alexander I himself, he hoped to translate some of his thoughts—most of all those relating to the liberation of the peasants—into legislation, and when the fifty-year-old dreamer realized that nothing could come of it, he took poison and died!" [24] This happened on the night of September 12, 1802.

Radishchev was one of the best informed persons of his day, not only in Russia but also in the entire world. Catherine II in her remarks on Radishchev's book had to concede that he "has considerable knowledge and has read many books." [25] His library comprised a valuable collection of scientific books, part of which was purchased after his death by the Commission on the Preparation of Laws.[26] Among foreign books it included the works of Montesquieu, Hume, Rousseau, Blackstone, Mably, Raynal, Verri, and Smith, books on natural and Roman law, on finances, political economy, the codes of law of England, France, Germany, Austria, and others.

Radishchev carefully studied contemporary Russian and western literature in various fields of knowledge. During his study at Leipzig University he became intimately acquainted with French materialism and other literature of the enlightenment, which ideologically prepared the way for the French bourgeois revolution. This literature, like the French revolution itself, had a definite influence on Radishchev, but it did not play a decisive role in the formation of his world outlook, of his socio-political and economic views.

For Radishchev the "first university," to use Pushkin's words, was the great Russian scholar, the founder of materialism in Russia, M. V.

[23] Radishchev, *op. cit.,* III, 247.

[24] A. I. Herzen, *Polnoe sobranie sochinenii i pisem* [Complete Collection of Works and Letters]. Edited by M. K. Lemke. (Prague: 1919), IX, 271.

[25] *Arkhiv kn. Vorontsova,* Bk. V, p. 407; Babkin, *op. cit.,* p. 157.

[26] See [Ia. L. Barskov], "Knigi iz sobraniia A. N. Radishcheva" [Books from the A. N. Radishchev Collection], *Dela i dni* [Problems and Days], Bk. I (1920), pp. 397–402.

Lomonosov. Even during Lomonosov's lifetime Radishchev received systematic instruction in Moscow, in the Agramakov family, which was closely tied to the university, and under the tutelage of professors of Moscow University. From Lomonosov came the materialistic ideas which became the foundation of Radishchev's world outlook. Not without reason does the *Journey from Petersburg to Moscow* end with "A word on Lomonosov," in which Radishchev shows how Lomonosov, "influencing his co-citizens in varied ways, pointed out to the common mind the path to knowledge."

The exposé of the defects of serfdom in the satirical journals of the second half of the eighteenth century and in the oral and literary pronouncements of the best people of that time—Polenov, the Kozelskii brothers, Novikov, Desnitskii, and others—could not help but have a positive influence on Radishchev. Especially important in this respect was Ia. P. Kozelskii's *Philosophical Propositions.*

Radishchev systematically and persistently studied the history of Russia, her economic problems, the development of agriculture, industry, trade, the condition of money circulation, finances, the tax burden of the toilers, and the situation of the peasantry and of other classes. Systematic analysis of economic and socio-political factors allowed Radishchev to evaluate critically the ideas of Russian and western enlightened literature and to make broad generalizations concerning the economy, the culture, and the socio-political life of Russia.

Of course, a strong and direct influence on Radishchev's revolutionary views was the Peasant War of 1773–1774, which reflected the growing inconsistencies between productive relations and productive forces. This upheaval jolted the entire autocratic-serf state and threatened its very existence.

Radishchev's scientific views found expression in his many literary works, a short list of which is given below. His celebrated book, *Journey from Petersburg to Moscow,*[27] depicts the political and economic

[27] Published by Radishchev's own press in 1790 in the amount of 650 copies. About twenty copies have been preserved, the remainder having been destroyed. In 1858 Herzen published the *Journey* in London, the first edition after Radishchev's, and distributed it illegally in Russia; in 1876 Kasprovich reprinted Herzen's edition in Leipzig. In Russia before the Revolution of 1905 tsarist censorship allowed the printing of one diluted version of the *Journey* edited by N. A. Shigin in 1868, 100 copies of the expensive edition of the *Journey* by A. S. Suvorin in 1888, and a bibliophile reprint by A. E. Burtsev, *Dopolnitelnoe opisanie bibliograficheski-redkikh khudozhestvenno-zamechatelnykh knig i dragotsennykh rukopisei* [Supplementary Description of Rare and Famous Books and Precious Manuscripts] (1899), vol. V. A two-volume edition of Radishchev's works by P. A. Efremov in St. Petersburg in 1872 (1985 copies) was destroyed in June, 1873. Not more than fifteen copies were preserved.

structure of Russia at the end of the eighteenth century and throws light on contemporary life. This work is one of the most outstanding revolutionary contributions to eighteenth century world literature. The epigram on the title page, "O grim monster savage, gigantic, hundred-mouthed, and bellowing (*Telemakhida*)," immediately prepares the reader for a critical attitude towards serfdom. The book seller Zotov, who was one of the witnesses in the Radishchev trial, said that it had created "a great curiosity among the public." [28] Frightened by its revolutionary character, Catherine II wrote to the Commandant of Petersburg, Bruce: "Inasmuch as this harmful book, *Journey from Petersburg to Moscow,* cannot be tolerated in a decent state, you are ordered to see that it is never printed or sold here under penalty of punishment commensurate with the crime." This tsarist censorship lasted for 115 years [29] until the 1905 revolution.

Radishchev's *Journey from Petersburg to Moscow* was correctly appraised by his contemporaries and later writers as a call to revolution. For example, Catherine II wrote that this book "is completely and clearly revolutionary"; Princess E. Dashkova believed that *Journey* was the "call to revolution." Pushkin characterized it as a "satirical call to indignation." Herzen, speaking about *Journey,* wrote: "These are our dreams, the dreams of the Decembrists." These words are significant. Herzen had traveled the road from revolutionary noble to revolutionary democrat. And when, in 1858, he praised Radishchev's ideas as "our dreams," this can only mean that Radishchev preceded even the dreams of revolutionary democracy in its struggle against autocracy and serfdom, and not merely "the dreams of the Decembrists," for Herzen was not a Decembrist.

In 1902 P. A. Kartavov printed 2900 copies of the *Journey*. This edition was destroyed in June, 1903. Only after the revolution of 1905 did it become possible for a wide reading audience to obtain *Journey from Petersburg to Moscow*. On the fate of various editions of the *Journey,* see *Literaturnoe nasledstvo* [Literary Heritage], Nos. 9–10 (1933), pp. 356–7; *Puteshestvie iz Peterburga v Moskvu. Materialy k izucheniiu 'Puteshestviia'* [Journey from Petersburg to Moscow. Materials for the Study of the 'Journey'] (Moscow-Leningrad: Academia, 1935), II, 322–46. At the present time the publication of Radishchev's literary heritage is complete in the Academy of Sciences' edition of his complete works (Vol. I in 1938, Vol. II in 1941, and Vol. III in 1952) as well as the publication of all the documents on Radishchev's trial by Babkin, *op. cit.*

[28] Readers paid twenty-five rubles to bookdealers to borrow this book. See *Literaturnoe nasledstvo,* Nos. 9–10 (1933), p. 354.

[29] Tsarist censorship of the XIX and XX centuries stood firmly behind the decree prohibiting the *Journey from Petersburg to Moscow* and "saw in Radishchev a writer who undermined all social foundations and who destroyed the church and the state." *Ibid.,* Nos. 9–10 (1933), p. 357.

Radishchev also wrote the revolutionary ode, "Vol'nost' " [Liberty], many poems, among them the epic "Bova," "Eighteen Centuries," "Historical Song," a number of shorter verses, and "Monument to a Dactyl-stropher Knight." The latter work, highly rated by Pushkin,[30] is a study of the necessity of making verse forms conform to the euphony of the Russian language. Here Radishchev appears as a follower of Lomonosov and develops the latter's ideas.

During his exile in Siberia Radishchev wrote one of the first scientific-philosophical treatises in Russia, "On Man, on His Mortality and Immortality." He is deservedly considered an originator of philosophical materialism in Russia, as Lomonosov was an originator of natural-scientific materialism. Radishchev distinguished himself as a philosophical-materialist, the heir of the tradition of Lomonosov, whom he very highly esteemed as the first great Russian scholar. He solved materialistically the basic question of philosophy—on the relations of existence and thought—and developed a materialistic theory of consciousness. In his philosophy significant individual attempts are made to explain dialectically the process of the development of nature.

Radishchev wrote about the development and variations in nature and society. On the whole, however, his materialism remained mechanical, clothed in the form of deism, and restricted by the level of development of science at the end of the eighteenth century. In his explanation of social development, Radishchev, for the most part, did not go beyond the limits of idealistic conceptions, differentiating the studies of social contract and natural law. However a distinguishing mark of Radishchev's studies on the social contract and natural law is the assertion of the sovereign right of a people to determine the forms of government structure.

But even in analyzing social phenomena in a number of cases, Radishchev rejected idealistic explanations. For his time, he thoughtfully defined the objective material conditions of those and other ideas and of human activity. "Expeditious reason," he wrote, "in man has always depended on life's demands and has been determined by environment. Those living near water invented boats and nets; those wandering in the forests and roving in the mountains invented bows and arrows and became the first warriors; those living in meadows, mottled with flowers and greens, domesticated useful animals and became cattle raisers . . . The cattle raiser began to imitate nature by seeding corn to feed his stock and later, eager for its abundance, planted grain. Agriculture resulted in the division of land into areas

[30] Pushkin, *op. cit.*, VII, 358.

and states, the building of villages and cities, and led to artisanships, handicrafts, trade, construction, laws, and governments. As soon as man said: this piece of land is mine! he rooted himself to the land and turned away from inhuman despotism, where one man orders another. He began to humble himself before the god he had invented and, clothing him in purple, set him on an altar above everyone else and burned incense to him; but having tired of his dreams and having shaken off his fetters and captivity, he defied the thing that he worshipped and destroyed it. This is the course of human reason." [31]

Radishchev shows in his philosophical treatises the historical development of the division of labor, the growth of social production, and the origin of private property. Thus he makes an interesting attempt to explain materialistically the origin of the division of society into classes, of exploitation and autocracy, on the basis of the appropriation of land by individuals. Here he repeats the thought he developed in the *Journey* and in the ode, "Liberty," the historical inevitability of the overthrow of autocracy and even of the execution of the Tsar.

The materialistic method of scientific research used by Radishchev is of great interest. He described his method of scientific investigation with the following words: "an inquirer should seek the cause of a matter, its deeds, or actions neither in his imagination, nor as did the ancient prophets, who deceived themselves and others in some invented fiction; by investigating the nature of things, deeds, and actions, he will discover their close and obscure ties with other things, deeds, or actions; he will connect similar and corresponding facts, he will dissect them, consider their similarities, and put them together for the conclusion issuing from them; going from one conclusion to another, from one action to another, he will attain and ascend to the general principle which, as the focal point of truth, illuminates all the paths leading into one." [32]

At the time of his affiliation with the Commission on Preparing Laws, Radishchev presented a number of legal projects and memoranda, such as, for example, the "Project on Separation of the Russian Code," the "Project for a Civil Code," [33] memoranda "On Legislation," [34] "On Prices for People Killed," "On the Right of Those Ac-

---

[31] Radishchev, *op. cit.,* II, 64.

[32] *Ibid.,* II, 40.

[33] Published for the first time in *A. N. Radishchev. Materialy i issledovaniia* [A. N. Radishchev. Materials and Studies] (Moscow-Leningrad: AS USSR, 1936).

[34] Published for the first time in *Golos minuvshego* [Heritage], December, 1916, pp. 74–96.

cused to Challenge the Judges and to Select Their Defender," and "Knowledge of Legislation." [35] In these works Radishchev expressed deeply progressive ideas in defense of civil freedom and in protest against all feudal-class limitations. He developed a number of important theoretical and practical economic propositions.

Of Radishchev's lesser publications, the ones which attract attention are "Letter to a Friend Living in Tobolsk by Reason of His Profession" [36] and "Conversation on What Constitutes a Son of the Fatherland." [37]

The "Fragment of a Journey to *** I *** T ***" is attributed to Radishchev with complete justification,[38] despite the fact that this has recently been questioned by G. Makogonenko and L. Krestova.[39] Makogonenko's main argument is based on the observation that in the "Fragment" none of the revolutionary conclusions peculiar to Radishchev are present, but, on the contrary, the idea of the contrast between the village of Ruin and the village of Well-Being appears. The weakness of this argument is obvious. The "Fragment" was published in 1772, prior to the Peasant War led by Pugachev, which had such a decisive influence on formulating Radishchev's revolutionary views. Before that war Radishchev had not yet asserted his revolutionary beliefs, had not called the people to armed insurrection, had only pointed out the burdens of serf exploitation. In the "Fragment" the pomeshchik-destroyers are not contrasted with the pomeshchik-"fathers," nor is the village of Well-Being with the village of Ruin. On the other hand, the very first page of the "Fragment" states with absolute clarity that Radishchev "stopped in almost every village and town . . . but in three days of this journey I found nothing worthy of praise. *Poverty* and *slavery* met my eyes everywhere in the shape of the peasants . . . I did not enter a single village without asking about

[35] All legal works of Radishchev are in the 3rd volume of *Polnoe sobranie sochinenii.*

[36] Published by Radishchev's own press in 1790. See *ibid.,* I.

[37] Published in *Beseduiushchii grazhdanin* [Talking Citizen], December, 1789. See also Radishchev, *op. cit.,* I.

[38] Published anonymously in *Zhivopisets* [Artist] (1772), Sheets 5 and 14; See also Radishchev, *op. cit., II; Russkaia proza XVIII veka* [Russian Prose of the XVIII Century] (Moscow-Leningrad: Gosizdat, 1950), I; *Satiricheskie zhurnaly N. I. Novikova* [N. I. Novikov's Satirical Journals] (Moscow-Leningrad: AS USSR, 1951).

[39] See Makogonenko, *op. cit.,* and also his article, "N. I. Novikov," *Russkaia proza XVIII veka,* I; L. V. Krestova, "Iz istorii zhurnalnoi deiatelnosti N. I. Novikova (Kto byl avtorom 'Otrivka Puteshestviia v ***' I. T. i 'Pisem k. Falaleiu'?)" [From the History of Journalistic Activity of N. I. Novikov (Who Was the Author of 'Fragment of the Journey to ***' I. T. and 'Letters to Falalei'?)], *Istoricheskie zapiski,* No. 44 (1953), pp. 253–87.

the reasons for peasant poverty. And listening to their answers, to my great distress I always found that the pomeshchiki themselves were the cause of it." [40] The entire "Fragment" contains a clear picture of the dreadful conditions of the peasant village of Ruin, and only in the last four lines does the traveller inform us that he set out the next day, suffering with impatience, to see the inhabitants of the village of Well-Being, because "my master had told me so many good things about the pomeshchik of that village." [41] These concluding lines of the "Fragment" should be considered an open refutation by Radishchev of the official pro-serfdom propaganda, which constantly distributed its version of the prevailing rule in the Russian village of good pomeshchik-"fathers" and fallaciously asserted that the peasantry in Russia lived better than that in other countries. As is known, Catherine II continually wrote and spoke on this matter. In her notes on Radishchev's *Journey* she wrote: "he decries the lamentable fate of the peasant condition, although it is indisputable that the fate of our peasants with good pomeshchiki is better than anywhere else." [42] This was continuously reaffirmed by Shcherbatov, Boltin, and other serf owners.

Radishchev demonstrated that, although "so much was told" to him about the well-being of pomestie peasants, he did not find in serf Russia the village of Well-Being, despite his attempts to reach it. Radishchev depicted in detail the village of Ruin, the condition and the exhausting labors of its peasants, but did not, and could not, describe the village of Well-Being—there is no such village in the picture he drew. Therefore he could not "contrast" these villages with each other.

When he negates Radishchev's authorship and assigns it to N. I. Novikov, Makogonenko ignores the remarks of Novikov himself in *The Artist:* this publisher and editor informs the reader that from the manuscript which he received from Mr. I. T. he deleted the last "conversation of the traveller with a peasant for several reasons: the intelligent reader himself can guess them. Besides, I assure my reader that this conversation would have satisfied his curiosity and would clearly have shown that the traveller had just cause to accuse the pomeshchik of the village of Ruin and those like him." [43] The edited version of "Fragment," as is clear from this note, was dictated by the censor's objections and softened Radishchev's sharp critique of serf-

[40] *Satiricheskie zhurnaly N. I. Novikova,* p. 295.
[41] *Ibid.,* p. 332.
[42] Babkin, *op. cit.,* p. 160.
[43] *Satiricheskie zhurnaly N. I. Novikova,* p. 332.

dom. Even the publisher of the "Fragment" affirms in this note that its contents are directed against serfdom. Why should it be necessary for Novikov to explain to the reader in detail his work on the manuscript if he himself were its author?

V. P. Semennikov presented broad and convincing evidence of Radishchev's authorship of the "Fragment." [44] Semennikov gave special attention to the similarity between the ideas of the "Fragment" and those of the chapter "Peshki" in *Journey from Petersburg to Moscow.*

In addition to the arguments of Semennikov, one can note a striking likeness in the ideas, content, and form of conversations between the traveller and peasants in the "Fragment" [45] and the conversations in the chapter "Liubani" from the *Journey from Petersburg to Moscow.*[46] In both places, the peasants are told that they are forced to work in their own fields on Sunday since they have to labor for the pomeshchik during the rest of the week; in both places the bestial system of unlimited barshchina is described: in both places the peasant hopes for "God's mercy" and believes that with a "good master" life would be better; in both places the traveller "thinks deeply" about the hard lot of the pomeshchik's peasants and about the fact that the pomeshchiki illegally drove them to "such an existence."

The mention of the "good" lord in the "Fragment" does not provide any basis for denying Radishchev's authorship of it. Radishchev describes typical pomeshchiki, bestially exploiting their serfs, and the reference by individual peasants to individual "good" pomeshchiki does not change the general tenor of Radishchev's sharply negative, revolutionary attitude towards serfdom, just as the occasional strong satire on "stupid" pomeshchiki by Novikov neither changes Novikov's generally liberal attitude towards serfdom, nor his faith in the "good" lord and the enlightened monarch.

Unconvincing also is the argument of L. Krestova. She ignores the testimony of P. A. Radishchev about his father, A. N. Radishchev, participating in *The Artist.* It is impossible to agree with Krestova's conclusion that from the period of his return from abroad in the

---

[44] V. P. Semennikov, *Radishchev. Ocherki i issledovaniia* [Radishchev. Outlines and Studies] (Moscow: 1923), pp. 319–64.

[45] Radishchev, *op. cit.,* II, 350–1; *Russkaia proza XVIII veka,* I, 446–7; *Satiricheskie zhurnaly N. I. Novikova,* pp. 331–2.

[46] Radishchev, *op. cit.,* I, 232–4. P. N. Berkov, *Istoriia russkoi zhurnalistiki XVIII veka* [History of Russian Journalism of the XVIII Century] (Moscow-Leningrad: AS USSR, 1952), p. 206, also points out the similarity between the content of the middle portion of the "Excerpt" and the chapter of the *Journey,* "Liubani," which he justly considers on elaboration of the original version presented in the "Excerpt."

autumn of 1771 to the writing of the first part of the "Fragment" in May, 1772, A. N. Radishchev had no opportunity to become basically acquainted with the conditions of the peasants. Was Radishchev then so completely unfamiliar with the life of the enserfed Russian peasants before his journey abroad? Had he not read the Russian satirical journals of the 1760's and 1770's? Had not documents on the skirmishes of pomeshchiki and peasants passed daily through his hands as recorder of the Senate? Farfetched also is Krestova's assertion that immediately upon his return to Russia Radishchev could not have turned to criticism of its faults because he came home with enthusiasm. But here Radishchev himself wrote that this enthusiasm died as soon as he returned.

Denying without foundation the validity of the comparison of the "Fragment," published in *The Artist,* with the chapters "Peshki" and "Liubani" from *Journey from Petersburg to Moscow,* Krestova acknowledges only differences between the chapter "Peshki" and the "Fragment" and, in regard to the chapter, "Liubani," remarks that this work has another ideological direction.

But the crucial point is that Radishchev made an enormous stride forward in the development of Russian social thought—from criticism of various aspects of serfdom to its revolutionary rejection. Eighteen years separate the publication of the "Fragment of a Journey to *** I *** T ***" from that of *Journey from Petersburg to Moscow.* During this time Radishchev's revolutionary convictions formed and matured, while N. I. Novikov was and remained a liberal critic of individual phases, but not of the *system,* of autocratic serfdom.

Krestova's major argument in attributing "Fragment of a Journey to *** I *** T ***" to N. I. Novikov is that in the *Moskovskii Sobesednik* of 1806, the reprinted text of "Fragment" and Novikov's article "An English Stroll" were placed together, one after the other, and that a correction was incorporated in "Fragment" which, in her opinion, could only have been made by the author. A detailed comparison of the texts does not convince us of Novikov's authorship, inasmuch as not only authors, but editors and publishers as well made and still make similar corrections. One should not ignore the adaptation of quotations from other texts as practiced in the eighteenth and the beginning of the nineteenth century. For example, one may cite M. D. Chulkov's *Historical Description of Russian Commerce.* In this work whole pages, paragraphs, and sentences are incorporated from the writings of other authors without any citations or quotation marks. Many similar examples can be found without difficulty. In reprinting the works of deceased authors, the editors, translators, and publishers made and still make corrections (and changes for greater accuracy) in the text, in the composition, and so on. Novikov was no exception to this rule, but he did not introduce radical alterations in the "Fragment" in the five editions of *The Artist* while Radishchev was still alive. Thus the contention that the author of "Fragment of a Journey to *** I *** T ***" was Novikov, and not Radishchev, is unconvincing.

In the works mentioned above, Radishchev emerged as a mature critic of the system of autocratic serfdom and an ardent defender of the oppressed people. He prepared a number of Russian translations of works of foreign literature. He translated from the Greek the pamphlet of A. Gika, entitled "The Desires of the Greeks Toward Christian Europe."[47] The pamphlet points out the past well-being and glory of the Greek people, "when our ancestors lived in a state of freedom." Radishchev prefaced his translation with a brief foreword in which he showed the impoverished condition of the Greek people languishing under the Turkish yoke.

He published a translation from the German of the book, *Officers' Manual.* This was a special handbook for officers, probably designed for use in the Russian army. It is possible that the initiative for the translation came from Count Bruce's staff, where Radishchev was then serving.

Of greater interest is the translation from the French by Radishchev in 1773 of the book of Mably, *Meditations on Greek History, or on the Causes for the Prosperity and Misfortune of the Greeks.* Mably considered private property to be the source of all evil in society.[48]

Radishchev's translation is remarkable for its treatment of individual words; for example, *despotisme*—autocracy, *tyran*—tormentor [*muchitel*], and so on, as well as for the comments by the translator himself. In notes to Mably's text, Radishchev makes apparent his own democratic convictions. On the word *despotisme* Radishchev gives the following comment: "Autocracy is a condition most repugnant to human nature. Not only can we not give anyone unlimited power over us; but even the law, a product of the general will, does not have the

---

47 Radishchev, *op. cit.*, II, 225–8.

48 Engels wrote of Mably the following: "Revolutionary uprisings by the still immature class were accompanied by the corresponding theoretical declarations; such were the utopian conceptions of an ideal social system in the XVI and XVII centuries and in the XVIII century already direct communist theories (of Morelli and Mably)." F. Engels, *Razvitie sotsializma ot utopii k nauke* [The Development of Socialism from Utopia to Science] (Moscow: 1953), pp. 34–5.

right to punish criminals except when it involves personal preservation. If we live under the authority of laws, that does not mean we must make them unalterable; but it means that we find some advantage in them. If we delegate to a law part of our rights and our natural authority, then that must be used to our advantage; we make a *tacit* contract with society in this regard. If the agreement is broken, then we too are freed from our *obligation*. The injustice of a sovereign gives the people, who are his judges, the same, or an even greater, right over him than the law gives him to judge criminals. *The sovereign is the first citizen of the people's commonwealth.*" [49] From this it is obvious that even in the year of the beginning of the Peasant War, 1773, Radishchev clearly expressed the idea of the right of a people to judge as a criminal a tsar who destroyed the interests of the people and their sovereignty.

Among Radishchev's economic works, those demanding attention are the "Letter on the Chinese Trade" and "Description of my Property," [50] also the "Note on the Taxes of the Petersburg gubernia," [51] and the uncompleted manuscript, "Trade." [52]

The "Letter on the Chinese Trade" is an investigation of foreign trade and its influence on the homeland's production. In this work Radishchev analyzed important aspects of political economy. He strengthened his theoretical position with abundant factual material from the customs reports and with direct observations on the development of production and trade in European Russia and in Siberia.[53]

Radishchev failed to complete his second economic work, "Description of My Property." The full title of this work—"A Description of My Property, Pomestie, Votchina, Village, or What You Will"—shows that here he deals with a typical estate of the central belt of Russia. From the plan of the work it is obvious that Radishchev intended to give a comprehensive picture of the peasant economy of an obrok pomestie village. This work has great value both for the revelation of Radishchev's economic views and for the description of the level of development in the Russian village at the end of the eighteenth century.

In the "Description of My Property" Radishchev gave the charac-

---

[49] Radishchev, *op. cit.*, II, 282, note.

[50] *Ibid.*, II.

[51] *Ibid.*, III.

[52] AS USSR, Archive of the Leningrad Branch of the Institute of History, *Sobranie Vorontsova* [Vorontsov's Collection], No. 398, Sheets 140–1.

[53] Radishchev noted his observations in diaries: "Notes on the Journey to Siberia" and "Notes on the Journey from Siberia." See Radishchev, *op. cit.*, III.

teristics of agricultural reserves and land utilization, an account of the means of production (buildings, cattle, tools) and their value, and prepared a balance of income and expenditures of the village and of the net income per individual of the population. He described all the agricultural labors and peasant industries, recommended measures for improving agricultural production, and revealed the socio-economic reasons for its low standard. This work is one of the first attempts in Russia to present a collated study on the economics of peasant-enserfed agriculture.

A number of important economic views, especially on the role of usurers and churchmen in the exploitation and ruination of the toilers, on trade in Siberia, and on the dreadful condition of the peasants are contained in Radishchev's recently published works, "Description of the Administration of Tobolsk," [54] "Note on the Taxes in the Petersburg Gubernia," and "Description of the Petersburg Gubernia." [55]

Radishchev was very interested in the economy of Siberia, in its native population, and the *"poselshchiki"* (settlers from Russia). "How rich is Siberia in its natural resources! What a powerful land! Centuries are still necessary; but as soon as it is settled, it is destined to play an important role in the chronicles of the world," he wrote to A. R. Vorontsov.[56]

Radishchev considered incorrect (especially in regard to Siberia) the division of Russia into gubernias without any consideration of the natural historical and economic development of her individual regions. In his opinion, a proper division of the Russian empire into gubernias "requires not bureaucratic art, but the heads and eyes of Palas, Georgi, and Lepekhin, even without glasses; attention must be paid to more than flowers and grasses." [57] Naming famous academicians and explorers of the natural wealth of Russia, Radishchev thereby emphasized the necessity of a scientific approach to the organization of the country into administrative regions.

Of great interest are Radishchev's views on tax policy and the influence of taxes on agriculture and peasant industries, to be found in "Note on the Taxes in the Petersburg Gubernia," "On the Tariff of 1766 and Its Duties," "On the Collection of the Head Tax," and

---

[54] *Ibid.* First published in a collection of articles *Sovetskaia etnografiia* [Soviet Ethnography], VI–VII (1947), 227–33.

[55] First published in the *Istoricheskii arkhiv,* V (1950), 220–73; Radishchev, *op. cit.,* III.

[56] *Ibid.,* III, 387. Letter to A. R. Vorontsov, July 24, 1791.

[57] *Ibid.,* III, 357. Letter to A. R. Vorontsov, March 15, 1791.

others.[58] These basic materials have great significance in the assessment of Radishchev's economic views. Their major importance lies obviously in the author's own clarification of a number of economic questions and in his observations on the legal situation of various layers in Russian serfdom in the eighteenth century. A significant part of these manuscripts can be viewed as preparatory work for "The Journey," and some of this material was used in "Description of My Property."

Radishchev studied in detail the condition of agriculture, particularly in Central Russia, the Petersburg gubernia, and Siberia. Everything interested him—the conditions of various groups of the peasantry and the kinds of taxes then in existence, the ways of collecting them, the burden of taxation on inhabitants of cities and villages, and the methods of "acquiring money" used by the peasants and craftsmen for payment of taxes. He sharply criticized the tax policy of the serf state.

The notes, "On the Tariff of 1766 and Its Duties" and "On the Bazaar," are directly linked to Radishchev's practical experience in his service in the Petersburg customs. His work in the field of foreign trade, in the Commerce College, and in the Petersburg Port Customs House is connected with a number of his writings, customs projects, and declarations.[59] Basically, these writings deal with the necessity for state regulation of imports and exports, for a protective tariff, and for measures against abuses in foreign trade.

About his economic occupations after assignment to service in the Commerce College, Radishchev wrote: "I felt it was my duty to acquire knowledge pertaining to trade in general, and so, in addition to my regular work, I read books pertaining to commerce, resumed my reading of history and travel, and tried to acquire [a knowledge—E. P.] of Russian legislation pertaining to trade in general." [60]

Radishchev's "Notes on a Journey to Siberia" and "Notes on a Journey from Siberia" [61] are important documentary testimonies on the life of the working classes. Like Radishchev's letters, they contain

---

[58] *Sobranie Vorontsova,* No. 398, 862, and 863. In the 3rd volume of Radishchev's works, his treatise "On Soul Tax" is included in "The Note on Taxes in St. Petersburg Gubernia" and his manuscript "On the 1766 Tariff . . ." is incorrectly labeled "A Project of a New General Customs Tariff."

[59] Radishchev, *op. cit.,* III, 51–93.

[60] Babkin, *op. cit.,* p. 188.

[61] Radishchev, *op. cit.,* III. In earlier editions the second work is entitled "A Diary of a Journey from Siberia."

important views on economic problems. Moreover, Radishchev produced a number of works and notes on historical themes, in which major attention is given to the conditions of life of the people, to their historical role, and to the causes which enabled the formation of the national character of the Russian people. Such is the nature of "An Abridged Narrative on the Acquisition of Siberia," [62] "Towards a History of Russia," [63] and others.

Radishchev's Struggle for the Overthrow of Autocracy

Radishchev did not separate the struggle against serfdom from the struggle for popular government; he stood for the revolutionary destruction of autocracy as a political form of the hegemony of the serfowner-pomeshchiki. This is self-evident.

Radishchev's revolutionary ideas developed in accordance with the growing demands for material improvement in society long before the abolition of serfdom took place in Russia. His deep and extensive criticism of serfdom and his proof of the necessity of a popular revolution for its destruction were far advanced. In "Conversation on What Constitutes a Son of the Fatherland" he criticized Aristotle, who had considered the order of things in which some reign and others are slaves to be established by nature. Radishchev wrote that nature was not so: if "a significant [large—E. P.] part of a generation of mortals is plunged into the darkness of barbarism, bestiality, and slavery," then "the cause of this is either that the generation has been cheated by life and circumstance, or has been compelled by somebody . . . or forced . . ." Radishchev understood that social conditions, and not nature, were responsible for the division of people into slaves and masters, into oppressors and oppressed. In this article the writer showed with compassion that in enserfed Russia the peasants are not considered people, that they are deprived even of the right to call themselves sons of their fatherland, that "they are not members of the state, they are not men, they are nothing more than machines moved by the tyrant . . . beasts of burden!"

Catherine was especially aroused by his expressions of hatred for autocracy and serfdom and by the idea of the revolutionary overthrow of autocracy and the destruction of serfdom. Having read "Letter to a Friend Living in Tobol'sk" after "Journey," she correctly interpreted these works: "It is obvious . . . his thoughts have been leading him

[62] *Ibid.,* II.
[63] *Ibid.,* III.

down this road for a long time." [64] As early as 1773, in a note on the word "autocracy," Radishchev revealed his democratic tendencies and defended the legality of popular judgment over the Tsar. In *Life of F. V. Ushakov,* published in 1789, Radishchev advanced the thought that man can bear much unpleasantness and persecution, but it is impossible to push him to the extreme. "The highest authority will be shattered by unreasonable strictness," wrote Radishchev, pursuing the same thought that excessive oppression will inevitably be destroyed by the people themselves. In the "Journey" he develops this idea fully.

Fear of the renewed and increased peasant movement within the country in the 1790's and of the possibility of the influence of the French Revolution was responsible for the special antagonism of Catherine towards the author of the ode, "Liberty," published in *Journey.* "This ode is completely and clearly seditious, since the Tsars are threatened with the block. The example of Cromwell is introduced with praise. These pages are of criminal intent, totally treasonable . . . ," [65] noted Catherine. The Empress read Radishchev's book almost a year after the fall of the Bastille. By persecution and rough justice for the revolutionary Radishchev and for the progressive Novikov, Krechetov, and Popov, and by prohibition of the distribution of the writings of Western enlighteners, Catherine sought to smother all "freedom of thought" and to save the autocratic-serf structure.

In "Liberty" Radishchev distinctly expressed a call to revolution and advanced the legality of a popular armed uprising and the justice of judgment over the tyrant-tsar; he praised a popular republic with a free union of the peoples of the multinational Russian empire. In this ode Radishchev directly presents "a prophecy on the future destiny of the fatherland," Russia; he clearly shows its difficult position and foresees its brilliant future. At the present time, Radishchev wrote, "the Tsar . . . sees in the people only foul creatures," and the people should thus come to an appropriate conclusion, throw out the tyrant, and destroy political oppression.

"Liberty" paints a stirring picture of the armed rebellion of the people and the overthrow of the autocracy. The people, having gained political power—"placed themselves on the throne"—gather in a meeting and proclaim a just popular judgment over the "crowned thief," sentencing him to death for his limitless evil-doing. The people charge the Tsar with abominating the labors of the people, detesting the toilers who till the soil, who extract metals from the earth, who forge

---

[64] For Catherine II's remarks on the *Journey from St. Petersburg to Moscow* see Babkin, *op. cit.,* p. 164.

[65] *Ibid.,* p. 163.

weapons for the army, and who cover the sea with ships, in a word, those who are responsible for the acquisition of wealth and well-being, and those who, not sparing their blood, protect the country from "external enemies." The people accuse the Tsar of taking away from the toilers the bits of food gained by their sweat and blood, ripping from the poorest their last rags, and gathering treasures for his court favorites. The people proclaim that they do not want to be "prisoners in their own fields" and prefer free labor on their land.

We present the most vivid verses of this remarkable ode:

10.

Let's examine the vast regions,
Where the tarnished throne of slavery rests,
Where all civil servants are peaceful
And see in the Tsar, God's image.
The Tsar's power protects religion here,
And in turn religion protects the Tsar;
They jointly oppress society;
The one attempts to fetter reason,
The other strives to destroy freedom;
"For the common good" they say.

13.

And we look on calmly,
As the ravenous dragon
Abuses incontestably
And poisons our joyful days.
Around the throne everyone
Kneels humbly upon his knees.
But tremble! The avenger nears;
He speaks, foretelling freedom,
And this report from land to land
Will flow, proclaiming freedom.

14.

A martial host will rise
To arm us all with hope;
And in the blood of the crowned tyrant
Each will hasten to wash his shame.
Everywhere I see the flash of sharp swords,
Death flying about in various forms;

It hovers over the proud head of the Tsar.
Rejoice chained people,
This nature's right of vengeance
Has called the Tsar to the scaffold.

22.

"Villain, the most cruel of all villains,
Evil has penetrated your head.
Criminal, first among them all,
Come forth, I summon you to judgment!
Enemy, all villainies are combined in you,
And not one will you escape
In your punishment.
Toward me you dared to turn your sting.
A single death is not enough;
Die! Die a hundred times!" [66]

Radishchev firmly believed that the time would come when the Russian people would not only overthrow the oppression of tsarism, but would free themselves also from "ecclesiastical authority"—the church. The victorious people would establish new laws based on freedom, equality for all, and an independent union of all peoples.

The process of the disintegration of the Russian empire and the formation of a union of peoples on a free basis are portrayed by Radishchev in "Liberty" and in commentaries on it in the chapter, "Tver," in the form of a "prophesy" about the future destiny of the fatherland, which "will disintegrate into its component parts," and then

From the depths of enormous ruin . . .
Will arise tiny stars,
And will adorn their immovable helms
With a crown of friendship,
And will direct the ship for the benefit of all,
And will crush the rapacious wolf . . .[67]

Radishchev's vision of a free union of peoples of the Russian empire on the basis of equality and for "the benefit of all" is especially remarkable for those times, when the autocratic-police regime ruling without limits inhumanly oppressed the so-called "natives."

---

[66] Radishchev, *op. cit.*, I, 3–4 and 5, 7.
[67] *Ibid.*, I, 16.

While he praised the examples of Cromwell, who executed the king and taught the people to avenge themselves, and also the war for independence in North America (1775–1783), Radishchev, at the same time, did not lose sight of the fact that the liberation of the American colonies from England's rule still did not extend to the entire American population. Slavery of the Negroes remained. Radishchev condemned with deep indignation the cruel treatment of the Indians by the American colonists, the inhuman exploitation of Negroes by the American slaveowners, and the colonial barbarism of the English in India.

The sympathetic attitude of Radishchev towards liberation movements of colonial peoples antagonized Catherine II. Pushkin described this displeasure: "The Empress, who strove to unite all the heterogeneous parts of the state, could not look with indifference on the separation of colonies from England's rule." [68]

On the basis of the experience of the Peasant War in Russia, the English revolution, and the war for independence in North America, Radishchev was convinced that no monarch would voluntarily surrender any of his power in the interests of the people.[69] Radishchev saw that in Russia "all those who could champion freedom, all great *otchinniki* [that is, men of property, people worried about their votchiny, about the acquisition of estates—E. P.], cannot be counted on to grant freedom, but only a very burdensome enslavement." [70]

Correctly understanding Radishchev's thought, Catherine II pointed out that he "placed hope on a revolution of peasants"; she judged Radishchev's book a work "serving the propagation of freedom and the elimination of the pomeshchiki." In her opinion, Radishchev "appointed himself as a leader to tear the sceptre from the hands of the Tsars by the book or some other manner . . ."

Radishchev developed a basis for the necessary destruction of autocracy and serfdom. "We are armed with the clubs of courage and nature for the overthrow of the hundred-headed monster . . . taking advantage, perhaps, of the autocrat's actions." [71] To Catherine it was clear that "he is a rebel worse than Pugachev." Pugachev had not rejected autocracy, and the popular masses had not risen as yet against the monarchy, but Radishchev was an irreconcilable enemy of the autocracy.

Radishchev firmly believed that the Russian people would cast off the hated yoke of autocracy and create a people's republic. From this

[68] Pushkin, *op. cit.*, VII, 355.
[69] Radishchev, *op. cit.*, I, 151.
[70] *Ibid.*, I, 352.
[71] *Ibid.*, I, 320.

point of view he criticized Montesquieu for his theory of the "separation of powers," which represented in essence the basis of an agreement between the ruling noble aristocracy and the bourgeoisie at the expense of the people. Radishchev also criticized Rousseau, who believed that a republican government was possible only in small states. Radishchev wrote: "Montesquieu and Rousseau have done harm with their philosophy. Having in mind the ancient republics, Asian governments, and France, the former advocated a separation of powers of the government. He forgot about his neighbors. The other, not accepting the lessons of history, thought that good government could exist only in small countries, but that in large ones force has to prevail." [72]

Radishchev also foresaw the possibility of civil war as a result of armed rebellion and the overthrow of the autocracy. He wrote: "the government with its dying breath will be on guard and will gather all its strength in order to deliver its final blow to crush rising liberty." The rebels, however, are invincible and the "oppressive government" will be destroyed. "The longed-for moment will come . . . O day! The chosen of all days!" Thus cried the poet-revolutionary, with the greatest faith in the future.

In addition, the revolutionary-republican called on the victorious people to be continually alert and to guard their freedom vigilantly:

> O! you, happy peoples,
> Where fate has granted you freedom!
> Guard the blessed gift of nature . . .
> Do not forget for even a moment
> That strength of power into cruel weakness,
> That light into darkness can be transformed.[73]

At the same time Radishchev understood that the revolution would not come at once, that the time was not yet ripe.

> But still years will pass
> Before this destiny is fulfilled;
> Far off, far off is still the end
> When all troubles will be extinguished.[74]

He wrote that even his grandsons would not see freedom, that before the fulfillment of his dreams a whole century might pass.

---

[72] *Ibid.*, III, 47.
[73] *Ibid.*, I, 14.
[74] *Ibid.*, I, 16.

Analysis and Revolutionary Criticism of Serfdom. Solution of the Land Question

The struggle to crush autocracy and to establish a people's republic Radishchev connected inextricably with the struggle against serfdom. Liquidation of serfdom was the basic theme in all of Radishchev's works. The absence in Russia of any state regulation of peasant obligations gave the pomeshchiki unlimited power over the serfs. The "Description of My Property" itemized the rights of a pomeshchik as follows: he can sell the peasant with his family or individually; he can compel him to work as much as the pomeshchik desires; he can punish the peasant as he wills, since he is both judge and executor of his sentences; the pomeshchik is the lord of all the peasant's possessions and of peasant children, and he arranges peasant marriages. "Thus the villager, if he makes use of anything, does so only by the lord's kindness." [75] The enserfed peasant cannot manage his work, his possessions, or even his own children.

Radishchev endeavored to prove theoretically his revolutionary position in his exposé of feudal methods of production. He considered it his duty as a citizen to show the harm for society of the enslavement of man by man and the contradiction of this enslavement both of natural law and of the economic interests of the country. Drawing his revolutionary conclusions about natural law from the teachings of the leaders of the enlightenment, Radishchev argued that peasants are human beings just like nobles: "they have limbs and feelings the same as you, and their right to use them should also be identical." [76] The enslavement of man by man he branded a cruel custom, a crime worthy of vengeance and punishment. It is impossible to consider a state prosperous where two-thirds of the population "is legally dead," deprived of civil rights. He opposed every form of slavery, and sharply deplored the brutal regime of exploiter-masters in America, where, in his words, a hundred proud citizens wallow in luxury, while their slaves are without shelter and other necessities of existence.

With great conviction Radishchev stressed the *economic arguments* against serfdom. He tried to reveal the inner content of the serf economy and the essence of those phenomena which he observed in society insofar as the level of science of that time permitted.

Analysing production under serfdom, he saw economic waste, especially in the *low productivity of the labor of the serfs.* He based this

---

[75] *Ibid.,* II, 187.
[76] *Ibid.,* I, 313.

view on the theory that the stimulus of human activity lies in man's interest in the results of his labor. "Because of this natural motivation, everything begun for oneself, everything that we do without coercion, we do well, with diligence and zeal. On the contrary, everything that is forced, everything that is not for our own benefit, is done lazily, badly, sloppily, and goes awry." [77] The enserfed peasants, by their role in production, were deprived of this incentive; they felt that it would "be sinful" for them to work with the same eagerness for the master as for themselves. "On the lord's ploughland a hundred hands feed one mouth, and on mine I have two to feed seven mouths . . . Even if you should work more at the master's work, he won't say thank you," said a peasant to the traveller. "The master doesn't pay taxes; he doesn't give up a sheep nor cloth nor a chicken nor butter." [78]

Radishchev showed the inequities in the distribution of the means of production and of consumer goods in an enserfed society. According to the nature of feudal property, neither the basic means of labor (land), nor the products of labor belong to the enserfed peasant. "The fields are not theirs, nor do the fruits of their labor go to them. And so they work lazily and do not care whether the land will turn into a wasteland during their work." [79]

Radishchev compared the work of the peasant on the lord's field with his work on land "given him by the arrogant owner, for most meagre subsistence." On his own alloted land the peasant, sparing no strength, overcomes all obstacles, works day and night and on holidays, "cares for himself, works for himself, and does things by himself." Radishchev defended forcefully this principle of personal material interest as one of the most important stimuli to the productivity of social labor in all branches of the national economy. The work of a toiler on his own behalf "gives him double satisfaction," but forced labor leads to a situation where "all fruits of farm labor are petrified or stunted; they would grow and be ample to satiate the citizens if the workers in the fields were zealous, if they were free." [80]

In the ode, "Liberty," Radishchev enthusiastically praised the constructive power, the grandeur, and the joy of free labor. The pomeshchik's land was, in the poet's simile, a grim stepmother and did not give a just reward for the peasant's labors. After the destruction of serfdom, after the abolition of pomeshchik land ownership and the

---

[77] *Ibid.*, I, 318–9.
[78] *Ibid.*, I, 233.
[79] *Ibid.*, I, 319.
[80] *Ibid.*

transfer of land to the peasants, the labor of the peasant and the result of his labor would be different.

> Under the shadow of slavery
> Golden fruits will not grow . . .
> But the spirit of freedom will warm the field,
> And joyfully the land will prosper at once,
> Everyone working and reaping for himself.[81]

Radishchev attributed the decline of Russian agriculture to serf exploitation and to the fact that "forced labor yields a smaller fruit." Such a system creates a deficit in the means of existence and impedes the growth of the population.

The pomeshchik frequently exacted not only the surplus, but also a part of the product which the peasant needed, and this demand lowered productivity. Characterizing this phenomenon, Radishchev wrote: "the producer does not give his surplus to society and does not have what he needs." [82] The amount of the "surplus," that is essentially, the surplus product, Radishchev placed in direct dependence on the method of production—on whether the producer worked for himself or for the exploiter—pomeshchik.

In Russian economic literature Radishchev was the first to offer a penetrating analysis of the question of the productivity of social labor. Pososhkov spoke about the necessity of "profit," but he did not relate its production with the social form of labor and proposed merely different rational methods of organizing labor, such as fixed tasks and others. Radishchev defended the free personal labor of the agriculturist on his own land and did not recognize any right of the landowners to appropriate the surplus labor of the peasant.

At the same time Radishchev did not view the peasantry as a homogeneous mass of toilers. He even then saw the beginning of the division of the peasantry. The rich peasants, as Radishchev showed, had an accumulation of cash, they hired farm hands for agricultural works, and bought land. They made up an insignificant upper class of the village at a time when the mass of the peasants was impoverished and could scarcely make ends meet. Explaining "the reasons for peasant poverty," Radishchev, in his own words, "always found that the pomeshchiki themselves were to blame."

Having analyzed the status and revealed the exploitative nature of the serf method of production, Radishchev clearly pointed out the vari-

---

[81] *Ibid.*, I, 4, 10.
[82] *Ibid.*, I, 315.

ous forms of serf exploitation in Russia. He studied the economic and legal position of various groups of peasants. He compared the burden of exploitation of state peasants with that of those assigned to factories and with that of pomestie peasants of both the obrok and barshchina types. He showed that the position of the state peasants was less burdensome than that of pomestie peasants. "The peasants in the St. Petersburg gubernia are property, as in the whole state," wrote Radishchev. "They are of two types: state and pomestie; a third type of peasants are colonists.

"The state peasants can be considered as assigned to the lands on which they live. They can be resettled by the director of household affairs under whose jurisdiction they fall. The land on which they live is considered state land, and they only have the use of it. The villages are given the right to buy land, but can this be called property?" [83]

Radishchev clearly saw that only a free man can realize the complete right of property, and the treasury (state) peasant under serfdom was not a free man. The tsars, by assigning state peasants to factories, gave them to various favorites, and courtiers continually transformed the state peasants into pomestie serfs. During her reign, Catherine II gave to her intimates 800,000 state peasants; Paul I turned over 600,000.

Radishchev compared the position of the state peasants with that of the pomestie-obrok peasants, who also had land for their own use, divided it among themselves in allotments, "set the obrok by measuring the land worked by them," decided all their internal problems "at meetings," and even "sometimes, with the permission of the pomeshchik, bought land." One essential difference existed between them. "There is only one difference, but a very important one, and that is that the state peasants pay a set tax which nobody can change without permission of the imperial majesty; the pomestie peasants, however, must pay whatever the lord wills." [84]

Radishchev's views indicate that the obrok form of exploitation of serf labor was easier for the peasant and contributed more to the country's economic development than the barshchina form. The obrok type permitted the expansion of crafts and insured the heavy manufacturing industry a working force of seasonal peasant workers.

Radishchev unmasked those serf owners who saw a major reason for the decline of agriculture in the obrok form of collection of feudal rents and who extolled the barshchina system as the best form of organization of the pomestie economy. He wrote with indignation that "the condition of the peasants tilling the soil for the master, or, to put it

[83] *Ibid.,* III, 130.
[84] *Ibid.,* III, 131.

more simply, living on his fields, is the most difficult . . . Indeed, if the lord has authority to give the peasants only as much land as the lord wants, if he is empowered to make them work as much as he wants, then with whom can you compare such an agriculturist? The only thing that saves the peasant from final exhaustion and death is the pomeshchik's greed. There is the peasant's protection." [85] In other words, if one could take the surplus product from the peasants without leaving them minimum subsistence, then the pomeshichiki would leave nothing to the peasant at all. But then the pomeshchik would be deprived of a source of wealth, a source of satisfaction of his avarice.

The so-called *mesiachina* [monthly] was an especially oppressive form of exploitation. Radishchev pointed out how the pomeshchik, in order to increase his income, "began to liken his peasants to tools without will or motivation." The pomeschik took the peasants from the fields and meadows and forced them to toil all day on manorial works. Radishchev showed that this mesiachina was tantamount to changing a serf into a slave. Mesiachina and transfer into household service deprived the peasants of any sort of economy of their own. They were thus dispossessed not only of immovable property, but also of movables. "Consequently those slaves had neither a cow, nor a horse, nor a ram, nor a sheep. The lord did not revoke permission to keep them, but took away the means to do so." [86] The peasant under mesiachina could not acquire property, because the pomeshchik had deprived him not only of the surplus product, but of all the means of labor. Not without reason he compared these peasants with the Lacedaemonians and called them slaves: they were like talking tools, like slaves in a slave system, divested of any means of production, turned into the complete property of the lord.

No different from mesiachina, and in many cases surpassing it in degree of exploitation, was the practice of a pomeshchik to lease whole villages or individual peasants to a creditor until the peasants worked off the debt of their pomeshchik. The peasants considered lease the worst form of work for the pomeshchik. "Now the tradition has grown up of giving villages in lease. And we [the peasants—E. P.] call it giving away our heads. The creditor skins the peasants; even in good times he leaves us nothing. In winter we cannot take leave, nor work in the town; all work for him, because he pays our head tax. It is an invention of the devil, to give one's peasants to a stranger to work," said a peasant to the traveller in the chapter, "Liubani." [87]

---

[85] *Ibid.*
[86] *Ibid.*, I, 325.
[87] *Ibid.*, I, 233.

Radishchev showed that in a serf village economy only the peasant is the direct producer. "The use of the natural powers of his peasants," that is, the exploitation of the labor of the enserfed peasants, is the source of the pomeshchik's wealth. The enserfed peasants "must work out of fear." Between the ruling class of pomeshchiki and the enserfed peasants *"the only tie is force,"* wrote Radishchev, noting the role of extra-economic compulsion under feudalism.[88]

Persistently and passionately opposed to slavery, Radishchev questioned not only the reactionary Russian representatives of the nobility, but also the conservative French spokesman of the Enlightenment, Voltaire, when they claimed that simple people, like oxen, always need drivers.

Similar in his views to the physiocratic school, Radishchev considered agriculture the basis of the Russian national economy. He affirmed that the poverty of the country emerged from the fact that the land was usurped by the pomeshchiki and that agriculture was not carried on in the interests of the people. "But the state," he wrote, "will prosper if agriculture is widespread and is directed to the benefit of the majority. But *if a small number of people usurp the land,* then commerce will profit and *the state will become poor,* as in the cases of Russia and Poland."[89]

Radishchev criticized sharply the feudal right of property, showed its historical limitation, and proved that only the agriculturist, the toiling peasant, should have the right of ownership of land, not the pomeshchik. He insistently defended the idea that only those who work the land should own it. "But who among us wears the chains, and who feels the burden of slavery? The agriculturist! the feeder of our empty stomachs, the satisfier of our hunger; he gives us health and prolongs our life yet has no right to dispose of what he works, nor what he produces. *Who then has more right to the field than its worker?*"[90]

Turning to history, Radishchev recalled that at one time the land was owned only by those who worked it "and he who cultivated it had exclusive use of it," in other words, the land and the product of labor belonged to the agriculturist. Contemporary society had deviated far "from the original practice regarding ownership" of land; social development led to the fact that "among us he who naturally has the right to it [ownership of land—E. P.] is not only completely excluded, but, while working alien fields, sees his own livelihood dependent on an-

---

88 *Ibid.,* I, 319. (Italics mine—E. P.)

89 *Sobranie Vorontsova,* No. 398, Sheet 140 (Italics mine—E. P.)

90 Radishchev, *op. cit.,* I, 314. (Italics mine—E. P.)

other's power." [91] Radishchev wrote that the seizure of the land by a few people led to the indigence of the majority of the population, and land ownership gave birth to serf relationships—"when man orders man."

Both in his immortal work, *Journey from Petersburg to Moscow,* and in later works, Radishchev persistently advocated the revolutionary theory of the peasants' inalienable right to land. In *Description of My Property* he continued to defend the peasant's right of ownership: "inasmuch as the settler pays a tax, by satisfying that requirement he should have the right of ownership." [92] He supported legislative guarantees of peasant ownership of land as a necessary step in the liberation of the peasants from personal dependence. Near the end of his life, in a special section of the "Project for a Civil Code," he considered property as a relationship between people, as an exclusive right of some over others.

Radishchev proved that the bourgeois right of ownership had no class distinction. "Anyone belonging to society can acquire property himself or through another only by reason of being a member of society." "Property is one of the objects which man had in view when he entered society; property became thereby a possession of every citizen, and to diminish his right to it would be a genuine violation of the original social contract." [93]

Radishchev's views on property were directed towards the abolition of feudal privileges, which strangulated the development of productive forces. He considered property the most important right of a citizen—of social man—while Diderot, Helvetius, and Quesnay recognized the right of property as a natural, given right of man.

According to Radishchev, the feudal form of ownership of land and of the peasant based on class monopoly was the major reason for social poverty in Russia and the chief hindrance to the development of economic power. To the end of his life he opposed serfdom and noble land ownership as a basis of serfdom, fought for equality of all citizens before the law, for laws promulgated "for the benefit of the millions," and not for a handful of lords, and struggled for the end to class privileges so that all citizens would have the same rights and obligations in society.

In his *Project for the Future* [94] "equality in possessions" should be interpreted not as an equal sharing of possessions, but as an equal

---

91 *Ibid.*, I, 315.
92 *Ibid.*, II, 187.
93 *Ibid.*, III, 204, 216.
94 *Ibid.*, I, chapter "Khotilov" in the *Journey.*

right of all citizens to acquire property. Radishchev wrote that future society must "clarify the acquisition and preservation of property . . . The boundary which divides the property of one citizen from another is deep, and seen, and reverently respected by all." [95]

Radishchev solved independently the important theoretical and practical questions relating to the forms of property. Realization of his solutions to the existing economic problems would have promoted the progressive development of Russia.

He propagandized for the democratic *right* of equal ownership, but not the equalization of possessions. In his various writings he demonstrated convincingly that equality in possessions among the peasants could not exist for the clear and simple reason that their incomes are not the same, even for portions of land identical in size. He used concrete examples to show that, in addition to the size of the land, a decisive influence on the amount of peasant income was wielded by the richness of the soil, the amount of labor which the peasant expended in cultivating the soil (and which depends on the size of the family and the quality of the tools), the proximity of markets, the presence or absence of nonagricultural industry, and so on. All these factors varied greatly in the immense Russian empire and contributed to the development of inequality of possessions among the peasantry. Therefore Radishchev excluded the possibility of equalizing possessions among the peasants and pressed for freedom of their economic activity and for liquidation of all feasible class restrictions. Such reforms, in his opinion, would improve the material prosperity of the people.

His views on equality represented, in essence, a bourgeois-democratic concept of equality profoundly revolutionary for the epoch of the struggle against serfdom. It was at the end of the eighteenth century that he saw not only the inequality of possessions among the peasantry, but even the beginning of the beginning of the process of its stratification. From among the peasants were emerging entrepreneurs —merchants and brokers, who enslaved the direct producers—hunters, fishermen, cattlemen, agriculturists, and craftsmen; the peasants received unequal income from agriculture and from trade. A large portion of the peasantry was poor, but there also were some rich men among them who had money "in the treasury." The latter hired farm hands and bought land, even if in the name of a pomeshchik.

Nowhere did Radishchev speak of the peasantry as a uniform mass, equally miserable throughout. He soundly evaluated the real processes of Russia's economic development as a result of an intensive study of

[95] *Ibid.*, I, 312.

agriculture, industry, and trade, and of the various classes then existing in society and of their irreconcilable contradictions. His contribution to the development of economic science was enormous. The materials which he collected and analyzed are of immense value in characterizing the Russian economic system in the second half of the eighteenth century.

The assertion in our literature that Radishchev favored the preservation of communal land ownership and common allotments of land is erroneous. He did not specially study the question of communal landownership. In his investigation of the agriculture of the Petersburg gubernia in the 1780's, Radishchev, a half century before Haxthausen,[96] the "discoverer" of the Russian commune, gave a description of all existing aspects of communal *land usage*. Haxthausen saw everything through the eyes of a very reactionary Prussian pomeshchik. Radishchev, however, showed the complete dependence of the enserfed commune on the pomeshchik and on the feudal-absolute state. Both the pomeshchik and the official of "household affairs" could, at any time, separate the commune member from the land, despite the existence of mutual responsibility which tied the peasant to the commune.

Radishchev wrote: "The state peasants administer themselves. They have heads, elders, and tenths, who manage the internal order; social affairs are decided in meetings: whatever the commune—that is, the meeting of the peasants—decides is respected as law. Division of land among themselves, allotment of taxes, drafting of recruits—all is done by agreement of the commune." Similarly, "the pomestie peasants, when their master obligates them by obrok, usually use all the land belonging to the village. They divide the land among themselves in allotments . . . Their ownership is in strips, and, especially with an increase in the population, it often happens that they make a new partition of land. They divide the meadows as they do the fields, but the forests are held in common. Sometimes with the pomeshchik's permission they buy land. They decide their internal affairs in meetings; they are administered by elders chosen by themselves, or by heads, administrators, or stewards appointed by the lords.[97] Here Radishchev pointed out the prevalence of the common use of land and of the reallotment of land among the state and pomestie obrok peasants.

---

[96] See A. Haxthausen, *Issledovaniia vnutrennikh otnoshenii narodnoi zhizni i v osobennosti selskikh uchrezhdenii Rossii* [Studies of Internal Relations of National Life and Especially Rural Institutions in Russia]. Translated from the German. (1847).

[97] Radishchev, *op. cit.*, III, 130–1.

His attitude towards communal utilization and division of land was dealt with in another work, "On the Collection of Head Tax." In his remarks on the margins he wrote: "Although the peasants pay for the land they hold, it is not similar in quality. In order to give everyone a like portion of good land, they divide it so that it is extremely poor for agriculture, but good for equality." [98] Radishchev noted the positive aspect of communal land use—the division of land by the members of the commune as a means of partially alleviating for a certain time the inequality of property among the peasants. Only in this sense were divisions a means of establishing equality. In the basic text to which the above footnote is appended Radishchev wrote about the actual extremes in the unequal burden of personal taxes which were collected from the peasant "soul" without consideration of his economic ability to pay.

Radishchev's remarks on the division of land were closely related to his generally negative appraisal of the tax policy of the autocracy. All personal feudal taxes, among which the head tax was the major one, had an external "mask of equality," but in essence they were extremely unequal, because the income of individual peasants was not uniform. Peasants were forced to adapt themselves to this state "equality" by their own methods of dividing the land periodically and thus temporarily mitigating the inequality of possessions. Only for this "equality" were divisions "good," in Radishchev's opinion. But divisions were "very bad for agriculture," since they curtailed the peasant's incentive to improve the land by using fertilizers.

It is generally recognized that this divisive system reduced the fertility of the soil and led to the decline of agriculture. Radishchev considered this a serious defect of the communal use of land. He could not study communal *landownership,* for in eighteenth century Russia land did not belong to the peasant communes, but to the pomeshchiki or the state treasury. The same thought was presented in the fragmentary note, "Annual Division of Lands Among the Peasants." "Who would have thought that our own times would accomplish in Russia a condition which the best legislators of antiquity had sought and about which the new ones do not think and on which the exquisite love of the Russian peasant for his dwelling depends?" [99]

Thus Radishchev had only a positive reaction to the division of land this major aspect of communal use of land—insofar as it allowed the peasants to release themselves from the actual inequality of their obligations to the state. *But Radishchev's program demanded the destruc-*

[98] *Sobranie Vorontsova,* No. 398, Sheet 59.
[99] Radishchev, *op. cit.,* III, 132.

tion of pomestie landownership and the establishment of private ownership of land by the peasants. It is not accidental that the *Journey* (1790), *Description of My Property* (1800–1801), and *Project for a Civil Code*" (1801–1802) do not have a single word about communal land ownership or the necessity of preserving divisions of land.

Radishchev criticized severely feudal land relationships. He defended the peasants' right of private property and the freedom of small independent producer-peasants from all forms of feudal dependence. Such a solution to the question of landownership corresponded with increasing material demands in Russia and exerted a most progressive influence on future economic development. The realization of Radishchev's reforms would have inevitably accelerated the development in Russia of capitalist production in all fields and would have promoted agriculture.

In essence, Radishchev was the first to recognize the necessity of a struggle on the part of the peasantry to attain an economic status that would enable it, in Lenin's words, "not to vegetate, not to pine away on the land, but to develop productive forces, to move agriculture forward." [100]

One should note here that, in his contention against serf exploitation of small producers and for the freedom of their economic activity, Radishchev did not understand, and at that time could not have understood, that small private ownership of the means of production in general and of land in particular inevitably produces a stratification of the peasantry into bourgeoisie and proletariat and gives rise to a new, capitalist form of exploitation. Radishchev defended the small producer from serf exploitation, and herein lies the progressiveness of his views.

In proposing and proving the proposition that land should be owned by those who cultivate it, Radishchev came close to the idea of the complete liquidation of pomestie land ownership—liquidation of the basic feudal method of production. This was Radishchev's greatest contribution. Not a single spokesman of the eighteenth century Enlightenment posed the land question as Radishchev did.

By showing that the seizure of land by a few, that is, the monopoly of pomestie ownership of land, was the basis of the exploitation of the enserfed peasants, Radishchev revealed the fundamental defect of feudalism: the enrichment of one class—the pomeschiki—at the expense of appropriating the labor of another class—the enserfed peasants. He disclosed also that the pomeshchiki, by realizing part of the products

[100] Lenin, *op. cit.*, XIII, 211.

of their economy on the market and by receiving monetary obrok, had "in their pockets the labor and sweat of their peasants for the whole year . . ." [101] From these conditions Radishchev drew his conclusion about the origin of the pomeshchik's wealth. *"The wealth of this vampire does not belong to him. It is earned by plundering,* an act which *deserves severe punishment by law."* [102] He invoked "humanity's vengeance" on the pomeshchiki and called them social thieves, greedy beasts, and insatiable leeches.

"How does the state benefit," asked Radishchev, "when several thousand quarters more grain a year are produced by those who are placed on a level with oxen and are assigned to plough a heavy furrow?" [103] Describing the horrible conditions of peasant huts, and the extremely low, wretched standard of living of the pomeshchik peasants, Radishchev said with bitterness: "These are what they justly consider the source of state abundance, strength, and might." [104]

Radishchev was the first in our economic literature to offer a well-developed analysis of peasant production on pomestie land. His data clearly confirm Lenin's words that serfdom was connected to a low, plodding stage of technique and extreme backwardness. Radishchev investigated the economics of the peasant agriculture of a pomestie obrok village which was typical of the central belt of Russia. He noted especially that the strip system and the remoteness of land—results of communal land usage by the peasants and of pomeshchik ownership of the land—impeded rational agriculture. He correctly pointed out the shortage of arable land and related it to the low level of technique in agricultural production as a whole, to the poor breeding of cattle, the primitiveness of tools and agricultural methods, the extreme poverty of "peasant capital" in buildings, cattle, and tools, and the immoderately inferior value of peasant labor. "Methods of production among us are not varied, and therefore grain is not produced in quantity. If the peasant is a family man, then he is close to being poor; if he is single, almost every peasant is rich, but, of course, not from agriculture." [105] Only a more rational management of agriculture would have been able to solve the problem of scanty arable land, but it was impossible under conditions of serfdom.

The method followed by Radishchev in his study of the village econ-

---

[101] Radishchev, *op. cit.*, II, 350.

[102] *Ibid.*, I, 326. (Italics mine—E. P.)

[103] *Ibid.*, I, 325–6.

[104] This hint is on physiocratic theories which considered agriculturists the only productive class.

[105] Radishchev, *op. cit.*, II, 179.

omy and his concrete analysis of serfdom deserve attention. Above all, he studied the level of development of productive forces. He supplied data on the land reserves, its distribution by premises and among individual owners, on the distribution of land from the point of view of proximity to or distance from the homestead, and on the quality of land. The three-field system was used. The land in all fields was divided into strips among individual peasant households according to the number of people, counting two people per peasant household (male and female).

He gave a description of all agricultural work and the calendar dates of its accomplishment. In the nonblacksoil gubernias the peasants plowed the land to be seeded with various grains two and three times, and in the south, where the soil was black, once. In the spring they sowed oats, buckwheat, barley, flax, and hemp; in the winter, rye. He described also the truck gardens where cabbages, radishes, cucumbers, onions, carrots, turnips, beets, and "potatoes or ground-apples" were grown. Radishchev calls all agricultural techniques "unproductive"; that is, primitive methods of cultivation were used, and yields were low.

In addition, he estimated the size of the working force and of households in the fields. Each household (two villagers with a horse) had four and two-thirds desiatiny of land. The detailed account of the work of a peasant horse for the summer is very interesting. "Each desiatina must be ploughed, let us say, twice and harrowed twice. Of the four and two-thirds desiatiny, two-thirds are cultivated in the year, that is, forty-seven sazhens wide and eighty long. Allowing three furrows to an arshin, there will be 423 furrows eighty sazhens in length; multiplying by two, the horse walks 270⅔ verst with the plow and thirty verst with the harrow, allowing two furrows per sazhen. Thus the horse covers 300 verst three times a year, that is in twelve days, twenty-five each day; add to this fifty trips for fertilizer, four for hay, of which two are of thirteen verst, and a whole harvest of grain—one is surprised at how peasant horses can do this work, considering that in winter their fodder consists of a little scattered straw, and in the summer, grass; add to this all the trips into the woods for firewood and other needs, transporting state and manorial officials . . ."[106] Pointing out the "bad fate" to which these horses were subjected, Radishchev was not so much concerned with horses, of course, as with the peasants, who did so much physical work.

---

106 *Ibid.*

Radishchev described other means of production—the work cattle, tools, buildings, and seed. He emphasized that "all cattle are of small size and poor stock." Utilization of cattle was far from full, and their care was very bad.

Having noted that "the first means for cultivating the land are work cattle," Radishchev wrote that "agricultural tools are the second means of cultivation. The same simple tools have been used for practically a hundred years"—the plow with two blunt plowshares, the wooden harrow with thirty-six teeth, the scythe, rake, sickle and spade for the garden. "With such unartful implements the land is cultivated here. Any innovation is opposed both by prejudice and by the insufficiency of peasant capital and the negligence of the agriculturists." [107]

In addition to the generally poor technical-economic standards, the buildings were in bad shape. "a closed court, very muddy in spring and fall. The cattle shed, the rather small hay shelter, and the usual barn for drying crops were dangerous structures . . ." [108]

Finally, the last means of production—the "deposits given to the land," that is, the seed and fertilizer, were inferior. The only type of fertilizer was manure, which scarcely covered one-seventh of the land, and "no other kind is known here."

After explaining the nature and sequence of agricultural work, the condition and level of technique, tools, and means of production, Radishchev described the economic results of the labor of peasants employed in agriculture and in crafts. He calculated the gross income from grain, flax, hemp, and work cattle. The harvest in the village was very low. He analyzed next the expenses of the village, which included all the state, communal, and manorial taxes, and also the demand for products within the village. One-fourth of the gross revenue of the village was spent in payment of money taxes and obrok alone. Internal needs for grain and other products comprised about three-fifths of the entire income.

Thus the economy of an enserfed obrok village at the end of the eighteenth century still had a clearly "natural" character. After the surplus products for the pomeshchiki and the state were deducted, the share retained by the peasants scarcely took the form of marketable goods. It was needed by the producers themselves within their own household. The peasants produced for themselves all their necessities and sold the products of their labor not because of their abundance, but because of the need to pay state and pomeshchik money taxes. Ex-

---

107 *Ibid.*, II, 181.
108 *Ibid.*

penditures for purchased goods comprised very paltry sums—only thirty rubles from the entire expenditure of 4,300 rubles for the whole village. By Radishchev's calculations, two rubles of net income from agriculture were received per capita of the population. By no means did this mean that every peasant had even the most insignificant surplus of income over expenditures. "This calculation, of course, is not exaggerated, for even if one can find ten households where they have a capital of from twenty-five to two hundred rubles, others do not have a kopek in the treasury." [109] Moreover, many peasants did not have enough grain for subsistence over the course of a year.

Radishchev also studied "handcrafts and other means of livelihood, outside of agriculture," [110] and various trades by which the peasants procured money for the payment of taxes and for food. Some peasants went "with sieves and tubs to the steppe grain centers, where they exchanged the goods for grain," [111] or left the town for the entire winter. Insecurity drove the peasant from the village; he was forced to seek other methods of earning money.

In his remarkable analysis of the economy of the enserfed village Radishchev did not limit himself merely to a description of the processes of production. As in all of his works, he connected this analysis with an explanation of the social conditions. On the first page of *Description of My Property,* the investigator pointed to the exploitative nature of the farm to be described. "Blessed be ye, blessed be ye, if all the fruits of your labors were only yours. But, oh sorrowful plight, the villager cultivates alien fields and himself is a stranger, alas!"

Radishchev examined in detail the peasant's obligations "toward his master" and toward the state. The power of the pomeshchik was so all-inclusive that the only thing "the lord cannot do is free his villager from state taxes . . . arrange marriage between relatives, and force them to eat meat during Lent." [112] Radishchev's analysis of the economy of the obrok serf village is a significant step forward in the development of Russian and world economic science. He applied completely the scientific method of investigation, showed thoroughly the low level of agricultural production, and, with precision and clarity unusual for those times, revealed its social bases.

Radishchev, like some of his predecessors and contemporaries, pro-

---

109 *Ibid.,* II, 183.
110 *Ibid.*
111 *Ibid.,* II, 186.
112 *Ibid.*

jected a series of measures for the intensification of agriculture and its rationalization. He felt that "truck gardening deserved more attention not only of village inhabitants, but of the government as well," [113] because a small area of land could give a greater yield.

He recommended fertilization of all plowed land with manure and mineral fertilizers, better rotation and seeding of grasses, improvement of agricultural tools, preliminary watering and treatment of seeds, row sowing, and so forth. He also took into consideration foreign methods, but he wrote that all these experiences and improvements were unattainable under an enserfed peasant economy.

Radishchev tried to reveal the causes for the backwardness of agriculture. The autocratic serfdom structure "is opposed to all innovations" and was the major impediment to economic development. He insisted that, even if there were an inventor who could demonstrate an easy and inexpensive method for "transforming all soil into black soil," despite the worthiness of his invention such an innovator would not receive recognition under existing conditions. "Our governments would not recognize his labors, and the life-giving new Heraclius would live out his life unesteemed, scorned, and in exile . . ." [114]

* * *

Radishchev recognized the need for the revolutionary destruction of serfdom at a time when it was prevalent not only in Russia, but also in a number of countries of Western Europe. In Prussia more than two-thirds of the population owed personal allegiance to a lord or were attached to the land; in Denmark the nobility estimated its wealth in a manner similar to the Russian pomeshchiki, according to the number of serfs owned; [115] in Hungary the barshchina was also without any limit; in France only a small number of peasants remained in personal dependence on feudalists, but a great number of feudal obligations and payments to the pomeshchiki and state barshchina were still preserved.

Radishchev believed in the justification of the peasant uprising led by Pugachev, and he also considered a popular revolution in general lawful and inevitable if a decisive and complete liquidation of serfdom were to be effected. He clearly saw that all previous proposals advanced by progressive people of Russia, such as Korobin, Kozelskii,

---

[113] *Ibid.*, II, 178.
[114] *Ibid.*, II, 192.
[115] Semevskii, *Krestiane v Rossii v tsarstvovanie Imperatritsy Ekateriny*, II, I, 19.

and the other deputies to the Legislative Commission of 1767, to limit the powers of the pomeshchiki over the person and possessions of the peasant met stubborn opposition on the part of the spokesmen of the nobles and their government. He did not consider Paul's decree of 1797 regarding a three-day barshchina a law, but merely a wish that fully corresponded with reality. The pomeshichiki were never called upon to answer for violation of this decree.

He pointed out the serf owners' instinctive fear of freedom for their dependents. He ironically quoted their arguments. "Agriculture will die; its tools will be ruined; arable land will become desert and will be covered with fruitless grass; the people, having no authority above them, will drowse into laziness and will become parasites and fall into discord. The cities will feel the crushing hands of ruin. Crafts will be foreign to the citizens; handiworkers will lose their diligence and zeal; trade will sink back into its source; wealth will cede its place to niggardly poverty; splendid edifices will decay; laws will be obscured and become covered with unreality. Then the great social structure will begin to tumble apart and will breathe its last, disunited from the whole; then the tsarist throne . . . will tumble; then . . . society will witness its own end." [116] It must be added that these same arguments were actually expressed by Prince M. M. Shcherbatov in defense of serfdom. [117, 118]

In refuting these arguments, Radishchev directly set the task of destroying the class of exploiters, which stood in the way of progress and suppressed national abilities. He expressed unshakeable confidence that the people, by overthrowing and destroying their tyrants, would take their fate into their own hands and produce out of their own midst more worthy leaders of the state and of social life than the parasitic representatives of the exploiting class. Radishchev viewed "the people" as the peasantry and artisans closely connected with the peas-

---

116 Radishchev, *op. cit.*, I, 275–6.

117 M. M. Shcherbatov, "Razmyshlenie o neudobstvakh v Rossii dat svobodu krestianam i sluzhiteliam, ili zdelat sobstvennost imenii" [Thoughts Concerning Inconveniences in Granting Freedom to Peasants and Servants in Russia or to Turn Estates into Personal Property], *Chteniia v Obshchestve istorii i drevnostei rossiiskikh,* Bk. III (1861).

118 In the noble-bourgeois literature a widely spread view prevailed even in the XIX century that peasants could not develop their farms without the pomeshchik's domination and supervision. This was ridiculed by Engelhardt: "The peasant is stupid and cannot organize himself by his own efforts. If no one will take care of him he will cut down all timber, will kill all birds, will catch all fish, will spoil all the land, and will die." A. N. Engelhardt, *Iz derevni. 12 pisem* [From the Village. 12 Letters] (Moscow: Sotsekgiz, 1937), p. 320.

antry and also with the workers engaged in manufacturing, for the most part made up of obrok peasants.

In *Journey from Petersburg to Moscow* (the chapter "Gorodnia") Radishchev wrote the inspired and prophetic words: "O! if the slaves, weighted down with fetters, raging in their despair, would with the iron that bars their freedom crush our heads, the heads of their inhuman masters, and redden their fields with our blood! What would the state lose by that? At once from their midst great men would rise from among them to replace the defeated generation; but they would be of other mind and without the right to oppress others. This is no dream, but my vision penetrates the dense curtain of time that veils the future from our eyes; I see through a whole century." [119]

The noble, and also the bourgeois, spokesmen slandered the people; they believed that the "rabble" would destroy all culture. The noble and bourgeois historians attributed to Radishchev a fear of popular anger; they stated that Radishchev advised the pomeshchiki to free the peasants because he dreaded peasant disturbances which would completely destroy all cultural achievements. Radishchev's remarkable statement, quoted above, fully disproves this slander. Radishchev openly called the oppressed people to revolution and saw within them the guarantee of progress in all areas of life.

While refuting the serfowners' contention that society would disintegrate without the nobles' authority over the peasants, Radishchev advanced one of the most important revolutionary propositions, in which is apparent his great faith in the strength and capability of the Russian people: the liberated people from their midst will produce most worthy and competent leaders of political and economic life. By assigning the decisive role in the historical process to the toiling people, and not to tsars and noble serfowners, Radishchev proves the necessity and lawfulness of popular revolution in Russia.

The economic anomalies which Radishchev revealed were to be destroyed together with serfdom. The greater the accumulation of these contradictions, the more powerful can be the indignant explosion of the exploited masses. "When the stream is blocked in its course it accumulates more power the firmer the block. And, once it breaks through the bulwark, nothing can oppose its flow. Such are our brothers, kept by us in chains. They await the occasion and the hour. The bell will toll . . . Death and scourge are promised us for our grimness and inhumanity." [120]

But Radishchev was not afraid of the explosion and considered the

---

[119] Radishchev, *op. cit.*, I, 368–9.
[120] *Ibid.*, I, 320.

punishment of the oppressors by the oppressed to be fully justified. In several places in his *Journey,* he turns directly to the peasants with a call to violent destruction of the hegemony of the serfowner-pomeshchik. "Break the tools of his agriculture; set fire to his threshers, his drying barns, his granaries; scatter the ashes over the fields on which his tyranny was perpetrated . . ." [121] The peasants had followed the "pretender" Pugachev because "they desire nothing except freedom from the yoke of their owners." [122] The revolutionary destruction of serfdom Radishchev considered as security and as a thrust of the mighty development of the country's productive forces, the flourishing of the economy, science, and culture.

Radishchev viewed the nobility as "destroyers . . . forging the chains and tightening the fetters of the most useful members of society." The *Journey* cited examples of the punishment by peasants of their pomeshchiki, their "elemental opposition . . . to the infernal domination." He justified the action of the peasants and felt that they "are not guilty before the law." Speaking of the pomeshchik-tyrant, he cried: "Everyone who has enough strength should take revenge on him for the offenses he committed." [123]

Radishchev well understood that his revolutionary ideas "are anathema to the nobles' society . . . anathema to the supreme government." He chose his revolutionary path consciously. Radishchev's works are permeated with active propaganda for a popular revolution, which, in his opinion, could be accomplished by the oppressed peasantry, the "entombed people," the "slaves bound with heavy chains," aroused by "the very burden of their enslavement." Exhorting the peasants to rebel, Radishchev did not realize that the spontaneous indignation of the peasantry against the serf oppression could not lead to victory, since it was not headed by the proletariat.

But Radishchev's greatest contribution is that he, the first in the history of Russia, appealed to the toiling people to overthrow serfdom and autocracy. Using contemporary scientific language, Radishchev was first to prove objectively the necessity to liquidate the base and the superstructure of feudal society by an aroused people and thus pave the way to a law of obligatory correspondence of productive relationships to the nature of productive forces.

Justice, however, demands that we note that, while being the first fighter for and propagator of popular revolution against autocracy and serfdom, Radishchev, at the same time, did not exclude the possibility

---

[121] *Ibid.,* I, 326.
[122] *Ibid.,* I, 320.
[123] *Ibid.,* I, 279.

of freeing the peasants by reforms from above. He advanced arguments, both economic and political, for such a move. He spoke of the poor productivity of forced labor and the disadvantages to the state of a low standard of living of the basic mass of the population—the peasantry—of the natural right of peasants to equality before the law, of the possibility of putting an end to peasant disturbances, and so on.

Moreover, in his study of the correlation of forces "at the summit," "and cognizant that the supreme power is incapable" of freeing the peasants at once, Radishchev "outlines the way . . . toward gradual liberation of the tillers of the soil in Russia." [124] This project consisted of the following. At first the household peasants were to be freed, and the pomeshchiki were to be prohibited from taking any agriculturists into their homes for service or work, and "should the pomeshchik take one . . . then the agriculturist becomes free." The peasants were to be allowed to enter into matrimony without asking their lord's consent.

Further, in the process of paving the way for the liberation of the peasants, Radishchev proposed a change in the laws of "ownership and protection of the agriculturists," which should be accomplished in the following way. "The portion of land that they cultivate must be their own property, for they themselves pay the head tax. The property acquired by a peasant should belong to him; nobody can deprive him of it arbitrarily." Thus, even before the liberation of the peasants from personal dependence, Radishchev proposed to deprive the pomeshchiki of the ownership of allotted land. Moreover, the peasant should have the right to acquire immovable property, that is land, not in the name of the pomeshchik, but in his own name. The peasant should have his civil rights restored and be guaranteed the right to protection of his person and possessions in court; "he should be judged by his peers, who should be chosen from among pomeshchik peasants"; punishment of a peasant without a trial should be forbidden, nor should he be deprived of property without due process of law. Prior to general liberation, individual peasants should be allowed "freely to acquire liberty, upon payment of a set sum to the lord."

The accomplishment of all the enumerated measures Radishchev regarded as preliminary steps in the liberation of all the peasants. "After this, the complete abolition of slavery will follow." [125] Such were the contents of Radishchev's project for the eventual emancipation of the peasants.

What does this project of Radishchev's mean in essence, and what place does it hold in his system? Most important and decisive in the

[124] *Ibid.*, I, 322.
[125] *Ibid.*

struggle of the enserfed peasants against the pomeshchiki was the destruction of the serf's dependence, the abolition of pomeshchik ownership of the land, and the overthrow of the pomeshchiki rule. Radishchev's "Project for the Future" expressed these democratic aspirations. In substance, it demanded: 1. Gratuitous transfer of all lands cultivated by the peasants (and in obrok estates all the land was usually being used by the peasants), that is, *full ownership*, to the peasants, without the shadow of a hint of any sort of compensation to the pomeshchiki. 2. Complete *abolition of the personal dependence* of all peasants on pomeshchiki without any possibility of a redemption payment. 3. *Destruction of the power of the pomeshchiki* ("Extinguish the barbarian custom, disintegrate the power of the tigers!"), restoration to the peasants of the rights of citizenship, and liquidation of all class privileges and priorities.[126]

All these demands were actually revolutionary, as they were aimed at the abolition of pomeshchik property and authority and the destrution of the entire political and economic structure. Therefore Radishchev himself did not believe that his project could be accomplished under eighteenth century conditions, and he called it a "Project for the Future." In this program the author saw "everywhere the citizen of the future." [127] It is not accidental that the "Project" for gradual liberation of Russian agriculturists was written *after* the revolutionary calls to forceful overthrow of pomeshchiki authority and to liquidation of their ownership of the land.

Recalling the peasant uprising under Pugachev, Radishchev wrote that even after their suppression the peasants "await the opportunity and the hour" to try again to free themselves "from the yoke of their owners," that "time will raise the scythe, it awaits the favorable hour, and the first adulator or humanitarian who rouses the unhappy ones will speed the moment. Wait and see." To help awaken the people and to stir them to revolution—this Radishchev regarded as his lifework.

Thus the content of his project for gradual liberation was prepared in the interests of the peasants and in no way sacrificed these interests to the benefit of the pomeshchiki, but its *method* of solution can be evaluated only as a vacillation towards liberalism. Similar vacillations to a greater or lesser degree were also made by other revolutionaries of the first generation.

Why did Radishchev, the revolutionary, propose the path of reform? The fact is that, being a materialist in his explanation of the develop-

---

[126] *Ibid.*, III, 406. "These divisions [into classes—E. P.] often in reality resemble monopolies." Letter to A. R. Vorontsov, November 26, 1791.

[127] *Ibid.*, I, 322.

ment of nature and thought, Radishchev remained an idealist in his understanding of the bases of social development and the nature of the power of the state. He explained the origin of the state by the idealistic theory of the social contract. Like all other eighteenth century enlighteners, he overestimated the power and role of human reason in overcoming social contradictions and rectifying social injustice. He did not believe in the beneficence of "enlightened absolutism." He hoped that it was possible somehow to compel, to oblige, and to persuade the representatives of the government to solve the peasant problem justly from the point of view of the peasantry. In the *Journey* he frequently appealed to the pomeshchiki of their own free will to liberate the peasants if not out of humanitarianism; if not out of understanding of the economic evils of enslavement of the producers, then at least out of fear of the inevitability of peasant insurrection. Radishchev foresaw that the longer the serfowners remained obstinate the stronger would be the explosion of peasant rage and vengeance. The peasants "await the opportunity and the hour . . . We will see around us the sword and the poison. Death and scourge will be our reward for your severity and inhumanity . . . That is what lies before us, and that is what we should expect. Ruin gradually brings grief, and the danger already hovers over our heads . . . Wait and see."[128]

It should be emphasized that this cycle of ideas by no means played as important, or as major, a role in Radishchev's system as has been judged by the bourgeois historians, who have pictured Radishchev as an ordinary noble liberal. Radishchev strengthened his project not so much by the arguments of logic as by the force of pressure "from below," the pressure of peasant upheaval. In essence, *his attitude towards reform was not conciliatory, but revolutionary*. Nowhere did he seek reconciliation of the interests of the opposing classes—the pomeshchiki and the enserfed peasantry—and he never sacrificed the interests of the exploited masses.

The question of *agrarian relationships* occupies a very important position in Radishchev's economic views. Not only because of his method of abolishing serfdom, that is, *popular* revolution, but also because of his solution of the agrarian question, the *transfer of land to the peasants,* Radishchev should be considered the originator of revolutionary and democratic ideas which received their full theoretical expression later in the works of the Russian revolutionary democrats. On the basis of the experience of the massive anti-feudal peasant move-

---

[128] *Ibid.,* I, 320–1.

ment which had shaken feudalism in the last third of the eighteenth century, Radishchev rose to the summit of revolutionary economic science of the time. The nobility's reaction succeeded temporarily in curbing peasant uprisings, in driving the "illness" within, but it did not eliminate its causes, and it failed to suppress the development of revolutionary theory, for which Radishchev laid the foundation.

In his literary works Radishchev expressed the general democratic tasks of the anti-feudal revolution. The realization of his program would have meant capitalistic development on the basis of a peasant economy free from the yoke of serfdom.

Radishchev's analysis of the feudal ownership of land, the interrelations of pomeshchiki and enserfed peasants, the causes of the low productivity of serf labor, and the sources of pomeshchik-serfowner wealth showed how deeply he delved into the problems of the feudal-serf society.

He did not limit himself to criticism of the feudal method of production. In his works he also developed a revolutionary program for solving the agrarian question and threw light on a number of other theoretical problems of political economy, such as the origin of the wealth of the owners of manufacturing and trading enterprises, the exchange and the price of goods, money, and credit, and feudal taxes. He devoted much attention to the subject of industrial development.

On the Development of Industry

Radishchev examined the problems of Russian industrial development in the light of the economic situation and the level of productive forces. From the time of Peter I Russia has rapidly forged ahead. Radishchev judged the economic policy of Peter I favorably and felt that he had earned the title "the Great" precisely because of his reforming activity, since he "was the first to give impetus to such an immense society, which had been motionless." [129] But Radishchev demonstrated that the productive forces of Russia, including her industry, would have had an incomparably greater range and the national well-being would have been significantly enhanced if the economy were not based on serfdom, but on the labor of personally free, direct producers, owners of the means of production. Although he recognized the merits of Peter's policy of developing industry and trade in Russia, at the same time Radishchev noted certain contraditions in it. In one of his historical notes Radishchev wrote: "Peter the First . . . directed his

[129] *Ibid.*, I, 150.

laws towards trade, manufacture, and naval and land forces. In the courts he established an order of business, but the axis, so to speak, on which everything had to turn remained as before." [130] With these words Radishchev very clearly indicated that Peter conducted his progressive reforms on the old feudal-serf basis. Radishchev pointed out that Peter I would have been even more famous if he had established "personal liberty."

In conformity with the economic development of Russia, Radishchev recognized agriculture as the foundation of its national economy, but he did not feel that social wealth was created solely in agriculture. "For even if the prime basis of all well-being is agriculture, something which hardly needs to be said about Russia . . . ," in Siberia whole regions engaged exclusively in "fur trade," and in other places "in handicrafts." The occupation of people "with their own handicraft" industry he viewed as a development "of real social significance," [131] that is, of production based on the social division of labor. Radishchev contrasted occupation in crafts and agriculture with trapping and hunting as indices of a low level of economic development. He advised "giving premiums to all who wish to abandon a life of trapping and living in the forest and to settled in productive areas and engage in agriculture," [132] that is, a transfer from a nomadic to a settled form of life.

Radishchev explained the specific character of the development of industry in Russia, which consisted of a wide distribution of industry in the form of home production in the village, and not in the form of heavy manufacturing. Inasmuch as crafts were still not separated from agriculture, the Russian peasants were engaged in occupations which in other countries had already become purely urban. Radishchev showed that "peasant handicrafts," with whose aid the obrok peasants "obtain money," were represented by silversmiths, goldsmiths, tanners, sawyers, bricklayers, stonemasons, sheepshearers, tailors, carpenters, wagoners, roadlayers, traders, and shoemakers. "The general handiwork of women is to spin and weave; they spin flax, wool, and hemp, and the cloth that they make is sold to merchants . . ."; they weave cloth and sacking for themselves and for sale. "In other countries, the above-enumerated crafts are practiced among the urban inhabitants, but in Russia the long winter, the low fertility of certain gubernias, and the bad agriculture transform many villages into towns." [133]

[130] *Ibid.*, III, 42.
[131] *Ibid.*, II, 10.
[132] *Ibid.*, II, 29.
[133] *Ibid.*, II, 184.

Studying the connection of each of these trades with agriculture, Radishchev observed an increasing separation of crafts from agriculture and the growth of the division of labor between town and village, with the result that many of the peasants "are already beginning to leave agriculture as a profession." The richer of them considered it advantageous to hire farm laborers to take their place in summer while they themselves went individually into salaried work, and those who had no tools joined those who had them "in partnership" or "in hire" for a share of the income. Thus sawyers always went in twos, sheepshearers took workers with them, and so forth. Sawyers traveled throughout the country (to Kiev, Kherson, Saratov, Astrakhan, and Petersburg). They "love this work, largely because they live in freedom," said Radishchev in pointing to the important positive aspect of the migratory trades of the obrok peasants—the relative independence from the pomeshchik's constant supervision, and a certain freedom of economic activity which helped to raise the productivity of labor. Radishchev showed that the development of peasant industry and of migratory trades strengthened the stratification of the peasantry.

The artel form of organization of peasant migratory occupations did not escape Radishchev's attention. At the same time, he demonstrated that in "partnerships" the lion's share of the common wage was appropriated by "masters," the owners of the tools, horses, and so forth.

Radishchev established that the greater part of the money income of the obrok peasants was not received from agriculture, but from migratory trades. He presented data which described the specialization of individual villages, small towns, and whole regions in one particular trade. This showed the comparatively high level of development of trades, which was one of the necessary conditions for the emergence and development of manufacturing.

The concrete evidence on peasant trades which Radishchev collected fully confirmed the pronouncements of one of his contemporaries who had studied with him in the Corps de Pages and in Leipzig University, P. I. Chelishchev.[134] In May, 1791, Chelishchev undertook a journey to northern Russia; he traveled 4,069 verst "by land" and water and in December of the same year returned to Petersburg. He gathered a mass of material covering the condition of the court, the peasants of the Olonetsk, Archangel, Vologda, and Novgorod gubernias, factories, peasant crafts, trade, shipbuilding, transportation, and natural resources in the north of European Russia.

Chelishchev noted the attempts made at the end of the eighteenth

[134] Catherine II at one time suspected even Chelishchev of co-authorship of the *Journey from Petersburg to Moscow.*

century to overcome technical backwardness and the introduction of "firing machines" (as steam machinery was then called) in Russia. He deplored the extreme lack of Russian industry and the rapacious exploitation of natural resources by foreign capitalists; he accused the government and the tsarist officials of lacking patriotic concern for the development of industry. "Why don't you develop the resources hidden in the bosom of the earth; we have so many of them, but we pay the English millions for them, the Nürnburgers thousands for needles alone; and we also pay much to the Dutch for herring, while we ourselves have sterlet, whitefish, sturgeon, salmon, and other treasures of the waters. Cannot Astrakhan and the Crimea supply us with wine, silk, and wool? Can the mineral deposits of the Urals and the vast gubernias of our beloved fatherland ever be exhausted? The firm, astute, and constructive reasoning of the Russians only needs encouragement in order to overshadow all the European nations in sciences, arts, and skill." [135] Chelishchev presented clear examples of the stratification of the peasantry in connection with the development of industry and the emerging capitalistic relationships. In many of his pronouncements the influence of Radishchev's ideas is distinctly evident.

Radishchev saw the need for the development of manufacturing and handicraft in Russia especially in connection with the task of abolishing serfdom, forming a class of small producers, and bettering the conditions of the peasantry. He assigned great importance to the promotion of peasant handicraft, which was tied to agriculture. He noted also the advantages of manufacturing:

> Ordinary manufactories, not including English and French, are useful in that they provide a livelihood to a large number of poor citizens, and for each two hundred, three hundred, five hundred, and one thousand men who receive their daily bread, one or two citizens become rich; silk handicraft, as it exists in the Moscow gubernia, does not enrich anyone, but, at least, it brings a comfortable existence to many individuals and to a great part of the village population.[136]

Radishchev, seeing the usefulness of manufactories in providing work for a great number of people, did not let it escape his attention that manufacturing was an undertaking which only enriched its owners. In this connection he noted the glaring discrepancies between the

---

[135] P. I. Chelishchev, *Puteshestvie po Severu Rossii v 1791 godu* [Journey in Northern Russia in 1791] (St. Petersburg: 1886), p. 274.

[136] Radishchev, *op. cit.*, II, 13.

material well-being of the factory workers and that of independent producers of goods.

Radishchev evaluated the role of industrial enterprises in the light of protecting the interests of the toilers, the direct producers, and of raising their standard of living. "If a trade, handiwork, art, or practice of any sort feeds a greater number of people, even though permitting a smaller amount of capital to circulate or producing numerically smaller wealth, then that art, handiwork, or practice, whatever it is, is preferable to one which, circulating great capital or producing more wealth, provides a livelihood for a smaller number of people . . . But if it can provide a livelihood to a great number of people, then it is all the more beneficial." [137] This opinion was shared by many statesmen of that time, including Radishchev's patron, Count A. R. Vorontsov, M. D. Chulkov, and others. It would be a mistake, however, to conclude from this that Radishchev had a negative attitude towards large-scale production. Radishchev gave preference to small independent production, but he did not deny the benefits of large-scale production as well.

In contrast to the argument of the serfowner Shcherbatov that the peasants, because of widespread "sensuality" among them, were drawn to nonagricultural work in search of an easy life, Radishchev pointed out that the agricultural worker was driven from the village by "the bony paw of hunger." The peasants, leaving their homes in the winter for trade and work in the cities, "not only accumulate money, but save in their absence that amount of bread which they would have consumed," [138] consequently they leave "to save bread," as was written later, in the nineteenth century, in populist literature. Still these seasonal trades did not take care of all the needs of the worker and his family. Therefore Radishchev proposed that for the country as a whole and for the peasantry in particular "the most beneficial utilization of winter occurs where this time, unproductive for agriculture, can be used for handiwork or in the factory." [139] He considered that it would be advantageous to build factories not only in large towns and capitals, but also where they could employ all those "who have not found work in distant places or do not want to leave home."

Radishchev showed that the combination of agriculture with trade was especially necessary in Russia, where "poor agriculture" did not provide the enserfed peasant with all his necessities and where the

[137] *Ibid.*, II, 20.
[138] *Ibid.*, III, 104.
[139] *Ibid.*, III, 105.

lack of "peasant capital" prevented the introduction of rational and profitable agriculture, because the pomeshchik robbed the peasant of everything "but the air." The long winter also aided the development of peasant crafts, as the peasant had much free time on his hands. "Manufacturing, factories, the fur trade, the carrier's trade, insofar as they are carried on in winter time, are very serviceable; our long winter season cannot be better used than for something useful or necessary." [140]

The idea of the utilization of wintertime for the development of industry was developed by Marx in *Das Kapital* in connection with his analysis of the brevity of the working season. He wrote: "It is easy to imagine what the loss would be for Russia if fifty million out of the sixty-five million inhabitants of her European area remained without employment during six or eight winter months when all field work must cease." [141]

In urging the omnifarious expansion of industrial production, Radishchev also turned serious attention to the extremely difficult condition of workers in manufacturing, especially votchina workers. It is known that pomeshchiki who exploited the forced labor of serfs in votchina factories usually did not pay the peasants any wages. The noble serf owners, "priding themselves on their science . . . in methods of enriching agriculture," elaborated both in the "Works of the Free Economic Society" and in "Instructions to Administrators of Estates," introduced various rationalizing measures to use the peasants in winter and summer work, but did not consider satisfying the needs of the worker and his family. Thus Radishchev demanded: "Give him work, but pay him for that work. Then he will have food, his home will be warm, and his children will not perish from nakedness and bad food." [142]

Insisting on the necessity of every encouragement of the peasants' "own handiwork," Radishchev proposed to secure raw materials for them, even if they had to be imported. As an example he cited the silk industry of the Moscow gubernia. "If it is advantageous to encourage handiwork indiscriminately, then the silk weavers deserve it even more. Silk handiwork in Russia is more useful because the greater part is carried on by village inhabitants at their own expense." [143] To obtain

---

140 *Ibid.*, II, 183. Regarding this Chelishchev wrote the following: "Look: throughout there is poverty, emptiness, boredom; everywhere is small gain and heavy work." Chelishchev, *op. cit.*, p. 273.

141 Marx, *Kapital,* II, 237.

142 Radishchev, *op. cit.*, III, 105.

143 *Ibid.*, II, 13.

raw materials for this branch of production, he considered it advantageous to import silk from China. The import of raw materials for processing in masters' home shops, and especially in Moscow manufactories, which supplied "all Russia" with their products, Radishchev viewed as one of the most important methods of developing the country's industry.

He also studied the problem of processing the country's own raw materials in Russian factories. Instead of exporting lambskins, he recommended raising sheep and establishing woolen factories; instead of exporting Russian leather, he proposed the construction of tanneries and footwear enterprises.

In backing a policy of protectionism, Radishchev took into account the fact that Russian industry had a broad distribution in the form of crafts and of peasant trades which were not yet fully separated from agriculture and which, even more than large-scale manufactures, needed protection from foreign competition. Using as an example the cessation of Chinese trade, he showed how manufactured and peasant production of textiles in Russia began to develop; he cited the tanning industry, the cultivation of flax and tobacco, and so on. He expressed regret that with the reopening of Chinese trade the lower price of Chinese textiles "will drive many Russian hand-produced and manufactured goods out of use in Siberia," [144] goods which had increased in production during the period of the cessation of Chinese trade. Observing some benefits from the temporary closing of Chinese trade, Radishchev did not endorse the stoppage of foreign trade with China, but urged the adoption of measures which would secure the growth of Russian industry.

It is known that the protection of industry by high customs tariffs was part of the economic policy of mercantilism. The mercantilists subordinated the problems of industrial production to the acquisition of wealth in the form of money through foreign trade. Radishchev, on the other hand, pressed for the omnifarious development of the country's industry in order to increase the internal demand for industrial goods and to raise the national prosperity. He recognized the benefit of large-scale production, but under conditions of enserfed Russia he could not understand its advantage over small production. Supporting the interests of the peasantry, Radishchev gave preference to small crafts. He did not know that on the basis of these crafts a new form of exploitation of the toilers—capitalistic manufacturing—would be born and develop.

---

[144] *Ibid.*, II, 33.

On Trade, Prices of Goods, and Profits

Radishchev devoted much attention to the production of goods under feudalism-serfdom. He thought that trade could develop only under conditions of "surplus of one's own products," in the presence of "domestic abundance," that is, under conditions of wide development of the country's production. "The more trade is spread, the more it will enrich the people." [145]

Radishchev offered a materialistic explanation of the origins of trade. He felt that trade arose when the volume of production began to exceed the demand of the immediate producers. "The surplus of goods and production forced people to exchange them for those of which there was a deficit. This led to trade." [146] Thus Radishchev demonstrated that at the base of the historical development of trade lies the division of labor. Deducing trade from conditions of production, he challenged its subordinate place in regard to production. Radishchev showed in detail in the example of the China trade "what stimulates it," how production of various goods "nourishes" trade, and how trade in turn influences the development of production.

He did not feel, as Adam Smith did, that the desire to exchange things is an eternal, natural characteristic of man. Radishchev showed that trade originates at a definite level of social production and is conditioned by it and not by the nature of man. He analyzed in detail how trade wtih China "can have a favorable influence on agriculture; . . . it can act to increase cattle breeding," how trade is needed for maintaining the production "of silk cloth and the spread of this handiwork in the Moscow gubernia." [147]

The necessity of freedom of internal trade, of unobstructed circulation of goods within a country, Radishchev regarded as an axiomatic truth, not demanding proof. He wrote that trade does not tolerate any obstacles and spontaneously, like a stream's waters, opens a path evading any ordinances and prohibitions, once production takes place.

Radishchev came close to defining the consumer value of goods and emphasized the necessary characteristic of goods—the ability to satisfy human demands—regardless of whether these products "like bread and shirts," satisfy indispensable needs or "just a fancy." [148]

He shows the dependence of production on demand. Even "a thing introduced into usage through fancy, and not through necessity . . ."

[145] *Sobranie Vorontsova,* No. 398, Sheet 140.
[146] Radishchev, *op. cit.,* I, 383.
[147] *Ibid.,* II, 22.
[148] *Ibid.,* II, 26.

cannot be "eliminated from use." Moreover, it is quite "impossible to eliminate something which we consider among the prime necessities, such as clothing in the northern climate." [149]

Radishchev considered as participants in the circulation of goods in the country not only the merchants themselves, but also the producers and the consumers of goods. From this it does not follow, of course, that every commodity always passes through "three hands." "Sometimes," he wrote, "the producer is also the seller of the commodity and delivers it to the place of its use. Sometimes a commodity passes through ten hands," but, in general, circulation always narrows down to the above-named "activity of three types of people." The producer, the merchant, and the consumer are owners of the goods; "they are its *possessors*"; they "are participants in trade and its stimulators." Those people who, in the process of trade, "temporarily handle" the commodity and do not become its owners in the process of circulation "are only its assistants." [150] By people who temporarily handle the commodity and do not become its owners, Radishchev meant trade workers, carriers, owners of premises, those renting storerooms for goods and taking goods into safekeeping, shipowners, and other agents of circulation. This division of all agents of commodity circulation into groups in accordance with the ownership of the commodities was undertaken in order to explain the process of price formulation and the distribution of profits.

Radishchev gave a detailed analysis of the influence on employment and income of various participants in trade through stoppage of circulation under conditions of simple commodity production. From such a stoppage those persons whose commodity "is not their property" lose the least. They are not deprived of capital and easily transfer their labors to other fields and "apply themselves to other things." "It is a completely different thing," wrote Radishchev, "to deprive a man of something from which he makes his profit than to deprive him of something that he owns; under those conditions, he in whose hands the commodity is left resembles a consumer: for although he does not want it, circulation of the commodity has stopped, and often it loses its value in his possession, as well as its price." [151] Thus those who are strictly merchants "can be deprived merely of profit and capital and that only temporarily and accidentally . . ." They lose more than their "helpers," however, from a cessation of circulation; but they comparatively easily transfer "their skill to another field."

---

149 *Ibid.*, II, 27–8.
150 *Ibid.*, II, 7–8.
151 *Ibid.*, II, 8–9.

The producers of goods suffer most of all from an obstruction in circulation. "However, the deprivation of profit falls most on the producers of [the commodity whose circulation is stopped—E. P.], . . . the producer is deprived of his craft or skill when he is no longer needed and cannot, like others, turn his skill to another occupation without prolonged training." [152]

Radishchev, however, saw benefit also in such a disturbance of trade, for, as a consequence, commodity production develops in new fields, new commodities and new directions of the flow of goods appear, ties are established in other areas, and the division of labor is strengthened. Then social production rises to a new, much higher stage.

In these considerations Radishchev turned his attention in essence to the results of stoppage of the act of T-D under simple goods production both for the producer of goods "when there is no need" for it [the commodity—E. P.] and for the Merchant, who "is like a consumer" because "the commodity remains in his hands." Radishchev wrote during the period of feudal-serf production, and therefore his judgment has great theoretical interest. His analysis of simple commodity production, Marx noted, already contained the possibility of crises, which is transformed into reality only under the hegemony of capitalistic methods of production.

Radishchev carefully collected material on domestic trade in Russia. In his diaries and letters for 1790–1797 he registered prices and the names of commodities and explained the conditions of their production and the direction of trade routes. He gave much attention to the large-scale centers of domestic trade—the Irbit and Makar'ev (later Nizhegorod) fairs.

In his study of the concentration of Russian and foreign goods in the Vyshnevolotsk canal, Radishchev considered also the major question which permeated all his work—the basic productive relationships of enserfed society. He showed that an abundance of goods in the stores and on the barges should not lead to rejoicing, because these goods are not created by free producers, but are a result of the misappropriation by pomeshchiki and merchants of the labor of enserfed peasants or the labor of American slaves—Negroes; these goods "have not yet dried off the sweat, blood, and tears of their production." [153]

On questions of the development of trade Radishchev defended the interests of the toilers and the small independent producers of goods, who "trade only in their own products." [154] The big merchants, "the

[152] *Ibid.*, II, 9.
[153] *Ibid.*, I, 324.
[154] *Ibid.*, II, 21.

big capitalists," "the prosperous brokers," monopolists, usurers, and speculators are portrayed in very negative terms.

It is necessary also to emphasize Radishchev's correct understanding of the importance of a broad national market both for establishing economic ties between separate areas of the country and for spreading culture and mutual enrichment of experience. "In regard to trade it is all the same whether it goes from right to left or from left to right, but this is not the case so far as education and enlightenment are concerned. The Siberians who have visited Moscow have acquired many concepts which they did not have before, and things that are learned in travel are never lost." [155] Having gained an intimate knowledge of Siberia during his exile, he pointed out that in many ways the Siberians were a whole century behind the population of Great Russia. Close trade ties with central Russia would serve as a method of eliminating this backwardness.

In various works Radishchev noted that poor transportation severely hindered the expansion of internal trade and the establishment of economic and cultural bonds between individual areas of Russia. "The roads, canals, and rivers must be free and maintained at the expense of the state, which derives its revenues from the population and from the wealth made more attainable by transportation." [156]

The lack of communications was responsible for the preservation of local closed markets, as a consequence of which great fluctuations occurred in the prices of one and the same commodity. Radishchev described such differences in prices and pointed out their negative influence. For example, inhabitants of the Barabinsk steppe, tied only loosely to markets, were dissatisfied with good harvests, because then the local prices of grain often fell and it was difficult for the peasants to secure sufficient money to pay their taxes.

In his description of the long and hard road by which Russian goods were sent to China and by which Chinese products were distributed, Radishchev expressed belief that in the future the Siberian population would change natural conditions and create a direct water route for communication with European Russia. In a letter from Siberia to A. R. Vorontsov, following Lomonosov Radishchev wrote about finding a possible direct water route along the northern shore of European Russia and Siberia through the Kara Sea and expressed the ardent wish that he might take part in the expedition for its discovery.

The construction of navigable canals he regarded as an important way of uniting separate parts of the country. In his opinion, the man

---

[155] *Ibid.*, II, 33.

[156] *Sobranie Vorontsova*, No. 398, Sheet 140.

who conceived "the making of a river by hand, so that all ends of different oblasts come together, is worthy of remembrance by future generations." [157] Radishchev outlined a program of wide investigation of the country's communication system in order to determine "methods of improving it."

Like many of his contemporaries, Radishchev considered foreign trade neither the sole, nor even the most important, source of state wealth. "Although foreign trade can be one of the sources of its [the state's—E. P.] wealth, nevertheless it cannot be considered the chief pillar of state power and might, and, therefore, it seems, in social benefit it can be replaced by something else . . ." [158] Foreign trade was still less a major source of prosperity for such a state as Russia. Even for Siberia, where hunting for fur-bearing animals was a basic occupation and where the welfare of the fur traders depended on profits from the sale of their pelts, foreign trade could not be regarded as essential for economic prosperity.

Foreign trade, in Radishchev's opinion, cannot be a basic source of wealth because foreign exchange is an equivalent one. "The truth is, no matter how little it is known and how little it is obvious, that a state only gives in trade exactly as much as it takes . . . If I receive a thing for a high price, then I am returning more for it . . ." [159] Radishchev did not recognize the possibility of ruining the state through foreign trade. In one note he asks: "Why do all trading states become rich? If those which buy more should lose, then they would grow poor. But this is not the case." [160] Radishchev considered foreign exchange equivalent, "because between nations money is like a commodity." [161]

From his position of believing in the equivalent exchange of foreign trade, Radishchev criticized the mercantilists. He saw wealth in the form of the accumulation of goods—of consumer goods; and he considered money a common representative of wealth. "For wine, sugar, and so on, Russia gives iron, tallow, hemp, and flax; Spain gives silver and gold. And why are these metals preferred in trade? Only because they are more widely used, and in common agreement they represent any commodity, and any commodity can be exchanged for them; for in the long run any trade is an exchange . . . Why, then, are they

[157] Radishchev, *op. cit.*, I, 323.
[158] *Ibid.*, II, 5–6.
[159] *Ibid.*, II, 31.
[160] *Sobranie Vorontsova*, No. 398, Sheet 141.
[161] *Ibid.*, Sheet 140.

preferred in trade to other goods, why are they considered as true wealth and sought after to the point of violating even the laws of reason? Is a piece of gold or silver more precious than wine or sugar cane . . . Oh, you who have paved the way by philosophizing on national prosperity, on social prosperity, on state prosperity, Plato, Montesquieu, can you imagine that at the customs gates the immortal products of your reason can be set on the same scale with the products of greed, extorted by blows from unfortunates drenched with bloody sweat! . . . such counsel shall not enter my heart." [162]

Although mercantilism was at that time already being opposed by the physiocrats and by representatives of English classical political economy, one cannot simply regard Radishchev as a belated critic of mercantilism. In the 1780's and 1790's the problem of money circulation and of the rate of exchange was acute in Russia. Various state commissions and individuals connected these difficulties with the lack of organization, with impediments in foreign trade, and with the leakage of gold and silver abroad as a consequence of "illegal" trade transactions. Radishchev opposed such a treatment of the causes of the decline of the rate of exchange and of the confusion in money circulation.

Radishchev viewed the liquidation of natural economy and the development of commodity production as an important means and a basic road to strengthening Russia's economic power. "I lack much data for determining the appraisable value of the benefits of foreign trade, which, in my opinion, is good only when it serves to stimulate internal trade," he wrote to A. R. Vorontsov.[163] In Russia at the end of the eighteenth century foreign trade transactions, in Radishchev's calculations, were in general very small in comparison with those of internal trade.

Radishchev knew well the economic theories of his times and was acquainted with the mercantilists, the physiocrats, and the works of Adam Smith. The French translation of Smith's book *Richesses des nations,* in two volumes, was in his library.[164] In one of his letters to A. R. Vorontsov he mentioned the book "of the Englishman Smith." [165] In "Letter on the Chinese Trade" Radishchev mentioned "the newest economists," particularly the English ones, who demanded freedom of foreign trade. "Two views on foreign trade prevail among political writers; both desire its improvement and extension, but their conclusions differ and the results stemming from them vary. The newest view

[162] Radishchev, *op. cit.,* II, 32.
[163] *Ibid.,* III, 376–7. Letter to A. R. Vorontsov, May 8, 1791.
[164] Barskov, *op. cit.,* p. 400.
[165] Radishchev, *op. cit.,* III, 370. Letter to A. R. Vorontsov, May 2, 1791.

of writers on foreign trade is that its freedom should not be limited by anything. The other view is the time-honored one generally in use . . . Regulations, institutions, tariffs, and customs are used. England with eight million inhabitants has with such institutions placed herself among the foremost states in Europe; but the English themselves now say and write that all barriers to trade are harmful; for it will maintain itself always in uncertain equilibrium." [166]

Contrasting and evaluating the differences between free traders and protectionists, Radishchev discussed them not abstractly from the point of view of theory in general, but as applicable to conditions in Russia, to the tasks of developing her productive forces. Concerned about her industrial backwardness and the urgent necessity of overcoming this situation, Radishchev criticized both the physiocrats and the new English economists for their demands for free trade, and he firmly averred that this principle was unsuitable for Russia.

He supported his rejection of free trade with a number of proofs and examples. Thus he stated that the English themselves began to talk and write about the harmfulness of all barriers to foreign trade only after England, with the help of a protective system and high customs tariff, had changed into a progressive industrial state.[167] Consequently, without these barriers English industry would not have attained such a high level, which at the time placed her above the competition of other countries.

Since Russian industry was significantly inferior to that of England, free importation of foreign goods would undermine and throttle the economic development of the country. "If a low price aids the import of these inexpensive goods, should we not recognize that they are harmful and that our products will not be taken in payment?" he asked.[168]

Radishchev knew what difficulty, destruction, bankruptcy, and mass unemployment the manufacturing industry in France experienced in the 1780's as a consequence of the flooding of her market with in-

[166] *Ibid.*, II, 6–7.

[167] The correctness of Radishchev's appraisal of English protectionism is fully supported by that offered by Engels: "Under the patronizing cover of protectionism there was created and developed in England in the last third of the XVIII century the system of contemporary heavy industry—production with the aid of machines propelled by steam . . .

Then the teaching of free trade by classical political economy acquired popularity—French physiocrats and their English followers—Adam Smith and Ricardo." Marx and Engels, *Sochineniia*, XVI, Pt. I, 311. It must be noted that in Radishchev's view the government should not strangulate "the natural freedom of action" within the country.

[168] Radishchev, *op. cit.*, II, 17.

expensive English goods. The import of inexpensive nankeen into Russia was detrimental, he argued, because it hindered the development of native flax and textile industries. The same was true of tobacco, the import of which at a lower price could destroy "the large harvests of this plant in the Irkutsk gubernia."

Radishchev tried to solve the problem of foreign trade not from the commercial or fiscal point of view, but from its influence on industrial production within the country and on the peasant economy.

Weighing the advantages and disadvantages of ceasing or reopening the Chinese trade, he concluded that from the cessation of this trade "the fur industry" and cattle raising had not suffered. Agriculture had actually gained, the spreading of flax production had increased, and the production of sheeting and the large-scale textile industry of Ivanov, Yaroslav, and other places had improved. Radishchev did not try to make a categorical conclusion as to whether it would be more advantageous to reopen that trade or not. On the whole, he found more benefits from the stoppage of many imports from China, as native industry had been stimulated.

Radishchev formulated his conviction of the necessity of protective tariffs for Russia and of the limitation of the freedom of foreign trade as early as the end of the 1770's and the beginning of the 1780's. This view was confirmed not only by his theoretical proposals, but by his practical activity as well.

Soon after he joined the Commerce College, he participated in the preparation of instructions to the Russian Consuls General in Hamburg, Lübeck, and Bremen. One of his earliest service documents directed the consuls "to guard the honor of the Russian flag," to protect the interests of Russian merchant vessels, and to give them all possible aid. In the interests of the development of export of "unprocessed [that is, raw materials—E. P.] and manufactured goods," it was recommended that impediments to Russian trade be removed, "that it grow year by year, and that goods be sold at as high a price as possible." With this aim in mind, one should be vigilant that Russian goods in German towns were not taxed at a greater rate than those of other states. Special attention was devoted to the export of canvas and hemp goods, inasmuch as "Russia is in a position to surpass all other nations in this regard." [169] It is interesting that Alexander Radishchev and Michael Chulkov were among the five officials of the Commerce College who signed this instruction in March, 1778.

As an administrative assistant in the 1780's and later as the Director

---

[169] Shmakov, *op. cit.*, p. 140–4.

of the St. Petersburg customs, through which passed three-fourths of the foreign trade turnover of Russia, Radishchev firmly and undeviatingly supported a protective tariff policy. This direction of economic policy Radishchev continually propagated in his numerous notes and projects on customs affairs.[170] He participated actively in preparing the tariff of 1782 which raised the duties on many goods. In his note, "On the Tariff of 1766 and Its Duties," Radishchev gave a general characterization of this tariff and its insufficiencies and pointed out in detail what should be preserved in a new tariff and what should be changed and made precise. He considered it beneficial to encourage "concessions in duties" to Russian merchants who shipped the country's goods abroad in Russian vessels.

Radishchev was a proponent of freedom of internal trade and showed the necessity of protecting the industrial development of Russia, which was without doubt a progressive demand for that time and which aided the strengthening of the country's economic independence.

In the history of economic science and in the explanation of the process of development of political economy Radishchev's theoretical views on the price of goods and on profits and their origin hold great interest. He was able to say something new in contrast to his predecessors, and he raised the development of political economy in Russia to a new level.

Radishchev differentiated between "true value" and "surplus value" of a commodity. "True value" included the losses in production and circulation. "Its true value, or that which it costs either the producer or the seller and the purchaser or anyone who has it temporarily in his hands, can never represent profit to anyone; because the original producer, in producing it, suffered a property loss; likewise, all those who sell, buy, or handle it suffer corresponding losses. This refers to all those who give money for the production of goods; for example, the agriculturist keeps cattle, tools, seeds, and so forth; the entrepreneur builds buildings and supplies; the merchant borrows money with interest, and so on; the carrier keeps a horse and fodder; the trader also." [171]

Consequently, the first element of "true value" in Radishchev's view is primarily the expenditures for the means of production, preservation, and transportation of goods to the place of consumption, that is, fixed capital expenditures, to employ the language of Marxist political economy.

---

[170] Radishchev, *op. cit.*, III.

[171] *Ibid.*, II, 8. Producer means in this case a hunter of fur-bearing animals.

The second element of "true value" is expenditures for actual human labor. Radishchev showed that in Russia, as a result of the enserfed nature of production, the labor of the serf did not cost the pomeshchik anything; he did not pay for it, and, therefore, the value of production was usually incorrectly determined. "In Russia (with few exceptions) only seeds are considered expenditures in production, tools and buildings sometimes, but labor never." [172]

His calculations included in the price of production expenditures not only for the means of production but also for the working force. To the value of the means of production, which were owned by the peasants in a village he described (cattle, agricultural tools, buildings, seeds), he added also the value of agricultural labor. "The *true value*" of a commodity in Radishchev's conception meant, thus, the costs of production.

"Surplus" or *"increased value of a commodity"* Radishchev called the entire surplus of the price of a commodity over and above the expenses of its production. Breaking down the value of a commodity into its component elements, Radishchev showed that the part of the price of a commodity which represented expenses could not be considered revenue or profit. "The entire surplus value of a commodity represents profit to everyone through whose hands the commodity has passed . . . Consequently the *increased value* of a commodity is turned into profit, and consequently the greater its increase is or the more expensive it becomes, the greater the profit from it." [173]

Thus, "surplus value" meant in essence the surplus value which was divided as profit among the participants in trade, the "owners" of the commodity—the entrepreneurs and merchants. Radishchev explained the advantages in augmenting the "increased value" of a commodity: "Not that there was a greater profit, but that it gave subsistence to a greater number." From this it is obvious that Radishchev was not an advocate of concentrating profits in the hands of a few entrepreneurs and merchants. He favored the greatest possible number of participants in the division of the "surplus value."

In the process of its passage from producer to consumer a commodity becomes more expensive. Radishchev understood this. The consumer "either consumes it or halts its circulation," he wrote; consequently, the consumer pays for the entire value of the commodity. In the process of circulation the commodity does not change either in its quantity or physical state as a consumer value, but it is changed in

---

[172] *Ibid.*, II, 174.

[173] *Ibid.*, II, 8. It is interesting to note that it was Radishchev who introduced into Russian economic science the term *"profitable price."*

price by the entire sum of the merchant's profit. "Usually, although exceptions may occur, a commodity increases in proportion to the number of hands through which it passes, not in its quantity or goodness, but in price, or to put it in other words: the more hands the commodity passes through, the more expensive it becomes." [174]

In Radishchev's opinion, the size of profit also depended on the speed of circulation. "The more rapid the circulation of a commodity, the more frequent and the greater their [the participants in the trade—E. P.] profits." Radishchev showed the influence also of supply and demand on the price of a commodity and the profit realized. "If sometimes the scarcity of a commodity makes it expensive, then sometimes also its extensive use keeps it at a high price." [175]

Radishchev defined the participation in the distribution of profits by agents of circulation as dependent upon their roles in production itself. Profit was divided between them "very unequally," he said. "Those to whom the commodity belongs" received more; "those who hold it temporarily" received less.[176] Thus Radishchev understood profit as that part of the value of a commodity which surpasses the cost of production and which is realized in the course of circulation. He showed the ways of realizing "surplus value." The question of where and by whom profit was created Radishchev answered with his deliberations on the origin of the wealth of owners of manufacturing enterprises and of merchants.

He proceeded from the assumption that the labor of man is the source of wealth, that the enrichment of the ruling classes comes from the appropriation of the labor of peasants and workers. It has already been shown how Radishchev explained the origin of the wealth of the pomeshchiki, and used the energies of "their peasants, assigning them to cultivate the land." The enserfed peasants "do not work for themselves," he wrote. As a result of peasant exploitation the pomeshchik had, in the form of money, "the accomplished labors and sweat of his peasants." [177] From this it is obvious that Radishchev understood the income of the pomeshchik to be the result of the gratuitous appropriation of the labor of the serfs.[178]

---

[174] *Ibid.*

[175] *Ibid.*, III, 358. Letter to A. R. Vorontsov, March 15, 1791.

[176] *Ibid.*, II, 8.

[177] *Ibid.*, II, 350.

[178] K. Marx later expressed in theoretical terms that, under barshchina labor, "the concurrence of surplus value with unpaid outside labor needs no analysis because it exists here in its obvious, tangible form . . ." Under obrok labor "the direct producer . . . must give his master . . . surplus forced labor, that is, unpaid, fulfilled without equivalent, labor in the form of surplus product, transformed into money" (K. Marx, *Kapital,* III, 804 and 810).

Radishchev revealed clearly enough the source of the wealth of owners of industrial enterprises—the manufacturers. He saw that their enrichment came at the expense of the labor of hired workers. The workers in Russian, English, and French manufacturing enterprises were the "poor citizens," wrote Radishchev. He was first in Russian literature to show that workers in industrial enterprises received for their work only "their daily bread," that is, that their working pay provided them with only the minimum means of subsistence, while the owners of manufacturing enterprises, of the means of production, were becoming rich by the labor of the thousands of hired workers who did not have their own means of production.

Radishchev showed that the small independent producers of goods were not in any better material position. Although they produced goods by their own labor with the aid of their own means of production, their insufficient finances and inability to sell their goods forced them to pay a significant share of the results of their labor to representatives of commercial capital.

Radishchev was the first to give special attention to the economic dependence of small producers on *speculators* and to an explanation of the sources of commercial profit. He saw that the merchant received profit directly from circulation, but he did not limit himself to this external aspect of the phenomenon. He revealed the essence of the relationships and saw the sources of the accumulation of commercial capital in the cruel exploitation of small producers. The merchants became rich by the labor of peasants, hunters, fishermen—such was Radishchev's conclusion.

In his study of the economy of Siberia, Radishchev wrote: "The Siberian peasants, with the exception of the Barabinsk settlers, live better and more abundantly than the pomestie peasants; they eat meat and, during Lent, fish, but it does not follow from this that they live in plenty. One out of a hundred or two hundred does not live in debt; others are all hired and work for the money given them. All their gains are mortgaged beforehand, and their labors are exploited by greedy and uncharitable traders." [179]

With indignation Radishchev described the predatory methods of merchants to enrich themselves at the expense of the fishermen and hunters. "Every summer these cruel usurers swindle from them [the fishermen—E. P.] their reserve food for a small price, and at the beginning of winter they sell it to them much more dearly." "The merchants going from village to village make agreements with peasants

[179] Radishchev, *op. cit.*, II, 29.

regarding the supplying of pelts and leave money as a deposit . . . by this method they take goods at such a low price that if they received only half of the agreed price they would be making a considerable profit." [180]

Thus Radishchev revealed the exploitative origin of the wealth both of the owners of manufacturing enterprises and of the merchants and showed that the source of profit, "of surplus value," was the labor of workers and peasants. Of course, under conditions of the Russian serf economy of the eighteenth century Radishchev could not disclose the principle of surplus value, but he paved the way for the development of revolutionary economic science.

Radishchev's statements on the origin of profits represented a new idea in Russian economic theory. Bourgeois science justified the appropriation of the product of labor by the owners of the means of production, their "direct interest in lowering the share of labor," that is, of the workers, in the social product. Radishchev viewed production and circulation from the opposite point of view—from the position of protecting the interests of the toilers. Therefore he criticized the exploitative system, not only of serfdom, but also of capitalistic production. Radishchev presented in essence certain aspects of that theory of the toilers which was developed by Chernyshevskii in the middle of the nineteenth century.

On Money and Credit

Radishchev developed original propositions in the theory of money and currency circulation, which under eighteenth century conditions was of great importance in the development of political economy. He viewed money, in the first place, as a means of circulation which eliminated the inconveniences of barter and, secondly, as a carrier of all wealth, of all "property." "The great difficulties of barter forced people to think about symbols to represent wealth and possession. Money was invented. Gold and silver, metals valuable because of their perfection and up to then serving as adornments, were transformed into symbols representing everything acquired." [181] In another work he wrote: "Money must be viewed as a symbol representing everything." [182]

Radishchev could not give a correct explanation of the origin of money, but he came close to understanding the essence of money. It

---

[180] *Ibid.*, III, 136–7.
[181] *Ibid.*, I, 383.
[182] *Sobranie Vorontsova,* No. 398, Sheet 140.

has been said above that Radishchev considered gold and silver to be like any other goods. But these goods, he wrote, have preëminence, since "by general agreement they represent any commodity and can be exchanged for any commodity." [183]

The preciousness of gold and silver is determined by their attributes, their rarity, and their difficulty of extraction. In "A Word on Lomonosov" Radishchev wrote with esteem about the works of the great teacher in natural sciences, especially metallurgy, and noted that with the transformation of gold into money conditions of accumulation were changed and the unlimited possibilities of accumulating wealth and the thirst for wealth appeared. "And only then was the heart of man ignited. Like an all-consuming flame the insatiable and loathsome passion for wealth is strengthened by constant feeding." [184] Gold and silver, which "in their natural form are merely lifeless treasure," [185] became the bearers of wealth when used as money, that is, with the development of commodity production and the designation of money as a general equivalent. Radishchev gave a rather detailed explanation of the functions of money. He called money "the measure of all goods which circulate in trade," a symbol "representing all possessions," all wealth, and he described it as "an instrument placing everything in circulation." [186]

In his analyses of exchange rate and credit Radishchev viewed money as a means of payment. He showed that in world currencies the weight of monetary metal is vital, not its national form. "If in one place a piece of silver costs the same as in another place, then the exchange, they say, is equal. But if in one place it costs more and in another less, then the exchange is unequal. But a piece of silver in essence, nevertheless, does not change; for example, one pound of silver in Russia and one in Holland have the same weight, although under different names." National currencies should be compared with each other only "according to their true weight." [187]

In the history of world economic science Radishchev was the first to give a clear definition of the nature of paper money as a representative of gold and to show its principal difference from metallic monies. "The fundamental coin in the world now is silver or gold; paper is an abbreviation of money; copper money is only scraps; both are tokens. Consequently all commercial calculations and transactions should be

---

[183] Radishchev, *op. cit.*, II, 32.
[184] *Ibid.*, I, 383.
[185] *Ibid.*, I, 385.
[186] *Ibid.*, III, 158–9.
[187] *Ibid.*, II, 16–7.

based on the price of silver and gold." [188] In other words, money as a measure of value can be only full-valued metallic money; paper money and small coins, on the other hand, fulfill their function in circulation as symbols of gold, as its representatives. Therefore the excessive issuance of paper money leads to the disorder of currency circulation and to a general rise of prices. Citing the activity of John Law in France as an example, Radishchev showed that excessive issuance of paper money, that is, inflation, was a "sham wealth, which in an instant can plunge a part of the state into ruin." [189]

As is known, Adam Smith did not see the major difference between paper money and gold money. He explained paper money simply as a more inexpensive means of circulation. Radishchev viewed it in essence as a symbol of value. "Paper currencies surpass in quantity copper, gold, and silver coins; they are treated as symbols, representing value, but metals are treated as commodities, because they are rarer." [190]

Referring to the dependence of paper money on "fundamental coin," Radishchev was first among the economists to try to explain the specific laws of paper-money circulation. He connected the circulation of assignats with the volume of commodity circulation and pointed out the destructive influence of inflation on the national economy. "A flood of paper money is evil; the stream from the broken dam drowns all commercial transactions; agriculture and handicrafts languish; the amount of paper money grows until the value of it is less than the sheet of paper on which it is printed." [191]

The issuance of paper money in excess of the needs of commodity circulation in Russia actually led to a decreasing circulation of gold and silver. For the thirty years of the reign of Catherine II the assets of the trade balance consisted of about four million rubles a year, and the total received, in Radishchev's calculation, was 120 million rubles of silver. "And in two or three years all this silver disappeared from circulation. The era of the decrease of silver money began with the war with Sweden. Is it possible that each year of war cost forty million? Perhaps, for with the increase of money the price of everything soared." [192] Radishchev showed that the increased issuance of paper money to cover the military expenditures of Catherine II resulted in

---

[188] *Ibid.*, II, 16.

[189] Radishchev was the first to introduce into Russian economic science the term "imaginary wealth." In the subsequent development of political economy the capital created by emission of paper notes was defined as "fictitious capital."

[190] *Sobranie Vorontsova,* No. 398, Sheet 141.

[191] Radishchev, *op. cit.*, III, 159.

[192] *Ibid.*, II, 31–2.

a price rise and the reduction of the amount of silver in circulation. The military expenditures for maintaining an army abroad and the growth of the parasitic demands of the imperial court and its circle changed the balance of payments to Russia's disadvantage. Within the country these expenses led to greater issuance of paper money and the fall of the exchange rate of the paper ruble. Part of the silver went, of course, into treasure hoards and into the reserves of the usurers and money changers. The foreign debt of the Russian state also grew. Radishchev remarked that unlimited printing of paper money did "not truly assist agriculture and hadicrafts," but enlarged government revenues; it would lead to the "disappearance of precious metals." [193]

In Radishchev's view "the issuing of money" should have no other aims than "bringing the wealth of the state into circulation." [194] He sharply criticized Catherine II for excessive issuance of paper money for "government profit" and for covering state expenditures. "The first banknotes represented money in circulation, but currently they are in excess," he said.[195] The excessive number of assignats "meant higher prices" and "instability" in the national economy, "especially in the years of bad grain harvests." As a consequence of the predatory financial policy of Catherine the "mining works, the mints, and the paper money are a national hydra," wrote Radishchev with indignation.

In revealing the antinational, ruinous nature of the autocratic financial policy, Radishchev offered a destructive criticism of the perpetrators of this policy: "the sovereign, who makes the money, is a social thief, and if not a thief, then a violator." [196] Radishchev argued that state revenue should have as its source not the issue of money above the necessary quantity for circulation, but the growth of industry and agriculture.

The method by which Radishchev attempted to reveal the laws of paper-money circulation was interesting. For this he calculated the volume of production of grain and "all other products"—manufactured goods—and determined the cost of production according to the prices existing at that time as expressed in money, which provides the volume of annual circulation. For verification he made another calculation: he took the amount of money in circulation multiplied by the amount of money exchanged and received the same "annual circulation," that is, the sum of the prices of goods. He checked the results of his calculations even a third time: the state budgetary revenue he took for a fifth

[193] *Ibid.*, III, 159.
[194] *Ibid.*, III, 548.
[195] *Ibid.*, III, 113.
[196] *Ibid.*

part of all monetary revenues in the country and thus determined the volume of the monetary revenue of the population for a year. If each coin were exchanged three times ("represented three things"), then the same sum of annual turnover would be received. In essence Radishchev was trying to establish the amount of money necessary for circulation. Of course, this is only one approach to the solution of the problem. But for the history of economic science the very presentation of the problem is of importance.

From his concept of the essence of money and monetary circulation Radishchev came to an explanation of the causes for the fall of the exchange rate. This problem was then very acute, and many statesmen considered the cessation of trade with China the reason for the fall of the exchange. Radishchev correctly pointed out that Chinese trade could not have had any influence on the exchange rate. In the first place, this trade was pure barter,[197] and, in the second, its share in the foreign trade turnover of Russia was then quite insignificant. The fall of the exchange rate Radishchev explained by the fall of the rate of the Russian assignat ruble. "If we take our ruble and compare it with Holland's money by its true weight, then its price will be thirty-five stivers or a little more. Why now are they giving twenty-seven or twenty-eight stivers for a ruble? Because they trade not in silver rubles, but in paper ones. Add to the paper ruble the exchange for silver [that is, the agio—E. P.], and then you will get the old ruble; or trade in silver money, and the exchange will be equal (*al pari*)." [198]

In another work Radishchev wrote: "The exchange rate here applies to silver money. Should you eliminate it and retain copper, then the exchange rate would become equal to it. Should you eliminate it, too, then the ruble will cost whatever can be bought for it." [199] He showed thereby that the value of the paper ruble can be expressed in money of full value or in goods.

The rate of exchange fell, according to Radishchev, for the same reason that prices of all goods in the country rose, namely, because of the increased issue of paper money to cover the growing military expenditures, which demanded forty million rubles per year in silver, that is, the entire sum of state revenues. Radishchev did not consider

---

[197] Pallas, Lepekhin and Chulkov wrote on the barter nature of the Kiakhta trade. Radishchev of course was familiar with their works.

In the barter trade at Kiakhta even later in the XIX century silver served only as "price measure," writes Marx, calling exchange of goods between Siberia and China "simple barter trade." Marx, *K kritike politicheskoi ekonomii,* p. 64.

[198] Radishchev, *op. cit.,* II, 17.

[199] *Ibid.,* III, 547.

the entire balance sheet of Russia, and therefore his solution of the problem was not exhaustive. But at the same time his indications of the connection of the fall of the rate of exchange with the excessive (in comparison with revenue) military expenditures of the country, especially abroad, and not just with the balance of foreign trade, were completely correct.

From his concept of money as a commodity, on the one hand, and, on the other, as capital, bringing income like any other property, Radishchev proceeded to his definition of credit and interest. He deduced credit relationships from commodity production on the basis of private ownership. In "Project for a Civil Code" he portrayed in detail the relationship of property with all the rights derived from it—of ownership, of usage, and of confiscation. "Like all other possessions one can change or sell it [money]; one can give it or lend it." [200] In his opinion one should not restrict freedom of the use of property, regardless of whatever form this property might take. In connection with this Radishchev posed "a vital question on profit." At that time the lending of money for interest by private persons—merchants, nobles, and officials—was widespread. Such usurers were sharply criticized in the satirical journals of Novikov and in the writings of Chulkov and others. Already under Elizabeth the government had decreed that the maximum interest rate was to be 6 per cent per annum.

Radishchev attempted to give an economic explanation of the very essence of interest and the right of collecting it. He did not defend the usurers, but proceeded from his understanding of the right of property, from the relationship of hard cash capital and the demand for it. One can borrow all kinds of things, but Radishchev considered only the money loan. The loan can be either charitable, that is, free of charge, or "with interest." Interest is the payment for use of something borrowed. "Interest in money is called percentage." [201]

Radishchev defined interest as *"the cost of money."* If it were permitted by law and not condemned by society for contracting parties by agreement "to name the price of property being transferred from hand to hand, then why is it not within the competence of contracting parties to name the price of money?" asked Radishchev.[202] He felt that the receipt of interest "is just and not disgraceful," like revenue from any capital property.

In a country with a weakly developed credit system and with a lack of accumulated money capital, Radishchev argued, the law on interest

---

200 *Ibid.*, III, 230–1.
201 *Ibid.*, III, 230.
202 *Ibid.*, III, 231.

would always be broken, and private persons who lend money will take for their risk a greater percent the stricter the prohibition. "Of course it would be better if money were cheap and interest rates low. But no law can set a price on it; where something is abundant, it will be cheap." [203] The rate of interest, he further wrote, was determined by the money market itself and by the relationship of the demand and supply of money capital, not by administrative interference on the part of the government. As was shown above, the representatives of the noble serfowning ideology sharply opposed the view of Radishchev, Chulkov, and other progressive economists that the creditor and borrower themselves should be permitted "to set the price of money" and to determine freely the rate of interest. The struggle to limit credit relationships was an attempt of the conservative nobility to preserve the seminatural character of the serf economy, the abolition of which the progressive spokesmen were urging.

Radishchev applied the general theoretical pronouncements on the nature of interest and the economic laws determining its rate to Russia, where the money market was not as yet well developed and where usury still prevailed. In Russia, despite governmental prohibition, interest was high because "accumulations of capital in ready money are few and because accumulated capital could be used much more profitably and safely in acquiring immovable properties. Examples of this are clearly evident among the brokers, contractors, and the merchants themselves." [204] Actually, the literature of the time contained many examples of the arbitrariness of the nobility and high officials towards their creditors, who, by various persecutions and law suits for dishonoring noblemen, were forced to renounce promissary notes, to give false receipts for payment of debts, and even to bribe, in order, they said, that the merchant could disengage himself inexpensively from the noble's claims. Therefore, Radishchev had every right to claim that it was less dangerous in Russia to invest money in property or in trade than to lend it.

As a result, in his analysis of money and money circulation Radishchev did not confine himself to posing the problems of economic policy as did his predecessors and contemporaries—Lomonosov, Rychkov, Chulkov, and others. He investigated theoretically the problems of money, currency circulation, and credit and offered an original solution.

In questions concerning the development of credit, as in all his economic proposals, Radishchev is first of all an opponent of feudal-

---

203 *Ibid.*, III, 232.
204 *Ibid.*

serf limitations and a champion of free economic activity of the small producers. "A commercial bank was never disadvantageous to a state," wrote Radishchev, "if only the government would not interfere in business." [205] But this interference in enserfed Russia always took place for the benefit of the nobility, and to the detriment of the merchants and the lower classes.

Radishchev's theory of money holds great interests in the development of economic science. In originality and thoroughness his monetary theory surpassed the teachings of all Russian economists before him and of the western bourgeois economists of the eighteenth century, including Adam Smith.

Criticism of State Tax Policy

Radishchev devoted much attention to the subject of taxes and tax policy, which, in his opinion, was one of the central problems of any economic policy. Petty, Pososhkov, the physiocrats, and Adam Smith were also concerned with these matters. A tax policy has either a stimulating or a retarding influence on the development of agriculture, industry, foreign and domestic trade, and finances. In the enserfed Russia at the end of the eighteenth century, as in all feudal and bourgeois states, almost the sole source of state revenues was the many direct and indirect taxes and collections from the taxed classes—the peasantry, merchants, and artisans. The nobility and clergy were exempt from personal taxes. Indirect taxes, duties on imports, and consumer taxes on vodka, salt, and other goods did not then play a decisive part in the state budget.

His special works, "On the Collection of Head Tax" and "On Taxes," recently published under the general title, "Note on Taxes of the Petersburg Gubernia," [206] are devoted to the study and criticism of the tax policy of the autocracy in the second half of the eighteenth century. Radishchev clearly defined his task: by using the example of the Petersburg gubernia, to study "all taxes," to show "the methods of satisfying them," to separate direct taxes, imposed on a member of society "by coercion," from indirect taxes, which are paid "in an unnoticed fashion" by consumers of goods, and to distinguish and compare "the burdens of the agriculturist and those of the city dweller."

Such a detailed and manifold tax study was undertaken by Radishchev for the first time in the history of Russian economic thought. He had a definite goal: "if possible, we shall point to the means to

[205] *Sobranie Vorontsova,* No. 398, Sheet 141.
[206] Radishchev, *op. cit.,* III.

assist the good and remove the bad." [207] After Radishchev the Decembrist, N. Turgenev, devoted the greatest attention to the problem of taxes.

Radishchev could limit himself with full justification to material on the Petersburg gubernia, because "people's taxes of the St. Petersburg gubernia are identical with those of other gubernias both in their essence and in the method of collection." [208] He approached his study historically, by explaining when each tax had been established and for what purpose, what brought about the introduction of this or that tax and what consequence it had, what influence it exercised on the economy of the country, and what effect it had on the material condition of the payers. From the detailed list of village land and city taxes prepared by Radishchev one can see the complex web of taxes by which the city and village population was burdened and the numerous abuses in taxation and collections which occurred "with and without permission."

For greater clarity Radishchev explained the class structure of the population and showed that the whole tax burden was borne by the peasants in the villages and the artisans in the towns. In his discussion of village taxes, Radishchev pointed out that only the state peasants were considered, "for it is impossible to calculate the burden of taxes on the settlers living on pomestie fields or, as they are called, the serfs. The tax of the peasant is at the whim of the pomeshchik and is measured by the extent of his greed or the lack of it." [209] The most clearly defined state tax on the enserfed peasant was the head tax. All remaining taxes depended only on the pomeshchik and went to benefit him.

The important "village land taxes" in money and in kind, on which Radishchev dwelt in detail, were the head and recruiting levies, the collection for stamped passports, the maintenance of roads, the quartering of soldiers, and the postal duty. The chief city taxes were the duty on the capital of merchants, the head tax for townspeople and guild artisans, the tax for the maintenance of roads, the collections for branding horse collars, the postal tax, and the tax on immovable property.

Of the indirect taxes the liquor and salt customs duties were evaluated in detail. To the general sum of treasury revenues from city taxes Radishchev added the value of the work of serfs assigned to *masters'* shops in state factories, in homes and gardens, and in the Admiralty, "each person contributing on the average sixty rubles per year in money." Thus Radishchev attempted here to determine the

---

[207] *Ibid.*, III, 97.
[208] *Ibid.*
[209] *Ibid.*, III, 118.

amount of the treasury's revenue which was created by appropriation of the labor of the serfs "assigned to masters' shops" in various fields.

In questions of tax policy as in other questions of economic theory and policy, Radishchev strictly maintained the position of a devastating critic of serfdom and defender of the interests of the people. The realization of his program would have led to the bourgeois-democratic development of the country.

The principle of equality of all citizens to acquire and dispose of property, established by Radishchev in *Journey* and in the *Project for a Civil Code,* was clearly emphasized in his discussions of tax policy. He opposed all forms of personal taxes and obligations and sought methods of transforming personal taxes into an income-property tax, which he considered just and which guaranteed equality to the citizens. All personal taxes seemed at first glance equal; actually "any tax distributed by the number of souls is in essence unequal . . ." [210] The inequities of all head levies consisted in their falling on an individual "without excluding from payment the youth or the old man, and placing on an equal the rich man and the poor man, without considering the ability of each . . ." [211] The head tax was levied uniformly on each payer, while the ability to pay and income varied greatly. The head tax, thus, was one of the factors contributing to economic inequality.

Radishchev's discussions on non-uniform incomes and the ability of the peasants to pay the tax are interesting. "For if one is to compare only two agriculturists, of whom one lives close to a large city and the other a hundred versts from it, one realizes quickly how their ability to acquire money differs. "If their fields yield unequal products, if one sows in black soil and the other in clay, then their harvests will vary. But their inequality can consist also in something else; one may sell a quarter of rye for five rubles, the other for two rubles, but the one may have grown twenty and the other four." [212]

Radishchev showed that the fertility of various plots of land, their location in relation to markets, and the difference of prices in local closed markets and in the more inclusive markets in large towns determined the profits of the agriculturists. As a result, some growers, according to Radishchev's calculation, paid one-fifteenth of their income for head tax, others one-tenth, and some even one-half.

What conclusion did Radishchev reach? He pointed out the injustice of equal taxation and demanded differentiation of taxes on the

---

[210] *Ibid.,* III, 108.
[211] *Ibid.,* III, 104.
[212] *Ibid.,* III, 121.

basis of income and possessions. Therein he saw the realization of the principle of the material equality of payers.

It will be recalled that the concept of equality was one of the most important ideas in all Radishchev's analyses: people are equal by the very nature of natural law; all members of society should be equal before the law; the law must be "the same for everyone"; the most important right of the citizen, to acquire property, should be the same for all people without any kind of class limitations. Moreover, the acquisition of property should be based on the personal labor of direct producers—peasants and artisans.

Such was Radishchev's understanding of equality. This is a bourgeois-democratic view. The demand for its realization was not only progressive, but even revolutionary in the struggle of the oppressed toilers, primarily the peasantry, against the feudal serf system. Radishchev did not advocate reactionary "equalitarianism" in possessions, that is, he did not want equalized incomes, but equality which, as Lenin wrote, has a "historical-absolute and historical-legal *content in the struggle with* serfdom." "These theories express progressive, revolutionary petit-bourgeois *democracy* . . . and serve as a banner in the most decisive struggle against the old serf Russia. The idea of equality is the most revolutionary idea in the struggle with the old order of absolutism in general—and with the old serf and big pomestie landownership in particular."[213] Radishchev's understanding of equality also expressed the peasants' interests.

Of course, Radishchev did not realize that his equality did not exclude, but definitely fostered, the exploitation of man by man and that it led to economic inequality, inasmuch as the small goods production which he advocated after the abolition of feudalism constantly and on a massive scale gives birth to capitalism. But in Russia at the end of the eighteenth century the defense of small-scale peasant and artisan production as a broad basis for the transition from feudalism to capitalistic production had a profoundly progressive character.

Proceeding from his understanding of equality, Radishchev also approached the concrete problem of the structure of tax policy, not on the basis of personal feudal obligations, but on the basis of an income-property tax. Showing the economic inequality of the head tax, Radishchev posed the problem: "On the transfer of the head tax into a material and land tax . . . Also quarters, bridges, and roads."[214] In Radishchev's opinion, such transformation of the feudal-serf head tax

[213] Lenin, *op. cit.,* XIII, 214.
[214] Radishchev, *op. cit.,* III, 549.

into a bourgeois income-property tax would mean the actual material "equalizing" of the payers. "Equalizing in this case will be, I think, not so difficult as many people believe," he wrote.[215]

He saw some beginnings in the distribution of taxes worked out by the peasants "among themselves according to their consent" in the allocation, at peaceful meetings, of the general sum of the tax assessed on the settlement, based not on individuals but on households or "families." The amount of "owned land," of income, and of the strength of the household was taken into account. If the tax were determined by the amount of land, Radishchev felt that "in this form this tax is sufficiently equalizing." [216]

In connection with this practice, the peasants also divided land "so that all will have an equal parcel of good land." Actual deviation from personal assessments towards land assessment according to the peasants' "consent" Radishchev viewed as only the first step in changing the tax system. It was necessary to go further and review and reconstruct all tax legislation. "Should we move one step forward, then what has been done in a small area we will spread to the whole." [217]

In Radishchev's opinion, the postal tax in the Petersburg gubernia could serve as an example of the correct distribution of a tax. Those areas closer to the capital paid more, and those farther away paid less, because the inhabitants of distant places did not use the postal roads as much, and their economy was less tied to the capital city. This tax was allocated not by persons, but according to the amount of business.

Showing the expedience and the economic necessity of an income-property system of assessment, Radishchev at the same time demanded the easement of the tax burden on agriculturists, industrialists, and merchants. This reform fully harmonized with Radishchev's general position, which was directed towards the all-round protection of peasant interests.

Having shown the essence and the unbearable burden of feudal personal taxes, Radishchev quite substantially corrected the views of Adam Smith on this question. The later viewed the head tax in the Russian empire in the 1770's as similar to that paid by the slave-owners in North America, India, and in ancient slave-owning states.

---

[215] *Ibid.*, III, 121.

[216] Actual departure from the legally established soul tax, if taxes were distributed, was advocated in Volynskii's "Instructions"; also in those of Chulkov and others, inasmuch as the collection of taxes was then placed on a more solid foundation.

[217] *Ibid.*, III, 122.

In Smith's opinion, this tax "represents, essentially, a tax on profit from a special form of capital dispersed in agriculture." [218]

As if answering Smith, Radishchev emphasized that it was not the pomeshchiki who paid the head tax, but the enserfed peasants themselves; that taxes and obligations took the lion's share of their income, and that this resulted in the ruin and degradation of peasant agriculture. The excessively high taxes led only to the "country's becoming poorer, because *the people will have less*. This is the only reasonable definition of poverty." [219]

The pomeshchiki-serfowners paid neither head nor land taxes, and their incomes from exploitation of the forced labor of the peasants were not subject to tax. The view of Adam Smith, who considered the head tax in Russia as a tax on capital as if it were paid by the pomeshchiki, was untrue both in form and content. Such a point of view led to a justification of personal taxes in the serf state. The revolutionary Radishchev, defending the interests of the oppressed peasantry, sharply condemned the greedy tax policy of the serf state, revealed its class nature, and found no economic justification for it.

On the question of indirect taxes Radishchev's position sharply differed from that of the bourgeois economists of the eighteenth century. For example, Adam Smith considered it beneficial for the people, for the simple workers, to abstain from consuming such taxed products as tea, sugar, tobacco, and meat. Justifying the high taxes on these and similar goods, Smith excluded them from the number of necessities for "the lower classes of the population." [220]

Radishchev was very disturbed by the fact that the toiling masses of enserfed Russia could not consume meat, sugar, and tea. With indignation he wrote of how, as a result of cruel exploitation, the peasants were forced to look on sugar as a "boyar food" and to consume meat only "during the first meal after a fast." Not abstention from consuming similar products, but indignation against the exploiter-serfowners and the autocracy which conducted economic policy in the interests of the pomeshchik was advocated by the first spokesman of popular revolution—Radishchev.

The entire tax policy of the state must "be based not on some sort of promises, but on national capital," wrote Radishchev.[221] In order to have a just concept of "national capital" in the country and "to estab-

---

218 Smith, *Issledovanie o prirode i prichinakh bogatstva narodov,* II, 369.
219 *Sobranie Vorontsova,* No. 398, Sheet 141.
220 Smith, *op. cit.,* II, 382–3, 386.
221 Radishchev, *op. cit.,* III, 159.

lish a certain legal rule on taxes, so that the people would know that it was immutable and no one would violate it," Radishchev recommended a statistical-economic investigation of Russia according to a definite program. The project shows how broadly Radishchev had understood the national economy and how profoundly he understood the interrelation of economic phenomena. He believed that only on the basis of a careful study of the status of production and circulation in different areas of the country could a firm and clear tax proposal be made. Such a method would not oppress the people, but would aid the further economic development of the country. Moreover, it would be necessary to advise the people how much each "should pay" in order to protect their interests better and oppose illegal extortions and persecutions.

The effect of each tax on village or town inhabitants Radishchev examined from the point of view of the "burden" of this tax and its influence on economic activity; "how much each branch of state revenue impedes the natural freedom of action and stifles the forces of freedom." [222] "Freedom of action" in Radishchev's understanding did not mean complete elimination of state interference in economic life, but abolition of feudal-serf forms and methods of this interference.

In his entire economic system, Radishchev showed the necessity of such state interference and of such an economic policy as, on the basis of the recognition of the bourgeois-democratic principle of equality of citizens, would aid the progressive development of industry, agriculture, and trade and would bring health to the financial structure and currency of Russia.

The Place of A. N. Radishchev in the History of Economic Thought

In the person of A. N. Radishchev the Russian people had an important scholar, the first spokesman of revolutionary Russia. A rebel from the nobility, he laid the foundation for developing the theory of national revolution; he was the most daring, decisive, and irreconcilable fighter against autocracy and serfdom in the eighteenth century.

Radishchev was the first in Russian literature to offer a systematic, profound, all-inclusive, and devastating criticism of the economic bases of serfdom. He showed that the peasants and the pomeshchiki were two opposed classes, whose interests were irreconcilable. Having revealed the contradictions of the serf method of production, Radishchev

[222] *Ibid.*, III, 113.

was the first to prove the necessity of its forceful abolition and the inevitability of national revolution in Russia.

Radishchev's revolutionary and democratic views were expressed both in the *method* of solving the major problem—the abolition of serfdom and autocracy by means of national revolution—and in the forms he proposed for the economic reorganization of society in the interests of the toiling people. Though essentially in favor of bourgeois methods of production, Radishchev proceeded not from the exploitative interests of the bourgeoisie, but from those of the toiling masses. His theoretical propositions cleared the road to revolutionary abolition of all forms of feudal oppression.

In his socio-political demands Radishchev towered above the members of the French Enlightenment of the eighteenth century. His ideal state structure was a popular republic which was to arise from an armed national uprising and the liquidation of all the feudal class limitations on property rights and the activities of members of society.

As a warm partisan of the national republic, advocating the sovereign right of a people to determine the form of government, Radishchev called on the masses not to await kindnesses from "enlightened monarchs," but by revolution to decide their own fate. All his works defended the interests of the peasants. His aim was to secure freedom and ownership of the land. Radishchev fought for the abolition of the landownership of the pomeshchiki on behalf of the peasants, for complete freedom of economic activity, and for destruction of all class privileges and limitations. Such goals demonstrate the enormous progressive significance of Radishchev's economic views.

He unwaveringly believed in the strength, might, and capability of the Russian people. Radishchev thus characterized the Russian people: "Firmness in undertakings and indefatigability in accomplishment are qualities which distinguish the Russian people . . . Enterprise and indestructibility in following undertakings are and were the first reasons for the success of the Russians: even under the very weight of the foreign yoke [in the period of Tartar-Mongol domination—E. P.] these qualities did not languish. O people destined for greatness and glory, if they would only turn towards you to achieve all this, what a social blessing that would be." [223]

Radishchev revealed the basis of the low productivity of enserfed labor and showed the importance of personal material interest as a stimulus to raising the productivity of social labor. In offering solutions to the agrarian problem, both in content and in method Radi-

---

[223] *Ibid.*, II, 146–7.

shchev foreshadowed the nineteenth century revolutionary democrats. In the area of industry and foreign trade he defended a policy of protectionism for Russia, and in the field of taxation he demanded the liquidation of all feudal taxes and the establishment of taxes of a bourgeois-democratic nature.

Russian economic conditions and special concern for the improvement of the peasantry's position left their stamp on Radishchev's views in regard to heavy industry. Defending in essence the transition to capitalistic production, Radishchev was unable to understand the revolutionizing role of heavy industry. He preferred production by small producers based on their personal labor to large-scale exploiting production.

Radishchev did not limit himself to criticism of serfdom and economic policy. In his works he also posed and clarified a number of large-scale theoretical problems of political economy, original for his time: feudal ownership of land; force as an extra-economic form of coercion to labor; the productivity of social labor and stimuli to improve it; the exploitative origin of the wealth of pomeshchiki, of owners of manufacturing enterprises, and of merchants; the price of commodities and profits; metallic and paper money; credit and interest; and so on. Radishchev was one of the first Russian economists to attempt an analysis of production. He proceeded to consider labor as the source of social wealth and constantly connected the problem of productivity of labor with its social form.

Radishchev was a major and original Russian thinker and the foremost economist of the eighteenth century.

The revolutionary demands and needs of the peasantry, expressed in Radishchev's works, could, under those conditions, not be strengthened by any organized form of revolutionary movement. Radishchev dreamed of popular support, but practically, like all the revolutionaries from the nobility, he was separated from the people, although he expressed their interests.

Beginning at the end of the eighteenth century and continuing throughout the nineteenth, the pomeshchiki serf-owners tried to relegate to oblivion not only the works, but even the very name of the writer-revolutionary. Noble-bourgeois historians, bowing before everything foreign, persistently spread the false rumors that Radishchev did not have any real roots in Russia, that he was only a student and follower of the western Enlightenment of the eighteenth century. Unfortunately the influence of noble-bourgeois historical literature found a place even in Soviet literature; here and there clear examples are still found of completely untrue evaluations of Radishchev in the spirit of cosmopolitanism. Instead of showing Radishchev's ideas as a reflection of the spontaneous uprising of the peasants against serfdom, some researchers continue to seek all possible influences from the West. This was done by Ia. L. Barskov in the article, "A. N. Radishchev: Life and Personality."[224]

An incorrect evaluation of the origin of Radishchev's ideas is given in the second edition of the textbook, *History of the USSR,* edited by the Academician Grekov. In the opinion of the author of the chapter of this textbook in which Radishchev is discussed, Radishchev borrowed everything from foreigners, did not create anything of his own, and was like a foreign body in the history of Russian social thought. The ideas of Radishchev were not conditioned by the economic processes and the class struggle in Russia and were not connected with the development of Russian economic thought. Doubtless, this sort of evaluation originated from the "Kazan pomeshchitsa," as Catherine II called herself; she wrote that Radishchev presented only "philosophizing appropriated from various semi-sages of his century, like Rousseau, Abbé Reynal, and similar hypochondriacs."[225]

Catherine II tried to create an image of "well-being" in her empire and to hide the sharp class conflicts. Therefore she attempted in every way to show the groundlessness of Radishchev's ideas in Russia by arguing that they were borrowed from the West. What Catherine said about Radishchev was repeated by all the noble and bourgeois spokesmen, and this continued right up to our own times.[226]

Radishchev struggled for the democratic development of Russia, which, in his opinion, national revolution could effect. He was the first to express this idea of national revolution and was a defender of the interests of the peasantry against autocracy and serfdom. Therefore it is impossible to agree with Plekhanov, who saw Radishchev as a representative of the interests of the third estate, that is, the bourgeoisie, and not of the peasantry.[227]

Profoundly vicious is the point of view of V. V. Sviatlovskii, who considered Radishchev the first spokesman of the "supra-class intelligentsia."[228] Even the concept of "supra-class intelligentsia" is untrue,

---

[224] *Ibid.,* II; *Materialy k izucheniiu "Puteshestviia,"* p. 93.

[225] Babkin, *op. cit.,* p. 160.

[226] Following his erroneous assertion about lack of independence in the development of Russian economic thought, Normano in his book writes that Radishchev's *Journey* contained English liberal ideas; see Normano, *The Spirit of Russian Economics,* p. 12. The American historian Laserson explains Radishchev's ideas as being influenced by American life. Laserson, *The American Impact on Russia* (New York: 1951).

[227] Plekhanov, *Sochineniia,* XXII, 74.

[228] Sviatlovskii, *Istoriia ekonomicheskikh idei v Rossii,* I, 84–90.

as the intelligentsia always reflects the interest of some class. It is also inapplicable to Radishchev, because he did not stand above classes, nor did he ever strive to reconcile the interests of opposing classes—the pomeshchiki and the peasants. M. N. Pokrovskii gave a basically incorrect characterization of Radishchev as a representative of the intelligentsia. Of Radishchev's literary works, Pokrovskii said: "This is a member of the intelligentsia who wrote for the intelligentsia"; "Radishchev did not think of appealing to the people." [229] Pokrovskii considered Radishchev a spokesman of the industrial bourgeoisie on the grounds that Radishchev was a protectionist. This evaluation corresponded with Pokrovskii's antiscientific attitude towards the social development of Russia.

No less fallacious is B. Syromiatnikov's characterization of Radishchev and the evaluation of *Journey from Petersburg to Moscow* in the Granat encyclopedic dictionary. Calling Radishchev "the first and most typical representative of the penitent nobility," Syromiatnikov related Radishchev's views to a bourgeois-liberal trend. Lowering Radishchev to the category of liberals, he argued that "in essence Radishchev was far from having any sort of revolutionary tendencies" and that he was "an enemy of civil war." Syromiatnikov evaluated the most revolutionary work of world literature of the eighteenth century as an appeal to Catherine II.

In their incorrect evaluation of Radishchev's class positions, V. Sviatlovskii, M. Pokrovskii, B. Syromiatnikov, and others followed in essence the bourgeois historian V. O. Kliuchevskii, who called Radishchev "an ultraliberal with a foreign university education." [230]

In recent years Soviet scholars have done much to overcome these wrong impressions. They have revealed the actual content of Radishchev's works and showed that his views had deep roots in those processes of Russian economic development and class struggle, among them also ideological struggles, which were being realized in the second half of the eighteenth century. The decisive influence on Radishchev of the Peasant War led by Pugachev had been made clear.

Even Radishchev himself noted the independent creative nature of his works. In "The Life of Fedor Vasil'evich Ushakov," saturated with autobiographical episodes, Radishchev wrote that his mind could not remain "so to speak, passive, engaged only in investigating the opinions of others." He did not follow that group of people who, in his

---

[229] M. N. Pokrovskii, *Russkaia istoriia v somom szhatom ocherke* [Russian History in a Concise Outline], (4th edition, Moscow: 1933), pp. 112–3.

[230] Kliuchevskii, *Kurs russkoi istorii,* V, 361.

expression, "adopt everything that reaches them, occupy themselves with others' publications." Radishchev belonged to those prominent Russian writers and scholars who, "having strengthened their natural capabilities by study, withdraw from the well-trodden paths and enter the unknown and unbroken ones."[231]

Having examined the influence of French leaders of the Enlightenment, Radishchev critically and creatively developed their ideas. He refused not only to bow before them, but, while respecting them, at the same time criticized decisively their erroneous positions and their narrowness regarding the protection of the interests of the toiling masses. This includes both the right and the left wing of the French Enlightenment, Voltaire and Rousseau, as well as Montesquieu and other contemporary authorities.

Radishchev could not agree with Voltaire either in his evaluation of the role of the enlightened monarchs or in his recognition of the eternal necessity of the whip and the driver for the common people. As was shown above, Radishchev criticized the "philosophizing" of Montesquieu and Rousseau on state structure, not agreeing with the individualistic philosophy of Rousseau, but asserting, on the contrary, that "man is a social being."[232] Regarding Rousseau's teachings on "the golden age" of the primitive savage he responded ironically: "Living in the huge Siberian forests among wild animals and tribes, frequently differing from them only by articulate speech, a faculty which they did not appreciate under the circumstances, I think that I too would become, in the end, the happy man of Rousseau and begin to walk on all fours."[233] Radishchev called Rousseau a very dangerous author for youth, "a skillful leader in the science of sensitivity," but this sensitivity "sometimes is not worth a broken kopek." Radishchev saw as a major defect in Rousseau's theories that in the end he "never had a sting,"[234] that is, he was never a revolutionary, a fighter for the forceful overthrow of serfdom and for the attainment of conditions of progressive development.

Radishchev's value as a thinker and a scholar lies in his profound knowledge of all the achievements of contemporary world socio-economic thought and his critical attitude towards it from the point of view of the applicability of these or other ideas to development in Russia. He was an enemy of all servility, including grovelling before

---

231 Radishchev, *op. cit.*, I, 180–1.
232 *Ibid.*, III, 478. Letter to A. R. Vorontsov June 3, 1795.
233 *Ibid.*, III, 428. Letter to A. R. Vorontsov February 17, 1792.
234 *Ibid.*, III, 429.

everything foreign. The unjust and unfounded lowering of Radishchev to the level of a simple imitator of Western European thinkers insults the feeling of patriotism and national pride of the Russian people.

Unmerited also is the neglect until recent times of the economic views of the first Russian revolutionary in general histories of economic theories. Thus in D. I. Rozenberg's *History of Political Economy* not only is the wealth of theoretical views of Radishchev ignored, but even his name is mentioned only once, in the chapter "Smithism in Russia." [235] The political viciousness of a similar type of obscurantism in the history of Russian science was brilliantly revealed by A. A. Zhdanov in his address to a philosophical discussion group in 1947. Lenin and Stalin placed Radishchev in the first rank of those revolutionary fighters for freedom who are the national pride of the great Russian people.

Under the conditions of serfdom and the reaction of the nobility Radishchev did not have the opportunity to finish many of the economic investigations that he began and to systematize his theoretical views. Autocratic-feudal Russia cut short Radishchev's life before his time, but the dominant exploiting classes could not throttle his revolutionary ideas, which tolled the alarm bell in the age-long struggle of the Russian people for their liberation.

Radishchev's economic views represent an important contribution to the development of worldwide economic science. He did not belong to any of the theoretical schools of the eighteenth century—neither to the mercantilists, the physiocrats, nor to the English classical school of bourgeois political economy.

Radishchev summed up and elevated to a new stage the struggle against serfdom in the eighteenth century. Being a direct predecessor of the Decembrists, he, at the same time, laid the foundation for those revolutionary ideas in Russian economic thought which subsequently were fully developed on a new, higher level by the nineteenth century revolutionary democrats, headed by Chernyshevskii. Therein lies the great scientific and political significance of Radishchev's economic views, his honorable place in, and immortal service to, the history of Russian and world economic thought.

---

[235] Rozenberg, *Istoriia politicheskoi ekonomii,* I, 142.

GLOSSARY

altyn—a monetary unit of medieval Russia. One *altyn* equaled six *dengas* or three *copecks.*

arshin—A Russian linear measure equal to about 28 inches.

barshchina—an obligation of a serf to work on his master's estate, often with his own stock and implements.

boyar—a member of the medieval Russian aristocracy, distinguished from the service nobility (*pomeshchiki* and *dvoriane*).

cheliad—a dependent class in medieval Russia who worked for a prince or a member of the nobility or the monasteries.

cheliadin—a member of the *cheliad.*

chetvert—a fourth; a quarter; a corn measure of about eight bushels.

copeck—a monetary unit which replaced the *denga* and *altyn,* used in medieval and modern Russia. A *copeck* equaled two *dengas.*

denga—a medieval Russian monetary unit borrowed from the Mongols which ceased to circulate after the seventeenth century. One *ruble* equaled 200 *dengas.* In modern Russia *dengi* denotes "money."

desiatina—a tithe; a land measure equal to 2.7 acres.

dolog—credit.

Domostroi—a sixteenth century literary document giving instructions to the master of the house concerning his conduct toward the members of his family.

druzhina—the retinue of Kievan princes, which helped them to trade, fight, and rule.

druzhinnik—a member of the *druzhina.*

dvorianin—a member of lower rank of a princely court; subsequently a member of the Russian nobility (*dvorianstvo*).

efimok—Joachimsthaler; a monetary unit used in seventeenth century Russia.

gosti—the highest ranking merchants of Moscow, appointed by the Tsar to handle his domestic and foreign trade in monopolized goods. *Gosti* could buy land and were also exempt from certain taxes.

gostinnaia sotnia—a merchants' association (guild) of lower rank merchants in Moscow in the sixteenth and seventeenth centuries. The membership of the association varied from 100 to 350 mombers, who, while influential, did not enjoy the same rights and privileges as did the *gosti.*

grivna—the basic monetary unit of Kievan Rus and of Moscow. It equaled ten *copecks.*

gubernia—an administrative unit in Russia introduced by Peter I and abolished by the Bolsheviks in 1923.

istoe—usurious capital.

izgoi—a feudal serf, bound to the owner and to the soil.

kabala—a form of servitude in medieval Russia under which an individual accepted an obligation to work for a definite and agreed period of time.

kabalnye knigi—slave registers.

kholop—a captive; a personal slave of the prince, the *boyar,* or the monastery.

kholopstvo—captivity; slavery; a surrender of freedom because of economic necessity.

kliuchnik—literally a possessor of keys; a house steward.

korm—a tax received by the administrators of Moscovite princes.

kormlenie—a system of local administration prevalent from the fourteenth through the sixteenth century in Moscow under which local administrators, who were appointed by the prince, received payment in kind from the local population.

kormlenshchik—a recipient of the *kormlenie;* a local administrator and tax collector and, as a rule, a member of the nobility.

kostka—a head tax on persons bringing merchandise to market.

kuna—a marten; also a monetary unit in Kievan Rus and later in Moscow.

kupa—a sum of money received by poor peasants from their masters upon fulfillment of an agreement.

lemekh—a plow or plowshare.

mesiachina—a form of peasant exploitation in fifteenth century Russia under which serfs became slaves.

mestnichestvo—an elaborate code in Muscovy regulating the quantity and quality of service which the Russian aristocracy rendered to the prince; a "trade union" founded upon genealogical principles.

muzhik—a Russian peasant.

myto—a transit and/or marketing tax.

naimit—servant; a hired laborer who in return for his work received a payment (*naim*).

namestnichestvo—a large administrative unit of medieval Russia.

namestnik—an administrator of a *namestnichestvo,* usually a high-born nobleman.

naspa—interest in kind on borrowed grain.

oblast—a province; an administrative unit of Russia.

obrok—payment in kind or money of a serf's obligations or dues to the nobleman; quit-rent.

obshchina—Russian peasant village commune; also known as *mir.*

ognishchanin—a man attached to the prince's household; a servant of the prince.

okniazhennaia zemlia—the land of free peasants which had been appropriated by a prince.

okolnichii—a courtier of the second rank attached to the person of the Tsar; the rank next to *boyar* in importance.

oprichnik—a member of the *oprichnina.*

oprichnina—a system of terror used by Ivan IV (1547–1584) to crush feudal aristocracy and thus to strengthen Russian autocracy.

ostrog—a fort and a blockhouse the Russians built along the rivers of Asia in their eastward expansion.

pismennye liudi—persons registered as taxpayers.

poltina—a monetary unit in medieval Russia equal to fifty *copecks.*

pomeshchik—a recipient, and later an owner, of an estate; a nobleman.

pomestie—an estate granted to a nobleman by a prince in return for service, usually of a military nature.

prikaz—an administrative department of the central government of Muscovy from the fifteenth through the seventeenth century.

prodazha—a fine in medieval Russia payable to the prince for various crimes (other than murder).

pud—a unit of weight equal to 36.113 lbs.

ratusha—town hall; city administration established by Peter I.

riadovich—a bondsman who worked for a master in accordance with a legally formulated agreement.

roleinyi zakup—land-indentured laborer of Kievan Rus.

rost—interest on money loans in medieval Russia.

ruble—a monetary unit introduced into Russia in the seventeenth century. Its value then was twelve to fifteen times greater than in the early part of the twentieth century, when it equaled 50 cents.

Russkaia Pravda—the civil code of Kievan Rus.

sazhen—a linear measure equal to seven feet.

skupshchik—a broker who as a rule came from among the peasants.

smerd—a free peasant of Kievan Rus who subsequently became obligated either to the prince or to a noble.

sobor—an assembly, usually of high church dignitaries.

sokha—a tax unit used in the thirteenth century; later a holding worked by two men; in the fifteenth century a tax base.

streltsy—professional soldiers of Russia in the sixteenth and seventeenth centuries.

sudebnik—a code of law introduced by Ivan II in 1497 and amended in 1550 by Ivan IV.

sukonnaia sotnia—textile association of Moscow's lower rank merchants in the sixteenth and seventeenth centuries.

tamga—an internal custom duty; a tax on a commodity calculated as a percentage of its value, i.e., *ad valorem.*

tiaglo—a tax or an obligation in kind or money, or both.

tiaglye liudi—people who were taxed in kind and in money.

tysiatsky—commander of the city militia in Novgorod who was elected by the *veche* and who acted as commander-in-chief in the absence of the prince.

tiun—a steward; an official of a prince.

tovar—goods; property; a product sold on the market.

tselovalnik—sworn man; a person who kissed the cross or the Bible; officials of local or central government in sixteenth and seventeenth century Russia.

uezd—a district; an administrative unit in Russia.

ukaz—an edict; a statute; an administrative decree.

Ulozhenie of 1649—the code of law approved by the *Zemskii Sobor* of 1649, which legalized serfdom in Russia and remained in force until the nineteenth century.

veche—a village or city assembly in medieval Russia which theoretically determined the domestic and foreign policy of the town, elected officials, and discharged certain judicial functions.

versta—a linear measure; a unit of distance equivalent to 0.6629 miles or about 3,500 feet.

vira—a fine in Kievan Rus payable to the prince for murder.

virnik—an official of the prince in charge of collecting fines for murders.

voevoda—a military as well as administrative leader of medieval Russia, usually a high-born member of the aristocracy.

voevodstvo—an administrative unit of medieval Russia presided over by a *voevoda*.

volost—a county; a district; an administrative unit in Russia.

votchina—patrimonial, hereditary form of landowning in medieval Russia.

votchinnik—an owner of a *votchina,* usually a *boyar.*

yarlyk—a charter granted by Mongol khans to Russian princes entitling them to rule their principalities.

yasak—a sign of subjection; a compulsory tax; a tribute paid by the conquered to their conquerors.

zakon—a legislative statute; a fundamental law.

zemskii sobor—a landed assembly in sixteenth and seventeenth century Russia composed of free landholders having authority to deal with such major issues as war and peace and the election of a new tsar.

zhalovanie—conditional landowning in return for a definite service; a fief which could neither be sold, bequeathed, nor alienated.

BIBLIOGRAPHY

A. Sources

Akty feodalnogo zemlevladeniia i khoziaistva XIV–XVI vekov [Acts of Feudal Landownership and Economy of the XIV–XVI Centuries]. Moscow: 1951.

Aristov, N. Ia., *ed. Khrestomatiia po russkoi istorii dlia izucheniia drevnerusskoi zhizni, pismennosti i literatury ot nachala pismennosti do XVI v.* [Selections in Russian History for the Study of Ancient Russian Life, Literature, and Education from the Beginning of Literacy to the XVI Century]. Warsaw: 1870.

Bakhrushin, S. B., *ed. Dukhovnye i dogovornye gramoty kniazei velikikh i udelnykh* [Testaments and Treaties of the Grand and Appanage Princes]. Moscow: 1909.

Bazilevich, K. V., *ed. Gorodskie vosstaniia v Moskovskom gosudarstve XVII v. Sbornik dokumentov* [Town Upheavals in the Moscovite State During the XVII Century. A Collection of Documents]. Moscow-Leningrad: 1936.

Biliarskii, P. S. *Materialy dlia biografii Lomonosova* [Materials for Lomonosov's Biography]. St. Petersburg: 1865.

Boltov, A. T. "Nakaz upraviteliu ili prikazchiku . . ." [An Instruction for the Administrator or Steward . . .], *Trudy Volnogo ekonomicheskogo obshchestva* [Works of the Free Economic Society], XVI (1770), pp. 69–230. Hereinafter cited as *TVEO.*

[Catherine II]. *Akty tsarstvovaniia Ekateriny II. Uchrezhdeniia dlia upravleniia gubernii i zhalovannye gramoty dvorianstvu i gorodam* [Acts of the Reign of Catherine II. Institutions for the Administration of Gubernias and Charters of the Nobility and Cities]. Moscow: 1907.

—— "Bumagi i perepiska" [Papers and Correspondence], *Sbornik Russkogo istoricheskogo obshchestva* [A Collection of the Russian Historical Society], Vols. 7, 10, 13, 17, 20, 23, 27, 42, 48, 51, 57, 87, 97, 135, and 145. Hereinafter cited as *SRIO.*

—— *Nakaz imperatritsy Ekateriny II . . .* [The Instruction of Catherine II . . .] Edited by N. D. Chechulin. St. Petersburg: 1907.

—— *Pisma i bumagi imperatritsy Ekateriny II khraniashchiesia v imperatorskoi Publichnoi biblioteke* [Letters and Papers of Empress Catherine II Preserved in the Imperial Public Library]. St. Petersburg: 1873.

—— *Zapiski Ekateriny II* [Notes of Catherine II]. St. Petersburg: 1907.

Chelishchev, P. I. *Puteshestvie po severu Rossii v 1791 godu. Dnevnik* [A Journey Through Northern Russia in 1791. A Diary]. St. Petersburg: 1886.

Chudinov, A. N., *ed. Russkaia klassnaia biblioteka* [Russian Classical Library]. St. Petersburg: 1902.

Chulkov, M. D. *Ekonomicheskie zapiski . . .* [Economic Notes . . .]. Moscow: 1788.

—— *Istoricheskoe opisanie rossiiskoi kommertsii pri vsekh portakh i granitsakh . . .* [A Historical Description of Russian Trade At All Harbors and Along the Frontiers . . .]. St. Petersburg-Moscow, 1781–8. 7 vols.

—— *Istoriia kratkaia rossiiskoi torgovli* [A Brief History of Russian Trade]. Moscow: 1788.

—— *Nastavlenie, neobkhodimo nuzhnoe dlia rossiiskikh kuptsov, a bolee dlia molodykh liudei, soderzhashchee pravila bukhgalterii* [An Instruction Necessary for the Russian Merchants and Especially for Young People Containing Also Accounting Rules]. Moscow: 1788.

—— *Slovar uchrezhdennykh v Rossii iarmarok izdannyi dlia obrashchaiushchikhsia v torgovle* [A Dictionary of Organized Fairs in Russia Issued for Those Who Are Engaged in Trade]. Moscow: 1788.

[Daniel of Russia]. *Zhite i khozhenie Danila Russkiia zemli igumena 1106–1108* [The Life and Journey of Daniel, the Abbot of Russian Lands in 1106–1108]. St. Petersburg: 1896.

Desnitskii, S. E. "Predstavlenie o uchrezhdenii zakonodatelnoi suditelnoi i nakazatelnoi vlasti v Rossiiskoi imperii (1768)" [A Proposal on the Organization of the Legislative, Judicial, and Executive Authority in the Russian Empire], *Zapiski imperatorskoi Akademii nauk po istoriko-filologicheskomu otdeleniiu* [Notes of the Imperial Academy of Sciences Historical-Philological Division], VII, No. 4 (1905), pp. 1–45.

Drukhovtsov, S. V. *Ekonomicheskii kalendar, ili nastavlenie gorodskim i drevenskim zhiteliam v raznykh chastiakh ekonomii . . .* [Economic Calendar, or an Instruction for Town and Village Inhabitants in Various Branches of Economy . . .]. Moscow: 1780.

Fokkerodt, I. G., and O. Pleir. *Rossiia pri Petre Velikom* [Russia Under Peter the Great]. Translated from the German by A. N. Shemiakhin. Moscow: 1874.

Gnevushev, A. M. *Akty vremeni pravleniia tsaria Vasiliia Shuiskogo* [Acts of the Reign of Tsar Vasilii Shuiskii]. Moscow: 1914.

Gnucheva, V. F., *ed. Materialy dlia istorii ekspeditsii Akademii nauk v XVIII–XIX vekakh* [Materials on the History of Expeditions of the Academy of Sciences During the XVIII–XIX Centuries]. Moscow-Leningrad: 1940.

Golitsyn, D. A. *De l'esprit des économistes ou les économistes justifiés d'avoir posé par leurs principes les bases de la Révolution Francoise.* Par le prince D . . . de G . . . Brunswick: 1796. 2 vols.

Grekov, B. D., and V. P. Adrianova-Perets, *eds. Khozhenie za tri moria Afanasiia Nikitina 1466–1472* [Afanasii' Nikitin's Journey Beyond Three Seas in 1466–1472]. Moscow-Leningrad: 1948.

Grekov, B. D., *ed. Pravda Russkaia* [Russian Law]. Moscow-Leningrad: 1940–7. 2 vols.

Gudzii, N., *ed. Khrestomatiia po drevnei russkoi literature XI–XVII vekov* [Selections on Ancient Russian Literature of the XI–XVII Centuries]. Moscow: 1947.

[Ivan IV]. *Poslaniia Ivana Groznogo* [The Messages of Ivan the Terrible]. Moscow-Leningrad: 1951.

Izbrannye proizvedeniia russkikh myslitelei vtoroi poloviny XVIII veka [Selected Works of the Russian Thinkers of the Second Half of the XVIII Century]. Moscow: 1952. 2 vols.

[Kiev University]. "Materialy dlia istorii votchinnogo upravleniia v Rossii" [Materials on the History of the *votchina* Administration in Russia], *Universitetskaia izvestiia* [University News] (1903–1910).

Kizevetter, A. A., *ed. Osnovnye zakonodatelnye akty kasaiushchiesia vysshikh gosudarstvennykh uchrezhdenii v Rossii XVIII i pervoi chetverti XIX stoletiia* [Basic Legal Acts Pertaining to Higher State Organs in Russia During the XVIII and the First Quarter of the XIX Centuries]. Moscow: 1909.

Khrapovitskii, A. V. *Dnevnik A. V. Khrapovitskogo 1782–1793* [A. V. Khrapovitskii's Diary, 1782–1793]. St. Petersburg: 1874.

Kotoshikhin, G. K. *O Rossii v tsarstvovanie Alekseia Mikhailovicha* [Russia During the Reign of Aleksei Mikhailovich]. St. Petersburg: 1840.

Kozelskii, Ia. *Mekhanicheskie predlozheniia . . . Predislovie* [Mechanical Proposals . . . Foreword]. St. Petersburg: 1764.

—— *Razsuzhdeniia dvukh indiitsov Kalana i Ibragima o chelovicheskom poznanii* [Discussions Between Two Indians, Kalan and Ibrahim, on Human Understanding]. St. Petersburg: 1788.

Kozmin, B. P., *ed. Sbornik materialov k izucheniiu istorii russkoi zhurnalistiki* [A Collection of Materials for the Study of History of Russian Journalism]. Moscow: 1952.

[Kurbskii, A.] *Sochineniia kniazia Kurbskogo* [Works of Prince Kurbskii]. St. Petersburg: 1914.

Lebedev, V. I., *ed. Reformy Petra I. Sbornik dokumentov* [The Reforms of Peter I. A Collection of Documents]. Moscow: 1937.

Lepekhin, I. *Dnevnye zapiski puteshestviia po raznym provintsiiam Rossiiskogo gosudarstva* [A Diary of a Journey Through Various Provinces of the Russian State]. St. Petersburg: 1771–1805. 4 vols.

Lomonosov, M. V. *Izbrannye filosofskie proizvedeniia* [Selected Philosophical Works]. Edited by G. S. Vasetskii. Moscow: 1950.

—— *Lomonosov. Sbornik statei i materialov* [Lomonosov. A Collection of Articles and Materials]. Moscow-Leningrad: 1940–1951. 3 vols.

—— *Lomonosovskii sbornik* [Lomonosov's Collection]. St. Petersburg: 1911.

—— *Polnoe sobranie sochinenii* [Complete Collection of Works]. Moscow-Leningrad: 1950–4. 7 vols.

—— *Sochineniia* [Works]. St. Petersburg: 1891–1902. 5 vols.

Malinovskii, A. F., and others, *eds. Sobranie gosudarstvennykh gramot i dogovorov khraniashchikhsia v gosudarstvennoi kolegii inostrannykh del* [A Collection of State Charters and Treaties Preserved in the State College for Foreign Affairs]. Moscow: 1813–1894. 5 vols.

Martynov, M., *ed. Vosstanie Emeliana Pugacheva. Sbornik dokumentov* [The Uprising of Emelian Pugachev. A Collection of Documents]. Leningrad: 1935.

Materialy po istorii krestianskoi promyshlennosti XVIII i pervoi poloviny XIX v. [Materials on the History of Peasant Industry During the XVIII and the First Half of the XIX Century]. Moscow-Leningrad: 1935–1950. 2 vols.

Materialy po istorii volnenii na krepostnykh manufakturakh v XVIII veke [Materials on the History of Upheavals in the Serf-worked Manufactories During the XVIII Century]. Moscow-Leningrad: 1937.

Materialy po istorii zemledeliia SSSR [Materials on the History of Agriculture of the USSR]. Moscow: 1952.

Meichik, D. M., *ed. Gramoty XIV i XV vv. Moskovskogo arkhiva Ministerstva iustitsii* [Charters of the XIV and XV Centuries in the Moscow Archives of the Ministry of Justice]. Moscow: 1883.

[Moscow Gubernia]. *Istoricheskoe i topograficheskoe opisanie gorodov Moskovskoi gubernii . . .* [A Historical and Topographic Description of the Towns of Moscow Gubernia . . .]. Moscow: 1787.

Nasonov, A., *ed. Pskovskie letopisi* [Pskov's Chronicles]. Moscow-Leningrad: 1941.

[Nizhnii Novgorod. Archival Commission]. *Deistviia Nizhnegorodskoi uchenoi arkhivnoi komissii. Sbornik* [Activities of the Archive Commission of Nizhnii Novgorod. A Collection]. Nizhnii Novgorod: 1912.

[Novgorod]. *Gramoty Velikogo Novgoroda i Pskova* [Charters of Great Novgorod and Pskov]. Moscow-Leningrad: 1949.

—— *Novgorodskaia pervaia letopis starshego i mladshego izvodov* [Early and Late Editions of the First Novgorod Chronicle]. Moscow-Leningrad: 1950.

Novikov, N. I., *ed. Ekonomicheskii magazin ili sobranie vsiakikh ekonomicheskikh izvestii, opytov, otkrytii, primechanii, nastavlenii, zapisok i sovetov . . .* [Economic Journal, or a Collection of Varied Economic News, Experiences, Discoveries, Remarks, Instructions, Notes, and Advises . . .]. Moscow: 1780–9. 40 vols.

—— *Izbrannye sochineniia* [Selected Works]. Moscow-Leningrad: 1951.

Olearii, Adam. *Opisanie puteshestviia v Moskoviiu i cherez Moskoviiu v Persiiu i obratno* [A Description of a Journey to Moscovy and Across Moscovy to Persia and Return]. Introduction, Translation, and Notes by A. M. Loviagin. St. Petersburg: 1906.

Onezhskie byliny zapisanye A. F. Gilferdingon letom 1871 goda [The Onega Tales Recorded by A. F. Hilferding in the Summer of 1871]. Moscow-Leningrad: 1949–51. 3 vols.

Pallas, P. S. . . . *Puteshestvie po raznym mestam Rossiiskogo gosudarstva* [A Journey Through Various Places of the Russian State]. St. Petersburg: 1773–88. 5 vols.

Pamiatniki drevnerusskogo kanonicheskogo prava [Memorials of Ancient Russian Canon Law]. St. Petersburg: 1908.

Pamiatniki drevnerusskoi literatury [Memorials of Ancient Russian Literature]. Leningrad: 1933.

Pamiatniki drevnei pismennosti [Memorials of Ancient Literature]. St. Petersburg: 1881.

Paterik Kievskogo Pecherskogo monastyria [The Lives of the Fathers of the Kiev Crypt Monastery]. St. Petersburg: 1911.

Pavlov, A., *ed. "Knigi zakonnye" soderzhashchie v sebe, v drevnerusskom perevode, vizantiiskie zakony zemledelcheskie, ugolovnye, brachnye i sudebnye* [Law Books Containing, in Ancient Russian Translation, the Byzantine Agricultural, Criminal, Marriage, and Legal Codes]. St. Petersburg: 1885.

[Peter I]. *Pisma i bumagi imperatora Petra Velikogo* [Letters and Papers of Emperor Peter the Great]. St. Petersburg: 1887–1948. 9 vols.

Pokrovskii, V. I., *ed. Sbornik svedenii po istorii i statistike vneshnei torgovli Rossii* [A Collection of Data on the History and Statistics of Russia's Foreign Trade]. St. Petersburg: 1902.

Pososhkov, I. T. *Kniga o skudosti i bogatstve* [A Book on Poverty and Wealth]. Moscow: 1951. (Also editions of 1842, 1911, and 1937)

——— *Zaveshchanie otecheskoe* [Father's Testament]. Moscow: 1873.

Povest vremennykh let [The Tale of Bygone Years]. Moscow-Leningrad: 1950.

[Pugachev, E.] *Emelian Pugachev v Nizhnem Povolzhe (dokumenty)* [Emelian Pugachev in the Lower Volga Region (Documents)]. Stalingrad: 1937.

——— *Pugachevshchina* [Pugachev's Period]. Moscow-Leningrad: 1926–31. 3 vols.

Radishchev, A. N. *Izbrannye filosofskie sochineniia* [Selected Philosophic Works]. Moscow: 1949.

——— *Izbrannye sochineniia* [Selected Works]. Moscow: 1952.

——— *A. N. Radishchev. Materialy i issledovaniia* [A. N. Radishchev. Materials and Studies]. Moscow-Leningrad: 1936.

——— *Polnoe sobranie sochinenii* [Complete Collection of Works]. Moscow: 1907. 2 vols.

——— *Polnoe sobranie sochinenii* [Complete Collection of Works]. Moscow-Leningrad: 1938–52. 3 vols.

——— *Puteshestvie iz Peterburga v Moskvu* [A Journey from Petersburg to Moscow]. Leningrad: 1949.

[Razin, Stepan]. *Krestianskaia voina pod predvoditelstvom Stepana Razina. Sbornik dokumentov* [Peasant War Under the Leadership of Stepan Razin. A Collection of Documents]. Moscow: 1954.

[Russia. Archeographic Commission.] *Akty istoricheskie* [Historical Acts]. St. Petersburg: 1841–2. 5 vols.

——— *Dopolneniia k aktam istoricheskim* [Supplements to the Historical Acts]. St. Petersburg: 1846–75. 12 vols.

——— *Krepostnaia manufaktura v Rossii* [Serf Manufacture in Russia]. Leningrad: 1930–4. 5 vols.

——— *Polnoe sobranie russkikh letopisei* [Complete Collection of Russian Chronicles]. St. Petersburg: 1841–1914. 24 vols.

—— *Russkaia istoricheskaia biblioteka* [Russian Historical Library]. St. Petersburg: 1875–1927. 39 vols.

[Russia. Church]. *Pamiatniki drevnerusskoi tserkovno-uchitelnoi literatury* [Memorials of Ancient Russian Church-Teaching Literature]. St. Petersburg: 1894–7. 3 vols.

[Russia. Foreign Office]. *Sobranie gosudarstvennykh gramot i dogovorov khraniashchikhsia v gosudarstvennoi kollegii inostrannykh del* [A Collection of State Charters and Treaties Preserved in the State College for Foreign Affairs]. Moscow: 1828.

[Russia. Imperial Society of Russian History and Antiquity]. "Chelobitnye dvorian i detei boyarskikh vsekh gorodov v pervoi polovine XVII v." [Petitions of the Nobility and of the Sons of Boyars of All Towns During the First Half of the XVII Century]. *Chteniia . . .*, Bk. III. Pt. 1 (1915), pp. 1–73.

[Russia. Russian Imperial Historical Society]. *Sbornik . . .* [Collection]. St. Petersburg: 1867–1916. 148 vols.

[Russia. Laws]. *Polnoe sobranie zakonov Rossiiskoi imperii s 1649 goda* [Complete Collection of Laws of the Russian Empire from 1649]. St. Petersburg: 1830. 44 vols.

—— *Sudebniki XV–XVI vekov* [Codes of the XV–XVI Centuries]. Moscow-Leningrad: 1952.

[Russia. Legislative Commission]. "Istoricheskie svedeniia o ekaterinskoi komissii dlia sochineniia proekta novogo Ulozheniia" [Historical Data on Catherine's Commission to Draft a New Code of Laws], *SRIO*, vols. 4, 8, 14, 32, 36, 43, 68, 93, 107, 115, 123, 134, 144, and 147.

[Russia. Senate]. *Senatskii arkhiv* [The Senate Archives]. St. Petersburg: 1888–1913. 15 vols.

[Russia. State Council]. *Arkhiv gosudarstvennogo soveta. Sovet v tsarstvovanie imperatritsy Ekateriny II (1768–1796)* [Archives of the State Council. Council During the Reign of Empress Catherine II (1768–1796)]. St. Petersburg: 1869.

[Russia. Free Economic Society]. *Trudy Volnogo ekonomicheskogo obshchestva* [Works of the Free Economic Society]. St. Petersburg: 1765–98. 52 vols.

Rychkov, P. I. "Nakaz dlia upravitelia ili prikashchika o poriadochnom soderzhanii i upravlenii dereven v otsutsvie gospodina" [An Instruction for the Administrator or a Steward on Orderly Maintenance in Administering Villages During the Lord's Absence], *TVEO*, XVI (1770), pp. 13–68.

—— "O manufakturakh iz khlopchatoi bumagi i iz verbliuzhei shersti" [About the Products from Cotton and Camel Hair], *ibid.*, II (1766), pp. 89–101.

—— "O sberezhenii i razmnozhenii lesov" [About the Conservation and Increase of Forests], *ibid.*, VI (1767), pp. 84–112.

—— "O sposobakh k umnozheniiu zemledeliia v Orenburgskoi gubernii" [About the Methods of Increasing Agriculture in the Orenburg Gubernia], *ibid.*, VII (1767), pp. 1–25.

—— "Otvety na ekonomicheskie voprosy, kasaiushchiesia do zemledeliia . . ."

[Replies to the Economic Questions Related to Agriculture . . .], *ibid.*, VII (1767), pp. 111–212.

—— "Perepiska mezhdu dvumia priiateliami o komertsii" [A Correspondence Between Two Friends About Commerce], *Ezhemesiachnye sochineniia* [Monthly Works], Feb., 1755, pp. 105–22; April, 1755, pp. 307–33; Dec., 1755, pp. 493–515.

—— "Pismo o uprazhnenii v derevenskom zhitii" [A Letter on Employment in Rural Life], *ibid.*, Nov., 1757, pp. 405–30.

—— "Primechaniia o prezhnem i nyneshnem zemledelii" [Remarks on Past and Present Agriculture], *TVEO*, VI (1767), pp. 56–68.

—— "Topografiia Orenburgskoi gubernii" [The Topography of the Orenburg Gubernia], *Sochineniia i perevody* [Works and Translations], January-June, 1762.

Rychkov, N. P. *Zhurnal ili dnevnye zapiski puteshestviia kapitana Rychkova po raznym provintsiiam Rossiiskogo gosudarstva 1769–1770 gg.* [Journal or Diary of a Trip by Captain Rychkov Through Various Provinces of the Russian State, 1769–1770]. St. Petersburg: 1770.

Shcherbatov, M. M. *Neizdannye sochineniia* [Unpublished Works]. Moscow: 1935.

—— "Razmyshleniia o neudobstvakh v Rossii dast svobodu krestianam i sluzhiteliam ili sdelat sobstvennost imenii" [Thoughts on Disadvantages in Russia of Granting Freedom to Peasants and Servants or Giving Them the Ownership of Land], *Chteniia*, Bk. 3 (1861).

—— *Sochineniia kniazia M. M. Shcherbatova* [Works of Prince M. M. Shcherbatov]. Edited by I. P. Khrushchev and A. G. Voronov. St. Petersburg: 1896–8. 2 vols.

Stoglav [100 Chapters]. Kazan: 1862.

Sumarokov, A. P. *Polnoe sobranie vsekh sochinenii v stikhakh i proze* [Complete Collection of All Works in Verse and Prose]. Moscow: 1781.

[Tartars]. *Istoriia Tatarii v materialakh i dokumentakh* [A History of the Tartar Region in Materials and Documents]. Moscow: 1937.

Tatishchev, V. N. *Izbrannye strudy po geografii Rossii* [Selected Works on Russian Geography]. Moscow: 1950.

—— *Leksikon Rossiiskoi istoricheskoi, geograficheskoi, politicheskoi i grazhdanskoi* [Russian Historical, Geographic, Political, and Civil Dictionary]. St. Petersburg: 1793.

—— "Nakaz shikhtmeisteru" [An Instruction for the Shaft Supervisor], *Istoricheskii arkhiv* [Historical Archives], VI (1951), pp. 199–240.

—— "Na pamiat o delakh astrakhanskikh" [Recollections About the Astrakhan Affairs], *ibid.*, VII (1951), pp. 403–7.

—— "Naprimer predstavlenie o kupechestve i remeslakh" [An Exemplary Proposal on Trade and Crafts], *ibid.*, VII (1951), pp. 410–26.

—— "Predlozhenie o razmnozhenii fabrik" [A Proposal on the Increase of Factories], *ibid.*, VII (1951), pp. 407–10.

—— "Zavodskii ustav" [The Mining Code], *Gornyi zhurnal* [Mining Journal], Bks 1–3, 5–10 (1831).

Topograficheskie izvestiia, sluzhashchie dlia polnogo geograficheskogo opisaniia Rossiiskoi imperii [Topographic News, Serving as a Complete Geographic Description of the Russian Empire]. St. Petersburg: 1771–4. 4 vols.

Tretiakov, I. *Rassuzhdenie o prichinakh izobiliia i medlitelnogo obogashcheniia gosudarstv* . . . [A Discourse on the Causes of Abundance and Lingering Enrichment of States . . .]. Moscow: 1772.

—— *Slovo o Rimskom pravlenii i o raznykh onogo peremenakh* . . . [A Treatise on Roman Administration and Its Various Changes . . .]. Moscow: 1769.

Tuchkov, S. A. *Zapiski Sergeia Alekseevicha Tuchkova, 1766–1808* [Notes of Sergei Alekseevich Tuchkov, 1766–1808]. St. Petersburg: 1908.

[Tver]. *Generalnoe soobrazhenie po Tverskoi gubernii izvlechennoe iz podrobnogo topograficheskogo i kameralnogo po gorodam i uezdam opisaniia 1783–1784 gg.* [A General View of the Tver Gubernia Based on a Detailed Topographic and Economic Description of Cities and Counties in 1783–1784]. Tver: 1873.

Veselovskii, S. B., *ed. Akty podmoskovnykh opolchenii i Zemskogo sobora 1611–1613* [Acts of the Sub-Moscow Armies and of the Zemskii Sobor of 1611–1613]. Moscow: 1911.

Viktorov, V., *ed. Krestianskoe dvizhenie XVII–XVIII vv. Sbornik dokumentov i Materialov* [Peasant Upheavals During the XVII–XVIII Centuries. A Collection of Documents and Materials]. Moscow: 1926.

[Vladimir. Archival Commission]. "Iz perepiski pomeshchika s krestianami vtoroi poloviny XVIII stoletiia . . ." [From a Correspondence Between a Pomeshchik and Peasants During the Second Half of the XVIII Century . . .], *Trudy Vladimirskoi uchenoi arkhivnoi komissii*, Bk. VI (1904).

Vladimirskii-Budanov, M. F., *ed. Khrestomatiia po istorii russkogo prava* [Selections on the History of Russian Law]. 3rd ed. Kiev; 1885.

[Vorontsov]. *Arkhiv kniazia Vorontsova* [The Archive of Prince Vorontsov] Moscow: 1872.

[Zemskii sobor]. *Akty otnosiashchiesia k istorii Zemskikh soborov* [Acts Pertaining to the History of Land Assemblies]. Moscow: 1909.

Zhdanov, I. N., *ed. Materialy dlia istorii Stoglavogo sobora* [Materials on the History of the Stoglav Assembly]. St. Petersburg: 1904.

Zuev, V. *Puteshestvennye zapiski ot St. Petersburga do Khersona v 1781–1782 godu* [Travel Notes from St. Petersburg to Kherson in 1781–1782]. St. Petersburg: 1787.

B. Monographic Literature

Afanasev, A. *Poeticheskie vozzreniia slavian na prirodu* [Poetic Views of the Slavs on Nature]. Moscow: 1868. 2 vols.

Andreevskii, I. *O dogovore Novgoroda s nemetskimi gorodami i Gotlandom, zakliuchennom v 1270 godu* [A Treaty Concluded in 1270 Between Novgorod and German Towns and Gotland]. St. Petersburg: 1855.

Anichkov, E. V. *Iazychestvo i drevniaia Rus* [Paganism and Ancient Rus]. St. Petersburg: 1914.

Anuchin, D. N. *Sudba pervogo izdaniia "Puteshestviia" Radishcheva* [The Fate of the First Edition of Radishchev's *Journey*]. Moscow: 1918.

Aristov, N. *Promyshlennost drevnei Rusi* [The Industry of Ancient Rus]. St. Petersburg: 1866.

Arkhangelskii, S. I. *Ocherki po istorii promyshlennogo proletariata Nizhnego Novgoroda i Nizhegorodskoi oblasti XVII–XIX vv.* [Outlines of the History of the Industrial Proletariat of Nizhnii Novgorod and of the Nizegorod oblast During the XVII–XIX Centuries]. Gorkii: 1950.

Babkin, D. S. *Protsess A. N. Radishcheva* [A. N. Radishchev's Trial]. Moscow-Leningrad: 1952.

Baburin, D. *Ocherki po istorii Manufaktur-kollegii* [An Outline of the History of the Manufacturing College]. Moscow: 1939.

Bak, I. S. *Ekonomicheskie vozzreniia M. V. Lomonosova* [The Economic Views of M. V. Lomonosov]. Moscow: 1946.

—— "Torgovoi kapital i genezis kapitalizma v Rossii" [Commercial Capital and the origins of Capitalism in Russia] in *Sbornik nauchnykh rabot vysshei torgovoi shkoly*. Moscow: 1955. Pp. 249–64.

Bakhrushin, S. V. *Ocherki po istorii remesla, torgovli i gorodov russkogo tsentralizovanogo gosudarstva XVI i nachala XVII vv.* [Outlines of the History of Crafts, Trade, and Towns of the Russian Centralized State of the XVI and the Beginning of the XVII Centuries]. Moscow: 1952.

Baranov, L. S. *Afanasii Nikitin—pervyi russkii puteshestvennik v Indiiu ("Khozhedenie za tri moria)* [Afanasii Nikitin—The First Russian Traveler to India (A Journey Beyond Three Seas)]. Kalinin: 1939.

Barats, G. M. *Kritiko-sravnitelnyi analiz dogovorov Rusi s Vizantiei . . .* [A Critical Comparative Analysis of Treaties Between Rus and Byzantium . . .]. Kiev: 1910.

Barskov, Ia. L. *Perepiska moskovskikh masonov XVIII veka, 1780–1792* [The Correspondence of Moscow's Masons of the XVIII Century, 1780–1792]. Petrograd: 1915.

Bartnev, P., *ed. Osmnadtsatyi vek* [The Eighteenth Century]. Moscow: 1868–9. 4 vols.

Bazilevich, K. V. *Elementy merkantilizma v ekonomicheskoi politike pravitelstva Alekseia Mikhailovicha (XVII v.)* [Mercantilist Elements in the Economic Policy of the Government of Alexis Mikhailovich (XVII Century)]. Moscow: 1940.

—— *Denezhnaia reforma Alekseia Mikhailovicha i vosstanie v Moskve v 1662 g.* [The Monetary Reform of Alexis Mikhailovich and the Upheaval in Moscow in 1662]. Moscow-Leningrad: 1936.

—— *Istoriia SSSR ot drevneishikh vremen do kontsa XVII veka. Kurs lektsii . . .* [History of the USSR from Ancient Times to the End of the XVII Century. Lectures . . .]. Moscow: 1950.

—— *Krupnoe torgovoe predpriiatie v Moskovskom gosudarstve v pervoi polovine XVII veka* [Large Commercial Enterprise in the Moscovite State During the First Half of the XVII Century]. Leningrad: 1933.

Beliaev, I. S. *Krestianin-pisatel nachala XVIII v. I. T. Pososhkov. Ego Zhizn i deiatelnost* [A Peasant Writer of the Beginning of the XVIII Century. I. T. Pososhkov. His Life and Activity]. Moscow: 1902.

Berkov, P. N. *Istoriia russkoi zhurnalistiki XVIII veka* [A History of Russian Journalism of the XVIII Century]. Moscow-Leningrad: 1952.

—— *Lomonosov i literaturnaia polemika ego vremeni, 1750–1765* [Lomonosov and the Literary Polemics of His Time, 1750–1765]. Moscow-Leningrad: 1936.

—— *Satiricheskie zhurnaly N. I. Novikova* [Satirical Journals of N. I. Novikov]. Moscow-Leningrad: 1951.

Bezsonov, P. *Russkoe gosudarstvo v polovine XVII veka. Rukopis vremen tsaria Alekseia Mikhailovicha* [The Russian State in the Middle of the XVII Century. A Manuscript of the Reign of Tsar Aleksei Mikhailovich]. Moscow: 1859–60.

Bilbasov, V. A. *Istoricheskie monografii* [Historical Monographs]. St. Petersburg: 1901. 4 vols.

Blagoi, D. *Aleksandr Radishchev, 1749–1949*. Moscow: 1949.

—— *Istoriia russkoi literatury XVIII v.* [A History of Russian Literature of the XVIII Century]. Moscow: 1951.

Blanqui, A. D. *Istoriia politicheskoi ekonomii v evrope s drevneishego do nastoiashchego vremeni* [A History of the Political Economy of Europe From Ancient to Present Times]. Translated by P. A. Bibikov. St. Petersburg: 1869. 2 vols.

Bliumin, I. G. *Ocherki ekonomicheskoi mysli v Rossii v pervoi polovine XIX veka* [An Outline of the Economic Thought in Russia During the First Half of the XIX Century]. Moscow-Leningrad: 1940.

Bochkarev, V. N. *Voprosy politiki v russkom parliamente XVIII v. Opyt izucheniia politicheskoi ideologii XVIII v. po materialam zakonodatelnoi komissii 1767–1768 gg.* [Problems of Politics in the Russian Parliament of the XVIII Century. A Study of Political Idealogy Through Documents of the Legislative Commission of 1767–1768]. Tver: 1923.

Bogoslovskii, M. *Oblastnaia reforma Petra Velikogo . . .* [The oblast Reform of Peter the Great . . .]. Moscow: 1902.

—— "Vvedenie podushnoi podati i krepostnoe pravo" [The Introduction of Soul Tax and Serfdom], *Velikaia reforma* [The Great Reform]. Moscow: 1911. I, pp. 52–65.

Bogoslovskii, A. *Upravlenie promyshlennostiu manufakturnoiu, gornozavodskoiu i torgovoiu v Rossii ot Petra Velikogo do nastoiashchego vremeni* [The Administration of Industrial, Mining, and Trade Manufacturing in Russia from Peter the Great to the Present]. Moscow: 1872.

Brückner, A. *Ivan Possoschkow. Ideen und Zustande in Russland zur Zeit Peters des Grossen*. Leipzig: 1878.

—— *Istoriia Ekateriny II* [A History of Catherine II]. St. Petersburg: 1885.

Budilovich, A., *ed. Lomonosov kak pisatel* [Lomonosov as a Writer]. St. Petersburg: 1871.

Budovnits, I. U. *Russkaia publitsistika XVI v.* [Russian Publicity in the XVI Century]. Moscow-Leningrad: 1947.

Bulich, N. *Sumarokov i sovremennaia emu kritika* [Sumarokov and His Contemporary Criticism]. St. Petersburg: 1854.

Bunge, N. Kh. *Ocherki politiko-ekonomicheskoi literatury* [Outlines of the Political-Economic Literature]. St. Petersburg: 1895.

Chaev, N. S. *Bulavinskoe vosstanie (1707–1708)* [The Bulavin Revolt (1707–1708)]. Moscow: 1935.

Chechulin, N. D. *Goroda Moskovskogo gosudarstva v XVI veke* [Towns of the Moscovite State During the XVI Century]. St. Petersburg: 1889.

Cherepnin, L. V. *Russkie feodalnye arkhivy XIV–XV vekov* [Russian Feudal Archives of the XIV–XV Centuries]. Moscow-Leningrad: 1948–51. 2 vols.

Chernyshev, I. V. *Agrarno-krestianskaia politika Rossii za 150 let* [The Agrarian-Peasant Policy of Russia for the Past 150 Years]. Petrograd: 1918.

Chernyshevskii, N. G. *Polnoe sobranie sochinenii* [Complete Collection of Works]. St. Petersburg: 1906.

Chistiakova, E. V. *Sotsialno-ekonomicheskie vzgliady A. L. Ordin-Nashchokina (XVII v.)* [Socio-Economic Views of A. L. Ordin-Nashchokin (XVII Century)] Voronezh: 1950.

Danilevskii, V. V. *Russkaia tekhnika* [Russian Technology]. Leningrad: 1948.

Dantsig, B. M. "Iz istorii russkikh puteshestvii i izucheniia Blizhnego Vostoka v dopetrovskoi Rusi" [From the History of Russian Journeys and Study of the Near East in the Pre-Petrine Rus], *Ocherki po istorii russkogo vostokovedeniia* [Outlines of the History of Russian Eastern Studies]. Moscow: 1953.

Diakonov, M. *Ocherki obshchestvennogo i gosudarstvennogo stroia grevnei Rusi* [Outlines of the Social and State Structure of Ancient Rus]. 2nd ed. St. Petersburg: 1908.

Ditiatin, I. *Ekaterinskaia komissiia 1767 g.* [Catherine's Commission of 1767]. Rostov-on-the-Don: 1905.

Druzhinin, N. M. *Gosudarstvennye krestiane i reforma P. D. Kiseleva* [State Peasants and the Reform of P. D. Kiselev]. Moscow-Leningrad: 1946.

Dubrovin, N. F. *Pugachev i ego soobshchniki* [Pugachev and His Associates]. St. Petersburg: 1884. 3 vols.

Engelman, I. *Sistematicheskoe izlozhenie grazhdanskikh zakonov soderzhashchikhsia v Pskovskoi sudnoi gramote* [A Systematic Presentation of Civil Codes Found in the Pskov Legal Charter]. St. Petersburg: 1855.

—— *O priobretenii prava sobstvennosti na zemliu po russkomu pravu* [The Acquisition of the Right of Landownership Under Russian Law]. St. Petersburg: 1859.

Engels, F. *Anti-Diuring* [Anti-Dühring]. Moscow: 1953.

—— *Krestianskaia voina v Germanii* [Peasant War in Germany]. Moscow: 1953.

Entsiklopedicheskii slovar Brokgauza . . . [Brockhaus Encyclopedic Dictionary . . .]. St. Petersburg: 1890–1904. 41 vols.

Firsov, N. N. *Istoricheskie kharakteristiki i eskizi* [Historical Characterizations and Sketches]. Kazan: 1922.

—— *Russkie torgovo-promyshlennye kompanii v pervoi polovine XVIII stoletiia* [Russian Commercial-Industrial Companies During the First Half of the XVIII Century]. 2nd ed. Kazan: 1922.

Florovskii, A. V. *Iz istorii ekaterinskoi zakonodatelnoi komissii 1767 g. Vopros o krepostnom prave* [The History of Catherine's Legislative Commission of 1767. The Serf Problem]. Odessa: 1910.

Gere, V. *Leibnits i ego vek. Otnoshenie Leibnitsa k Rossii i Petru Velikomu . . .* [Leibnitz and His Age. Leibnitz' Attitude Towards Russia and Peter the Great . . .]. St. Petersburg: 1871.

Golikov, I. I. *Deianiia Petra Velikogo . . .* [The Activities of Peter the Great . . .]. Moscow: 1837–43. 15 vols.

Golubinskii, E. *Istoriia russkoi tserkvi* [A History of the Russian Church]. Moscow: 1880–1.

Gorbunov, M. A. *Filosofskie i obshchestvenno-politicheskie vzgliady A. N. Radishcheva* [Philosophic and Socio-Political Views of A. N. Radishchev]. Moscow: 1949.

Gorbunov, A. N. *Lgotnye gramoty, zhalovalnye monastyriam i tserkvam v XIII, XIV i XV vekakh . . .* [Charters Granted to Monasteries and Churches in the XIII, XIV and XV Centuries . . .]. St. Petersburg: 1860–9.

Gorchakov, M. *O zemelnykh vladeniiakh vserossiiskikh metropolitov, patriarkhov i sviatogo Sinoda* [Land Holdings of the All-Russian Metropolitans, Patriarchs, and the Holy Synod, 988–1738]. St. Petersburg: 1871.

Gote, Iu. V. *Istoriia oblastnogo upravleniia v Rossii ot Petra I do Ekateriny II* [A History of the oblast Administration in Russia from Peter I to Catherine II]. Moscow: 1913. 2 vols.

—— *Ocherk istorii zemlevladeniia v Rossii* [An Outline of the History of Landownership in Russia]. Sergeev Posad: 1915.

Grekov, B. D., *et al. Istoriia SSSR* [History of the USSR]. Moscow: 1947.

—— *Kievskaia Rus* [Kievan Rus]. Moscow: 1949.

—— *Krestiane na Rusi s drevneishikh vremen do XVII v.* [Peasants in Rus from Ancient Times to the XVII Century]. Moscow: 1952.

Hennin, Wilhelm. *Opisanie uralskikh i sibirskikh zavodov, 1735* [A Description of the Ural and Siberian Mills in 1735]. Moscow: 1937.

Herman, K. *Statisticheskie issledovaniia otnositelno Rossiiskoi imperii* [Statistical Studies of the Russian Empire]. St. Petersburg: 1819.

Higgs, H. *Fiziokraty. Frantsuzskie ekonomisty XVIII veka* [The Physiocrats. French Economists of the XVIII Century]. St. Petersburg: 1899.

Herberstein, Sigizmund. *Zapiski o moskovitskikh delakh* [Notes About the Moscovite Affairs]. St. Petersburg: 1908.

Herzen, A. I. *Polnoe sobranie sochinenii i pisem* [Complete Collection of Works and Letters]. Petrograd: 1919.

Iakushkin, V. *Ocherki po istorii russkoi pozemelnoi politiki v XVIII i XIX v.*

[Outlines of the History of Russian Land Policy in the XVIII and XIX Centuries]. Moscow: 1890.

—— *Radishchev i Pushkin* [Radishchev and Pushkin]. Moscow: 1886.

Iakovtsevskii, V. N. *Kupecheskii kapital v feodalno-krepostnicheskoi Rossii* [Commercial Capital in Feudal-Serf Russia]. Moscow: 1953.

Iasnopolskii, L. N. *Ocherki russkogo biudzhetnogo prava* [Outlines of the Russian Budgetary Law]. Moscow: 1912.

Ilin, M. "Afanasii Nikitin," *Liudi russkoi nauki* [Individuals of Russian Science]. Moscow-Leningrad: 1948. I, pp. 515–24.

Iofa, L. S. *Sovremenniki Lomonosova—I. K. Kirilov i V. N. Tatishchev* [I. K. Kirilov and V. N. Tatishchev—Lomonosov's Contemporaries]. Moscow: 1949.

Istoriia kultury drevnei Rusi [A History of the Culture of Ancient Rus]. Moscow-Leningrad: 1948. Vol. I.

Istoriia russkoi literatury [A History of Russian Literature]. Moscow-Leningrad: 1941–8. 3 vols.

[Iulaev, S]. *Salavat Iulaev, k 200-letiu so dnia rozhdeniia* [Salavat Iulaev, 200th Birthday Anniversary]. Ufa: 1952.

Iushkov, S. V. *Istoriia gosudarstva i prava SSSR* [A History of the State and Law of the USSR]. 3rd ed. Moscow: 1950.

—— *Russkaia Pravda. Proiskhozhdenie, istochniki i ee znachenie* [Russkaia Pravda. Its Origins, Sources, and Significance]. Moscow: 1950.

Ivaniukov, I. *Politicheskaia ekonomiia kak uchenie o protsese razvitiia ekonomicheskikh iavlenii* [Political Economy as a Study of the Process of the Development of Economic Phenomena]. 3rd ed. Moscow: 1891.

Iz istorii russkoi filosofii XVIII–XIX vekov [The History of Russian Philosophy of the XVIII–XIX Centuries]. Moscow: 1952.

Kafenganz, B. B. *Istoriia khoziastva Demidovykh v XVIII–XIX vv.* [A History of the Demidov Estates During the XVIII–XIX Centuries]. Moscow-Leningrad: 1949.

—— *I. T. Pososhkov. Zhizn i deiatelnost.* [I. T. Pososhkov. Life and Activity]. 2nd ed. Moscow: 1951.

Kalugin, F. *Zinovii, inok Otenskii i ego bogoslovsko-polemicheskie i tserkovno-uchitelnye proizvedeniia* [Zinovei, An Otensk Monk and His Theological-Polemic and Church-Informative Works]. St. Petersburg: 1894.

Kashintsev, D. *Istoriia metallurgii Urala* [A History of Metallurgy in the Urals]. Moscow-Leningrad: 1939.

Kaufman, I. I. *Serebrianyi rubl v Rossii ot ego vozniknoveniia do kontsa XIX veka* [The Silver Ruble in Russia from its Origins to the End of the XIX Century]. St. Petersburg: 1910.

Keltuiala, V. A. *Kurs russkoi literatury* [A Course of Russian Literature]. St. Petersburg: 1906–11.

Kirilov, *Prepodobnyi Nil Sorskii, pervoosnovatel skitskogo zhitiia v Rossii i ustav ego o zhitelstve skitskom* [The Reverend Nil Sorskii, Founder of the Hermitic Life in Russia and His Rules of Hermitic Life]. n.p.: 1891.

Kizevetter, A. A. *Istoricheskie ocherki* [Historical Sketches]. Moscow: 1912.

Khodnev, A. I. *Istoriia imperatorskogo Volnogo ekonomicheskogo obshchestva s 1765 do 1865 g.* [A History of the Imperial Free Economic Society from 1765 to 1865]. St. Petersburg: 1865.

Khromov, P. A. *Ekonomicheskie razvitie Rossii v XIX–XX vekakh* [The Economic Development of Russia During the XIX–XX Centuries]. Moscow: 1950.

—— "Nekotorye voprosy razvitiia russkoi ekonomicheskoi mysli" [Some Problems of the Development of Russian Economic Thought], *Iubileinaia sessiia Akademii nauk SSSR*. Moscow-Leningrad: 1947. II, pp. 659–69.

Kliuchevskii, V. O. *Kurs russkoi istorii* [A Course of Russian History]. Moscow: 1937. 5 vols.

—— "Podushnaia podat i otmena kholopstva v Rossii" [The Soul Tax and the Abolition of Slavery in Russia], *Opyty i issledovaniia* [Essays and Studies]. Petrograd: 1918. Pp. 268–357.

—— *Sbornik statei posviashchennykh V. O. Kliuchevskomu* [A Collection of Articles in Honor of V. O. Kliuchevskii]. Moscow: 1909.

Klochkov, M. V. "Pososhkov o krestianakh" [Pososhkov About the Peasants], in *Velikaia reforma* [The Great Reform]. Moscow: 1911. I, pp. 66–79.

Kogan, Iu. Ia. "Svobodomyslie Ia. P. Kozelskogo" [The Freethinking of Ia. P. Kozelskii], in *Voprosy istorii religii i ateizma* [Problems of the History of Religion and Atheism], Moscow: 1950. Pp. 155–87.

Koialovich, M. O. *Istoriia russkogo samosoznaniia po istoricheskim pamiatnikam i nauchnym sochineniam* [A History of Russian Self-consciousness Based on Historical Memorials and Scholarly Works]. St. Petersburg: 1884.

Korkunov, N. M. *Istoriia filosofii prava* [A History of the Philosophy of Law] 4th ed. St. Petersburg: 1908.

Kostomarov, N. I. *Ocherk domashnei zhizni i nravov velikorusskogo naroda v XVI i XVII stoletiiakh* [An Outline of the Daily Life and Customs of the Great Russian People in the XVI and XVII Centuries]. St. Petersburg: 1906.

—— *Ocherk torgovli Moskovskogo gosudarstva v XVI i XVII stoletiiakh* [An Outline of the Trade of the Moscovite State in the XVI and XVII Centuries]. St. Petersburg: 1905.

—— *Russkaia istoriia v zhizneopisaniiakh ee glavneishikh deiatelei* [Russian History in the Biographies of Its Main Participants]. St. Petersburg: 1913. 3 vols.

—— *Velikorusskie religioznye volnodumtsy v XVI veke. Matvei Bashkin i ego suchastniki. Feodosii Kosoi* [The Great Russian Religious Free Thinkers of the XVI Century. Matvei Bashkin and His Contemporaries. Feodosii Kosoi]. St. Petersburg: 1903.

Kozlovskii, I. P. *Pervye pochty i pervye pochtmeistery v Moskovskom gosudarstve* [The First Post Offices and the First Postmasters in the Moscovite State]. Warsaw: 1913.

Krepostnaia manufaktura v Rossii [Serf Manufacturing in Russia]. Leningrad: 1930–2. 3 vols.

Kulakova, L. *A. N. Radishchev. Ocherk zhizni i tvorchestva* [A. N. Radishchev. An Outline of His Life and Activity]. Leningrad: 1949.

Kulisher, I. M. *Istoriia russkogo narodnogo khoziaistva* [A History of Russian National Economy]. Moscow: 1925.

—— *Ocherk istorii russkoi torgovli* [An Outline of the History of Russian Trade]. Petrograd: 1923.

—— *Ocherk istorii russkoi promyshlennosti* [An Outline of the History of Russian Industry]. Petrograd: 1922.

Kunin, K. I. *Puteshestvie Afanasiia Nikitina* [Afanasii Nikitin's Journey]. Moscow: 1947.

Kurts, B. G. *Sochinenie Kulberga o russkoi torgovle v tsarstvovanie Alekseia Mikhailovicha* [Kulberg's Work About Russian Trade During the Reign of Aleksei Mikhailovich]. Kiev: 1915.

—— *Sostoianie Rossii v 1650–1655 gg po doneseniam Rodesa* [Conditions in 1650–1655 According to Rodes' Reports]. Moscow: 1915.

Lamanskii, V. I. *Lomonosov i Peterburgskaia akademiia nauk* [Lomonosov and the Petersburg Academy of Sciences]. Moscow: 1865.

Lappo-Danilevskii, A. S. *Ocherk vnutrennoi politiki imperatritsy Ekateriny II* [An Outline of Domestic Policy of Empress Catherine II]. St. Petersburg: 1898.

—— *Organizatsiia priamogo oblozheniia v Moskovskom gosudarstve so vremen smuti do epokhi preobrazovanii* [The Organization of Direct Taxation in the Moscovite State from the Time of Troubles to the Period of Reforms]. St. Petersburg: 1890.

—— *Russkie promyshlennye i torgovye kompanii v pervoi polovine XVIII v.* [Russian Industrial and Commercial Companies During the First Half of the XVIII Century]. St. Petersburg: 1899.

Latkin, V. N. *Zakonodatelnye komissii v Rossii v XVIII stoletii* [Legislative Commissions in Russia in the XVIII Century]. St. Petersburg: 1887.

Lebedev, D. M. *Geografiia v Rossii XVII veka (dopetrovskoi epokhi)* [Geography in Russia of the XVII Century (the Pre-Petrine Period)]. Moscow-Leningrad: 1949.

—— *Geografiia v Rossii petrovskogo vremeni* [Geography in Russia During Peter's Time]. Moscow-Leningrad: 1950.

Lebedev, V. I. *Krestianskaia voina pod rukovodstvom Emeliana Pugacheva* [The Peasant War Under the Leadership of Emelian Pugachev]. Moscow: 1951.

Lenin, V. I. *Sochineniia* [Works]. Moscow: 1941–9. 35 vols.

Leshkov, V. "Drevniaia russkaia nauka o narodnom bogatstve i blagosostoianii" [Ancient Russian Teaching About National Wealth and Prosperity], *V vospominanie 12 ianvaria 1855* [In Commemoration of the 12th of January, 1855]. Moscow: 1855.

Levshin, A. *Istoricheskoe i statisticheskoe obozrenie uralskikh kazakov* [Historical and Statistical Review of the Ural Cossacks]. St. Petersburg: 1823.

Liashchenko, P. I. *Istoriia narodnogo khoziaistva SSSR* [History of the National Economy of the USSR]. Moscow: 1952. 2 vols.

—— *Ocherki agrarnoi evolutsii Rossii* [Outlines of the Agrarian Evolution of Russia]. 4th ed. Leningrad: 1925.

Librovich, S. F. *Istoriia knigi v Rossii* [A History of Book Publishing in Russia]. Moscow: 1914.

Likhachev, D. S. *Natsionalnoe samosoznanie drevnei Rusi . . .* [National Consciousness in Ancient Rus . . .]. Moscow-Leningrad: 1945.

—— *Russkie letopisi i ikh kulturno-istoricheskie znachenie* [Russian Chronicles and their Historic-Cultural Significance]. Moscow-Leningrad: 1947.

—— *Slovo o polku Igoreve. Istoriko-literaturnyi ocherk* [The Tale of Igor's Host. A Historical-Literary Outline]. Moscow-Leningrad: 1950.

—— *Vozniknovenie russkoi literatury* [The Origins of Russian Literature]. Moscow-Leningrad: 1952.

Listopadov, A. M. *Donskie istoricheskie pesni* [Historical Songs of the Don]. Rostov-on-the-Don: 1946.

Liubimenko, I. *Istoriia torgovykh snoshenii Rossii s Angliei* (XVI v) [A History of Trade Relations Between Russia and England (XVI Century)]. Iuriev: 1912.

Liubomirov, P. G. *Ocherki po istorii metallurgicheskoi i metalloobrabatyvaiushchei promyshlennosti v Rossii (XVII, XVIII i nachalo XIX vv.)* [Outlines of the History of the Metallurgic and Metal-Processing Industry in Russia (XVII, XVIII and the Beginning of the XIX Centuries)]. Leningrad: 1937.

—— *Ocherki po istorii russkoi promyshlennosti, XVII–XVIII i nachalo XIX vv.* [Outlines of the History of Russian Industry of the XVII–XVIII and the Beginning of the XIX Ceuturies]. Moscow: 1947.

Lodyzhenskii, K. *Istoriia russkogo tamozhennogo tarifa* [A History of Russian Custom Tariff]. St. Petersburg: 1886.

Longinov, A. V. *Mirnye dogovory russkikh s grekami, zakliuchennye v X veke* [Peaceful Treaties Concluded Between the Russians and the Greeks in the X Century]. Odessa: 1904.

Longinov, M. N. *Novikov i moskovskie martinisty* [Novikov and Moscow's Martinists]. Moscow: 1867.

Lozanov, A. N., *ed. Pugachev v Srednem Povolzhe i Zavolzhe* [Pugachev in the Central and Trans-Volga Regions]. Kuibyshev: 1947.

Maikov, L. *O bilinakh Vladimirova tsikla* [The Legends of the Vladimir Cycle]. St. Petersburg: 1863.

[Makarii, the Archbishop of Kharkov]. *Istoriia Russkoi tserkvi . . .* [A History of the Russian Church . . .]. St. Petersburg: 1868. 2 vols.

Makogonenko, G. *Nikolai Novikov i russkoe Prosveshchenie XVIII v.* [Nikolai Novikov and Russian Enlightenment of the XVIII Century]. Moscow-Leningrad: 1951.

—— *A. N. Radishchev. Ocherk zhizni i tvorchestva* [A. N. Radishchev. An Outline of His Life and Activity]. Moscow: 1949.

Malinin, V. *Starets Eleazarova monastyria Filofei i ego poslaniia* [Elder Filofei of the Eleazarov Monastery and His Teachings]. Kiev: 1901.

Manuilov, A. A. *Politicheskaia ekonomiia. Kurs lektsii* [Political Economy. Lectures]. Moscow: 1914.

Martysevich, I. D. *Pskovskaia sudnaia gramota. Istoriko-iuridicheskoe issledovanie* [Legal Charter of Pskov. A Historical-Legal Study]. Moscow: 1951.

Marx, K. *Formy, predshestvuiushchie kapitalisticheskomu proizvodstvu* [Forms Preceding Capitalist Production]. Moscow: 1940.

—— *Kapital* [Capital]. Moscow: 1953–4. 4 vols.

—— *Secret Diplomatic History of the Eighteenth Century*. London: 1899.

—— and F. Engels. *Arkhiv Marksa i Engelsa* [The Archives of Marx and Engels]. Moscow: 1938–1946. 8 vols.

—— *Nemetskaia ideologiia* [German Ideology]. Moscow: 1934.

—— *Sochineniia* [Works]. Moscow: 1929–43. 24 vols.

Meshalin, I. V. *Tekstilnaia promyshlennost krestian Moskovskoi gubernii v XVIII i pervoi polovine XIX veka* [The Textile Industry of Peasants of Moscow Gubernia in the XVIII and the First Half of the XIX Century]. Moscow-Leningrad: 1950.

Miakotin, V. A. *Iz istorii russkogo obshchestva* [The History of Russian Society]. St. Petersburg: 1906.

Mikhalevskii, F. I. *Ocherki istorii deneg i denezhnogo obrashcheniia* [Outlines of the History of Money and Monetary Circulation]. Moscow: 1948.

Miliukov, P. N. *Glavnye techeniia russkoi istoricheskoi mysli* [The Main Trends of Russian Historical Thought]. Moscow: 1898.

—— *Gosudarstvennoe khoziaistvo Rossii v pervoi chetverti XVIII stoletiia i reforma Petra Velikogo* [The State Economy of Russia During the First Quarter of the XVIII Century and the Reform of Peter the Great]. 2nd ed. St. Petersburg: 1905.

—— *Ocherki po istorii russkoi kultury* [Outlines of the History of Russian Culture]. Moscow: 1901–3.

—— *Spornye voprosy finansovoi istorii Moskovskogo gosudarstva* [Disputed Problems of the Financial History of the Moscovite State]. St. Petersburg: 1892.

Miliutin, V. *O nedvizhimykh imushchestvakh dukhovenstva v Rossii* [The Immovable Property of the Clergy in Russia]. Moscow: 1862.

Milkov, F. N. *P. I. Rychkov. Zhizn i geograficheskie trudy* [P. I. Rychkov. His Life and Geographic Works]. Moscow: 1953.

Miller, O. S. *Opyt istoricheskogo obozreniia russkoi slovesnosti khrestomatieiu, raspolozhennoiu po epokham* [A Historical Study of Russian Literature Through Selections Divided into Periods]. St. Petersburg: 1865.

Miller, V. F. *Istoricheskie pesni russkogo naroda XVI–XVII vv.* [Historical Songs of the Russian People of the XVI–XVII Centuries] Petrograd: 1915.

Mindalev, P. *Molenie Danila Zatochnika i sviazannye s nim pamiatniki* [The Prayer of Danilo Zatochnik and Its Related Memorials]. Kazan: 1914.

Modzalevskii, L. B., and A. I. Andreev, *eds. Lomonosov. Sbornik statei i materialov* [Lomonosov. A Collection of Articles and Materials]. Moscow-Leningrad: 1946.

Modzalevskii, L. B. *Rukopisi Lomonosova v Akademii nauk SSSR* [Lomonosov's Manuscripts in the Academy of Sciences of the USSR]. Moscow-Leningrad: 1937.

Morozov, A. A. *Mikhail Vasilevich Lomonosov, 1711–1765*. Leningrad: 1952.

[Moscow]. *Istoriia Moskvy* [A History of Moscow] Moscow: 1952.

[Moscow University]. *Biograficheskii slovar professorov i prepodavatelei imperatorskogo Moskovskogo universiteta . . . [1755–1855]* [Biographic Dictionary of Professors and Lecturers of the Imperial Moscow University . . . (1775–1855)]. Moscow: 1855. 2 pts.

—— *Rechi, proiznesennye v torzhestvennykh sobraniiakh imperatorskogo Moskovskogo universiteta russkimi professorami onogo* [Speeches Delivered at Solemn Meetings of the Imperial Moscow University by Its Russian Professors]. Moscow: 1820. 2 pts.

Muliukin, A. S. *Ocherki po istorii iuridicheskogo polozheniia innostrannykh kuptsov v Moskovskom gosudarstve* [Outlines on the History of the Legal Position of Foreign Merchants in the Moscovite State]. Odessa: 1912.

Nechkina, M., *ed. Istoriia SSSR* [A History of the USSR]. Moscow: 1949. Vol. 2.

Nakrasov, I. S. *Opyt istoriko-literaturnogo issledovaniia o proiskhozhdenii drevnerusskogo 'Domostroia'* [A Historical-Literary Essay on the Origins of Ancient Russian 'Domostroi']. Moscow: 1873.

Nevolin, K. A. *Istoriia rossiiskikh grazhdanskikh zakonov* [A History of Russian Civil Laws]. St. Petersburg: 1857.

Nikitin, S. A. *Istochnikovedenie istorii SSSR XIX v.* [The Study of the Sources of History of the USSR in the XIX Century]. Moscow: 1940.

Nikolskii, N. M. *Istorii russkoi tserkvi* [A History of the Russian Church]. 2nd ed. Moscow-Leningrad: 1931.

Nisselovich, L. N. *Istoriia zavodsko-fabrichnogo zakonodatelstva Rossiiskoi imperii* [A History of the Factory-Mill Legislation of the Russian Empire]. St. Petersburg: 1883–4. 2 pts.

Obnorskii, S. P. *Ocherki po istorii russkogo literaturnogo iazyka starshego perioda* [Outlines of the History of the Russian Literary Language of the Ancient Period]. Moscow: 1946.

Ocherki istorii SSSR. Period feodalizma. IX–XV vv. [Outlines of the History of the USSR. Feudal Period. IX–XV Centuries]. Moscow: 1953. 2 vols.

Oncken, A. *Istoriia politicheskoi ekonomii do Adama Smita* [A History of Political Economy Before Adam Smith]. Translated from the German. St. Petersburg: 1908.

Orlov, A. S. *Drevniaia russkaia literatura XI–XVI vv.* [Ancient Russian Literature of the XI–XVI Centuries]. Moscow: 1953.

—— *Vladimir Monomakh*. Moscow-Leningrad: 1946.

Orlov, Vl. *Radishchev i Russkaia literatura* [Radishchev and Russian Literature]. Moscow: 1949.

—— *Russkie prosvetiteli 1790–1800–kh godov* [Russian Men of Enlightenment of the 1790–1800's]. 2nd ed. Moscow: 1953.

Osherovich, B. S. *Ocherki po istorii russkoi ugolovno-pravovoi mysli (2 polovina XVIII i 1 chetvert XIX v.* [Outlines of the History of Russian Criminal-Legal Thought (Second Half of the XVIII and the First Quarter of the XIX Centuries]. Moscow: 1946.

Osokin, E. *Vnutrennie tamozennye poshliny Rossii* [The Internal Custom Dues of Russia]. Kazan: 1850.

Patlaevskii, I. *Denezhnyi rynok v Rossii ot 1700 do 1762 g.* [The Money Market in Russia from 1700 to 1762]. Odessa: 1868.

Pavlenko, N. I. *Razvitie metallurgicheskoi promyshlennosti Rossii v pervoi polovine XVIII veka* [The Development of the Metallurgic Industry of Russia During the First Half of the XVIII Century]. Moscow: 1953.

Pavlov, A. *Istoricheskii ocherk sekuliarizatsii tserkovnykh zemel v Rossii* [An Historical Outline on the Secularization of Church Lands in Russia]. Odessa: 1871.

Pavlov-Silvanskii, N. P. *Feodalizm v udelnoi Rusi* [Feudalism in Appanage Rus]. St. Petersburg: 1910.

—— *Immunitet v udelnoi Rusi* [Immunity in Appanage Rus]. St. Petersburg: 1900.

—— *Ocherki po russkoi istorii XVIII–XIX vv.* [Outlines of Russian History of the XVIII–XIX Centuries]. St. Petersburg: 1910.

—— *Proekty reform v zapiskakh sovremennikov Petra Velikogo* [Reform Projects in the Notes of the Contemporaries of Peter the Great]. St. Petersburg: 1897.

Pazhitnov, K. A. *Polozhenie rabochego klassa v Rossii* [Condition of the Working Class in Russia]. 2nd ed. Leningrad: 1925. Vol 1.

—— *Problema remeslennykh tsekhov v zakonodatelstve russkogo absoliutizma* [The Problem of Craft Guilds in the Legislation of Russian Absolutism]. Moscow: 1952.

—— *Promyshlennyi trud v krepostnuiu epokhu* [Industrial Labor During Serfdom]. Leningrad: 1924.

Pekarskii, P. *Nauka i literatura pri Petre Velikom* [Science and Literature Under Peter the Great]. St. Petersburg: 1862. 2 vols.

—— *Zhizn i literaturnaia perepiska Petra Ivanovicha Rychkova* [Life and Literary Correspondence of Peter Ivanivich Rychkov]. St. Petersburg: 1867.

Penchko, N. A. *Osnovanie Moskovskogo universiteta* [The Founding of Moscow University]. Moscow: 1953.

Perevalov, V. A. *Lomonosov i Arktika* [Lomonosov and the Arctic]. Moscow-Leningrad: 1949.

Petrov, S. *Pugachev v Penzenskom krae* [Pugachev in the Penza Region]. Penza: 1950.

Petukhov, E. *Serapion Vladimirskii, russkii propovednik XIII veka* [Serapion of Vladimir, Russian Preacher of the XIII Century]. St. Petersburg: 1888.

Picheta, V. I. "Finansovaia i ekonomicheskaia politika Petra i gosudarstvennoe khoziaistvo Rossii kontsa XVII i nachala XVIII veka" [The Financial and Economic Policy of Peter and State Economy of Russia at the End of the XVII and the Beginning of the XVIII Century], *Tri veka* [Three Centuries]. Ed. by V. V. Kalash. Moscow: 1913. IV, pp. 43–61.

—— *Istoriia krestianskikh volnenii v Rossii* [A History of Peasant Upheavals in Russia]. Minsk: 1923.

Platonov, S. F. *Ivan Groznyi (1530–1584)* [Ivan the Terrible, 1530–1584). Petrograd: 1923.

—— *Lektsii po russkoi istorii* [Lectures on Russian History]. 10th ed. Petrograd: 1917.

Plekhanov, G. V. *Sochineniia* [Works]. Moscow-Leningrad: 1925. 24 vols.

Pokrovskii, M. N. *Ocherk istorii russkoi kultury* [An Outline of the History of Russian Culture]. 4th ed. Moscow: 1921.

—— *Protiv istoricheskoi kontseptsii M. N. Pokrovskogo. Sbornik statei* [Against the Historical Concept of M. N. Pokrovskii. A Collection of Articles]. Moscow-Leningrad: 1939.

—— *Russkaia istoriia s drevneishikh vremen* [Russian History From Ancient Times]. Moscow: 1933. Vol. I.

Pokrovskii, S. A. *Vneshniaia torgovlia i vneshniaia torgovaia politika Rossii* [Foreign Trade and the Foreign Trade Policy of Russia]. Moscow: 1947.

Pokrovskii, V. *Aleksandr Nikolaevich Radishchev. Ego zhizn i sochineniia* [A. N. Radishchev. His Life and Works]. Moscow: 1907.

Pokrovskii, V. S. *Istoriia russkoi politicheskoi mysli* [A History of Russian Political Thought]. Moscow: 1952.

—— *Obshchestvenno-politicheskie i pravovye vzgliady A. N. Radishcheva* [Socio-Political and Legal Views of A. N. Radishchev]. Kiev: 1952.

Ponomarev, N. V. *Istoricheskii obzor pravitelstvennykh meropriiatii k razvitiiu selskogo khoziaistva v Rossii ot nachala gosudarstva do nastoiashchego vremeni* [A Historical Survey of Governmental Measures in the Development of Rural Economy in Russia from the Founding of the State to the Present Time]. St. Petersburg: 1888.

Popov, N. *V. N. Tatishchev i ego vremiia* [V. N. Tatishchev and His Time]. Moscow: 1861.

Presniakov, A. *Kniazhoe pravo v drevnei Rusi* [Princely Law in Ancient Rus].

—— *Moskovskoe tsarstvo* [Moscovite Tsardom]. Petrograd: 1918.

Prikazchikova, E. V. *Ekonomicheskie vzgliady A. N. Radishcheva* [The Economic Views of A. N. Radishchev]. Moscow-Leningrad: 1949.

Ptukha, M. *Ocherki po istorii statistiki XVII–XVIII vekov* [Outlines of the History of Statistics of the XVII–XVIII Centuries]. Moscow: 1945.

Pushkin, A. S. *Polnoe sobranie sochinenii* [Complete Collection of Works]. Moscow-Leningrad: 1951.

Rashin, A. G. *Formirovanie promyshlennogo proletariata v Rossii* [The Formation of the Industrial Proletariat in Russia]. Moscow: 1940.

Remezov, I. *Moskovskii krestianin Ivan Tikhonovich Pososhkov* [A Moscovite Peasant, I. T. Pososhkov]. St. Petersburg: 1883.

Romanovich-Slavatinskii, A. *Dvorianstvo v Rossii ot nachala XVIII v. do otmeny krepostnogo prava* [The Nobility in Russia from the the Beginning of the XVIII Century to the Abolition of Serfdom]. 2nd ed. Kiev: 1912.

Rozhdestvenskii, S. V. *Sluzhiloe zemlevladenie v Moskovskom gosudarstve*

XVI v. [Service Landownership in the Moscovite State in the XVI Century]. St. Petersburg: 1897.

Rozenberg, D. I. *Istoriia politicheskoi ekonomii* [A History of Political Economy]. Moscow: 1940.

Rozhkov, N. A. *Gorod i derevnia v Russkoi istorii* [Town and Village in Russian History]. Petrograd: 1918.

—— *Russkaia istoriia v sravnitelno-istoricheskom osveshcheni (osnovy sotsialnoi dynamiki* [A Comparative-Historical View of Russian History (The Foundations of Social Dynamics)]. Moscow-Leningrad: 1928. 2 vols.

—— *Selskoe khoziaistvo Moscovskoi Rusi v XVI veke* [The Village Economy of Moscovite Rus in the XVI Century]. Moscow: 1899.

Russkaia proza v XVIII veke [Russian Prose of the XVIII Century]. Moscow-Leningrad: 1950. Vol. I.

[Russia. Senate]. *Istoriia pravitelstvuiushchego senata za dvesti let, 1711–1911* [A History of the Governing Senate for the Past 200 Years, 1711–1911]. St. Petersburg: 1911.

Russkii biograficheskii slovar [Russian Biographic Dictionary]. St. Petersburg: 1896–1918. 25 vols.

Russkoe narodnoe poeticheskoe tvorchestvo [Russian National Poetic Creativeness]. Moscow-Leningrad: 1953.

Rybakov, B. A. *Remeslo drevnei Rusi* [The Craft of Ancient Rus]. Moscow: 1948.

Rzhiga, V. *Mikula Selianinovich.* Moscow: 1929.

—— *Peresvetov I. S.–publitsist XVI veka* [I. S. Peresvetov–A Publicist of the XVI Century]. Moscow: 1908.

Sadikov, P. A. *Ocherki po istorii oprichniny* [Outlines of the History of the oprichnina]. Moscow-Leningrad: 1950.

Samokvasov, D. Ia. *Istoriia russkogo prava. Lektsii* [A History of Russian Law. Lectures]. Moscow: 1906.

Semennikov, V. P. *Knigoizdatelnaia deiatelnost N. I. Novikova i tipograficheskoi kompanii* [The Book-publishing Activity of N. I. Novikov and of the Printing Company]. Petrograd: 1922.

—— *Novyi tekst "Puteshestviia iz Peterburga v Moskvu" Radishcheva* [A New Text of Radishchev's "Journey from Petersburg to Moscow"]. Moscow: 1921.

—— *Radishchev. Ocherki i issledovaniia* [Radishchev. Sketches and Studies]. Petrograd: 1923.

Semenov, A. *Izuchenie istoricheskikh svedenii o Rossiiskoi vneshnei torgovle i promyshlennosti s poloviny XVII stoletiia po 1858 god* [A Study of Historical Data on Russian Foreign Trade and Industry from the Middle of the XVII Century to 1858]. St. Petersburg: 1859. 3 pts.

Semevskii, V. I. *Krestiane v tsarstvovanie imperatritsy Ekateriny II* [Peasants During the Reign of Empress Catherine II]. St. Petersburg: 1901–3.

—— *Krestianskii vopros v Rossii v XVIII i pervoi polovine XIX veka* [The Peasant Problem in Russia in the XVIII and the First Half of the XIX Century]. St. Petersburg: 1888.

Serbina, K. N. *Ocherki iz sotsialno-ekonomicheskoi istorii russkogo goroda. Tikhvinskii posad v XVI–XVIII vv.* [Outlines of the Socio-Economic History of a Russian Town. Tikhvinsk Settlement in the XVI–XVIII Centuries]. Moscow-Leningrad: 1951.

Sidorov, S. *O zaslugakh Petra Velikogo otnositelno russkoi promishlennosti* [Peter the Great's Contribution to Russian Industry]. Moscow: 1852.

Shchapov, A. *Golos drevnei Russkoi tserkvi ob uluchshenii byta nesvobodnykh liudei* [The Teachings of the Ancient Russian Church About the Improvement of the Conditions of Non-Free People]. Kazan: 1859.

Shchepetov, K. N. *Krepostnoe pravo v votchinakh Sheremetevykh (1708–1885)* [Serfdom on Sheremetev Estates (1708–1885)]. Moscow: 1947.

Shetyrev, S. *Istoriia imperatorskogo Moskovskogo universiteta . . . 1755–1855* [A History of the Imperial Moscow University . . . 1755–1855] .Moscow: 1855.

Shklovskii, V. *Chulkov i Levshin* [Chulkov and Levshin]. Leningrad: 1933.

Shliapkin, I. A. *Ermolai Pregreshnyi. Novyi pisatel epokhi Groznogo i ego sochineniia* [Ermolai Pregreshnyi. A New Writer of the Time of Ivan the Terrible and His Works]. St. Petersburg: 1911.

Shmakov, A. *Radishchev v Sibiri* [Radishchev in Siberia]. Irkutsk: 1952.

Shmurlo, E. *Petr Velikii v otsenke sovremennikov i potomstva (XVIII vek)* [Peter the Great in the Opinion of Contemporaries and Posterity (XVIII Century)]. St. Petersburg: 1912.

Shultse-Gevernits, G. *Ocherki obshchestvennogo khoziaistva i ekonomicheskoi politiki Rossii* [Outlines of the Public Economy and Economic Policy of Russia]. Translated from the German. St. Petersburg: 1901.

Smirnov, I. I. *Vosstanie Bolotnikova 1606–1607* [Bolotnikov's Uprising of 1606–1607]. Moscow: 1951.

Smirnov, M. A. *Rossiia i Turtsiia v XVI–XVII vv.* [Russia and Turkey During the XVI–XVII Centuries]. Moscow: 1946. 2 vols.

Smirnov, P. *Posadskie liudi i ikh klassovaia borba do serediny XVII veka* [The Settlement People and Their Class Struggle up to the Middle of the XVII Century]. Moscow-Leningrad: 1947.

Smolianov, I. D. *Velikii pisatel-revolutsioner Aleksandr Nikolaevich Radishchev* [The Great Writer-Revolutionary A. N. Radishchev]. Pskov: 1949.

Solovev, S. *Istoriia Rossii s drevneishikh vremen* [A History of Russia from Ancient Times]. Moscow: 1851–1895. 29 vols.

Speranskii, M., *ed. Byliny* [Legends]. Moscow: 1916.

Spiridonova, E. V. *Ekonomicheskaia politika i ekonomicheskie vzgliady Petra I* [The Economic Policy and Economic Views of Peter I]. Moscow: 1952.

Stalin, I. V. *Ekonomicheskie problemy sotsializma v SSSR* [The Economic Problems of Socialism in the USSR]. Moscow: 1952.

—— *Marksizm i voprosy iazykoznaniia* [Marxism and Problems of Linguistics]. Moscow: 1952.

—— *Sochineniia* [Works]. Moscow: 1946–53. 13 vols.

—— *Voprosy leninizma* [Problems of Leninism]. Moscow: 1952.

Streis, Ia. Ia. *Tri puteshestviia* [Three Journeys]. Moscow: 1935.

Stepanov, T. *Zapiski o politicheskoi ekonomii* [Notes on Political Economy]. St. Petersburg-Kharkov: 1844–8. 2 pts.

Strumilin, S. G. *Dogovor zaima v drevnerusskom prave* [Credit Agreement in Ancient Russian Law]. Moscow: 1929.

—— *Istoriia chernoi metallurgii v SSSR* [A History of the Black Metallurgy in the USSR]. Moscow: 1954.

Sukhomlinov, M. I. *Issledovaniia i stati po russkoi literature i prosveshcheniiu* [Studies and Articles in Russian Literature and Education]. St. Petersburg: 1889. Vol. I.

—— *Istoriia Rossiiskoi akademii* [A History of the Russian Academy]. St. Petersburg: 1875.

Sviatlovskii, V. I. *Istoriia ekonomicheskikh idei v Rossii* [A History of Economic Ideas in Russia]. Petrograd: 1923.

—— *K istorii politicheskoi ekonomii i statistiki v Rossii* [On the History of Political Economy and Statistics in Russia]. St. Petersburg: 1906.

—— *Ocherk po istorii ekonomicheskikh vozzrenii na zapade i v Rossii* [An Outline of the History of Economic Views in the West and in Russia]. St. Petersburg: 1913.

Tikhanov, P. N. *Pamiatniki drevnei pismennosti* [Memorials of Ancient Literature]. St. Petersburg: 1892.

Tikhomirov, M. N. *Drevnerusskie goroda* [Ancient Russian Towns] Moscow: 1946.

—— *Issledovanie o Russkoi Pravde. Proiskhozhdenie tekstov* [An Examination of the Russian Law. The Origin of Texts]. Moscow-Leningrad: 1941.

—— *Istochnikovedenie istorii SSSR s drevneishikh vremen do kontsa XVIII v.* [A Study of the Sources of History of the USSR from Ancient Times to the End of the XVIII Century]. Moscow: 1940.

—— *Posobie dlia izucheniia Russkoi Pravdy* [An Aid for the Study of the *Russkaia Pravda*]. Moscow: 1953.

Tikhonravov, N. S. *Russkaia literatura XVIII i XIX vv.* [Russian Literature of the XVIII–XIX Centuries]. Moscow: 1898.

Tolstoi, D. *Istoriia finansovykh uchrezhdenii v Rossii so vremeni osnovaniia gosudarstva do konchiny Ekateriny II* [A History of Russia's Financial Institutions from the Founding of the State to the Death of Catherine II]. St. Petersburg: 1848.

Tretiakov, P. N. *Vostochno-slavianskie plemena* [The Tribes of Eastern Slavs]. Moscow: 1953.

Trubetskoi, S. P. *Zapiski kniazia S. P. Trubetskogo* [The Notes of Prince S. P. Trubetskoi]. St. Petersburg: 1907.

Tugan-Baranovskii, M. *Russkaia fabrika v proshlom i nastoiashchem* [The Russian Factory in the Past and at the Present]. St. Petersburg: 1898.

Udintsev, V. *Istoriia zaima* [A History of Credit]. Kiev: 1908.

[Ukraine]. *Istoriia Ukrainskoi SSSR* [History of the Ukrainian SSR]. Kiev: 1953.

Ustrialov, N. *Istoriia tsarstvovaniia Petra Velikogo* [A History of the Reign of Peter the Great]. St. Petersburg: 1858–63. 6 vols.

—— *Skazaniia kniazia Kurbskogo* [The Sayings of Prince Kurbskii]. 3rd ed. St. Petersburg: 1868.

Valk, S. N. *Sovetskaia arkheografiia* [Soviet Archeography]. Moscow-Leningrad: 1948.

Vasetskii, G. and Iovchuk, M. *Ocherki po istorii russkogo materializma XVIII i XIX vv.* [Outlines of the History of Russian Materialism of the XVIII and XIX Centuries]. Moscow: 1942.

Vasilchikov, A. *Zemlevladenie i zemledelie v Rossii i drugikh evropeiskikh gosudarstvakh* [Landownership and Agriculture in Russia and Other European States]. St. Petersburg: 1881.

Veidemeier, A. *Dvor i zamechatelnye liudi v Rossii vo vtoroi polovine XVIII stoletiia* [The Court and Important People in Russia in the Second Half of the XVIII Century]. St. Petersburg: 1846. 2 pts.

Velikaia reforma [The Great Reform]. Moscow: 1911. 8 vols.

Vernadskii, I. *Ocherk istorii politicheskoi ekonomii* [An Outline of the History of Political Economy]. St. Petersburg: 1858.

Veselago, F. *Ocherk russkoi morskoi istorii* [An Outline of Russian Maritime History]. St. Petersburg: 1875.

Veselovskii, S. B. *K voprosu o proiskhozhdenii votchinnago regima* [On the Question of the Origin of the Votchina System]. Moscow: 1926.

—— *Soshnoe pismo* [Plough Letter]. Moscow: 1915–6. 2 vols.

Viatkin, M. P. *Emelian Pugachev*. Leningrad: 1951.

Vipper, R. Iu. *Ivan Groznyi* [Ivan the Terrible] Moscow-Leningrad: 1944.

Vitashevskaia, M. *Puteshestvie za tri moria Afanasiia Nikitina* [Afanasii Nikitin's Journey Beyond the Three Seas]. Moscow: 1949.

Vitchevskii, V. *Torgovaia, tamozhennaia i promyshlennaia politika Rossii so vremen Petra Velikogo do nashikh dnei* [The Trade, Customs, and Industrial Policy of Russia from Peter the Great to our Times]. Translated from the German. St. Petersburg: 1909.

Vladimirskii-Budanov, M. F. *Obzor istorii russkogo prava* [A Review of the History of Russian Law]. 3rd ed. Kiev-St. Petersburg: 1900.

Voprosy istorii otechestvennoi nauki [Problems of the History of Native Science]. Moscow-Leningrad: 1949.

Zagorovskii, A. *Istoricheskii ocherk zaima po russkomy pravy do kontsa XIII stoletiia* [An Historical Outline of Credit Under Russian Law up to the End of the XIII Century]. Kiev: 1875.

Zagoskin, N. *Ocherki organizatsii i proiskhozhdeniia sluzhilogo soslovia v dopetrovskoi Rusi* [Outlines of the Organization and Origin of Service Nobility in the Pre-Petrine Rus]. Kazan: 1875.

—— *Ustavnye gramoty XIV–XVI vv. opredeliaiushchie poriadok mestnogo pravitelstvennogo upravleniia* [The XIX–XVI Centuries Charters Determining the Order of Local Administration]. Kazan: 1875–6.

Zamiatnin, V. V. *Sotsialno-ekonomicheskie vzgliady A. N. Radishcheva (1749–*

1949) [Socio-Economic Views of A. N. Radishchev (1749–1949))]. Voronezh: 1949.

Zaozerskaia, E. I. *Manufaktura pri Petre I* [*Manufactures Under Peter I*]. Moscow-Leningrad: 1947.

Zaozerskii, A. I. *Tsarskaia votchina XVII v. Iz istorii khoziaistvennoi politiki tsaria Alekseia Mikhailovicha* [Tsar's Estate in the XVII Century. A History of the Household and Departmental Policy of Tsar Aleksei Mikhailovich]. Moscow: 1937.

Zhizhka, M. V. *Emelian Pugachev.* 2nd ed. Moscow: 1950.

C. Periodical Literature

Adrianova-Perets, V. P. "Krestianskaia tema v literature XVI veka" [The Peasant Theme in XVIth Century Literature], *Trudy otdela drevnerusskoi literatury* [Works of the Department of Ancient Russian Literature], X (1954), pp. 200–11. Hereinafter cited as *TODL.*

Afanasev, A. "Gosudarstvennoe khoziaistvo pri Petre Velikom" [State Economy Under Peter the Great], *Sovremennik* [Contemporary], No. 6–7 (1847).

Alefirenko, P. "Ekonomicheskie vzgliady V. N. Tatishcheva" [Economic Views of V. N. Tatishchev], *Voprosy istorii* [Problems of History], No. 12 (1948), pp. 89–96.

—— "Sotsialno-politicheskie vozzreniia V. N. Tatishcheva" [Socio-Political Views of V. N. Tatishchev], *ibid.,* No. 10 (1951), pp. 103–14.

Aleksandrov, S. S. "Ekonomicheskie i politicheskie vzgliady V. N. Tatishcheva" [Economic and Political Views of V. N. Tatishchev], *Izvestiia Akademii Nauk SSSR. Otdelenia ekonomiki i prava* [Bulletin of the Academy of Sciences of the USSR. Department of Economics and Law], No. 4 (1951), pp. 186–207. Hereinafter cited as *Izvestiia AN USSR.*

Bak, I. S. "S. E. Desnitskii–vydaiushchiisia russkii sotsiolog" [S. E. Desnitskii An Outstanding Russian Sociologist], *Voprosy filosofii* [Problems of Philosophy], No. 1 (1955), pp. 58–67.

—— "Dmitri Alekseevich Golitsin (Filosofskie, obshchestvenno-politicheskie i ekonomicheskie vozzreniia" [D. A. Golitsin (Philosophic, Socio-Political and Economic Views)], *Istoricheskie zapiski* [Historical Notes], No. 26 (1948), pp. 258–72.

—— "Ia. P. Kozelskii. Filosofskie, obshchestvenno-politicheskie i ekonomicheskie vozzreniia" [Ia. P. Kozelskii. Philosophic, Socio-Political, and Economic Views], *Voprosy istorii,* No. 1 (1941), pp. 83–100.

—— "Ekonomicheskie vozzreniia M. V. Lomonosova" [Economic Views of M. V. Lomnosov], *Problemy ekonomiki* [Problems of Economics], No. 4 (1940), pp. 131–43.

—— "A. Ia. Polenov. Filosofskie, obshchestvenno-politicheskie i ekonomicheskie vzgliady" [A. Ia. Polenov. Philosophic, Socio-Political, and Economic Views] *Istoricheskie zapiski,* No. 28 (1949), pp. 182–202.

—— "Economicheskie vozzreniia P. I. Rychkova" [Economic Views of P. I. Rychkov], *ibid.*, No. 16 (1945), pp. 126–38.

—— "Obshchestvenno-ekonomicheskie vozzreniia I. A. Tretiakova" [Socio-Economic Views of I. A. Tretiakov], *Voprosy istorii,* No. 9 (1954), pp. 104–13.

—— "Vozniknovenie russkoi selsko-khoziaistvennoi ekonomii" [The Emergence of Russian Rural Economy], *Sotsialisticheskoe selskoe khoziaistvo* [Socialist Rural Economy], No. 9 (1945).

Bakrushin, S. "Ivan Groznyi" [Ivan the Terrible], *Bolshevik,* No. 13 (1943), pp. 48–61.

Baklanova, N. A. "Ian de-Gron, prozhekter v Moskovskom gosudarstve XVII v." [Jan de-Gron, A Project Maker in the Moscovite State of the XVII Century] *Uchenye zapiski Instituta istorii RANION* [Scientific Notes of the Institute of History of the RANION], IV (1929), pp. 109–22.

Barskov, Ia. L. "Literaturnoe nasledstvo A. N. Radishcheva i N. I. Novikova" [The Literary Heritage of A. N. Radishchev and N. I. Novikov], *Literaturnoe nasledstvo* [Literary Heritage], No. 9–10 (1933), pp. 340–58.

Bazilevich, K. V. "Kollektivnye chelobitia torgovykh liudei i borba za russkii rynok v pervoi polovine XVII veka" [Collective Petitions of Merchants and the Struggle for the Russian Market in the First Half of the XVII Century], *Izvestiia AN USSR,* No. 2, Series VII (1932), pp. 91–123.

—— "Novotorgovoi ustav 1667 g. K voprosu o ego istochnikakh" [The New Commercial Code of 1667. Its Sources], *ibid.,* No. 7, Series VII (1932), pp. 589–622.

—— "Opyt periodizatsii istorii SSSR feodalnogo perioda" [An Essay on the Periodization of the Feudal Period of the USSR's History], *Voprosy istorii,* No. 11 (1949), pp. 65–90.

Betiaev, Ia. "Politicheskie i filosofskie vzgliady A. N. Radishcheva" [Political and Philosophic Views of A. N. Radishchev], *Pod znamenem marksizma* [Under the Banner of Marxism], No. 8 (1938), pp. 81–110.

Bezobrazov, V. P. "O vlianii ekomomicheskoi nauki na gosudarstvennuiu zhizn v sovremennoi Evrope" [The Influence of Economic Science on State Life in Contemporary Europe], *Russkii vestnik* [Russian Herald], January, 1867, pp. 113–41.

Bibikov, G. N. "Rassloenie krepostnogo krestianstva v barshchinnoi votchine v kontse XVIII i nachale XIX v." [Stratification Among the Serfs on the Barshchina Estates at the End of the XVIII and the Beginning of the XIX Centuries], *Istoricheskie zapiski,* No. 4 (1938), pp. 76–112.

Borovoi, S. Ia. "Kreditnaia politika tsarizma v usloviiakh razlozheniia krepostnichestva" [The Credit Policy of Tsarism During the Disintegration of Serfdom], *Voprosy istorii,* No. 2 (1954), pp. 129–38.

Brikner, A. G. "Kniaz M. M. Shcherbatov kak chlen Bolshoi komissii 1767 g." [Prince M. M. Shcherbatov as a Member of the Main Commission of 1767], *Istoricheskii vestnik* [Historical Herald], Oct., 1881, pp. 217–49.

Budovnits, I. U. "'Izbornik' Sviatoslava 1076 g. i 'Pouchenie' Vladimira Monomakha i ikh mesto v istorii russkoi obshchestvennoi mysli" [Sviatoslav's 'Collection' of 1076 and Vladimir Monomakh's 'Testament' and their Place in the History of Russian Social Thought], *TODL,* X (1954), pp. 44–75.

Bunge, N. "Issledovanie nachal torgovogo zakonodatelstva Petra Velikogo" [An Inquiry into the Origins of Trade Legislation of Peter the Great] *Otechestvennye zapiski* [Fatherland Notes], Pt. II (1850), pp. 1–30.

Cherepnin, L. V. and A. I. Iakovlev, "Pskovskaia sudnaia gramota" [The Legal Charter of Pskov], *Istoricheskie zapiski,* No. 6 (1940), pp. 235–99.

Cherepnin, L. V. "Osnovnye etapy razvitiia feodalnoi sobstvennosti na Rusi (do XVII v.)" [Basic Phases in the Development of Feudal Ownership in Rus (Before the XVII Century)], *Voprosy istorii,* No. 4 (1953), pp. 38–63.

Danilov, V. V. "K kharakteristike 'Khozhdeniia' igumena Danila" [The Nature of Abbot Daniel's Journey], *TODL,* X (1954), pp. 92–105.

Danilova, L. V. and V. T. Pashuto, "Tovarnoe proizvodstvo na Rusi (do XVII v.)" [The Commodity Production in Rus (Before the XVII Century)], *Voprosy istorii,* No. 1 (1954), pp. 117–36.

Drakokhrust, E. I. "Rassloenie krepostnogo krestianstva v obrochnoi votchine XVIII v." [Stratification Among Serfs on the obrok Estates in the XVIII Century], *Istoricheskie zapiski,* No. 4 (1938), pp. 113–40.

Druzhinin, N. "O periodizatsii istorii kapitalisticheskikh otnoshenii v Rossii" [The Periodization of History of Capitalist Relations in Russia], *Voprosy istorii,* No. 11 (1949), pp. 90–106.

Fedorov, G. B. "Unifikatsiia russkoi monetnoi sistemy i ukaz 1535 g." [The Unification of the Russian Monetary System and the ukaz of 1535] *Izvestiia AN USSR,* VII, No. 6 (1950), pp. 547–58.

Filipov, M. "Sovremennye russkie ekonomisty" [Contemporary Russian Economists], *Nauchnoe obozrenie* [Scientific Review], Nos. 7–12 (1899), No. 3 (1900).

Finkelshtein, N. A. "Pismo o 'Kitaiskom torge' Radishcheva" [Radishchev's Letter on Chinese Trade], *Uchenye zapiski Sverdlovskogo gosudarstvennogo pedagogicheskog instituta* [Scholarly Notes of the Sverdlovsk State Pedagogical Institute], 1939, pp. 261–76.

Gaisimovich, A. I. "Tsekhi v Rossii v XVIII veke" [The Guilds in Russia in the XVIII Century], *Izvestiia AN USSR,* No. 5, Series VII (1931), pp. 523–68.

Goltsev, V. A., "Dvizhenie russkoi ekonomicheskoi nauki" [Progress of Russian Economic Science], *Russkaia zhizn* [Russian Life], No. 3 (1885).

Gorbunov, M. A. "Filosofskie i sotsiologicheskie vozzreniia A. N. Radishcheva" [Philosophic and Sociological Views of A. N. Radishchev], *Uchenye zapiski Akademii nauk pri TsKVKP(b)* [Scientific Notes of the Academy of Sciences at the CC of the CPSU(b)], Issue V (1949), pp. 36–68.

Gussov, V. M. "Istoricheskaia osnova moleniia Danila Zatochnika" [The Historical Foundation of the Prayer of Daniel Zatochnik], *TODL,* VII (1949), pp. 410–8.

Grekov, B. D. "Opyt obsledovaniia khoziaistvennykh anket XVIII v." [A Study of Economic Questionnaires of the XVIII Century], *Letopis zaniatii Arkheograficheskoi komissii za 1927–1928,* Issue 35 (1929), pp. 39–104.

Ikonnikov, V. S. "Blizhnii boiarin Afanasii Lavrentievich Ordin-Nashchokin odin iz predshestvennikov petrovskoi reformy" [The Friendly Boyar A. L. Ordyn-Nashchokin, One of the Forerunners of Peter's Reform], *Russkaia starina,* [Russian Antiquity], No. 10 (1883), pp. 17–66; No. 11 (1883), pp. 273–308.

Karataev, N. K. "P. I. Rychkov—vydaiushchiisia russkii ekonomist XVIII v." [P. I. Rychkov—An Outstanding Russian Economist of the XVIII Century] *Vestnik Akademii Nauk SSSR,* No. 3 (1950), pp. 84–93.

Karnovich, E. "Krestiane i pomeshchiki po ideiam Ivan Pososhkova . . ." [Peasants and Nobles in the Eyes of Ivan Pososhkov . . .], *Sovremennik,* No. 10 (1858), pp. 33–80.

Kazakevich, T. A. "Mirovozzrenie A. N. Radishcheva [A. N. Radishchev's World Outlook], *Vestnik Leningradskogo universiteta,* No. 10 (1948).

Kizevetter, A. A. "Osnovnaia tendentsiia drevnerusskogo Domostroia" [The Main Tendency of the Ancient Russian Domostroy], *Russkoe bogatstvo,* January, 1896, pp. 39–59.

Khalanskii, M. "K byline pro Mikulu Selianovicha" [The Legend About Mikula Selianovich], *Russkii filologicheskii vestnik,* No. 6 (1881), pp. 270–3.

Khromov, P. A. "K istorii russkoi ekonomicheskoi mysli" [The History of Russian Economic Thought], *Bolshevik,* No. 6 (1944), pp. 36–45.

Kliuchevskii, V. O. "A. L. Ordin-Nashchokin, moskovskii gosudarstvennyi chelovek XVII v." [A. L. Ordin-Nashchokin, A Moscovite Statesman of the XVII Century] *Nauchnoe slovo,* Bk. 3 (1904), pp. 121–38.

Kolpanev, A. I. "O 'kupliakh' Ivana Kality" [About the Purchases of Ivan Kalita], *Istoricheskie zapiski,* No. 20 (1946), pp. 24–37.

Krylova, T. K. "K istorii torgovoi politiki Petra I v Iugo-Zapadnoi Evrope" [The History of Peter the I's Trade Policy in Southwestern Europe] *Uchenye zapiski Leningradskogo gosudarstvennogo pedagogicheskogo instituta,* Vol. 19 (1939), pp. 135–44.

Kulomzin, A. "Gosudarstvennye dokhody i raskhody v tsarstvovanie Ekateriny II 1762–1796" [State Revenues and Expenditures During the Reign of Catherine II, 1762–1796], *Russkii vestnik,* Vol. 84 (1869), pp. 108–51.

Lapshina, R. G. "Feodosii Kosoi—ideolog krestianstva XVI v." [Feodosii Kosoi —Peasant Spokesman of the XVI Century], *TODL,* IX (1953), pp. 235–50.

Lebedev, V. "Bulavinskoe vosstanie (1707–1708 gg.)" [The Bulavin-Led Upheaval (1707–1708)], *Istorik-marksist* [Marxist Historian], No. 3 (1933), pp. 45–64.

Liashchenko, P. I. "Krepostnoe selskoe khoziaistvo Rossii v XVIII v." [Serf Village Economy in Russia in the XVIII Century], *Istoricheskie zapiski,* No. 15 (1945), pp. 97–127.

Likhachev, D. S. "Nekotorye voprosy ideologii feodalov v literature XI–XIII vekov" [Some Questions of the Ideology of the Feudalist in the Literature of the XI–XIII Centuries], *TODL,* X (1954), pp. 76–91.

——— "Sotsialnye osnovy stylia "Molenia" Danila Zatochnika" [Social Foundations of the Style of Danilo Zatochnik's "Prayer"], *ibid.,* X (1954), pp. 106–19.

Lipshits, E. E. "Vizantiiskoe krestianstvo i slavianskaia kolonizatsiia (preimushchestvenno po dannym Zemledelcheskogo zakona)" [Byzantine Peasantry and Slavic Colonization (Based Mainly on the Data of the Land Code)], *Vizantiiskii zbornik* [Byzantine Collection], 1945, pp. 96–143.

Liubomirov, P. G. "Rol kazennogo, dvorianskogo i kupecheskogo kapitala v stroitelstve krupnoi promyshlennosti Rossii v XVII–XVIII vv." [The Role of the State, Nobility, and Commercial Capital in the Organization of Heavy Industry in Russia in the XVII–XVIII Centuries], *Istoricheskie zapiski,* No. 16 (1945), pp. 65–99.

Meichik, D. "Russko-Vizantiiskie dogovory" [Russo-Byzantine Treaties] *Zhurnal Ministerstva narodnogo prosveshcheniia* [Journal of the Ministry of Public Instruction], LVII (June, 1915), pp. 349–72; LIX (October, 1915) pp. 292–317; LX (November, 1915), pp. 132–63. Hereinafter cited as *ZhMNP.*

Mikhailov, A. V. "K voprosu o redaktsiiakh 'Domostroia,' ego sostave i proiskhozhdenii" [The Problem of the 'Domostroi's' Editions, Its Content and Origin], *ibid.,* CCLXI (February, 1889), pp. 294–324; CCLXII (March, 1889) pp. 125–76; CCLXX (1890), pp. 332–69.

Moroshkin, F. L. "Ob uchasti Moskovskogo universiteta v obrazovanii otechestvennoi iurisprudentsii" [Participation of Moscow's University in the Organization of Native Jurisprudence], *Uchenye zapiski Moskovskogo universiteta,* No. 8 (1834).

Moskalenko, F. "Velikii predshestvennik dekabristov" [The Great Forerunner of the Decembrists], *Literaturnyi Voronezh,* No. 4 (1940), pp. 150–68.

M-v, E. "Neskolko myslei o Pososhkove kak ekonomiste XVIII stoletiia" [Some Thoughts About Pososhkov as an Economist of the XVIII Century], *Zapiski imperatorskogo Kazanskogo ekonomicheskogo obshchestva,* II, Pt. 2 (1859), pp. 31–50.

Nikitin, N. P. "Zarozhdenie ekonomicheskoi geografii v Rossii. Obzor materialov XVIII v." [The Founding of Economic Geography in Russia. A Review of Documents of the XVIII Century], *Voprosy geografii,* Collection 17 (1950), pp. 43–104.

"Ocherki russkoi zhurnalistiki, preimushchestvenno staroi" [Outlines of Russian Journalism, Primarily Ancient], *Sovremennik,* Nos. 1, 2, and 3 (1851).

Oreshnikov, A. V. "Denezhnye znaki domongolskoi Rusi" [Monetary Signs of the Pre-Mongol Rus], *Trudy Gosudarstvennogo istoricheskogo muzeia,* Issue 6 (1936).

Panchenko, B. A. "Krestianskaia sobstvennost v Vizantii. Zemledelcheskii Zakon i monastyrskie dokumenty" [Peasant Ownership in Byzantium. The Agricultural Code and Monastery Documents], *Izvestiia russkogo arkheologicheskogo instituta v Konstantinople,* IX, Issue 1–2 (1904).

Pankratova, A. M. "O roli tovarnogo proizvodstva pri perekhode ot feodalizma k kapitalizmu" [Role of Commodity Production During Transition from Feudalism to Capitalism], *Voprosy istorii,* No. 9 (1953), pp. 59–77.

Pashkov, A. "Ekonomicheskie vzgliady I. T. Pososhkova" [Economic Views of I. T. Pososhkov], *Izvestiia AN USSR,* No. 4 (1945).

—— "K izucheniiu istorii russkoi ekonomicheskoi mysli" [On the Study of the History of Russian Economic Thought], *Voprosy ekonomiki,* No. 7 (1948), pp. 75–89.

—— "U istokov russkoi ekonomicheskoi mysli" [At the Sources of Russian Economic Thought], *ibid.,* No. 1 (1952), pp. 46–62.

Pashuto, V. and L. Cherepnin. "O periodizatsii istorii Rossii epokhi feodalizma" [On the Periodization of the Feudal Period of Russian History], *Voprosy istorii,* No. 2 (1951), pp. 52–80.

Pavlov, A. S. "Po voprosu o vremeni, meste i kharaktere pervonachalnogo perevoda vizantiiskogo zemledelchskogo ustava na slavianskii iazyk" [The Problem of the Time, Place, and Nature of the First Translation of the Byzantine Agricultural Code into the Slavic Language], *ZhMNP* (September, 1886), pp. 98–125.

Pavlov-Silvanskii, N. P. "Novye izvestiia o Pososhkove" [New Data on Pososhkov] *Izvestiia Otdeleniia russkogo iazyka i slovesnosti Imperatorskoi Akademii nauk,* IX, Bk. 3 (1904), pp. 105–48.

Pogodin, M. "Krestianin Ivan Pososhkov—gosudarstvennyi muzh vremen Petra Velikogo" [Peasant Ivan Pososhkov—A Statesman of Peter the Great's Time], *Moskvitianin,* No. 3 (1842), pp. 68–104.

—— "Pososhkov po vnov otkrytym dokumentam" [Pososhkov in the Light of the Newly Discovered Documents], *Russkii vestnik,* Vol. 45 (1863), pp. 763–90.

Pokrovskii, S. A. "Falsifikatsiia russkoi obshchestvennoi mysli" [A Falsification of Russian Social Thought], *Voprosy istorii,* No. 3 (1948), pp. 100–6.

—— "Ucheniie S. E., Desnitskogo ob obshchestve i gosudarstve" [S. E. Desnitskii's Teaching About the Society and State], *Trudy Voronezhskogo gosudarstvennogo universiteta,* Issue 2 (1947), pp. 78–101.

Polenov, D. V. "A. Ia. Polenov—russkii zakonoved XVIII veka" [A. Ia. Polenov—Russian Jurist of the XVIII Century], *Russkii arkhiv* 1865, pp. 704–36.

Polianskii, F. Ia. "O tovarnom proizvodstve v usloviakh feodaliza" [On Commodity Production Under Feudalism], *Voprosy istorii,* No. 1 (1953), pp. 40–60.

Prussak, A. V. "Zavody rabotavshie na Pugacheva" [Factories Which Worked for Pugachev], *Istoricheskie zapiski,* No. 8 (1940), pp. 174–207.

[Pugachev, E.] "Dopros E. Pugacheva v Tainoi ekspeditsii v Moskve v 1774–1775 gg." [The Interrogation of E. Pugachev in the Secret Office in Moscow in 1774–1775], *Krasnyi arkhiv,* Vols. 69–70 (1935), pp. 159–237.

—— "Dopros pugachevskogo atamana A. Khlopushi" [The Interrogation of Pugachev's Ataman A. Khlopusha], *ibid.,* Vol. 68 (1935), pp. 162–71.

—— "Doprosy Pugacheva" [Pugachev's Interrogations], *Chteniia,* Bk. 2 (1858), pp. 1–52.

—— "Novye materialy ob uchasti krestian Povolzhia v vosstanii E. I. Pugacheva" [New Materials on the Volga Region Peasants' Participation in the Uprising of E. I. Pugachev], *Istoricheskii arkhiv,* VIII (1953), pp. 278–332.

Pypin, A. N. "Russkaia nauka i natsionalnyi vopros v XVIII veke" [Russian

Science and the National Problem in the XVIII Century], *Vestnik Evropy,* May, 1884, pp. 212–56; June, 1884, pp. 548–600.

Razgon, A. M. "Promyshlennye i torgovye slobody i sela Vladimirskoi gubernii vo vtoroi polovine XVIII v." [Industrial and Commercial Settlements and Villages of Vladimir Gubernia in the Second Half of the XVIII Century] *Istoricheskie zapiski,* No. 32 (1950), pp. 133–72.

Romanov, B. A. "K voprosu o zemelnoi politike Izbrannoi Rady. St. 85 Sudebnika 1550 g." [The Question of Land Policy of the Chosen Council. Article 85 of the Code of 1550], *ibid.,* No. 38 (1951), pp. 252–69.

—— "Sudebnik Ivana Groznogo" [The Code of Ivan the Terrible], *ibid.,* No. 29. (1949), pp. 200–35.

Rubinshtein, N. L. "Nekotorye voprosy formirovaniia rynka rabochei sily v Rossii XVIII veka" [Some Problems of the Formation of a Labor Force Market in Russia in the XVIII Century], *Voprosy istorii,* No. 2 (1952), pp. 74–101.

—— "Ulozhennaia komissiia 1754–1766 gg. i ee proekt novogo ulozheniia" [The Legislative Commission of 1754–1766 and Its Project of a New Code], *Istoricheskie zapiski,* No. 38 (1951), pp. 208–51.

Rychkov, N. D. "Zapiski Petra Ivanovicha Rychkova" [P. I. Rychkov's Notes], *Russkii arkhiv,* No. 10 (1905), pp. 289–340.

Rzhiga, V. F. "Literaturnaia deitelnost Ermolaia-Erazma" [Literary Activity of Ermolai-Erazm], *Letopis zaniatii Arkheograficheskoi komissii za 1923–1925 gody,* 1926, pp. 103–99.

—— "Opyty po istorii russkoi publitsistiki XVI veka. Maksim Grek kak publitsist" [Essays on the History of Russian Publicity in the XVI Century. Maksim the Greek as a Pamphleteer], *TODL,* I (1934), pp. 5–120.

Sakketti, A. L. "Politicheskaia programma I. S. Peresvetova" [The Political Program of I. S. Peresvetov], *Vestnik Moskovskogo universiteta,* 1951, pp. 107–17.

Samoilov, V. "Khozhenie Afanasiia Nikitina v Indiiu" [Afanasii Nikitin's Journey to India], *Istoricheskii zhurnal,* No. 3 (1940), pp. 76–86.

Semevskii, V. I. "Iz istorii obshchestvennykh techenii v Rossii v XVIII i pervoi polovine XIX veka" [A History of Social Movements in Russia in the XVIII and the First Half of the XIX Century], *Istoricheskoe obozrenie* IX (1897), pp. 244–99.

—— "Ocherk upravleniia manufakturnoi promyshlennosti ot Petra I do Ekateriny II [An Outline of the Administration of Manufacturing Industry from Peter I to Catherine II], *ZhMNP,* No. 103 (September, 1859), pp. 193–232.

Sergeevich, V. I. "Otkuda neudachi Ekaterinskoi zakonodatelnoi komissii?" [Why Did Catherine's Legislative Commission Fail?], *Vestnik Evropy,* I (1878), pp. 138–64.

Sivkov, K. V. "K istorii zemlevladeniia v Rossii v nachale XVIII v." [A History of the Landownership in Russia in the Beginning of the XVIII Century], *Izvestiia AN SSSR,* No. 3, Series VII (1933), pp. 195–224.

—— "Obshchestvennaia mysl i obshchestvennoe dvizhenie v Rossii v kontse

XVIII v." [Social Thought and Social Movement in Russia at the End of the XVIII Century], *Voprosy istorii,* Nos. 5–6 (1946), pp. 90–5.
—— "Podpolnaia politicheskaia literatura v Rossii v poslednei treti XVIII v." [Underground Political Literature in Russia in the Last Third of the XVIII Century], *Istoricheskie zapiski,* No. 19 (1946), pp. 63–101.
Shapiro, A. L. "K istorii krestianskikh promyslov i krestianskoi manufaktury v Rossii XVIII v." [A History of Peasant Industries and Peasant Manufactures in Russia in the XVIII Century], *ibid.,* No. 31 (1950), pp. 136–53.
—— "Zapiski o Petersburgskoi gubernii A. N. Radishcheva" [A. N. Radishchev's Notes on Petersburg Gubernia], *Istoricheskii arkhiv,* V (1950), pp. 190–287.
Shatilova, T. "Rabotnye liudi v svete deputatskikh nakazov 1767 g." [The Working People in the Light of the Delegates' Instructions of 1767], *Arkhiv istorii truda v Rossii,* Bk. 8 (1923), pp. 123–34.
Shchepkin, M. "Ekonomicheskie poniatiia v Rossii v kontse XVIII v." [Economic Concepts in Russia at the End of the XVIII Century], *Moskovskie vedomosti* Nos. 142, 143, 154, 172, and 177 (1859).
Shmakov, A. "Neizvestnye sluzhebnye bumagi A. N. Radishcheva" [Unknown Service Papers of A. N. Radishchev], *Iuzhnyi Ural,* Nos. 11–12 (1954–5).
Shtrange, M. M. "Frantsuzskaia burzhuaznaia revolutsiia 1789–1794 gg. i raznochinnye sloi russkogo obshchestva" [The French Bourgeois Revolution of 1789–1794 and the Commoners of Russian Society], *Istoricheskie zapiski,* No. 39 (1952), pp. 98–120.
Smirnov, I. I. "Sudebnik 1550 goda" [The Code of 1550], *ibid.,* No. 24 (1947).
Stieda, W. "Peter der Grosse als Merkantilist," *Russische Revue,* Bd IV, Heft 3 (1874).
Stolpianskii, P. "Odin iz nezametnykh deiatelei Ekaterinskoi epokhi Iakov Pavlovich Kozelskii" [Ia. P. Kozelskii—One of the Lesser known Statesmen of Catherine's Period], *Russkaia starina,* Vol. 128 (Dec., 1906), pp. 567–87.
Sudeikin, V. T. "Ekonomicheskaia politika Petra Velikogo" [The Economic Policy of Peter the Great], *Russkii vestnik,* Vol. 285 (1903), pp. 56–84.
Syromiatnikov, B. I. "S. E. Desnitskii—osnovatel nauki russkogo pravovedeniia" [S. E. Desnitskii—The Founder of Russian Legal Studies], *Izvestiia AN USSR,* No. 3 (1945), pp. 33–40.
Tarasov, I. "Ivan Pososhkov," *Iuridicheskii vestnik,* No. 10 (1880), pp. 179–209.
Tikhomirov, M. N. " 'Napisanie' Danila Zatochnika" [The Writing of Danilo Zatochnik], *TODL,* X (1954), pp. 269–79.
—— "Vasilii Nikitich Tatishchev," *Istorik-marksist,* No. 6 (1940), pp. 43–56.
Tikhomirov, I. A. "O trudakh M. V. Lomonosova po politicheskoi ekonomii" [M. V. Lomonosov's Works on Political Economy], *ZhMNP,* Feb., 1914, pp. 249–64.
Topilin, P. K. "Pervye shagi russkoi ekonomicheskoi mysli" [The First Steps of Russian Economic Thought], *Trudy Saratovskogo ekonomicheskogo instituta,* I (1948).
Ustiugov, N. V. "Remeslo i melkoe tovarnoe proizvodstvo v Russkom gosu-

darstve XVII v." [Crafts and Small Commodity Production in the Russian State of the XVII Century], *Istoricheskie zapiski,* No. 34 (1950), pp. 166–97.

Vasilevskii, V. G. "Zakonodatelstvo ikonobortsev" [The Legislation of the Iconoclasts], *ZhMNP* October-November, 1878.

Veretennikov, V. I. "K istorii sostavleniia dvorianskikh nakazov v Ekaterinskuiu komissiiu 1767 g." [A History of the Composition of the Nobility's Instructions to Catherine's Commission of 1767], *Zapiski Kharkovskogo Universiteta,* Bk. 4 (1911), pp. 1–32.

Veselovskii, A. N. "Iuzhno-russkie byliny" [South-Russian Legends], *Sbornik Otdeleniia russkogo iazyka i slovesnosti Imperatorskoi Akademii nauk,* No. 2, Vol. 22 (1881); No. 3, Vol. 36 (1884).

Vilenskaia, E. S. "Ob osobennostiakh formirovaniia russkoi osvoboditelnoi mysli v XVIII v." [About Particularities in the Formation of Russian Emancipating Thought in the XVIII Century], *Voprosy filosofii,* No. 2 (1951), pp. 114–28.

—— "Radishchev-pervyi ideolog krestianskoi revolutsii" [Radishchev—The First Spokesman of Peasant Revolution], *Istoricheskie zapiski,* No. 34 (1950), pp. 288–320.

"Voprosy istorii russkoi ekonomicheskoi mysli" [Problems of the History of Russian Economic Thought], *Voprosy ekonomiki,* No. 10 (1953), pp. 104–14.

Zagriatskov, M. "Obshchestvenno-politicheskie vzgliady S. E. Desnitskogo" [S. E. Desnitskii's Socio-Political Views], *Voprosy istorii,* No. 7 (1949), pp. 101–12.

Zimin, A. A. "O politicheskoi doktrine Iosifa Volotskogo" [The Political Doctrine of Joseph Volotskii], *TODL,* IX (1953), pp. 159–77.

INDEX

Lightning Source UK Ltd.
Milton Keynes UK
UKHW032137190922
409103UK00005B/571